Family Law
Third Edition

William P. Statsky

WEST PUBLISHING COMPANY
St. Paul   New York   Los Angeles   San Francisco

■ **PHOTO CREDITS**

48 Courtesy of Lawyers Cooperative Publishing Company   49 Lawyer Cooperative Publishing Company   51 **top** American Bar Association   51 **bottom** Bureau of National Affairs   52 **bottom** *Index to Legal Periodicals*, 1988–1989, copyright © 1989 by the H.W. Wilson Company. Material reproduced by permission.   53 **top** Information Access Company   55 **top** Mead Data Central, Inc.   55 **bottom** Used with permission of Martindale-Hubbell, a division of Reed Publishing (USA) Inc. *MARTINDALE-HUBBELL*® is a registered trademark of Reed Publishing (USA) Inc.   56 **bottom** Matthew Bender & Company, Inc.   57 **top** Callaghan & Company   57 **bottom** Matthew Bender & Company, Inc.   161 William P. Statsky   163 Wide World Photos, Inc.   353 Georgia Office of Child Support   370 Library of Congress   371 Robert Eckert, EKM Nepenthe   460 National Organization for Women   461 National Right to Life

■ **PRODUCTION CREDITS**

Cover Design: Kristen Weber
Cover Image: *Family Group* by Henry Moore,
    1948–49. Bronze, Photo by Lee Boltin.
    Reproduced with permission from the
    Hakone Open-Air Museum,
    Kanagawa-ken, Japan.
Text Design: Roslyn Stendahl
Copyediting: Margaret Jarpey
Composition: Parkwood Composition Services, Inc.

COPYRIGHT ©1978,
1984   By WEST PUBLISHING COMPANY
COPYRIGHT © 1991 By WEST PUBLISHING COMPANY
                 610 Opperman Drive
                 P.O. Box 64526
                 St. Paul, MN 55164-0526

Printed in the United States of America

98 97 96 95 94 93   8 7 6 5 4 3

Library of Congress Cataloging-in-Publication Data

Statsky, William P.
    Family Law/William P. Statsky.—3rd ed.
        p.   cm.
    ISBN 0-314-71851-6
    1. Domestic relations—United States.   I. Title
    KF505.S83 1991
    346.7301'5—dc20
    [347.30615]

                                                    90-12361
 CIP

For Gabriel, who just made tenderfoot.

Summary Table of Contents

Table of Contents

By the Same Author:

Case Analysis and Fundamentals of Legal Writing, 3d ed. St. Paul: West Publishing Company, 1989 (with J. Wernet)

Essentials of Paralegalism. St. Paul: West Publishing Company, 1988

Inmate Involvement in Prison Legal Services: Roles and Training Options for the Inmate as Paralegal. American Bar Association, Commission on Correctional Facilities and Services, 1974

Introduction to Paralegalism: Perspectives, Problems and Skills, 3d ed. St. Paul: West Publishing Company, 1986

Legal Desk Reference. St. Paul: West Publishing Co., 1990 (with B. Hussey, Michael Diamond & R. Nakamura).

The Legal Paraprofessional as Advocate and Assistant: Roles, Training Concepts and Materials. Center on Social Welfare Policy and Law, 1971 (with P. Lang)

Legal Research and Writing: Some Starting Points, 3d ed. St. Paul: West Publishing Company, 1986

Legal Thesaurus/Dictionary: A Resource for the Writer and Computer Researcher. St. Paul: West Publishing Company, 1985

Legislative Analysis and Drafting, 2d ed. St. Paul: West Publishing Company, 1984

Paralegal Employment: Facts and Strategies for the 1990s, St. Paul: West Publishing Company, 1988

The Regulation of Paralegals: Ethics, Professional Responsibility, and other Forms of Control, St. Paul, West Publishing Company, 1988

Torts: Personal Injury Litigation, 2d ed. St. Paul: West Publishing Company, 1990

Rights of the Imprisoned: Cases, Materials and Directions. Indianapolis: Bobbs-Merrill Company, 1974 (with R. Singer)

What Have Paralegals Done? A Dictionary of Functions. National Paralegal Institute, 1973

A Note to the Student:
The Meaning of "Your State"

Throughout the skills assignments of this book, you will see reference to the phrase, "your state," e.g., the state code of your state. The objective of many of these assignments is to help you relate the law outlined in the chapters of this book to the specific law of a particular state: "your state." The phrase, "your state" can have several meanings:

- the state where you intend to use your skills—where you hope to be employed;
- the state where you are studying (which may be different from the state where you will be employed);
- the state where you are now working (which may be different from the state where you hope to be employed).

Ask your teacher which meaning of "state" to use. If the choice is yours and you know the state where you will be employed, it is highly recommended that you select this state as the focus of the assignments in this book.

The selection of a state may depend in part on the availability of certain law books. In Chapter Two, p. 47, there is a list of the library law books dealing with Family Law to which you should have access.

CHAPTER ONE

The Scope and Skills of a Family Law Practice

■ Chapter Outline

F amily law encompasses a wide variety of legal problems. In addition to the obvious areas of divorce, custody, and support, the family law practitioner must know something about criminal law, contract law, property law, tort law, civil procedure law, evidence law, juvenile law, tax law, estate law, etc. Our study of each of these areas of the law will have two dimensions: knowledge of what the law is, and skills to use that knowledge. A number of these skills will take you into the law library, where the technique of *cartwheeling* will be very helpful. This technique is designed to generate numerous words and phrases that should be checked in indexes and tables of contents.

Next, twelve skills are described that will be the basis of assignments throughout the remaining chapters of the book. Along with their description, you will be given general instructions about how to use them in completing assignments.

A great deal of the family law is contained in the state statutory code of your state. The *state-code assignments* will train you to use these codes effectively. And once you find law in the codes, the next step is to apply it to concrete sets of facts. The *legal-analysis assignments* focus on this skill of application, primarily by asking you to identify and apply elements.

In the *complaint-drafting assignments,* you will spend a good deal of time with the critical pleading that initiates litigation by stating a cause of action. One way to avoid bitter litigation is to encourage the parties to agree on how to handle controversies that have arisen or that might arise. The *agreement-drafting assignments* will increase your appreciation of this aspect of family law.

Next to statutory law, the largest volume of law we will study comes from the courts in the form of common law. Many of the *court-opinion assignments* will ask you to find common law, although some of them will also ask you to find opinions that have interpreted statutory law. A practical method of handling statutory law and common law is to translate both into checklists. The *checklist-formulation assignments* will introduce you to this skill.

Next come three fact-gathering skills, all of which use the technique of fact particularization. First is the skill of formulating a plan of gathering new facts and substantiating ones you already have (the *investigation-strategy assignments*). Second is the skill of obtaining information in person from one individual (the *interview assignments*). Third is the skill of drafting written questions that will be sent to the other side (the *interrogatory assignments*).

Two assignments ask you to provide a step-by-step overview of how something is done. The first involves a legal proceeding in a court or in an administrative agency (the *flowchart assignments*); the second, a system of accomplishing a particular task in a law office (the *systems assignments*).

Finally, the chapter covers the skill of determining the status of proposed laws in the legislature that affect the family law practitioner. This skill is used in completing the *legislative-monitoring assignments*.

Section A. The Scope of Family Law

Family law is sometimes referred to as the law of domestic relations. What kinds of problems are covered in this area of the law? Suppose that you are a paralegal working for Karen Smith, an attorney in your state. One of the clients of the office is Susan Miller who lives out of state. The attorney receives the following telegram from Ms. Miller:

2/7/90

Karen Smith:

I am leaving the state in a week to come live with my mother. She will help me move everything so that we can start a new life. I must see you as soon as I arrive. My husband has threatened me and the children. I will bring the twins with me. I don't know where my oldest boy is. He is probably with his father getting into more trouble.

Susan Miller

A checklist is provided below of many of the questions that are potentially relevant to the case of Susan Miller. As a paralegal, you might be asked to conduct preliminary interviews and field investigation on some of the questions. Others may require legal research in the law library. (For an overview of paralegal responsibilities in family law, see the job descriptions in Appendix A, page 555.) As you can see from the list, the scope of the law covered in a family law practice can be very broad.

Criminal law

■ Has Mr. Miller committed a crime? What kind of threats did he make? Did he assault his wife and children?

- Has he failed to support his family? If so, is the nonsupport serious enough to warrant criminal action against him?
- Even if he has committed a crime, would it be wise for Ms. Miller to ask the district attorney to prosecute?
- Is there any danger of further criminal acts by her husband? If so, what can be done, if anything, to prevent them?

Divorce/separation/annulment law

- What does Ms. Miller want?
- Does she know what her husband wants to do?
- Does she have grounds for a divorce?
- Does she have grounds for an annulment? (Were the Millers validly married?)
- Does she have grounds for a judicial separation?
- Does Mr. Miller have grounds for a divorce, annulment, or judicial separation against his wife?

Law of custody

- Does Ms. Miller want permanent custody of all three children? (Is she the natural mother of all three? Is he their natural father? Are there any paternity problems?) Will Mr. Miller want custody? What is the lifestyle of the parent or parents seeking custody? Is joint custody an option?
- If she does not want a divorce, annulment, or judicial separation, how can she obtain custody of the children?
- Does she want anyone else to be given temporary or permanent custody of any of the children (e.g., a relative)? Will such a person make a claim for custody *against* Ms. Miller?

Support law

- Is Mr. Miller adequately supporting his wife?
- Is he adequately supporting the three children?
- Can Ms. Miller obtain a court order forcing him to support them while she is deciding whether she wants to terminate the marital relationship?
- If she files for divorce, annulment, or judicial separation, can she obtain a temporary support order while the case is in progress?
- If she files for divorce, annulment, or judicial separation and loses, can she still obtain a support order against him?
- Would a support order do any good? Does Mr. Miller have assets (personal property or real property) against which a support order can be enforced?
- If he cannot be relied upon for support and she cannot work, does she qualify for public assistance?

Contract/agency law

- While she is living apart from her husband, can she enter into contracts with merchants for the purchase of food, clothing, furniture, transportation, etc., and make *him* pay for them?

■ Has she already entered into such contracts?

■ Has she ever worked for him or otherwise acted as his agent?

■ Has he ever worked for her or otherwise acted as her agent?

■ Have the children (particularly the older child) entered into any contracts under their own names? If so, who is liable for such contracts? Can they be cancelled or disaffirmed?

Real and personal property law

■ Do either or both of them own any real property, e.g., land? If so, how is the real property owned? Individually? As tenants by the entirety? Who provided the funds for the purchase?

■ What rights does she have in his property?

■ What rights does he have in her property?

■ What is his income? Can his wages be garnished? What pension rights does he have?

■ What other personal property exists—cars, bank accounts, stocks, bonds, furniture? Who owns this property?

Tort law

■ Has he committed any torts against her (e.g., assault, conversion)?

■ Can one spouse sue another in tort?

Civil procedure/conflict of law

■ If a court action is brought (e.g., divorce, custody, separate maintenance), what court would have jurisdiction? A court in this state? A court in the state where he resides?

■ How can service of process be made?

■ If she sues and obtains a judgment in this state, can it be enforced in another state?

Evidence

■ What factual claims will Ms. Miller be making, e.g., that Mr. Miller has money that could be used to support the family?

■ What testimonial evidence (oral statements of witnesses) exists to support her claims?

■ How much of this evidence is admissible in court?

■ How much of the admissible evidence is likely to be believed by a judge or jury?

■ What other relevant evidence should be pursued, e.g., documentary evidence such as marriage and birth certificates, records of purchases?

■ Whose depositions should be taken, if any?

Juvenile law

■ Can a neglect petition be brought against Mr. Miller? Against Ms. Miller?

- Why is she upset about her eldest son? Has he committed any "acts of delinquency"? How old is he?
- Is he a Person in Need of Supervision (PINS)?

Tax law

- Have Mr. Miller and his wife filed joint tax returns in the past?
- Are there any refunds due (or money owed) on past returns?
- In a property settlement following a divorce or separation, what would be the most advantageous settlement for Ms. Miller from a tax perspective?
- What arrangement might Mr. Miller seek in order to obtain the best tax posture? What is negotiable? What will he be willing to give up in order to obtain his tax objectives? Will he, for example, cooperate in allowing her to have sole custody of the children in exchange for her cooperation in ensuring that his alimony payments are deductible?

Estate law

- Do they both have their own wills? If so, who are the beneficiaries? If there is no divorce, can he leave Ms. Miller out of his will entirely?

Professional responsibility/ethics

- Is Mr. Miller represented by counsel? If so, can we contact Mr. Miller directly, or must all communications to him be made through his attorney? If he is not yet represented, are there limitations on what we can and cannot say to him?
- If Ms. Miller can find her eldest son, can she simply take him away from her husband when the latter is not around? Would this be illegal? What is the ethical obligation of an attorney whose client is about to do something illegal?

Miscellaneous

- Can Mr. Miller be forced to pay her legal fees that grow out of present and future difficulties together?

The purpose of this book is to examine many of the above questions that could arise in a case such as *Miller v. Miller*. More specifically, the purpose is to equip you with the skills needed to be able to raise and to answer such questions that could arise in your state.

Section B. The Skills Assignments: General Instructions

The study of law should always have two components:

- *Knowledge* of what the law is
- *Skills* to use that knowledge on behalf of clients as part of a legal service delivery team

Knowledge without skills is as useless (and as potentially dangerous) as skills without knowledge. To help you develop such skills, this book provides various *assignments* throughout, the nature of which will be discussed later in this chapter. Many of these assignments will ask you to examine some law books containing family law material such as:

manuals	formbooks
codes	digests
encyclopedias	treatises

One of our major objectives is to increase your ability to use such books. Indeed, they constitute the entire subject matter of chapter 2.

In the practice of family law, the lawyer and the paralegal would use these materials to:

- Find a standard form in a practice book that will have to be adapted to the needs of a current client.
- Check the court rules to determine how many days a client has to file a court document.
- Check the state statutory code to determine the grounds for a divorce.
- Find case law to determine whether your state courts have ever rendered a decision on a set of facts similar to the facts of a current client.
- (etc.)

The assignments in this book are designed to train you to accomplish such tasks while you are studying the basic principles of family law.

Each law book (or set of law books) has its own peculiar features. Unfortunately, a common feature of many books is the poor organization of the material in them. *If, however, you are able to use the index and the table of contents of these books, 70 percent of the battle has been won.* Using the index and the table of contents is a skill in itself. The CARTWHEEL (Exhibit 1–1) is a technique designed to assist you in acquiring this skill. Its objective can be simply stated: to develop in you the habit of trying to phrase every word involved in the client's problem *fifteen to twenty different ways!* When you go to the index or table of contents of a law book, you naturally begin looking up the words and phrases that you think should lead you to the relevant material in the book. If you do not find anything on point, two conclusions are possible.

- There is nothing on point in the law book.
- You checked the wrong words in the index and table of contents.

Most people make the mistake of coming to the first conclusion. Nine times out of ten, though, the second conclusion is accurate. The solution is to phrase a concept in as many different ways and in as many different contexts as possible. Hence, the CARTWHEEL.

Suppose that the problem of the client involved, among other things, a wedding. The structure of the CARTWHEEL for this example is illustrated in Exhibit 1–1.

The first step would be to look up the word "wedding" in the index and table of contents of any law book. Assuming that you are not successful with this word (either because the word is not in the index and table or because

☐ **EXHIBIT 1–1** The CARTWHEEL: using the index and table of contents of law books

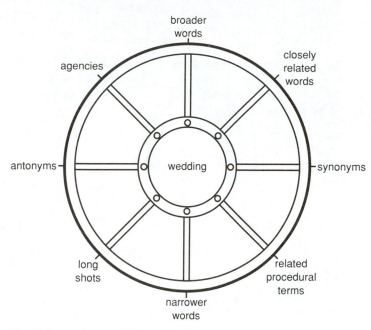

1. Identify all the *major words* from the facts of the clients's problem, e.g., wedding (most of these facts can be obtained from the intake memorandum written following the initial interview with the client). Place each word or small set of words in the center of the CARTWHEEL.
2. In the index and table of contents, look up all of these words.
3. Identify the *broader* categories of these major words.
4. In the index and table of contents, look up all of these broader categories.
5. Identify the *narrower* categories of these words.
6. In the index and table of contents, look up all of these narrower categories.
7. Identify all *synonyms* of these words.
8. In the index and table of contents, look up all of these synonyms.
9. Identify all of the *antonyms* of these words.
10. In the index and table of contents, look up all of these antonyms.
11. Identify all *closely related* words.
12. In the index and table of contents, look up all of these closely related words.
13. Identify all *procedural* terms related to these words.
14. In the index and table of contents, look up all of these procedural terms.
15. Identify all *agencies*, if any, which might have some connection to these words.
16. In the index and table of contents, look up all of these agencies.
17. Identify all *long shots*.
18. In the index and table of contents, look up all of these long shots.

Note: The above categories are not mutually exclusive.

☐ A paralegal in the
law library

the page or section references after the word in the index and table do not
lead you to relevant material in the body of the book), the next step is to think
of as many different phrasings and contexts of the word "wedding" as possible.
This is where the eighteen steps of the CARTWHEEL can be useful.

If you applied the steps of the CARTWHEEL to the word "wedding,"
here are some of the words and phrases that you would check:

1. *Broader words:* celebration, ceremony, rite, ritual, formality, festivity, etc.

2. *Narrower words:* civil wedding, church wedding, golden wedding, proxy
wedding, sham wedding, shotgun marriage, etc.

3. *Synonyms:* marriage ceremony, nuptial, etc.

4. *Antonyms:* alienation, annulment, divorce, separation, legal separation,
judicial separation, etc.

5. *Closely related works:* matrimony, marital, conjugal, domestic, husband,
wife, bride, license, anniversary, custom, children, blood test, premarital, spouse,
relationship, family, home, consummation, cohabitation, sexual relations, betrothal, minister, wedlock, oath, contract, community property, name change,
domicile, residence, etc.

6. *Procedural terms:* action, suit, statute of limitations, complaint, discovery,
defense, petition, jurisdiction, court, superior court, county court, etc.

7. *Agencies:* Bureau of Vital Statistics, County Clerk, Department of Social
Services, License Bureau, Secretary of State, Justice of the Peace, etc.

8. *Long shots:* dowry, common law, single, blood relationship, fraud, religion,
illegitimate, remarriage, antenuptial, alimony, bigamy, pregnancy, gifts, chas-
tity, impotence, incest, virginity, support, custody, consent, paternity, etc.

As indicated in the chart, there may be some overlapping of categories; they are not mutually exclusive. Also, it is not significant whether you place a word in one category or another so long as the word comes to your mind as you comb through the index and table of contents. The CARTWHEEL is, in effect, a *word association game* that should become second nature to you with practice. Perhaps some of the word selections in the above categories seem a bit far-fetched. You will not know for sure, however, whether a word will be fruitful until you try it. Be imaginative, and take some risks.

Assignment 1.1

Cartwheel the following words:

(a) cruelty

(b) support

(c) paternity

Assignment 1.2

(a) The statutory code of your state probably has a number of different statutes that deal with "children." Use its indexes and tables of contents to help you find as many of these as you can (up to a maximum of ten). Use the CARTWHEEL to help you think of many different phrasings and contexts for the word "children." Give a brief summary of what each statute says about children.

(b) Repeat the above assignment for the word "woman."

Throughout the chapters of this book, you will find twelve major kinds of skill assignments:

On the pages where these assignments are found, you will be given *specific instructions.* In addition, a set of *general instructions* will be available for each of the twelve categories of assignments. These general instructions are in chapter one and will be discussed next. Hence, throughout the remaining chapters of this book, you will be referred back to this chapter for *general instructions* for all assignments.

☐ Some typical state
statutory codes

☐ **State-Code Assignment**

A great deal of family law grows out of the statutory law of your state written by your state legislature. This law will be found within a multi-volume state statutory code.

It is important that you become acquainted with the family law sections of your statutory code. Many of the assignments in the chapters of this book ask you to examine this code on a particular family law topic.

The general instructions for all statutory code assignments are as follows:

☐ General Instructions
for the State-Code
Assignment

 General Instructions for the State-Code Assignment

1. The first step is to make sure that you know the name and location of the statutory code for your state. Some states have more than one code—each from a different publisher.
2. Be sure that you are using the latest edition of the state code.
3. Use the CARTWHEEL technique (page 7) to help you use the various indexes and tables of contents in the code. (There is often a general index at the end of the code volumes as well as smaller indexes after each volume or set of volumes covering the same topic area.)
4. Statutes can be changed or repealed, and new statutes can be added. Be sure that you are aware of such modifications by:
   ■ Checking the pocket part, if any, of every volume you use
   ■ Checking replacement volumes, if any
   ■ Checking supplement volumes or pamphlets, if any

- Shepardizing the statute. To *shepardize* a statute means to go to the set of *Shepard's Citations* covering your state code and examine all of the references provided on your statute, e.g., amendments, repeals, opinions interpreting the statute. Find the citation of your statute in black bold print within each pamphlet and bound volume. The references, if any, will be found in columns immediately beneath the citation of your statute.

5. Give a complete citation to every statute that you think covers the assignment. Ask your teacher to explain the standard citation format used in your state. It will often include components such as:
   - The title or chapter number of the statute
   - The abbreviated name of the code
   - The section number of the statute
   - The subsection number, if any
   - The date of the code (use the date you find on the spine of the volume, or the date you find on the title page, or the latest copyright year—in this order of preference).

6. When you quote from a statute, always put quotation marks around the language you are quoting.

7. If the assignment asks you to apply the statute to the facts of a problem in the assignment, follow the General Instructions for the Legal-Analysis Assignment, page 24.

8. When you need help in understanding a statute, use the following approaches:
   - See if there are definition statutes that define some of the words in the statute you are examining (if such definition statutes exist, they will usually precede the statute you are examining at the beginning of the cluster of statutes on that topic.)
   - Examine cases that have interpreted the statute. You can obtain leads to these cases, if any exist, by checking the *Notes to Decisions,* which are summaries of cases and are found immediately after the text of the statute in annotated editions of the code. (*Annotated* simply means organized by subject matter with research references such as Notes to Decisions or other commentary.) You can also find cases interpreting the statute by shepardizing the statute.

9. If you cannot find what you are looking for in the statutory code, proceed as follows:
   - Repeat step 3 above. Frequently, the difficulty is the failure to use the indexes and tables of contents creatively. Do the CARTWHEEL exercise again to try to come up with more words and phrases to be checked in the indexes and tables of contents of the statutory code.
   - Check the court rules of your state courts to determine whether they treat the topic you are pursuing.
   - Check the constitution of your state to determine whether it treats the topic you are pursuing.
   - Find out if any court opinions have been written by your state courts on the topic you are pursuing. For the techniques of finding court opinions, See General Instructions for the Court-Opinion Assignment, page 31.

Assignment 1.3

(a) What is the name of the state code of your state?

(b) Who publishes it?

(c) How is it updated? Pocket parts? Supplemental pamphlets? Both?

(d) Use the indexes of the code to find any statute on the grounds for divorce in your state. Give the citation of this statute. See instruction 5 in the General Instructions for the State Code Assignment on the information that should be included in your citation. (See also Assignment 13.1, page 372.)

(e) In addition to printing the text of the statute you have selected, what other information does the code provide about the statute, e.g., summary of cases interpreting the statute? historical data about the statute? Give an overview of the kinds of information provided.

(f) In question "c" you indicated how your code is updated. Use all of these updating features to determine whether there have been any changes in the statute you identified in question "d" since the bound volume containing the statute was published.

(g) What is the name of the set of *Shepard's* that will enable you to shepardize the statutes of your state code?

(h) Assume that your state legislature passed a statute on family law two weeks ago. Since the statute is so recent, it may not be mentioned anywhere in your state code. Later, it will be included in one of the code's updating features. Assume further, however, that you want to read this statute now. You could call the legislature and ask that a copy of the new statute be sent to you. What other ways exist in your state to obtain recently enacted statutes? Ask your librarian to help you.

☐ **Legal-Analysis Assignment**

What is legal reasoning or legal analysis? The process can be diagrammed as follows:

Facts: George and Helen are married. One day after a big argument, George walks out of the house and says, "Good-by. Find someone else to take care of you." He does this resolving to stay away forever.

Rule: One spouse *abandons* another by leaving without any intention of returning.

Application of rule to facts: When George walked out of the house resolving to stay away forever, he left "without any intention of returning." This is abandonment.

Unlike this example, however, applying a rule to the facts is often the most difficult part of legal analysis. This can be due to a number of reasons, including:

■ A word or phrase in the rule is ambiguous.

■ You feel that you need more facts than you are given.

Ambiguity in the Rule

Facts: George and Helen are married. One day after a big argument, George walks out of the apartment and says, "Goody-by. Find someone else to take care of you." He does this resolving to stay away forever. He moves downstairs to a vacant, never-used room in the same building he and his wife jointly own. The room has its own exit to the street.

Rule: One spouse *abandons* another by leaving without any intention of returning.

There is an ambiguity in the rule. What does "leaving" mean? At least two interpretations are possible:

- Moving out of the entire dwelling.
- Moving out of whatever part of the dwelling in which both spouses normally live together.

Which is the correct definition of "leaving"? The difference in the definitions is critical. Depending on which definition is adopted, a different result is reached:

- According to the first definition, George has not abandoned Helen because he did not move out of the entire dwelling.
- According to the second definition, George did abandon Helen since he moved out of the rooms where they both normally lived; under this definition, he can commit abandonment without moving out of the entire building.

Your task in legal analysis is to be sensitive to such ambiguity in the rules that you are trying to apply to facts. Unfortunately, most students are not. They do not like to search for ambiguity; they accept language at face value. To combat this tendency, you should look at every word in the rule that you are applying and ask yourself: "What is the definition of this word? Is more than one definition possible? If my initial answer is no, think harder! Am I sure that both sides of the controversy would agree on the definition of the word I am examining?"

When you are writing an interoffice memorandum or a school examination, one of the biggest mistakes you can make is to hit the reader over the head with one conclusion. Do not try to impress the readers of your analysis with its certitude and inevitability. Where ambiguity exists, find it and write about it. Good legal analysis articulates both sides of the controversy. If you personally favor one side over the other, you may state your opinion, but only after you have placed yourself in the shoes of both sides and presented the best argument for each.

Once you have identified ambiguity in the rule being applied and have carefully spelled out how each side to the controversy would handle the ambiguity, what do you do next? How do you *resolve* the ambiguity? You would have to do legal research, e.g., to find out whether any courts have interpreted any words/phrases that are ambiguous. Has a court ever defined the word "abandons" in our rule? If so, you need to find the opinion containing the definition. For purposes of the legal-analysis assignments in this book, however, you will not do any legal research unless the instructions in the assignment (or your teacher) tell you otherwise.

The Need for More Facts

In the process of trying to connect rules to facts, you may sometimes feel that more facts than those given in the assignment are needed to more accurately assess whether the rule applies. If so, state what additional facts you would like to have and *state why they may be helpful to your analysis.*

In the example involving George and Helen, suppose we are told that George said to Helen, "Good-by. Find someone else to take care of you," but we are not told whether he walked out. In your analysis you would have to point out that the facts do not state what George did immediately after he made this statement to Helen. You need additional facts. You need to know whether he left the building or any part of the building after he made the statement. The rule refers to "leaving," and you do not know whether or how he left.

Also, if the facts do not clearly show that George left with the intent of never returning, you would need additional facts to help resolve the intent issue. For example:

- Did he take his clothes with him?
- Did he speak to anyone else after he left about what he was doing?
- How far away did he go when he left?
- Did he change his address officially, e.g., at the post office?
- Did he call Helen or otherwise contact her after he left? If so, how long after he left, how often, and about what?
(etc.)

State why you need the additional facts. For example, if George took his clothes with him when he left, it would be some indication that his departure was permanent, i.e., that he had no intention of returning when he left. This should be stated as such in your legal analysis.

Analysis of Elements

One of the most important skills of legal analysis is the ability to break down any rule into its elements. An element of a rule is defined as follows.

Element

1. A *portion* of a rule that can be conveniently discussed separately from the other elements, and
2. A *precondition* of the applicability of the entire rule (if one of the elements of the rule does not apply, the entire rule does not apply).

To a very large extent, legal analysis proceeds by element analysis. Element analysis is also of major importance to the structure of a memorandum of law, as we shall see. In addition, element analysis is used as an aid in performing other tasks. For example:

- When drafting a complaint, the drafter often tries to allege enough facts to establish each element of the cause of action. (A cause of action is a legally acceptable reason for suing.)
- When a trial judge gives instructions to a jury (the charge), he or she must cover all of the elements of the cause of action and of the defenses. When counsel submits proposed instructions to the judge, the elements must likewise be covered.
- When an attorney is conducting a deposition, he or she will frequently organize the questions around the elements of the causes of action and defenses in the case.

- The organization of an exam answer will often follow the list of elements of the rules being discussed.

A major characteristic of *sloppy* legal analysis is that it does not clearly take the reader through the elements of a rule. Good analysis discusses every element, with an emphasis on the element(s) in contention. No element is passed over.

Suppose you are analyzing the following rule found in a statute:

> § 25–403.   A pharmacist must not sell prescription drugs to a minor.

Note that the rule is not broken down into elements. You must identify the elements on your own. The elements of § 25–403 are as follows:

Elements of § 24–403

1. Pharmacist
2. Selling
3. Prescription drugs
4. Minor

No violation exists unless all four elements of the statute are established.

If a pharmacist sells simple aspirin (a nonprescription drug), he or she is not liable under the statute. The third element cannot be established. Hence no violation, since one of the elements (preconditions) cannot be met.

For a number of reasons, rules such as statutes and regulations can be difficult to break into elements. For example, the rule may be long or may contain:

- lists
- alternatives
- exceptions or provisos

Nevertheless, the same process is used. You must take the time to dissect the rule into its component elements. Examine the following rule and its elements.

> **§ 5.**   While representing a client in connection with contemplated or pending litigation, a lawyer shall not advance or guarantee financial assistance to his client, except that a lawyer may advance or guarantee court costs, expenses of investigation, expenses of medical examination, and costs of obtaining and presenting evidence provided the client remains ultimately liable for such expenses.

Elements of § 5.

1. A lawyer
2. Representing a client in connection with contemplated litigation or in connection with pending litigation.
3. Advances financial assistance to his client or guarantees financial assistance to his client, except that the following is proper:
   a. lawyer advances or guarantees court costs, or
   b. lawyer advances or guarantees expenses of investigation, or
   c. lawyer advances or guarantees expenses of medical examination, or

  d. lawyer advances or guarantees costs of obtaining evidence, or

  e. lawyer advances or guarantees costs of presenting evidence,

so long as the client remains ultimately liable for all expenses ("a"–"e").

When an element is stated in the alternative, list all the alternatives within the same element. Alternatives related to one element should be kept within the phrasing of that element. The same is true of exception or proviso clauses. State them within the relevant element since they are intimately related to the applicability of that element.

In the above example, the most complicated element is the third—(3). Within it there are lists, alternatives, an exception, and a proviso. But they all relate to the same point of the propriety of financial assistance. None of the subdivisions of the third element should be stated as a separate element. You sometimes must do some unraveling of a rule in order to identify its elements. This certainly had to be done with the third element of § 5. Do not be afraid to pick the rule apart in order to cluster its thoughts around unified themes that should stand alone as elements. Diagram the rule for yourself as you examine it.

If more than one rule is involved in a statute, regulation, constitutional provision, charter, ordinance, etc., treat one rule at a time. Each rule should have its own elements, and, when appropriate, each element should be subdivided into its separate components.

Once you have broken the rule down into its elements, you have the structure of the anaylsis in front of you. Each element becomes a separate section of your analysis. You discuss one element at a time, concentrating on those that pose the greatest difficulties.

Assignment 1.4

Break the following rules into their elements:

(a) § 52. A court of this State shall not exercise its jurisdiction under this Act if at the time of filing the petition a proceeding concerning the custody of the child was pending in a court of another state exercising jurisdiction substantially in conformity with this Act, unless the proceeding is stayed by the court of the other state because this State is a more appropriate forum or for other reasons.

(b) § 10.2. With respect to a child who has no presumed father under Section 4, an action may be brought by the child, the mother or personal representative of the child, the appropriate state agency, the personal representative or a parent of the mother if the mother has died, a man alleged or alleging himself to be the father, or the personal representative or a parent of the alleged father if the alleged father has died or is a minor.

(c) § 107(b). When the mental or physical condition (including the blood group) of a party, or a person in the custody or under the legal control of a party, is in controversy, the court in which the action is pending may order the party to submit to a physical or mental examination by a physician or to produce for examination the person in his custody or legal control. The order may be made only on motion for good cause shown and upon the notice to the person to be examined and to all parties and shall specify time, place, manner, conditions, and scope of the examination and the person or persons by whom it is to be made.

In order to do legal analysis, you must identify the *legal issue*. A legal issue is simply a question. Its answer will tell whether a particular rule applies to a particular set of facts. To fail to identify the issue would be like trying to steer a ship without a rudder or to drive a car without the steering wheel: your legal analysis would drift aimlessly.

A legal issue has two components:

1. A brief quote from the element of the rule in contention
2. The major facts to which the element is being applied

In formal legal analysis, both components should be present in your statement of the legal issue.

Every element of a rule is potentially the basis of a separate issue. A rule with five elements, for example, could constitute five separate issues, each structured around whether the element applies. It is rare, however, for every element to lead to a separate issue. This is because every element of a rule will probably not be in contention. For an element to be *in contention* you must be able to make a reasonable prediction that the parties to the dispute will probably disagree on whether the element applies. If it is clear that both parties will agree on the applicability or nonapplicability of a particular element, then it would be a waste of time to construct an issue around that element and to spend time analyzing it.

At the time you write your memorandum, you may not know for certain what the other side will eventually say about the applicability of a rule. You must do your best to anticipate what your opponent might argue about the rule and any element within it.

There are two main kinds of disagreements that the parties can have about an element:

1. *Disagreement about the facts.* If you anticipate that the other side will disagree over whether the facts fit within an element, you should contruct an issue around that element. In a child custody case, for example, each parent may present numerous conflicting facts on whether it would be in the "best interest" of the child to be placed with one parent or the other. An issue clearly exists on the element of "best interest."

Sometimes fact gaps will interfere with your ability to indentify issues. (See the discussion above on the importance of articulating the need for more facts, page 13.) If, for example, a tax deduction can be taken for alimony payments, but we are not told in the problem whether the alimony was in fact paid by the ex-husband, we have a fact gap. We will not know whether there is an alimony-tax issue until we close this gap by finding out.

2. *Disagreement about definitions.* If you anticipate that the other side will disagree over the definition of an element, you should construct an issue around that element. We saw an example of this earlier when we asked whether "leaving" in the abandonment rule meant moving out of the entire dwelling or moving out of that part of the dwelling in which both spouses normally live together (page 13).

Let's return to the pharmacy example:

§ 25–403. A pharmacist must not sell prescription drugs to a minor.

Suppose the following facts are involved:

Facts: Fred Jones owns a drugstore and is a licensed pharmacist. One day he sells tetracycline to Phil, a nineteen-year-old male.

Has Fred violated § 25–403? Step one in answering this question is to break § 25–403 down into its elements:

Elements of § 25–403

1. Pharmacist
2. Selling
3. Prescription drugs
4. Minor

These elements become a checklist from which we begin to explore the presence of legal issues.

Elements 1 and 2 are not realistic candidates for legal issues. There is no reasonable doubt over whether Fred is a pharmacist and over whether he engaged in selling. The facts clearly tell us that he is a pharmacist who did make a sale.

What about element 3? Should it become the basis of a legal issue? Did Fred sell a 'prescription drug'? Is tetracycline such a drug? There is a factual gap that hinders our ability to answer the question at this point. The facts do not tell us whether tetracycline is sold over-the-counter or whether Phil purchased it by prescription. Further interviewing or investigation is needed on this factual question. This is a "next step" that should be listed at the end of the memo.

Element 4 clearly poses some ambiguity. What is a minor? Is a nineteen-year-old a minor? It is not clear. This ambiguity should prompt the preliminary draft of a legal issue:

Is a nineteen-year-old a "minor" within the meaning of § 25–403?

An alternate (more formal) phrasing of the issue would be as follow:

When a pharmacist sells tetracycline to a nineteen-year-old, has the pharmacist violated § 25–403 which prohibits sales of "prescription drugs" to "a minor"?

Every element is part of a checklist that must be examined in the above manner. If one element is glossed over, a potential legal issue may be missed. Recall again the components of a legal issue:

- A brief quote from the element in contention
- The major facts to which the element is being applied

We have just explored how you go about determining whether an element is in contention. The next question is, how do you know which facts are major? Fortunately, the process of determining when an element is in contention will also tell you which facts are major. A fact is major, and therefore should be included in the phrasing of a legal issue, when that fact raises doubt or ambiguity in your mind on whether the element is in contention. The fact that Phil is a nineteen-year-old is a major fact because this is the fact that prompted us to ask the question, what is a minor? Hence, the reason for the first phrasing of the above issue:

Is a nineteen-year-old a "minor" within the meaning of § 25–403?

Note that the fact that Phil was a male was left out of the statement of the issue. It does not appear to be relevant to the applicability of § 25–403 that the buyer is a male or female. Sex is not major, but age is.

The alternative (more formal) phrasing of the above issue does contain more facts:

> When a pharmacist sells tetracycline to a nineteen-year-old, has the pharmacist violated § 25–403, which prohibits sales of "prescription drugs" to "minors"?

More facts are included in this statement of the issue, e.g., pharmacist, selling, tetracycline. Two reasons account for phrasing the issue in this way:

- The issue raises the question of the applicability of the entire rule rather than simply one of the elements of the rule.
- The issue contains facts that provide a context to an understanding of the issue even if all of the facts are not major to the element primarily in contention.

Both reasons can justify a longer statement of a legal issue provided the issue does not become so lengthy that it is too awkward to read, and provided the added facts will not detract from the focus on the element primarily in contention. Neither of these difficulties appears present in the alternative phrasing of the issue provided above.

Examine the following statements of legal issues.

- Does § 504 apply?
- The issue is the admissibility of the confession.
- Does he have the burden of proof?

Avoid phrasing issues in this way. First, they are weak because of the absence of facts. Legal disputes do not arise in the abstract. There must be a set of facts in order for a legal dispute to exist. One cannot comprehend the issue until one knows the facts that give rise to that issue. This does not mean that the statement of the issue must contain a statement of all the facts; again, only the major facts (i.e., those that give rise to the issue) need to be stated, along with perhaps a limited number of additional facts that help give context to the issue. Second, the three statements of issues above are incomplete because they do not quote the pertinent language in the element of the rule that is in dispute (i.e., that is ambiguous) when applied to the major facts.

To summarize, the two guidelines that should govern the phrasing of issues are as follows:

1. The legal issue should contain a statement of the major facts from the problem that raise the ambiguity in the language of an element (a limited number of context facts may also be added).
2. The legal issue should also contain a brief quotation from the language of the element that is ambiguous in view of the major facts of the problem.

The components of the legal issue do not have to be stated in the above order—so long as both components are present in the legal issue.

Assignment 1.5

In each of the following situations, you are given a fact situation plus a rule in the form of a statute. Phrase the legal issue involved in each situation.

(a) *Facts:*   Smith files a complaint against Jones at the board on Wednesday. On the following Tuesday, the board serves a copy of the complaint against Jones and begins its investigation. Jones claims the investigation is improper.

Statute: § 31(b).   No investigation can be commenced by the board until it has served a copy of the complaint on the person against whom the complaint is directed within five days after the complaint has been filed with said board.

(b) *Facts:*   Jane and her two children by a former marriage receive Aid to Families with Dependent Children (AFDC). Jane's friend, Jack, who is a traveling salesperson, stays at Jane's apartment during his monthly business trips. This allows him to stay in town five to ten days at a time.

Statute: § 11351.   Whenever an unrelated adult male resides with a family applying for or receiving AFDC, he shall be required to make a financial contribution to the family which shall not be less than it would cost him to provide himself with an independent living arrangement.

One format in which you present your legal analysis to your supervisor is the interoffice memorandum of law (Exhibit 1–2).

☐ **EXHIBIT 1–2** Interoffice Memorandum

```
                    INTEROFFICE MEMORANDUM
TO:                 Mary Adams
FROM:               George Wilson
DATE:               March 13, 1990
NAME OF CASE:       Hagerty v. Hagerty
OFFICE FILE NO.:    90-49
COURT DOCKET NO.:   B-408-90
RE:                 ''Serious marital discord'' and the re-
                    fusal to seek alcoholism treatment un-
                    der § 402(b)
```

Statement of Assignment
    You have asked me to determine whether our client, Linda Hagerty, can prevent her husband from dissolving the marriage on the ground of irretrievable breakdown under § 402(b).

Issue
    Whether ''serious marital discord'' constituting an ''irretrievable breakdown'' of a marriage exists under § 402(b) when one party believes that the marriage can

Continued

☐ **EXHIBIT 1–2** Interoffice Memorandum   (Continued)

be saved if the other party seeks treatment for alcoholism which the latter refuses to do?

Facts

Paul Hagerty has filed for dissolution of the marriage on
the ground of ''irretrievable breakdown'' of the marriage.
Linda and Paul Hagerty have been married for four years. They
have two children. Paul has a serious drinking problem according to our client. While intoxicated, he breaks furniture
and is abusive to the children and his wife. She has repeatedly asked him to seek rehabilitation treatment through AA or
some other counseling service. Two months ago she told him to
leave unless he seeks treatment. He did leave but has refused
treatment. She now insists that he return and undergo treatment. He has filed for a dissolution of the marriage on the
ground of an ''irretrievable breakdown of the marriage.'' He
feels that their marriage is hopeless. Our client wants to
defend the action and prevent the dissolution.

Analysis

Section 402(b) provides as follows:

A court may make a finding that there has been an irretrievable breakdown of the marriage relationship if
the finding is supported by evidence of serious marital discord adversely affecting the attitude of the
parties toward the marriage.

Two elements must be present before a court will declare the
existence of an ''irretrievable breakdown'' of the marriage:

(1) serious marital discord;
(2) adversely affecting the attitude of the parties
toward the marriage.

Section 402(b) has been in existence for less than a year. No
case law exists defining the terms of § 402(b), and no other
statutes exist providing these definitions.

(1) Serious Marital Discord

Two definitions of the phrase are possible. Mr. Hagerty
will argue that ''serious marital discord'' exists if either
party to the marriage feels that there is no likelihood of
reconciliation. Our client, on the other hand, should argue
that both parties must agree that reconciliation is unlikely,
or at least that evidence of marital collapse must exist in
addition to the views of only one of the spouses. Under Mr.
Hagerty's definition, there is ''serious marital discord''
because one party (himself) feels that there is no likelihood of reconciliation. Our client feels that a reconciliation is likely if her husband will seek treatment for his
alcoholism.

Our client can argue that ''marital discord'' was meant
to refer to the opinions of two people--the partners to the

Continued

☐ **EXHIBIT 1–2** Interoffice Memorandum   (Continued)

marriage. The agreement of both sides on the likelihood of reconciliation is critical to a determination of whether the marriage can survive. The lack of such a likelihood in the minds of <u>both</u> spouses amounts to an ''irretrievable breakdown.''

But our client is convinced that the marriage <u>is</u> retrievable. A court should not rule otherwise when one of the parties takes this position. In her view, Mr. Hagerty is sick and is in no position to judge whether a reconciliation is possible. His refusal to seek treatment for this sickness of alcoholism should disqualify him from making meaningful assessments as to whether the marriage can survive. The legislature could not have intended that a marriage would end simply at the whim of one of the parties, particularly when the party who wants out is too ill to make a considered judgment on the likelihood of reconciliation.

She can further argue that § 402(b) does not state that either party can obtain a dissolution of the marriage simply because one of the spouses says he or she wants it. The statute calls for ''evidence'' of ''serious marital discord.'' There must be a showing of irreconcilability. This must mean that a court is required to look at the underlying evidence of whether there is hope. A mere statement by one of the parties that there is no hope is not enough ''evidence.'' More is required. The court should examine Mr. Hagerty's condition and listen to whatever expert witnesses she may be able to call. She will want an opportunity to prove through such witnesses that hope does exist because of treatment. This opportunity is destroyed if the court accepts Mr. Hagerty's statement at face value that the marriage cannot be saved. Section 402(b) calls for a more thorough probe by a court.

Mr. Hagerty, on the other hand, will argue that our client is using the wrong definition of ''serious marital discord'' for purposes of establishing an ''irretrievable breakdown.'' If <u>either</u> side feels that there is no likelihood of reconciliation, a court should find evidence of ''serious marital discord'' for purposes of establishing an ''irretrievable breakdown.'' Otherwise, one of the parties could force a dead marriage to continue out of stubbornness, unreasonableness, or malice. The legislature could not have intended such a result.

Mr. Hagerty will argue that our client told him to leave and to enter treatment. We can probably assume from the facts that Mr. Hagerty does not want to enter treatment or that he thinks treatment will not be effective. In any event, Mrs. Hagerty has laid down a condition that Mr. Hagerty says cannot be met. He will argue that to force him into treatment would be as unproductive as to force him to continue his marriage.

He will further try to argue that our client's actions demonstrate that even <u>she</u> feels that ''serious marital dis-

Continued

☐ **EXHIBIT 1–2** Interoffice Memorandum   (Continued)

cord'' exists. <u>She</u> threw him out, and <u>she</u> insisted on an unacceptable condition. She may say that she thinks the marriage is salvageable, but her actions point to the opposite
conclusion.

(2) <u>Adversely Affecting the Attitude of the Parties Toward
the Marriage</u>
    It is unlikely that this element will be in contention.
Both parties will probably argue that the difficulties have
adversely affected their views of the marriage. The phrase
''adversely affecting'' is not defined in the statute or in
any court opinions. An ''attitude'' that has been ''adversely'' affected means no more than negative feelings toward something——the marriage. Even Mrs. Hagerty cannot deny
that she has negative feelings about the marriage as a result
of the controversy surrounding alcoholism. She may not think
the marriage is hopeless, but her feelings are certainly negative as evidenced by the fact that she told him to leave the
house.
    It might be significant to note that the second element
refers to ''parties''——in the plural. The statute does not
say ''attitude of one of the parties.'' This point might bolster Mrs. Hagerty's argument on the first element that the
legislature intended <u>both</u> parties to feel that reconciliation
was not possible.

<u>Conclusion</u>
    The only element in contention will be the first. I think
that Mr. Hagerty has the stronger argument. If Mr. Hagerty
feels that the treatment for his alcoholism will not help the
marriage and if he refuses to undergo this treatment, it is
difficult to avoid the conclusion that the parties to the
marriage cannot be reconciled. The main argument favoring our
client is that the legislature may not have intended a marriage to be terminated this easily.

NEXT STEPS
    There are two things that I have not yet done on this
case:
    (1) I have not yet checked the legislative history of
§ 402(b) to determine whether it will provide any guidance on
the meaning of § 402(b).
    (2) I have not yet checked the statutes of other states
to see if they have the same language as our § 402(b). If
such statutes exist, then I need to check cases interpreting
these statutes as potential persuasive authority for our
case.

Assignment 1.6

    Bill and Pat were married in state A on March 13, 1943, where they continue to
live. They have one child, Brenda, age fifteen. Since 1950, Bill and Pat have been having

marital difficulties. Bill is a traveling salesman who spends a good deal of time away from State A. From 1951 to 1954, he did not see his family at all. He returned on February 4, 1955. He and Pat attended martial counseling sessions for about three months. By the summer of 1955, problems again arose. Bill left home. On the day he left he said to Pat, "If you can straighten yourself out, I'll consider coming back." He packed all of his clothes and books, but left behind the high school trophy he received for swimming. Although the departure was bitter, both sides agreed to maintain their joint checking account. Bill made deposits in the account. Pat wrote checks on the account to cover house expenses. In September of 1955, Bill contacted a real estate broker in State B about renting an apartment for six months in that state. The broker suggested tax advantages of buying a condominium in State B as opposed to renting. Bill was persuaded. He had been in State B only once or twice for his job, but wanted to explore the possibility of more extensive business opportunities there. On October 1, 1955, the broker called to inform Bill of a good condominium prospect in State B. On October 5, 1955 Bill was killed in an automobile accident on a highway in State B while on the way to examine the condominium for the first time.

State B wants Bill's estate to pay a state inheritance tax on the theory that at the time of death, Bill was domiciled in State B. The representative of Bill's estate disagrees and claims that Bill was domiciled in State A at the time of death.

In state B the following statute exists, which is the basis of State B's claim:

> **§ 14.**   Inheritance taxes are owed by persons who die domiciled in this state which exists when the decedent had a physical presence in the state with the intent of making the state a permanent home.

Prepare an interoffice memorandum of law on the question of State B's right to inheritance taxes. Do not do any legal research on the problem. Do the memo solely on the basis of the information provided above.

The office file number is 82-421. There is no court docket number since no court action has yet been initiated. The Tax Department of State B has taken the position that inheritance taxes are due under § 14.

The law office where you work has been retained by the representative of Bill's estate, who does not want to pay the inheritance tax to State B. Since the inheritance tax rate for State A is lower than for State B, it would be to the advantage of the estate to obtain a ruling that at the time of death, Bill was domiciled in State A.

For purposes of this assignment, you can assume following definitions apply:

- *Physical presence:* actually being in a place
- *Intent of making the state a permanent home:* the desire to live in the state indefinitely; the place to which one intends to return when away (a person can have only one permanent home)

☐ General Instructions for the Legal-Analysis Assignment

General Instructions for the Legal-Analysis Assignments

1. The starting point in the legal-analysis exercise is a set of facts referred to in the assignment. It is to this set of facts that you must apply the rule or rules.

2. How do you find the rule or rules to apply to the facts?
   - By examining the text of the chapter immediately preceding the assignment

■ By examining the state code of your state—if you are told to do so in the assignment.

3. Carefully examine each word/phrase in the rule being applied. Break the rule into its elements, and concentrate on those elements in contention.

4. Define each important word/phrase in each element.

5. Determine whether more than one definition exists for each important word/ phrase.

6. If more than one definition is possible, state each definition and show what effect the different definitions would have on the result of the analysis. How would each side use the definition that is favorable to itself?

7. State the legal issue(s).

8. Carefully examine each of the facts given to you in the assignment.

9. Note any differences in the fact situation given in the assignment with comparable fact situations discussed in the text of the chapter immediately preceding the assignment. You will have to assess for yourself whether such fact differences are significant.

10. If you determine that you need more facts to provide the analysis, state what facts you need and why you would like to have the additional facts. Specifically, how will the additional facts assist in completing the analysis?

11. Analyze the facts from the perspective of both sides. Do not be dogmatic in your analysis. Whenever possible, show how the facts might be interpreted differently by both sides.

12. Give your answers in the format of an interoffice memorandum of law as presented in Exhibit 1–2 on page 20.

13. Do not do any legal research on the assignment unless you are specifically instructed to do so; e.g., see instruction 2 above.

☐ Complaint-Drafting Assignment

A complaint (Exhibit 1–3) is a document filed in court by a party suing another party that states a grievance—called a *cause of action*—against the other party. When this document is filed in court and served on the other party, the litigation has formally begun. A cause of action is simply a legally acceptable reason for suing. In many of the assignments of this book, you will be asked to draft a complaint.

General Instructions for the Complaint-Drafting Assignment

☐ General Instructions for the Complaint-Drafting Assignment

1. Your objective is to draft a complaint that would be acceptable to a trial court in your state.

2. Go to your state statutory code and read everything you can about complaints in general and about complaints involving divorce and other domestic relations matters in particular. To help you find material in the statutory code, use the CARTWHEEL technique, page 7.

3. Go to the court rules of the courts of your state and read everything you can about complaints in general and about complaints involving divorce and other domestic relations matters in particular. To help you find material in the court rules, use the CARTWHEEL technique.

4. Some state codes and court rules have standard form complaints which may be helpful. Caution, however, must be exercised in using standard forms. See How to Avoid Abusing a Standard Form, page 28.

5. Many states have practice manuals, formbooks, or other practice materials written by attorneys. On identifying such texts for your state, see infra page 48. These materials often contain standard form complaints which may be helpful. See How to Avoid Abusing a Standard Form.

6. In the complaint-drafting assignments of this book, you will often need additional facts in order to do the complaint, e.g., the names of the parties, their addresses, the docket number of the case, some of the basic facts that prompted the plaintiff to file the complaint, etc. You can make up the facts that you need so long as your facts are consistent with the limited facts that are provided in the assignment.

7. Normally, the caption of the complaint contains:

   ■ The name of the court

   ■ The parties' names and litigation capacity (plaintiff, defendant, etc.)

   ■ The docket number assigned by the court

   ■ The title of the pleading (complaint for . . .)

8. Each paragraph is usually numbered separately. The content of each paragraph should be limited to a single allegation or to a small number of allegations that are closely related.

9. Find out what the commencement or beginning of the complaint should contain (see instructions 1–5 above). Some states require a citation to the statute giving the court subject-matter jurisdiction (its power to hear this kind of case—see page 395) and a statement of basic facts that cover the residency of the plaintiff and the existence of a marriage.

10. The body of the complaint contains a statement of the plaintiff's cause of action. In a divorce action, for example, this would consist of the facts constituting the grounds for the divorce.

11. The cause of action should be stated briefly and concisely. Avoid long recitations of the facts.

12. You cannot draft a complaint unless you know every component or element of the cause of action. For a divorce on the ground of separation, for example, there must be a voluntary living apart for a designated period of time, and the . time apart must be consecutive. There should be allegations of fact in the complaint that cover each of these elements of the ground.

13. With the exception of the citation to the statute on subject-matter jurisdiction referred to above in instruction #9, you do not give citations to statutes, court rules, or opinions in the complaint. Limit yourself to the statement of facts—the essential facts.

14. If you are not sure of a fact, you can state it "on information and belief."

15. If the plaintiff has more than one cause of action or theory of recovery, you should state all of them. Each should be separately stated and numbered, I, II, III, etc. Each separate theory or cause of action is called a *Count*.

16. The prayer for relief should contain everything the plaintiff is asking the court to do.

17. The verification is a sworn statement that the contents of the pleading are true.

☐ **EXHIBIT 1–3** The basic structure of a complaint

Caption

STATE OF _____
COUNTY OF _____
FAMILY COURT BRANCH

Mary Smith, Plaintiff
        v.   Civil Action No. _____

Fred Smith, Defendant

Commencement

                    COMPLAINT FOR ABSOLUTE DIVORCE

The plaintiff, through her attorney, alleges:

    (1) The jurisdiction of this court is based upon section _____ , title _____ of the State Code (1978).

    (2) The plaintiff is fifty years old.

    (3) The plaintiff is a resident of the State of _____ , County of _____ . She has resided here for five years immediately preceding the filing of this complaint.

    (4) The parties were married on March 13, 1973 in the State of _____ , County of _____ .

Body

    (5) There are no children born of this marriage.

    (6) The plaintiff and defendant lived and cohabitated together from the date of their marriage until February 2, 1988 at which time they both agreed to separate because of mutual incompatibility. This separation has continued voluntarily and without cohabitation for more than two years until the present time.

    (7) Since the separation, the plaintiff has resided at _____ _____ , and the defendant has resided at _____ .

    (8) There is no reasonable likelihood of reconciliation.

WHEREFORE, the plaintiff PRAYS:

Prayer For Relief

(1) For an absolute divorce.

(2) For alimony and a division of property.

(3) For restoration of her maiden name.

(4) For reasonable attorney's fees and costs.

(5) For such other relief as this Court may deem just and proper.

_____   _____

Linda Stout   Mary Smith, Plaintiff

Attorney for Plaintiff
234 Main St.
_____ , _____ 07237

Verification

STATE of _____
COUNTY of _____

    Mary Smith, being first duly sworn on oath according to law, deposes and says that she has read the foregoing complaint by her subscribed and that the matters stated therein are true to the best of her knowledge, information and belief.

                                      _____

                                      Mary Smith

Subscribed and sworn to before me on this _____ day of _____ , 19 _____ .

                                      _____

                                      Notary Public

My commission expires _____

You will often have the need to check a *standard form* before you begin your own drafting. This can be useful so long as you know how to avoid abusing the form.

A standard form is a frequently used format for a document or instrument, e.g., pleading, contract, or other agreement. Standard forms are found in a number of places, including formbooks, manuals, practice texts, some statutory codes, some court rules. Many legal stationery stores print and sell them. Most are written by private attorneys. Occasionally, however, a standard form will be written by the legislature or by the court as the suggested or required format to be used.

Considerable care must be exercised in the use of standard forms. They can be very deceptive in that they appear to require little more than a filling in of the blanks, whereas, intelligent use of the forms usually requires much more. The guidelines in the following list should be kept in mind.

How to Avoid Abusing a Standard Form

1. The cardinal rule is to *adapt* the form to the particulars of the client's case on which you are working.

2. Do not be afraid of changing the printed language of the form if you have a good reason for doing so. Whenever you make such a change, bring it to the attention of your supervisor for approval.

3. Forms often have boilerplate language, e.g., "wherefore," "hereinafter," "party of the first part." You should know the difference between essential language and such boilerplate.

4. You should never use a standard form unless and until you have satisfied yourself that you know the meaning of every word and phrase on it, whether it is boilerplate or essential. The great temptation of most form users is to ignore what they do not understand because the form has been used so often in the past without any apparent difficulty. Do not give in to this temptation. Find out what everything means by:
   - Asking your supervisor
   - Asking other knowledgeable people
   - Doing other legal research
   - Using a legal dictionary

5. You need to know whether the entire form or any part of it has ever been litigated in court. To find out, you must do legal research in the area of the law relevant to the form.

6. Once you have found a form that appears useful, look around for another form that covers the same topic. Analyze the different forms available. Which one is preferable? Why? The important point is to keep questioning the validity of the form. Be very skeptical about the utilization of any form.

7. Do not leave any blank spaces on the form.

8. If the form was written for another state, be sure that it is adapted to the law of your state.

9. Occasionally you may go to an old case file to find a document in that file that might be used as a model for a similar document that you need to draft on a current case. All of the above cautions apply equally to the adaptation of documents from closed case files.

☐ Looking for "model" documents in the closed case files

☐ Agreement-Drafting Assignment

Several times in this book, you will be asked to draft an agreement, e.g., a separation agreement. The general instructions on this assignment follow:

General Instructions for the Agreement-Drafting Assignment

☐ General Instructions for the Agreement-Drafting Assignment

1. You will need additional facts in order to draft the agreement, e.g., you may need the names of the parties, their addresses, the property they own, how they own it, other economic facts. There are two ways in which you will obtain these facts:

   ■ Conduct a mock legal interview of fellow students according to the guidelines in the General Instructions for the Interview Assignment, page 36.

   ■ Make up any of these facts that you need, provided they are reasonable within the context of the circumstances of the assignment.

   Your instructor will let you know which option to take.

2. It is always useful to obtain copies of similar agreements that were written in the past for other clients and/or to obtain copies of model agreements commonly found in formbooks, manuals, practice books, etc. Such material may provide effective starting points for your own drafting. Caution, however, must be exercised in using such material. See How to Avoid Abusing a Standard Form, page 28.

3. It is critical that you know the law of the area covered by the agreement. What can and cannot be accomplished by the agreement? What legal pitfalls must be avoided? Research in the area of the law, therefore, is an essential precondition of drafting.

4. For purposes of the agreement-drafting assignments in this book, however, you do not have to do any legal research unless your instuctor tells you to do so. You should find all the law that you need by reading the chapter text immediately preceding the drafting assignment you are doing.

5. When tax considerations are relevant, they should be taken into consideration in drafting the agreement.

6. Know what the client wants to accomplish by the agreement. Know the specific client objectives. (See instruction 1 above on how to obtain such facts.) It is too general, for example, to say that the client wants to divide the property of the spouses in an equitable manner. A more specific and acceptable example of an objective would be to have the other spouse use the vacation home for ten years or until she remarries, whichever occurs earlier. Have all the specific objectives in mind when you draft. Each clause in the agreement should relate to one or more of the objectives. Your drafting guide is your statement of objectives.

7. At the beginning of the agreement, label the kind of agreement that it is, e.g., *Separation Agreement.* Also at the beginning, state the names and addresses of the parties entering the agreement.

8. Number each paragraph consecutively (1, 2, 3, etc.). Limit the subject matter of each paragraph to a single topic or to closely related topics. Be as narrow as possible in selecting the topic of a paragraph. For example, in a separation agreement dealing with the disposition of the property that the spouses accumulated during the marriage, each paragraph should cover a separate category of property. Similarly, there should be separately numbered paragraphs covering custody of the children, visitation rights, alimony, etc.

9. A major mistake made by drafters is to assume that everyone will have the same definition of words. Major words should always be defined. A *major word* is any important word that could have more than one meaning. The word "property," for example, has several meanings, e.g., real property, personal property, property in one's possession now, property to be received in the future, etc. What meaning did the parties intend for the word, "property"? Such words should be carefully defined in the agreement.

10. One sign of an effective agreement is fairness. It does not make much sense to try to take unfair advantage of the other side in the drafting of the agreement since the result may be an unworkable agreement leading to considerable delay, animosity, and litigation expense. The cooperation of both sides is necessary to make the agreement work. An important incentive to such cooperation is a feeling of both parties that the agreement is fair.

☐ Court-Opinion Assignment

There are two reasons why you need to know how to locate court opinions on family law topics:

- To find the *common law*, which is judge-made law created in the absence of controlling statutory law. A considerable amount of family law comes from the common law.

- To find court opinions that have interpreted statutes on family law.

General Instructions for the Court-Opinion Assignment

1. The objective of the assignment is to find opinions on the family law issue being studied. In the law library there are a number of books that can provide you with leads to such opinions. The major leads (which will be explained in greater detail below) are:

   ■ Notes to decisions found within most statutory codes

   ■ The state digest or the regional digest covering opinions of your state, or the American Digest System

   ■ *American Law Reports*

   ■ Footnote references in formbooks, hornbooks, manuals, legal encyclopedias, legal periodical literature, etc.

   ■ *Words and Phrases*

   ■ Attorneys and paralegals experienced in family law

2. You may not be familiar with all the law books mentioned above. If that is the case, do not wait for a course in legal research before starting to learn how to use them. Start *now* by asking questions about the books. Ask librarians, fellow students, teachers, practicing attorneys, and paralegals, etc. Above all, browse through them as often as you can. With a little practice and determination, you will soon be able to obtain basic information from the books.

3. Notes to Decisions. To know how to use these Notes to Decisions, you must first know how to use a statutory code. (Review the General Instructions for the State-Code Assignments, page 10). The Notes contain summaries of opinions that have interpreted statutes. Hence in order to find these Notes you must first find a statute that covers the topic under examination. If opinions exist interpreting this statute, they will be summarized in the Notes to Decisions following the statute. Be sure to check for more recent Notes in the pocket parts of the code. If the Notes covering a particular statute are extensive, an index to the Notes is often included.

4. Digests. Digests are volumes of small paragraph summaries of court opinions. A digest is, in effect, a massive index to court opinions and are consequently often called "case finders." There are three kinds of digests—all of which contain the same basic material and format:

   ■ State Digest. Most states have their own digests, i.e., small paragraph summaries of all the opinions written by courts in a particular state.

   ■ Regional Digest. There are a number of regional digests covering the opinions written by the state courts of several neighboring states. If you have access to such digests, find out if there is one that covers the opinions of your state courts.

   ■ American Digest Systems. This is the most comprehensive digest of all, covering the opinions of almost every court in the county. Under a digest topic and number, you will find summaries of opinions organized alphabetically by state. Under any such topic and number, look for the abbreviation of your state.

   Whatever digest you use, your starting point should be the indexes (e.g., the Descriptive Word Index volumes) of the digest. To use these indexes effectively, apply the CARTWHEEL technique.

5. *American Law Reports.* These volumes contain the full text of selected court opinions plus extensive research material following the opinions. This material is called an *annotation.* Within these annotations there often is a state-by-state breakdown of the legal issues treated in the annotation. Hence, when you find an annotation on a family law topic, you can look for court opinions from your state on that topic. There are several units of the *American Law Reports* volumes: ALR, ALR2d, ALR3d, ALR4th, and ALR Fed. Each unit has its own index features. For all these indexes, use the CARTWHEEL technique to gain access to the volumes.

6. Footnote references in other books. Often the most valuable part of formbooks, hornbooks, manuals, legal periodical literature, and legal encyclopedias are the footnotes. These footnotes usually give citations to court opinions on the topics being discussed in the body of the text. Use the CARTWHEEL technique to find discussions in these books on the family law topic you are examining. Once you find such discussions, see if there are any footnotes provided, and if so, see if there are any references (citations) to court opinions of your state. In a set of books that has extensive footnotes, such as either of the major legal encyclopedias (*Corpus Juris Secundum* and *American Jurisprudence 2d*), the courts opinion references in the footnotes may be organized alphabetically by state, which will make it easier for you to determine if opinions of your state are provided.

7. *Words and Phrases.* This is a multi-volume set of books containing thousands of definitions of legal terms. The definitions are quotations from court opinions. Try to find definitions of words from court opinions of your state on the family law topic under examination.

8. Experienced Attorneys and Paralegals. Never be reluctant to go to attorneys and paralegals in the field of family law to ask them for a lead to a court opinion of your state on a particular topic or to ask them for suggestions on how you might go about finding such an opinion. (For purposes of the assignments in this book, do not seek such suggestions until after you follow instructions 3–7 above on your own).

Assignment 1.7

Answer the following questions by going to the nearest large law library to which you have access (on locating libraries, see page 45):

(a) Give the name of every reporter in the library that will obtain the full text of court opinions written by state courts of your state. Who publishes each reporter? What courts are covered in each?

(b) Give the name of every digest that will provide small paragraph summaries of the court opinions of your state.

(c) Go to one of the digests you mentioned in "b" above. Use the index features of this digest to locate a key topic and number for *any* five family law subjects. (Select five different subject areas.) What are the key topics and numbers? Give the cite of the first opinion summarized under each key topic and number you have selected.

☐ **Checklist-Formulation Assignment**

It is important that you learn how to write checklists that could become part of a manual. Every rule that you are told about or that you read about can be "translated" into a checklist. Checklist formulation should eventually become second nature to you. The sooner you start thinking in terms of do's, don'ts, tasks, etc., the better.

Suppose that you have before you the following statute of your state:

§ 1742. No marriage shall be solemnized without a license issued by the county clerk of any county of this state not more than thirty days prior to the date of the solemnization of the marriage.

One way to handle this statute is to create a checklist of questions that you would ask a client in order to determine whether the statute applies. Some of the questions would be:

1. Did you have a marriage license?
2. Where did you get the license? Did you obtain it from a county clerk in this state?
3. On what date did you obtain the license?
4. On what date did you go through the marriage ceremony (*solemnization*)? (You want to determine if there were more than thirty days between the date the client received the license and the date of the ceremony.)

These are the questions that must be asked as part of a large number of questions concerning the validity of a particular marriage. If you were creating a manual, the above four questions in your checklist for § 1742 could go under the manual topic of "Marriage Formation" or "Marriage License." Most laws can be translated into checklists in this way.

To be sure, there are client checklists written by others already in existence. You will often find them in published manuals or similar practice books. Why create your own? The goal is not to come up with a substitute for those in manuals which you are encouraged to use extensively. Your checklists are intended to *supplement* those prepared by others. More significantly, two of the best ways for you to learn how to use already prepared manuals are (1) to write checklists of your own and (2) to see the connection between the law (e.g., a statute) and the guidelines and questions within a checklist. Your understanding of the checklists will be increased if you begin to see how they relate to the law itself. Thus, the emphasis placed on checklists (particularly within the assignments of this book) is intended in large measure to increase the effectiveness of your use of manuals and practice books in the area of family law.

General Instructions for the Checklist-Formulation Assignment

☐ General Instructions for the Checklist-Formulation Assignment

1. The starting point in all the checklist-formulation assignments will be a rule. The rule usually will be found within a statute or a court opinion to which you will be referred.
2. Your objective is to make a list of questions that you would ask yourself, a client, or a witness for the purpose of determining whether the rule might apply.

3. Make sure that you understand the rule. Closely analyze it. Make inquiries about what you do not understand in the rule. Consult a legal dictionary. Read closely related rules in order to see the rule you are examining in context. Read the rule again.

4. Break the rule down into elements as discussed on page 14.

5. For each element of the rule, design a question or a series of questions.

6. Every time the rule says that something must be done or that something must not be done, create a question or a series of questions designed to determine whether it was done.

7. Every time the rule imposes a precondition (i.e., *if* such and such occurs, *then* . . .), create a question or a series of questions designed to determine whether the precondition occurred.

8. Be alert to the word "and" in the rule. It usually refers to additional requirements. Create questions designed to determine whether all the additional requirements were met.

9. Be alert to the word "or" in the rule. It usually refers to alternative requirements. Create questions designed to determine which, if any, of the alternatives were met.

10. If you have been diligent in creating checklists, you will be taking major steps toward the creation of your own manual. Even if you do not create manuals, however, checklist creation is valuable as a practical way of thinking about any law. (For other components of such a manual, see the General Instructions for the Systems Assignment, page 41.)

The Fact-Gathering Assignments

The next three categories of assignments cover various facets of the fact-gathering process in the area of family law. A cardinal principle in this process is the necessity of obtaining relevant factual detail. This is achieved through a technique called *fact particularization*. Once you identify the facts collected in the case thus far, you assume that these facts are woefully incomplete. For example, they fail to give more than one version of what happened. Then you identify a large number of basic who, what, where, why, when, and how questions that, if answered, will provide as complete a picture of what happened as is possible at this particular time.

Suppose you are working on a child custody case. To particularize this case, you ask a series of questions centered on the following interrelated and overlapping clusters: participant details, incident details, place details, time details, and verification details.

1. *Participant Details.* Who is involved in the case? Obtain the names of children, parents, grandparents, other relatives, neighbors, government agency workers connected with the case, friends of the children and of the parents, teachers and ministers who know the family, employers of the parents, medical personnel who have treated the children, witnesses to specific events, etc. What does each participant know about the current and past family living conditions? How do you know? What have they said? What is the age and the educational background of each participant? Etc.

2. *Place Details.* Where do the children live? Where else have they lived? Where do they go to school, religious services, recreational activities, medical

care, cultural events, etc? For each place, give the address, how far away from home it is, how the children get there, what costs are involved, who pays them, what happens there, what the feelings of the children are about the place, what they have said about it, what other participants think about the place, etc.

3. *Time Details*. On an average day how much time do the children spend on their normal activities? When did any of the important events mentioned above occur, e.g., abuse? How long did it last? Has it occurred more than once in the past? When?

4. *Incident Details*. What happened? What events are relevant to the well-being of the children and the fitness of the parents to be guardians? Explain ordinary and extraordinary occurrences in their day-to-day lives.

5. *Verification Details*. Every fact that you have obtained has a source, e.g., the client, a record. Assume that you wanted to obtain an additional source to verify the original source of every important fact. Where would you go? Whom would you ask? What additional records would you try to obtain? How would you try to obtain them? Assess the believability of each source. Etc.

As indicated, the above categories of questions are interrelated. You will be simultaneously probing for details on people, incidents, places, dates, etc. There may be considerable overlap in your questions. This is not significant so long as you achieve comprehensiveness in factual detail, i.e., so long as you achieve factual particularity. Also, the above list of questions is just the tip of the iceberg. Scores and scores of additional questions in the same mold must be pursued. Given the complexity of human events and of human relationships, a great deal of factual detail is needed before you are able to achieve factual comprehensiveness. The objective of fact particularization is to get you into the habit of going beneath the surface in order to be able to look at people and events from a variety of perspectives. Nothing is taken at face value.

☐ **Investigation-Strategy Assignment**

In many cases, the number of facts to be gathered and verified can be enormous. To keep from becoming overwhelmed, a plan of action must be developed. The investigation-strategy assignment is designed to help you construct such a plan in order to give the investigation some direction. The instructions for this assignment are as follows:

General Instructions for the Investigation-Strategy Assignment

☐ General Instructions for the Investigation-Strategy Assignment

1. The starting point in this assignment is a set of facts on a case that you are given in the assignment. Assume that you have entered the case after these facts have been collected by someone else.

2. Assume further that these facts are inadequate because *many* more facts are needed. Review the material on fact particularization, page 34.

3. Closely, examine the facts that you have. Are they arranged chronologically? If not, rearrange them chronologically so that the facts tell a story with a beginning, middle, and end. Of course, there will be many gaps in the story. Your task will be to identify these gaps and to raise the questions that the investigator would have to ask in order to try to fill or close the gaps. These

questions will become the investigator's strategy or plan for further investigation.

4. The focus of these questions will be on what you *don't* know about the facts that you have.

5. Isolate the facts that you have into small clusters of facts, e.g., the child is unhappy, the husband left the house in a rage. For each small set of facts that you identify or isolate in this way, make a *large* list of questions that fall into two categories.

   ■ Ask questions in order to obtain additional facts that will help you compile a much more detailed picture of what happened. To aid you in this list, ask the basic who, what, where, why, when, how questions about every fact. (See material on fact particularization.)

   ■ Ask questions in order to obtain additional facts that will help substantiate (or prove) the facts that you already have.

   There is no rigid formula that you must follow in making these lists of questions. The goal is a comprehensive list of questions which, if answered, would provide a comprehensive picture of what happened.

6. Consider structuring questions to elicit details on participants, incidents, places, times, and dates.

7. Be particularly scrupulous about dates. Ask questions about the dates that you have and also about the dates that are missing.

8. In your questions on participants, try to identify a diversity of *versions*. Make a list of every person who is involved or who could be involved in the facts. Assume that each person potentially has a different version of the facts or of a critical incident or series of incidents. Structure questions that will elicit these different versions.

9. Preceding most of the assignments there will be a discussion of some legal principles or rules of law governing family law topics. Include questions on the elements of any relevant rules of law. (On breaking rules into their elements, see page 14; See also General Instructions for the Checklist-Formulation Assignment.)

10. The list of questions in this assignment does not have to be written in any particular order. Select any format that is readable.

11. In some of the chapters you will find lists of interviewing questions and investigation tasks. If these lists are relevant to the area of the assignment, expand on them. Use the lists as points of departure for further fact particularization.

□ **Interview Assignment**

The interview assignment heavily relies on some of the skills covered earlier, especially fact particularization and checklist formulation. Interviewing is deceptive in that many students feel that it is relatively easy to do. It isn't. The instructions for the interview assignment are as follows:

□ General Instructions for the Interview Assignment

General Instructions for the Interview Assignment

1. In this assignment, you are asked to interview another person, e.g., a fellow student, someone at home.

2. Review the material on fact particularization, page 407. One of your objectives is to obtain substantial factual specificity. As the interviewer, you should strive for a comprehensive picture of the people and events involved in the assignment.

3. In some of the chapters, you will find lists of interviewing questions. If the lists are relevant to the area of the assignment, expand on them. Use the lists as points of departure for further fact particularization.

4. After you complete the interview, prepare an intake memorandum from your notes. The heading of the memo should say "Intake Memorandum." Indicate who wrote the memo (you), who will receive the memo (your teacher or supervisor), the name of the person interviewed (the interviewee), the date of the interview, and the date you turned in the memo. The first paragraph of the memo should state the assignment (e.g., "You have asked me to interview (name of the interviewee) in order to (state the purpose of the interview assignment).

5. In preparation for your interview, identify every rule of law that might be relevant to the fact situation (see the discussion in the text preceding the assignment). Break down each rule into its elements (see page 14). Be sure to ask questions that are relevant to the applicability of every element. (See also the General Instructions for the Checklist-Formulation Assignment, page 33).

6. Try to arrange the facts in your intake memo in roughly chronological order so that the facts unfold as a story with a beginning, middle, and end.

7. *Instructions to Interviewee:* you can make up facts as you go along so long as the facts are reasonably consistent with the facts initially provided. Do not volunteer any information. Simply answer the questions asked.

8. Your teacher may decide to role play the interview in front of the class. If so, the class may be asked to comment on how the interview was conducted, e.g., did the interview follow the assignment, was there adequate fact particularization, did the interview ramble, was the interviewee placed at ease, how could the interview have been improved?

☐ **Interrogatory Assignment**

Interrogatories are a written set of questions addressed by one party in litigation to another before trial. The purpose of the interrogatories is to obtain factual information about the other party's case in order to prepare for trial. The instructions for the interrogatory assignment are as follows:

General Instructions for the Interrogatories Assignment

☐ General Instructions for the Interrogatories Assignment

1. Your objective in writing the questions, i.e., the interrogatories, is to obtain as much information as possible from the other side in order to assist you in preparing a case. See the material on particularizing facts, page 34. The material on preparing investigation strategies, page 35, should also be helpful in drafting interrogatories.

2. The interrogatories that you draft should be acceptable in your state, which means that you should know whatever restrictions exist in statutes and in the court rules of your state on the scope and format of interrogatories in family law cases. For example, is there a limited number of questions that can be sent?

3. The scope of questions you can ask is usually quite broad. The test is whether the question is reasonably calculated to lead to evidence that will be admissible in court. This is a much broader standard than whether the answer itself would constitute admissible evidence.

4. Avoid unduly long or oppressive interrogatories.

5. Avoid questions that violate the privilege against self incrimination (e.g., "Did you burn your house on purpose?").

6. Avoid questions that violate the attorney-client privilege (e.g., "What did you tell your attorney about the child?").

7. Avoid questions that violate the doctor-patient privilege (e.g., "What did you tell your doctor about the pain?").

8. Avoid questions that violate the husband-wife privilege (e.g., "What did you tell your wife about the pain?").

9. Avoid questions that violate the attorney work-product rule (e.g., "Does your attorney think my client has a valid claim?").

10. In many states it is permissible to ask a question that would involve the application of law to fact—sometimes called "contention interrogatories." For example, "Do you contend that Mr. _____ had no intent to marry you at the time of the wedding ceremony?" or, "Is it your position that Ms. _____ took the child out of the state in order to avoid complying with the custody decree?" If you ask such a question, be sure to follow it with a series of detailed questions that seek the factual reasons for the possible answers that could be given.

11. Be careful about the verb tense used in questions. Present tense (e.g., "is") is used to determine facts that are still current. Past tense (e.g., "was") is used to determine events that are over. If a question relates to past and present tense, break the question down into several questions.

12. It can be useful to try to find sample interrogatories in manuals, formbooks, and other practice materials. Such interrogatories, of course, would have to be adapted to the particular needs of the client's case on which you are currently working. On the dangers of using such forms, see How to Avoid Abusing a Standard Form, page 28.

13. It can also be useful to go to the closed case file of another case that contains interrogatories in order to try to adapt them. Again, the use of such materials is but a point of departure. Great care must be used in determining what, if anything, can be borrowed from other interrogatories.

14. Before you draft your interrogatories, you should know the case (on which you are working) inside and out. You should read all pleadings filed to date, e.g., complaint, answer, all the correspondences in the file, the intake memorandum, etc. Many ideas for questions will come from this knowledge. For purposes of the assignments in this book, however, you will not have access to such data since the assignments will be based on hypothetical cases.

15. Litigation involves causes of action and defenses. Each of these causes of action and defenses can be broken down into elements (page 14). Each of these elements should become the basis of a checklist. Ask questions that seek facts that could potentially be used to support each of the elements. (See also the General Instructions for the Checklist-Formulation Assignment, page 33).

16. It is sometimes useful to ask your questions in such a way that the "story" of the facts unfolds chronologically.

17. Be constantly concerned about dates, full names, addresses, exact amounts, etc.

18. Always ask what witnesses the other side intends to rely on to support its version of the facts at the trial. Ask for the names and addresses of such witnesses.

19. Ask what documentation, physical things, or exhibits the other side will rely on to support its version of the facts. You may want to ask that such items be sent

along with the answers to the interrogatories (or that such items be brought to a later deposition).

20. Avoid questions that call for simple "yes" or "no" answers unless you immediately follow up such questions with other questions that ask for details.

21. Include a definition or abbreviation section at the beginning of the interrogatories to avoid confusion and undue repetition in the later questions. This section will define words and phrases that you intend to use in more than one question. For example: "A 'medical practitioner' as used in these interrogatories is meant to include any medical doctor, osteopathic physician, podiatrist, doctor of chiropractic, naturopathic physician, nurse, or other person who performs any form of healing art."

22. Phrase the questions so that the person answering will have to indicate whether he or she is talking from first-hand knowledge, second-hand knowledge (hearsay), etc.

23. As to each fact, ask questions calculated to elicit the respondent's ability to comment on the fact, e.g., how far away was he or she, does he or she wear glasses, how long has he or she known the party, in what capacity, etc.

24. Avoid complicated and difficult-to-read questions. Be direct and concise.

☐ **Flowchart Assignment**

A flowchart is a step-by-step account of any process such as a particular kind of litigation, e.g., a divorce, or a particular kind of administrative proceeding, e.g., a workers' compensation hearing. A number of assignments in this book ask you to prepare a flowchart on the legal process under discussion. The instructions for this assignment are as follows:

General Instructions for the Flowchart Assignment

☐ General Instructions for the Flowchart Assignment

1. Design the flowchart based upon the law of your state. The chart will give an overview of how something is done in your state, e.g., how to adopt a child, how to change your name.

2. The two primary sources of information for the flow chart are your state code and the court rules for the courts in your state. See General Instructions for the State-Code Assignment page 10. See also the CARTWHEEL technique for using codes and court rules page 7.

3. It is also possible for you to obtain information for the flowchart from manuals, formbooks, and other practice material. It is recommended, however, that you try to obtain the information directly from the code and the court rules. The practice materials may be out of date. Furthermore, the intelligent use of practice materials requires that you know how to check the accuracy and timeliness of such materials by going to the primary sources—the code and the court rules (and occasionally, the state constitution).

4. The flowchart must be chronological, moving from the first step of the process to the last step.

5. The structure and graphics of the flowchart can be varied:
   - It may be presented as a series of boxes (one step per box) with all the boxes connected by arrows to show the progression of the process.
   - It may be presented in the form of a list of brief paragraphs with each numbered paragraph stating one step.

- It may be presented in the form of an outline with the major headings being the key phrases of the process, e.g., agency contact, pretrial, etc.

You will note that one of the flowcharts presented in this book is structured as numbered steps (page 422). It is not necessary that this structure be used for all the flowchart assignments. Again, use your imagination in designing the sequence of events involved.

6. The information in the flowchart must be procedural. The concern is to obtain all the mechanics of the process. The flowchart should not contain information on substantive liability matters, e.g., the definition of cruelty as a ground for divorce.

7. For each item of information in the flowchart, state your source, e.g., the citation to the statute or court rule that provided you with the procedural information you used in the flowchart.

8. Statutory codes and court rules often have sections that deal with litigation in general. Such sections are often listed in the index and tables of contents of the codes and court rules under broad topics such as "Civil Procedure," "Actions," "Court Procedures," "Courts," etc. You should check these sections to see what, if anything, they say about the topic of your flowchart.

9. In addition, there may be special sections of your statutory code and court rules that cover the procedural steps that are peculiar to the topic of your flowchart. Check these as well.

10. The major phases of litigation are as follows: pretrial; trial; appeal; and enforcement. Within these phases, the number of specific steps can be numerous. Some of the steps that you may have to cover are as follows:

- What agency, if any, has jurisdiction over the case?
- What is the application process at the agency?
- What court(s) have jurisdiction?
- How is service of process made?
- How is venue determined?
- Must any special format to be used for the complaint?
- How is the complaint served and filed?
- Must any special format be used for the answer?
- How is the answer served and filed?
- Are there any special rules for raising counterclaims?
- Are there any special motions that can be made, e.g., motion to dismiss?
- What rules govern pretrial discovery:

    deposition;

    interrogatories;

    requests for admissions;

    court ordered examinations (physical and mental)?

- What sanctions can be imposed for violation of the discovery rules?
- What preliminary orders can be requested, and how must the request be made?
- When and how can a request for a jury be made?
- What rules govern the issuing of the final judgment?
- How many days does a party have to appeal?

- What court has jurisdiction to hear the appeal?
- How can a judgment be enforced?

(etc.)

Again, the above list is not exhaustive. If there are other steps or more detailed steps that apply to the process you are flowcharting for your state, you should accurately list them.

☐ Systems Assignment

Great skill is required to design and implement an effective system. A good way to start learning this skill is to identify and describe a system (or lack of a system) in the work lives of others. The systems assignment is designed to help you make such a start. The instructions for this assignment are as follows:

General Instructions for the Systems Assignment

☐ General Instructions for the Systems Assignment

1. Your goal is to interview practicing attorneys, paralegals, and legal secretaries who handle family law cases in order to identify their system for providing legal services on a certain kind of case.

2. You are seeking the following kinds of information on the case involved in this assignment:

   - Who does what on the case? What does the attorney do? The paralegal? The secretary?
   - In what sequence is it all done?
   - How long does the process take from beginning to end? Does the time involved differ from case to case? If so, what are the main factors causing the differences?
   - What equipment, if any, is used, e.g., fax machines, computers?
   - What computer software, if any, is used, e.g., word processing, spreadsheet?
   - Are any standard forms used?
   - Are there any manuals that are particularly helpful? If so, were they written by the office or by someone else?
   - Has the office recently changed its system for handling this kind of case? What were the changes and why were they made?
   - Does anyone have any problems with how the present system works? If so, what are they and what recommended improvements are contemplated?

3. If possible, try to interview someone from another firm that handles the same kind of case so that you can compare the systems used.

4. How do you find practicing lawyers, paralegals, and secretaries in the field of family law?

   - There may be fellow classmates who are secretaries or paralegals.
   - Check with your paralegal association.
   - Check with an association of legal secretaries.
   - Ask your teacher for leads.

5. Another person who would have valuable information for this assignment is the law office manger or legal administrator of the larger firms.

6. Everyone is busy, particularly those working in a law office. You must not give the impression that you are going to take up a lot of time of the people you interview. Have a checklist of questions ready. Be prepared. Guard against giving an impression that you are not sure what you want.

☐ **Legislation-Monitoring Assignment**

Frequently your state legislature will be considering changes in the family law of your state. A paralegal may be asked to follow the progress of such proposed legislation—to monitor its ongoing status in the legislature. The following guidelines point out how you can accomplish this task as well as obtain background information on the area involved.

☐ General Instructions for the Legislation Monitoring Assignment

 General Instructions for the Legislation-Monitoring Assignment

1. Begin with the legislature. Find our what committee in each house of the legislature (often called the senate and house or assembly) is considering the proposed family law legislation. Also determine whether there are more than two committees considering the entire bill or portions of it.

2. Ask committee staff members to send you copies of the bill in its originally proposed form and in its amended form.

3. Determine whether the committees considering the proposed legislation have written any reports on it and, if so, whether copies are available.

4. Determine whether any hearings have been scheduled by the committees on the bill. If so, try to attend. For hearings already conducted, see if they have been transcribed (a word-for-word recording).

5. Find out the names of people in the legislature who are working on the bill: legislators "pushing" the bill, legislators opposed to it, staff members of the individual legislators working on the bill, staff members of the committees working on the bill.

6. The local bar association is probably interested in the bill and may have taken a position on it. Call the association and find out what committee of the bar is involved with the subject matter of the bill. This committee may have written a report on the position of the bar on the bill. If so, try to obtain a copy.

7. Is there an administrative agency of the government involved with the bill? Do any of these agencies have jurisdiction over the subject matter of the bill? If so, find out who in the agency is working on the bill and whether any written reports of the agency are available.

8. Who else is lobbying for or against the bill? What organizations are interested in it? Find out if they have taken any written positions.

9. What precipitated consideration of the bill by the legislature? Was there a court opinion that prompted the legislative action? If so, you should know what the opinion said.

10. Are any other legislatures in the country contemplating similar legislation? Some of the ways of finding out follow:

    ■ Look for law review literature on the subject matter of the bill. Check the *Index to Legal Periodicals, Current Law Index,* and the *Legal Resource Index;*

- Check loose-leaf services, if any, covering the subject matter of the bill—these services often cover proposed legislation in the various legislatures;
- Check with organizations such as bar associations, public interest groups, business associations, etc.; they often assign staff members to do this kind of state-by-state research on what the legislatures are doing. Such organizations may be willing to share this research with you;
- Find out if their is a Council of State Governments in your area—it may have done the same research mentioned in the preceding point, or it may be able to lead you to such research.

Key Chapter Terminology:

Domestic Relations Law
Cartwheel
Statutory Code
Shepardize
Citation
Annotated
Legal Analysis
Element
Element in Contention
Legal Issue
Interoffice Memorandum of Law
Complaint
Cause of Action

Standard Form
Court Opinion
Common Law
Digests
Checklists
Fact Particularization
Investigation Strategy
Legal Interviewing
Interrogatories
Flowchart
Systems
Monitoring Legislation

CHAPTER TWO

Law Books and Legal Institutions: A Guide to the Family Law of Your State

■ Chapter Outline

L aw books are critical tools of a lawyer. The same should be true of the paralegal. Since there is so much law, and since a good deal of it is changing every day, no one—including an experienced judge—can be expected know all the family law of a particular state. In a child-support case, for example, the question is not so much, "What is the law of child support?" as it is "What is the law of child support *today*?" Understanding general principles is helpful as a starting point, but more is usually needed in the actual practice of law. And the ticket of admission to current law is the law library.

In this chapter, we will cover some of the fundamentals of the law library from the viewpoint of the family law practitioner. The chapter is not intended as a substitute for a full course in legal research, nor does it assume that you have already had such a course. Rather, we will highlight some of the basics in order to reinforce what you may have learned elsewhere, or to give you a headstart on what you will be learning for the first time elsewhere.

After listing the major places where law libraries are located, we will examine the distinction between primary and secondary authority. This background will be the basis of an overview of some of the more commonly used resources in a law library. These resources will become the starting point of your bibliography of family law. Finally, we will briefly identify the kinds of courts and administrative agencies that have the ultimate responsibility of applying this law.

Section A. Finding a Law Library

The availability of law libraries depends to a large degree on the area in which you live, study, or work. Rural areas will have fewer possibilities than larger cities or capitals.

Twelve different law library possibilities are listed below. Find out which ones exist in your area. You may need permission to use some of them. (This is certainly true of a private law firm's library.) If a law school or university library is a *depository library*, it is required by law to let you use it, or at least to use those sections of the library that contain the government documents that the library receives free of charge.

- Law school library
- General university library (may have a law section)
- Law library of a bar association
- State law library (in the state capital and perhaps in branch offices in counties throughout the state)
- Local public library (may have a law section)
- Law library of a court
- Law library of the legislature or city council
- Law library of the city solicitor or corporation counsel
- Law library of a private law firm
- Law library of the district attorney or local prosecutor
- Law library of the public defender
- Law library of a federal, state, or local administrative agency (particularly in the general counsel's office of the agency)

You may have to use some ingenuity to locate these libraries and to gain access to them. Try more than one avenue of entry. Do not become discouraged when the first person you contact tells you that the library is for members or private use only. Some students adopt the strategy of walking into a library— particularly a library supported by public funds—and acting as if they belong. Rather than asking for permission, they wait for someone to stop them or to question their right to be there. Other students take the wiser course of seeking permission in advance. Yet, even here, some creativity is needed in the way that you ask for permission. The bold question, "Can I use your library?" may be less effective than an approach such as, "Would it be possible for me to use some of your law books for a short period of time for some important research that I must do?"

There is one other law library that you need to consider: your own. It is not too soon for you to start collecting your own law books, beginning with your course books on law. Never buy a practice book or manual without checking with at least two lawyers or paralegals on the *practical* value of the book. Ask them how often they consult the book. Remember, it is not necessarily wise to purchase a book simply because it treats an area of the law you need to know something about. Also be prepared for "sticker shock" when you find out what some of these books cost.

Section B. The Law Books on Family Law: Compiling A Bibliography

Two kinds of law books are relevant to family law practice: those books containing *primary authority* and those containing *secondary authority*.

Primary Authority

Primary authority is the law itself: *statutes* written by legislatures, *constitutions* written by the founders of the nation or of a state, *opinions* written by the courts, and *regulations* written by administrative agencies. What law books contain primary authority?

Statutes

Statutory codes, session laws, statutes at large, etc.

Constitutions

The beginning volumes of a statutory code

Opinions

Reporters, reports, advance sheets, loose-leaf services, etc.

Regulations

Code of the Federal Regulations (CFR) loose-leaf services

Court Rules

A volume called *Court Rules* (may also be found within the statutory code)

Secondary Authority

Secondary authority contains leads to and information about primary authority. Examples follow.

Digests

Small paragraph summaries of court opinions

Practice Manuals

Summaries of the law with an emphasis on "how-to-do-it"

Legal Encyclopedias, Hornbooks, Treatises, Law Reviews

More scholarly summaries and commentary on the law

Legal Newspapers

Current events in the local courts and other legal matters

Shepard's

This set of books will give you references to the subsequent history of opinions, statutes, constitutional provisions, etc. For example, you will be told whether an *opinion* has been cited by other opinions, whether a *statute* has been amended by the legislature or interpreted in opinions, etc.

Essential Questions to Ask about Law Books

For every law book that you use, determine the answers to the following questions.

1. What kind of primary authority does the book contain?
2. If the book contains secondary authority, who is the author and/or editor?
3. Who published the book?
4. Has there been more than one edition of the book? If so, what edition are you examining?
5. What is the latest date on the copyright page?
6. Is the book kept up to date? Through pocket parts? Through supplemental volumes?
7. If the book is part of a set, how many volumes are there in the set?
8. Is there a general index? If so, where is it located? Are there also more narrow indexes in the book? If so, where are they located?
9. Same questions as in no. 8 with reference to table of contents.
10. Are there any other tables in the book, e.g., abbreviation tables? cross-reference tables? If so, locate and describe the purpose of each.
11. Does the book contain a preface or other introductory/explanatory features? If so, where are they located, and how useful are they?

Most Important Publications for Family Law Practitioners

The most important law books that a family law practitioner should have access to are as follows:

Your State Code

The statutes of the legislature govern many aspects of the substantive and procedural law of this area. Family law statutes will probably be found in three or four volumes of your state. (See page 10 for more about using state codes.)

Court Rules

You will need access to the court rules of those courts with jurisdiction over the subject matter of family law cases. More than one state court may have this jurisdiction.

State Court Opinions and Digests

There are usually several sets of reporters containing the opinions of your state courts, particularly the highest state court. There may be an official reporter published by the state itself. In addition, there is a regional reporter published by a private company (West) containing the opinions of the highest state courts (and some lower courts) of a cluster of states in the same region of the country. You need to find out what region your state is in so that you can use that regional reporter.

Almost every state has a digest that contains small paragraph summaries of the court opinions of that state. Most of the regional reporters also have regional digests that give summaries of the opinions in their respective regional reporter. The largest digest covering every state is the *American Digest System*. You need to have access to your individual state digest, or to your regional digest (if one exists for your region), or to the *American Digest System*.

On using reporters and digests, see page 31.

Practice Manual

Many states have a general practice manual covering a variety of topics such as Family Law, Probate Law, Corporate Law, etc. There may also be an individual manual on Family Law. Such manuals usually contain practical information, e.g., forms, checklists.

Legal Newspapers

The legal newspaper gives current cases, docket calendars for local courts, news on what the legislature and bar association are doing, etc.

Descriptions of Specific Publications and Related Tools

We will now briefly examine some important publications relevant to a family law practice. These are texts that cover the law of more than one state. As you gain experience in the field, you will want to add to the list and perhaps substitute other texts for those listed here. We will also highlight a few of the widely used technological tools employed in the practice of law such as the computer database used for research.

□ *American Jurisprudence 2d (Am.Jur.2d),* published by Lawyers Co-operative Publishing Company

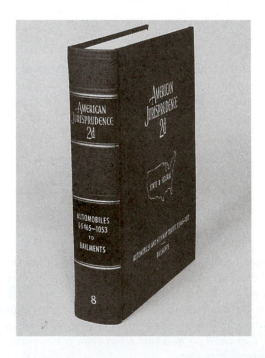

American Jurisprudence 2d (Am.Jur.2d)

This is a national encyclopedia that summarizes every major area of the law. (Its competition is *Corpus Juris Secundum*.) The encyclopedia is excellent for obtaining background information on a family law topic as well as for obtaining leads to court opinions of your state.

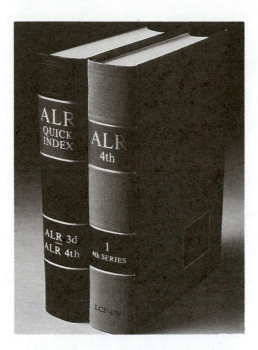

☐ *American Law Reports*, published by Lawyers Co-operative Publishing Company

American Law Reports

This is a reporter containing selected opinions followed by extensive research papers (called *annotations*) on issues within the opinions. The annotations try to cover the law of every state. There are five units to the system:

ALR	*American Law Reports*, First Series
ALR 2d	*American Law Reports*, Second Series
ALR 3d	*American Law Reports*, Third Series
ALR 4th	*American Law Reports*, Fourth Series
ALR Fed	*American Law Reports*, Federal Series

Since these volumes are so extensive, covering almost all areas of the law, you are almost certain to find at least one annotation on the family law case you are researching. Examples of such annotations follow.

"Right of child to enforce provisions for his benefit in parents' separation or property settlement agreement," 34 ALR 3d 1357.

"Award of custody of child where contest is between child's father and grandparent," 25 ALR 3d 7.

Beyond the Best Interests of the Child, by J. Goldstein, A. Freud, and A. Solnit

Beyond the Best Interests of the Child is a very influential book on child custody. A major theme of the book is the "psychological parent" vs. the biological parent (see page 323).

☐ *Community Property in a Nutshell,* by R. Mennell, published by West Publishing Company

Community Property in a Nutshell

This paperback provides an overview of the law of community property.

☐ *Corpus Juris Secundum (CJS),* published by West Publishing Company

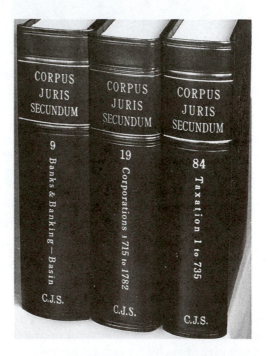

Corpus Juris Secundum (CJS)

CJS is a national legal encyclopedia that summarizes almost every area of the law. Many family law topics are included. The encyclopedia is excellent for obtaining background information on a family law topic as well as for obtaining leads to court opinions of your state through the extensive footnotes that are provided.

□ *Family Law Quarterly* and *Family Advocate*, published by the American Bar Association

Family Advocate

Family Advocate is a legal periodical of the Section of Family Law of the American Bar Association. Its emphasis is the practical dimension of a family law practice.

Family Law Quarterly

This legal periodical is published by the Section of Family law of the American Bar Association. It is devoted to topics that are relevant to the family law practitioner.

□ *Family Law Reporter*, published by the Bureau of National Affairs (BNA)

Family Law Reporter

A loose-leaf service, *Family Law Reporter* is regularly updated. It contains summaries of important family law cases from every court in the country. Supreme Court opinions are printed in full. It also reports on what the legislatures are doing in this area of the law and provides articles for the practitioner. (See photo on previous page.)

□ *Family Law Tax Guide,* published by Commerce Clearing House

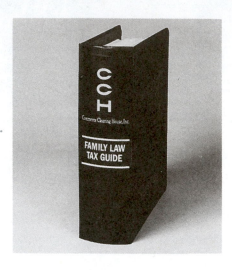

Family Law Tax Guide

This is a loose-leaf service on tax laws and strategies. In the areas of separation, divorce, estates, and gifts, the service covers the preparation of current returns as well as tax-planning ideas.

□ *Index to Legal Periodicals,* published by H. W. Wilson Company (Sample issue and page excerpt)

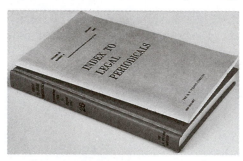

Choosing one's family: can the legal system address the breadth of women's choice of intimate relationship?. B. J. Cox. 8 *St. Louis U. Pub. L. Rev.* 299-337 '89
The justification for conciliation. J. G. Hall, D. F. Martin. 133 *Solic. J.* 1318-20 O 20 '89
La reforma del derecho de familia en España (1952 a 1987). D. Espín Cánovas. 22 *Rev. Jur. U.I.P.R.* 17-28 S '87/Ag '88
Unpacking the "rational alternative": a critical review of family mediation movement claims. M. J. Bailey. 8 *Can. J. Fam. L.* 61-94 Fall '89
The use of abstention and the automatic stay to allow state courts to decide domestic relations matters. 6 *Bankr. Dev. J.* 371-402 '89
Domestic violence
    See also
      Battered women
      Child abuse
An impossible balancing act?. M. Wright. 139 *New L.J.* 1488+ N 3 '89

Indexes: Periodicals

Legal periodicals (often called *law reviews,* or *law journals*) are an excellent source of literature on the law. They contain articles on current trends in the law, case notes on recent important court opinions, book reviews, etc. Periodicals are published by law schools, bar associations, and private companies. There are two main kinds of periodicals, specialty and general. Specialty periodicals cover one major area of law or practice. In this bibliography, we look at a number of legal periodicals on the family law speciality: *Family Advocate, Family Law Quarterly, Journal of Family Law.* General periodicals such as the *Harvard Law Review* and the *Louisiana Bar Journal* cover a much broader spectrum of legal topics, including family law.

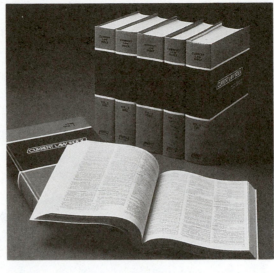

MARITAL counseling *see*
    Marriage counseling
MARITAL property
    see also
    Separate property
                    -analysis
Report from the ABA level: on the cutting edge of
    the law. by Paul J. Buser
                    26 Advocate (Idaho) 14(3) March '83
Legal recognition of unmarried cohabitation: a
    proposal to update and reconsider common-law
    marriage. by David S. Caudill
                    49 Tennessee Law Review 537-575 Spr '82
                    -cases
To have and to hold: property rights in a graduate
    degree. (case note) Saint-Pierre v. Saint-Pierre 357
    N.W.2d 250 (S.D. 1984) by Alice Rokahr
                    30 South Dakota Law Review 690-701 Summ '85
Domestic relations - contractual agreements as a
    means of avoiding equitable distribution. (case
    note) Buffington v. Buffington 317 S.E.2d 97
    (1984) by Peter M. Jennings
                    21 Wake Forest Law Review 213-241 Spr '85
                    -comparative method
Married women's rights under the matrimonial
    regimes of Chile and Colombia: a comparative
    history. by Edith E. Scott
                    7 Harvard Women's Law Journal 221-249 Spr '84
                    -economic aspects
Equal shares or fair shares in Australian family
    property law? by Frank Bates
                    Conveyancer 19-30 Jan-Feb '86
                    -evidence
Lay witnesses can value assets; how lawyers can use
    their testimony in matrimonial cases. by Arnold H.
    Rutkin and Kathleen A. Hogan
                    22 Trial 33(3) June '86
                    -law and legislation
New probate and non-probate property elections
    under Wisconsin's Marital Property Act; part 2. by
    Howard S. Erlanger and June Miller Weisberger
                    59 Wisconsin Bar Bulletin 13(6) Nov '86
                    575

□ *Current Law Index,*
published by Informa-
tion Access Company
(Sample issue and
page excerpt)

How do you find out about the literature in legal periodicals? Suppose you are researching a family law issue and you want to locate legal periodical literature on that issue.

You would turn to one of three main index systems:

1. *Current Law Index* (CLI) published by Information Access Company
2. *Index to Legal Periodicals* (ILP) published by H. W. Wilson Company
3. *Legal Resource Index* (LRI) published by Information Access Company

LRI is a microfilm version of CLI. The latter is also contained on a laser disk-computer system called InfoTrac. Unlike ILP, the other two index systems cover legal newspapers in addition to legal periodicals. Sample issues and page excerpts are included above for CLI and ILP.

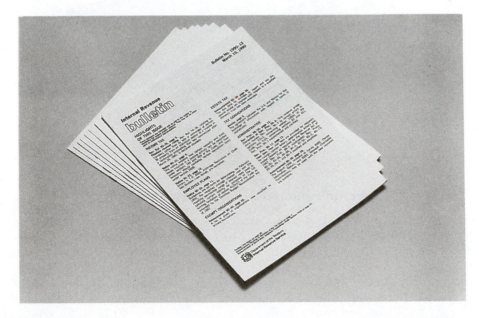

□ *Internal Revenue Bulletin,* published by the Internal Revenue Service (IRS)

Internal Revenue Bulletin

This bulletin prints official rulings and procedures of the IRS on tax matters. It is published weekly. (See photo on previous page.)

□ *Journal of Family Law,* published by the University of Louisville School of Law

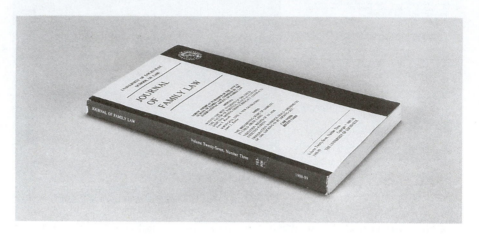

Journal of Family Law

This legal periodical contains articles and notes on family law topics, summaries of recent family law court opinions, and reviews of books in this area of the law.

□ *The Law of Domestic Relations in the United States,* by H. Clark, published by West Publishing Company

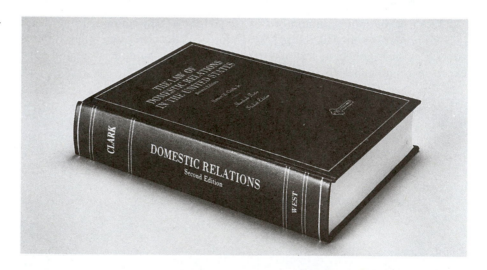

The Law of Domestic Relations in the United States

This is a hornbook that summarizes most areas of family law. There are extensive footnotes to court opinions. Most hornbooks are national in scope. They do not cover the law of any individual state in depth. Because of the extensive footnotes, however, you can often find citations to opinions of particular states in the footnotes. Some hornbooks, such as Clark's, are highly respected and are often relied on by courts and practitioners.

□ *Lexis*[1] by Mead Data Central, Inc.

Lexis

It is possible to do a significant amount of legal research by computer if you are lucky enough to have access to one. The computer, however, does not replace the researcher. Nor does it eliminate the need for the researcher to learn the conventional techniques of legal research. Competent use of the computer requires an understanding of the basic structure of the law books and how they are used in the traditional way.

Lexis is a computerized legal research system. You can use it to find case law on numerous topics such as alimony, joint custody, surrogate mothers, etc. It will also enable you to locate statutory law and some administrative law. The other major computer research system is Westlaw (see entry for Westlaw).

□ *Martindale-Hubbell Law Directory*, published by Reed Publishing Company

Martindale-Hubbell Law Directory

This directory is an annual listing of lawyers and law firms in America. The last volume in this set is the digest volume. It contains summaries of the

---

[1]Reprinted with the permission of Mead Data Central, Inc. LEXIS® and NEXIS® are registered trademarks for information products and services of Mead Data Central, Inc.

law of every state and of every country (including family law). In addition, this volume prints many of the uniform laws, e.g., Uniform Child Custody Jurisdiction Act.

☐ Newsletters (left to right) published by Leader Publications, the National Association of Counsel for Children, and the National Legal Research Group.

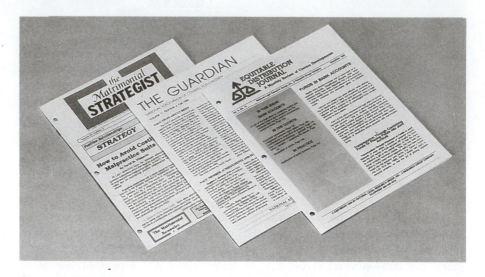

Newsletters

There are a number of newsletters devoted to various aspects of family law. Their primary audience is the day-to-day practitioner who needs current information about a particular specialty. The newsletters presented above are published by Leader Publications (*The Matrimonial Strategist*), the National Association of Counsel for Children (*The Guardian*), and the National Legal Research Group (*Equitable Distribution Journal*).

☐ *Separation Agreements and Antenuptial Contracts,* by A. Lindey, published by Matthew Bender.

Separation Agreements and Antenuptial Contracts

This standard text provides summaries of the law and numerous clauses for separation agreements, antenuptial agreements, and cohabitation agreements between parties who do not plan to marry.

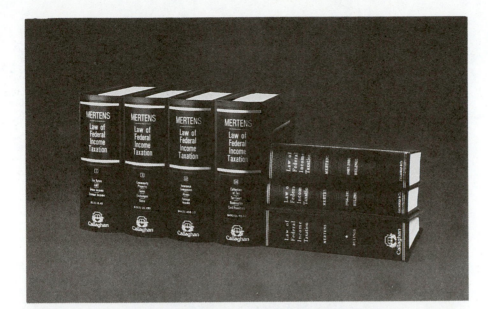

☐ Treatises published by Callaghan & Company and Matthew Bender

Treatises

A treatise (not to be confused with a *treaty*) is any book written by a private individual (or by a public official writing in a non-official capacity) that gives a summary of a particular topic and usually a commentary on that topic as well. If the topic is on the law, the book is called a legal treatise. We have already seen some examples of legal treatises, e.g., *The Law of Domestic Relations in the United States*. Example of others are *Law of Federal Income Taxation* published by Callaghan & Company, and *Family Law and Practice* published by Matthew Bender.

☐ *Uniform Laws An-*
notated published by
West Publishing
Company

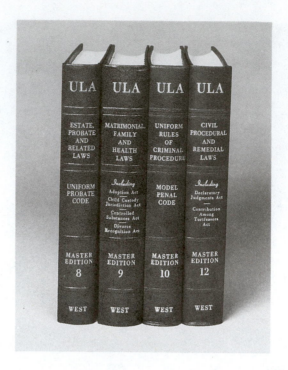

Uniform Laws

The National Conference of Commissioners on Uniform State Laws is an organization of individuals appointed by each state. The conference drafts *proposed* legislation to be considered by the legislatures of the various states. The states, of course, are free to reject these proposals, adopt them in toto, or modify them. One of the goals of the conference is to encourage uniformity in areas of the law where this is needed. To find out if any of the uniform laws have been enacted in your state, you would check your state code. All of the uniform laws are printed in a set of books called *Uniform Laws Annotated*, Master Edition, published by West. (Try to find this set for purposes of Assignment 2.1). Some of the uniform laws are also printed in the digest volume of *Martindale-Hubbell's Law Directory*.

☐ *A Uniform System*
of Citation published
by the Harvard Law
Review Association

A Uniform System of Citation

Often called "the blue book," this small pamphlet tells you how to cite statutes, cases, regulations, treatises, and any other document that you might want to cite in your legal writing. To many people, this "blue book" is the bible of citation form. Whenever you are submitting a memo or brief to a supervisor you should find out in advance whether that supervisor wants you to follow it.

Westlaw

Westlaw is a computerized legal research system. You can use it to find case law on numerous topics such as alimony, joint custody, surrogate mothers, etc. It will also enable you to locate statutory law and some administrative law.

☐ *Westlaw* by West Publishing Company

Words and Phrases

This is a multi-volume legal dictionary. The definitions of the words and phrases come mainly from court opinions. Hence, the dictionary can serve as a case finder. Almost all of the family law concepts discussed in this book are defined in this dictionary.

☐ *Words and Phrases*, published by West Publishing Company

Assignment 2.1

Make a list of every book mentioned above, beginning on page 49. (Ask your teacher if he or she wants you to add any other law books to this list, e.g., practice books for your state.) Go to the nearest large law library to which you have access. Find out if the law library has the book (or set of books). If so, give its location in the library. If the library does not have the book, inquire about other libraries in the area that might have it. You do not have to go to these other libraries; simply list them as possibilities to be checked at another time. Compile a chart similar to that presented below. The format of the chart is not important so long as you include all of the basic information. Your chart will become a checklist for you to use in this course and in your legal career. It is important that you become acquainted with these books as soon as possible.

There are three main ways for you to obtain the information that you will need for each book:

■ Using the card catalog of the law library
■ Browsing in the library
■ Asking the librarian or other library staff

Name of library:

Address and phone number:

Hours:

Name of law book	Check if available	Location/ call no.	Other libraries to check

Section C. Legal Institutions that Apply Family Law

Courts

Here our concern is as follows: what courts in your state have jurisdiction (sometimes called *subject-matter jurisdiction*) over family law problems? These courts may have different names in different states, e.g., Family Court, Domestic Relations Court, Juvenile Court, Superior Court, District Court, Circuit Court, etc. The word *jurisdiction* refers simply to the *power* of the court to handle certain kinds of cases. If a court has concurrent jurisdiction over a matter, it means that more than one court in the state can hear the case. *Exclusive jurisdiction*, on the other hand, means that only one court can hear the particular kind of case.

How can you determine which courts in your state have jurisdiction over family law problems and what the limitations are, if any, on that jurisdiction? Several ways exist:

1. Examine all state statutes in the statutory code on the judicial system of your state.
2. Examine all constitutional provisions in the state constitution on the judicial system of your state.
3. Examine the court rules of each court in your state.
4. Ask court clerks, experienced lawyers, and experienced paralegals.
5. Examine practice manuals.

While the latter two sources of information (4 and 5) can be quite reliable, it is highly recommended that you learn to consult the primary sources of information: statutes, constitutions, and court rules (1, 2, and 3 above).

Assignment 2.2

What courts in your state have trial court jurisdiction over family law problems? For each court, make a list of the kinds of family law problems it can hear. (See General Instructions for the State-Code Assignment in chapter one.)

Administrative Agencies

Unlike other areas of the law, administrative agencies are minimally involved in family law. The courts are the primary institutions that resolve family law conflicts. Some of the agencies that do play a role are the Bureau of Vital Statistics, Adoption Department, Child Welfare Agency, Marriage Conciliation Bureau, etc.

Assignment 2.3

Make a list of every state agency in your state that handles children in trouble, husband-wife difficulties, or any other family law problem. Select any two of these agencies. Write, call, or visit these two agencies and ask for copies of the following:

- Program literature describing the services of the agency
- Sample application forms that the public uses to obtain the benefits and services of the agency
- Examples of the agency's regulations

As you collect this data, exchange it among your classmates for agencies that you have not checked yourself. Be prepared to give a class presentation on the workings of a particular agency and its relationship to the topics you will be studying in this course.

Key Chapter Terminology

Depository Library
Primary Authority
Statutes
Constitutions
Opinions
Regulations
Secondary Authority
Digests
Shepard's
Practice Manual
Legal Newspaper
Am.Jur.2d
American Law Reports
Annotations
Hornbook

CJS
Legal Periodicals
Lexis
Legal Newsletters
Treatise
National Conference of Commission-
    ers on Uniform State Laws
A Uniform System of Citation
Blue Book
Westlaw
Words and Phrases
Jurisdiction
Concurrent Jurisdiction
Exclusive Jurisdiction

CHAPTER THREE

The Dynamics of Working in a Family Law Office

■ Chapter Outline

A law office can be a hectic environment in which to work. Survival may well depend on the new employee's ability to take advantage of numerous on-the-job learning opportunities. A wealth of information and technique can be acquired and developed this way.

First, ask lots of questions about the instructions you are given. Repeat the instructions back to your supervisor, and write them down in a notebook. Whenever possible, segment the instructions into separate tasks, and make a checklist of all the steps needed to perform each task. Find out if there are other relevant checklists and manuals already in the office. Look for a model of what you have been asked to prepare. Do some independent research in the law library on several of the instructions you have been given. Solicit the assistance of experienced secretaries and paralegals. If possible, find out from your supervisor if you are proceeding properly before the due date of the assignment. Participate in training programs conducted in the office and by outside associations. Seek regular evaluations of your work.

There are three potential interferences with effective communication between a client and a law office. The first is the personal bias of office workers. Since the cases handled in a family law practice can be emotionally charged, the need for professionalism is clear, particularly if the office is defending a client who has done something that clashes with a worker's personal values. A second interference is the inarticulateness of some clients. Clients are not always sure what they want until options are presented to them. A third interference is the pigeonholing that results from legal workers letting their specialized training and experience block out client problems that fall outside that training and experience.

Violence is another potential issue in family law. Perhaps more that in any other area of law practice, there is a potential for violence between spouse and spouse, and sometimes between defendant and opposing counsel.

Section A. How to Be Supervised

The central question of this chapter is, how does a new paralegal survive in a busy law office handling a substantial number of family law cases? The first rule of survival is to have a realistic understanding of what you could find during your first month on the job. The following list outlines possible problems.

- The family law you learned in school is not enough to enable you to handle every assignment you are given on the job.

- Your supervisors give you numerous, hard-to-follow instructions, assuming that you know a lot more than you do.

- When you receive your first few assignments, you panic momentarily with the strange feeling that you don't remember anything you learned.

- Your supervisor tells you to forget everything you learned because "we do things differently here."

- Some of the attorneys are suspicious of paralegals—they are not quite sure what you are trained to do; you've got to prove yourself.

- One or more of the secretaries, who have been at the firm some time, are suspicious and perhaps resentful of your presence—they think that they should have been upgraded into the job you were given.

- The office moves at a frantic pace with seemingly no time for you to think. (etc.)

What should you do when confronted with such situations? One solution is to learn *how to be supervised.*

Supervision—whether given or received—does not come naturally to most of us. Unfortunately, very few people know how to supervise effectively.[1] This includes lawyers, and paralegals who are sometimes required to supervise secretaries, clerks, and other paralegals. The skill of *being* supervised is no easier to acquire, even though most of us have more experience at it. This skill requires:

1. Carrying out an assigned responsibility according to the instructions of the supervisor

2. Taking maximum advantage of each assignment to develop knowledge and skills.

---

[1]See Statsky, *Techniques for Supervising Paralegals,* 22 The Practical Lawyer 81 (June 1976).

Both of these objectives may sound relatively easy to accomplish. You may feel that you are already an expert at carrying out assigned tasks and at learning while doing. Are you?

If you asked a supervisor to assess the quality of the people he or she has supervised, you might be told that one in twenty is a "good worker." Are you the one in twenty? Most people get fifteen to twenty minutes of productive work time out of each work hour. How much productive time are you able to get? Possibly 99 out of 100 of us *do not know what our supervisors really think of us.*

Assignment 3.1

Think of the last five people who have supervised you in an employment setting. (If you have not yet worked enough to have had five work supervisors, select other settings in which others had to supervise you, e.g., school/church projects, other volunteer activity.) For each supervisor, answer the following questions:

(a) What would that person's general impression be of you as a worker?

(b) What negative comments would he or she make about you as a worker?

(c) If any of the supervisors could have replaced you before you left, would they have done so? Why or why not?

Most of us would have great difficulty answering the questions of Assignment 3.1 objectively. When we think about our prior work settings that have been less than satisfactory, our inclination is to blame someone else for what went wrong. While it may be true that others deserve some blame, we need to look at our own participation, our own shortcomings, our own responsibility for what happened.

Step one, therefore, in the process of learning how to be supervised is to try to answer the questions, "Who am I as a worker?" "What are my strengths and weaknesses?" "Would I hire myself?" "Where do I need improvement?" "Does my ego interfere with my performance?" "Am I afraid to say, 'I don't understand'?" "Do I know how to ask for help?" Your ability to give honest and positive answers to questions such as these will be much more important in determining your success as a paralegal than the amount of family law you learn in this course.

We now turn to a number of concrete suggestions to maintain a healthy supervisor-supervisee relationship.

King's Clothes

Don't play king's clothes with the instructions that you receive. Recall the story in which the king was naked, but everybody kept admiring his beautiful wardrobe. As new people arrived, they saw that he had no clothes, but they heard everyone talking as if he were fully dressed. Not wanting to appear stupid, they, too, began admiring the king's wardrobe. Paralegals play king's clothes when they pretend they understand all the instructions they are receiving when in fact they do not. For obvious reasons, this is a serious mistake.

Whenever you are given an assignment in a new area, there should be a great deal that you do not understand. This is particularly true during your first few months on the job when everything is new! Don't pretend to have knowledge and skills that you do not yet have. Constantly ask questions about new things. Don't be reluctant to ask for explanations. Learn how to ask for help. *It will not be a sign of weakness.* Quite the contrary. People who want to make sure that they fully understand all their instructions soon gain a reputation for responsibility and conscientiousness.

Repetition of Instructions

Repeat the instructions to your supervisor before you leave the room. Once your supervisor has told you what he or she wants you to do, do not leave the room in silence or with the general observation, "I'll get on that right away." First make sure you are on the same wavelength by repeating the instructions back to the supervisor *as you understand them.* This will be an excellent opportunity for the supervisor to determine what you did and did not understand and to provide you with clarifications where needed.

Supervisors are not always sure what they want. Discussing instructions with you provides the supervisor with the opportunity to think through, and possibly even change, what he or she wants done.

Written Instructions

Write your instructions down. Never go to your supervisor without pen and paper. Preferably, keep an Instructions Notebook in which you record the following information:

- Notes on what you are supposed to do
- The date you are given the assignment
- The date the supervisor expects you to complete all or part of the assignment
- Later changes made by your supervisor on your assignment
- Dates you actually complete the assignment

The notes will serve as your memory bank. If questions arise about what you were supposed to do, you have something concrete to which to refer.

Separation of Tasks

If the instructions appear to be complicated, ask your supervisor to segment them into separate tasks and give priorities to each one. Many supervisors do not give instructions in clear logical patterns. They may talk in a rambling, stream-of-consciousness fashion. When you feel overwhelmed by the instructions, simply say: "OK, but can you break that down for me a little more in terms of what you want me to do first? I'll be able to do the entire assignment, but it would help if I approach it one step at a time. Where do you want me to start?"

Your Own Checklists

As often as possible, write your instructions and what you do in the form of checklists. A methodical mind views a project in "do-able" steps that can be tackled one at a time. You need a methodical mind in order to function in a busy law office. One of the best ways to develop such a mind is to think in terms of checklists. A checklist is simply a chronological sequencing of tasks that must be performed in order to complete a project. We have already seen how to translate a rule into a checklist (page 33). This same process can be used to convert the instructions from your supervisor into a detailed checklist.

To be sure, it can be time-consuming to draft checklists. Keep in mind, however, that:

- The checklists can be invaluable for other employees who are given similar assignments in the future.
- The checklists will be a benefit to you in organizing your own time and in assuring completeness.

You will not be able to draft checklists for everything that you do. Perhaps you will not be able to write more than one checklist a week. Perhaps you will have to use some of your own time to write the checklists. Whatever time you can devote to checklists will be profitably spent so long as you are serious about using them. They may have to be rewritten or modified later. This should not deter you from the task, since most things that are worth doing require testing and reassessment.

Once you have a number of checklists, you have the makings of a how-to-do-it manual that you have written yourself. If you want to see the face of your supervisor light up, watch his or her reaction upon discovering that you are this organized!

Office Manuals and Checklists

Don't reinvent the wheel. If manuals and checklists already exist in your office on the topic of your assignments, you should find and use them, adapting what you find to the particular assignment on which you are working. Unfortunately, the how-to-do-it information is usually buried in the heads of the attorneys, paralegals, and secretaries of the office. No one has taken the time to write it all down.

Models

One of the best ways of making sure you know what the supervisor wants is by asking whether any models exist that you could use as a guide for what you are being asked to do. Such models may be found in closed case files, manuals, formbooks, practice texts, etc. As pointed out in Chapter 1, however, great care is needed in using such material. Every new legal problem is potentially unique. What will work in one case may not work in another. A model is a guide, a starting point, and nothing more.

Legal Research

Do some independent legal research on your own on the instructions you are given. Often you will be told what to do without being given more than a cursory explanation of why it needs to be done that way. However, all of the instructions you are given have a basis in the law. A complaint, for example, is served on an opposing party in a designated way because the law has imposed rules on how such service is to be made. You will be asked to serve a complaint in a certain way without being told what section of the state code (or of your court rules) *requires* it to be served in that way. It would be highly impractical for you to be able to read all the law that is the foundation for the instructions you are given. It is not necessary to do so, and you would not have time to do so.

What you *can* do, however, is select certain instructions on certain assignments and do some background legal research in order to gain a greater appreciation for why the instructions were necessary to accomplish the task. You will probably have to do such legal research on your own time unless the assignment you are given includes some legal research. The research can be time-consuming, but you will find it to be enormously educational. It can place a totally new perspective on the assignment and, indeed, on your entire job.

Secretaries and Paralegals

Secretaries and other paralegals who have worked in the office for a long period of time can be very helpful to you if you approach them properly. Everybody wants to feel important. Everybody wants to be respected. Avoid asking for something in such a way as to give the impression that you are *entitled* to what is being sought—even if you are. Think of how you would like to be approached if you were in the position of the secretary or other paralegal. What would you turn off? What would make you want to go out of your way to cooperate with and assist a new paralegal employee who needs your help? Your answers (and sensitivity) to questions such as these will go a long way toward enabling you to draw on the experience of others in the office.

Feedback before Due Date

Unless the assignment you are given is a very simple one, do not wait until the date that it is due to communicate with, and obtain feedback from, your supervisor. Of course, if you are having trouble with the assignment, you will want to check with your supervisor as soon as possible and as often as necessary. It would be a mistake, however, to contact the supervisor only when trouble arises. To be sure, you should limit your contacts with any busy supervisor to essential contacts. You could take the following approach in your discussions: "Everything seems to be going fine on the project you gave me. I expect to have it in to you on time. I'm wondering, however, if you could give me a few moments of your time so that I can bring you up to date on where I am so that you can let me know if I am on the right track?"

Perhaps this "perception check" could take place on the phone or during a brief office visit. Suppose that you have gone astray on the assignment without knowing it? It is obviously better to discover this before the assignment is due. The more communication you have with your supervisor, the more likely it is that you will catch such errors before much time is wasted.

Ongoing Education

Sometimes there are training sessions for new attorneys conducted in the law firm. You should ask that you be included in some or all of such sessions.

Bar associations and paralegal associations often conduct all-day seminars on legal topics relevant to your work. Seek permission to attend them if they are held during work hours.

Regular Evaluations

Ask to be evaluated regularly. For a number of reasons, evaluations are either not given or are unhelpful when they are given:

- Evaluations can be time-consuming.
- Evaluators are reluctant to say anything negative, especially in writing.
- Most people don't like to be evaluated; it's too threatening to their egos.

The major anitdote is to let your supervisor know that you want to be evaluated and that you can handle criticism. If you are defensive when you are criticized, you will find that the evaluations of your performance will take place behind your back. Such a work environment is obviously very unhealthy.

Consider this approach that a paralegal might take with a supervisor: "I want to know what you think of my work. I want to know where you think I need improvement. That's the only way I'm going to learn. I also want to know when I'm doing things correctly, but I'm mainly interested in your suggestions on what I can do to increase my skills." If you take this approach *and mean it,* the chances are good that you will receive some very constructive criticism. Futhermore you demonstrate your responsibility and maturity when you take the initiative in obtaining evaluations of your performance.

In addition to the occasional oral evaluations that you might ask for, you may want to use an evaluation form that could be filled out in a short period of time by each of your supervisors. A sample of such a form is shown in Exhibit 3–1. You will note that the form is centered around basic legal skills.

The advantage of this form is that it takes only moments to fill in. All that is needed is the circling of a small number of words. The disadvantage is that there is not much detail provided by the evaluation. Most supervisors, however, are not going to have time to provide you with lengthy, narrative evaluations. During conversations with your supervisor, you should be able to receive more comprehensive assessments of strengths and weaknesses. The form might be a catalyst for such conversations.

The form lists a number of "areas being evaluated." Other areas could be added, and some of the areas listed can be broken down into narrower areas. You can adapt the form to the particular needs of the law office setting in which you find yourself. The objective is to find an evaluation instrument that is not burdensome to supervisors, that helps them organize their thoughts about what you have been doing, and that provides you with some useful information about your current standing.

Section B. Assessing Your Own Biases

Your involvement in a domestic relations case may come at a number of stages:

- You might do the comprehensive client interview after the attorney has decided to take the case and has established the attorney-client relationship

☐ **EXHIBIT 3–1** Performance evaluation form

PERFORMANCE EVALUATION

Employee:

Supervisor completing this evaluation:

Date this evaluation was completed:

Period covered by this evaluation:

Instructions: for each item in column one, circle the appropriate word in each of the three corresponding columns

Areas Being Evaluated	To What Extent Has Paralegal Been Given Tasks in This Area	Complexity of Paralegal Tasks in Area	Evaluation of Paralegal's Performance in area
1. Fact Analysis; Fact Organization	Extensive Minimal None	Very Complex Average Complexity Simple	Excellent Good Fair Needs Improvement
2. Writing Ability, e.g., digest reports, drafts of pleadings	Extensive Minimal None	Very Complex Average Complexity Simple	Excellent Good Fair Needs Improvement
3. Outside Contact, e.g., clients, witnesses, agencies, vendors	Extensive Minimal None	Very Complex Average Complexity Simple	Excellent Good Fair Needs Improvement
4. Field Investigation	Extensive Minmal None	Very Complex Average Complexity Simple	Excellent Good Fair Needs Improvement
5. Using the Law Library	Extensive Minimal None	Very Complex Average Complexity Simple	Excellent Good Fair Needs Improvement
6. Ability to work independently	Extensive Minimal None	Very Complex Average Complexity Simple	Excellent Good Fair Needs Improvement
7. Working with Others in the Office	Extensive Minimal None	Very Complex Average Complexity Simple	Excellent Good Fair Needs Improvement
8. Time Management/ Working under Pressure	Extensive Minimal None	Very Complex Average Complexity Simple	Excellent Good Fair Needs Improvement
9. Following Instructions	Extensive Minimal None	Very Complex Average Complexity Simple	Excellent Good Fair Needs Improvement
10. Showing Initiative	Extensive Minimal. None	Very Complex Average Complexity Simple	Excellent Good Fair Needs Improvement
11. Motivation			Excellent Good Fair Needs Improvement
12. Overall Abilities			Excellent Good Fair Needs Improvement

through a contract called the *retainer* (specifying the fee, the scope of the representation, etc.).

- You might do field investigation in order to uncover and verify facts relevant to the case.
- You might handle intermediate client contact in order to obtain and exchange needed information.
- You might be asked to undertake legal research on the case and prepare drafts of certain documents, e.g., the divorce complaint.
- You might schedule client appointments, conduct witness interviews, and make a variety of arrangements centered around certain court dates.

No matter what stage of a case you are working on, you need to be aware of how your personal feelings might effect your work on the case. How would you answer the following question: "Are you objective enough that you can assist a person even though you have a personal distaste for what that person wants to do or what that person has done?" Many of us would quickly answer "yes" to this question. We all like to feel that we are levelheaded and not susceptible to letting our prejudices interfere with the job we are asked to accomplish. Most of us, however, have difficulty ignoring our personal likes and dislikes.

Assignment 3.2

The following fact situations involve aspects of domestic relations cases. To what extent might an individual be hampered in delivering legal services because of personal reactions toward the client?

(a) Mr. Smith, the client of your office, is being sued by his estranged wife for custody of their two small children. Mr. and Mrs. Smith live separately, but Mr. Smith has had custody of the children during most of their lives while Mrs. Smith has been in the hospital. Mrs. Smith has charged that Mr. Smith often yells at the children, leaves them with neighbors and day care centers for most of the day, and is an alcoholic. Your investigation reveals that Mrs. Smith will probably be able to prove all these allegations in court.

(b) Mrs. Jones is being sued by Mr. Jones for divorce on the ground of adultery. Mrs. Jones is the client of your office. Thus far your investigation has revealed that there is considerable doubt over whether Mrs. Jones did in fact commit adultery. During a recent conversation with Mrs. Jones, however, she tells you that she is a prostitute.

(c) Jane Anderson is seeking an abortion. She is not married. The father of the child wants to prevent her from having the abortion. Jane comes to your office for legal help. She wants to know what her rights are. You are a devout Catholic assigned to work on the case.

(d) Tom Donaldson is a client of your office. His former wife claims that he has failed to pay her court-ordered alimony payments and that those payments should be increased substantially because of her needs and his recently improved financial status. Your job is to help Tom collect a large volume of records concerning his past alimony payments and his present financial worth. There is no one else in the office who is available to do this record gathering but you. It is clear, however, that Tom does not like you. On a number of occasions, he has indirectly questioned your ability.

Having analyzed the fact situations involved in the above assignment, do you still feel the same about your assessment of your own objectivity? Clearly, we cannot simply wish our personal feelings away or pretend that they do not exist. Nor are there any absolute rules or techniques that apply to every situation that you will be asked to handle. Nor are the following admonitions very helpful: "Be objective," "be dispassionate," "don't get personally involved," "control your feelings." Such admonitions are too general, and when viewed in the abstract, may appear to be not needed, since we want to believe that we are always objective, dispassionate, detached, and in control.

Perhaps the best we can do is to recognize that there are facts and circumstances that arouse our emotions and that tempt us to impose our own value judgments. Perhaps if we know where we are vulnerable, we will be in a better position to prevent our reactions from interfering with our work. It is not desirable for you to be totally dispassionate and removed. A paralegal who is cold, unfeeling, and incapable of empathy is not much better than a paralegal who self-righteously scolds a client. It is clearly not improper for a paralegal to express sympathy, surprise, and perhaps even shock at what unfolds from the client's life story. If these feelings are genuine and if they would be normal reactions to the situation at a given moment, then they should be expressed. Again, however, the problem is *how to draw the line* between expressing these feelings, and reacting so judgmentally that you interfere with your ability to communicate with the client now and in the future. Again, there are no absolute guidelines. As you gain experience in the art of dealing with people, you will hopefully develop styles and techniques that will enable you to avoid going over that line too often. The starting point in this development is the recognition of how easy it is to go over the line. The main antidote available to you is your own willingness and ability to assess when you are in the danger zone.

Assignment 3.3

(a) Think about your past and present contacts with people who have irritated you the most. Make a specific list of what bothered you about these people. Suppose that you are working in a law office where a client did one of the things on your list. Could you handle such a case?

(b) In the relationship among husband, wife, and child, many things can be done that would be wrong (i.e., illegal, immoral, improper) according to your personal system of values. Make a list of the ten things that could be done by husband, wife, or child to another family member (e.g., husband to wife, child to parent, etc.) which would be most offensive to your sense of values. Assume that a client in the office where you work has done one of these ten things and is being challenged in court by someone because of it. Your office is defending the client against this challenge. What difficulties do you see for yourself in being able to assist this client?

Section C. What Does the Client Want?

There are a number of assumptions that can be made about many clients with family law problems:

- The client is not sure what he or she wants in spite of what he or she says.
- The client is not aware of his or her legal or nonlegal options.
- The family law problem probably involves other legal problems about which the client is unaware and about which even you may be unaware at the outset.

Suppose that a client walks into the office and says "I want a divorce." The following observations *might* be possible about the client:

1. The client has an incorrect understanding of what a divorce is.

2. The client says she wants a divorce because she thinks that this is the only legal remedy available to solve her problem.

3. If the client knew that other remedies existed (e.g., annulment, judicial separation, a support order) she would consider these options.

4. What the client is really troubled about is the fact that her husband beats the kids; a divorce is the only way she thinks she can stop it.

5. The client does not want a divorce. She is being pressured by her husband to institute divorce proceedings. He has threatened her with violence if she refuses.

6. The client consciously or unconsciously wants and needs an opportunity to tell someone how badly the world is treating her, and if given this opportunity, she may not want to terminate the marriage.

7. If the client knew that marriage counseling was available in the community, she would consider using it before taking the drastic step of going to a law office for a divorce.

If any of these observations is correct, think of how damaging it would be for someone in the law office to take out the standard divorce forms and quickly fill them out immediately after the client says, "I want a divorce." This response would not be appropriate without first probing beneath the statement to determine what in fact is on the client's mind. Some clients who speak only of divorces and separation agreements, would be receptive to and even anxious for reconciliation. The danger exists that the client might be steered in the direction of a divorce because no other options are presented to her, because no one takes the time to help her express the ideas, intentions, and desires that are lurking beneath the otherwise clear statement, "I want a divorce."

This is not to say that you must be prepared to psychoanalyze every client or that you must always distrust what the client initially tells you. It is rather a recognition of the fact that *most people are confused about the law and make requests based upon misinformation as to what courses of action are available to solve problems.* Common sense tells us to avoid taking all statements at face value. People under emotional distress, particularly in situations of family conflict, need to be treated with sensitivity. We should not expect them to be able to express their intentions with clarity all the time in view of the emotions involved and the sometimes complicated nature of the law.

Assignment 3.4

In the case of the following three statements made by a client, what areas do you think would be reasonable to probe in order to determine if the statement is an accurate reflection of what the client wants? What misunderstandings do you think the client might have? What further questions would you want to ask in order to be sure that you have identified what the client wants?

(a) "I want to commit my husband to a mental institution."

(b) "I can't control my teenage son anymore. I want him placed in a juvenile home."

(c) "I want to put my baby daughter up for adoption."

Section D. The Pigeonhole Mentality

A great deal of specialization exists in the practice of law. Lawyers often concentrate on certain kinds of cases, e.g., bankruptcy, criminal law, tax law, and, of course, family law. Many paralegals do the same if they happen to work for specialists. The danger of specialization is "pigeonholing:" seeing everything in terms of the specialty and blocking out what does not fall within it. A bankruptcy lawyer may overlook a tax problem, and tax lawyer may overlook a bankruptcy problem. The following article by Marc Ullom examines this problem from the perspective of the paralegal:

What You Hear is What You Get by Mark Ullom

THE PARALEGAL FORUM 5, Philadelphia Association of Paralegals
(March 1988).

Scenario A:

"It was a typically successful day. Two clients came to the door with divorce agreements amicably outlined. Another brought in bankruptcy creditor lists [that were] complete to the last name and address. Another came in with perfect liability in a personal injury case, carrying stacks of medical bills neatly catalogued for each doctor who treated the injuries. Each consultation took fifteen minutes, and the first three paid their fees in full. My paralegal took the paperwork, transferred it into the pleadings and we had time left over for the staff to take a long lunch at our favorite restaurant."

Scenario B:

"Then I woke up. The alarm hadn't gone off. I almost missed my nine o'clock appointment with a divorce client who then said she couldn't afford to start the case. Then I had to rush down to a bankruptcy hearing for a guy who got hurt at work, fell behind on his bills, and then was laid off from his job because he couldn't afford to get his car fixed."

So much for the textbook cases with neatly packaged issues. Hope as we might for the "Scenario A" days of our dreams, the "Scenario B" days are as common as calendar pads.

Attractive as the first scenario might seem, the practice of law would become dull indeed if everything were so convenient. More importantly, if my days ever begin to seem simple, I'll know I'm not listening to my clients as well as I should.

In these times of specialization, we do oversimplify things. We tend to shoehorn the client's needs into the skills we have to fit them. Bankruptcy specialists notice only bankruptcy problems. Divorce people see only the domestic issues. If that is the skill we have, that is the service we will provide. But in so doing, both we and the client stand to lose. The client loses when the real problems are only partly solved. The law firm loses when we overlook an opportunity to serve effectively, be properly paid for it, and win a client who will have the confidence to return with legal needs in the future.

So why say this to the paralegal community? The answer is as close as the telephone you pick up first. It is as obvious as the answers you relay to the client on the attorney's behalf.

Consider the number of client contacts that are handled by the paralegal rather than the attorney. Clients mention facts to you in brief conversation that they do not think are important enough to "bother" the lawyer. If you are well attuned to the client's words, you will be alerting the attorney to issues even if they are not in your area of specialty.

How well are you attuned to the client? Take a moment to reread "Scenario B." How many cases are really there? Nobody knows until the lawyer asks a few more questions, but try these: divorce, financial problems due to accumulated debt of a separated spouse, financial problems due to child support arrearages, money problems due to illness, injury or job layoffs, bankruptcy, worker's compensation injury, [other] personal injury claims . . ., auto accident, unemployment compensation. There may even be more, but the most important fact is that nobody knows until the appropriate follow-up questions are asked.

As a paralegal, there is much you can do to help your attorney spot all the needs of the client:

1. Listen to the casual comments of the client, such as: "can't make it in today— got hurt," or "looking for a house."

2. Notice changes in the client's mood, in comments like: "why does it take so long," "my friend's case went smoother," "money getting tight," and "spouse doesn't agree with you" (when it's not a divorce case!).

3. Alert the attorney first, so the attorney can decide what action is appropriate, if any.

4. Document your contact in the casefile, too, so that the attorney will remember your contact when reviewing the file.

5. Defer any comment to the client until the attorney makes a decision how to proceed.

6. Brush up on other areas of procedure, too, especially those areas that most often touch the edges of your practice.

Properly handled, your communications with the client—which are usually more frequent than those of the attorney—will tell the client [you are interested in] all the client's legal needs, and stand ready to serve. . . .

Section E. Violence Directed at Attorneys

As the following article indicates, attorneys practicing family law can be the targets of physical violence from emotionally distraught people involved with their clients.

On the Firing Line by D. Weikel

CALIF. LAWYER 22 (November 1988).

When divorce and romantic discord turn to war, lawyers are sometimes the first casualties. Orange County attorney William M. Swain, for example, will never use his left hand again—a grim reminder of the heights to which violence can rise during a divorce case.

While taking a court-ordered inventory of a Fullerton pawn shop on May 6, 1985, Swain was shot twice by Victor Pahl, the estranged husband of Swain's client. Swain lost his spleen and part of his pancreas. He also suffered a punctured stomach and lung as well as permanent damage to his hand.

Pahl admitted pulling the trigger, but was acquitted in December 1987 of attempted murder, assault and attempted manslaughter charges. Jurors said they believed the defense contention that Pahl, depressed by his pending divorce, was in a "zombielike" state and did not know what he was doing.

Swain's experience may be extreme, yet the risks he faced are not uncommon for attorneys handling dissolutions, palimony cases and restraining orders. No statistics reveal the number of times family lawyers have been threatened or assaulted. But the frequency of family-related violence means that family law attorneys often get caught on the firing line. Roughly a third of all female homicide victims are killed by husbands or boyfriends, according to the FBI and the state attorney general's office. And crime figures show that 20 percent of all murders involve some kind of family relationship.

"It really doesn't matter if the violence happens in 1 percent or 100 percent of your cases," says Margaret Anderson of Santa Rosa, chair of the State Bar's Family Law Section. "One percent can do a lot of damage."

Although the problem has been discussed by local and state bar associations, attorneys and judges say there are few solutions except restraining orders, training for lawyers, and beefed-up security.

Some courthouses across the state have increased the number of bailiffs in domestic law courts, and a few have installed metal detectors to screen everyone, lawyers included.

Santa Clara County Superior Court installed its metal detector after a bailiff found a gun in a lunch box brought into court by an estranged husband. "The sheriff and the judges have finally realized how dangerous family law can be," says San Jose attorney Lynne Yates-Carter, who sits on the executive committee of the State Bar's Family Law Section. In some counties, lawyers and clients threatened by ex-spouses can request bailiffs to escort the threatened ones around the courthouse or to their cars.

To help attorneys cope with potentially violent situations, some bar associations sponsor seminars on how to keep client emotions under control. Divorce lawyers say they regularly consult therapists. With experience, attorneys can become adept at identifying potential problems and avoiding catastrophes.

When that can't be done, some attorneys have old-fashioned ways to deal with the situation.

Lisa Hughes, a petite family law practitioner in Santa Ana, keeps a loaded .38-caliber pistol in her office. The door to her firm has a peephole.

"I have had hundreds of clients beaten and threatened, and I have had at least six death threats," Hughes says. "On two occasions I have had a coroner call and say they had someone in the morgue with my card in their pocket. They were not my clients. Perhaps they would have been."

Key Chapter Terminology

Supervision	Skills
King's Clothes	Bias
Evaluation	Objectivity
Retainer	

Ethics and Malpractice

■ Chapter Outline

Two of the worst things that can happen to a lawyer are (1) to be disciplined by the bar association for unethical conduct; (2) to be sued in court by a client for malpractice. In this chapter, we will examine both concerns. All employees of a firm must be aware of them in order to help prevent either from occurring.

Ethical rules govern the conduct of lawyers. The violation of these rules can lead to the ultimate sanction of disbarment. There are, however, no ethical rules governing paralegals that are backed by sanctions. Yet lawyers can be sanctioned for what paralegals do in the law office. A lawyer has an ethical obligation to give proper supervision to paralegals.

There are twelve major catagories of ethical violations. It is unethical for a lawyer to fail to have the knowledge and skill that is reasonably necessary to represent a particular client; to charge an unreasonable fee, or to charge most forms of contingent fees in a domestic relations case; to reveal information relating to the representation of a client; to represent a client to whom the lawyer cannot give undivided loyalty; to commingle general law firm funds with client funds in the same account; to withdraw from a case improperly;

to make false statements to a tribunal or to fail to disclose certain information to the tribunal; to communicate with the other side without the permission of the latter's lawyer; to fail to inform paralegals and other employees of the lawyer's ethical responsibilities; to solicit prospective clients improperly; to advertise in a false or misleading manner; and to assist a nonlawyer engage in the unauthorized practice of law.

Closely related to (and often overlapping) these ethical violations, are other kinds of wrongdoing by lawyers. For example, a lawyer can be sued for breach of contract, fraud, malicious prosecution, and most importantly, negligence. In addition, the lawyer is liable, under the doctrine of *respondeat superior,* for similar wrongdoing committed by a paralegal within the office. The paralegal is also individually liable for such wrongdoing. The client can sue the paralegal, the supervising lawyer, or both until the client's damages have been paid.

Section A. Ethics

Ethics are standards of conduct embodied within rules that govern an organization, an occupation, or a profession. There are two main kinds of ethical rules: those that are backed up by sanctions for violating the rules, and those that are not.

All lawyers are subject to rules of ethics, often called *canons of ethics, codes of ethics,* or *rules of professional responsibility.* They are promulgated and enforced by the courts, usually through the state bar association. Sanctions exist for violating the rules, e.g., reprimand, suspension, disbarment.

At the present time, no ethical rules governing paralegals are backed by sanctions. Some of the paralegal associations have codes of ethics, but there is no enforcement mechanism behind them. Paralegals, like all citizens, are governed by other kinds of rules, such as criminal statutes on the unauthorized practice of law, that *are* backed by sanctions. You can go to jail for practicing law without a license! But no paralegal can be reprimanded, suspended, or "disbarred" for unethical behavior, since there is no paralegal ethical code in existence that is enforced by an organization that can impose these sanctions.

When a paralegal works for a lawyer, is the paralegal governed by the ethical rules that apply to lawyers? Only indirectly. Since a paralegal cannot be a full member of a bar association, he or she cannot be disciplined by the bar association or by the courts for ethical violations. But a *lawyer* can be disciplined for paralegal conduct in the office. As we shall see, one of the ethical obligations of a lawyer is to supervise paralegal employees properly. A lawyer can be sanctioned for improprieties of the paralegal that could have been prevented by proper supervision.

Assignment 4.1

(a) Give the full citation to the ethical rules that govern the conduct of lawyers in your state.

(b) What is the name of the bar association committee in your state that has jurisdiction over the ethical standards of lawyers? What disciplinary powers does this committee have over lawyers?

(c) If a lawyer is dissatisfied with the ruling of the above committee concerning his or her ethical conduct, to what court can the lawyer appeal? (To find answers to the above questions, check your state statutory code and your state constitution. See General Instructions for the State-Code Assignment in chapter one. In addition, you may want to contact your state bar association. Ask it to send you any descriptive literature available on the system for disciplining lawyers.)

(d) Draft a flowchart of all the procedural steps that must be taken to discipline a lawyer for unethical conduct. (See also General Instructions for the Flowchart Assignment in chapter one.)

The American Bar Association (ABA) is a voluntary national bar association; lawyers are not required to belong to it. Although the ABA publishes ethical rules, it does not discipline lawyers for unethical conduct. As previously indicated, such conduct is subject to sanction by the state court and the state bar association. The role of the ABA is merely to *propose* ethical rules for consideration by the various states. A state is free to adopt, modify, or reject the ethical rules recommended by the ABA. In view of the prestige of the ABA, many states have adopted its proposals with very little change.

The most recent proposals of the ABA are found within the very influential *Model Rules of Professional Conduct*. The following overview is based on these rules. Rule numbers are given for those that are quoted or summarized.

Ethical issues for the family law practitioner arise in the following major areas:

☐ **Competence**

☐ **Fees**

☐ **Confidentiality of information**

☐ **Conflict of interest**

☐ **Safekeeping Property**

☐ **Withdrawal**

☐ **False statements/failure to disclose**

☐ **Communication with the other side**

☐ **Nonlawyer assistants**

☐ **Solicitation**

☐ **Advertising**

☐ **Unauthorized practice of law**

☐ **Competence**

> **Rule 1.1** A lawyer shall provide competent representation to a client.

A classic example of incompetent lawyer is one who accepts more cases than his or her office can handle. As a consequence, court dates and other filing deadlines are missed, documents are lost, and the lawyer fails to determine what law governs each case. Such a lawyer is practicing law "from the hip"—unethically.

Many, if not most, graduates of law school need a good deal of on-the-job study and guidance before they are ready to handle client cases of any complexity. A law school education does little more than help ensure that the lawyer is equipped to go out and *continue* learning through legal research and experience. A good lawyer is always learning the law.

A *competent* lawyer is one who has the *knowlege* and *skill* deemed reasonably necessary to represent a particular client. The amount of knowledge and skill required depends on the complexity of the case. A great deal of knowledge and skill, for example, may be needed by a lawyer representing a wife in a divorce case where the issue is the present value of the husband's partially vested pension or his partnership interest in a foreign business.

How do ethical lawyers obtain this knowledge and skill? They draw on the general principles of analysis learned in law school. But more importantly, they take the time needed to *prepare* themselves. They spend time in the law library. They talk with their colleagues. In some instances, they formally associate themselves with more experienced lawyers in the area. A lawyer who fails to take these steps is acting unethically if his or her knowledge and skill are not what is deemed reasonably necessary to properly represent a particular client.

☐ Fees

> **Rule 1.5(a).**   A lawyer's fee shall be reasonable.
>
> **Rule 1.5(d).**   A contingent fee in a domestic relations case is prohibited if the payment or amount of the fee is dependent on securing a divorce, on the amount of alimony obtained, on the amount of support obtained, or on the amount of a property settlement in lieu of alimony or support.

There is no absolute rule on when a fee is excessive and therefore unreasonable. A number of factors must be considered: the amount of time and labor involved, the complexity of the matter, the experience and reputation of the lawyer, the customary fee in the locality for the same kind of case, etc.

The basis or rate of the fee should be communicated to the client before or soon after the lawyer starts to work on the case. This is often done in the contract of employment called the *retainer*.

At one time bar associations published a list of "recommended" fees for designated kinds of services. These minimum fee schedules have now been prohibited by the United States Supreme Court, *Goldfarb v. Virginia State Bar*, 421 U.S. 773, 95 S.Ct. 2004, 44 L.Ed.2d 572 (1975). Such schedules constitute illegal price fixing by the bar.

There are two main kinds of fees: fixed or contingent. A *fixed fee* is one that is paid regardless of who wins the case. It may be a flat sum, an hourly rate, or a combination. A *contingent fee* is dependent on the outcome of the case, e.g., a lawyer receives 30 percent of a jury award in a negligence case, but nothing if the client loses the case.

Under the *Model Rules*, and in most states, contingent fees are unethical if they are directly tied to obtaining a divorce, or to the amount of alimony, support, or property settlement. A main argument against contingent fees in such cases is that the lawyer might be so anxious to obtain the divorce or a certain amount from the other side that he or she might interfere with possibilities of reconciliation between the parties—since the contingent fee is not paid if the parties get back together again.

Contingent fees for representing defendants in criminal cases are also unethical.

Fee splitting involves a single bill to the client covering the fee of two or more lawyers who are not in the same firm. For example:

> Jones, Esq. and Smith, Esq. both work on behalf of a husband seeking custody of his children. The husband receives one bill for the work of both lawyers even though they work for different law firms.

The lawyers, in effect, are splitting or dividing the fee between them. This arrangement is proper under certain conditions, e.g., the total fee is reasonable, the client does not object to the participation of all the lawyers involved.

☐ Confidentiality of Information

Rule 1.6. A lawyer must not reveal information relating to the representation of a client unless (a) the client consents to the disclosure, or (b) the lawyer reasonably believes the disclosure is necessary to prevent a client from committing a criminal act that is likely to result in imminent death or substantial bodily harm.

Rule 5.3 (Comment). Lawyers must instruct and supervise their paralegals and other nonlawyer assistants on the obligation not to disclose information relating to the representation of a client.

The confidentiality rule applies to *all* information relating to the representation of a client, whatever its source. The prohibition in the *Model Rules* is not limited to so-called secrets or matters explicitly communicated in confidence. A lawyer or paralegal at a party, for example, should not tell an acquaintance that the law firm is representing a certain divorce client who does not want the divorce, or that another client is adopted and is trying to force the state to reveal the names of the natural parents. An even more blatant example of a breach of confidentiality would be to carelessly leave an open client file on a desk where a stranger (e.g., another client) can read it in whole or in part. The rule on confidentiality makes it unethical for lawyers (1) to reveal client information themselves, and (2) to fail to prevent their nonlawyer employees from revealing such information.

The rule is designed to encourage clients to discuss their cases fully and frankly with their lawyers, including embarrassing or legally damaging information. Arguably, a client would be reluctant to tell a lawyer everything if the client had to worry about whether the lawyer might reveal the information to others.

The *attorney-client privilege* serves a similar function as the ethical rule on confidentiality. The two doctrines overlap. The attorney-client privilege is an *evidentiary* rule that applies to judicial and other proceedings in which a lawyer may be called as a witness or otherwise required to produce evidence concerning a client. Under the attorney-client privilege, the client can refuse to disclose, and can prevent the lawyer from disclosing, communications between them whose purpose was to facilitate legal services for the client. The rule on confidentiality we have been discussing is an *ethical* rule that can lead to the imposition of sanctions on lawyers for disclosing client information.

The attorney-client privilege, on the other hand, applies when someone is trying to force evidence from the lawyer or client.

Of course, a client can always consent to a lawyer's disclosure about the client—*if* the client is properly consulted about the proposed disclosure in advance. Some disclosures are impliedly authorized by the client in view of the nature of the case. In a dispute over alimony, for example, the lawyer would obviously have to disclose certain financial information about the client to a court or to opposing counsel.

Another instance where a lawyer can ethically disclose client information involves criminal conduct and imminent danger. For example:

> A lawyer represents a husband in a bitter divorce action against his wife. During a meeting at the law firm, the husband shows the lawyer a gun which he says he is going to use to kill his wife later the same day.

Can the lawyer tell the police what the husband said? Yes. It is not unethical for a lawyer to reveal information about a client if the lawyer reasonably believes the disclosure is necessary to prevent the client from committing a criminal act that could lead to someone's imminent death or substantial bodily harm.

Finally, suppose the lawyer later sues the client for nonpayment of fee, or the client sues the lawyer for malpractice. In such proceedings, a lawyer can reveal information about the client if the lawyer reasonably believes the disclosure is necessary to present the claim against the client or to defend the claim made by the client against the lawyer.

☐ Conflict of Interest

Rule 1.7. A lawyer should avoid a conflict of interest with his or her client.

A conflict of interest means being pulled in two different directions at the same time, creating a significant possibility that a person to whom you owe individual loyalty will be placed at a disadvantage. Such conflicts can exist in many settings. For example, assume that a salesman does part-time work selling the same kind of products of two competing companies. The salesman has a conflict of interest. How can he serve two masters with the same loyalty? How does he divide his customers between the two companies? There is an obvious danger that he will favor one over the other. The fact that he may try to be fair in his treatment of both companies does not eliminate the conflict of interest. A "significant possibility" or potential certainly exists that one of the companies will be disadvantaged. It may be that the two companies are aware of the problem and are not worried. This does not mean that there is no conflict of interest; it simply means that the affected parties are willing to take the risks involved in the conflict. As we shall see, consent is usually a valid defense to a conflict-of-interest charge.

In a law office, a number of conflict-of-interest issues can arise:

- Multiple representation
- Former client/present adversary
- Law firm disqualification

- Business transactions with a client
- Gifts from a client
- Loaning money to a client

We will explore these issues through a series of fact situations involving lawyers and clients in a family law practice.

Multiple Representation

> Bob and Patricia Fannan are separated, and they both want a divorce. They disagree over who should have custody of the children and how the marital property should be divided. Mary Franklin, Esq., is a lawyer that Jim and Mary know and trust. They decide to ask Franklin to represent both of them in the divorce.

Franklin has a conflict of interest in this case of multiple representation, also referred to as *common representation*. How can she give her undivided loyalty to both sides? On the custody question, for example, how can Franklin vigorously argue that Bob should have custody, and at the same time vigorously argue that Patricia should have custody? A client is entitled to the *independent professional judgment* of a lawyer. How can Franklin act independently for two different people who are at odds with each other? The difficulty is not solved by Franklin's commitment to be fair and objective in giving her advice to the parties. Her role as lawyer is to be a *partisan advocate* for the client. It is impossible for Franklin to play this role for two clients engaged in such a dispute. A clear conflict of interest exists. In every state, it would be unethical for Franklin to represent both Jim and Mary in this case.

Suppose, however, that the divorce case involved different facts:

> Jim and Mary Smith are separated, and they both want a divorce. They have been married only a few months. There are no children and no martial assets to divide. George Davidson, Esq., is a lawyer that Jim and Mary know and trust. They decide to ask Davidson to represent both of them in the divorce.

Can Davidson ethically represent both sides here? There are some states that *will* allow him to do so on the theory that there isn't much of a conflict between the parties. Hence the potential for harm in multiple representation is almost nonexistent. Other states, however, disagree. They frown on multiple representation even in so-called "friendly divorces" of this kind.

There is no absolute ban on all multiple representation in the ABA *Model Rules of Professional Responsibility,* although such representation is certainly discouraged. The rule is as follows:

> **Rule 1.7.**   A lawyer shall not represent a client if the representation of that client will be directly adverse to another client, *unless:*
>   (1) the lawyer reasonably believes the representation will not adversely affect the relationship with the other client, *and*
>   (2) both clients consent after consultation about the risks of the multiple representation.

In the Smith divorce, both conditions can probably be met. Such a divorce is little more than a paper procedure since there is no real dispute between the parties. Hence Davidson *would* be reasonable in believing that his representation of Jim would not adversely affect Mary, and vice versa. Davidson can represent both sides so long as Jim and Mary consent to the multiple representation after Davidson clearly explains to both of them whatever risks might be involved in doing so.

Nevertheless, lawyers are urged to avoid multiple representation even when ethically proper. The divorce may have been "friendly" when granted, but years later, one of the ex-spouses may well attack the lawyer for having had a conflict of interest. When reminded that both parties consented to the multiple representation, the ex-spouse will inevitably respond by saying, "I didn't understand what I was being asked to consent to."

The coming of no-fault divorce (page 370) has in part been due to a desire to take some of the animosity out of the divorce process. A full adversarial confrontation is not needed in every case, particularly where there is no custody dispute and few assets to divide. Hence there are pressures on the bar associations and the courts to relax the conflict-of-interest rules in divorce cases where the actual disputes between the parties are minimal or nonexistent. The legal profession is sensitive to the criticism that a too-strict application of the rules in such cases simply results in more business for more lawyers. Yet the cautious lawyer remains understandably reluctant to take chances.

Former Client/Present Adversary

> Jessica Winters, Esq., represented Gregory Noonan in his divorce action against his former wife, Eileen Noonan. In this action, Eileen received custody and alimony. Five years later, Eileen wants to reopen the case in order to obtain more alimony. Winters no longer represents Gregory who now has a different lawyer. Eileen hires Winters in her action for increased alimony.

A former client is now an adversary. Winters once represented Gregory; she is now suing him. Without the consent of the former client (Gregory), it is unethical for Winters to "switch sides" and represent Eileen against him [Rule 1.9(a)]. Consent is needed whenever the second case is the same as the first one, or when the two are substantially related. It is not necessary that the two cases involve the same set of parties. Without Greogory's consent, it would be equally unethical for Winters to represent one of his children who later sues the father for support to force him to pay college expenses. Such an action would be substantially related to the original divorce action.

If the cases are the same or are substantially related, the likelihood is strong that the lawyer will use information learned in the first case to the detriment of the former client in the second case. Winters undoubtedly found out a good deal about Gregory when she represented him in the divorce case. She might now be able to use this information *against* him in Eileen's attempt to increase her alimony or in the child's attempt to force him to pay college expenses.

Winters had a duty of loyalty when she represented Gregory. This duty does not end once the lawyer's fees are paid. The duty continues if the same case arises again or if a substantially related case arises later—even if the lawyer no longer represents the client. A conflict of interest would exist if Winters subsequently acquires a new client who goes against Gregory in the same case or in a substantially related case. Her new duty of loyalty to the second client would clash with her continuing duty to the former client in such a case.

Suppose however, that the second case against a former client is totally unrelated to the first. There is still an ethical obligation on the lawyer to refrain from using any information relating to the representation in the first case to the disadvantage of the former client in the second case [Rule 1.9(b)]. There is no ban on taking the case, but if there is any information in the office relating to the first case, that information cannot be used against the former client in the second case.

Law Firm Disqualification

> Two years ago, John Farrell, Esq., represented the father in a custody dispute with the child's maternal grandparent. The father won the case, but the grandmother was awarded limited visitation rights. The grandmother now wants to sue the father for failure to abide by the visitation order. She asks John Farrell to represent her . (The father is now using a different law firm.) John declines because of a conflict of interest, but he sends her to his law partner down the corridor.

If a lawyer is disqualified from representing a client because of a conflict of interest, every lawyer in the *same law firm* is also disqualified unless the client being protected by this rule consents to the representation. In the above example, the *father* would have to consent to the representation of the grandmother by the partner, or indeed, by John Farrell himself. [Rule 1.10].

Business Transactions with a Client

> Paul Kelly, Esq., is Ed Johnson's lawyer in a divorce case. Johnson owns a cleaning business for which Kelly does some of the legal work. Johnson offers to allow Kelly to buy a 30 percent interest in the business. Kelly would continue as Johnson's lawyer.

Assume that the business runs into difficulties and Johnson considers bankruptcy. He goes to Kelly for advice on bankruptcy law. Kelly has dual concerns: to give Johnson competent legal advice, and to protect his own 30 percent interest in the business. Bankruptcy may be good for Johnson, but disastrous for Kelly's investment. How can he give Johnson independent professional advice when the advice may go against Kelly's own interest?

This is not to say, however, that it is always unethical for a lawyer to enter a business transaction with a client. If certain strict conditions are met, it can be proper. The rule is as follows:

> **Rule 1.8(a).** A lawyer shall not enter a business transaction with a client, *unless*
> (1) the terms of the business transaction are fair and reasonable to the client and are fully disclosed to the client in understandable language in writing, *and*
> (2) the client is given reasonable opportunity to seek advice on the transaction from another lawyer who is not involved with the transaction or the parties, *and*
> (3) the client consents to the business transaction in writing.

In our example, Johnson must be given the chance to consult with an attorney other than Kelly on the prospect of letting Kelly buy a 30 percent interest in the business. Kelly would have to give Johnson a clear, written explanation of their business relationship. And the relationship must be fair and reasonable to Johnson.

Gifts from a Client

> William Stanton, Esq., has been the family attorney of the Tarkinton family for years. At Christmas, Mrs. Tarkinton gave Stanton a television set and told Stanton to change her will so that Stanton's daughter would receive funds for a free college education.

Generally, attorneys are allowed to accept a gift from a client. If, however, a document must be prepared in order to carry out the gift, it is unethical for the lawyer to prepare that document. A conflict of interest would exist. In our example, it would probably be in Mrs. Tarkinton's interest to have the will written so that she could retain maximum flexibility on how much she would pay for the college education and so that she could change her mind if she wanted to. Yet it would be in Stanton's interest to try to write the will so that it would be difficult for her to back out of her commitment.

Thus, a lawyer cannot prepare a document such as a will, a trust fund, a contract, etc., that results in any substantial gift from a client to the lawyer, or to the lawyer's children, spouse, parents, brothers, or sisters. If a client wants to make such a gift, another lawyer must prepare the document. There is, however, one exception. If the client is *related* to the person receiving the gift, the lawyer can prepare the document [Rule 1.8(c)].

There does not appear to be any ethical problem in taking the gift of the television set. No documents are involved.

Loaning money to a Client

> Henry Harris, Esq., is Barbara Atkinson's attorney in a divorce action against her husband. While the case is pending, Harris agrees to lend Atkinson living expenses and court filing fees.

It can be a conflict of interest for a lawyer to give financial assistance to a client in connection with current or planned litigation. A loan covering litigation expenses, however, is an exception to this rule. In our example, the main difficulty is the loan to cover the client's living expenses. Suppose that the husband makes an offer to settle the case with Barbara. There is a danger that Harris's advice will be colored by the fact that he has a financial interest in Barbara—he wants to have his loan on living expenses repaid. The offer to settle from the husband may not be enough to cover the loan. Should he advise Barbara to accept the offer? It may be in Barbara's interest to accept the offer, but not in his own interest. Such *divided loyalty* is the essence of a conflict of interest.

As indicated, a major exception concerns the expenses of litigation such as filing fees and other court costs. It is not unethical for a lawyer to lend the client money to cover such expenses.

☐ Safekeeping Property

> **Rule 1.15.**   A lawyer shall hold client property separate from the lawyer's own property.

Client funds—or the funds of others connected with a client's case—should be kept in a separate account, and complete records should exist on the funds.

The lawyer should not *commingle* or mix general law firm funds with client funds. It is unethical for a lawyer to place everything in one account no matter how good the records are on who owns the amounts in the account. In a commingled account, the danger is simply too great that client funds will be used for nonclient purposes.

☐ **Withdrawal**

> **Rule 1.16(a).** A lawyer must withdraw from a case if continuing would result in a violation of the law or of these ethical rules. The lawyer must also withdraw if discharged by the client, and if the lawyer's physical or mental condition materially impairs his or her ability to represent the client.

Lawyers are not required to take every case. Furthermore, once lawyers begin a case, they are not obligated to stay with a client until the case is over. If, however, the lawyer has been appointed to the case, or if the case has already begun in court, withdrawal must usually be with the permission of the court.

There are circumstances in which a lawyer must not accept a case or must withdraw from a case:

- The representation of the client would violate the law, e.g., the lawyer is asked for advice on how to defraud the Internal Revenue Service.

- The representation of the client would violate ethical rules, e.g., the lawyer discovers he or she has a conflict of interest with the client that cannot be cured by consent.

- The client fires the lawyer.

- The lawyer's physical or mental condition has deteriorated (e.g., alcohol problems, depression due to grief) to the point where the lawyer's ability to represent the client has been materially impaired.

A lawyer has the option of withdrawing if the client insists on an objective that the lawyer considers "repugnant" (e.g., the client wants to pursue litigation solely to harass someone), or "imprudent" (e.g., the client insists that a motion be refiled which the lawyer feels is an obvious waste of time and is likely to incur the anger of the court) [Rule 1.16(b)(3)].

☐ **False Statements/Failure to Disclose**

> **Rule 3.3(a).** A lawyer shall not knowingly: (1) make a false statement of material fact or law to a tribunal, (2) fail to disclose a material fact to a tribunal when disclosure is necessary to avoid helping a client commit a criminal or fraudulent act, (3) fail to tell a tribunal about laws or other authority that go directly against the position of the lawyer's client if this law or authority is not disclosed by opposing counsel, or (4) offer evidence that the lawyer knows is false.

One of the reasons the legal profession is held in low esteem by the general public is the perception that lawyers do not always comply with Rule 3.3(a).

The implications of subsection 3 of the rule are particularly startling.

> Karen Singer and Bill Carew are attorneys opposing each other in a bitter case involving a large sum of money. Singer is smarter than Carew. Singer knows about a very damaging but obscure case that goes against her client. But because of sloppy research, Carew does not know about it. Singer never mentions the case and it never comes up during the litigation.

Singer may pay a price for her silence. She is subject to sanctions for a violation of her ethical obligation of disclosure under Rule 3.3(a)(3).

☐ Communication with the Other Side

> **Rule 4.2.** In representing a client, a lawyer shall not communicate with a party on the other side about the subject of the case if the lawyer knows that the party is represented by another lawyer. The latter lawyer must consent to such a communication.

> **Rule 4.3.** If the other side is not represented, a lawyer must not give him or her the impression that the lawyer is uninvolved. The lawyer should not give this person advice other than the advice to obtain his or her own lawyer.

The great fear is that a lawyer will take advantage of the other side.

> Dan and Theresa Kline have just separated and are thinking about a divorce. Each claims the marital home. Theresa hires Thomas Darby, Esq., to represent her. Darby calls Dan to ask him if he is interested in settling the case.

It is unethical for Darby to contact Dan about the case if Darby knows that Dan has his own lawyer. Darby must talk with Dan's lawyer. Only the latter can give Darby permission to communicate with Dan. If Dan does not have a lawyer, Darby can talk with Dan, but he must not allow Dan to be mislead about Darby's role. Dan must be made to understand the fact that Darby works for the other side. The only advice Darby can ethically give Dan in such a situation is to obtain his own lawyer.

☐ Nonlawyer Assistants

> **Rule 5.3.** A lawyer must make reasonable efforts to ensure that paralegals, secretaries, and other nonlawyers working in the office are aware of and act in accordance with the lawyer's ethical responsibilities.

As we said earlier, a lawyer acts unethically if he or she does not properly supervise nonlawyers working in the office. Such supervision must include "appropriate instruction" on the ethical rules governing a lawyer's conduct.

□ Solicitation

> **Rule 7.3.** A lawyer may not solicit employment from a prospective client with whom the lawyer has no family or prior professional relationship when a significant motive for doing so is the lawyer's monetary gain.

> Frank Ellis, Esq., stands outside the office of a marriage counselor and gives a business card to any depressed, angry, or otherwise distraught husband or wife coming out of the office after a therapy session. The cards says that Ellis is a lawyer specializing in divorce cases.

Ellis's way of looking for prospective divorce clients is pejoratively referred to as "ambulance chasing." There is no indication that Ellis is related to any of the people coming out of the therapy sessions, nor that he has any prior professional relationship with them, e.g., as former clients. Ellis appears to have one goal: finding a source of fees. His conduct is therefore unethical under Rule 7.3. It would make no difference if the solicitation were made on the phone, through the mail, or in person so long as the target is a specific person who is known to need legal services. Direct, one-on-one solicitation of clients in this way is not allowed. The concern is that a lawyer who approaches a stranger in trouble may exert undue influence on him or her. Citizens should not be pressured into using the legal system or into using any particular lawyer at a time when they may be vulnerable to such pressure.

A different result would follow if Ellis engaged in proper *advertising*, a topic to which we now turn.

□ Advertising

> **Rule 7.2.** A lawyer may advertise services on radio, on TV, in the newspaper, or through other public media so long as the ad is neither false nor misleading and does not constitute improper solicitation under Rule 7.3.

There was a time when almost all forms of advertising by lawyers were disallowed. In 1977, however, the United States Supreme Court stunned the legal profession by holding that truthful advertising cannot be completely prohibited. *Bates v. State Bar of Arizona*, 433 U.S. 350, 97 S.Ct. 2691, 53 L.Ed.2d 810 (1977). The first amendment protects such advertising. Furthermore, truthful and nonmisleading advertising to the general public does not pose the same danger of undue pressure on specific persons by lawyers who are primarily interested in money.

The *Bates* opinion has had a dramatic impact on the legal profession. Prior to the opinion, traditional lawyers considered any form of advertising to be highly offensive to the dignity of the profession. Many still do. While *Bates* forced the profession to change, the scope of this change is still the subject of debate, since the Supreme Court did not prohibit all regulation of lawyer advertising. Consequently, states differ on what regulations should be imposed.

☐ **Unauthorized Practice of Law**

> **Rule 5.5(b).** A lawyer shall not assist someone who is not a member of the bar in the unauthorized practice of law.

Lay people can represent themselves. It is not the unauthorized practice of law, therefore, for a lawyer to give assistance to such people in their endeavor. Suppose, however, that a lawyer assists a nonlawyer to help *others* with their legal problems:

> Sam Grondon is a nonlawyer who sells Do-It-Yourself Divorce Kits. A kit contains all the forms for a divorce in the state, plus written instructions on how to use the forms. Paulene Unger, Esq., writes the kits and obtains a royalty from Sam on every sale. She never talks to any buyers of the kits. Most customers make their purchase by mail without talking to Sam. A few customers go to Sam's house to buy the kits. Occasionally, Sam will answer some simple questions to help these buyers fill out the forms in the kits.

Has Paulene assisted a nonlawyer in the unauthorized practice of law? Yes, but only with respect to the customers that come to Sam's home and receive in-person instruction on filling out the forms. Such activity is the unauthorized practice of law, and a lawyer must not assist someone to engage in it. It is proper for a nonlawyer to sell (and indeed, to write) how-to-do-it texts, and to give written instructions on using the material in the texts—so long as the instructions are not directed at a particular person. Giving generalized legal instructions to the public at large is not the practice of law. Kits on divorcing yourself, suing your landlord, incorporating, etc., are illegal only when personal legal advice is provided along with the kits—as when Sam helped particular buyers fill out the forms. An attorney acts unethically to the extent that he or she is associated with a nonlawyer engaged in such activity.

Assignment 4.2

Smith is a lawyer who works at the firm of Johnson & Johnson. He represents Ralph Grant, who is seeking a divorce against his wife, Amy Grant. In their first meeting, Smith learns that Ralph is an experienced carpenter who is out of work and has very little money. Smith's fee is $150 an hour. Since Ralph has no money and has been having trouble finding work, Smith tells Ralph that he won't have to pay the fee if the court does not grant him the divorce. One day while Smith is working on another case involving Helen Oberlin, he learns that Helen is looking for a carpenter. Smith recommends Ralph to Helen, and she hires him for a small job.

Six months pass. The divorce case is dropped when the Grants reconcile. In the meantime, Helen Oberlin is very dissatisfied with Ralph's carpentry work for her; she claims he didn't do the work he contracted to do. She wants to know what she can do about it. She tries to call Smith at Johnson & Johnson, but it told that Smith does not work there anymore. Another lawyer at the firm, Georgia Quinton, Esq., helps Helen.

Are there any ethical violations involved in this situation? See the General Instructions for the Legal-Analysis Assignment, in chapter one.

Section B. Other Wrongdoing[1]

The following list provides an overview of the major ways that lawyers can be sanctioned. These sanctions are in addition to bar discipline if unethical conduct is also committed. The phrase "legal malpractice" usually refers to the last item on the list—negligence.

- Contempt of court
- Criminal action
- Breach of contract
- Fraud
- Malicious prosecution
- Abuse of process
- False arrest or false imprisonment
- Defamation
- Negligence

While our primary emphasis in this section will be the last sanction—a civil negligence action (see Exhibit 4–1 on the Predominant Errors in Family Law)—a brief mention of the others is appropriate.

Contempt of Court

A lawyer can be cited for contempt of court for conduct such as insulting a judge in open court, flagrantly disobeying a court order, etc. The punishment for such conduct can be a fine or imprisonment.

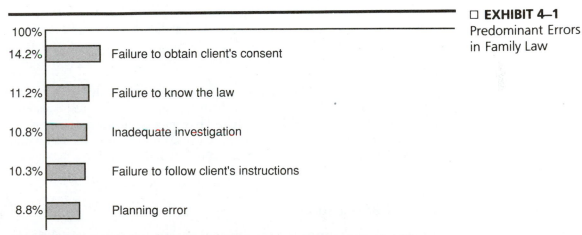

□ **EXHIBIT 4–1**
Predominant Errors in Family Law

Source: Ameircan Bar Association, Standing Committee on Lawyers' Professional Liability, National Legal Malpractice Center, *History of Statistical Analysis* (1985).

---

[1]See W. Statsky, TORTS: PERSONAL INJURY LITIGATION (2d ed. 1989).

Criminal Conduct

A lawyer, like any citizen, can be convicted of a crime. Stealing a client's funds, for example, can lead to a larceny conviction. Obstruction of justice and certain kinds of income tax evasion can similarly be prosecuted.

Breach of Contract

There are two possible theories under which a breach-of-contract action could be brought by a client against his or her lawyer.

1. Breach of an express warranty or guarantee given by the lawyer to the client to produce a certain result, *or*

2. Breach of an *implied* condition that the lawyer will use reasonable skill in rendering professional services.

It is rare that a lawyer will give any guarantees. Hence, a breach-of-contract action based on breach of warranty or on an unfulfilled guarantee is unlikely. In a few states, however, courts will *imply* a contractual condition or promise in the lawyer-client relationship that the lawyer will use reasonable care in providing legal services. A failure to provide such care will then become the basis of a breach-of-contract action against the lawyer. Other states will not imply such a condition and hence will not permit a contract action unless the lawyer has given a specific warranty or guarantee that has been broken. When a lawyer fails to provide reasonable care in such states, the theory of liability is the *tort* of *negligence* rather than the breach-of-contract action.

Does it make any difference whether the client sues a lawyer in a *contract* action based upon a breach of implied promise to use reasonable care or in a *tort* action for negligence? Essentially, it makes no difference since in both kinds of actions the main question will be whether the lawyer used reasonable care, as we shall see below. One possible difference might be the statute of limitations, which in a given state may differ for the two types of actions.

Fraud

When a lawyer gives false legal advice that is intentionally or knowingly false, a civil fraud or deceit action can be brought. In some states, consumer fraud statutes have been held to apply to lawyers who, for example, misrepresent their experience in order to attract clients. (Futhermore, the fraud may be serious enough to lead to a criminal fraud action in *addition* to the civil fraud action.)

Malicious Prosecution

Malicious prosecution is a tort brought against someone for maliciously instituting legal proceedings against you. Here is an example of how a lawyer could become a defendant in a malicious prosecution action:

> After a bitter divorce proceeding, Diana is awarded custody of the only child of the marriage. George, her ex-husband, asks his lawyer to institute proceedings against Diana to remove custody of the child from her because she is a prostitute. It is clear to the lawyer, however, that Diana is not a prostitute and that George wants to bring the action solely to "get even" with her. Nevertheless,

the lawyer agrees to go ahead. The strategy they decide to take is to file a criminal neglect case against Diana because of the prostitution. Then they will ask the court to take the child away from her. George is the complaining witness against Diana in the criminal neglect proceeding.

The prosecutor loses the criminal case, and Diana is acquitted of criminal neglect.

Diana now brings a malicious prosecution civil suit against *both* George and his lawyer. She will win if she can prove malice—that George and his lawyer knew that the criminal case was without any foundation. She must show that it was not brought in the good faith belief that it could be won.

Abuse of Process

Suppose an attorney advises a client to institute an otherwise valid criminal action against an individual solely for the purpose of pressuring that individual to settle a pending civil action on favorable terms. The lawyer and the person initiating the criminal action may both be liable for the separate tort called *abuse of process.* They both misused the criminal court process: forcing someone to settle a civil suit is not one of the purposes of the criminal law.

False Arrest or False Imprisonment

As with the torts discussed above, the client as well as the lawyer may both be liable if they have wrongly brought about the arrest or confinement of a person. In most situations, however, only the lawyer's client is sued.

Defamation

In the course of heated litigation, it would not be uncommon for a lawyer to defame one of the parties, a nonparty witness, or the other attorney. If, however, the defamation occurs in connection with a court proceeding, the defaming lawyer enjoys the defense of absolute privilege.

Negligence

One in every seventeen lawyers will be sued for negligence. This is a dramatic increase from only a short time ago. In this section, we will examine the nature of a negligence suit against a lawyer. In these suits, the test for the standard of care against which the lawyer's conduct will be measured is the *reasonable person,* with the qualification that since the lawyer holds him or herself out as a person with special skills, the standard of care will be a reasonable person possessing such skills. The lawyer will not be liable simply because he or she made a mistake or lost a case. Unless the lawyer specifically guarantees a result, the standard of care will be reasonableness, not warranty. Expressed in greater detail, the standard is as follows:[2]

> An attorney who acts in good faith and in an honest belief that his advice and acts are well founded and in the best interest of his client is not answerable for a mere error of judgment or for a mistake in a point of law which has not

---

[2]*Hodges v. Carter,* 239 N.C. 517, 519–20, 80 S.E.2d 144, 145–46 (1954).

been settled by the court of last resort in his State and on which resonable doubt may be entertained by well-informed lawyers.

Conversely, he is answerable in damages for any loss to his client which proximately results from a want of that degree of knowledge and skill ordinarily possessed by others of his profession similarly situated, or from the omission to use reasonable care and diligence, or from the failure to exercise in good faith his best judgment in attending to the litigation committed to his care.

A distinction should be made between:

- A mistake that could have been made by any lawyer in good standing using the skill and knowledge normally possessed by lawyers, and
- A mistake that would not have been made by a lawyer in good standing using the skill and knowledge normally possessed by lawyers.

Only the latter category of mistake is considered unreasonable and hence will lead to liability for negligence. The test is not whether the *average* lawyer would have made the mistake. The focus is on the lawyer *in good standing* using the knowledge and skills *ordinarily* or *normally* found in lawyers.

It is important to keep in mind that the lawyer is the *agent* of the client. While the lawyer is representing the client (within the scope of the lawyer's "employment"), the client is bound by what the lawyer does—and this includes both successes and mistakes. Therefore, if the lawyer makes a mistake and the client loses the case as a result, the recourse of the client is to sue the lawyer and try to establish that an unreasonable mistake was made that would not have been made by a lawyer in good standing using the skill and knowledge normally possessed by lawyers.[3]

 Mistakes of Lawyers

Kind of Mistake

Technical/mechanical mistake *not* involving the exercise of judgment.

Examples
- Lawyer forgets to file an action and client is thereby barred by the statute of limitations.
- Lawyer forgets to appear in court and client thereby has a default judgment entered against him or her.

Negligence Consequences of This Kind of Mistake

It is relatively easy for a client to win a negligence action against a lawyer based on this kind of mistake. (See, however, the discussion on causation starting on page 95.)

---

[3]Depending upon the kind of mistake the lawyer made, some courts might permit the client to "undo" the error by correcting it, e.g., permit a client to file a document even though the client's lawyer had negligently allowed the deadline for its filing to pass. It is rare, however, that the courts will be this accommodating. A client will have to live with the mistakes of his or her lawyer and seek relief solely by suing the lawyer for negligence. See R. Mallen and V. Levit, LEGAL MALPRACTICE, 45ff (1977).

Kind of Mistake

Tactical mistake involving the exercise of judgment and discretion in a relatively uncomplicated area of the law.

Examples

- Lawyer decides not to call a certain witness who would have been able to provide valuable testimony.
- Lawyer does not object to the introduction of certain evidence at trial from the other side and thereby waives the right to object on appeal.

Negligence Consequences of This Kind of Mistake

It is difficult for a client to win a negligence action against a lawyer based on this kind of mistake unless what the lawyer did or failed to do was blatantly contrary to what would be considered good or competent practice. (See the discussion on causation below.)

Kind of Mistake

Tactical mistake involving the exercise of judgment and discretion in a complicated area of the law.

Examples

- Lawyer fails to challenge the constitutionality of a statute.
- Lawyer calls an expert witness on the value of a complex pension plan, and the witness gives very damaging testimony to the client of the lawyer who called this witness.

Negligence Consequences of This Kind of Mistake

It is almost impossible for a client to win a negligence action against a lawyer based on this kind of mistake. This is so not only because of the complexity of the area of the law, but also because of the difficulty of proving causation, i.e., that the mistake caused the client any harm (See the discussion on causation.)

Causation

To win a negligence case against a lawyer, it is not enough to establish that the lawyer made an unreasonable mistake; causation must also be proven. For certain kinds of lawyer errors, a "trial within a trial" must occur. For example:

> Bill hires Clara Bonner, Esq. to represent him in a suit against his ex-wife Patricia for defrauding him out of $10,000 which he had received as an inheritance from his uncle. He claims that she did this while they were married. (Assume that the intrafamily tort immunity would not bar this action, page 543.) Unfortunately, Bonner forgets to file the action within the statute-of-limitations period. Bill can no longer sue Patricia for fraud; the action is barred. Bill now sues Bonner for negligence in letting the statute of limitations run. Assume that Bonner's error was quite unreasonable. What can Bill recover from his lawyer? $10,000? Is that what he lost? Did the lawyer *cause* $10,000 in damages? The answer is yes—but only if Bill can establish (1) that he would have won his fraud case against Patricia, and (2) that he would have been able to recover $10,000 from her. In Bill's negligence suit against Bonner, Bill must establish that he would have won the suit against Patricia if it had not been barred by the statute of limitations. He must show that he had a meritorious fraud case. This is the "suit within a suit" or the "trial within a trial."

The difficulty of establishing causation can be further complicated: suppose that Patricia no longer has the $10,000 or is bankrupt. Even if Bill could have won a $10,000 judgment against her, he would have been able to *collect* nothing or very little. Hence it cannot be said that Bonner's negligence in waiting too long to file the fraud action caused Bill a $10,000 loss.

Note on Indemnity

Indemnity is the right to have another person pay you the amount you were forced to pay. In tort law, when one party is liable to a plaintiff solely because of what someone else has done (e.g., employer is liable because of what employee did), the party who is liable and who pays as a result of the liability can often receive indemnity from the person whose conduct produced the liability. Assume that a lawyer is representing a *defendant* in a suit brought against the latter. Assume further that the defendant loses the suit and must pay the judgment solely because of the negligence of the lawyer representing the defendant. In some states, such a client can ask a court to force the lawyer to *indemnify* him or her based upon the above definition of indemnity.

The following guidelines address the problem of escalating malpractice claims against lawyers.

Avoiding Malpractice: Practice Guide

Reprinted with permission from ABA/BNA's Lawyer's Manual on Professional Conduct (Trial Practice Series), p. 301:1001. Copyright 1989 by The Bureau of National Affairs, Inc., jointly with the American Bar Association.

With the dramatic increase in the number of malpractice claims that are being asserted against lawyers, the need for methods of reducing a lawyer's potential exposure to liability is obvious. There are a variety of practices lawyers can institute to improve their chances of avoiding malpractice:

- Decline representation of prospective clients whose legal matter, expectation about the legal system, or personality gives a strong impression of trouble.
- Use a system to screen prospective clients' cases for actual and potential conflicts of interest.
- If a prospective client's business is declined, put that decision in writing and send a non-engagement letter to the would-be client.
- Establish what services the client wants and shape the client's expectations to encourage an understanding of what the lawyer and legal system can and cannot accomplish, and how long it may take to resolve the matter.
- Do not make promises or guarantees of results unless they can be fulfilled.
- Always use a written representation agreement that sets out both the objects of the retainer and the details of the fee arrangement.
- Maintain rapport with the client and keep him informed of all the significant occurrences in his case.
- Bill the client regularly and detail the services rendered.
- Research both the facts and law of the client's case before commencing legal action on his behalf.
- Have an effective time and docket control system.

- Refer cases to, or associate with, more experienced counsel when necessary, but check the other lawyer's qualifications first to assure his good standing and expertise.
- Do not withhold legal services on the sole basis that the client has not paid your fee.
- Stay out of business deals with clients.
- Think twice before suing a client to recover payment of your fee.
- Be aware of situations in which liability to non-client third parties could arise.

Section C. Paralegals

Our concern is twofold: when is the paralegal liable for his or her wrong-doing, and when is the employing lawyer liable for the wrongdoing of the paralegal? The governing principle of employer liability is *respondeat superior*. According to this concept, the employer is responsible for the torts of its employees so long as they were acting in the scope of their employment at the time they did the acts leading to the torts. Assume that George Rothwell is a paralegal working for Helen Farrell, Esq. In the course of George's job, he does some negligent work that harms a client. Helen Farrell, Esq., is liable to the client for the negligence even if she did nothing wrong or negligently herself. She is vicariously liable.

It is important to keep in mind, however, that employees are *also* responsible for their own torts. The client in the above example could elect to bring a direct action against the paralegal, George Rothwell, for negligence.

Respondeat superior is simply a basis upon which liability can be imposed on the employer in the event that the client decides not to sue the employee directly or decides to sue both the employer and the employee. Of course, the client cannot obtain double damages by suing the master (employer) and the servant (employee). There can only be one recovery. The choice is usually to pursue "the deep pocket"—the person who has the most money from which a judgment can be collected. Most often, of course, this is the employer.

Intentional Torts and Criminal Activity

If a paralegal commits an intentional tort, e.g., deceit, battery, malicious prosecution, the paralegal is personally liable to the injured party. If the paralegal commits a crime, the criminal act may also be the basis for a civil action against the paralegal. What about the employing attorney? Is he or she also liable for the employee's intentional torts or for the civil wrong growing out of the paralegal's criminal act?

The answer depends, in part, on whether the paralegal was attempting to further the "business" of his or her employing lawyer at the time. If so, then the lawyer is liable to the client under the doctrine of *respondeat superior*. The tortious activity in such cases will be considered within the scope of employment. For example, suppose that while trying to collect an unpaid law firm bill, the paralegal assaults or slanders the client. Such activity would probably be considered within the scope of employment since the incident centered on a law firm matter—the client's bill. Quite a different result, however, might be reached if the paralegal happens to meet a law firm client at a bar and assualts or falsely imprisons the client following an argument over a football game.

Negligence

It is often much easier to establish that the paralegal's negligence was within the scope of employment (making the employer vicariously liable under *respondeat superior*) than it is to prove that intentional torts fall within this scope.

When the paralegal allegedly makes a negligent mistake, what is the standard of care? Is the paralegal held to the standard of care of a lawyer or of a paralegal? The basic standard of care is reasonableness under the circumstances. If the person is engaged in a trade or profession and thereby possesses greater skills than the average citizen, then the standard of care will be the reasonable person possessing such skills. According to the *Restatement of Torts*.[4]

> **§ 299A. Undertaking in Profession or Trade** Unless he represents that he has greater or less skill or knowledge, one who undertakes to render services in the practice of a profession or trade is required to exercise the skill and knowledge normally possessed by members of that profession or trade in good standing in similar communities.

The implication of § 299A is that if the paralegal "represents" him or herself as having more skill than most paralegals, he or she will be held to the higher skill standard. Suppose, for example, that the paralegal (or secretary or law clerk) deals directly with a client and does not make clear to the client that he or she is *not* a lawyer. Assume that by the manner in which the paralegal acts, the clients justifiably is under the impression that the paralegal is the lawyer. The paralegal then makes a negligent mistake. If the client brings a negligence action against the paralegal, the standard of care against which the paralegal's conduct will be measured will be that of a lawyer since the paralegal, in effect, represented him or herself to the client as a lawyer. If, on the other hand, the paralegal makes clear to the client that he or she is not a lawyer and that he or she has less training and skill than a lawyer, then the standard of care, under § 299A, is "the skill and knowledge normally possessed" by paralegals.

Suppose, however, that the paralegal never deals directly with the client. The entire work product of the paralegal in such situations blends into the work product of the lawyer. Therefore, the legal services are represented to the client as the work product of the lawyer. Hence, even though the negligent act about which the client is complaining was committed by the paralegal, that standard of care will be the reasonable *lawyer* under the circumstances, since the client had every right to believe it was receiving the services of a lawyer.

---

[4]American Law Institute, RESTATEMENT (SECOND) OF TORTS, § 299A (1965).

Assignment 4.3

In this assignment you will be asked to determine whether there are any court opinions in your state in which lawyers have been sued for designated causes of action. (See General Instructions for the Court-Opinion Assignments in chapter one.) For each of the causes of action listed below, give the citation to at least three court opinions, if any, written by a state court of your state in which a lawyer was sued for:

(a) Breach of contract

(b) Fraud

(c) Malicious prosecution

(d) Abuse of process

(e) False arrest or false imprisonment

(f) Negligence

Briefly describe the facts of one case under each category.

Assignment 4.4

Joe Smith, Esq., represents Jim Noonan in the preparation of a will. It was Jim's intent that his friend Ralph Skidmore receive a bequest of $10,000. Joe Smith drafts the will. After Jim dies, it is discovered that Joe Smith made a mistake in drafting the will with the result that Ralph received nothing.

(a) Make an argument that Joe Smith did not *cause* a $10,000 loss to Ralph. Assume that Jim died at the age of thirty-five, one year after the will was drafted, and that his death was a surprise to everyone—including Jim.

(b) Are there any other problems that might prevent Ralph from being able to bring a negligence action against Joe Smith?

(See General Instructions for the Legal-Analysis Assignments in chapter one.)

(c) Draft a complaint for Ralph against Joe Smith.

(See General Instructions for the Complaint-Drafting Assignment in chapter one.)

Key Chapter Terminology

Ethics
Canons of Ethics
Rules of Professional Responsibility
Sanctions for Unethical Conduct
American Bar Association (ABA)
*Model Rules of Professional
    Responsibility*
Lawyer Competence
Fees
Retainer
Minimum Fee Schedule
Price Fixing
Contingent Fee
Fee Splitting
Client Confidentiality

Attorney-Client Privilege
Conflict of Interest
Multiple Representation
Common Representation
Independent Professional Judgment
Disqualification
Switching Sides
Divided Loyalty
Commingling Funds
Withdrawal of Attorney
Communication with Other Side
Nonlawyer Assistants
Solicitation
Advertising
Unauthorized Practice of Law

Legal Malpractice
Contempt of Court
Fraud
Malicious Prosecution
Abuse of Process
False Imprisonment
Negligence
Standard of Care

Good Standing
Technical Mistake
Tactical Mistake
Indemnity
Non-Engagement Letter
Paralegal Negligence
Respondeat Superior

CHAPTER FIVE

Preliminary Legal Interview: Background Information

■ Chapter Outline

T he central theme of this chapter is factual comprehensiveness. While many issues can arise in a divorce proceeding, the major question is often, who gets what? To represent a client effectively on this question, the law firm must know a great deal about the financial assets and liabilities of the client and of the other spouse. One way to start collecting the data is by conducting a thorough preliminary client interview.

The interview should also cover nonfinancial matters such as the identity and health of all the participants, and prior contacts with other attorneys. But the focus of the interview is usually financial. How have the parties supported themselves in the past? What are their expenses? What kinds of property do they own? How did this property come into the marriage? Where is this property now? These broad topics will be pursued through scores of detailed questions that are designed to provide evidence and leads to evidence that will be used as the case unfolds.[1]

Questions and checklists on other areas, e.g., on the grounds for divorce, on separation agreements, will be presented in the chapters on these topics. Later, when we examine interrogatories, we will also see how similar information, particularly financial information, is sought from an opponent (page 213).

The questions are not necessarily listed in the order in which they would be asked. In most law firms, such questions would be asked during an initial client interview after the client has signed a retainer, the document that, in effect, hires the firm. Some lawyers, however, prefer to send the questions home with the client to be answered in a more relaxed setting where the client can check his or her records.

Intake Memorandum

FROM: __(name of interviewer)__   CASE NUMBER # _____

TO: __(name of supervisor)__   OFFICE FILE NUMBER _____

DATE OF INTERVIEW: _____

You have asked me to conduct an interview of our client _____ in order to obtain comprehensive financial and related information.

I. Introductory Facts

(Use other side or attach additional sheets
if more space is needed for any of the questions

1. Client's full name _____
2. Maiden name (if woman) _____
3. Other names used (if any) _____
4. Current address _____
5. Length of time lived at this address _____
6. Other residences (if any) and the amount of time lived at each _____
   _____
   _____
7. Home phone _____ Business phone _____
8. Business address _____
9. Occupations _____
10. Other addresses and phone numbers where client can be reached _____
    _____
11. Age _____

---

[1]Many of the questions are adapted from L. Brown, *A Family Legal Information Check List,* 3 THE PRACTICAL LAWYER 60, no. 6 (October 1957), and L. Barrett, *The Initial Interview with a Divorce Client,* 23 THE PRACTICAL LAWYER 75, no. 4 (June 1977). Copyright by the American Law Institute. Reprinted with the Permission of *The Practical Lawyer*. See also L. Brown, MANUAL FOR PERIODIC CHECKUP (1983).

I. Introductory Facts—Continued

12. Place of birth _____

13. Location of birth certificate _____

14. Name of spouse _____

15. Address _____

16. Home phone _____

17. Business address _____

18. Business phone _____

19. Other addresses and phone numbers where spouse can be reached _____

    _____

20. Age of spouse _____

21. Place of birth _____

22. Names and addresses of other attorneys (if any) who have been contacted about
    this case _____

    _____

II. Marital Facts

23. Date current marriage entered _____

24. Place of marriage _____

                          (City)   (County)   (State)

25. Marriage license dated _____

26. Marriage license granted by _____

27. Certified copy of license kept at _____

28. Marriage ceremony performed by _____

29. Marriage certificate dated _____

30. Certified copy kept at _____

31. Names and addresses of witnesses to ceremony _____

    _____

32. Has there ever been a common law spouse? If so, give details. _____

    _____

33. Is the current marriage the client's first marriage? _____

34. If not, answer questions 23–32 as to each prior marriage. _____

    _____

    _____

35. Indicate how each prior marriage terminated _____

    _____

    _____

    _____

36. Was current spouse ever married before? _____

37. If so, give names of prior spouses and how each prior marriage terminated ___

    _____

    _____

    _____

II. Marital Facts—Continued

38. List all children, if any. For each child, give full name, date of birth, current address, means of support, names of natural parents, names of adoptive parents, if any, names of guardians, if any _____

_____

_____

_____

_____

III. Prior Contracts Between Spouses

39. Was there an antenuptial contract? _____

40. If so, on what date was it signed _____

41. Give the names and addresses of the attorneys, if any, who prepared it _____

_____

42. Contract kept at _____

43. Is there a waiver by the wife of dower or other rights? _____

_____

44. Is there a clause on the manner of holding title to real property? If so, explain.

_____

_____

45. Is there a clause on life insurance? If so, explain. _____

46. Is there a clause on waiving future claims to each other's property? If so, explain.

_____

47. Summarize other important clauses _____

_____

_____

_____

48. Is there a separation agreement already in existance? _____

49. If so, on what date was it signed? _____

50. Give the names and addresses of the attorneys, if any, who prepared it _____

51. Was this agreement made after you separated? _____

52. Attach a description of how the agreement divided property between the spouses.

53. Support provisions in the agreement for spouse and children (attach description of terms).

54. Custody of children (attach description of terms)

55. Summarize other important clauses _____

_____

_____

_____

56. Separation agreement kept at _____

IV. Itemized Monthly Expenses

	Yourself	Children
57. Mortgage or rent		
58. Taxes		
59. Insurance on house		
60. Gas/oil		
61. Electric		
62. Water & Sewer		
63. Telephone		
64. Maintenance of house or apartment		
65. Maintenance of swimming pool		
66. Groceries		
67. School tuition		
68. Life insurance		
69. Clothing		
70. Shoes		
71. Maintenance for clothing—tailors, laundry, etc.		
72. Maid		
73. Babysitter		
74. Gasoline for car		
75. Tolls		
76. License		
77. Registration		
78. Maintenance for car		
79. Payments on car		
80. Insurance on car		
81. Doctors		
82. Drugs		
83. Health insurance		
84. Haircuts/hairdresser		

IV. Itemized Monthly Expenses—Continued

		Yourself	Children
85.	Miscellaneous toiletries—soap, cold cream, etc.		
86.	Pets—care and food		
87.	Entertainment		
88.	Cash allowance		
89.	Vacation allowance		
90.	Contribution to church		
91.	Charity (other)		
92.	Subscriptions		
93.	Club membership, musical instruments and lessons		
94.	Totals		

V. Health Information

95. Describe your present health. Give details on prior health problems, if any. Names of doctors. Dates of treatment _____

_____

_____

_____

_____

96. Same questions as to your spouse _____

_____

_____

_____

_____

97. Same questions as to each dependent child _____

_____

_____

_____

_____

VI. Wills

98. Do you have your own will? _____

99. Date will signed _____

100. Name of lawyer who prepared will _____

101. Address _____

102. Initial executor _____

Wills—Continued

103. Successor executor _____

104. Is guardian named for children? _____

105. Specific bequests, if any:

    What property or amount? To whom (attach description) _____

    _____

    _____

    _____

    _____

106. Remainder bequest:

    To whom _____

If will contains testamentary trust:

107. Name of initial trustee _____

108. Successor trustee _____

109. Attach a description of the property that will go into the trust.

110. Lifetime beneficiaries _____

111. Remainder beneficiaries _____

112. Where is original will kept? _____

Codicils or amendments:

113. Date codicil signed _____

114. Attach description of contents of codicil _____

115. Where is original codicil kept? _____

116. Does your spouse have a separate will? _____

117. Significant provisions in spouse's will _____

    _____

    _____

    _____

    _____

118. Do you and your spouse have a joint will? If so, questions 99–115 should be answered as to the joint will.

VII. Client's Business

119. Nature of business _____

If sole owner of business:

120. Name of business _____

121. Address _____

If partnership:

122. Name of partnership _____

123. Address _____

124. Names of other partners _____

125. Percentage interest of client _____

126. Is there a written agreement? _____

VII. Client's Business—Continued

127. General or limited partnership? _____

128. Date of agreement _____

129. Termination provision _____

130. Any provision for purchase or sale of partnership interest during lifetime of partners? If so, attach description.

131. After death of partner? If so, attach description.

If corporation:

132. Name of corporation _____

133. State of incorporation _____

134. Total issued shares _____

135. Number of shares client owns _____

136. Position in corporation _____

137. Member of board of directors? _____

     Total number of members _____

138. Is client an officer of the corporation? _____ Which office? _____

     Is there a written agreement among stockholders? _____

     If so, state:

139. Date of agreement _____

140. Names of parties and stock ownership of each _____

141. Is there provision for purchase of sale of stock during lifetime?

     _____

142. After death of a stockholder? _____

143. For other corporations, attach answers to questions 132–142 for each.

VIII. Spouse's Business

144. Answer questions 119–143 for spouse (attach answers).

IX. Client's Employment

145. Social Security Number _____

Present employment:

146. Employer's name _____

147. Address _____

148. Salary _____

149. Present employment started on _____

150. Nature of present employment—brief job description _____

     _____

     _____

     _____

Union membership:

151. Name of union _____

152. Address _____

IX. Client's Employment—Continued

153. Date became member _____
154. Dues _____
155. Payable _____

List and briefly describe employment benefits client may have, such as:

156. Life insurance _____
157. Medical insurance _____
158. Dental insurance _____
159. Paid vacations _____
160. Paid holidays _____
161. Illness leave _____
162. Severance pay _____
163. Credit union _____
164. Pension plan _____
165. Profit-sharing plan _____
166. Attach brief description of last three jobs.

X. Spouse's Employment

167. Social Security Number _____

Present Employment:

168. Employer's name _____
169. Address _____
170. Salary _____
171. Present employment started on _____
172. Nature of present employment—give a brief job description _____
_____
_____
_____

Union Membership:

173. Name of union _____
174. Address _____
175. Date became member _____
176. Dues _____
177. Payable _____

List and briefly describe employment benefits spouse may have, such as:

178. Life Insurance _____
179. Medical insurance _____
180. Dental insurance _____
181. Paid vacations _____
182. Paid holidays _____
183. Illness leave _____
184. Severance pay _____

X. Spouse's Employment—Continued

185. Credit union _____

186. Pension plan _____

187. Profit-sharing plan _____

188. Attach brief description of last three jobs.

XI. Real Property

On separate sheets of paper, answer questions 189 to 210 for *each* item of real property owned by the client, the spouse, or together. Examples of real property include: current residence(s), vacation home, fixtures on the land, undeveloped land, business buildings, land held for business, leased real property, etc.

189. Describe the nature of the property.

190. Location of the property.

191. Original cost.

192. Was property received by will or via intestacy?

193. If so, from whom and to whom?

194. If purchase, who paid for the property?

195. Where did the money come from that was used to purchase the property?

196. In whose name was the property taken?

197. Where are the documents of sale located?

198. Date of sale.

199. Name and address of seller.

200. Describe any improvements made to the property. Include the dates of the improvements.

201. What funds were used to pay for the improvements?

202. Does any insurance exist on the property?

203. If so, who pays the premium, with what funds, and who is the beneficiary?

204. Are any taxes paid on the property?

205. If so, who pays them and with what funds?

206. Is any money owed on the property?

207. If so, to whom?

208. Who pays and with what funds?

209. Who uses the property now?

210. Other information relevant to this property.

XII. Personal Property (Other Than Securities and Cash)

On separate sheets of paper, answer questions 211 to 232 for *each* item of personal property (with a value of over $100) owned by the client, the spouse, or together. Examples of personal property include: cars, trucks, boats, furniture, jewelry, clothing, business inventory, business equipment, etc. (Attach a brief description of all other property with a value of under $100.)

211. Describe the nature of the property.

212. Location of the property.

213. Original cost.
214. Was property received by will or via intestacy?
215. If so, from whom and to whom?
216. If purchased, who paid for the property?
217. Where did the money come from that was used to purchase the property?
218. In whose name was the property taken?
219. Where are the documents of sale located?
220. Date of the sale.
221. Name and address of seller.
222. Describe any improvements made to the property. Include the dates of the improvements.
223. What funds were used to pay for the improvements?
224. Does any insurance exist on the property?
225. If so, who pays the premium, with what funds, and who is the beneficiary?
226. Are any taxes paid on the property?
227. If so, who pays them and with what funds?
228. Is any money owed on the property?
229. If so, to whom?
230. Who pays and with what funds?
231. Who uses the property now?
232. Other information relevant to this property.

XIII. Stocks/Bonds/Accounts/Deposit Boxes

(If you have more than five of any item, answer the same questions on separate sheets of paper for the sixth, seventh, etc.)

Stocks

233.	Name of corporation					
234.	Name of owner as shown on certificate					
235.	Number of shares					
236.	Certificate number					
237.	Date acquired					
238.	Cost of shares					
239.	Source of funds used to purchase					

Bonds

240.	Name of corporation or obligor					
241.	Name of owner as shown on bond					
242.	Face amount due at maturity					
243.	Bond number					
244.	Date acquired					
245.	Cost					
246.	Source of funds used to purchase					
247.	Maturity date					
248.	Rate of interest					
249.	When is interest payable?					
250.	Are coupons attached?					

Savings Certificates

251.	Name of bank or institution					
252.	Address					
253.	Type of certificate					
254.	Name(s) on certificate					
255.	Amount					
256.	Rate of interest					
257.	Source of funds to purchase					
258.	Date purchased					
259.	Dates renewed					

Savings and Checking Accounts

260.	Name of bank or savings institution					
261.	Address of bank					
262.	Type of account					
263.	Name(s) on account					
264.	Persons authorized to draw on account					
265.	Date account opened					
266.	Amounts currently in account					

Safe Deposit Boxes

267.	Name of bank or institution					
268.	Address					
269.	Number of box					
270.	In whose name was the box opened?					
271.	Who is authorized to enter box?					
272.	Date box obtained					
273.	Contents					

XIV. Insurance

Life Insurance

274. Name of the person whose life is insured _____

275. Insurance company _____

276. Address _____

277. Place where policy is kept _____

278. Kind of policy _____

XIV. Insurance—Continued

279. Date of issue _____

280. Face amount _____

281. Policy number _____

282. Premium _____

283. When payable? _____

284. Who pays and what funds are used? _____

285. Beneficiary or beneficiaries _____

_____

286. Owner of policy _____

287. Has policy been assigned? If so, when and to whom? _____

_____

288. Loans against policy? If so, when made and in what amount? _____

_____

Accident and Health Insurance

289. Company _____

290. Address _____

291. Kind of policy _____

292. Date of issue _____

293. Number of policy _____

294. Premium _____

295. When payable? _____

296. Who pays and what funds are used? _____

Fire or Homeowner Insurance

297. Name of insured _____

298. Company _____

299. Address _____

300. Kind of policy—coverages in addition to fire _____

301. Amount of coverage _____

302. Property covered _____

303. Date of issue _____

304. Date of expiration _____

305. Premium _____

306. Who pays and what funds are used? _____

307. Policy number _____

Automobile Insurance

308. Name of insured _____

309. Company _____

310. Address _____

(*answer for each automobile*):

311. Make _____

XIV. Insurance—Continued

312. Model _____
313. Year _____

Coverage of Policy:

314. Bodily injury liability _____
315. Each person _____
316. Each occurrence _____
317. Medical payments _____
318. Property damage liability _____
319. Comprehensive loss or damage _____
320. Collision _____
321. Other _____
322. Date of issue _____
323. Date of expiration _____
324. Premium _____
325. Who pays and what funds are used? _____
326. Policy number _____

XV. Miscellaneous Income

327. Income from trusts (you) _____
328. Income from trusts (spouse) _____
329. Royalty income (you) _____
330. Royalty income (spouse) _____
331. Rental income (you) _____
332. Rental income (spouse) _____
333. Other income (specify recipient and source) _____
    _____

XVI. Liabilities

334. Mortgages _____
335. Property that is mortgaged _____
336. Who pays? _____
337. Promisory note or other credit transactions (include amounts outstanding on all credit cards) _____
    _____
    _____
338. Who pays? _____
339. Other debts _____
    _____

XVII. Tax Returns

Income Tax	Year	Year	Year	Year	Year
U.S. Return					
340. Separate or joint					
341. Amount of gross income					
342. Amount of tax paid					
State Return					
343. Separate or joint					
344. Amount of gross income					
345. Amount of tax paid					
City Return					
346. Separate or joint					
347. Amount of gross income					
348. Amount of tax paid					
Gift Tax					
349. Date filed					
350. Name of recipient(s) and the amount of the gift(s)					
351. Gift tax paid, if any					

XVIII. Persons Familiar With Client's Affairs

For each of the following, state name, address, and extent of relationship:

352. Business associates _____

353. Close relatives _____

354. Other lawyers consulted _____

355. Doctor _____

356. Clergy _____

357. Accountants _____

358. Bankers _____

XVIII. Persons Familiar With Client's Affairs— Continued

359. Insurance agents _____

360. Stockbrokers _____

361. Others we should know about _____

_____

Authorization to Represent and Compensation Agreement

(Retainer)

Authorization to Represent and Compensation Agreement

1. I hereby request and authorize you to represent me as my Attorney in fact and in law as related to:

and against all additional persons, firms, or corporations who may appear to be related to this case.

2. As compensation for your services as my Attorney, I agree to pay you as follows:

3. I understand that it is impossible at this time to specify the exact nature, extent, and difficulty of the contemplated services and the time involved. You as my Attorney shall exert your best effort at all times to represent my interests and rights.

4. In connection with the services rendered, it is agreed that you as my Attorney shall be compensated for additional work not contemplated in the above noted estimate at a minimum rate of $ _____ per hour. I understand that telephone calls and conferences are billed as office charges.

I understand I am to reimburse you in all events for any sums actually paid by you for investigation, preparing claims for trial, court costs, and your expenses.

Dated: _____

_____
                                                Signature

We agree to act as Attorney on the above stated basis.

Dated: _____

                              By _____

Retainer paid _____

_____

Assignment 5.1

Interview a married person. Cover the questions outlined in this chapter as well as any additional questions that you think should be included. Tell the person you interview:

(a) To assume that he or she is about to file for divorce and has hired the law firm where you work as a paralegal.

(b) To assume that during the marriage the spouses acquired considerable wealth.

(c) To make up answers to all the questions that you ask.

(See General Instructions for the Interview Assignment in chapter one. Instructions 5 and 6 in these General Instructions do not apply to Assignment 5.1.)

Key Chapter Terminology

Client Interview
Intake Memorandum
Marital Facts
Itemized Expenses
Real Property

Personal Property
Retainer
Income
Liabilities

Breach of Promise to Marry, the Heart-Balm Statute, and Contracts Restraining Marriage

■ Chapter Outline

When two people promise to marry each other, a *contract* is created so long as the parties have the legal capacity to enter a contract, and the elements of a valid contract exist—offer, acceptance, and consideration. Years ago, if one of the parties refused to enter the marriage, and thereby breached the contract, the other party could bring a *heart-balm* cause of action for breach of promise to marry. Many states, however, have enacted heart-balm statutes that abolish this contract action because of the difficulty of assessing damages, the danger of blackmail, and the inappropriateness of trying to force someone to enter a marriage he or she no longer wants.

Fraud is an alternative cause of action a plaintiff can bring against a defendant who reneges on a promise to marry. The elements of fraud are a deliberately false statement of present fact by the defendant, intent to have the plaintiff rely on the statement, actual reliance by the plaintiff on the statement, and resulting harm. Not all states, however, will allow a fraud suit. They have interpreted the heart-balm statute as abolishing both the contract action and the fraud action.

In states where a suit is still possible, under a contract or a fraud cause of action, the usual remedy is for the plaintiff to seek compensatory *damages*. The damage award may be increased by aggravated damages for special circumstances, or by punitive or exemplary damages intended to punish the defendant and deter others from similar conduct. Mitigating circumstances, on the other hand, will decrease the award.

When a planned marriage does not occur, any gifts that have already been exchanged are considered irrevocable (do not have to be returned) provided that all the elements of a gift exist: delivery, voluntary transfer, intent to relinquish title and control, no consideration, intent to have the gift take effect immediately, and acceptance by the donee. If, however, a court concludes that the donor would not have made the gift except for the anticipation of marriage, then the gift is considered conditional and thus must be returned.

Finally, a contract that imposes a total or a near total prohibition on marriage is an unenforceable, general restraint on marriage. On the other hand, contracts that impose reasonable limitations on one's right to marry can be enforceable.

Section A. Breach of Promise to Marry

For centuries, one of the sacred principles in law has been the stability of contracts. An organized society depends on the faithful performance of contractual commitments. Hence courts are available to force parties to abide by their contracts. In the business world, thousands of contracts are made every hour. Merchants invest large amounts of money and other resources in reliance on these contracts. Consequently, the law will not allow one merchant to avoid performing its contract simply because it is now having second thoughts about the agreement reached or because it can now obtain a better deal elsewhere. But does the sacred principle of contractual stability apply to broken promises to marry, and should courts be used to force parties to honor such contracts? Before answering this question, we need an understanding of the basic law of contracts:

Contract

A contract is an agreement that is enforceable by law.

Elements of a Contract

1. There must be an *offer*.
2. There must be an *acceptance* of the offer.
3. There must be *consideration*. (Consideration is something of value that is given or exchanged.)
4. The parties must have the *capacity* to enter a contract. (Capacity means the legal power to do something.)
5. Some contracts must be in *writing* in order to comply with the Statute of Frauds.

Example:

John, age thirty-four, has been dating Mary, an independently wealthy woman of thirty-three, who proposes to him. John accepts, and they both agree on a wedding date. The next day Mary changes her mind and tells John that she no longer wants to marry him. Does a contract exist that is enforceable by John against Mary?

1. *Offer*. Mary offered to marry John.
2. *Acceptance*. John agreed to marry her (he accepted her offer).
3. *Consideration*. Something of value was exchanged by both parties; they both exchanged *promises* to marry each other. This mutual *exchange of promises* was the consideration for the contract.

4. *Capacity*. There was no indication that either John or Mary lacked the capacity to enter the contract. For example, when the offer was accepted, neither was a minor and neither appeared to be mentally incapable of understanding the nature of their agreement.

5. *Writing*. Mutual promises to marry do not have to be in writing to be enforceable; the Statute of Frauds does not apply to this kind of contract.

All of the requirements for a contract, therefore, appear to have been met. Does John have a *cause of action* (i.e., a legally acceptable reason for bringing a suit) against Mary? Years ago, the answer was yes. The suit for breach of promise to marry was referred to as a *heart-balm* cause of action. (Later in this book we will consider two other heart-balm causes of action: alienation of affections and criminal conversation.)

The tide has begun to turn against heart-balm actions such as the breach of promise to marry. Many states have abolished the action through *heart-balm statutes* such as the following:

> **§100.** Breach of contract to marry shall not constitute an injury or wrong recognized by law, and no action, suit or proceeding shall be maintained therefor.

These statutes were enacted for a number of reasons. The tensions involving a refusal to marry are usually so personal, intense, and possibly bitter that a court did not appear to be a proper setting to handle them. As one judge said, the "courtroom scene" should not be "transposed into a grotesque marketplace whose wares would be the exposure of heart-rending episodes of wounded pride, which should be best kept private rather than public." Courts were also afraid of being flooded with breach-of-promise lawsuits. Another major problem concerned the *remedy* that an aggrieved party might seek. In the business world, a possible remedy for a breach of contract is *specific performance*, which forces the wrongdoer to perform the contract. For the marriage contract that is breached, the remedy of specific performance would mean that the court would force the reluctant party to go through with the marriage contract. The obviously unacceptable concept of a compulsory marriage under these circumstances led many states to abolish the cause of action altogether. Another possibly remedy is the payment of *damages*, i.e., money, to compensate for the breach, which many states have concluded is equally inappropriate.

Assignment 6.1

(a) In your state code look for heart-balm statutes for breach of contract to marry. If such statutes exist, give their citation and summarize what they say. (See General Instructions for the State-Code Assignment in chapter one.)

(b) Find a court opinion written by one of your state courts that tells whether or not a heart-balm action for breach of contract to marry can be brought. Briefly state the facts and conclusion of this opinion. (See General Instructions for the Court-Opinion Assignment in chapter one.)

(c) If your state allows heart-balm actions for breach of contract to marry, draft a complaint alleging such a breach. In the hypothetical situation involving John and Mary (page 120), assume that John is bringing the complaint against Mary for breach of contract to marry in your state. (See General Instructions for the Complaint-Drafting Assignment in chapter one.)

(d) If your state allows heart-balm actions for breach of contract to marry, prepare a flowchart of the procedural steps necessary to bring such an action. (See General Instructions for the Flowchart Assignment in chapter one.)

Assignment 6.2

Assume that you live in a state where heart-balm actions can be brought. Dan asks Carol to marry him. Carol says yes. The date is set for the wedding. Two weeks before the wedding, Carol learns that Dan has just married Linda. At the time Dan was engaged to Carol, she was already married to Bill, but Dan did not know this. Carol was in the process of divorcing Bill and hoped to have had the divorce finalized before her marriage to Dan. Carol wanted to wait until the divorce was final before telling Dan about the prior marriage and divorce. Dan did not learn about any of this until after his marriage to Linda. When Carol's divorce to Bill became final, she sued Dan. The cause of action stated in Carol's complaint against Dan is breach of promise to marry. Should Carol be allowed to bring this action? Why or why not? (See General Instructions for the Legal-Analysis Assignment in chapter one.)

Assume that a woman lives in a state where it is still possible to sue for breach of promise to marry. Today even these states would not grant her the remedy of specific performance if she won. No court will order a marriage to occur. What then does a court victory mean? For what can she be compensated? What has she lost? What are her damages? The very difficulty of answering these questions has been partly responsible for the abolition of the cause of action in most states. Yet where the action can be brought, the jury must be given instructions on the standards to use in arriving at an amount of money (damages) that the defendant must pay a plaintiff who has successfully convinced the court that the defendant breached a promise to marry the plaintiff. Four aspects of damages need to be considered.

1. *Compensatory damages* cover what the plaintiff has lost. The jury can consider:

- Out-of-pocket expenses. Money spent by plaintiff in purchasing a trousseau, a hall, rings, etc.
- Loss of income. The plaintiff may have lost income by leaving a job in order to marry the defendant.
- Physical and mental health deterioration due to worry, publicity, and humiliation.
- Injury to the plaintiff's reputation and chances of obtaining a new marriage proposal.
- Destroyed financial expectations. If the defendant was wealthy and the plaintiff was poor, the plaintiff has obviously lost a great deal in terms of potential standard of living. Note, however, that most states will not allow damages for this kind of loss.

2. *Aggravated damages* covers special circumstances that could increase the damage award. For example:

- Sexual intercourse due to seduction.
- Pregnancy, miscarriage.
- An unusual degree of publicity and resulting humiliation.

3. *Punitive or exemplary damages* covers conduct that calls for an increase in the damage award in order to punish the defendant and to deter others from similar conduct. For example:

- Fraud. The defendant never intended to marry the plaintiff in spite of the promise made.
- Malice. The defendant wanted to hurt and humiliate the plaintiff, or the defendant recklessly disregarded the impact of the breach of promise.

4. *Mitigating circumstances* covers circumstances which, in fairness, warrant a reduction in damages. Some states allow a jury to consider these circumstances in order to lessen the amount of damages it would otherwise impose on the defendant. For example:

- Plaintiff never loved the defendant. Plaintiff was trying to marry for money only.
- Plaintiff was unchaste before meeting the defendant.
- Defendant broke the promise to marry, but with some sensitivity to the feelings of the plaintiff.

There was a time when juries returned very high verdicts against defendants in breach-of-promise actions, e.g., $250,000. More recently, however, the trend has been toward smaller verdicts. Some states will limit damage awards to out-of-pocket losses, e.g., the cost of wedding preparation, and will not compensate the victim for more speculative harm such as that caused by humiliation.

Interviewing and Investigation Checklist

Factors Relevant to the Promise to Marry (C = client; D = defendant)

Legal Interviewing Questions

1. On what date did you and D first agree to be married?

2. Where were you at the time of this agreement? Were you in this state? If not, what state?

3. How old were you at the time? How old was D?

4. What specific language did D use when he or she promised to marry you? What specific language did you use when you accepted? (Try to obtain exact quotations.)

5. Was a date set for a wedding? If so, what date? If not, why not?

6. Were any preparations made, e.g., church or caterer contacted?

7. Did D send you any letters ("love letters") about the engagement? Did you send D any?

8. Did D ever repeat his or her promise to marry you? If so, under what circumstances?

9. If D never used specific words to agree to marry you, what actions did D take to indicate to you that D wanted to marry you? How much time did you spend together? Did you live together? (Where? How long?) Did you talk about children? Did you meet each other's parents?

10. When did you first learn that D no longer wished to marry you? What specifically was said and done?

11. What reason did D give?

12. What did you say or do when you learned about this? Did you give any indication to D that you did not want to marry D? Were you angry? How was it expressed?

13. Was there anything about your life prior to the time that D promised to marry you that D did not know but which D now feels you should have revealed, e.g., information about a prior marriage, about your age, about your prior sex life?

14. What expenses did you have in order to prepare for the wedding? (clothes, church, etc.)

15. Were you employed before the engagement? Did you leave your job? How did the cancellation of the marriage affect your job, if at all?

16. Describe your standard of living before the cancellation, e.g., kind of dwelling, car, travel, entertainment interests, etc.

17. Describe the standard of living of D.

18. If D had married you, describe what you think your financial standing and standard of living would have been.

19. Describe the effect of D's breach of promise on your physical and mental health, e.g., did you lose any sleep, were there any special mental problems?

20. When D broke the promise to marry you, who knew about it? Was there any publicity?

21. Were you humiliated? Describe the reasons why.

22. Since the engagement to D was broken, have you been dating others? When they find out about the broken engagement, what is their reaction? Do you think that your chances of marrying in the future are diminished because of D's breach of promise? Why?

23. Did you have sexual relations with D? Were you seduced by D? Did D impregnate you? (If so, inquire into pregnancy problems, abortion, miscarriage, delivery.)

24. Do you have any reason to believe that at the time D promised to marry you, D never intended to do so? Explain.

25. Do you have any reason to believe that D wanted to hurt you? Explain.

26. Could D say that you never loved D?

27. Did D ever give you any gifts?

28. On what date did you receive each gift? Was it before or after the engagement?

29. What were D's exact words when D gave you each gift? What did you say to D?

30. When did each gift come into your possession?

31. Answer questions 27–30 for any gifts you gave D.

32. Did you or D receive any shower gifts of wedding gifts from others before the engagement was broken? Explain.

Possible Investigation Tasks

- Obtain birth certificates to verify ages.
- Try to reach anyone who may have heard about D's promise to marry C. Obtain witness statements.
- Contact church, caterer, etc., to determine if wedding preparations were made. Obtain witness statements.

- Help C locate all letters from D.

- Locate all receipts of expenses due to wedding preparation. If not available, contact merchants and others to whom money was paid in order to obtain new receipts or copies.

- Obtain financial records, e.g., bank statements, to show the financial worth and standard of living of C before the engagement was broken. Try to obtain the same kind of records for D.

- Obtain medical records to document the physical and mental strain caused C when D broke the promise to marry, e.g., hospital records, doctor bills.

- Determine what kind of publicity, if any, accompanied the news that D had broken the engagement, e.g., newspaper clippings.

- Attempt to determine whether D had broken any other marriage engagements.

- Draft an inventory of every gift in any way connected with D's relationship with C. For each gift, identify the donor, donee, date of gift, kind and value of gift, and the circumstances surrounding the gift. If the donor has asked for the gift back, determine the response of the donee, the present location of the gift, etc.

The breach-of-promise cause of action is considered by some to be merely a device for *blackmailing* the defendants into agreeing to a substantial settlement to avoid the publicity of a trial. For this and other reasons, a number of states, as indicated earlier, have enacted heart-balm statutes to abolish this cause of action altogether.

Some plaintiffs have tried to get around this statutory prohibition by bringing a *tort* cause of action for *fraud* rather than the breach-of-contract cause of action.

Elements of The Tort of Fraud
(Sometimes called misrepresentation or deceit)
1. There must be a *false statement* of present fact by the defendant (D).
2. The D must *know* that it is false.
3. The D must *intend* that the plaintiff (P) rely upon the statement.
4. The P must *rely* on the statement of the D and be reasonable in so relying.
5. The P must suffer *harm* due to the reliance.

In a case of a broken engagement, an example of a fraud cause of action, if allowed, would be as follows: D told P that he wanted to marry P. At the time D made this *statement,* it was *false* because D never wanted to marry P. D *knew* that the statement was a lie and *intended* to use the statement to get P to do something (e.g., lend D money, have sexual relations with D). P believed that D wanted to marry her and *relied* on D's statement (e.g., by giving D money; by having sex with D). P suffered *harm* because of this reliance (e.g., humiliation, unwanted pregnancy).

Can such a fraud cause of action be brought in a state that has abolished the breach-of-contract cause of action? The question is whether the heart-balm statute was intended by the legislature to eliminate both causes of action even though the act may specifically mention only the contract action. Some states allow the fraud action. Others have said that the heart-balm statute eliminates both the contract and the tort action.

Assignment 6.3

On July 4, 1987 in your state, Jim Smith asked Linda Jones to marry him. Jim has a middle-class background, while Linda is independently wealthy. Linda told Jim that she had never loved any other man in her life. This was not true, but she felt that unless she told this to Jim, he would never have proposed to her. On July 25, 1987, Linda told Jim that she would marry him, but on August 19, 1987, she informed him that she had changed her mind. Jim is very upset. On October 4, 1989, he filed suit against her in your state.

(a) On behalf of Jim, draft a complaint against Linda for breach of promise to marry. If you live in a state that has abolished breach-of-promise actions, draft the complaint on a fraud cause of action. Assume that fraud causes of action have not been abolished in such situations even though the breach of promise causes of action have been. (See General Instructions for the Complaint-Drafting Assignment in chapter one.)

(b) Every state has statutes of limitations, which specify the time limits within which suits must be brought. If they are not brought within the statutory time period, they will be barred forever. In assignment "a", you drafted Jim's complaint. In answer to that complaint, would Linda be able to raise the defense that Jim's suit is barred by the statute of limitations? Check your state code to find out what the statute of limitations would be for this cause of action. (See General Instructions for the State-Code Assignment in chapter one.)

(c) Draft a set of interrogatories to be sent to Jim. Concentrate on questions calculated to uncover facts that might be used to assess damages. (See General Instructions for the Interrogatories Assignment in chapter one.)

Section B. The Problem of Gifts

It is not commonly known that once a gift is made, it is *irrevocable*—the giver (called the donor) cannot reclaim the gift from the person to whom it was given (called the donee). For a gift to be irrevocable in this way, all of the elements of a gift must be present.:

Elements of Irrevocable Gift

1. There must be a *delivery* of the property.[1]
2. The transfer must be *voluntary*.
3. The donor must intend to relinquish *title* and *control* of what is given.
4. There must be *no consideration* (e.g., payment by the donee).
5. The donor must intend that the gift take effect *immediately;* there must be a *present* intention to give an *unconditional* gift.
6. The donee must *accept* the gift.

If Pat says to Bill "I'll give you my car next year," no gift has been given. There was no intent that an immediate transfer occur, and hence there was no delivery. If Pat says to Bill, "You have borrowed my pen; maybe I'll give it to you tomorrow," again there is no gift since there was no intent by Pat

---

[1]The delivery of the gift of a house or of the contents of a safety deposit box can be accomplished by a symbolic act such as giving the donee the key to the house or box.

to relinquish her title and dominion over the pen now. This is so even though Bill already had possession of the pen.

Suppose that Pat says to Bill, "I'll give you this desk if it rains tomorrow." No gift has occurred because a condition exists which must be fulfilled before the gift becomes effective, i.e., it must rain tomorrow. There is no present intention to relinquish title and dominion. Suppose that Frank and Judy exchange engagement rings after they both agree to be married. One or both of them then change their minds. Did a legally binding gift occur? It appears that all of the elements of a binding gift existed, so either Frank or Judy can refuse to return the ring. Yet, should we not *infer* a condition that the parties intended the gift to be binding only if the marriage took place? They never explicitly said this to each other, but it is reasonable to infer that this is what they had in mind, i.e., that this is what they would have intended if they had thought about it. Courts often find that such an *implied intention* exists, thereby forcing a return of premarital gifts.

Examine the following sequence of events:

January 1, 1990:	Mary and Bob meet.
January 2, 1990:	On a date, Bob gives Mary a bracelet.
March 13, 1990:	Mary and Bob become engaged; they exchange rings. The marriage date will be November 7, 1990.
March 26, 1990:	This is Mary's birthday; Bob gives Mary a new car.
June 5, 1990:	Bob and Mary change their minds about marriage.

Bob wants the bracelet, ring, and car back. When Mary refuses, Bob sues her, contending in court that the elements of a gift were not present when he gave Mary the items, because he intended her to keep them only if they married. Should the court infer this condition of marriage? The answer depends on what Bob's intention was *at the time* he gave each of the items to Mary.

The exchange of rings poses the least problem. Most courts would agree that a condition of marriage was implied and permit their return. At the time the bracelet was given, however, the parties were not engaged. A jury might conclude that Bob's intent was to please Mary, but not necessarily to win her hand in marriage. The bracelet was given the day after they met when it is unlikely that marriage was on anyone's mind. It would be rare, therefore, for a court to rule that the gift of the bracelet was conditional and force Mary to return it.[2] The birthday gift of the car is the most troublesome item. Again the central question is, what was Bob's intent at the time he gave her the car? Mary would argue that there was no condition of marriage attached to the gift. She would say that a birthday gift would have been given whether or not they were engaged. Bob, on the other hand, would argue that the value of the new car is strong evidence that it would not have been given as a birthday gift unconnected with the impending marriage. His argument is probably correct. Do you agree?

---

[2]On the other hand, the facts show that two months after the bracelet was given, the parties became engaged. This short time period does raise the possibility, however slight, that marriage *was* on Bob's mind when he gave Mary the bracelet, i.e., that the gift was conditional. More facts would be needed in order to determine whether this argument has merit.

Assignment 6.4

What further facts would you seek in order to assess whether the car was a gift in the case of Bob and Mary above? See General Instructions for the Investigation-Strategy Assignment in chapter one.

Suppose that Bob unilaterally broke the engagement without any plausible reason or justification. In such a situation, many courts would consider Bob a wrongdoer who should not be able to profit from his wrong by reclaiming any of the gifts. In such courts, the donor can have the conditional gifts returned only if the engagement ended by mutual agreement or if it were the donee who broke the engagement without justification.

Third parties, e.g., relatives and friends, often send gifts in contemplation of the coming marriage. When the marriage does not take place, these parties can force a return of the gifts since courts almost always will conclude that such gifts were conditional.

In the prior section we saw that some states passed heart-balm statutes that abolished the cause of action for breach of promise to marry. Some of these statutes are worded so broadly that courts might interpret them to mean that *any* cause of action growing out of a broken engagement will not be allowed, including a cause of action to obtain the return of conditional gifts.

Assignment 6.5

Examine the following sequence of events:

February 13, 1988:	Jim says to Bob, "Please introduce me to Joan. I want to meet her because I know that she is the girl I want to spend the rest of my life with." Bob does so. Jim is so happy that he gives Bob a gold wristwatch and says to him, "I want you to have this. Thanks for being my friend. I want you to wear this watch to my wedding some day."
March 1, 1988:	Joan brings Jim home to meet her mother. When the evening is over, Jim gives Joan's mother an expensive family Bible.
June 23, 1988:	Jim loans Joan $1,000 to pay a medical bill of Joan's youngest brother, giving her one year to pay back the loan without interest.
July 23, 1988:	Joan pays back the $1,000.
September 5, 1988:	They agree to marry. The wedding date is to be February 18, 1989. On the day that they agree to marry, Jim gives Joan a diamond bracelet, saying, "I want you to have this no matter what happens."
December 14, 1988:	They both agree to break the engagement.

Jim asks Bob for the wristwatch back. Bob refuses. Jim asks Joan's mother for the Bible back. The mother refuses. Jim asks Joan for one month's interest at 10 percent on the $1,000 loan and also asks for the bracelet back. Joan refuses both requests.

(a) Assume that the law office where you work represents Jim. Conduct a legal interview of Jim. (See General Instructions for the Interview Assignment in chapter one.)

(b) Can Jim obtain any of these items from Bob, the mother, or Joan? (See General Instructions for the Legal-Analysis Assignment in chapter one.)

(c) Draft a complaint against Joan in which Jim seeks the return of the bracelet and one month's interest. (See General Instructions for the Complaint-Drafting Assignment in chapter one.)

(d) Prepare a flowchart of the steps necessary to litigate the matter raised in the complaint that you drafted in "c" above. (See General Instructions for the flowchart Assignment in chapter one.)

Section C. Contracts Restraining Marriage

In this section we consider contracts of private parties that have the effect of restraining marriage. The state, of course, also restrains the formation of marriages through regulations on obtaining licenses, blood tests, etc. The legality of these regulations will be considered later.

The law looks with disfavor on attempts to limit the right to marry, even with the consent of the person subject to the limitation. Not all restrictions, however, are invalid. A distinction must be made between a *general restraint* on marriage and a *reasonable limitation* on marriage.

General Restraint

Consider the following situations:

- In exchange for a large sum of money to be given to her by her father, Mary agrees never to marry.

- As John goes off to war, Jane says, "It is you that I want to marry, and even if you don't want to marry me, even if you marry someone else, even if you die, I promise you that I will never marry anyone else as long as I live." John leaves without promising to marry Jane.

A general restraint on marriage is a total or near total prohibition against marriage, and is unenforceable. Mary's father cannot sue her to hold her to her agreement never to marry, nor can Jane be sued by John for breach of her promise should she marry someone other than him. People may decide on their own never to marry, but no court will force them to abide by that decision.

The John/Jane agreement is unenforceable for another reason. You will recall that for a contract to exist, there must be consideration. Jane's consideration was her promise never to marry anyone but John. John, however, gave no consideration in exchange. Hence, Jane's promise is unenforceable because she received no consideration; there was no contract to breach.

Reasonable Limitation

A reasonable limitation or restraint on marriage is one that (1) is a partial rather than a general prohibition, (2) serves what the court feels is a useful purpose, and (3) is not otherwise illegal. Consider the following situations:

- John enters a contract in which he promises that he will never marry a woman who is not of his religious faith.

- Mary enters a contract in which she promises never to marry anyone who has a criminal record.

- Jane enters a contract in which she promises that she will not marry before she turns eighteen, and that she will obtain the permission of her parent if she decides to marry between the ages of eighteen and twenty-one.

- Linda enters a contract in which she promises that she will not marry until she completes her college education.

Assume that John, Mary, Jane, and Linda received consideration for their promises. Are their promises enforceable? If John, Mary, Jane, and Linda later decide to marry contrary to their promises, can they be forced through litigation to abide by those promises? Not all states will answer this question in the same way, but generally the answer is yes. The restraints on marriage to which they agreed are enforceable. All of the restraints are *partial:* they do not totally prohibit marriage or come near such a total prohibition. All of the restraints arguably serve a *useful purpose:* to protect a person or a valuable tradition. Do you agree? There is no *illegality* evident in any of the restraints, e.g., no one is being asked to refrain from marriage in order to engage in adultery or fornication (which are crimes in some states). Hence, all of the restraints could be considered reasonable limitations on one's right to marry and are enforceable in most states.

Suppose school teachers sign a contract containing a clause that they will quit if they marry. This is not a general restraint on marriage, but is it enforceable as a reasonable limitation? Is there a useful or beneficial purpose to the restriction? Many courts have said yes, although this conclusion has been criticized. Can you see any useful purpose in forcing a teacher to resign under these circumstances? Do not answer this question by saying that people should be forced to do what they have agreed to do. Answer it on the basis of whether you think any person, tradition, value, etc., is being protected by holding the teacher to his or her contract.

Thus far we have been examining *contracts* that restrain marriage. Suppose, however, that the attempted restriction on marriage came as a condition attached to a *gift* rather than through a contract. For example:

- In Bob's will, he promises to give $100,000 to Fran so long as she remains unmarried. When Bob dies, Fran is not married. She is given the gift (bequest) of $100,000. One year later, Fran marries. Bob's estate brings a suit against Fran to have the money returned.

- John has a deed drafted which states, "I convey all my property to my widowed sister, Joan, to be owned and used by her until she remarries, at which time all remaining property shall go to the Red Cross."

The same rules on marriage restrictions should apply to such gifts as apply to contracts. If a person is going to lose a substantial gift upon marriage, the gift obviously operates to restrain marriage. In theory, the same rules do apply. In fact, however, some courts are more inclined to find the restrictions to be reasonable (and hence enforceable) when gifts are involved than when the restraint is embodied in a contract.

Assignment 6.6

Examine each of the following hypotheticals closely. Determine which restraints on marriage, if any, are enforceable. Give specific reasons you think the restraint is or is not enforceable. (See General Instructions for the Legal-Analysis Assignment in chapter one.)

(a) John is married to Brenda. John enters a contract with Brenda's father stating that if children are born from the marriage and if Brenda dies before John, John will never remarry. In exchange, John is given the father's large farm to live in for life without having to pay any rent. Children are born, and Brenda does die first. John then marries Patricia. Brenda's father then sues to evict John from the farm. Does John have a defense to this suit?

(b) Joan enters a contract with her aunt stating that she will not have children before she turns twenty-one. In exchange, Joan is given a sum of money. Before she turns twenty-one, Joan has a baby (out of wedlock). The aunt sues Joan for breach of contract. Does Joan have a defense?

(c) Fred enters a contract with his father in which the father agrees to pay for Fred's entire medical education if Fred agrees to marry a doctor or a medical student if he decides to marry. When Fred becomes a doctor, he marries Sue, an electrician. The father sues Fred for the cost of the medical education. Does Fred have a defense?

(d) Bill and Jean are not married. They live together, sharing bed and board. They enter a contract by which Jean promises to continue to live with Bill and to care for him. Bill agrees to place $500 per month in a bank account for Jean so long as she carries out her promise. Jean cannot receive the money until Bill dies. Also, if she marries before Bill dies, she forfeits the right to all the money in the account. After living with Bill for twenty years, Jean leaves him to marry Tom. Can Jean sue Bill to recover $120,000, (plus interest), the amount in the account at the time she married Tom?

Key Chapter Terminology

Breach of Promise to Marry	Punitive Damages
Contract	Exemplary Damages
Offer	Mitigation of Damages
Acceptance	Blackmail
Consideration	Fraud
Capacity to Contract	Reliance
Statute of Frauds	Marital Gifts
Minor	Delivery of Gift
Cause of Action	Donor
Heart Balm	Donee
Remedy	Symbolic Delivery
Specific Performance	Implied Intention
Aggrieved Party	Conditional Gift
Damages	Contract Restraining Marriage
Compensatory Damages	General Restraint on Marriage
Out-of-Pocket Damages	Reasonable Restrictions on Marriage
Aggravated Damages	

CHAPTER SEVEN

Antenuptial Agreements and Contract Cohabitation

■ **Chapter Outline**

An *antenuptial agreement* is a premarital contract that defines certain rights and obligations during marriage and upon the termination of marriage by death or divorce. To be enforceable, the agreement must be in writing; must meet the requirements for a valid contract; must be based on full disclosure of assets; must be fair to the prospective wife; and must not be against public policy. Depending upon what the parties exchange in such an agreement, a gift tax may have to be paid.

Contract cohabitation refers to an agreement between two unmarried parties covering property and other rights while they live together as husband and wife without being married. Some states will enforce such agreements so long as they are not based solely on meretricious sexual services, or so long as the sexual aspect of their agreement is severable from the rest of the agreement. When one party sues the other for breaching the agreement, the media's misleading phrase for the litigation is *palimony suit*.

If the aggrieved party cannot establish the existence of an express or implied cohabitation contract, other theories might be used by the court to avoid the unfairness of one of the parties walking away from the relationship with nothing. These theories include quantum meruit, resulting trust, constructive trust, partnership, joint venture, and the putative-spouse doctrine.

Section A. Antenuptial Agreements

An antenuptial agreement (also called a *prenuptial* or *premarital agreement*) is a contract made by two individuals about to be married. It is quite different from a *cohabitation agreement* made by individuals living together who do not plan to be married (page 146), and from a *separation agreement* made by married individuals who no longer wish to live together and will probably seek a divorce (page 205).

The major function of an antenuptial agreement is to define rights and obligations during the contemplated marriage as well as upon the termination of the marriage by divorce or death. Why, you might ask, would two individuals about to enter the blissful state of marriage discuss such matters as "who gets what" if there is a divorce? The kinds of people who tend to make antenuptial agreements are usually:

- Older
- Have substantial property of their own
- Have been married before and already have children

Such individuals may want to make clear that the new spouse is not to have any claim on designated property, or that the children of the former marriage have first claim to property acquired before the second marriage.

An awareness of the large number of marriages that end in divorce causes some people to seek a measure of advance protection through an antenuptial agreement, particularly men and women who have separate careers and have lived together before marriage.

> Changing lifestyles, skyrocketing divorce rates and increased awareness about prenuptial agreements have prompted more middle-aged, middle income and young professionals to clamor for such protection from their soon-to-be-spouses. Matrimonial lawyers across the country say they are doing double or triple the number of prenuptial agreements compared to the volume during the previous five to ten years.[1]

Parties, however, cannot completely reshape the nature of their marital status through a contract. While antenuptial agreements tend to promote marital harmony and hence are favored by the courts, there are limitations and requirements that we need to explore:

- ☐ **Written contract**
- ☐ **Valid Contract**
- ☐ **Disclosure**
- ☐ **Fairness to Prospective Wife**
- ☐ **Public Policy**

☑ **Written Contract**

In most states, the Statute of Frauds requires that the agreement be in writing.

---

[1]Nance, *Prenuptial Pacts: "Till Some Breach Doth Them Part,"* 1 NATIONAL LAW JOURNAL at 26 (November 7, 1988).

☐ Valid Contract

For the antenuptial agreement to be enforceable, it must be a valid contract. Offer, acceptance, and consideration[2] are necessary (page 120). The parties must have the legal capacity to contract, and they must do so freely without fraud or duress. Some states impose other requirements, e.g., that the contract be formally notarized or acknowledged.

Assignment 7.1

What are the requirements for entering a valid antenuptial agreement in your state? (See General Instructions for the State-Code Assignment, in chapter one.)

☐ Disclosure

The prospective spouses must make a full and frank disclosure of assets. This standard is one of the most important. The concern is that a spouse will agree to certain property arrangements on the basis of an erroneous understanding of the other's worth at the time of the antenuptial agreement. The wife, for example, may have known that the husband was "well to do" or, alternatively, that his means enabled him to live "modestly." This degree of information, however, is generally not considered adequate. The husband must see to it that the wife has the details of his financial worth, his bank accounts, his holdings, his other property, etc. Furthermore, when the husband makes these disclosures, there must be no *under-valuation of assets*. Some states require proof that the wife (or husband) had the benefit of the advice of *independent counsel* before accepting the terms of the agreement. In short, prospective spouses must not deal with each other at arm's length. They have the equivalent of a *fiduciary* or trust responsibility to each other.

Assignment 7.2

Jim and Mary are engaged to be married. Mary is very wealthy; Jim is a poor laborer. As part of an antenuptial agreement, Jim waives his right to a full disclosure of the kind, quantity, and value of Mary's assets. Years later, following a divorce, Mary tries to enforce the antenuptial agreement. Jim responds by claiming that the agreement is invalid because Mary did not provide him with full disclosure. What result? (See General Instructions for the Legal-Analysis Assignment in chapter one.)

☐ Fairness to Prospective Wife

This standard is more controversial. Not all states require that the agreement be fair, particularly if the husband has fully complied with the standard of disclosure mentioned above, and the wife will not be left destitute or become a public charge. A great deal depends on one's view of the status of women.

---

[2]The consideration can be the marriage itself. See § 2 of the Uniform Premarital Agreement Act, 9B UNIFORM LAWS ANNOTATED (1987).

There was a time when the law assumed that the man was always the dominant force in a relationship with a woman and that the latter thus needed special protection. Almost by definition, a woman would not know how to take care of herself and, therefore, would be taken unfair advantage of by her husband or husband-to-be. According to this view, the law should protect a woman who signs a bad agreement even if there was full disclosure and no fraud by the man. The state, in effect, becomes a third party to the antenuptial agreement in order to ensure that the woman receives a fair and reasonable deal. The view in other states, however, is that in today's society, women can take care of themselves, are capable of bargaining on their own behalf, and, if they make a bad bargain in an antenuptial agreement, should be held to it—so long as there was full disclosure and so long as they will not be left destitute.

Most states fall somewhere in between these two extremes. Unfortunately, the courts within a given state are not always consistent in handling such claims by a woman that the antenuptial agreement she signed should be invalidated because of unfairness. Although the trend is toward rejecting such claims, many cautious attorneys take extra steps to try to prevent a "fairness" challenge. For example, one attorney, having videotaped the signing of an agreement, asked the jury, "Does she look like she's under duress; does she [look like] she knows what she is doing? Does she look happy? A picture is worth a thousand words."[3]

When fairness is an issue, it is important to note that an antenuptial agreement must be fair *at the time someone tries to enforce it* whether or not it was fair at the time it was signed. An attorney who fails to make this distinction runs the risk of being subject to a malpractice action when it eventually becomes clear years later that the antenuptial agreement is inadequate to meet current financial needs. Some attorneys recommend using an *escalation clause* under which the amount of alimony a spouse receives increases according to the number of years the parties were married; the longer the marriage, the more alimony provided by the antenuptial agreement.[4]

☐ Public Policy

Care must be taken to avoid provisions in an antenuptial agreement that are illegal because they are against public policy. For example, the parties cannot agree in advance that neither will ever make a claim on the other for the support of any children that they might have together. The livelihood of children cannot be contracted away by such a clause. So, too, it would be improper to agree never to contest a future divorce action or other suit initiated by the other side. It is against public policy to discourage the use of the courts in this way, since legitimate grievances might go unheard.

Assignment 7.3

Would the following provisions in an antenuptial agreement be legal in your state? (see General Instructions for the Court-Opinion Assignment in chapter one):

(a) A clause designating how much support one spouse will receive from the other during the marriage

---

[3]S. Nance, *Prenuptial Pacts: "Till Some Breach Doth Them Part,"* 1 NATIONAL LAW JOURNAL at 27 (November 7, 1988).

[4]Ibid.

(b) A clause stating that the husband will never have to wash the dishes

(c) A clause stating that the children from a prior marriage will not live with the parties

(d) A clause stating that any children born to the couple will not attend formal services of any religion

(e) A clause stating a minimum number of times that the parties will engage in sexual intercourse per month.

Very often the antenuptial agreement will specify alimony and other property rights in the event of a *divorce*. Many courts once considered such provisions to be against public policy because they *facilitate* (or encourage) *divorce*. The theory is that a party will be more inclined to seek a divorce if he or she knows what funds or other property will be available upon divorce, particularly, of course, if the financial terms upon divorce are favorable. Most courts, however, are moving away form this position. Divorces are no longer difficult to obtain in view of the coming of no-fault divorce laws. There is less pressure from society to keep marriages together at all costs. A spouse who wants a divorce can obtain one with relative ease and probably does not need the inducement of a favorable antenuptial agreement to terminate the marriage. Hence some (but by no means all) courts have upheld provisions in antenuptial agreements that provide a designated amount of alimony, or indeed that provide no alimony in the event of a divorce. A major concern of the court will be whether the agreement is otherwise fair to the spouse and whether the disclosure requirement has been met.

As indicated, however, this approach is not taken in all states. Some courts refuse to enforce *any* antenuptial agreement that tries to define rights in the event of a divorce. They will enforce only non-divorce clauses such as one covering the disposition of property upon death. Other courts distinguish between an alimony-support clause and a property-division clause in an antenuptial agreement. When the parties eventually divorce and one of them tries to enforce the antenuptial agreement, such courts are more likely to enforce the property-division clause than the alimony-support clause. These courts are reluctant to relinquish the flexibility they need to make sure that one of the spouses does not become destitute and a public charge because this person unwisely agreed to low or no alimony in an antenuptial agreement years ago.

Assignment 7.4

(a) The property division clause in the antenuptial agreement of George and Jane provides that in the event of a divorce George will receive $750,000 and Jane will receive all other property acquired during the marriage. Is this clause legal? (See the General Instructions for the Legal-Analysis Assignment in chapter one.)

(b) Assume that George and Jane live in a community property state where it is legal for the parties to agree to treat community property as separate property so that each is no longer entitled to 50 percent of that property. The property division clause in their antenuptial agreement provides that in the event of a divorce, all community property will be treated as separate property and will go to the party who has title to the property at the time of the divorce. Is this clause legal? (See General Instructions for the Legal-Analysis Assignment in chapter one.)

Death clauses in antenuptial agreements are less controversial. Parties often agree to give up the rights they may have (e.g., dower, page 453) in the estate of their deceased spouse. If the antenuptial agreement is not otherwise invalid, such terms are usually upheld by the courts.

The *Uniform Premarital Agreement Act*, which has been adopted in about a fourth of the states, has a very liberal view of what the parties can cover in an antenuptial agreement:

Uniform Premarital Agreement Act 9B Uniform Laws Annotated (1987)
§ 3. Content

(a) Parties to a premarital agreement may contract with respect to:

  (1) the rights and obligations of each of the parties in any of the property of either or both of them whenever and wherever acquired or located;

  (2) the right to buy, sell, use, transfer, exchange, abandon, lease, consume, expend, assign, create a security interest in, mortgage, encumber, dispose of, or otherwise manage and control property;

  (3) the disposition of property upon separation, marital dissolution, death, or the occurrence or nonoccurrence of any other event;

  (4) the modification or elimination of spousal support;

  (5) the making of a will, trust, or other arrangement to carry out the provisions of the agreement;

  (6) the ownership rights in and disposition of the death benefit from a life insurance policy;

  (7) the choice of law governing the construction of the agreement; and

  (8) any other matter, including their personal rights and obligations, not in violation of public policy or a statute imposing a criminal penalty.

(b) The right of a child to support may not be adversely affected by a premarital agreement.

Interviewing and Investigation Checklist

Factors Relevant to the Validity of the Antenuptial Agreement

(C = client; D = defendant)

Legal Interviewing Questions

1. On what date did you begin discussing the agreement?

2. Whose idea was it to have an agreement?

3. On what date did you first see the agreement?

4. Who actually wrote the agreement?

5. Did you read the agreement?

6. Did you understand everything in the agreement?

7. Describe in detail what you thought was in the agreement.

8. Did you sign the agreement? If so, why?

9. Were there ever any changes made in the agreement? If so, describe the circumstances, the nature of the change, who proposed it, etc.

10. Do you recall anything that was said during the discussions on the agreement that was different from what was eventually written down?

11. Was anyone present at the time you either discussed or signed the agreement?

12. Where is the agreement kept? Were you given a copy at the time you signed?

13. Before you signed the agreement, did you consult with anyone, e.g., attorney, accountant, relative?

14. If you did consult with anyone, describe that person's relationship, if any, with your spouse.

15. What were you told by the individuals with whom you consulted? Did they think it was wise for you to sign the agreement? Why or why not?

16. How old were you when you signed the agreement? How old was your spouse?

17. How much did you know about your spouse's background before you agreed to marry? What generally did you think D's wealth and standard of living was?

18. How did you obtain this knowledge?

19. While you were considering the antenuptial agreement, describe what you specifically knew about the following: D's bank accounts (savings, checking, trust), insurance policies, home ownership, business property, salary, investments (e.g., stocks, bonds), rent income, royalty income, inheritances (recent or expected), cars, planes, boats, etc. Also, what did you know about D's debts and other liabilities? For each of the above items about which you had knowledge, state how you obtained the knowledge.

20. When did you first learn that D owned (_____) at the time you signed the agreement? (Insert items in parentheses that C learned about only after the agreement was signed.)

21. Do you think you were given an honest accounting of all D's assets at the time you signed? Why or why not?

22. Do you think the agreement you signed was fair to you and to the children you and D eventually had? Why or why not?

Possible Investigation Tasks

- Obtain copies of the antenuptial agreement and of all drafts of the agreement, if any, reflecting changes.

- Contact and interview anyone who has knowledge of or was present during the discussions and/or signing of the agreement.

- Try to obtain bank records, tax records, etc., that would give some indication of the wealth and standard of living of D and of C at the time they signed the antenuptial agreement.

- Prepare an inventory of every asset C *thought* D owned at the time the agreement was signed, and an inventory of every asset your investigation has revealed D *in fact* owned at the time of the signing.

Section B. Special Tax Consequences

As we have seen, *consideration* is something of value that is exchanged between parties. In an antenuptial agreement, the consideration is usually an exchange of promises, such as a promise to relinquish the right to inherit a designated portion of the spouse's real property. While such consideration

"It's a prenuptial agreement silly! I'm asking you to *marry* me!"

Source: Mark Hannabury, 90 CASE AND COMMENT 34 (March–April 1985).

may be sufficient for *contract* purposes, it may not be sufficient to avoid a *gift tax*.

A gift tax must be paid if there is a transfer that is not made for "an adequate and full consideration in money or money's worth" Internal Revenue Code, § 2512(b). If all that is exchanged in the antenuptial agreement is a promise to refrain from claiming certain rights that the law gives one spouse in the other, a gift tax may have to be paid, since "a relinquishment or promised relinquishment" of "marital rights in the spouse's property or estate, shall not be considered to any extent a consideration 'in money or money's worth' " Treasury Regulations, § 25.2512-8.

This result does *not* apply to exchanges made between spouses pursuant to a separation agreement leading to a divorce. The tax consequences of such agreements will be discussed later (page 428).

Assignment 7.5

(a) Find an opinion written by a court in your state that discusses the fairness of an antenuptial agreement. Give the facts and result of the opinion. If no such opinion exists in your state, try to find one written by a neighboring state. According to the opinion, what standards are used in the state to assess the fairness of the antenuptial agreement? (See General Instructions for the Court-Opinion Assignment in chapter one.)

(b) Pretend that you are about to be married, and draft an antenuptial agreement for you and your future spouse. You can assume anything you want (within reason) about the financial affairs and interests of your spouse-to-be and yourself. Number each clause of the agreement separately and consecutively. Try to anticipate as many difficulties as possible that could arise during the marriage and state in the agreement how you want them resolved. (See General Instructions for the Agreement-Drafting Assignment in chapter one.)

(c) After your instructor makes note of the fact that you have drafted an agreement, you will be asked to exchange agreements with another member of the class. You are to analyze the agreement written by your classmate. Go through each numbered clause in the agreement and determine whether it is valid or invalid according to the standards identified in this chapter and/or according to the law governing antenuptial agreements in your state. When you cannot apply a standard, in whole or in part, because you need more facts, simply list the factual questions to which you would like answers in order to be able to assess the validity of the clause in question. (See General Instructions for the Legal-Analysis Assignment in chapter one.)

Section C. Sample Antenuptial Agreement Clauses

Sample Antenuptial Agreement Clauses

B. Stone, Modern Legal Forms
§§ 4493ff., p. 220ff., (West Publishing Co., 1977)

(I)
Antenuptial Agreement—Release of Husband's Rights in Wife's Property

Agreement made this _____ day of _____ , 19 __ , between John Day, of _____ , and Jane Kent, of _____ .

Whereas a marriage is shortly to be solemnized between the parties hereto;

Whereas Jane Kent now owns a large amount of property and expects to acquire from time to time additional property under a trust established for her by her father, _____ ;

Whereas John Day has agreed that all of the property now or in the future owned by Jane Kent, or her estate, shall be free of all rights that he might acquire by reason of his marriage to her.

It is agreed as follows:

Wife Retains Full Control of Property

1. Jane Kent shall have full right and authority, in all respects the same as she would have if unmarried, to use, enjoy, manage, convey, mortgage, and dispose of all of her present and future property and estate, of every kind and character, including the right and power to dispose of same by last will and testament.

Husband Releases All Right in His Wife's Property

2. John Day releases to Jane Kent, her heirs, legal representatives and assigns, every right, claim, and estate, actual, inchoate, or contingent, that he might have in respect to said property by reason of his marriage to Jane Kent.

Deceased Minor Child's Property

3. In the event any child of said marriage shall survive Jane Kent and shall then die a minor, John Day releases every right, claim, and estate he might inherit by reason of death of such minor child, and agrees that the property of such minor child shall be subject to any bequest or devise thereof made by Jane Kent.

Additional Instruments

4. John Day further agrees that upon the request of Jane Kent he will execute, acknowledge and deliver any additional instruments that may reasonably be necessary to carry out more effectually the purpose of this agreement.

Representatives Bound

This agreement shall bind the parties and their heirs, legal representatives and assigns.

In Witness Whereof, etc.

(II)
Clause Releasing Husband's Interest in Wife's Property for a Lump Sum Payable on Wife's Death

Now, therefore [Wife] agrees that she will, upon her decease, cause to be paid to [Husband,] if he is then living, $ _____ , within one year after her death; and [Husband] agrees that he will, upon the death of [Wife,] take the said $ _____ in full of all rights of curtesy, homestead, survivorship, inheritance, separate maintenance, widower's award, or otherwise in or to her estate, and in full of all other rights, interests, claims or allowances which he might be entitled to but for this agreement, and that on payment to him of the $ _____ he will release, quitclaim and discharge to her representatives or heirs all rights of curtesy, homestead, survivorship, inheritance, separate maintenance, widower's award, and all other rights, claims or interests which he might have in her estate but for this agreement.

(III)
Antenuptial Agreement—Release of Wife's Interest in Husband's Property—Present Payment of a Lump Sum

Agreement made this day _____ day of _____ , 19 __ , between John Day, of _____ , and Jane Kent, of _____ , witnesseth:

Whereas the parties contemplate entering into marriage relations:

Whereas John Day is the owner of property listed on the memorandum attached hereto; and

Whereas John Day desires to make suitable provision for Jane Kent in lieu of dower or other interest in his property which she otherwise might have.

Now, therefore, the parties agree as follows:

Payment of Lump Sum

1. John Day agrees to pay to Jane Kent, immediately after the solemnization of said marriage, the sum of _____ dollars, the said sum to be her sole and separate property.

Wife Releases Rights in Husband's Property

2. Jane Kent agrees that she will accept the said sum in lieu of any and all claims of dower, inheritance and descent in and to the property of John Day, now owned or that may hereafter be acquired by him, and in lieu of any and all other claims which might otherwise arise or accrue to her by reason of said marriage.

Management of Lump Sum

3.   In view of the nature of the property set forth in the memorandum attached hereto, the nature and extent of which property is fully understood by Jane Kent, it is the desire of Jane Kent, and it is therefore agreed, that John Day shall take over the management of the _____ dollars this day given by him to the end that its value may be preserved and made productive.

Wife to Join in Conveyances

4.   Jane Kent agrees that upon the request of John Day, she will execute all and any proper instruments of conveyance in order to enable John Day to sell or convey real estate now owned or afterward acquired by him.

In Witness Whereof, *etc.*

(IV)
Antenuptial Agreement—Release of Marital Rights in Husband's Estate—Payment of Lump Sum Out of Husband's Estate

This agreement, made this _____ day of _____ , 19 __ , between John Day, of _____ , and Jane Kent, of _____ .

Whereas, a marriage is about to be solemnized between the parties to this agreement, who have made a full disclosure to each other as to their property, and are desirous that Jane Kent should have a cash payment instead of an interest in the estate of John Day.

Now, therefore, if Jane Kent survives John Day, Jane Kent agrees to accept from the estate of John Day the sum of _____ dollars in lieu of dower and her distributive share of the personal property, and John Day shall hold all the real estate which he now owns or may hereafter acquire free from any claim of dower, inchoate or otherwise; in consideration whereof John Day agrees that Jane Kent shall be paid said sum of _____ dollars as soon after his decease as may be practicable.

In Witness Whereof, *etc.*

(V)
Clause Providing for Monthly Payment to Wife After Husband's Death

Now, therefore, the Husband agrees that the representative of his estate shall pay to the Wife the sum of _____ dollars ($ _____), payable as follows: _____ dollars ($ _____) _____ days after the decease of the Husband and a like amount each _____ days thereafter, until the full sum is paid in full, which cash payment shall be a lien on any real estate owned by the husband at the time of his decease, provided, however, that at his option the Husband, during his life, may purchase an annuity for a like sum payable in monthly installments in any good and solvent insurance company, which annuity shall be received by the Wife as a substitute for said cash payment. Provided also that if the Wife shall predecease the Husband, this agreement shall terminate upon her death.

(VI)
Antenuptial Agreement Releasing Husband's Interest in Wife's Estate and Limiting Wife's Interest in Husband's Estate

Whereas, _____ , of _____ , herein called the Husband, and _____ , of _____ , herein called the Wife, contemplate entering into marriage relations; and whereas, the Husband has a large estate and has children by a former marriage; and whereas, the Wife is possessed of property in her own right and has a child by a former marriage; and whereas, the said parties desire to prescribe, limit, an determine the interest and control which each of them may have in the estate of the other party; therefore the following agreement is entered into:

Know all men by these presents: That we, _____ and _____ , being about to enter into the marriage relations, do hereby agree:

Husband Releases His Rights in Wife's Estate

1. In the event of the death of the Wife during the continuance of said marriage relations, the Husband surviving her, then the Husband shall receive from the estate of the Wife the sum of five dollars; such sum when paid by the executors or administrators of the estate of the Wife to be in full for all claims and demands of every kind and character which the Husband shall have against the estate of the Wife.

Wife Limits Her Rights in Husband's Estate

2. In the event of the death of the Husband during the said marriage relations, the Wife agrees that her claim upon the estate of the Husband shall be limited to $ _____ , and a payment by the executors or the administrators of the estate of the Husband to the Wife, her heirs or legal representatives, of the sum of $ _____ shall be in full for all claims and demands of every kind and character which the Wife shall have against the estate of the Husband.

During Marriage Each to Have Full Control of Own Property

3. During the continuance of said marriage relations, each of the parties is to have full right to own, control, and dispose of his or her separate property the same as if the marriage relations did not exist, and each of the parties is to have full right to dispose of and sell any and all real or personal property now or hereafter owned by each of them without the other party joining, and said transfer by either of the parties to this contract shall convey the same title that said transfer would convey had the marriage relations not existed. This contract limits the right of either party to participate in the estate of the other, whether the marriage relation is terminated by death or legal proceedings.

Purpose of Contract to Limit Rights

4. The purpose of this agreement is to define and limit the claims and demands which each of the parties shall have against the estate of the other. Should either party die during the pendency of this contract, or should the contract be terminated by legal proceedings, the claims herein stipulated and defined shall be the limit which either party may have against the other party or his or her estate.

Contract Made with Full Knowledge

5. This agreement is entered into with full knowledge that each of the parties has a separate estate, and no claim or demand can be predicated upon the fact that there has been any misrepresentation or concealment as to the amount and condition of said separate estate, it being expressly agreed that each of the parties considers the amount hereinabove fixed to be sufficient participation in the estate of the other, and it being expressly stated that each of the parties has sufficient general knowledge of the condition of the estate of the other to justify making and entering into this agreement.

In Witness Whereof, *etc.*

_____

(VII)
Antenuptial Agreement Each Relinquishing Interest in Other's Property

Agreement made the _____ day of _____ , 19 __ , between John Day, of _____ , and Jane Kent, of _____ .

Whereas, the parties contemplate entering into the marriage relation with each other, and both are severally possessed of real and personal property in his and her own right, and each have children by former marriages, all of said children being of age and possessed of means of support independent of their parents, and it is desired by the parties that their marriage shall not in any way change their legal right, or that of their children and heirs, in the property of each of them.

Therefore it is agreed:

Home

1. John Day agrees that he will provide during the continuance of the marriage a home for Jane Kent, and that the two children of Jane Kent may reside in such home with their mother so long as said children remain unmarried.

Husband Releases Rights in Wife's Property

2. John Day agrees, in case he survives Jane Kent, that he will make no claim to any part of her estate as surviving husband; that in consideration of said marriage he waives and relinquishes all right or curtesy or other right in and to the property, real or personal, which Jane Kent now owns or may hereafter acquire.

Wife Releases Rights in Husband's Property

3. Jane Kent agrees, in case she survives John Day, that she will make no claim to any part of his estate as surviving wife; that in consideration of said marriage she waives and relinquishes all claims to dower, homestead, widow's award, or other right in and to the property, real or personal, which John Day now owns or may hereafter acquire.

Intent that Marriage Shall Not Affect Property

4. It is declared that by virtue of said marriage neither one shall have or acquire any right, title, or claim in and to the real or personal estate of the other, but that the estate of each shall descend to his or her heirs at law, legatees, or devisees, as may be prescribed by his or her last will and testament or by the law of the state in force, as though no marriage had taken place between them.

Agreement to Join in Conveyances

5. It is agreed that in case either of the parties desires to mortgage, sell or convey his or her real or personal estate, each one will join in the deed of conveyance or mortgage, as may be necessary to make the same effectual.

Full Disclosure between the Parties

6. It is further agreed that this agreement is entered into with a full knowledge on the part of each party as to the extent and probable value of the estate of the other and of all the rights conferred by law upon each in the estate of the other by virtue of said proposed marriage, but it is their desire that their respective rights to each other's estate shall be fixed by this agreement, which shall be binding upon their respective heirs and legal representatives.

In Witness Whereof, *etc.*

(VIII)
Antenuptial Agreement Each Relinquishing Interest in Other's Property—Another Form

This Agreement made the _____ day of _____ , 19__ , between John Day, of _____ , and Jane Kent, of _____ .

Whereas, the parties contemplate legal marriage under the laws of the State of _____ ; and

Whereas, it is their mutual desire to enter into this agreement whereby they will regulate their relationships toward each other with respect to the property each of them own and in which each of them has an interest.

Now, therefore, it is agreed as follows:

1. That all properties of any kind or nature, real, personal or mixed, wherever the same may be found, which belong to each party, shall be and forever remain the personal estate of said party, including all interest, rents and profits which may accrue therefrom.

2. That each party shall have at all times the full right and authority, in all respects the same as each would have if not married, to use, enjoy, manage, convey and encumber such property as may belong to him or her.

3. That each party may make such disposition of his or her property as the case may be, by gift or will during his or her lifetime, as each sees fit; and in the event of the decease of one of the parties, the survivor shall have no interest in the property of the estate of the other, either by way of inheritance, succession, family allowance or homestead.

4. That each party, in the event of a separation, shall have no right as against the other by way of claims for support, alimony, attorney fees, costs, or division of property.

In Witness Whereof, *etc.*

(IX)
Antenuptial Agreement Each Relinquishing Interest in Other's Property—Another Form

This agreement is made the _____ day of _____ , 19 __ , between _____ , of _____ , and _____ , of _____ .

Whereas, a marriage is intended to be shortly after the date hereof solemnized between the said _____ and _____ ; and

Whereas, each of the parties is possessed of considerable property, and has made a full and frank disclosure to the other in relation to its character and amount, and they have been advised as to their respective rights therein in the event of their marriage and in the absence of any agreement between them:

Now, therefore, the [*bridegroom*] and [*bride*], hereby declare it to be their intention that during their marriage each of them shall be and continue completely independent of the other as regards the enjoyment and disposal of all property, whether owned by either of them at the commencement of the marriage or coming to them or either of them during the marriage. Accordingly, they agree that all property belonging to either of them at the commencement of the marriage or coming to either of them during the marriage shall be enjoyed by him or her, and be subject to the dispositions of him or her, as his or her separate property, and after the death of either it shall be free from any claim by the other on account of dower, curtesy, or other statutory right, in the same manner as if the marriage had never been celebrated.

In Witness Whereof, *etc.*

(X)
Antenuptial Property Settlement Providing for Pooling of Property

This agreement made this the _____ day of _____ , 19 __ , between _____ , of _____ , and _____ , of _____ .

Whereas, the parties are contemplating marriage and establishing a home together; and

Whereas, the parties upon their marriage desire to pool their resources for the benefit of each other; and

Whereas, this agreement is made in order to avoid any future conflict as to their rights and interests in said property.

Now, therefore, the parties agree as follows:

1.   The parties shall enter into the marriage relation and live together as husband and wife.

2.   On or before the date of marriage all property belonging to the parties, including bonds, bank accounts and realty, shall be reissued, redeposited and deeds drawn so that each party shall be the joint owner, with right of survivorship, of all of the property at present owned and held by the parties individually.

3.   Each party obligates himself to purchase and hold all property, present and future, jointly with the other party and agrees to execute any instrument necessary to convey, sell, or encumber any property, real or personal, when it is to the best interest of both parties that same be conveyed, sold, or encumbered.

4.   At the death of either party the property belonging to both shall become the absolute property of the other, free from claims of all other persons. To make effective this section of the agreement a joint will of the parties is made and is placed in their safety deposit box in the _____ Bank in the City of _____ , _____ .

5.   Should either party file a divorce against the other, then the party so filing shall by such filing forfeit to the other all right, title, and interest in all the property, real, personal or mixed, jointly held and owned by them.

6.   The parties agree that the original of this instrument shall be deposited in escrow with _____ to be held by him.

7.   This agreement cannot be revoked except by written consent of both parties and the holder in escrow shall not deliver the original to anyone except a court of competent jurisdiction or to the parties to this instrument upon their mutual demand for the surrender thereof.

8.   This agreement is made in triplicate with each party hereto retaining a copy thereof, but the copy shall not be used in evidence or serve any legal purpose whatsoever if the original is available.

In Witness Whereof, *etc.*

Section D. Contract Cohabitation

Compare the following two situations:

> Jim hires Mary as a maid in his house. She receives weekly compensation plus room and board. For a three-month period Jim fails to pay Mary's wages, even though she performs all of her duties faithfully. During this period, Jim seduces Mary. Mary sues Jim for *breach of contract* due to nonpayment of wages.
>
> Bob is a prostitute. Linda hires Bob for an evening but refuses to pay him his fee. Bob sues Linda for *breach of contract* due to nonpayment of the fee.

The result in the second situation is clear. Bob cannot sue Linda for breach of contract. A contract for sex is not enforceable in court. Linda promised to pay money for sex. Bob promised and provided sexual services. This was the consideration he gave in the bargain. But sex for hire is illegal in most states. In fact, fornication (sex between unmarried persons) and adultery (sex between a married person and someone with whom he or she is not married) are crimes in some states even if there is no payment involved. Bob's consideration was *meretricious sexual services* and, as such, cannot be the basis of a valid contract. Meretricious means vulgar or unlawful.

☐ **EXHIBIT 7-1** How Families Have Changed, 1970–1986

	1970	1980	1986	Percent Change 1970–1986	
Population	205,100,000	227,700,000	241,078,000	Up	17.5
Marriages performed	2,159,000	2,413,000	2,401,000	Up	11.2
Divorces granted	708,000	1,182,000	1,590,000	Up	124.6
Married couples	44,728,000	48,643,000	51,704,000	Up	15.6
Married couples with children	25,541,000	24,501,000	24,630,000	Down	3.6
Unmarried couples with children present	196,000	424,000	612,000	Up	212.2
Single-parent families	6,800,000	10,435,000	12,625,000	Up	85.7
Unmarried couples	523,000	1,600,000	2,200,000	Up	320.6
Births	3,731,000	3,598,000	3,371,000	Down	9.6
Births to unmarried women	398,000	600,000	828,000	Up	108.0

Source: Bureau of the Census. *U.S. Statistical Abstract*, 1988. (Washington, DC: Government Printing Office, 1988).

The result in the first situation above should also be clear. Mary has a valid claim for breach of contract. Her sexual relationship with Jim (even if she consented to it) is incidental and, therefore, irrelevant to her right to collect compensation due her as a maid. She did not sell sexual services to Jim. There is no indication in the facts that the parties bargained for sexual services or that she engaged in sex in exchange for anything from Jim, e.g., continued employment, a raise in pay, lighter work duties. Their sexual involvement with each other is a fully *severable* part of their relationship and should not affect her main claim. Something is severable when what remains after it is removed can survive separately.

Now we come to a more difficult case:

> Dan and Helen meet in college. They soon start living together. They move into an apartment, pool some or all of their resources, have children, etc. Fifteen years after they entered this relationship, they decide to separate. Helen now sues Dan for a share of the property acquired during the time they lived together. At no time did they ever become married either through a marriage ceremony or a common-law marriage, page 157.

Child support is not an issue in this case. Natural parents have a duty to support their children whether or not they are married. What about the adults— Dan and Helen? They cohabited (lived together and acted as husband and wife) but they never married. They built a relationship, acquired property together, and helped each other over a long period of time. What happens now that they have separated?

This is not an academic question. By the late 1980s, over 2 million unmarried heterosexual couples were living together in nontraditional family units, a 320 percent increase over a fifteen-year period.[5] See Exhibit 7-1 for an overview.

---

[5]During this same period, there were about one and a half million gay and lesbian couples living together. B. Strong and C. DeVault, THE MARRIAGE AND FAMILY EXPERIENCE, 4th ed., p. 161 (1989).

For years, the law has denied any rights to an unmarried person who makes financial claims based upon a period of cohabitation. The main reasons for this denial are as follows:

- To grant financial or property rights to unmarried persons would be to treat them as if they were married. There is a fundamental difference between being married and not being married. Our laws favor the institution of marriage. To recognize unmarried relationships would denigrate marriage and discourage people from entering it.
- Sexual relations are legal and morally acceptable within marriage. If the law recognizes unmarried cohabitation, then illicit sex is being condoned. The relationship is not much different from *prostitution*.

These two arguments are still dominant forces in the law of many states. In 1976, however, a major decision came from California: *Marvin* v. *Marvin* 18 Cal.3d 660, 134 Cal.Rptr. 815, 557 P.2d 106 (1976). This case held that parties living together would not be denied a remedy in court upon their separation solely because they never married. Although all states have not followed *Marvin,* the decision has had a major impact in this still-developing area of the law.

The parties in *Marvin* lived together for seven years without marrying. The plaintiff alleged that she entered an oral agreement with the defendant that provided (1) that he would support her, and (2) that while "the parties lived together they would combine their efforts and earnings and would share equally any and all property accumulated as a result of their efforts whether individual or combined." She further alleged that she had agreed to give up her career as a singer in order to devote full time to the defendant as a companion, homemaker, housekeeper, and cook. During the seven years that they were together, the defendant accumulated in his name over $1 million in property. When they separated, she sued for her share of this property.

The media viewed her case as an alimony action between two unmarried "ex-pals" and dubbed it a "palimony" suit. Palimony, however, is not a legal term. The word *alimony* should not be associated with this kind of case. Alimony is a court-imposed obligation of support that grows out of a failed marital relationship. Such a relationship was not involved in the *Marvin* case.

One of the first hurdles for the plaintiff in *Marvin* was the problem of "meretricious sexual services." The defendant argued that even if a contract did exist (which he denied), it was unenforceable because it involved an illicit relationship. The parties were not married but were engaging in sexual relations. The court, however, ruled that

> "[A] contract is unenforceable only *to the extent* that it *explicitly* rests upon the immoral and illicit consideration of meretricious sexual services. . . . The fact that a man and woman live together without marriage, and engage in a sexual relationship, does not in itself invalidate agreements between them relating to their earnings, property, or expenses."

The agreement will be invalidated only if sex is an express condition of the relationship. If the sexual aspect of their relationship is severable from their agreements or understandings on earnings, property, and expenses, the agreements or understandings will be enforced. An example of an *un*enforceable agreement would be a promise by a man to provide for a woman in his will in exchange for her agreeing to bear his children. This agreement is *explicitly* based on a sexual relationship. Thus sex cannot be separated from the agreement and is *not* severable.

The next problem faced by the plaintiff in *Marvin* was the theory of *recovery*. The main reason married parties have financial rights in each other is their *marital status,* which gives rise to duties imposed by law. What about unmarried parties? The *Marvin* court suggested several theories of recovery for such individuals:

- Express contract
- Implied contract
- Quantum meruit
- Resulting trust
- Constructive trust
- Partnership
- Joint venture
- Putative-spouse doctrine

To the extent that any of the theories are based on an express or implied agreement, the phrase *contract cohabitation* is sometimes used to describe the relationship between the parties.

Before we examine the theories, several points need to be emphasized. First, as indicated earlier, not all states agree with the *Marvin* doctrine that there are circumstances when unmarried cohabiting parties should be given a remedy upon separation. Second, the above list of eight remedies is not exhaustive. The *Marvin* court recognized that new theories may have to be developed to achieve justice in particular situations. Third, all of the theories will be to no avail, even in states that follow *Marvin,* if it can be shown that "meretricious sexual services" were at the heart of the relationship and cannot be separated from the other aspects of the relationship.

Express Contract

In an *express contract,* the parties expressly tell each other what is being "bargained" for, e.g., household services in exchange for a one-half interest in a house to be purchased, or companion services (nonsexual) in exchange for support during the time they live together. There must be an offer, acceptance, and legal consideration. The latter is the exchange of promises.

While this is the cleanest theory of recovery, it is often difficult to prove. Rarely will the parties have the foresight to commit their agreement to writing, and it is equally rare for witnesses to be present when the parties make their agreement. Ultimately the case will turn on which party the court believes.

Implied Contract

An *implied contract* exists when it is clear from the circumstances that there was an agreement between the parties even though its terms were never expressly discussed. Consider the following example:

> Someone delivers bottled milk to your door daily, which you never ordered. You consume the milk every day, place the empty bottles on the front door, exchange greetings with the delivery person, never demand that the deliveries stop, etc.

At the end of the month when you receive the bill for the milk, you will not be able to hide behind the fact that you never expressly ordered the milk. Under traditional contract principles, you have entered an "implied contract" to buy the milk, which is as binding as an express contract. Unless the state has enacted special laws to change these principles, you must pay for the milk.

In the case of unmarried individuals living together, we must similarly determine whether an implied contract existed. Was it clear by the conduct of the parties that they were entering an agreement? Was it obvious under the circumstances that they were exchanging something? Did both sides expect "compensation" in some form for what they were doing? If so, an implied contract existed, which can be as enforceable as an express contract.

Quantum Meruit

In *quantum meruit*, again there is no express contract. It cannot be said that the terms of an agreement have been communicated. Yet, the following occurred:

- The plaintiff conferred a nonmeretricious benefit on the defendant, e.g., providing household services.
- The plaintiff conferred this benefit with the expectation of compensation.
- The defendant expressly or impliedly requested this benefit.
- The defendant would be unjustly enriched if the plaintiff is not compensated.

When these factors are present, the theory of quantum meruit may allow the plaintiff to recover the reasonable value of the services (or other benefit) that he or she provided, less the reasonable value of any support that the plaintiff received during the time involved. An example might be a man who arranges for a foreign woman to come to this country to live in his home and provide domestic services.

Resulting Trust

A *trust* exists when one person holds property for the benefit of another. At times, the law will hold that a trust is implied. An example of an implied trust is a resulting trust. Assume that Tim and Sandra, an unmarried couple, decide to buy a house. They use the funds in a joint account to which both contribute equally. The deed to the house is taken in Tim's name so that he has legal title. On such facts, a court will impose a resulting trust for Sandra's benefit. She will be entitled to a half-interest in the house through the trust. A theory of resulting trust might also be possible if Sandra contributed services rather than money toward the purchase of the property. A court would have to decide what her interest in the property should be in light of the nature and value of these services.

Constructive Trust

A *constructive trust* is another example of a trust that is imposed by law. Assume that a party obtains title to property through fraud or an abuse of confidence. The funds used to purchase the property come from the other party. A court will impose a constructive trust on the property if this is necessary to avoid the unjust enrichment of the person who obtained title in this way. This person will be deemed to be holding the property for the benefit of the party defrauded or otherwise taken advantage of.

Partnership

A *partnership* is a voluntary contract between two (or more) persons to use their resources in a business or other venture, with the understanding that they will proportionately share losses and profits. A court might find that an unmarried couple entered a partnership and thereby acquired rights and obligations in the property involved in the partnership.

Joint Venture

A *joint venture* is like a partnership, but on a much more limited scale. It exists when there is an express or implied agreement between parties to embark on an enterprise for a common purpose, e.g., to purchase property for speculation. Under a joint venture, each party has a mutual right to control the enterprise. A court might use this theory to cover some of the common enterprises entered into by two unmarried individuals who were living together at the time, e.g., the purchase of a home. Once a joint venture is established, the parties have legally enforceable rights in the fruits of their endeavors.

Putative-Spouse Doctrine

In limited circumstances, the *putative-spouse doctrine* might provide a remedy. This doctrine applies when the parties attempt to enter a marital relationship, but a legal *impediment* existed to the formation of the marriage, e.g., one of the parties was under age or was married to someone else. If at least one of the parties is ignorant of this impediment, the law will treat the "marriage" as otherwise valid (page 175). Upon separation, the innocent party will be entitled to a share of the property accumulated by their joint efforts.

Another theory, to be considered in the following chapter, is common-law marriage which is still recognized in some states.

 Interviewing and Investigation Checklist

Factors Relevant to the Property Rights of Unmarried Couples

Legal Interviewing Questions

1. When and how did the two of you meet?

2. When did you begin living together?

3. Why did the two of you decide to do this? What exactly did you say to each other at the time?

4. Did you discuss the living arrangement together? If so, what was said?

5. What was said or implied about the sexual relationship between you? Describe this relationship.

6. What was your understanding about the following matters: rent, house purchase, house payments, furniture payments, food, clothing, medical bills?

7. Did you agree to keep separate or joint bank accounts? Why?

8. What other commitments were made, if any? For example, was there any agreement on providing support, making a will, having children, giving each other property or shares in property? Were any of these commitments put in writing?

9. Did you ever discuss marriage? If so, what was said by both of you on the topic?

10. What did you give up in order to live with him or her? Did he or she understand this? How do you know?

11. What did he or she give up in order to live with you?

12. What other promises were made or implied between you? Why were they made?

13. How did you introduce each other to third persons?

14. Did you help each other in your businesses? If so, how?

15. What were your roles in the house? How were they decided upon? Through agreement? Explain.

16. Did he or she ever pay you for anything you did? Did you ever pay him or her? Explain the circumstances.

17. If no payment was ever made, was payment expected in the future? Explain.

18. Were the two of you "faithful" to each other? Did either of you ever date others? Explain.

19. Did you use each other's money for any purpose? If so, explain the circumstances. If not, why not?

Possible Investigation Tasks

- Obtain copies of bank statements, deeds for property acquired while the parties were together, loan applications, tax returns, etc.

- Interview persons who knew the parties.

- Contact professional housekeeping companies to determine the going rate for housekeeping services.

Assignment 7.6

(a) Shepardize *Marvin* v. *Marvin* to determine whether the case has been cited in any opinion written by a court in your state. Pick any three opinions in your state that cited *Marvin* v. *Marvin* and state how each used *Marvin*. Did it agree with, disagree with, or expand upon *Marvin?* (If your state is California where the case was decided, you should shepardize *Marvin* to find three other California cases that have cited *Marvin* v. *Marvin*. How they expand or narrowed *Marvin?)*

(b) What crime or crimes, if any, can unmarried people in your state commit when they engage in sexual intercourse? (See General Instructions for the State Code Assignment in chapter one.)

(c) Helen Smith and Sam Jones live together in your state. They are not married and do not intend to become married. They would like to enter a contract that spells out their rights and responsibilities. Specifically, they want to make clear that the house in which they both live belongs to Helen even though Sam has done extensive remodeling work on it. They each have separate bank accounts and one joint account. They want to make clear that only the funds in the joint account belong to both of them equally. Next year they hope to have or adopt a child. In either event, they want the contract to specify that the child will be given the surname, "Smith-Jones" which is a combination of their own last names. Draft a contract for them. Include any other clauses that you think appropriate, e.g., on making wills, the duration of the contract, on the education and religion of children. (See General Instructions for the Agreement-Drafting Assignment in chapter one.)

(d) Tom and George are gay. They live together. George agrees to support Tom while the latter completes engineering school, at which time Tom will support George while the latter completes law school. After Tom obtains his engineering degree, he leaves George. George now sues Tom for the amount of money that would have been provided as support while George attended law school. What result? (See General Instructions for the Legal-Analysis Assignment in chapter one.)

(e) Richard and Lea have lived together for ten years without being married. This month, they separated. They never entered a formal contract, but Lea says that they had an informal understanding that they would equally divide everything acquired during their relationship together. Lea sues Richard for one-half of all property so acquired. You work for the law firm that represents Lea. Draft a set of interrogatories for Lea that will be sent to Richard in which you seek information that would be relevant to Lea's action. (See General Instructions for the Interrogatories Assignment in chapter one.)

Section E. Sample Cohabitation Agreement

Cohabitation Agreement
W. Mulloy, WEST'S LEGAL FORMS, 2d
§ 3.54, pp. 225–229 (1983).

I
Intention of the Parties

_____ and _____ declare that they are not married to each other, but they are living together under the same roof, and by this agreement intend to protect and define each other's rights pertaining to future services rendered, earnings, accumulated property and furnishings and other matters that may be contained herein. It is expressly set forth herein that the consent of either party to cohabit sexually with the other is not a consideration, either in whole or in part, for the making of this agreement. It is further expressly set forth herein that the general purpose of this agreement is that the earnings, accumulations and property of each party herein shall be the separate property of the person who earns or acquires said property, and shall not be deemed community property, joint property, common law property, or otherwise giving the non-earning or non-acquiring party an interest in same.

II
Representations to the Public

It is agreed that should either or both of the parties to this agreement represent to the public, in whatever manner, that they are husband and wife, that said representation shall be for social convenience only, and shall in no way imply that sexual services are a consideration for any party of this agreement, nor shall it imply that sexual cohabitation is taking place.

III
Property, Earnings, and Accumulations

It is agreed that all property of any nature or in any place, including but not limited to the earnings and income resulting from the personal services, skill, effort, and work of either party to this agreement, whether acquired before or during the term of this agreement, or acquired by either one of them by purchase, gift or inheritance during the said term, shall be the separate property of the respective party, and that neither party shall have any interest in, and both parties hereby waive any right or interest he or she may have in the property of the other.

IV
Services Rendered

It is agreed that whatever household, homemaking, or other domestic work and services that either party may contribute to the other or to their common domicile shall be voluntary, free, and without compensation, and each party agrees that work of this nature is done without expectation of monetary or other reward from the other party.

V
Debts and Obligations

It is agreed that all debts and obligations acquired by either party which is to the benefit of that party shall be the debt or obligation of that party only, and that the other shall not be liable for same. Should one party be forced to pay a debt rightfully belonging to and benefitting the other, the other promises to reimburse, indemnify and hold harmless the one who has paid said debt or obligation.

Those debts and obligations which are to the benefit of both parties, such as utilities, garbage, local telephone service, rent, and renters insurance shall be paid in such sums and in such proportion by each party as shall be mutually agreeable.

VI
Money Loaned

All money, with the exception of mortgage or rent payments, transferred by one party to the other, either directly or to an account, obligation, or purchase of the other, shall be deemed a loan to the other, unless otherwise stated in writing. This shall include such things as downpayments on a home or vehicle, and deposits in either party's separate bank account.

VII
Rented Premises

It is agreed that should the parties share rented premises, said rented premises shall "belong" to the person who first rented the same, and should the parties separate, the second one shall leave taking only such belongings as he or she owned prior to moving in or purchased while living together.

If the parties both rent the premises from the beginning, then it is agreed that they will have a third person flip a coin to see who "owns" the premises, and the winner will have the option to remain while the loser leaves.

VIII
Rent or Mortgage

It is agreed that the parties may split the rent or mortgage payments in whatever proportion they choose, each contributing such sum as is mutually agreeable. It is also agreed that if one party contributes to the mortgage payment of a premises belonging to or being purchased in the name of the other party, that such contribution shall be deemed rent only, and shall be non-refundable and shall not create in the person who is living in the premises owned or being purchased by the other, any interest in said property or in the equity therein.

IX
Business Arrangements

A.   It is agreed that should one party hereto contribute services, labor, or effort to a business enterprise belonging to the other, that the party contributing said services, labor or effort shall not acquire by reason thereof any interest in, ownership of, or claim to said business enterprise, nor shall said person be compensated in any way for said services, labor, or effort, unless the terms of said compensation are expressly agreed to by both parties.

B.   Should the parties share services, labor or effort in a jointly owned business enterprise the relative interests of each party shall be apportioned according to a separate partnership agreement, or, if there is no express agreement, then in proportion that each contributed thereto.

C.   It is agreed that the business known as _____ is the individual and separate business of [*Name of Owner*], and is not to be deemed a jointly owned business of both parties.

X
Separate Accounts

In conformity with the intentions of the parties set forth herein, both parties agree to maintain separate bank accounts, insurance accounts (except "renter's" insurance to insure the contents of an apartment, house, etc., which the parties may jointly hold), tax returns, credit accounts, credit union accounts, medical accounts, automobile registration and ownership, and deeds to property, and to make all purchases of personal property, including furniture, appliances, records, books, works of art, stereo equipment, etc., separate, in order to avoid confusion as to the ownership of same, and also in order to avoid nullifying the general intent of this agreement.

XI
Duration of this Agreement

This agreement shall remain in effect from the date the parties start cohabiting until either party leaves or removes himself or herself from the common domicile with the intention not to return, or until they marry, or until they make a new written agreement which is contrary to the terms of this agreement.

XII
Attorneys Fees and Costs

Each party agrees to act in good faith with the provisions of this agreement, and should one party breach the agreement or fail to act in good faith therewith, such party agrees to pay to the other such attorneys fees and costs as may be reasonable in order to properly enforce the provisions herein.

XIII
No Common Law Marriage Intended

Even though the parties hereto are cohabiting under the same roof and may give the appearance of being married, or from time to time represent to the public that they are husband and wife, they do not intend by such acts to acquire the status of "common law" marriage, and expressly state herein that this is not an agreement to marry, that they are not now married, and that they understand they are not married to each other during the term of this agreement.

XV
Waiver of Support

Both parties waive and relinquish any and all rights to "alimony," "spousal support," or other separate maintenance from the other in the event of a termination of the living together arrangement.

Dated: _____

_____
[*Name and Signature of Party*]

_____
[*Name and Signature of Party*]

Key Chapter Terminology

Antenuptial Agreement	Contract Cohabitation
Prenuptial Agreement	Breach of Contract
Premarital Agreement	Meretricious Sexual Services
Statute of Frauds	Severable
Disclosure of Assets	Prostitution
Financial Worth	*Marvin v. Marvin*
Valuation of Assets	Palimony
Independent Counsel	Express Contract
Fiduciary Duty	Implied Contract
Fairness	Quantum Meruit
Escalation Clause	Unjust Enrichment
Public Policy	Resulting Trust
Child Support	Constructive Trust
Facilitation of Divorce	Partnership
Uniform Premarital Agreement Act	Joint Venture
Gift Tax	Putative-Spouse Doctrine
Consideration	Impediment to Marriage
Relinquishment of Marital Rights	

CHAPTER EIGHT

The Formation of Ceremonial Marriages and Common-Law Marriages

▪ Chapter Outline

Marriage is a coming together for better or for worse, hopefully enduring and intimate to the degree of being sacred. It is an association that promotes a way of life, not causes; a harmony in living, not political faiths; a bilateral loyalty, not commercial or social projects. Yet it is an association for as noble a purpose as any involved in our prior decisions.

Griswold v. Connecticut, 381 U.S. 479, 486, 85 S.Ct. 1678, 1682, 14 L.Ed.2d 510 (1965)—Justice Douglas.

Many material benefits derive from being married, particularly when a spouse dies, e.g., social security and pension benefits. To claim these benefits, one must establish the existence of a valid ceremonial marriage, or, in states that allow them, common-law marriage.

Requirements that must be fulfilled to enter a ceremonial marriage include obtaining a license, waiting a designated period of time, going through a physical examination, having the ceremony performed by an authorized person, having witnesses to the ceremony, and recording the license in the proper public office. Yet in most states, the failure to comply with such requirements is not a ground for an annulment.

In states where common-law marriages are still possible, the requirements are a present agreement to enter a marital relationship, living together as husband and wife (cohabitation), and an openness about living together as man and wife. As with ceremonial marriages, the parties must have the legal capacity to marry and must intend to marry. The latter conditions will be considered in Chapter 9.

The validity of a marriage is governed by the state in which it was entered or contracted. Hence if a couple enters a common-law marriage in a state where it is valid, but moves to a state where such marriages have been abolished, the latter state will recognize the marriage as valid.

Occasionally an impediment exists to an otherwise valid common-law marriage, e.g., one of the parties is still married to someone else. If the impediment is removed while the parties are still openly living together, a valid common-law marriage will be established as of the date of the removal.

Same-sex marriages are invalid in every American state. No legislature has passed a statute recognizing them, and all of the arguments made in court to force recognition have been unsuccessful. In some states, however, homosexuals have achieved limited rights in this area, e.g., to enter contracts governing nonsexual aspects of living together, to adopt a gay adult, to be considered a "family" for purposes of rent control, and to register as "domestic partners" for purposes of being entitled to bereavement leave upon the death of one of the partners.

Section A. Raising the Marriage Issue

A client is not likely to walk into a law office and ask, "am I married?" The existence of a marriage becomes an issue when the client is trying to obtain some other objective, such as:

- A divorce (you can't divorce someone to whom you are not married)
- Pension benefits as a surviving spouse of a deceased employee
- Social security survivor benefits through a deceased spouse
- Worker's compensation death benefits as the surviving spouse of an employee fatally injured on the job
- Assets as the spouse of a deceased person who died without a valid will (i.e., who died intestate)
- Assets under a clause in a will that gives property "to my wife" or "to my husband"
- A forced share of a deceased spouse's estate in lieu of what the latter provided (or failed to provide) in the will for the surviving spouse
- Entrance to the United States (or avoidance of deportation) as a result of being married to a U.S. citizen

Section B. Regulating Who Can Marry

Marital status may be achieved through one of two possible methods: ceremonial marriage or common-law marriage. As we shall see in the next section, however, many states have abolished common-law marriage.

The United States Supreme Court has held that marriage is a fundamental right. Consequently, a state is limited in its power to regulate one's right to marry. For example, a state cannot prohibit *miscegenation,* the marriage of persons of different races. Nor can it withhold a marriage license pending proof that child-support payments (from an earlier marriage) are being met, and that any children due such payments are not likely to become public charges. Only "reasonable regulations that do not significantly interfere with decisions to enter into the marital relationship may legitimately be imposed" *Zablocki v. Redhail,* 434 U.S. 374, 386, 98 S.Ct. 673, 681, 54 L.Ed.2d 618 (1978).

States have imposed two major kinds of requirements for entering marriage: (1) technical or formal requirements for ceremonial marriages, e.g., obtaining a license, and (2) more basic requirements relating to the capacity to marry that apply to both ceremonial and common-law marriages, e.g., being of minimum age to marry, and not being too closely related to the person you want to marry. The latter requirements will be discussed in Chapter 9. Here our focus is primarily on the technical or formal requirements.

Section C. Ceremonial Marriage

The requirements for a *ceremonial marriage,* found within the statutory code of your state, usually specify the following:

- Marriage license (Exhibit 8–2)
- Ceremony performed by an authorized person (Exhibit 8–1)
- Witnesses to the ceremony (Exhibit 8–1)
- Waiting period
- Physical examination of the two parties
- Recording of the license in a designated public office following the ceremony

Not all states have the same requirements, and some may impose additional ones.

Interviewing and Investigation Checklist

Factors Relevant to a Ceremonial Marriage

Legal Interviewing Questions

1. On what date did you apply for the marriage license? On what date was it issued?
2. Did you both go to fill out the application?
3. Where did you go to obtain the license?
4. Describe the person who iussed the license to you.
5. What happened after you obtained the license?
6. State the address and phone number of the person who performed the wedding ceremony.
7. How did you know that this person was authorized to perform the ceremony?

8. Give names, addresses, and phone numbers of all witnesses at the wedding ceremony, other than guests. Did anyone else have a role at the ceremony? If so, describe it.

9. On what date did the ceremony take place?

10. Did you both take physical or medical examinations before you were issued the license? If so, where, who performed them, and what were the results?

11. Do you know whether your marriage license was recorded?

12. Where, when, and by whom was your license recorded?

Possible Investigation Tasks

- Obtain a copy of the marriage license.

- Determine if a receipt exists for payment of the license fee, if any.

- If requested, obtain statements (affidavits) from the witnesses and from the person performing the ceremony concerning the circumstances of the ceremony.

- Go to where marriage records are kept in the county and copy all facts pertaining to the marriage.

- Obtain a copy of the medical record of the physical examination after the client signs an authorization to release this record to you.

□ **EXHIBIT 8–1**

Authorization to celebrate or witness a marriage

Number _____ .

To _____ , authorized to celebrate (or witness) marriages in the state of _____ , greeting:

You are hereby authorized to celebrate (or witness) the rites of marriage between _____ , of _____ , and _____ , of _____ , and having done so, you are commanded to make return of the same to the clerk's office of _____ within ten days under a penalty of fifty dollars for default therein.

Witness my hand and seal of said court this _____ day of _____ , anno Domini _____ .

_____ Clerk.

By _____ Assistant Clerk.

Number _____ .

I, _____ , who have been duly authorized to celebrate (or witness) the rites of marriage in the state of _____ do hereby certify that, by authority of a license of corresponding number herewith, I solemnized (or witnessed) the marriage of _____ and _____ , named therein, on the _____ day of _____ , at _____ , in said state.

Assignment 8.1

Go to your state statutory code and determine whether there are statutes relating to (1) marriage licenses, (2) persons who can perform the ceremony, (3) witness requirements for the ceremony, (4) waiting periods, (5) physical examination, and (6) filing or recording of the license, (7) other technical requirements.

For each statute, or portion thereof, answer the following three questions:

(a) What does the statute tell you about the topic? (Give a brief summary.)

(b) What, if anything, is ambiguous, unclear, or unanswered in the statute?

☐ EXHIBIT 8–2
A Marriage License

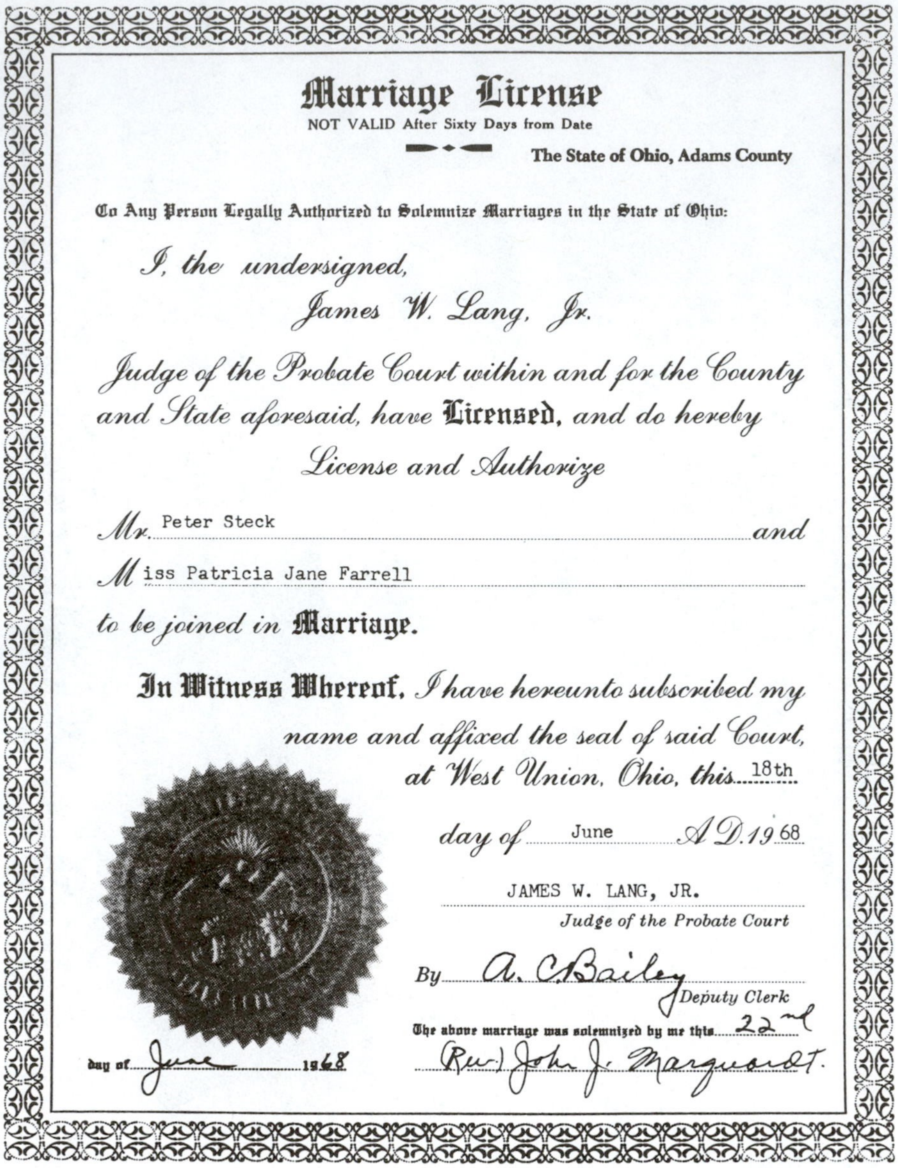

Marriage License
NOT VALID After Sixty Days from Date

The State of Ohio, Adams County

To Any Person Legally Authorized to Solemnize Marriages in the State of Ohio:

I, the undersigned,
James W. Lang, Jr.
Judge of the Probate Court within and for the County and State aforesaid, have **Licensed**, *and do hereby License and Authorize*

Mr. Peter Steck *and*

*M*iss Patricia Jane Farrell

to be joined in **Marriage.**

In Witness Whereof, *I have hereunto subscribed my name and affixed the seal of said Court, at West Union, Ohio, this* 18th *day of* June *A.D. 19*68

JAMES W. LANG, JR.
Judge of the Probate Court

By A. C. Bailey
Deputy Clerk

The above marriage was solemnized by me this 22nd day of June 1968

(Rev.) John J. Marquardt.

(c) What specific questions would you ask a client in order to determine whether the statute applies?

(See General Instructions for the State-Code Assignment and General Instructions for the Checklist-Formulation Assignment in chapter one.)

Assignment 8.2

In Assignment 8.1 above, you identified all of the requirements for a ceremonial marriage in your state. In this assignment, you are to interview someone who was married in your state in order to determine whether all the requirements for a ceremonial marriage were met. You may interview your spouse or a married relative, friend, class-mate, etc. Before you conduct the interview, draft a checklist of questions necessary to determine if the marriage is in compliance with state requirements. (These should be questions that could be part of a manual.) Make notes of the interviewee's answers. For all answers, ask the interviewee if any documents or other evidence exists to sub-stantiate (or corroborate) information given. (See General Instructions for the Checklist-Formulation Assignment in chapter one.) Hand in to your instructor a written account to the interview, (including the questions you asked). Remember that one of the primary characteristics of such written work products should be specificity; the details of names, addresses, dates, who said what, etc., can be critical. (See General Instructions for the Interview Assignment in chapter one.)

Suppose that the technical requirements for a ceremonial marriage have been violated. What consequences follow?

Assume, for example, that a statute requires a ten-day waiting period between the date of the issuing of the license and the date of the ceremony. Joe and Mary want to be married right away, and find a minister who marries them on the very same day they obtained the license. What result? Are they validly married? In most states, the marriage is *valid* even when there has been a failure to comply with one of the requirements (discussed in this chapter) for a ceremonial marriage. In such states, noncompliance with the requirements for a ceremonial marriage cannot later be used as a ground for annulment or divorce. Keep in mind, however, that we are *not* discussing age or relationship requirements that involve the *legal capacity* of parties to marry nor are we discussing requirements relating to intent to marry. Violations of such re-

☐ Over 2,000 follow-ers of the Rev. Sun Myung Moon go through a ceremonial marriage in Madison Square Garden, New York City.

quirements can indeed be grounds for annulment or divorce, as we will see in the next chapter.

While noncompliance with technical requirements does not affect the validity of the marriage in most states, other consequences may result. The parties, for example, might be prosecuted for perjury if they falsified any public documents in applying for the marriage. The person who performed the marriage ceremony without the authority to do so may be subjected to a fine. Other sanctions similar to these might also apply.

Assignment 8.3

(a) In your state, is the validity of the marriage affected by a violation of any of the technical requirements for a ceremonial marriage that you identified in Assignment 8.1?

(b) What penalties can be imposed for the violation of any of the technical requirements for a ceremonial marriage in your state?

To answer the above two questions, you may have to check both statutory law and case law. See General Instructions for the State-Code Assignment and for the Court-Opinion Assignment in chapter one.

Assignment 8.4

Suppose that a statute in a state provides as follows:

> **§ 10.**   No marriage shall be invalid on account of want of authority in any person solemnizing the same if consummated with the full belief on the part of the persons so married, or either of them, that they were lawfully joined in marriage.

George and Linda read a newspaper article stating that five of seven ministers connected with the Triple Faith Church in their state had been fined for illegally performing marriage ceremonies. A week later, they are married by Rev. Smith, who is in charge of Triple Faith Church but who has no authority to marry anyone. Can the validity of their marriage be called into question under § 10? (See General Instructions for the Legal-Analysis Assignment in chapter one.) Would it be invalid in your state? (See General Instructions for the State-Code Assignment in chapter one.)

Note on Proxy Marriage

Some states sanction a proxy marriage in which the ceremony takes place with one or both parties being absent (e.g., the groom is overseas). A third-party agent must be given the authority to act on behalf of the missing party or parties during the ceremony.

Section D. Common-Law Marriage

A *common-law marriage* is a marital union of two people who have not gone through a wedding ceremony or complied with the requirements for a ceremonial marriage. In our society a vast number of people live together in what some of the religions refer to as "the state of sin." Such individuals can enter a common-law marriage even thought they may never have heard of this kind of marriage. If the conditions of a common-law marriage have been fulfilled, the marriage is as valid as a ceremonial marriage. Children born during a common-law marriage, for example, are legitimate. To end such a marriage, one of the parties must die or they both must go through a divorce proceeding in the same manner as any other married couple seeking to dissolve a marriage.

Many states have abolished common-law marriages (see Exhibit 8–3). Even in such states, however, it is important to know something about common-law marriages for the following reasons:

1. Parties may enter a common-law marriage in a state where such marriages are valid and then move to another state that has abolished such marriages.

□ **EXHIBIT 8–3** Common-Law Marriage

State	Valid in state? (A date indicates it is invalid if entered after date shown)	Recognized if currently valid where contracted	State	Valid in State? (A date indicates it is invalid if entered after date shown)	Recognized if currently valid where contracted
Alabama	Yes	Yes	Montana	Yes	Yes
Alaska	1/1/64	Yes	Nebraska	1923	Yes
Arizona	No	Yes	Nevada	1943	Yes
Arkansas	No	Yes	New Hampshire	No	Yes
California	1895	Yes	New Jersey	1939	Yes
Colorado	Yes	Yes	New Mexico	No	Yes
Connecticut	No	†	New York	1933	Yes
Delaware	No	Yes	North Carolina	No	Yes
Dist. of Columbia	Yes	Yes	North Dakota	No	Yes
Florida	1/1/68	Yes	Ohio	Yes	Yes
Georgia	Yes	Yes	Oklahoma	Yes	Yes
Hawaii	No	Yes	Oregon	No	Yes
Idaho	Yes	Yes	Pennsylvania	Yes	Yes
Illinois	1905	†	Rhode Island	Yes	†
Indiana	1/1/58	†	South Carolina	Yes	Yes
Iowa	Yes	Yes	South Dakota	7/1/59	†
Kansas	Yes	Yes	Tennessee	No	Yes
Kentucky	No	Yes	Texas	Yes	Yes
Louisiana	No	†	Utah	No	Yes
Maine	No	†	Vermont	No	†
Maryland	No	Yes	Virginia	No	Yes
Massachusetts	No	Yes	Washington	No	Yes
Michigan	1/1/57	Yes	West Virginia	No	Yes
Minnesota	1941	†	Wisconsin	1913	†
Mississippi	4/5/56	†	Wyoming	No	Yes
Missouri	1921	†			

†Legal status unclear.
Source: U.S. Department of Labor, Women's Bureau.

Under traditional conflicts-of-law principles, as we shall see, the second state may have to recognize the marriage as valid. In our highly mobile society, parties who live together should be aware that if they travel through states that recognize common-law marriages for vacations or for other temporary purposes, one of the parties could later claim that they entered a common-law marriage in such a state.

2. It may be that your state once recognized common-law marriages as valid, but then, as of a certain date, abolished all such marriages for the future. A number of people may still live in your state who entered valid common-law marriages before the law was changed, and hence, their marriages are still valid

For people who have not entered ceremonial marriages, the question of whether they were married by common-law usually arises after one of the parties has died and the survivor is seeking:

- A share of the deceased's will
- Dower or curtesy rights (page 453)
- An intestate share if the deceased did not leave a valid will (page 267)
- A suit for wrongful death of his or her "spouse"
- Social security benefits or worker's compensation benefits through the deceased (etc).

Assignment 8.5

Is there a statute in your state abolishing common-law marriages? If so, what is its effective date? If not, are common-law marriages valid in your state? Check court opinions for the answer. See General Instructions for the State-Code Assignment in chapter one, and General Instructions for the Court-Opinion Assignment in chapter one.

What conditions must exist for a valid common-law marriage (in states that recognize such marriages)? Not all states have the same requirements. Generally, however, the following conditions must be met.

Common-Law Marriage

1. The parties must have legal capacity to marry (page 120).
2. There must be a present agreement to enter a marital relationship—to become husband and wife to each other. (Some states require an express agreement; others infer an agreement from the manner in which the man and woman relate to each other.)
3. The parties must actually live together as husband and wife, i.e., there must be cohabitation.
4. There must be an openess about the relationship; the parties must make representations to the world that they are husband and wife. (See interviewing questions in checklist below.)

In some states, there is a reluctance on the part of the courts to find all these elements present in a particular case. Common-law marriages may be disfavored by the court *even in a state where such marriages are legal.* The fear is as follows: two people will decide to live together solely for sexual reasons; one will die and the survivor will claim that they were really married in order to take advantage of benefits available only to surviving spouses. Such courts often require "clear and convincing" evidence that all the elements existed.

Interviewing and Investigation Checklist

Factors Relevant to the Formation of a Common Law Marriage Between C (Client) and D (Defendant)

Legal Interviewing Questions

1. On what date did you first meet D?

2. When did the two of you first begin talking about living together? Describe the circumstances. Who said what, etc.

3. Did you or D ever discuss living together with anyone else?

4. On what date did you actually move in together? How long have you been living together?

5. In whose name was the lease to the apartment or the deed to the house in which you lived?

6. Do you have separate or joint bank accounts? If joint, what names appear on the account?

7. Who pays the rent or the mortgage?

8. Who pays the utility bills?

9. Who pays the food bills?

10. Since you have been living together, have you filed separate or joint tax returns?

11. Have you ever made a written or oral agreement that you and D were going to be married?

12. Why didn't you ever go through a marriage ceremony?

13. Did you ever introduce each other as "my husband" or "my wife?"

14. Name any relatives, neighbors, business associates, friends, etc., who think of you and D as husband and wife.

15. Did you and D ever discuss making individual or joint wills?

16. Did you and D ever separate for any period of time? If so, describe the circumstances.

17. Did you and D ever have or adopt any children? If so, what last name did the children have?

18. On insurance policies, is either of you the beneficiary? How is the premium paid?

19. During your life with D, what other indications exist that the two of you treated each other as husband and wife?

Possible Investigation Tasks

- If C indicates that C or D discussed their moving in together with anyone else, obtain witness statements (affidavits) from such individuals.

- Obtain a copy of the lease or deed.

- Obtain copies of bills, receipts, tax returns, etc., to determine how the names of C and D appear on them.
- Obtain copies of any agreements between C and D.
- Interview anyone C indicates would think of C and D as husband and wife.
- Obtain birth certificates of children, if any.

Two situations remain to be considered: *conflict of law* and *impediment removal.*

Conflict of Law

Bill and Pat live in State X, where common-law marriages are legal. They enter such a marriage. Then they move to State Y, where common-law marriages have been abolished. A child is born to them in State Y. Bill is injured on the job and dies. Pat claims worker's compensation benefits as the "wife" of Bill. Will State Y recognize Pat as married to Bill? Is their child legitimate?

The law where a marriage was contracted will generally govern its validity. Pat and Bill's marriage was contracted in State X, where it is valid. Since the marriage was valid where it was contracted, State Y will accept the marriage as valid (even though it would have been invalid had they tried to enter it in State Y). Pat is married to Bill and their child is legitimate. (Later, we will discuss the problem of parties moving to another state solely to take advantage of its more lenient marriage laws and returning to their original state after the marriage, page 195.)

Impediment Removal

In 1969 Ernestine enters a valid ceremonial marriage with John. The begin having marital troubles and separate. In 1975 Ernestine and Henry begin living together. Ernestine does not divorce John. She and Henry cohabitate and hold each other out as husband and wife in a state where common-law marriages are valid. Except for the existence of the 1969 marriage to John, it is clear that Ernestine and Henry would have a valid common-law marriage. In 1981 John obtains a divorce from Ernestine. Henry and Ernestine continue to live together in the same manner as they had since 1975. In 1989, Henry dies. Ernestine claims death benefits under the Worker's Compensation Act as his surviving "wife." Was she ever married to Henry?

Ernestine and Henry never entered a ceremonial marriage. Until 1981 a serious impediment existed to their being able to marry: Ernestine was already married to someone else. When the marriage was dissolved by the divorce in 1981, the impediment was removed. The issue is (1) whether Ernestine and Henry would be considered to have entered a valid common-law marriage at the time the impediment was removed, or (2) whether at that time they would have had to enter a *new* common-law marriage agreement, express or implied. In most states, a new agreement would not be necessary. An earlier agreement to marry (by common law) will carry forward to the time the impediment is removed so long as the parties have continued to live together openly as husband and wife. Accordingly, Ernestine automatically became the wife of Henry when the impediment of the prior marriage was removed, since she and

Henry continued to live together openly as husband and wife after that time. As one court puts it:

> "It is not to be expected that parties once having agreed to be married will deem it necessary to agree to do so again when an earlier marriage is terminated or some other bar to union is eliminated." *Matthews v. Britton*, 303 F.2d 408, 409 (D.C.Cir.1962).

In the states that reach this conclusion, it makes no difference that either or both of the parties knew of the impediment at the time they initially agreed to live as husband and wife.

Assignment 8.6

Examine the following sequence of events:

1. Ann and Rich meet in State Y where they agree to live together as husband and wife forever. They do not want to go through a marriage ceremony, but they agree to be married and openly represent themselves as such. State Y does not recognize common-law marriages.

2. Rich accepts a job offer in State X, where common-law marriages are legal, and they both move there.

3. After three years in State X, Rich and Ann move back to State Y. One year later, Rich dies. In his will, he leaves all his property "to my wife." Ann is not mentioned by name in his will.

4. From the time they met until the time of Rich's death, they lived together as husband and wife, and everyone who knew them thought of them as such.

(a) Can Ann claim anything under the will? State Y provides tax benefits to "widows." Can Ann claim these benefits? (See the General Instructions for the Legal-Analysis Assignment in chapter one.)

(b) What further information would you like to have about this case? (See the General Instructions for the Investigation-Strategy Assignment in chapter one.)

Assignment 8.7

Vivian Hildenbrand and Tom Hildenbrand began living together in Oregon in 1975 and continuously did so until Tom's death in 1984. During this time, pursuant to mutual agreement, they cohabited and held themselves out as husband and wife, but never went through a marriage ceremony. They purchased real property in their joint names as husband and wife. On four different occasions, they went on vacation fishing trips to a resort in Idaho, where they registered as husband and wife, held themselves out as such, and lived together during their stay. Two trips in 1977 were of three days' duration each. Two trips were of seven days' duration each, one in 1978 and one in 1979. Oregon does not recognize common-law marriages. Idaho does.

(a) Were the parties married in 1984? (See General Instructions for the Legal-Analysis Assignment in chapter one.)

(b) Assume that Tom Hildenbrand died while he was working for the Oregon XYZ Chemical Company, due to an on-the-job accident. Vivian claims Oregon worker's compensation benefits. The state Worker's Compensation Board denies these benefits on the ground that she was not his wife. Draft a complaint for Vivian against the board. (See General Instructions for the Complaint-Drafting Assignment in chapter one.)

Section E. Homosexual "Marriages"

Given the recent movements for civil rights, gay liberation, and sexual freedom generally, the question has arisen as to whether a man can marry a man, and a woman marry a woman. Traditional marriage statutes neither specifically prohibit nor approve same-sex marriages. Such marriages, however, have been denied by the courts on the theory that marriage has always contemplated a man and a woman. When the legislatures wrote the marriage statutes, they must have had opposite-sex marriages in mind since that was the standard assumption. If same-sex marriages are to be legal, specific legislation will have to be enacted.

Denmark is one of the few countries of the world that has specifically authorized same-sex marriages. The parties, however, do not have all the rights of traditional marriages. For example, they cannot adopt minor children.

Proponents of same-sex marriages in America have attempted a number of strategies—all without success:

1. *Equal protection.* Since individuals of the opposite sex can marry, why treat gay individuals differently? Is this unequal treatment unconstitutional? Thus far the courts have said no.

2. *Fundamental right to marry.* The Supreme Court has said that there cannot be unreasonable restrictions on the right to marry since this is a fundamental right. (*Zablocki,* page 159) No court, however, has yet held that the prohibition against same-sex marriages is unreasonable.

3. *Common-law marriage.* If gay people cannot enter ceremonial marriages, can they enter a common-law marriage if all of the conditions for such a marriage are present, e.g., open cohabitation, intent to marry (page 166)? No. Where this theory has been used, the courts have still insisted on a man-woman relationship.

4. *Putative-spouse doctrine.* Here the parties acknowledge a legal impediment to the marriage but argue that they had a good-faith belief that they were legally married (page 175). Courts, however, have said that homosexuals could not possibly have such a good-faith belief.

In many states, homosexual conduct among adults is a crime even if it is consensual. The United States Supreme Court has held that it is constitutional for states to impose criminal penalties for such conduct. *Bowers v. Hardwick,* 478 U.S. 186, 106 S.Ct. 2841, 92 L.Ed.2d 140 (1986). Such states obviously have little sympathy for the argument that homosexuals should be allowed to marry.

Suppose that one of the parties is a transsexual (an individual, usually a man, who has had a sex-change operation). Can such an individual marry a man? Most courts would not permit the marriage, arguing that both parties to the marriage must have been *born* members of the opposite sex. There are a few courts, however, that take the opposite position and allow such marriages.

A number of other special circumstances need to be considered in this area of the law:

■ Two homosexuals can enter a *Marvin*-type contract in which they agree to live together and share property acquired during the relationship. The major issue (as in a heterosexual relationship) is whether sexual services were an integral and inseparable part of the agreement. If so, as we have seen, the contract will not be enforced (page 148).

- In some states a gay adult can adopt another gay adult.

- Assume that two lesbians live together. One is artificially inseminated and bears a child. In a few states, the other lesbian may be able to adopt the child, who then has two legal parents of the same sex.

- In the above situation, if the other lesbian does not adopt the child and the adults separate, can the other lesbian be granted visitation rights? If the women had entered a *co-parenting agreement* in which they agreed to raise and support the child together, would such an agreement be enforceable? In the absence of adoption, it is unlikely that a court would be sympathetic to the lesbian seeking visitation rights or asserting other parental rights under a co-parenting agreement.

- Our immigration laws grant preferential treatment to spouses of U.S. citizens wishing to enter this country. Courts addressing the question of whether a homosexual U.S. citizen can "marry" a homosexual alien and thereby confer on him or her the status of a "spouse" have said no.

- The University of California at Berkeley has refused to allow gay student couples to live in married student housing, even if they can prove they are financially and domestically interdependent. The university has taken the position that it has no authority to recognize unmarried couples.

- Assume that two homosexuals live together in a rent-controlled apartment, only one of whom is the tenant of record. The latter dies of AIDS. The landlord tries to evict the survivor on the theory that he is not entitled to the protection of the regulation that forbids eviction of "the surviving spouse of the deceased tenant or some other member of the deceased tenant's family who has been living with the tenant." Is the eviction valid? The answer depends on whether the regulation is interpreted to include a broader definition of "family" than the traditional one. A recent New York case surprisingly adopted such an interpretation:

Braschi v. Stahl Associates, Co.

New York Court of Appeals
74 N.Y.S.2d 201 (1989)

Titone, J.

Appellant, Miguel Braschi, was living with Leslie Blanchard in a rent-controlled apartment located at 405 East 54th Street from the summer of 1975 until Blanchard's death in September of 1986. . . .

Appellant and Blanchard lived together as permanent life partners for more than 10 years. They regarded one another, and were regarded by friends and family, as spouses. The two men's families were aware of the nature of the relationship, and they regularly visited each other's families and attended family functions together, as a couple. Even today, appellant continues to maintain a relationship with Blanchard's niece, who considers him an uncle.

In addition to their interwoven social lives, appellant clearly considered the apartment his home. He lists the apartment as his address on his driver's license and passport, and receives all his mail at the apartment address. Moreover, appellant's tenancy was known to the building's superintendent and doormen, who viewed the two men as a couple.

Financially, the two men shared all obligations including a household budget. The two were authorized signatories of three safe-deposit boxes, they maintained joint checking and savings accounts, and joint credit cards. In fact, rent was often paid with a check from their joint checking account. Additionally, Blanchard executed a power of attorney in appellant's favor so that appellant could make necessary decisions—financial, medical and personal—for him during his illness. Finally, appellant was the named beneficiary of Blanchard's life insurance policy, as well as the primary legatee and coexecutor of Blanchard's estate. Hence, a court examining these facts could reasonably conclude that these men were much more than mere roommates. . . .

Contrary to [the position of the landlord], we conclude that the term family, . . . should not be rigidly restricted to those people who have formalized their relationship by obtaining, for instance, a marriage certificate or an adoption order. The intended protection against sudden eviction should not rest on fictitious legal distinctions or genetic history, but instead should find its foundation in the reality of family life. In the context of eviction, a more realistic, and certainly equally valid, view of a family includes two adult lifetime partners whose relationship is long term and characterized by an emotional and financial commitment and inter-

dependence. This view comports both with our society's traditional concept of "family" and with the expectations of individuals who live in such nuclear units. . . . In fact, Webster's Dictionary defines "family" *first* as "a group of people united by certain convictions or common affiliation" (Webster's Ninth New Collegiate Dictionary 448 [1984]; *see*, Ballantine's Law Dictionary 456 [3d ed 1969] ["family" defined as "(p)rimarily, the collective body of persons who live in one house and under one head or management"]; Black's Law Dictionary 543 [Special Deluxe 5th ed 1979]). Hence, it is reasonable to conclude that, in using the term "family," the Legislature intended to extend protection to those who reside in households having all of the normal familial characteristics. . . .

Of course, this opinion did not authorize homosexual marriages. As indicated, any change in the law forbidding same-sex marriages will have to come through new legislation. Courts are not willing to make the change on their own. Furthermore, changes in the law are likely to be gradual as the government slowly starts to recognize same-sex relationships for certain limited purposes. For example, San Francisco recently considered amending its administrative code to authorize city workers and their live-in lovers to sign a "Declaration of Domestic Partnership" (Exhibit 8–4) and file it with the county clerk. *Domestic partners* are "two people who have chosen to share one another's lives in an intimate and committed relationship of mutual caring, who live together and have signed a Declaration of Domestic Partnership in which they have agreed to be jointly responsible for basic living expenses incurred during the Domestic Partnership." If they want to end this new legal relationship, they would file a "Declaration of Termination" with the county clerk. The effect of the legislation would have been to extend to such partners a number of benefits and rights that formerly applied only to traditional spouses, e.g., health benefits, hospital visitation rights, bereavement leave. A local church attacked the legislation for allowing "pseudo-marriages" and being a "frontal assault on marriage and the family as we know it." The controversy caused such a stir that it was placed on the ballot for voter approval and was defeated by a narrow margin.

Domestic partners have had greater luck in New York City, where a similar program was enacted into law by the mayor through an Executive Order (see Exhibit 8–5).

☐ **EXHIBIT 8–4** Declaration of Domestic Partnership

Name _____

Address _____

_____

Title/Party _____

City and County of San Francisco—State of California
DECLARATION OF DOMESTIC PARTNERSHIP

If filed with County Clerk, original Declaration No. _____ READ CAREFULLY BEFORE YOU SIGN. By signing this, you take on serious obligations. If you choose to file your Declaration with the San Francisco County Clerk, this Declaration becomes a PUBLIC RECORD. You must file an Amendment any time your address changes.

I DECLARE, UNDER PENALTY OF PERJURY:
1. I am not married;
2. I am not related to my partner in any way which would bar marriage in California;
3. I reside together with my partner, and I agree to be jointly responsible for our basic living expenses (see Definitions included in Domestic Partners information packet).
4. We are each other's Domestic Partner;
5. I have not, within the last six months, been a member of a different domestic partnership;
6. I am 18 years of age or older;
[Complete #7 if you want to file this Declaration with the County Clerk:]
7. (a) My partner and I both reside together in the City and County of San Francisco;
   (b) (Name) _____ works in the City and County of San Francisco.
I understand that if we stop residing together, or if either of us decides to end the Domestic Partnership, we must file a Notice of Termination, send a copy to each other and to any third party to whom either of us has given a copy of this Declaration to obtain benefits or rights. I declare under penalty of perjury under the laws of the State of California that the statements above are true and correct.

Signature _____   Signature _____
Print Name: _____   Print Name: _____
Signed on _____, 19___   Signed on _____, 19___
in _____   in _____
Residence Address: Residence Address:
_____   _____
_____   _____

☐ **EXHIBIT 8—5** New York City's Executive Order Regarding Domestic Partnership

Executive Order No. 123
August 7, 1989

BEREAVEMENT LEAVE FOR CITY EMPLOYEES
WHO ARE MEMBERS OF A DOMESTIC PARTNERSHIP

WHEREAS, there have been significant changes in our society resulting in diverse living arrangements among individuals and an expanded concept of what constitutes a family unit; and

WHEREAS, many of these living arrangements involve long-term committed relationships between unmarried persons; and

WHEREAS, the death of one individual in such a relationship, or the death of that individual's parent or child or other relative residing in the household, would have a profound personal impact upon the other individual in such a relationship;

NOW, THEREFORE, by the power vested in me as Mayor of the City of New York, it is hereby ordered:

Section 1. Bereavement Leave Established. Bereavement leave for all City employees is hereby established in the event of the death of a ''domestic partner'', as defined in Section 2, or the death of a parent or child of such domestic partner, or the death of a relative of such domestic partner residing in the household, and shall be afforded in accordance with existing rules and regulations and the terms of this Executive Order.

Section 2. Domestic Partnerships Defined. Domestic partners are two people, both of whom are 18 years of age or older and neither of whom is married, who have a close and committed personal relationship involving shared responsibilities, who have lived together for a period of one year or more on a continuous basis at the time of registration, and who have registered as domestic partners and have not terminated the registration in accordance with procedures to be established by the Department of Personnel of the City of New York.

Section 3. Registration. The Department of Personnel of the City of New York is directed to establish procedures and develop forms for the registration and termination of domestic partnerships. The Department of Personnel shall not register a domestic partnership if either member is currently a member of another domestic partnership or was previously a member of another domestic partnership and less than one year has expired since the termination of that domestic partnership.

Section 4. Effective Date. This Order shall take effect immediately.

Edward I. Koch
M A Y O R

Note on Putative Marriages

A few states (e.g., Louisiana, Texas), recognize putative marriages, page 151).

> "A putative marriage is one which has been contracted in good faith and in ignorance of some existing impediment on the part of at least one of the contracting parties. Three circumstances must occur to constitute this species of marriage: (1) There must be bona fides. At least one of the parties must have been ignorant of the impediment, not only at the time of the marriage, but must also have continued ignorant of it during his or her life. (2) The marriage must be duly solemnized. (3) The marriage must have been considered lawful in the estimation of the parties or of that party who alleges the bona fides." *United States Fidelity & Guarantee Co.* v. *Henderson,* 53 S.W.2d 811, 816 (Tex.Civ.App.1932).

Key Chapter Terminology

Ceremonial Marriage
Miscegenation
Marriage License
Waiting Period
Physical Examination
Solemnization of Marriage
Proxy Marriage
Common-Law Marriage

Legitimacy of Children
Conflicts of Law
Impediment Removal
Same-Sex Marriages
Transsexual
Co-parenting
Domestic Partnership
Putative-Spouse Doctrine

Annulment

■ Chapter Outline

A divorce is a termination of a valid marriage. An annulment is an acknowledgement that the parties were never married, whether they lived together (and acted as if they were married) for thirty minutes or for thirty years after the "marriage" ceremony. To obtain an annulment, a party must establish *grounds,* and must have *standing,* which is the right to go into court and ask for relief. Two categories of grounds exist: grounds relating to the legal capacity to marry, and grounds relating to the intent to marry. Some of these grounds will render the marriage void, while others will render it voidable.

There are four grounds relating to the legal capacity to marry:

1. *Prior existing marriage.* At the time of the marriage, a prior marriage had not been terminated.

2. *Consanguinity and affinity.* The parties married in violation of a prohibition against the marriage of certain individuals who are already related to each other.

3. *Nonage*. A party was underage at the time of the marriage.

4. *Physical disabilities*. A party had a specified disease or was impotent at the time of the marriage

There are four grounds relating to the intent to marry:

1. *Sham marriage*. The parties never intended to live together as husband and wife.

2. *Mental disability*. At the time of the marriage, a party was incapable of understanding the nature of the marriage relationship.

3. *Duress*. A party was forced into the marriage.

4. *Fraud*. A party intentionally misrepresented or concealed certain facts from the other party that were either essential to the marriage or were material to the decision to enter the marriage.

Under conflicts-of-law principles, if a marriage is valid in the state where it was entered, another state (to which the parties move) must recognize the marriage as valid—even if the marriage would have been invalid if it had been entered in the latter state. An exception to this principle is made if the recognition of such a marriage would violate a strong public policy of the state to which the parties moved. There are statutes that invalidate a marriage entered in a state solely to evade the marriage law of another state.

In an annulment proceeding, the court must award custody of the children and provide for their support. (Children born from an annulled marriage are usually considerate legitimate.) If the state does not allow alimony, the court may use a theory such as quasi-contract (discussed in this chapter) to divide property acquired during the time the parties were together.

Given the nature of annulment, a court must sometimes address special problems. For example, suppose a divorced spouse remarries and thereby loses certain benefits granted by the divorce. But the second marriage is annulled. Are the divorce benefits revived? Not all states answer this and related questions in the same way. Other issues that arise involve inheritance, bigamy, tort liability, evidence, and income tax status.

Section A. Annulment, Divorce, and Legal Separation

An *annulment* is a declaration that the marriage never existed. In a sense it is technically incorrect to refer to an "annulled marriage." The word "marriage" means the legal union of two people as husband and wife. If reasons (i.e., grounds) exist to substantiate the initial *illegality* of the union, then no marriage ever existed in spite of the license, the ceremony, consummation, and perhaps even children. While you will frequently see the phrase, "suit to annul a marriage," it would be more technically accurate to use the phrase, "suit to annul an attempted marriage," or "suit to declare the validity or invalidity of a marriage."

A *divorce,* on the other hand, is a legal dissolution of a marriage that once validly existed. In a divorce there is something to dissolve; in an annulment, there is simply a judicial statement or declaration that no marital relationship existed between the parties at the outset.

A *legal* or *judicial separation* is a court order that the parties can live apart, i.e., that there can be a termination of the "bed-and-board" relationship between the parties. Parties so separated are still legally married; they cannot remarry unless they later obtain a divorce.

Section B. The Void/Voidable Distinction

As we study the grounds for annulment, we will see that certain grounds will render the marriage *void*, while other grounds will render it only *voidable*. *Void* means the marriage is invalid whether or not any court ever declares its invalidity. *Voidable* means the marriage is invalid only if a court declares that it is invalid.

If no one brings an action to invalidate a voidable marriage, it will always be considered a valid marriage. If a court declares a voidable marriage to be invalid, the invalidity generally "relates back" (discussed later under section H) to the moment when the marriage was attempted. No court action is needed to declare the invalidity of a void marriage. Also, a void marriage is considered invalid from the time the parties tried to enter it. A void marriage is referred to as *void ab initio*, i.e., invalid from the very beginning.

States use different terminology to describe the proceeding:

- Action for annulment.
- Suit to annul.
- Libel for annulment.
- Action for declaratory judgment (i.e., for a court pronouncement) that the marriage is invalid.
- Action to affirm the validity of a marriage.

(etc.)

If the marriage is voidable, it is essential that an annulment action (or whatever the proceeding is called in your state) be brought. If it is not brought, as indicated above, the marriage will be considered valid. Suppose, however, that the marriage is void. Technically, there is no need to bring any court action since the marriage is void whether or not a court has declared it so. Nevertheless, parties still use the courts to seek judicial declarations of void marriages in order to remove any doubt that the marriage is invalid.

Section C. Who Can Sue?

As we study each of the grounds for annulment, one of the questions we must ask ourselves is, who can be the plaintiff to bring the annulment action? The wrongdoer (i.e., the party who knowingly did the act that constituted the ground for the annulment) may *not* be allowed to bring the action. This party will lack *standing* to bring the action. If the *innocent* party refuses to bring the action, it may be that the marriage can never be annulled. The wrongdoing party, in effect, is prevented (sometimes called *estopped*) from getting out of what might clearly be an invalid marriage. Such a marriage is sometimes referred to as a *marriage by estoppel*. The wrongdoing party has *"dirty hands"* by reason of his or her wrongdoing and should not be allowed to "profit" from this wrongdoing through a court action seeking an annulment. Whether a wrongdoing party will be estopped from bringing the annulment action may depend on whether the marriage is void or voidable.

Section D. Overview of Grounds for Annulment

✗ There are essentially two kinds of grounds for annulment. First are those that relate to a party's *legal capacity* to marry:

1. Preexisting marriage
2. Improper relationship by blood or by marriage
3. Nonage
4. Physical disabilities
5. Sex of the parties

✗ Second are those that focus on whether a party with legal capacity to marry formed the requisite *intent* to marry:

1. Sham marriages
2. Mental disabilities
3. Duress
4. Fraud

Assignment 9.1

List the grounds for annulment in your state. (See General Instructions for the State-Code Assignment in chapter one.)

Note on Grounds for a Church Annulment

The Roman Catholic Church has its own separate system of annulment, defined as "a declaration by a competent tribunal of the Church that what had the appearance of marriage was in fact invalid according to canon law." The annulment, or *declaration of nullity*, is "granted as a result of some impediment or on various grounds related to defective consent or lack of form. The most frequent grounds for marriage nullity is *defective consent*, especially lack of due discretion and lack of due competence." [emphasis added] *Huels*, THE PASTORAL COMPANION: A CANON LAW HANDBOOK FOR CATHOLIC MINISTRY, 259 (1986). To determine whether grounds for annulment exist according to *canon law*, the following questions are critical:

First, when [the couple] said their vows, did both partners freely accept and clearly understand the lifelong commitment they were making? And secondly, at that time, did both partners have the personal capacity to carry out consent, to form a community of life with the chosen partner? CATHOLIC UPDATE, UPD 100 (St. Anthony Messenger Press, 1980)

The annulment procedure includes a formal hearing presided over by a tribunal judge. An advocate presents the case of the petitioner seeking the annulment. Also present is a "defender of the bond" who monitors the proceeding to ensure that rights are protected and Church law properly observed. The hierarchy in Rome has criticized American bishops for allowing too many church annulments. In 1985, for example, 80 percent of the 45,632 annulments granted worldwide were granted by church tribunals in the United States.

Section E. Grounds Relating to the Legal Capacity to Marry

Prior Existing Marriage (Bigamy)

Here we will consider both the criminal and the civil consequences of entering a second marriage when the first marriage has not ended—*bigamy*.

Crime

Entering a second marriage or even attempting to enter such a marriage when the first marriage has not ended by death, annulment, or divorce is a felony in most states. *Polygamy*[1] or *bigamy* is a crime.

In some states, if a spouse has disappeared for a designated number of years, he or she will be presumed dead. This presumption is the foundation for what is called the *Enoch Arden* defense, which will defeat a bigamy prosecution following a second marriage. States may differ on the elements of the Enoch Arden defense, e.g., differences as to the length of the disappearance, differences on the requirement of diligence in trying to locate the missing spouse before remarrying, etc.

Annulment: The Civil Action

Our next concern is the existence of a prior undissolved marriage as a ground for an annulment of a second (attempted) marriage. In most states, a bigamous marriage is void; in only a few states is it voidable.

When a claim is made in an annulment proceeding that a second marriage is invalid because of a prior undissolved marriage, one of the common responses or defenses to this claim is that the *first* marriage was never valid or that this earlier marriage ended in a divorce or annulment. Yet marriage records, particularly old ones, are sometimes difficult to obtain, and for common-law marriages, there simply are no records. Consequently, proving the status of a prior marriage can be a monumental task. Was it properly contracted? Was it dissolved? To assist parties in this difficult situation, the law has created a number of *rebuttable presumptions*, including:

- A marriage is presumed to be valid.
- When more than one marriage exists, the latest marriage is presumed to be valid.

---

[1]Polygamy is the practice of having more than one spouse at the same time, usually more than two.

The effect of the second presumption is that the court will treat the first marriage as having been dissolved by the death of the first spouse, by divorce, or by annulment. Note, however, that the presumption is *rebuttable*, which means that the party seeking to annul the second marriage can attempt to rebut (i.e., attack) the presumption by introducing evidence (1) that the first spouse is still alive, or (2) that the first marriage was *not* dissolved by divorce or annulment. The presumption favoring the validity of the latest marriage is so strong, however, that some states require considerable proof to overcome or rebut it.

Finally, we need to consider the impact of *Enoch Arden* in annulment cases. We have already looked at Enoch Arden as a defense to a criminal prosecution for bigamy. We now examine the consequences of Enoch Arden on the second marriage in a civil annulment proceeding. Paul marries Cynthia. Cynthia disappears. Paul has not heard from her for fifteen years in spite of all his efforts to locate her. Paul then marries Mary in the honest belief that his first wife is dead. Mary does not know anything about Cynthia. Suddenly Cynthia reappears, and Mary learns about the first marriage. Mary immediately brings an action against Paul to annul her marriage to him on the ground of a prior existing marriage (bigamy). The question is whether Paul can raise the defense of Enoch Arden. Can Paul contest the annulment action against him by arguing that he had a right to presume that his first wife was dead? The states differ in their answer to this question. Here are some of the different approaches:

- Enoch Arden applies only to criminal prosecutions for bigamy; the presumption of death does not apply to annulment proceedings.

- Enoch Arden does apply to annulment proceedings; the missing spouse is presumed dead. The second marriage is valid and cannot be annulled even if the missing spouse later appears.

- Enoch Arden does apply to annulment proceedings; the missing spouse is presumed dead. If, however, the missing spouse later appears, the second marriage can be annulled. Hence, the Enoch Arden defense is effective only if the missing spouse stays missing.

Summary of Ground for Annulment: Prior Existing Marriage

Definitions: The existence of a prior valid marriage that has not been dissolved by divorce, annulment, or the death of the first spouse.

Void or Voidable: In most states, the establishment of this ground renders the second marriage void.

Who Can Sue: In most states, either party to the second marriage can bring the annulment action on this ground.

Major Defenses: 1. The first spouse is dead or presumed dead (Enoch Arden).
2. The first marriage was not validly entered.
3. The first marriage ended by divorce or annulment.
4. The plaintiff has "dirty hands" (available in a few states).

Is this annulment ground also a ground for divorce? Yes, in some states (see page 381.)

Consanguinity and Affinity Limitations

There are two ways that you can be related to someone: by blood or by marriage. If you are related by blood, you are related by *consanguinity;* if you are related by marriage, you are related by *affinity.*

Examples of a marriage of individuals related by consanguinity would be:

- Father marries his daughter.
- Sister marries her brother.

Examples of a marriage of individuals related by affinity would be:

- Man marries his son's former wife.
- Woman marries her stepfather.

State statutes prohibit certain individuals related by consanguinity and related by affinity from marrying. Violating these prohibitions can be a ground for annulment of the marriage.

States generally agree that certain relationships are *incestuous:* marriage of parent and child, brother and sister, grandparent and grandchild, etc. Some disagreement exists in the area of cousin-cousin marriages and affinity relationships.

The *crime* of incest is committed mainly by designated individuals related by consanguinity. Surprisingly, however, the crime can also be committed in some states by designated individuals related by affinity.

Assignment 9.2

In the following list, you will find pairs of individuals. For each pair, check your state code and answer three questions: can the individuals marry; what code section gives you the answer; and if the marriage is prohibited, is it void or voidable? (See General Instructions for the State-Code Assignment, page 10.)

(a) Mother/son. Can they marry? _____ Void or voidable? _____ Code section
_____ .

(b) Father/daughter. Can they marry? _____Void or voidable? _____ Code section
_____ .

(c) Brother/sister. Can they marry? _____Void or voidable? _____ Code section
_____ .

(d) Grandparent/grandchild. Can they marry? _____ Void or voidable? _____
Code section _____ .

(e) Uncle/niece or aunt/nephew. Can they marry? _____ Void or voidable? _____
Code section _____ .

(f) First cousin/first cousin. Can they marry? _____ Void or voidable? _____ Code
section _____ .

(g) Second cousin/second cousin. Can they marry? _____ Void or voidable? _____
Code section _____ .

(h) Half brother/half sister. Can they marry? _____ Void or voidable? _____ Code
section _____ .

(i) Father-in-law/daughter-in-law or mother-in-law/son-in-law. Can they marry? ____
Void or voidable? _____ Code section _____ .

(j) Brother-in-law/sister-in-law. Can they marry? _____ Void or Voidable? _____
Code section _____ .

(k) Stepparent/stepchild. Can they marry? _____ Void or Voidable? _____ Code section _____ .

(l) Adoptive parent/adoptive child. Can they marry? _____ Void or Voidable? ____ Code section _____ .

(m) Godparent/godchild. Can they marry? _____ Void or Voidable? _____ Code section _____ .

(If your state code does not provide a direct answer to any of the above questions, you may have to check court opinions. See General Instructions for the Court-Opinion Assignment in chapter one.)

Assignment 9.3

(a) Locate the sections in your state code that define criminal behavior. Determine how many, if any, of the marriages mentioned in Assignment 9.2 "a" through "m" would subject the parties to criminal prosecution. (See General Instructions for the State-Code Assignment in chapter one.)

(b) Draft a flowchart of the procedural steps that would constitute a criminal prosecution for any of the crimes you identified in part "a" of Assignment 9.3 (See General Instructions for the Flowchart Assignment in chapter one.)

Notes on Consanguinity and Affinity

1. Assume that a prohibition to a marriage exists because of an affinity relationship between the parties. What happens to the prohibition when the marriage ends by the death of the spouse who created the affinity relationship for the other spouse? Can the surviving spouse *then* marry his or her in-laws? Some states allow such marriages, while others maintain the prohibition even after the death of the spouse who created the affinity relationship for the other spouse.

2. The Uniform Marriage and Divorce Act (§ 207) would prohibit all marriages between ancestors and descendants, would prohibit brother-sister marriages, would prohibit adopted brother-sister marriages, would permit first-cousin marriages, and would permit all affinity marriages.

3. States differ on whether two adopted children in the same family can marry.

4. As indicated above, the Supreme Court has held that marriage is a fundamental right and only "reasonable regulations" that interfere with the decision to enter a marriage can be imposed. (*Zablocki*, page 159). It is anticipated that some of the rules mentioned above regarding who can marry will be challenged as unreasonable regulations—particularly those rules prohibiting the marriage of individuals related by affinity.

Summary of Ground for Annulment: Prohibited Consanguinity or Affinity Relationship

Definition: State statutes declare that persons lack the legal capacity to marry if they are related by consanguinity (blood) or by affinity (marriage) in the manner specified in those statutes.

Void or Voidable: In most states the prohibited marriage is void.

Who Can Sue: Either party can be the plaintiff in the annulment action.

Major Defenses: 1. The parties are not prohibitively related by blood or marriage.

2. The spouse who created the affinity relationship for the other spouse has died (this defense is available only for affinity relationships and only in some states).

Is this annulment ground also a ground for divorce? Yes, in most states (see page 381).

Nonage

In order to marry, a party must be a certain minimum age. This age may differ, however, depending upon whether:

- Parental consent exists.
- The female is already pregnant.
- A child has already been born out of wedlock.

In some states, a court may have the power to authorize a marriage of parties under age even if a parent or guardian has refused to consent to the marriage. In these states, the court will consider such factors as the maturity of the parties, their financial resources, whether children (to be born or already born) would be illegitimate if the marriage were not authorized, etc. Still another variation in some states is the authority in the courts to require that underage individuals go through premarital counseling as a condition of their being able to marry.

There was a time when states imposed different age requirements for males and females. Most states have changed this either by statute or by a court ruling that this kind of sex discrimination is unconstitutional.

Assignment 9.4

What age restrictions apply to marriages in your state? (See General Instructions for the State-Code Assignment in chapter one.)

Summary of Ground for Annulment: Nonage

Definition: At the time of the marriage, one or both of the parties was under the minimum age to marry set by statute.

Void or Voidable: In most states, the marriage is voidable.

Who Can Sue: Usually, only the underaged party is allowed to bring the annulment action. In some states the parent or guardian of the underaged party can also sue.

Major Defenses: 1. The parties where of the correct statutory age at the time of the marriage.
2. The underaged party affirmed or ratified the marriage by cohabitation after that party reached the statutory minimum age.
3. The wrong party is bringing the suit.
4. Even though the parties failed to obtain parental consent as specified in the statute, the absence of this consent is not a ground for annulment (note, however, that this is so only in some states);

5. The male-female age distinctions in the statute, if any, are illegal because they violate the equal protection clause of the constitution.

Is this annulment also a ground for divorce? Yes, in some states (see page 381).

Physical Disabilities

The major physical incapacities or disabilities mentioned in marriage statutes are *communicable venereal disease* and *incurable impotence*. While several other physical problems are sometimes involved (e.g., epilepsy and pulmonary tuberculosis in advanced stages), most of the litigation centers on venereal disease and impotence.

As indicated in Chapter 8, most states have a statutory requirement that parties contemplating marriage go through a medical examination as a condition of obtaining a marriage license. A major objective of this exam is to determine whether either or both of the parties have communicable venereal disease. Suppose that either or both of the parties do have such a disease at the time of their marriage. It may be that the medical exam failed to show this, or that they failed to take the exam (and entered a common-law marriage in a state where such marriages are valid), or that they were able to falsify the results of the medical exam. States differ as to the consequences of marrying where one or both of the parties have the disease. While in most states the marriage is valid, there are several states in which the marriage is not and in which a ground for annulment can arise as a result. Futhermore, a state may make it a crime knowingly to marry or have sexual intercourse with someone who has an infectious venereal disease.

Issues related to a discussion of impotence include:

- Inability to copulate (i.e., to have sexual intercouse)—incurable
- Inabilitiy to copulate—curable
- Inability to have children (*sterility*)
- Refusal to have sexual intercourse

In most states, only the first situation—an incurable inability to copulate—is a ground for annulment. The standard for incurability is not the impossibility of a cure; rather, it is the present unlikelihood of a cure. The standard for copulation is the ability to perform the physical sex act naturally, without pain or harm to the other spouse. The "mere" fact that a spouse does not derive pleasure from the act is not what is meant by an inability to copulate. The *refusal* to copulate is not an inability to copulate, although the refusal is sometimes used as some indication of (i.e., as evidence of) the inability to copulate. In most states, it makes no difference whether the inability is due to physical (organic) causes or to psychogenic causes, nor does it matter that the person is impotent only with his or her spouse. If normal coitus is not possible with one's spouse, whatever the cause, the ground exists.

It is a defense to an annulment action that the party seeking the annulment knew of the party's impotence at the time of the marriage and yet still went through with the marriage. Also, continued cohabitation (living as husband and wife) long after the party learned of the other partner's impotence may constitute the equitable defense of *laches* (i.e., waiting an unreasonably long time to bring the suit) and thus bar the annulment action.

Note on Testing for AIDS

At one time Illinois mandated that the "medical examination shall include tests to determine whether either of the parties to the proposed marriage has been exposed to human immunodeficiency virus (HIV) or any other identified causative agent of acquired immunodeficiency syndrome (AIDS)" ILL. REV. STAT. ch. 40, § 204(b). The requirement was eventually repealed. Large numbers of people avoided the test by traveling to neighboring states to obtain a marriage license:

> "During the first 6 months of legislatively mandated premarital testing for human immunodeficiency virus in Illinois, 8 of 70,846 applicants for marriage licences were found to be seropositive, yielding a seroprevalence of 0.011%. The total cost of the testing program for 6 months is estimated at $2.5 million or $312,000 per seropositive individual identified. Half of the reported seropositive individuals reported a history of risk behavior. During the same period, the number of marriage licenses issued in Illinois decreased by 22.5%, while the number of licenses issued to Illinois residents in surrounding states increased significantly. We conclude that mandatory premarital testing is not a cost-effective method for the control of human immunodeficiency virus infection" Turnock and Kelly, *Mandatory Premarital Testing for Human Immunodeficiency Virus: The Illinois Experience*, 261 J. OF THE AMER. MED. ASSOC. 3415 (June 16, 1989).

Summary of Ground for Annulment: Physical Disabilities (Impotence)

Definition: The incurable inability to copulate without pain or harm to the spouse.

Void or Voidable: Voidable.

Who Can Sue: Either party.

Major Defenses: 1. The impotence is curable.
2. The nonimpotent party knew of the other's impotence at the time of the marriage.
3. Statute of limitations or laches (the plaintiff waited too long to bring this annulment action).

Is this annulment ground also a ground for divorce? Yes, in some states (see page 381).

Homosexual "Marriages"

Since people of the same sex cannot legally marry, annulment can never be an issue, since there is no accepted marital union to annul. See the earlier discussion of homosexual "marriages" on page 170.

 ## Section F. Grounds Relating to the Intent to Marry

Sham Marriages

An essential element of a marriage contract is the intent to enter a marriage. With this in mind, examine the following "marriages":

- Dennis and Janet enter a marriage solely to obtain permanent resident alien status for Dennis, who is not a U.S. citizen. Janet is a citizen. Dennis wants to use his marriage status to avoid deportation by immigration officials.

- Edna dares Stanley to marry her following a college party. After a great deal of laughing and boasting, they go through all the formalities (obtaining a license, having the blood test, etc.) and complete the marriage ceremony.
- Frank and Helen have an affair. Helen becomes pregnant. Neither wants the child to be born illegitimate. They decide to be married solely for the purpose of having the child born legitimate.
- Robin and Ken have been dating for a number of months. They decide to get married "just to try it out." They feel that this a more modern and rational way of determining whether they will want to stay together forever. It is fully understood by both that there will be "no hard feelings" if either of them wants to dissolve the marriage after six months.

All four of the above couples go through all the steps required to become married. To any reasonable outside observer of their outward actions, nothing unusual is happening. They all intended to go through a marriage ceremony; they all intended to go through the outward appearances of entering a marriage contract. Subjectively, however, they all had "hidden agendas."

According to traditional contract principles, if individuals give clear outward manifestations of mutual assent to enter a contract, the law will bind them to their contract even though their unspoken motive was *not* to enter a binding contract. Most courts, however, apply a different principle to marriage contracts than to other contracts. The situations involving the first three couples above are totally sham marriages. The parties never intended to live together as husband and wife; they had a limited purpose of avoiding deportation, of displaying braggadocio, or of "giving a name" to a child. Most courts would declare such marriages to be void and would grant an annulment to either party so long as the parties did not consummate their union or otherwise cohabit *after* the marriage. If, however, the couples in these three cases lived together as husband and wife even for a short period after the marriage, most courts would be reluctant to declare the marriage void. The subsequent cohabitation would be some evidence that at the time they entered the marriage they *did* intend to live as husband and wife. The central question is always this: what intention did the parties have at the time they entered the marriage? Did they intend to be married or not? It is, of course, very difficult to get into their heads to find out what they were thinking. Hence, the law must rely on objective conduct as evidence of intent. If parties cohabit after marriage, this is certainly some evidence that they intended to be married at the time they appeared to enter a marriage contract.

In the first three hypothetical cases, assume that the couples did not cohabit after they entered the marriage. Most courts would, therefore, find that at the time they entered the marriage contract, they did not have the intention to be married, i.e., to assume the duties of a marriage. It should be pointed out, however, that some courts, applying a *different* rule, would hold that the marriage is valid whether or not cohabitation followed the marriage ceremony—so long as the parties went through all the proper procedures to be married.

What about the fourth hypothetical case, in which the parties entered a *"trial marriage"*? The fact that the parties cohabited is evidence that they did intend to be married at the time they entered the marriage contract. Most courts would find that this marriage is valid and deny an annulment to anyone who later claims that the parties never intended to assume the marital status. It cannot be said that they married in jest or that they married for a limited purpose. The fact that they did not promise to live together as husband and wife forever does not mean that they lacked the intent to be married at the time they entered the marriage.

Summary of Ground for Annulment: Sham Marriage

Definition: The absence of an intention to marry in spite of the fact that the parties voluntarily went through all the formalities of a marriage.

Void or Voidable: Void.

Who Can Sue: Either party.

Major Defense: The parties did have the intention to marry at the time they entered the marriage ceremony. A major item of evidence that this intention existed is that they cohabited after the ceremony. (NOTE: in some states, the annulment will be denied if the parties went through all the outward formalities of the marriage in spite of what their unspoken objective was.)

Is this annulment ground also a ground for divorce? Usually not.

Assignment 9.5

(a) Elaine is twenty years old, and Philip, a bachelor, is seventy-five. Philip asks Elaine to marry him. Philip has terminal cancer and wants to die a married man. He and Elaine know that he probably has less than six months to live and that he will spend the rest of his life in a hospital bed. Under their arrangement, she does not have to continue as his wife after six months if he is still alive. They go through all the formal requirements to be married. On the day after the marriage ceremony, Elaine changes her mind and wants to end the marriage. Can she obtain an annulment? (See General Instructions for the Legal-Analysis Assignment in chapter one.)

(b) Interview Elaine. (See General Instructions for the Interview Assignment in chapter one.)

(c) Draft a complaint for Elaine for her annulment action. (See General Instructions for the Complaint-Drafting Assignment in chapter one.)

(d) Draft a set of interrogatories from Philip to Elaine. (See General Instructions for the Interrogatory Assignment in chapter one.)

Mental Disabilities

Two related reasons have been attributed to the existence of *mental disability* as a ground for annulment. First, it is designed to prevent people from marrying who are incapable of understanding the nature of the marriage relationship. Second, it is designed to prevent or at least discourage such individuals from reproducing, since it is argued that many mentally ill parents are likely to be poor parents and their children are likely to become public charges.

A great deal of difficulty exists in defining mental disability. The various state statutes use different terms to describe this condition: insane, idiot, weak-minded, feebleminded, unsound mind, imbecile, lunatic, incapable of consenting to a marriage, mentally ill or retarded, legally incompetent, mental defective, etc. One court provided the following definition:

While there has been a hesitancy on the part of the courts to judicially define the phrase "unsound mind," it is established that such term has reference to the mental capacity of the parties at the very moment of inception of the marriage contract. Ordinarily, lack of mental capacity, which renders a party incapable of entering into a valid marriage contract, must be such that it deprives him of the ability to understand the objects of marriage, its ensuing duties and undertakings, its responsibilities and relationship. There is a general agreement of the authorities that the terms "unsound mind" and "lack of mental capacity" carry greater import than eccentricity or mere weakness of mind or dullness or intellect. Johnson v. Johnson, 104 N.W.2d 8, 14 (N.D.1960).

Not all states would agree with every aspect of this definition of mental disability, although in general it is consistent with the definitions used by most courts.

Suppose that a person is intoxicated or under the influence of drugs at the time the marriage contract is entered. In most states, this, too, would be a ground for annulment if the alcohol or drugs rendered the person incapable of understanding the marriage contract.

While the issue of mental health usually arises in annulment actions—when someone is trying to dissolve the marriage—it also becomes relevant in some states at the license stage. Before a state official can issue a license to marry, he or she may be required by statute to inquire into the prior mental difficulties, if any, of the applicants for the license, e.g., to ask whether either applicant has ever been in a mental institution. In these states, the license to marry may be denied to any mentally disabled person unless that person is sterilized or the woman involved in the proposed marriage is over forty-five years old. (For more on sterilization, see page 460). It is generally conceded, however, that these license restrictions have been ineffective in preventing the marriage of people with serious mental problems. They are also of questionable constitutionality in view of the *Zablocki* opinion, page 159.

Whenever the mental health question arises (at the license stage or as part of an annulment proceeding), it is often very difficult to prove that the "right" amount of mental illness is present. All individuals are presumed to be sane unless the contrary has been demonstrated. Suppose that someone was once committed to a mental institution and, upon release, seeks to be married. Surely, the fact of prior institutionalization does not conclusively prove that the person is *presently* incapable of understanding the marriage contract and the marriage relationship at the time he or she attempts to marry.

Assume that a person is mentally disabled but marries during a brief period of mental health before relapsing again to his or her prior state of mental disability. The marriage took place during what is called a *lucid interval,* and many states will validate such a marriage if there was cohabitation. Furthermore, some states will deny the annulment if the parties cohabited during a lucid interval at any time *after* the marriage was entered even if one or both parties was not "lucid" at the time of the marriage. The problems, however, of trying to prove that any "interval" was "lucid" can be enormous.

Notes on Mental Illness

1. A state may have one standard of mental illness that will disable a person from being able to marry, another standard that will disable a person from being able to enter an ordinary business contract, and still another standard that will disable a person from being able to write a will.

2. Mental illness is, of course, also relevant in criminal proceedings where the defense of *insanity* is often raised in an attempt to relieve a defendant of criminal

responsibility for what was done. Within criminal law, a great debate has always existed as to the definition of insanity. The *M'Naghten "right-wrong"* test is as follows: "at the time of the committing of the act, the party accused was laboring under such a defect of reason, from disease of the mind, as not to know the nature and quality of the act he was doing, or if he did know it that he did not know he was doing what was wrong." 10 Clark & F. 200, 8 Eng.Rep. 718 (1843). The *Durham "diseased mind"* test is as follows: "an accused is not criminally responsible if his unlawful act was the product of mental disease or mental defect." Durham v. United States, 214 F.2d 862, 874–75 (D.C.Cir. 1954). See also United States v. Brawner, 471 F.2d 969 (1972). The *Model Penal Code* test is as follows: "A person is not responsible for criminal conduct if at the time of such conduct as a result of mental disease or defect he lacks substantial capacity either to appreciate the criminality (wrongfulness) of his conduct or to conform his conduct to the requirements of the law." §4.01.

Summary of Ground for Annulment: Mental Disability

Definition: The inability to understand the marriage contract and the duties of marriage at the time the parties attempt to enter the marriage due to mental illness, the influence of alcohol, or the influence of drugs.

Void or Voidable: Voidable in most states.

Who Can Sue: In some states, only the mentally ill person (or his or her parent or guardian) can sue for the annulment. In other states, only the mentally healthy person can sue. In many states, either can sue.

Major Defenses: 1. The person was never mentally disabled.
2. The marriage occurred during a lucid interval.
3. After the marriage began, there was a lucid interval during which the parties cohabited.
4. The plaintiff has no standing to bring this annulment action.

Is this annulment ground also a ground for divorce? Yes, in most states, if the mental disability arises after the marriage commences (see page 381).

Duress

If someone has been forced to consent to marry, then it clearly cannot be said that that person had the requisite *intent* to be married. The major question of *duress* is what kind of force will be sufficient to constitute the ground for annulment. Applying physical force or threatening its use is clearly sufficient. If an individual is faced with a choice between a wedding and a funeral, and chooses the wedding, the resulting marriage will be annulled as one induced by duress. The same is true if the choice is between bodily harm and marriage. Suppose, however, that the choice does not involve violence or the threat of violence. The most common example is as follows:

> George is courting Linda. They have had sexual relations several times. Linda becomes pregnant. Linda's father becomes furious at George and threatens to "turn him in" to the county district attorney to prosecute him for the crimes of seduction and bastardy. (If Linda is underage, the charge of statutory rape may be involved as well.) Furthermore, Linda and her father will sue George in the county civil court for support of the child. On the other hand, no criminal

prosecution will be brought and no civil action will be initiated if George agrees to marry Linda. George agrees, and the "shotgun wedding" promptly takes place. After the wedding, it becomes clear that Linda was not pregnant; everyone made an honest mistake. George then brings an action to annul the marriage on the ground of duress.

Here the threat is of criminal prosecution and of bringing a civil support action. If such threats are made *maliciously*, they will constitute duress and be a ground for annulment. The threat is malicious if it has no basis in fact. If the threats are not malicious, no annulment action can be based on them.

In most states, marriages induced by duress are voidable rather than void, but only the innocent party will have standing to bring the annulment action on that ground. If, however, this innocent party voluntarily cohabited with the "guilty" party (i.e., the one who did the coercing) after the effects of the duress have worn off, then the annulment action will be denied on the theory that the marriage has been ratified.

Assignment 9.6

Do you think that any of the following marriages could be annulled on the ground of duress? (See General Instructions for the Legal-Analysis Assignment in chapter one.)

(a) Rita married Dan after Dan threatened to kill Rita's second cousin if she did not marry him. The only reason Rita married Dan was to save her cousin's life.

(b) Tom married Edna after Tom's very domineering father ordered him to marry her. Tom had been in ill health lately. Tom married Edna solely because he has never been able to say no to his father.

(c) Paula married Charles after Paula's mother threatened suicide if she would not marry him. Paula married Charles solely to prevent this suicide.

Summary of Ground for Annulment: Duress

Definition: The consent to marry was induced by (a) physical violence, or (b) threats of physical violence, or (c) malicious or groundless threats of criminal prosecution, or (d) malicious or groundless threats of civil litigation.

Void or Voidable: Voidable in most states.

Who Can Sue? The party who was coerced.

Major Defenses: 1. There was no physical violence or threat of it.
2. The plaintiff did not believe the threat of violence and hence was not coerced by it.
3. There was no threat of criminal prosecution or of civil litigation.
4. The threat of criminal prosecution or of civil litigation was not malicious; it was made in the good-faith belief that it could be won.
5. This is the wrong plaintiff (e.g., this plaintiff has "dirty hands" since this is the party who used duress).
6. The plaintiff freely cohabited with the defendant after the effect of the duress had gone (ratification).

Is this annulment ground also a ground for divorce? Yes, in some states (see page 381).

Fraud

The theory behind *fraud* as a ground for annulment is that if a party consents to a marriage where fraud is involved, the consent is not real. A party does not have an *intent to marry* if the marriage has a foundation in fraud. The party intends one thing and gets another! Generally, for this ground to succeed, the defendant must intentionally misrepresent or conceal a fact that is essential or material to the marriage and the person deceived must reasonably rely upon this fact in the decision to enter the marriage.

Not every fraudulent representation will be sufficient to grant an annulment. As one court put it:

> Surely every representation leading up to marriage cannot be material,—the fact that a brunette turned to a blond over night, or that the beautiful teeth were discovered to be false, or the ruddy pink complexion gave way suddenly to pallor, or that a woman misstated her age or was not in perfect health, would lead no court to annul the marriage for fraud. Ryan & Granfield, *Domestic Relations,* 136 (1963).

What kind of fraud is ground for an annulment? Most courts have used an *essentials* test: *The fraud must involve the essentials of the marital relationship, usually defined as those aspects of the marriage that relate to sex and children.* For example, a man misrepresents his intent to have children. This would clearly go to the essentials of the marriage.

A much broader definition of fraud (making annulment easier to obtain on this ground) is the *materiality* test: *The fraud must be material, meaning "but for" the fraudulent representation (whether or not it relates to sex and children) the person deceived would not have entered the marriage.* Fewer courts use the materiality test than those that continue to insist on the essentials test.

Although, in theory, the essentials test is usually deemed to be the stricter of the two tests, in reality, the two tests often overlap and are frequently applied inconsistently by the courts. If children have been born from the union, for example, courts often strain the application of the tests in order to deny the annulment since preserving the marriage may be the only way to legitimize the children in some states. Also, if the marriage has never been consummated, courts tend to be more liberal in finding fraud. Oddly, a few courts treat an unconsummated marriage as little more than an engagement to be married.

The state of mind of the deceiving party is critical. In most states there must be an *intentional misrepresentation* of fact or an *intentional concealment* of fact. Consider the following methods by which false facts are communicated:

 Forms of Communication

1. Just before their marriage, Joe tells Mary that he is anxious to have children with her. In fact, he intends to remain celibate after their marriage.

2. Joe says nothing about his planned celibacy since he knows that if he tells Mary, she will not marry him. He says nothing about children or celibacy, and the subject never comes up prior to their marriage.

1. Joe's statement about children is an *intentional misrepresentation* of fact.

2. Joe's silence is an *intentional concealment* of fact.

3. Joe does not tell Mary that he intended to remain celibate because he incorrectly assumed that Mary already knew.

4. Just before their marriage, Joe tells Mary that since he is physically unable to have sexual intercourse, he will have to stay celibate. To his surprise, Joe later finds out that he is not impotent.

5. One hour after Joe marries Mary, he gets on a bus and disappears forever. They never had sexual intercourse before or after marriage, and never discussed the subject.

3. Joe's silence is an *innocent* (or *good-faith*) *nondisclosure* of fact.

4. Joe's statement is an *innocent* (or *good-faith*) *misrepresentation* of fact.

5. From Joe's conduct we can draw an *inference* that at the time he married Mary, he probably never intended to consummate the marriage.

Generally, only the first, second, and fifth form of communication mentioned in the above chart will support an annulment on the ground of fraud. *Innocent nondisclosure* or *innocent misrepresentation* will not be sufficient in most states. It should be pointed out, however, that in some states the innocence of the communication is not relevant so long as the other elements of fraud are present.

Summary of Ground for Annulment: Fraud

Definition: The intentional misrepresentation or concealment of a fact that is essential or material to the marriage and that the person deceived reasonably relies upon in the decision to enter the marriage.

Void or Voidable: Voidable in most states.

Who Can Sue: The innocent party only.

Major Defenses: 1. The fraud was not about an essential fact.
2. The fraud was not material: the plaintiff did not rely on the fraud in his or her initial decision to marry.
3. The fraud arose after the marriage was entered (again, no reliance).
4. The plaintiff may have relied on the fraud, but he or she was unreasonable in doing so.
5. After plaintiff discovered the fraud, he or she consummated the marriage or otherwise cohabited with the fraudulent party *(ratification)*.
6. The misrepresentation or nondisclosure was innocent—made in good faith with no intention to deceive.
7. This plaintiff has no standing to bring the annulment action since the plaintiff was the deceiver.
8. This plaintiff has "dirty hands" (e.g., in a case involving fraud relating to pregnancy, the plaintiff had premarital sex with the defendant).

Is this annulment ground also a ground for divorce? Yes, in a few states (see page 381).

Section G. Conflicts of Law

When a conflicts-of-law question exists, the law of two states must be compared. The law that exists where the parties were married (the *state of celebration*) must be compared with the law that exists where the parties now live (the *state of domicile* or *domiciliary state*). A *domicile* is the place where a party has been physically present with the intention of making that place a permanent home (page 390). The question arises as follows:

> Jim and Jane marry in State X where their marriage is valid. They then move to State Y. If they had married in state Y, their marriage would not have been valid. Jim sues Jane in state Y for an annulment. What annulment law does the court in State Y apply: the law of State X or the law of State Y?

State "X" is the state of celebration or the state of contract, i.e., the state where the parties entered the marriage contract. State "Y" is the domiciliary state, i.e., the state where the parties are domiciled. State "Y" is also called the *"forum state,"* meaning the state where the suit is being brought. Specifically, the forum is the court hearing the case. In this case the domiciliary state happens to be the same of the forum state.

To place this problem in a concrete perspective, assume that Jim dies without a valid will, i.e., *intestate*. Under the intestacy laws of most states, his spouse and heirs receive designated portions of his estate. If there is no spouse, the heirs obviously have more of an estate to share. Hence, it is in the interest of the heirs to claim that Jane is not the surviving spouse of Jim since they were never validly married. The success of this claim may depend on which law applies: that of State X or State Y.

Before examining the question of what law applies, we need to keep in mind the public policy favoring marriages. Legislatures and courts tend to look for reasons to validate a marriage, rather than create circumstances that make it easy to invalidate it. This is all the more so if the parties have lived together for a long time and if children have been born from the union. We have already seen that the law has imposed a presumption that a marriage is valid. The public policy favoring marriage, however, is not absolute. Other public policies must also be taken into account. The conflicts-of-law rules are a product of a clash of public policies.

> **General Conflicts-of-Law Rule in Annulment Actions**   If the marriage is valid in the state of celebration (even though it would have been invalid if it had been contracted in the domiciliary state), the marriage will be recognized as valid in the domiciliary state *unless* the recognition of the marriage would violate some strong public policy of the domiciliary state.

Thus, in the case of Jim and Jane above, the general rule would mean that State Y would apply the law of State X unless to do so would violate some strong public policy of State Y. Assuming that no such policy would be violated, the annulment would be denied, since the marriage was valid in the state of celebration, State X. Assuming, however, that a strong public policy is involved, State Y would apply its own law and grant the annulment.

What do we mean by a strong public policy, the violation of which would cause a domiciliary state to apply its own marriage law? Some states provide that if the marriage would have been *void* (as opposed to merely voidable) had it been contracted in the domiciliary state, then the latter state will not recognize the marriage even though the state of celebration recognizes the marriage as valid. In other words, it is against the strong public policy of a domiciliary state to recognize what it considers a void marriage regardless of the fact that other states consider the marriage valid. As we have seen, states differ on which annulment grounds will render a marriage void or voidable. A marriage that the domiciliary state would consider bigamous or incestuous is usually not recognized. In such cases, the domiciliary state will apply its own marriage law and grant the annulment even though the marriage may have been valid in the state of celebration. When other grounds for annulment are involved, states differ as to whether they, as domiciliary states, will apply their own marriage law or that of the state of celebration.

Marriage-Evasion Statutes

Suppose that a man and woman live in a state where they cannot marry, e.g., they are underage. They move from their domiciliary state to another state solely for the purpose of entering or contracting a marriage since they can validly marry under the laws of the latter state, e.g., they are not underage in this state. They then move back to their domiciliary state. If an annulment action is brought in the domiciliary state, what law will be applied? The marriage law of the domiciliary state or that of the state of celebration? If the annulment action is brought in the state of celebration, what law will be applied? Again the conflicts question becomes critical because the annulment will be granted or denied depending upon which state's marriage law governs. Note that the man and woman went to the state of celebration in order to *evade* the marriage laws of the domiciliary state. Several states have enacted *marriage-evasion* statutes to cover this situation. In such states, the choice of law depends upon the presence or absence of an intent to evade. The statute might read as follows:

> **§ 1.** If any person residing and intending to continue to reside in this state who is disabled or prohibited from contracting marriage under the laws of this state shall go into another state or country and there contract a marriage prohibited and declared void by the laws of this state, such marriage shall be null and void for all purposes in this state with the same effect as though such prohibited marriage has been entered into in this state.
>
> **§ 2.** No marriage shall be contracted in this state by a party residing and intending to continue to reside in another state or jurisdiction if such marriage would be void if contracted in such other state or jurisdiction and every marriage celebrated in this state in violation of this provision shall be null and void.[2]

It is sometimes very difficult to prove whether the parties went to the other state with the intent to evade the marriage laws of their domiciliary state. It

---

[2] National Conference of Commissioners on Uniform State Laws, "Uniform Marriage Evasion Act." The Uniform Commissioners withdrew the Uniform Marriage Evasion Act in 1943 because so few states had adopted it. There are states, however, that still have statutes the same as or similar to the Uniform Act quoted in the text.

may depend on how long they remained in the state of celebration, whether they returned to their initial domiciliary state or established a domicile in another state altogether. The interviewing and investigation checklist below is designed to assist you in collecting evidence on intent:

Interviewing and Investigation Checklist

Factors Relevant to the Intent to Evade the Marriage Laws[3]
Legal Interviewing Questions

1. How long have the two of you lived in State X?
2. Why didn't you get married in State X?
3. When did you decide to go to State Y?
4. Have you or D ever lived in State Y?
5. Do you or D have any relatives in State Y?
6. Were you or D born in State Y?
7. On what date did you and D go to State Y?
8. Did you sell your home or move out of your apartment in State X?
9. When you left State X, did you intend to come back?
10. After you arrived in State Y, when did you apply for a marriage license?
11. On what date were you married?
12. While you were in State Y, where did you stay? Did you have all your clothes and furniture with you?
13. Who attended the wedding ceremony in State Y?
14. Did you and D have sexual relations in State Y?
15. Did you or D work in State Y?
16. How long did you stay in State Y?
17. Did you ever vote or pay taxes in State Y?
18. Did you open a checking account in any bank in State Y?
19. Where did you go after you left State Y?

Possible Investigation Tasks

- Obtain copies of all records that tend to establish the kind of contact that the parties had with State Y, e.g., motel receipts, bank statements, rent receipts, employment records.
- Interview friends, relatives, and associates of the parties to determine what light they can shed on the intent of the parties in going to State Y.

Thus far our main focus has been on marriages that are valid in the state of celebration but invalid and annullable in the domiciliary state if they had been contracted in the latter state (see Exhibit 9–1). Suppose, however, that

---

[3]See also the interviewing and investigation checklist for establishing domicile, page 391.

the marriage was invalid in the state of celebration. The parties then move to a new state where they establish a domicile. If they had been married in their new domicile state, their marriage would have been valid. An annulment action is brought in their new domicile state (Exhibit 9–2).

Our question now becomes, if a marriage is invalid where contracted, can it ever be considered valid in any other state? Will a present domiciliary state validate a marriage that is invalid according to the law of the state of celebration? Surprisingly, the answer is often yes. In some states, a domiciliary state will deny an annulment of a marriage that would have been valid if contracted in the domiciliary state but that is clearly invalid in the state where it was actually contracted. Such states take this position, in part, because of the public policy (and indeed the presumption) favoring the validity of marriages.

Assignment 9.7

(a) Is there a statute in your state that deals with marriages contracted out of state? If so, give its citation and state how it handles such marriages. (See General Instructions for the State-Code Assignment in chapter one.)

(b) Find a court opinion written by a state court in your state that involved an annulment action brought in your state concerning a marriage that was contracted in another state. (If no such action has ever been brought in your state, pick an opinion from any state.) Answer the following questions about the opinion you found:

1. In what state was the marriage contracted?
2. What was the ground for the annulment?
3. What marriage law was applied in the opinion?
4. What reason did the court give for applying that law?

5. Was the annulment granted? Why or why not?

(See the general instructions for the court-opinion assignment in chapter one.)

Summary of Conflicts-of-Law

1. A marriage will be considered valid in a domiciliary state if (a) the marriage is valid according to the state where it was contracted, and (b) recognizing the validity of the marriage would not violate any strong public policy of the domiciliary state. If both conditions are met, the domiciliary state will deny the annulment even though the marriage could have been annulled if it had been contracted in the domiciliary state.

2. Generally, if a marriage would have been void had it been contracted in the domiciliary state, the latter state will not apply the law of the state of celebration where the marriage is valid.

3. Some states have statutes that invalidate marriages contracted in other states solely to evade its marriage laws.

4. Some states have statutes that invalidate marriages contracted in their own state solely to evade the marriage laws of other states.

5. Some states will validate a marriage contracted in another state (even though the marriage is invalid in the state where it was contracted) so long as the marriage would have been valid if it had been contracted in the state where the parties are now domiciled. In effect, such a state will deny the annulment even though the state of celebration would have granted it.

Section H. Consequences of an Annulment Decree

In theory, an annulled marriage never existed. The major question that always arises as a result of this theory is, what effect does the annulment have on events occurring after the "marriage"?

The old rule was that once a marriage was declared invalid, the declaration "related back" to the time the parties attempted to enter the marriage. This *"relation back"* doctrine meant that the annulment decree was retroactive. The doctrine, when strictly applied, resulted in some very harsh consequences. Children born to parents before their marriage was annulled were, in effect, born out of wedlock and were illegitimate. Suppose that a woman lives with a man for forty years before their marriage is annulled. She would not be entitled to any alimony or support payments since a man has no duty to support someone who was never his wife. Clearly, these were unfair consequences, and steps were taken in many states to offset them. What follows is an overview of the present law in this area.

Legitimacy of Children from an Annulled Marriage

With few exceptions, the states have passed statutes that *legitimize* children from an annulled marriage. Some of the statues, however, are not absolute, e.g., the statute might say that the children are legitimate only if one or more of the parents honestly believed that their marriage was valid when they entered it, or the statute might legitimize all the children born from an annulled marriage *except* when the annulment was granted on the ground of a prior existing marriage (bigamy).

Alimony and Disposition of Property Acquired before the Marriage Was Annulled

In some states, *alimony* cannot be awarded in annulment proceedings. In other states, however, statutes have been passed that allow alimony in such actions. This includes *temporary alimony* pending the final outcome of the action, and permanent alimony following the annulment decree. It may be, however, that alimony will be denied to the "guilty" party, e.g., the party who committed the fraud or who forced the other party to enter the marriage.

Another limitation on alimony in some states is that only defendants can receive it. By definition, the plaintiff seeking the annulment is saying that no marriage ever existed. A few courts say that it is inconsistent for the plaintiff to take this position and also to ask for alimony.

Where alimony is authorized, counsel or *attorney fees* are also awarded. The spouse able to pay, usually the husband, must pay the fees of the attorney for the other spouse in defending or initiating the annulment action.

Suppose that it is clear in a particular state that alimony cannot be awarded in the annulment action. Courts have devised various theories to provide the woman with some kind of relief:

1. *Punative spouse theory (in community property states)*. A putative spouse is one whose marriage is invalid. In some community-property states (page 249), the *innocent* putative spouse (i.e., the one who believed in good faith that the marriage was valid) is entitled to a *division of the property* acquired during the marriage—sometimes referred to as the *quasi-marital property*.

2. *Quasi-contract theory*. The elements of a valid contract have been discussed earlier (page 120). An annulled marriage is an invalid contract. Generally, a party whose contract has been wrongfully breached cannot recover any money (i.e., *damages*) if it turns out that the contract was invalid. This can be quite unfair to the innocent party, especially if this party invested a good deal of time and resources and if the other party benefited thereby. To avoid such *"unjust enrichment,"* the law establishes the fiction of a *quasi contract*, according to which the party who has been enriched must pay to the other party the reasonable value of the goods and/or services received. This doctrine has been applied to annulled marriages as a device to provide resources to a wife who is not entitled to alimony. Some states use this doctrine to require the husband to pay the wife the reasonable value of the services she rendered during the marriage.

3. *Quasi-partnership or joint-venture theory*. Here the theory is that during the marriage the husband and wife were somewhat like business partners engaged in a joint business venture. The partnership is over, and there should now be a fair distribution of assets of the participants.

4. *Resulting-trust or constructive-trust theory*. A trust is property held by one person for the benefit of another. Carefully drafted trust agreements specify

who the trustee is, what the *trust res* (i.e., the trust property) is, who the beneficiaries are, etc. When such trust instruments are not in existence, the law might rule that the existence of a trust is implied when fairness, justice, and equity seem to require it. Such trusts are called *resulting* or *constructive trusts*. In states that use this device, the husband of the annulled marriage can be considered the "trustee" of property acquired during the marriage. The wife, as "beneficiary" of this "res" would receive whatever portion of the property that a court deems fair.

As you can see, all of these theories rely upon fictions, since:

- A putative "spouse" is technically not a spouse.
- A quasi "contract" is technically not a contract.
- A quasi "partnership" is technically not a partnership.
- A resulting or constructive "trust" is technically not a trust.

Here is another instance where the law will "bend" in order to achieve an equitable result.

Problems of Revival

> Bob is validly married to Elaine. They go through a valid divorce proceeding, which provides that Bob will pay Elaine alimony until she remarries. One year later, Elaine marries Bill; Bob stops his alimony payments. Two years later, Elaine's marriage to Bill is annulled.

In this case, what is Bob's obligation to pay alimony to Elaine? Several possibilities exist:

1. Bob does not have to resume paying alimony; his obligation ceased forever when Elaine married Bill; the fact that the second marriage was annulled is irrelevant.
2. Bob does not have to resume paying alimony; Bill must start paying alimony if the state authorizes alimony in annulment actions.
3. Bob must resume paying alimony from the date of the annulment decree; the annulment of the second marriage *revived* his earlier alimony obligation.
4. Bob must resume paying alimony for the future and for the time during which Elaine was "married" to Bill; the annulment *revived* the alimony obligation.

The last option is the most logical since the technical effect of an annulment decree is to say that the marriage never existed; the decree is retroactive to the date when the parties entered the marriage that was later annulled. While the last option is perhaps the most logical of the four presented, it is arguably as unfair to Bob as the first option is unfair to Elaine. States take different positions on this problem. Most states, however, adopt the second or third option mentioned above.

Custody and Child Support

When children are involved, whether considered legitimate or not, courts will make temporary and permanent custody decisions in the annulment proceeding. Furthermore, child-support orders are inevitable when the children are minors. Hence the fact that the marriage is terminated by annulment usually has little effect on the need of the court to make custody and child-support orders (page 291).

Inheritance

To die *testate* is to die leaving a valid will. Either spouse, of course, can make a will and leave property to each other. Suppose, however, that one of the spouses of the annulled marriage dies *intestate*, i.e., dies without a valid will. In this event, the state's intestacy laws operate to determine who inherits the property of the deceased. The intestacy statute will usually provide that so much of the deceased's property will go to the surviving spouse, so much to the children, etc. If the marriage has already been annulled, there will be no surviving spouse to take a spouse's intestate share of the decedent's estate. An annulment, as well as a divorce, terminates mutual intestate rights between the former spouses.

Social Security and Worker's Compensation Benefits

Earlier we discussed the problem of revival in connection with alimony payments. The same problem exists with respect to certain statutory entitlement benefits. Suppose, for example, that Jane is entitled to social security or worker's compensation benefits following the death of her husband, Jim. Assume that these benefits will cease if and when she remarries. Jane then marries Tom, and the benefits stop. The marriage with Tom, however, is subsequently annulled. Are the benefits now revived on the theory that Jane was never married to Tom? Case law is split on this question with some cases holding that the benefits do revive, and others concluding the opposite.

Criminal Law Consequences

Ed marries Diane. He leaves her without obtaining a divorce. He now marries Claire. This marriage is then annulled. He is charged with the crime of bigamy. Can he use as a defense the argument that since his marriage with Claire was annulled, he was never married to Claire? Most of the cases that have answered this question have said that the subsequent annulment is *not* a defense to the bigamy charge.

Interspousal Immunity in Tort Actions

As we shall see later, in some states one spouse cannot sue another for certain personal torts. This prohibition is called the *interspousal tort immunity*. For example, if George assaults his wife, Paulene, she would not be able to sue him for the tort of assault. (She might be able to initiate a criminal action against him for the crime of assault and battery, but she could not bring a *civil* assault action against him.) An annulment of the marriage would not change this result. Even if George's marriage with Paulene was later annulled, she would still not be able to bring this tort action against him for conduct that occurred while they were together. The annulment does not wipe out the vestiges of the interspousal tort immunity.

The Privilege for Marital Communications

At common law, one spouse was not allowed to give testimony concerning *confidential communications* exchanged between the spouses during the marriage. The details of this prohibition will be explained later (page 410). For now, our question is as follows:

> Sam is married to Helen. Their marriage is annulled. A year later Sam is sued by a neighbor who claims that Sam negligently damaged the neighbor's property. The alleged damage was inflicted while Sam was still married to Helen. At the trial, the neighbor calls Helen as a witness and asks her to testify as to what Sam told her about the incident while they were still living together. According to the privilege for marital communications, Helen would be prohibited from testifying about what she and her husband told each other during the marriage. Their marriage, however, was annulled so that in the eyes of the law they were never married. Does this change the rule on the privilege? Can Helen give this testimony?

The answer is not clear; few cases have considered the issue. Of those that have, some have concluded that the annulment does not destroy the privilege, while others have reached the opposite conclusion.

Tax Return Status

A husband and wife can enjoy the advantages of income splitting by filing a joint return so long as they were married during the taxable year. Suppose, however, that after ten years of marriage and ten years of filing joint returns, the marriage is annulled. Must the parties now file amended returns for each of those ten years? Should the returns now be filed as separate returns rather than joint ones, again on the theory that the annulment meant that the parties were never validly married? According to the Internal Revenue Service, Publication 504, *Tax Information for Divorced or Separated Individuals*, p. 1 (1988 Edition):

> You are considered unmarried for the whole year [if you have] . . . obtained a decree of annulment which holds that no valid marriage ever existed. You also must file amended returns claiming an unmarried status for all tax years affected by the annulment not closed by the statute of limitations.

Assignment 9.8

Answer the following questions by examining the statutory code of your state.

(a) Is there a statute on the question of whether the children of annulled marriages are legitimate? If so, give the citation to the statute and explain how it resolves the question.

(b) Is there a statute on the question of whether temporary and permanent alimony can be granted in annulment proceedings? If so, give the citation to the statute and explain how it resolves the question.

(See General Instructions for the State-Code Assignment in chapter one.)

Assignment 9.9

How would the following two problems be resolved in your state? You may have to check both statutory law and case law. (See General Instructions for the State-Code

Assignment in chapter one and General Instructions for the Court-Opinion Assignment in chapter one.)

(a) Fred and Jill are married. Fred is killed in an automobile accident with the ABC Tire Company. Jill brings a wrongful-death action against the ABC Tire Company. The attorney of ABC learns that Jill was married to someone else at the time she married Fred. The attorney claims that Jill cannot bring the wrongful-death action since she was never validly married to Fred.

(b) Bob and Mary are married. Bob dies intestate (i.e., without leaving a valid will). Mary claims Bob's estate (i.e., his property) pursuant to the state's intestate law. Bob's only other living relative, Fred, claims that he is entitled to Bob's estate. Fred argues that Mary is not entitled to any of Bob's property because the marriage between Bob and Mary was invalid and should be annulled.

Assignment 9.10

(a) What is the name of the court in your state that can hear annulment actions?

(b) How does this court acquire jurisdiction over the subject matter of annulment actions, e.g., residence or domicile requirements, place of celebration, etc?

(c) To what court(s) can a party appeal a trial court judgment on annulment?

(See General Instructions for the State-Code Assignment in chapter one.)

Assignment 9.11

Prepare a flowchart of annulment litigation in your state. (See General Instructions for the Flowchart Assignment in chapter one.)

Key Chapter Terminology

Annulment
Divorce
Legal Separation
Judicial Separation
Void Marriage
Voidable Marriage
Void ab Initio
Suit to Annul
Declaratory Judgment
Standing to Sue
Estoppel
Marriage by Estoppel
Dirty Hands
Grounds
Legal Capacity to Marry
Intent to Marry
Church Annulment
Canon Law
Defective Consent

Bigamy
Polygamy
Enoch Arden
Rebuttable Presumption
Consanguinity
Relationship by Affinity
Incest
Nonage
Parental Consent
Physical Disabilities
Communicable Disease
Impotence
Sterility
Sham Marriage
Consummation
Cohabitation
Trial Marriage
Mental Disability
Mental Illness

Lucid Interval
Insanity
Right/Wrong Test
Duress
Fraud
Essentials Test
Materiality Test
Misrepresentation
Conflicts of Law
Domicile
Domiciliary State
State of Celebration
Marriage Evasion
Public Policy
Relation Back
Legitimacy of Children
Alimony
Property Division

Temporary Alimony
Attorney Fees
Putative Spouse
Quasi Contract
Quasi-Martial Property
Damages
Unjust Enrichment
Quasi Partnership
Joint Venture
Resulting Trust
Constructive Trust
Trust Res
Revival
Testate
Intestate
Interspousal Tort Immunity
Marital Communications
Confidential Communications

Separation Agreements: Legal Issues and Drafting Options

■ Chapter Outline

C hapter 10 begins our comprehensive study of the separation agreement. Parts of Chapter 11 (on child custody), Chapter 12 (on child support), and Chapter 15 (on taxation) also cover important dimensions of the separation agreement. Chapter 10, however, examines the document as a whole, setting the stage for the other chapters.

A major goal of the law office is to prepare an effective separation agreement that will avoid litigation. Many factors influence the ultimate shape of the agreement that the parties negotiate, e.g., the standard of living of the parties before the separation, their future earning capacity, plans for remarriage, if any.

The first step is the collection of extensive information, particularly financial information pertaining to everyone involved. Elaborate checklists can be helpful in this effort, as well as detailed interrogatories sent to the other spouse.

For a separation agreement to be valid, the parties must have the capacity to contract. The agreement must not violate public policy by inducing the parties to divorce, and it must not be the product of collusion, duress, or fraud. Finally, the consideration for the agreement must be proper.

The separation agreement should clearly distinguish alimony from property division. The distinction can be relevant in a number of areas, e.g., the effect of bankruptcy, the effect of remarriage and death, the availability of contempt, the power of the court to modify terms, and federal tax treatment. The distinction is not simply a matter of labels. The question is, what did the parties intend?

In negotiating alimony, the parties should consider a number of factors, e.g., method of payment, coverage, relationship to child support, modification, termination, and security. The principal focus of the court will be the needs of the recipient, the length of the marriage, and the ability of the payor to pay. Marital fault is usually not relevant.

In negotiating property division, the first step is to categorize all the property to be divided as personal or real. What resources were used to acquire it? How is title held? The division that is made depends on the bargaining process and on whether the parties live in a community-property state or in a common-law-property state. Pension assets can be divided, particularly through a Qualified Domestic Relations Order (QDRO). Businesses are also divisible, including their goodwill. Not all states agree, however, as to whether a license or degree can be divided.

The parties also need to consider the continuation of insurance policies, debts incurred before and after the separation agreement is signed, the payment of taxes, whether wills need to be changed, the payment of counsel fees, and the need for a nonmolestation clause.

Child-custody and child-support terms of a separation agreement are modifiable by a court, unlike property-division terms. Spousal-support terms are often modifiable, particularly if the separation agreement has been incorporated and merged into the divorce decree.

When problems arise that involve an interpretation of the separation agreement, the parties may decide to submit the controversy to arbitration or mediation in lieu of litigation. If the parties reconcile and resume cohabitation after they sign the separation agreement, the spousal-support terms (but not the property-division terms) are automatically canceled in some states. In others, both support and property-division terms are canceled if they are executory.

Chapter 10 closes with a description of computer software helpful in family law, and a series of sample separation-agreement clauses.

Our focus here and in the next two chapters will be on the nature of the separation agreement, the drafting options available, and the response of a court when the parties are not able to reach an agreement.

Section A. Separation Agreements and Litigation

The negotiation and drafting of the separation agreement are among the most important and difficult tasks of the family law practitioner. A *separation agreement* is a post-nuptial contract between a husband and wife governing their rights and obligations toward each other while they are separated. Generally, a divorce is contemplated by both parties when they enter the agreement. This, however, is not always the case. Some separation agreements are written by parties who never divorce and hence never remarry.

Separation agreements find their way into court in the following kinds of situations:

- One party sues the other for breach of contract, i.e., for violation of the separation agreement; the plaintiff in this suit wants the original separation agreement enforced.

- The parties file for a divorce and ask the court either (1) to approve the terms of the separation agreement, or (2) to approve them *and* to incorporate them into the divorce decree so that the decree and the agreement become merged.

- After the divorce, one of the parties brings a suit to set aside the separation agreement, e.g., because it was induced by fraud.

The law encourages the parties to enter separation agreements. So long as certain basic public policies (to be discussed below) are not violated, the law gives a great deal of leeway to the parties to resolve their difficulties and, in effect, to decide what their relationship will be on such vital matters as alimony, property division, custody and visitation of the children, etc. The role of the lawyer and paralegal is to assist the client in this large endeavor.

A high priority of the family law practitioner must always be to avoid litigation. Litigation is often extremely time-consuming, expensive, and emotionally draining on everyone involved. The marital breakdown of the parties was probably a most painful experience for the entire family. Litigation tends to remind the parties of old sores and to keep the bitterness alive. While a separation agreement will not guarantee harmony between the spouses, it can help keep their disputes on a constructive level.

If a *written* separation agreement does not exist, will everything inevitably end up in litigation? Not necessarily. It is extremely unwise, however, for the parties to rely exclusively on their *oral* understandings of what they agreed to do about accumulated property, future expenses, custody, visitation of the children, etc. Misunderstandings can easily arise as to "who was supposed to get what" and "who was supposed to do what." A well-drafted separation agreement can avoid many such controversies. A written agreement is therefore wise, even in states that enforce oral separation agreements.

Section B. Negotiation Factors

What is a "good" or effective, separation agreement? Obviously, this will vary according to the individual circumstances of each party, indeed, of each family. Nevertheless, some general observations can be made about the characteristics of an effective separation agreement.

 Characteristics of an Effective Separation Agreement

1. *Comprehensive.* It covers all major matters. Should something "new" arise, months or years later, the parties will not have to say, "We never thought of that when we drafted the agreement."

2. *Fair.* If the agreement is not fair to both sides, it may be unworkable, which will force the parties into expensive and potentially bitter litigation. Hence the worst kind of legal assistance a law office can provide is to "outsmart" the other side into "giving up" almost everything. Little is accomplished by winning the war, but losing the peace.

3. *Accurate.* The agreement should accurately reflect the intentions of the parties. What they orally agreed to do in formal or informal bargaining sessions should be stated in the written agreement.

4. *Legal.* There are certain things that can and cannot be done in a separation agreement; the agreement must not attempt to do that which is illegal.

5. *Readable.* The agreement should be written in language that the parties can understand without having to hire a lawyer every time a question arises.

An effective separation agreement is achieved through bargaining or negotiation, either by the parties on their own or, more commonly, through lawyers representing them. From a broader perspective, however, the separation agreement is a product of who the parties are, what their personalities are, what their sensibilities tell them should or should not be done, what their upbringing and moral instincts tell them is fair.

The separation agreement can be a complex document. In Exhibit 10–1, the myriad of factors that can influence the separation agreement are presented. As you can readily tell, the factors can have an infinite variety of relationships with each other. In some cases, for example, certain factors predominate over others. In the next several chapters, we will examine some of the individual factors in greater detail in order to see how they are often interrelated in the process of creating the agreement.

Section C. Checklists for Preparation of a Separation Agreement

Before an intelligent separation agreement can be drafted, a great deal of information is needed. First of all, a series of detailed lists should be compiled on the following items:

- All prior agreements between husband and wife, e.g., antenuptial agreements, loan agreements

□ **EXHIBIT 10–1** Factors Influencing the Content of Separation Agreement

Guilt feelings on who caused the marriage to fail

Extent of present indebtedness

Perceptions of what is best for the children

Competence of lawyers

Whether either or both want a divorce

The likelihood that the husband will go bankrupt in future

Whether either side wishes to remarry (and if so, when)

The extent of prior and present bitterness between the parties

What the law will and will not permit the parties to do

Ages of the children

Cost of lawyers

Tax consequences

Health of the parties and of the children

Personalities of the parties

Ages of the parties

Future earning capacity of both parties

Present standard of living

THE SEPARATION AGREEMENT

The place where the bargaining takes place

The likelihood the husband will fall behind in payments later

The knowledge each party has of the other's assets

Whether either side is in a hurry to "get it over with"

Prior education and employment of the parties

Advice given by relatives, friends, minister, etc.

The desires of the children

Whether either lives an unorthodox life style

Present state of the economy

The cost of trying to force the other to abide by the agreement

Whether each party presently has a "cool head"

Whether a divorce action, if any, will be contested

- All property held by the husband in his separate name
- All property held by the wife in her separate name
- All property in one person's name that really "belongs" to the other
- All property held jointly—in both names
- All property acquired during the marriage
- All contracts during the marriage for the sale of real property
- All insurance policies currently in force
- All debts currently outstanding, with an indication of who incurred each one
- All income from any source earned by the husband
- All income from any source earned by the wife
- Projected future income of either party, e.g., pension rights, royalties, loans that will be repaid, future trust income, expected inheritance
- All present living expenses of the husband
- All projected living expenses of the husband
- All present living expenses of the wife
- All projected living expenses of the wife
- All present living expenses of the children
- All projected living expenses of the children

In addition to such lists, the following data should be collected:

- Names and addresses of both spouses and of the children
- Data on all prior litigation, if any, between the parties
- Name and address of spouse's present attorney
- Names and addresses of prior attorneys, if any, retained by either party
- Copies of tax returns filed in prior years
- Character references (if needed on questions of custody or credibility)
- Names and addresses of individuals who might serve as arbitrators, or mediators
- Documentation of prior indebtedness
- Copy of will(s) currently in force, if any

The preliminary client interview in Chapter 5 (page 101) includes a great number of questions that should provide much of this background information within the knowledge of the client. The interrogatories in the next section focus on obtaining information from the *opposing* spouse, and are also designed to identify critical information needed to negotiate and draft a separation agreement.

Study the following checklist before examining the law governing individual clauses of a separation agreement and the drafting options available for each clause. This checklist is an overview of topics that need to be considered by the parties. Some of the headings in the checklist are commonly used in the separation agreement itself.

1. *Alimony:*
   - Who pays

- How much
- Method of payment
- Frequency of payment
- Whether it terminates on remarriage or death of either spouse
- Tax consequences
- Whether it fluctuates with income of husband
- Whether it is modifiable
- Security for payment
- Method of enforcement

2. *Child support:*
   - Who pays
   - How much
   - Whether it is modifiable
   - Method of payment
   - Security for payment
   - Frequency of payment
   - Tax consequences
   - Whether it terminates when the child reaches a certain age
   - Whether it terminates if the child is otherwise emancipated
   - College expenses

3. *Custody:*
   - Who obtains custody and what kind, e.g., sole custody, joint custody, split custody
   - Visitation rights to noncustodial parent
   - Visitation rights to others, e.g., grandparent
   - Summer vacations and special holidays
   - Removal of child from state (temporary or permanent)
   - Changing the surname of children
   - Consultation on major educational and medical decisions
   - Religious practice and training

4. *Health expenses (custodial parent and children):*
   - Medical
   - Dental
   - Drugs
   - Special needs
   - Other
   - Who pays

5. *Insurance:*
   - Life
   - Health
   - Automobile

- Disability
- Homeowner's

6. *Wills:*
   - Wills already in existence (individual or mutual)
   - Changes to be made in existing wills

7. *Debts still to be paid:*
   - Incurred by whom
   - Who pays

8. *Personal property:*
   - Cash
   - Joint and separate bank accounts (savings, checking, certificates of deposit, etc.)
   - Stocks
   - Bonds
   - Motor vehicles
   - Art works
   - Household furniture
   - Jewelry
   - Rights to receive money in the future, e.g., retirement pay, stock options, royalties, rents, court judgment awards
   - Other

9. *Real property:*
   - Residence
   - Vacation home
   - Business real estate
   - Tax shelters
   - Leases
   - Other

10. *Income tax returns*
11. *Attorney fees and court costs*
12. *Incorporation of separation agreement into divorce decree*
13. *Arbitration*
14. *What happens to agreement if parties reconcile*

Section D. Uncovering Financial Assets: Interrogatories

Gaining access to all the personal and financial information that the attorney needs to negotiate a separation agreement or to prepare for trial is not always easy. In fact, one of the major reasons that separation agreements are later challenged is that one of the parties did not have a complete inventory of the other spouse's financial assets before signing. Discovery devises such as depositions (page 407) and interrogatories (page 407) are sometimes used to obtain this kind of information. *Interrogatories* are written questions sent to the opposing party seeking information relevant to the controversy, particularly facts on financial assets.

The following comprehensive set of interrogatories are part of a law office's strategy to uncover facts. Reading them will give you a good idea of the kind of information that is the foundation of effective negotiation and drafting of a separation agreement. Without answers to the following questions *prior* to negotiation, an attorney would, in most cases, not be able to negotiate and draft the agreement competently.

```
SUPREME COURT OF THE STATE OF _____
COUNTY OF _____
_____X

                        Plaintiff,              INTERROGATORIES
        -against-                    Index No.:

                        Defendant.
_____X
```

The plaintiff, requests that the defendant answer under oath, in accordance with Section _____ , the following interrogatories:

NOTE: Questions concerning marriage and children are with relation to the other party to this suit, unless otherwise indicated. Where a question or part of a question is inapplicable, indicate same.

1. State your full name, age, residence and post office address, home telephone number, social security number, business address and business phone number.

2. State:
   (a) The names, birth dates and present addresses of all children born or adopted during the marriage, indicating whether any children are emancipated, and who has legal custody of each unemancipated child.
   (b) Whether any dependent child is in need of unusual or extraordinary medical or mental care or has special financial needs, giving a detailed description of the condition which requires such care and the treatment required, to the best of your knowledge, including, but not limited to:
      (i)   Nature of treatment;
      (ii) Name of treating doctor(s) and/or other professionals;
      (iii) Cost of care; and
      (iv) Estimated length of treatment.

3. As to yourself state:
   (a) Your present health;
   (b) Whether you have any need of unusual or extraordinary medical care or special financial needs;
   (c) Educational background, giving all schools attended and years of attendance, any degrees conferred, as well as any special training courses and employment skills;

(d) If you were married at the time you attended school or any special training course, indicate whether your spouse contributed to the cost of your education and/or support and living expenses and the amount thereof, and, if your spouse did not contribute to these, who paid for your education and/or support and living expenses;

(e) If you own or have been granted a license to practice any profession in this or any other state, indicate the nature of such license(s) and the approximate monetary value of each license.

4. If you have any disability(ies) which at any time renders or rendered you unable to perform work or limits or limited your ability to perform work, either now, in the past, or in the future, state:

(a) The nature of the disability(ies);

(b) The name and address of each treating physician for the past ten years for said disability(ies);

(c) The frequency of said treatment;

(d) The cost of said treatment;

(e) The nature of said treatment;

(f) The method of payment for said treatment, including the name of the payor.

*Attach any medical reports concerning this disability(ies).

PRIMARY AND MARITAL RESIDENCES

5. State your primary residence addresses for the past five (5) years, up to the present time, indicating periods of residence at each address.

6. If you are not currently residing with your spouse, state the names, ages and relationship to you of those persons with whom you reside at the above address, either on a permanent or periodic basis.

7. If your primary residence is rented or leased, state:

(a) The monthly rental and term of the lease or agreement;

(b) To whom the rental is paid, including name and address;

(c) Whether any other persons are contributing to the rental, the amount of the contribution, and the names of any such persons.
*Attach copies of cancelled rent checks for the last twelve (12) months and a copy of your lease or rental agreement.

8. If your present primary residence is owned by you, state:

(a) The date the residence was acquired;

(b) From whom it was purchased;

(c) The purchase price;

(d) The downpayment;

(e) The source of the downpayment, showing contribution by both spouses, as well as any other persons;

(f) The amount of the original mortgage(s);

(g) The amount of the mortgage(s) as of the date of the separation of the parties;

(h) The amount of the mortgage(s) at the present time if different than (g) above;

(i) The name and address of the mortgagee(s) and the mortgage number(s), if any;

(j) The market value of the property at the time of the separation of the parties;

(k) The present market value of the property, if different than in (j) above;

(l) The tax basis of the house when acquired;

(m) The adjusted tax basis of the house at the time of the separation of the parties;

(n) The current adjusted tax basis, if different from your answer to (m) above;

(o) The nature and dollar amount of any liens and/or encumbrances on the property not indicated in a previous answer(s);

(p) The current assessed valuation assigned the property for real property taxation purposes.
*Attach copies of closing statement of purchase, deeds, and a copy of any appraisals obtained, as well as the most recent bill or bills for real estate taxes.

9. If the residence referred to in question 8 above is not the ''marital residence'', then supply the same information as requested in questions 8(a) through 8(p) above for the ''marital residence''.

*Attach copies of closing statement of purchase, deeds, and a copy of any appraisals obtained, as well as the most recent bill or bills for real estate taxes.

10. Who has been paying the mortgage and/or tax payments from the date of the separation of the parties?

REAL ESTATE

11. If you have an interest in any real property other than indicated in the previous section, for each such piece of real property, state:

(a) Street address, county and state where the property is located;

(b) Type of property, deed references and your interest in the property (full or partial; type of tenancy; restraints on alienation);

(c) Zoning of the property;

(d) Date same was acquired;

(e) From whom it was purchased;

(f) The downpayment;

(g) The source of the downpayment, showing the contribution of both spouses and others;

(h) The amount of the original mortgage(s);

(i) The purchase price;

(j) The amount of the mortgage(s) as of the date of the separation of the parties;

(k) The amount of the present mortgage(s);

(l) The name and address of the mortgage(s) and the mortgage number(s), if any;

(m) The present market value of the property;

(n) The nature and dollar amount of any liens and/or encumbrances on the property which are not listed in a previous answer;

(o) The names and addresses of all co-owners and their interest in the property;

(p) Itemize all operation expenses, including but not limited to taxes, mortgage payments, insurance, fuel oil, gas, electric, water and maintenance;

(q) The present assessed valuation assigned the property for real property taxation purposes;

(r) The exact nature and extent of your interest, if not listed in question 11(b);

(s) The tax basis on the property when acquired;

(t) The adjusted tax basis at the time of the separation of the parties;

(u) The names and mailing addresses of all tenants and occupants and the annual and/or monthly rental paid by each, and their relation- ship to you, if any;

(v) The source and amount of any income produced by the property, if not previously indicated.

*Attach copies of the closing statement of purchase, deeds and a copy of any appraisals obtained.

12. If you have sold or otherwise disposed of any real property in which you have had an interest within the last ten (10) years, state for each property, in detail, the same information as asked in interrogatory 11 above.

*Attach copies of each closing statement of purchase and deed.

13. If you have executed any contracts to buy or sell real property within the last ten (10) years, indicate the location of the property, terms of the sale, and whether you were the purchaser or seller, and the name of the other party or parties.

*Attach a copy of each such contract.

14. If you are the holder of any real property not disclosed in a previous interrogatory, state for each:
(a) The type of such property (whether real or personal);
(b) The location of the such property;
(c) The date acquired;
(d) The net monthly rental to you from each piece of property;
(e) The gross monthly rental to you from each piece of property;
(f) The present value of such property.

INCOME AND EMPLOYMENT

15. State the names, addresses and telephone numbers of all employers for the last ten (10) years and give the dates of such employment, position held, reason for termination, and salary.

16. As to your present employment, state;
(a) Name and address of your employer;
(b) Type of work performed, position held and nature of work or busi- ness in which your employer is engaged;
(c) Amount of time you have been employed in your present job;
(d) Hours of employment;
(e) Rate of pay or earnings, setting forth specifically your gross and net average weekly salary, wages, commissions, overtime pay, bo- nuses and gratuities.

*Attach copies of all evidence of above payments, including pay stubs, W-2 forms, etc. for the past year.

17. State what benefits your employer provides for you and/or your family inclusive but not limited to all of the following. Include a brief de- scription of the benefit and whether your family is a beneficiary of the particular benefit.
(a) Health insurance plan;
(b) Life insurance coverage;
(c) Pension, profit sharing or retirement income program;
(d) Expense and/or drawing accounts;
(e) Credit cards (include reimbursement for business expenses placed on your personal credit cards);
(f) Disability insurance coverage;

(g) Stock purchase options;

(h) Indicate whether you are required to pay for all or any part of the benefits listed in this interrogatory and the amount of those payments and/or contributions.

18. If you are furnished with a vehicle by any person, employer or other entity, state:

(a) The year, make, model, and license number;

(b) The name and address of the legal owner;

(c) The name and address of the registered owner;

(d) The date you were furnished with such vehicle or replacement vehicle;

(e) The amount paid for gas, repairs, maintenance, and insurance costs by you personally and by anyone other than yourself. Indicate whether you are reimbursed directly or indirectly for the expenses paid by you personally.

*If said automobile is leased, attach a copy of said lease.

19. Describe any other property or other benefit furnished to you as a result of your present employment.

20. State and itemize all deductions taken from your gross weekly earnings or other emoluments, including but not limited to taxes, insurance, savings, loans, pensions, profit sharing, dues and stock options.

21. State if you have an employment contract with any company, corporation, partnership, and/or individual at the present time or at any time during the last three (3) years. If there is or was such a contract of employment, state the terms thereof, or if written, attach a copy hereto.

22. As a result of your employment at any time during the marriage, are you entitled to receive any monies from any deferred compensation agreement? If so, for each agreement state:

(a) The date such agreement was made, or if in writing, executed. If written, attach a copy.

(b) The parties making or executing such agreement.

(c) The amount you are to receive under such deferred compensation agreement and when you are to receive same. Attach copies of evidence of such payment.

23. State whether you have filed Federal, State and/or Local income tax returns during the last five (5) years. If so, indicate the years during which the same was filed and whether Federal, State or Local.

*Attach copies of all such returns filed during the past five (5) years.

24. State in which bank savings account or checking account your salary or other compensation is deposited, giving the name of the bank, branch and account number. If said salary, bonus or other compensation checks are cashed or negotiated rather than deposited, indicate the name and branch of the bank(s) where said checks are regularly cashed or negotiated.

25. State whether you have received or are receiving any form of compensation, monetary or otherwise, from any work and/or services performed for other individuals, companies, corporations and/or partnerships outside the business in which you are regularly engaged. If so, state:

(a) The name and address of the individual, company, corporation and/or partnership from whom you are receiving or have received such compensation during the last five (5) years;

(b) The amount of the compensation received;

(c) The nature of the services rendered by you for said compensation.

  *Attach copies of all 1099 forms, ''miscellaneous income'' received as a result of such work and/or services during the last five (5) years.

26. State whether your salary or other compensation will increase during the next year and/or contract period as a result of any union contract and/or employment contract or as the result of any regular incremental increase, or as a result of a promotion which you have received which is not yet effective.

27. Itemize all income benefits and other emoluments not already included in your answers to the preceding interrogatories, including but not limited to any other sources of income such as pensions, annuities, in-heritances, retirement plans, social security benefits, military and/or veterans' benefits, lottery prizes, bank interest, dividends, showing the source, amount and frequency of payment of each. Indicate whether each income benefit and/or other emolument is taxable or non-taxable.

SELF-EMPLOYMENT

28. If you are self-employed or conduct a business or profession as a sole proprietor, partner or corporation, state the type of entity it is. (For purposes of this question, a corporation includes any corporation in which your interest exceeds twenty percent (20%) of the outstanding stock).

29. If a partnership, list the names and addresses of all partners, their relationship to you and the extent of their interest and yours in said partnership.

  *Attach copies of any partnership agreements in effect at any time dur-ing the last five (5) years and all partnership tax returns filed dur-ing this period.

30. If a corporation, list the names and addresses of all directors, offi-cers and shareholders and the percentage of outstanding shares held by each. If any of the foregoing people are related to you, indicate the relationship.

  *Attach copies of all corporate tax returns filed by the corporation during the past five (5) years.

31. State whether you have had an ownership interest(s) in any other corpo-ration, partnership, proprietorship or limited venture during the course of the marriage. If so, state:

(a) The nature of such interest(s);

(b) The market value of such interest(s);

(c) The position held by you with respect to such interest(s) including whether you were an officer, director, partner, etc.;

(d) The date of acquisition of your interest(s) and the market value of said interest(s) when acquired;

(e) The value of said interest(s) on the date of your marriage if such interest(s) were acquired before your marriage;

(f) The date of termination of your ownership interest, if terminated;

(g) The total sales price of the business enterprise, if terminated;

(h) The amount of the compensation received by you and the form of the compensation if other than cash or negotiable instrument as a re-sult of the sale and/or transfer;

(i) The terms of each agreement of sale;

(j) The income received by you from the business during the last year prior to the sale and/or transfer.

32. State for each business, partnership, corporation and/or other enter-
    prise in which you have an interest, the following:
    (a) The amount of your contribution to the original capitalization;
    (b) The amount of your contribution for any additional capitalization
        or loans to the business entity;
    (c) The source from which monies were taken for capitalization and/or
        loans;
    (d) The market value of the business entity at the time of the separa-
        tion of the parties;
    (e) The present market value of the business if different than (d)
        above;
    (f) The market value of your share of the business entity at the time
        the separation of the parties if different than (d) above;
    (g) The present market value of your share of the business entity if
        different than (f) above;
    (h) The market value of your share of, and the total value of the busi-
        ness entity at the time of your marriage;
    (i) Amount of loans and/or reimbursement of capitalization paid you by
        the business entity, at any time during the past five (5) years,
        stating the amount received, the date received, and the disposition
        of the proceeds;
    (j) The present amount maintained in the capital account;
    (k) The name and address of all banks in which the business has or has
        had, during the past five (5) years, checking and/or savings ac-
        counts, the account numbers of each account, the amount presently
        contained in each, the amount contained in each at the time of the
        separation of parties and the amount contained in each six months
        prior to the separation of the parties. If an account was closed
        prior to the time periods mentioned in this question, that is,
        prior to six months before the separation of the parties, indicate
        the amounts in each such account for a three-year period prior to
        the closing account. State the destination of the amount that was
        in the account when closed;
    (l) The total value of your capital account;
    (m) The total value of all accounts receivable;
    (n) The dollar value of all work in progress;
    (o) The appreciation in the true worth of all tangible personal assets
        over and above book value;
    (p) The total dollar amount of accounts payable;
    (q) A list of all liabilities.

33. State the name and address of the following:
    (a) All personal and business accountants consulted during the last
        five (5) years;
    (b) All personal and business or corporate attorneys consulted during
        the past five (5) years (except those attorneys representing you in
        this action);
    (c) Your stockbroker(s);
    (d) Your investment advisor(s).

PERSONAL ASSETS

34. Itemize all bank and savings and loan association accounts, time depos-
    its, certificates of deposit, savings clubs, Christmas clubs and check-
    ing accounts in your name or in which you have an interest presently or
    have had an interest during the past five (5) years, stating for each:
    (a) The name and address of each depository;
    (b) The balance in those accounts as of the date of the separation of
        the parties;

(c) The present balance;

(d) The balance four (4) months prior to the separation of the parties;

(e) If there is any difference between your answers to (b), (c) and (d) above, specify when the withdrawals were made, who received the benefit of the withdrawals, who made the withdrawal and where the proceeds of the withdrawals went;

(f) The name and address in which each account is registered, account numbers and the present location and custodian of the deposit books, check registers and/or certificates.

*Attach copies of the monthly statements of such accounts for the past five (5) years and copies of savings account books or savings books and check registers.

35. State whether you have a safe deposit box either in your name individually, or in the name of a partnership, or corporation and to which you have access, stating the following:

(a) The location of the box and box number;

(b) The name in which it is registered and who, in addition to yourself, has access to the box;

(c) List the contents of said box in which you or your spouse claim an interest.

36. If you have any cash in your possession or under your control in excess of one hundred dollars ($100), specify:

(a) The amount of the cash;

(b) Where it is located;

(c) The source of said cash.

37. For each vehicle of any nature in which you have any interest, including, but not limited to, automobiles, trucks, campers, mobile homes, motorcycles, snowmobiles, boats and/or airplanes, state:

(a) The nature of each vehicle;

(b) Your interest therein;

(c) The name in which the vehicle is registered;

(d) The make, model and year of each;

(e) The price paid and the date acquired;

(f) The principal operator of the vehicle since its purchase;

(g) The present location of the vehicle;

(h) The name and address of any co-owners;

(i) The present value of said asset.

38. State whether you own any horses or other animals with a value in excess of two hundred fifty Dollars ($250). If so, state:

(a) The date of purchase and purchase price of same;

(b) The type of animals;

(c) The market value at the time of the separation of the parties;

(d) The present market value if different from (c);

(e) The names and addresses of any co-owners and the percentage of their interest in the same.

39. List all household goods, furniture, jewelry and furs with a value in excess of two hundred fifty dollars ($250), in which you have an interest, stating for each:

(a) The nature of each;

(b) Your interest therein;

(c) The price paid and the date acquired;

(d) The present value of the asset;

(e) Whether the asset is ''marital property,'' ''separate property,'' or ''community property.'' If you claim the asset is separate property, state your reasons therefor.

40. State whether you own or have an interest in any collections or hobbies, including but not limited to art, stamps, coins, precious metals,
antiques, books and/or collectibles with an aggregate value in excess
of two hundred fifty dollars ($250). If so, state:
    (a) The nature of each;
    (b) Your interest therein and the interest of any co-owners. Also state
        the names and addresses of all co-owners;
    (c) A complete itemization of each such collection, showing the price
        paid and the date acquired of each such collection.
    (d) The present value of each element of the asset; An ''element''
        means a unit which is capable of being sold by itself;
    (e) The value of each such element, if owned prior to the marriage, at
        the time of the marriage.

41. State whether you are receiving or are entitled to receive any royalty
income. If so, state:
    (a) The basis for such income, including the nature of any composition,
        copyright, work or patent from which such income arose;
    (b) The amount of such income yearly during the past five (5) years;
    (c) The terms of any agreement in relation to such composition, work,
        patent, etc.
        *Attach copies of any royalty statement or other invoice verifying
        such income.

42. State whether you have any legal actions pending for money damages, or
whether you are entitled to receive any legal settlements or insurance
recoveries. If so, state:
    (a) The amount of money which you are demanding in your pleadings, or
        to which you are entitled as an insurance recovery or legal
        settlement;
    (b) The court in which the action is or was pending, the caption of the
        case and the index or docket number;
    (c) Whether any other person has an interest in the insurance recovery,
        legal settlement, or pending action and, if so, state their name,
        address and the nature of their interest;
    (d) The circumstances resulting in your becoming entitled to the insur-
        ance recovery or legal settlement, or the commencement of the legal
        action.

43. State whether you have any HR10 or IRA arrangements. If so, state:
    (a) The date of the creation of each such plan;
    (b) The amounts contributed by you or on your behalf to each such plan;
    (c) The current value of your account under each such plan.

44. State whether you are entitled to receive, or have received during the
past five (5) years any gambling awards or prizes, indicating the nature thereof, the amount, when you are to receive the same, and the
date you became entitled to the award or prize.

45. State the names and addresses of all persons who owe you money not indicated in previous interrogatories. Also state as to each;
    (a) The amount thereof;
    (b) When said sum is due;
    (c) The nature of the transaction that entitled you to receive the
        money and when the transaction took place.

STOCK ASSETS

46. Itemize all shares of stock, securities, bonds, mortgages and other investments, other than real estate revealed in previous interrogatories,
stating for each:
    (a) Identity of each item as to type and amount of shares;

(b) Whose name they are registered in and the names of any co-owners and their interest therein;

(c) The source of the monies from which you purchased the item;

(d) The original price of each item;

(e) The market value at the time of the separation of the parties;

(f) The present market value of each item if different from (e) above;

(g) The amount of any dividends and/or other distribution received on a yearly basis;

(h) The present location and custodian of all certificates or evidences of such investments.

*Attach hereto monthly statements of these securities for the past five (5) years.

47. State whether any of the shares of stock owned by you and listed in any of your previous answers to interrogatories is subject to any cross purchase or redemption agreement. If so, state:

(a) The date of such agreements;

(b) The parties to such agreements;

(c) The event that will bring about the sale or transfer under the agreement;

(d) The sale price under such agreement.

48. Itemize all shares of stock, securities, bonds, mortgages and other investments, other than real estate and business entities previously listed in your name or in which you have an interest, which you have sold in the last five (5) years, stating for each:

(a) The identity of each item as to type and amount of shares;

(b) Whose name they were registered in, including the names of any co-owners and their interest therein;

(c) The source of the monies from which you purchased each item;

(d) The original price of each item and date of purchase;

(e) The market value at the time of the separation of the parties;

(f) The amount of dividends or other distribution received on a yearly basis;

(g) The date each was sold or transferred;

(h) To whom each was sold or transferred;

(i) The amount received for each such sale or transfer;

(j) The disposition and destination of the proceeds of said sale;

(k) If applicable, the value of each such item at the time of your marriage.

49. Itemize all shares of stock, securities, bonds, mortgages and other investments which you have purchased but which is held nominally by third persons, stating for each:

(a) The manner in which the person is holding said investment;

(b) The identity of each item as to type and amount of shares;

(c) Whose name they are registered in, including the names of any co-owners and their interest therein;

(d) The source of the monies from which you purchased each item;

(e) The original price of each item;

(f) The market value at the time of the separation of the parties;

(g) The present market value of each item;

(h) The value, if applicable, at the time of your marriage;

(i) The present location and custodian of all certificates or evidence of such investments;

(j) The amount of dividends or other distribution received on a yearly basis.

*Attach hereto monthly statements of these securities for the past three (3) years.

50. Are you the holder of any mortgages, accounts receivable, notes or other evidence of indebtedness not indicated in your answer to previous interrogatories? If so, for each such instrument, state:
   (a) The type of instrument;
   (b) The date of maturity of such instrument;
   (c) The amount of interest payable to you yearly under such instrument;
   (d) The nature of the sale or transaction (including the type of merchandise sold) from which the said instrument arose;
   (e) The date the instrument was acquired by you.

51. State whether you have any money invested in any business ventures not answered in previous interrogatories. For each such investment state:
   (a) The nature of such investment;
   (b) Your share of the interest therein;
   (c) The original cost of such investment and the source of monies used for said investment;
   (d) The amount of income yielded from the said investment;
   (e) The present value of said investment.

52. If, during the course of your marriage, you have received any inheritances, state:
   (a) From whom you inherited;
   (b) The nature and amount of the inheritance;
   (c) The disposition of any of the assets of the inheritance, tracing them if possible, to the time of the separation of the parties;
   (d) The value of the inheritance at the time of the separation of the parties;
   (e) The present value of the inheritance.

53. State whether you expect to receive any inheritances. If so, state:
   (a) From whom you expect to inherit;
   (b) The nature and amount of inheritance.

54. State whether you have, during the last five (5) years, sold or transferred any interest in personal property valued in excess of two hundred fifty dollars ($250) and for each such sale or transfer state:
   (a) The nature of the property;
   (b) The date of the sale or transfer;
   (c) The method of transfer;
   (d) The name and address of each purchaser or person receiving title;
   (e) The amount received for said transfer or sale;
   (f) The disposition of proceeds of said sale or transfer.

55. State whether you have made any gift of any money and/or personal property to friends, relatives or anyone else during the past five (5) years of a value in excess of two hundred fifty dollars ($250). If so, state:
   (a) The name and address of said person and the relationship of that person to you;
   (b) The nature and value of the gift or the amount of money given;
   (c) The date each gift was given;
   (d) The reason for such gift.

TRUSTS

56. State whether you are the grantor, beneficiary or holder of a power of appointment for any trust created by you, the members of your family, or any other persons or corporations. If so, state:
   (a) The date of the trust instrument;
   (b) The name of the settlor of each trust;
   (c) The name of the beneficiary(ies) of each trust;
   (d) The present amount of each trust corpus;

(e) The amount of the trust corpus at the time of the separation of the parties;

(f) The amount of the trust corpus at the time of your marriage, if applicable.

(g) Any restrictions on alienation to which such corpus is subject;

(h) The terms of each trust instrument;

(i) The income earned by the trust during the past five (5) years.
    *If there is a trust instrument, attach a copy hereto. If the trustee has rendered an accounting during the past five (5) years attach a copy hereto.

57. List any and all property, assets or things of a value in excess of two hundred fifty Dollars ($250) which you hold in trust for anyone, stating as to each:

(a) A description of the property, its location, and the name and address of the person for whom you hold same;

(b) The conditions or terms of the trust, including whether or not you are paid any commissions or other compensation for holding such property;

(c) How such property was acquired by you and whether you paid any part of the consideration therefor.

58. List any and all property or things of value of every nature or kind with a value in excess of two hundred fifty dollars ($250) which is held in trust for you or which is in the care and/or custody of another person, corporation or entity for you, stating for each:

(a) The nature of the property, its location and custodian;

(b) The name and address of the trustee, if different than above;

(c) The conditions or terms of the trust;

(d) How such property was acquired and who paid the consideration therefor;

(e) The original cost;

(f) The value at the time of the separation of the parties;

(g) The present value if different than (f) above.
    *Attach copies of any trust instruments or writings evidencing the above.

INSURANCE

59. List each life insurance policy, annuity policy, disability policy or other forms of insurance not disclosed in a previous interrogatory, stating for each:

(a) The name and address of the insurance company;

(b) The policy number;

(c) The type of policy;

(d) The name and address of the owner of the policy;

(e) The name and address of the present beneficiary of the policy;

(f) If there has been a change of beneficiary in the last five (5) years, give the date of each change and the name and address of the former beneficiary;

(g) The date the policy was issued;

(h) The face amount of the policy;

(i) The annual premium and the name and address of the person paying the premium currently and for the past five (5) years;

(j) The cash surrender value of said policy;

(k) If any loans have been taken out against the policy, the date of each such loan, the person making such loan, the amount of the loan and the purpose for which the proceeds were utilized;

  (l) If said policy has been assigned, the date of the assignment, the name and address of each assignee;

  (m) The present custodian of the policy;

  (n) If any policy is supplied by an employer, whether it is a condition of employment and under what conditions it terminates.

60. State whether you have surrendered, transferred, or in any way terminated any form of insurance policy for the last five (5) years. If so, state:

  (a) The name and address of the insurance company;

  (b) The number of the policy;

  (c) The type of policy;

  (d) The name and address of the last and/or current owner of the policy;

  (e) The name and address of the last and/or present beneficiary of the policy;

  (f) The face amount of the policy;

  (g) The cash surrender value of the policy at present or just prior to its being surrendered, transferred, or terminated;

  (h) The person transferring, surrendering, or terminating said policy;

  (i) If any cash was realized from the said transfer, termination, or surrender, the amount realized and for what purposes the proceeds were used.

PENSION AND DISABILITY

61. State whether you are entitled to any pension, profit sharing and/or retirement plan. If so, state:

  (a) The nature of the plan;

  (b) The name and address of the entity or person providing the plan;

  (c) Whether your interest in the plan is vested and, if not, the date and conditions under which the plan will vest;

  (d) Whether the plan is contributory or non-contributory and, if contributory, the amount you contributed during the marriage;

  (e) The amount you earned in the plan during the marriage;

  (f) If you have the right to withdraw any monies from the plan, how much money you may withdraw and when;

  (g) If you have withdrawn and/or borrowed any monies from the plan, indicate when and how much was borrowed and whether the money must be returned or repaid;

  (h) If there are any survivor benefits, and if so, give a brief description thereof.

  *Attach copies of all writings concerning the plan(s) in your possession or which are readily available from your employer or pension payor.

62. If you are entitled to any disability benefits, state:

  (a) The nature of the disability;

  (b) The dollar amount of the award;

  (c) The date of payment of the award;

  (d) Whether there are any survivor benefits, giving a brief description thereof;

  (e) Whether any benefits or awards are presently being claimed by you, litigated or are being reviewed, indicating the amount thereof if not included above.

EXPENSES

63. Itemize your average monthly expenses in detail [see chart on page 226]. If any of the expenses include support of any other person

outside your immediate family, set forth the name and address of such person, and the portion of each expense attributable to each such person supported. (NOTE: All weekly expenses must be multiplied by 4.333 to obtain the monthly expense.) If certain expenses are paid by your employer, spouse or another party, so indicated by footnoting.

*   *   *   *   *

MONTHLY BUDGET EXPENSE
(See interogatory 63)

Food _____
Clothing _____
Mortgage(s) _____
Property taxes _____
Rent _____
Utilities _____
Fuel oil _____
Telephone _____
Garbage collection _____
Water _____
Plumbing _____
Electrician _____
Doctors _____
Dentists _____
Orthodontists _____
Psychiatrists _____
Attorney fees _____
Drugs _____
Hair Care _____
Dry Cleaners _____
Laundry _____
Veterinarian _____
Newspapers _____
Magazines _____
Insurance _____
    Homeowners' _____
    Renter's _____
    Automobile _____
    Life _____
    Hospitalization _____
    Floaters _____
    Umbrella _____
    Disability _____
    Other _____
Professional dues _____
Club dues _____
Babysitters _____
Domestics _____
Burglar alarm service _____
Voluntary/court ordered support ____

PAST DUE INSTALLMENT OBLIGATIONS
    Credit cards _____
    Auto Loans _____
    Personal Loans _____
    Charge Accounts _____

Credit Card Fees _____

Education _____
Allowances _____
Sports & hobbies _____
Dancing lessons _____
Music lessons _____
Sport lessons _____
Auto expenses _____
    Gas _____
    Maintenance _____
    Commuting _____
    Parking _____
    License & Registration ____
    Transportation _____
Camp _____
Household improvements _____
Household repairs _____
Apartment maintenance _____
Garden maintenance _____
Pool maintenance _____
Termite/pest service _____
Tree service _____
Water softener _____
Furniture & appliances _____
Furnishings _____
Contributions _____
Vacations _____
Christmas tips _____
Christmas presents _____
Chanukah presents _____
Other presents _____
Entertainment _____
Misc. Spending money _____
Emergencies _____
Cable TV _____

DETAIL ALL OTHER EXPENSES BELOW:

_____
_____
_____
_____
_____
_____

TOTAL MONTHLY EXPENSES _____

64. State whether anyone contributes to your support, income and/or living expenses who has not been included in a previous interrogatory. If so, state:
    (a) Their names and address;
    (b) Their relationship to you;
    (c) The amount of support, income and/or living expenses received by you during the last five (5) years and the frequency of said support, income and/or living expenses;
    (d) The reason for said support;
    (e) The nature of said support.

LIABILITIES

65. Set forth a list of all credit card balances, stating:
    (a) The name of the obligor;
    (b) The total amount due at the present time and the amount due at the time of the separation of the parties;
    (c) The minimum monthly payment;
    (d) The name in which the card is listed, and the names of all persons entitled to use the card;
    (e) The exact nature of the charges for which the money is owed;
    (f) Who incurred each obligation.
        *Attach copies of all credit card statements for the past twelve (12) months.

66. Set forth in detail any outstanding obligations, including mortgages, conditional sales contracts, contract obligations, promissory notes, and/or government agency loans not included in your answers to any previous interrogatories, stating for each:
    (a) Whether the obligation is individual, joint, or joint and several;
    (b) The names and addresses of each creditor;
    (c) The form of the obligation;
    (d) The date that the obligation was incurred;
    (e) The consideration received for the obligation;
    (f) A description of any security given for the obligation;
    (g) The amount of the original obligation;
    (h) The date of interest on the obligation;
    (i) The present unpaid balance of the obligation;
    (j) The date and the amount of each installment repayment due;
    (k) An itemization of the disposition of the funds received for which the obligation was incurred.

67. List all judgments outstanding against you and/or your spouse not included in your answer to a previous interrogatory, and for each state:
    (a) The names of the parties and their respective attorneys;
    (b) The courts in which same were entered and the index or docket number assigned to each case;
    (c) The amount of each judgment.

68. If there is a wage execution, judgment and/or order to pay out of income and earnings, state:
    (a) How much is taken from your earnings each week;
    (b) The obligor;
    (c) The balance due.

69. State the nature of any lien or security interest not indicated in your answer to a previous interrogatory to which any of the assets listed by you in previous interrogatories are subject, indicating for each:
    (a) The name and address of the holder thereof;
    (b) The holder's relationship to you;

(c) The amount and frequency of the payments you make thereon;
(d) The balance due.

MISCELLANEOUS

70. If any money, property and/or asset was acquired by you either before the marriage or after the separation of the parties; state for each with a value in excess of two hundred fifty dollars ($250) the following:
    (a) The nature of the property;
    (b) The date acquired;
    (c) The source of the acquisition;
    (d) Your interest therein;
    (e) The present market value.

71. If any other money, property, or assets described in the above interrogatory was sold, transferred and/or disposed of, state for each:
    (a) The manner of the disposition;
    (b) The date of the disposition;
    (c) To whom sold, transferred or disposed and their relationship to you;
    (d) The amount received.

72. List all gifts received by you from your spouse with a value in excess of one hundred dollars ($100), giving for each:
    (a) The date received;
    (b) The nature of the gift;
    (c) The market value of the gift.

73. List all gifts received by you from your family, your spouse's family, or any other party or entity, with a value in excess of one hundred dollars ($100), giving for each:
    (a) The name of the donee and the relationship of the donee to you;
    (b) The date received;
    (c) The nature of the gift;
    (d) The market value of the gift.

74. If you have prepared a financial statement of your assets and liabilities, either individually or for any business in which you have an interest within the past five (5) years, state:
    (a) The dates of all such statements;
    (b) The name and address of the person, firm, company, partnership, corporation, or entity for whom they were prepared;
    (c) The name and address of all persons who worked on the preparation of such statements.
    *Attach copies of all said statements.

75. Sate what counsel fees you have paid and/or agreed to pay for services rendered in connection with the separation of the parties.

76. State whether you have made application for any loans with any lending institutions, individuals, companies and/or corporations during the past five (5) years. If so state for each:
    (a) The name and address of the lending institution, individual, company or corporation;
    (b) The date of the application;
    (c) The amount of the loan;
    (d) Whether your application was approved or denied.
    *Attach a copy of all such loan applications.

77. List any contributions made by you in excess of two hundred fifty dollars ($250) within the past five (5) years. For each such gift or con-
tribution state:
(a) The name of the donee;
(b) The reason for the contribution;
(c) The amount of such contribution.

Section E. The Beginning of the Separation Agreement

On the assumption that the law firm has a comprehensive picture of the assets of the client (see Chapter 5) and of the opposing spouse (see interrogatories, earlier in this chapter), we turn now to the separation agreement itself.

It is good practice in the drafting of a separation agreement to number each paragraph separately (1, 2, 3, etc.) after the introductory clauses, and to use headings for each major topic, e.g., alimony, custody.

Separation Agreement

THIS AGREEMENT, entered into this _____ day of _____ , 19 __ , by Fred Jones (referred to in this agreement as the Husband), residing at _____ , and by Linda Jones (referred to in this agreement as the Wife), residing at _____ ,

Witnesseth:

WHEREAS, the parties were married on _____ , 19 __ in the state of _____ , city of _____ , and

WHEREAS, _____ children were born of this marriage: (here list each child with date of birth)

WHEREAS, as a result of irreconcilable marital disputes, the parties have been voluntarily living apart since _____ , 19 __ which both parties feel is in their own best interests and that of their children, and

WHEREAS, both parties wish to enter this agreement for the purpose of settling all custody, support, and property rights between them and any other matter pertaining to their marriage relationship, and

WHEREAS, both parties acknowledge that they have had separate and independent legal advice from counsel of their own choosing on the advisability of entering this agreement, that they have not been coerced or pressured into entering the agreement and that they voluntarily decide to enter it.

NOW THEREFORE, in consideration of the promises and the mutual commitments contained in this agreement, the parties agree as follows:

(the full text of the agreement goes here in numbered paragraphs; sample clauses are found at the end of this chapter, page 275)

★ A number of issues relating to these introductory clauses need to be discussed:

☐ **Public policy and collusion**

☐ **Capacity to contract**

☐ **Duress and fraud**

☐ **Consideration**

☑ Public Policy and Collusion

The above agreement between Fred and Linda Jones is careful to:

■ Point out that a separation has already occurred, and

■ Avoid mentioning divorce—at least at the beginning of the agreement.

So long as the parties are still living together and separation is not imminent due to a recent decision to separate, the law operates on the assumption that there is still hope. By definition, a separation agreement attempts to provide *benefits* to the parties in the form of money, freedom, etc. The very existence of such an agreement is viewed as an *inducement* to obtain a divorce unless the parties have already separated or are about to do so shortly. A separation agreement between two parties who are still living together and who intend to remain together indefinitely might be declared unenforceable. It would be the equivalent of one spouse saying to another, "If you leave me now, I'll give you $25,000." The agreement is invalid because it is conducive to divorce, i.e., it encourages the parties to separate. This is against *public policy*.

Another kind of illegal agreement is an attempted "private divorce." Suppose a husband and wife enter the following brief separation agreement:

> "We hereby declare that our marriage is over and that we will have nothing to do with each other henceforth. As we part, we ask nothing of each other."

Assume further that this agreement is not shown to anyone. To permit parties to make such a contract would be to enable them to divorce themselves without the involvement of a court. At the time the parties attempted to enter this contract, it may have seemed fair and sensible. Suppose, however, that months or years later, the wife finds herself destitute. If she sues her husband for support or alimony, he cannot defend the action by raising her contract commitment not to ask anything of him. If either of them later tries to marry someone else, he or she will have no defense against a charge of bigamy.

A more serious kind of illegal agreement between husband and wife involves *collusion*. Collusion is fraud committed on the court by agreeing on a story to be told to the court that both parties know to be untrue, e.g., the plaintiff in a divorce action falsely asserts that the defendant deserted her on a certain date, and the defendant falsely admits to this, or he remains silent even though he knows that the assertion is false. The objective is usually to *facilitate* the granting of the divorce. Before no-fault divorce became part of our legal system (page 370), this kind of falsehood was common. Another example is a separation agreement providing that if either party later seeks a divorce, the other party will not appear or will not raise any defenses to the divorce action even if the parties know that such defenses exist. Such an agreement would be invalid because it is *collusive,* improperly inducing divorce.

The rule that separation agreements are invalid if they are conducive to divorce has been criticized as unrealistic since it is difficult to imagine a mutually acceptable separation agreement involving future divorce that does *not* facilitate or encourage the parties to go through with the divorce. Nevertheless, courts continue to watch for improper facilitation and collusion. It may be that the coming of no-fault divorce will lessen a court's inclination to invalidate a separation agreement for these reasons. Since divorce has been made much easier to obtain because of no-fault grounds, courts should be more reluctant to try to save the marriage at all costs and more willing to let the separation agreement be the vehicle through which the parties confront the inevitable. This is not to say that courts will no longer be concerned with collusion and agreements that are conducive to divorce. These prohibitions are still on the books. The atmosphere, however, has changed with no-fault. Most of the court decisions on these prohibitions were decided before the arrival of no-fault. It is questionable how willing a court may be to follow all of those decisions today.

Below there are a series of clauses sometimes found in separation agreements with comments on how the courts have treated the issues of divorce facilitation and collusion raised by the clauses.

> "The wife agrees that she will file for a divorce against the husband within three months."
>
> "None of the terms of this separation agreement shall be effective unless and until either of the parties is granted a divorce."

The first clause is invalid; a party cannot promise to file for a divorce. The clause does not merely encourage divorce, it makes it almost inevitable. The second clause appears to be as bad as or worse than the first. Neither of the parties will obtain any of the benefits in the separation agreement unless one of them obtains a divorce. Arguably, this clause encourages one of the parties to file for divorce and the other party to refrain from contesting the divorce. Oddly, however, the courts have not interpreted the second clause in this way. It *is* legal to condition the entire separation agreement on the granting of a divorce. The logic of this result is not entirely clear, but the courts so hold.

> "The wife agrees that if the husband files for divorce, she will not raise any defenses to his action."
>
> "In the event that the wife travels to another state to file for divorce, the husband agrees to go to that state, appear in the action, and participate therein."

The first clause is collusive. If a party has a defense, it is improper to agree not to assert it. Even if you are not sure whether you have a defense, it is collusive to agree in advance to refrain from asserting whatever defense you *might* have. Courts consider this as improper as an agreement to destroy or to conceal important evidence.

The second clause above is more troublesome. Here the parties are clearly contemplating an out-of-state divorce, perhaps because they both realize that they would have difficulty establishing the grounds for divorce in their own state. Such *migratory divorces* were once quite common. Is a clause conducive to divorce if it obligates the defendant to appear in the foreign divorce action? Some states think that it is and would invalidate the agreement. Other states, however, would uphold the agreement.

Assignment 10.1

Determine whether any of the following clauses improperly facilitate divorce or are collusive. (See General Instructions for the Legal-Analysis Assignment in chapter one.)

(a) "In the event that the wife files a divorce action, the husband agrees not to file any defenses to said action if and only if it is clear to both parties that the husband has no defense."

(b) "In the event that the wife files a divorce action, the husband will pay in advance all expenses incurred by the wife in bringing said action."

(c) "In the event that the wife files for a judicial separation, for separate maintenance, or for an annulment, the husband agrees to cooperate fully in the wife's action."

Assignment 10.2

(a) Locate a digest containing small paragraph summaries of court opinions from your state. (For the kinds of digests that exist, see page 48.) Find those parts of the digest that deal with separation agreements. List any ten key topics and key numbers that cover any aspect of separation agreements.

(b) Are there any statutes in your state code dealing with separation agreements? If so, briefly summarize them. (See General Instructions for the State-Code Assignment in chapter one.)

☑ Capacity to Contract

There was a time in our history when the very thought of a wife entering a contract with her husband was anathema. A married woman lacked the *capacity to contract* with her husband. At common law, the husband and wife were one, and "the one," was the husband! You cannot make a contract with yourself. This rule, of course, has been changed. A wife can enter a contract with her husband (although the Internal Revenue Service and the husband's creditors are often suspicious of such contracts, especially when the result is to place property purchased by the husband in the name of the wife). Linda Jones is no longer denied the right to enter a separation agreement with Fred Jones simply because she is his wife.

Today, the major question of capacity involves mental health. A separation agreement is invalid if either party lacked the capacity to understand the agreement and the consequences of signing it. The traditional test is as follows: The person must understand the nature and consequences of his or her act at the time of the transaction. This understanding may not exist due to insanity, mental retardation, senility, temporary delirium due to an accident, intoxication, drug addiction, etc.

☐ Duress and Fraud

In the excerpt from the Jones separation agreement above (page 229) you will note that several times at the beginning of the agreement the parties mention that they are entering it "voluntarily." According to traditional contract principles, if a party enters a contract because of *duress*, it will not be enforced. Suppose that a wife is physically threatened if she does not sign the separation agreement. Clearly the agreement would not be valid. The husband could not sue her for breaching it or attempt to enforce it in any other way.

Of course, simply because the separation agreement says that the parties enter it "voluntarily" does not necessarily mean that no duress existed: either spouse could have been forced to say the agreement was signed voluntarily. But to have the agreement say that it was "voluntarily" signed is at least *some* indication (however slight) that no duress existed, although an aggrieved party can introduced evidence to the contrary.

During discussions and negotiations, if a husband lies about a major asset that he possesses, the separation agreement can be set aside for fraud. If he fails to disclose all of his assets, many courts will again invalidate the agreement unless its terms are deemed to be fair to the wife.

If the wife later becomes destitute, or near-destitute, some courts will come to her rescue and not let her suffer the consequences of the bad bargain that she made when she signed the agreement, even if there is no clear evidence of duress or fraud. A few courts will go so far as to *presume* that the husband has taken an unfair advantage of his wife until he demonstrates otherwise, e.g., by proving that she had independent advice, by proving that he disclosed everything to her (e.g., prior tax returns, bank statements). In most situations, a husband will not be allowed to treat his wife "at arm's length" as he would a competitor in a commercial transaction. This is not to say, however, that a wife will never have to suffer the consequences of failing to be as shrewd as she could have been in negotiation. Suppose that she is currently living comfortably but that she would be able to live even *more* comfortably if she could renegotiate the separation agreement. Will a court allow her to do so? If she had the benefit of independent advice and is not facing a serious financial crisis, most courts will not force the husband to pay her more than the separation agreement provides. We will return to this theme again later in the chapter when we discuss alimony.

The last WHEREAS clause in the beginning of the Jones separation agreement (page 229) recites that both Fred and Linda had the benefit of separate legal advice on the advantages and disadvantages of signing the agreement. As indicated, this fact can be very significant in a court's deliberation on whether to set the agreement aside on a ground such as duress. The husband is in a much better position if his wife had her own lawyer even though, as we shall see, the husband may have to pay her legal expenses.

The following case of *Bell v. Bell*, contains some of the factors that a court will consider when the validity of a separation agreement is called into question:

Bell v. Bell

Court of Special Appeals of Maryland, 1977.
38 Md.App. 10, 379 A.2d 419.

Diane M. Bell, the appellant, appeals from an order from the Circuit Court for Montgomery County which dismissed her bill of complaint for cancellation of a separation and property settlement agreement between her and her husband, Stanley A. Bell, the appellee, and the cancellation of eleven deeds executed pursuant to that agreement. She raises [this question . . .] on appeal: was the chancellor's decision clearly erroneous when he found that the agreement and deeds were not obtained by duress or undue influence. * * *

The facts that gave rise to this suit are as follows. Diane Bell consulted an attorney in July of 1975, concerning the preparation of a separation agreement. The agreement was prepared and Mrs. Bell presented it to Mr. Bell at home on the morning of August 27, 1975. After examining the agreement at his place of business

Mr. Bell inserted several changes and gave it to his secretary for retyping. Two significant changes were made in the agreement. The original provided for child support in the amount of $700 per month. This figure in the amended agreement was reduced to $300. Mr. Bell's agreement also provided for the disposition of the eleven houses owned by the parties as tenants by the entireties. Under his agreement Mrs. Bell was to receive one of the houses while he retained the other ten. After his agreement was completed he telephoned the appellant and asked her to come to his office in Wheaton to sign the agreement. At that time no mention was made of the changes.

When Mrs. Bell arrived, Mr. Bell suggested that they go to the nearby offices of Ralph Duane Real Estate Co. so that they could discuss the agreement in private. Prior to Mrs. Bell's arrival Mr. Bell had prepared a series of sixteen 3 x 5 cards containing phrases such as "the man," "the kids," "his carrier," "your name," and "Ingrid (accessory)." During the course of the meeting he used these cards to inform the appellant of an investigation of her activities by private detectives and his knowledge of her adulterous affair with a police lieutenant. He also informed her that he knew that many of the contacts occurred at the apartment of her friend, Ingrid Gibson. He then presented his version of the separation agreement and made it clear that unless she signed it he would reveal her relationship to the Internal Affairs section of the police department and to the newspapers. Several times during the course of the conversation Mrs. Bell threatened to leave or requested an opportunity to consult with her attorney, but on each occasion, Mr. Bell threatened to "start the ball rolling" if such attempts were made before the agreement was signed. Mr. Bell placed a tape recorder in the office and recorded the entire conversation without the knowledge of Mrs. Bell. The tape was introduced into evidence.

After Mrs. Bell registered several protests, she read through the agreement and negotiated with Mr. Bell to make several changes. Among these changes was the receipt of a total of $15,000 in cash in addition to the one house. Under the agreement that was signed Mr. Bell received approximately $163,000 worth of property that was previously owned as tenants by the entireties while Mrs. Bell settled for approximately $45,000 in cash and property.*

The appellant argues that a confidential relationship existed between the parties and the burden was on the appellee to show the agreement was fair in all respects. In order to establish a confidential relationship one must show that by virtue of the relationship

between them, he is justified in assuming the other party will not act in a manner inconsistent with his welfare. Unlike many jurisdictions, Maryland does not presume the existence of a confidential relationship in transactions between husband and wife. * * * In Maryland there has been a presumption that the husband is the dominant figure in the marriage. In Manos v. Papachrist, 199 Md. 257, 262, 86 A.2d 474, 476 (1951), the Court noted:

"Ordinarily the relationship of husband and wife is a confidential one. Of course, in any given case it is a question of fact whether the marital relationship is such as to give the husband dominance over his wife or to put him in a position where words of persuasion have undue weight. Generally, however, on account of the natural dominance of the husband over the wife, and the confidence and trust usually incident to their marriage, a court of equity will investigate a gift from a wife to her husband with utmost care, especially where it strips her of all her property; and the burden of proof is on the husband to show that there was no abuse of confidence, but that the gift was fair in all respects, was fully understood, and was not induced by fraud or undue influence."

We noted the questionable foundation upon which this presumption rests in light of Article 46 of the Maryland Declaration of Rights, better known as the Equal Rights Amendment, in Trupp v. Wolff, 24 Md.App. 588, n. 15, 335 A.2d 171 (1975). * * * Since that decision, the Court of Appeals has held that sex classifications are no longer permissible under the amendment. * * * Consequently, the presumption of dominance cannot stand.

When the presumption is disregarded the question of whether a confidential relationship exists between husband and wife becomes a question of fact. Among the various factors to be considered in determining whether a confidential relationship exists are the age, mental condition, education, business experience, state of health, and degree of dependence of the spouse in question. * * *

The testimony shows that Mrs. Bell was born in Europe, moved to this country when she was eleven years old, and left school at the age of fifteen. Although she is employed as a beautician, she has relatively little experience or expertise in business matters. On the other hand, Mr. Bell is an experienced businessman, possesses a real estate license, and has a college degree. The chancellor considered these facts, but found that no confidential relationship existed primarily because Mrs. Bell negotiated several changes in the agreement and questioned other provisions, as is clearly shown by the tape recording. He found there was a lack of trust and confidence in the other party necessary to the establishment of a confidential relationship. We

---

*The property Mr. Bell received had a gross value of $597,000 but was subject to mortgages totalling $434,339.

are unable to say his decision on this issue was clearly erroneous. Md. Rule 1086.

Absent proof of a confidential relationship between the parties, separation agreements, not disclosing any injustice or inequity on their face, are presumptively valid and the burden is on the party challenging the agreement to show its execution resulted from coercion, fraud, or mistake. Cronin v. Hebditch, 195 Md. 607, 74 A.2d 50 (1950). * * *

The only inequity claimed by the appellant is that she relinquished her one half interest in approximately $210,000 worth of real estate for approximately $45,000 in property and cash. This disparity in consideration is not sufficient to show that the agreement was unjust or inequitable. The cases which have found agreements to be unjust or inequitable on their face involved agreements that were completely lacking in any reasonable consideration. Cronin v. Hebditch, supra; Eaton v. Eaton, 34 Md.App. 157, 366 A.2d 121 (1976). In Cronin the wife signed an agreement releasing all her rights in property totalling more than $700,000 for a mere $10,000 and the Court of Appeals voided the agreement. More recently, in Eaton we struck down an agreement in which rights in $200,000 to $250,000 worth of property were released for $4,300. There we said:

> " '[The] defendant in this case has ostensibly purchased far more cheaply than a Court of Equity can condone all of the plaintiff's rights "of whatsoever kind or nature originating in and growing out of the marriage status." ' " 34 Md.App. at 162, 366 A.2d at 124.

As we are unable to say the agreement in question was lacking in any reasonable consideration, Cronin and Eaton cannot be used to relieve the appellant from proving the agreement was the product of duress or undue influence.*

---

*We are aware that some cases in other jurisdictions have created a presumption of invalidity where the consideration given is grossly disproportionate to the consideration received or is otherwise unfair. See Le Bert-Francis v. Le Bert-Francis, 194 A.2d 662 (D.C.1963) (where separation agreement is unfair it is presumed to be invalid and the burden is on the party seeking to enforce it to prove otherwise); Demaggio v. Demaggio, 317 So.2d 848 (Fla.App.1975) (presumption of fraud created where agreement was grossly disproportionate, husband concealed assets, and wife was unrepresented by counsel); Davis v. Davis, 24 Ohio Misc. 17, 258 N.E.2d 277 (1970) (where provisions are disproportionate burden is on party seeking to uphold agreement to show there was full disclosure and the agreement was signed voluntarily).

In the absence of a confidential relationship, we see no reason to shift the burden of proof because the parties were husband and wife and one of them made a bargain which now seems unfair, but is not grossly unfair.

The appellant's claim of duress or undue influence rests on the threats of Stanley Bell to notify the Internal Affairs section of the Police Department and the newspapers of her adulterous relationship unless the agreement was signed. Mr. Bell also stated that such disclosures would ruin the career of her lover and Ingrid Gibson, as well as her reputation in the community. The chancellor construed these statements as being no more than a threat to institute a divorce action on the grounds of adultery.

In order to establish duress there must be a wrongful act which deprives a person of the exercise of his free will. * * * Although we have found no Maryland case discussing the issue whether a threat to institute a civil suit can furnish a legally sufficient basis for duress, the question has been considered by a number of courts in other jurisdictions. Under these cases such suits do not form a legally sufficient basis for duress where the threat to institute the suit is made in good faith. * * * The courts have stated the assertion of a claim with the knowledge there is no reasonable belief of success or that it is false, amounts to bad faith and is a sufficient basis for a claim of duress. * * * Even though a particular act is legal, if it is wrongful in the moral sense a number of authorities have held that it can be used to establish a claim of duress. * * * Link v. Link, 278 N.C. 181, 179 S.E.2d 697 (1971). * * *

The appellant argues that a threatened civil suit can be wrongful in a moral sense where it is used to coerce a settlement in a transaction unrelated to the subject matter of the suit. In support of this argument she relies on Link v. Link, supra. In Link the husband threatened to institute divorce proceedings against the wife and seek custody of their children unless the wife signed an agreement transferring her individual property to the husband. In deciding the case the Court noted the general rule that threats to institute civil proceedings are not wrongful but went on to state:

> "The law with reference to duress has, however, undergone an evolution favorable to the victim of oppressive action or threats. The weight of modern authority supports the rule, which we here adopt, that the act done or threatened may be wrongful even though not unlawful, per se; and that the threat to institute legal proceedings, criminal or civil, which might be justifiable, per se, becomes wrongful, within the meaning of this rule, if made with the corrupt intent to coerce a transaction grossly unfair to the victim and not related to the subject of such proceedings." 179 S.E.2d at 705.

* * *

We find the reasoning of Link to be persuasive. Applying this approach to the case before us we think there was a legally sufficient basis for a finding of duress.

Mr. Bell threatened an action for divorce on the grounds of adultery to force a property settlement between the parties. Although the threatened action and the separation agreement both relate to the marital status of the parties, their substance is significantly different. A court in an action for divorce does not have jurisdiction to settle the property rights of the parties to real estate. Md.Code, Courts and Judicial Proceedings Article § 3–603. * * * Mr. Bell's threats of a civil suit for divorce were unrelated to the dispute over the property and were made to obtain Mrs. Bell's signature on an agreement.

Even though the chancellor concluded that there was no wrongful conduct he went on to note in his opinion that even if the actions were considered wrongful, they did not deprive Mrs. Bell of her free will. * * * In support of this finding he noted that Mrs. Bell actively negotiated with Mr. Bell concerning various provisions in the agreement. At one point in the conversation she stated:

"Umn, I'm just trying to get you know as much as I can which is, you have to admit, you'd do the same thing."

Although there was testimony that Mrs. Bell was extremely upset after the agreement was signed, there was other testimony to the contrary. The chancellor considered this evidence and concluded:

"[T]he negotiations and the tenor of the parties' meeting indicate quite clearly that the Plaintiff, in order to avoid an embarrassing incident involving her and close friends, freely and voluntarily negotiated with her husband."

The question of whether Mrs. Bell was deprived of her free will was one of fact and as there is ample evidence to support this finding, we are unable to say it was clearly erroneous. * * * In other words, there is no rule of law that precludes a woman from giving away a substantial portion of her property to save her reputation, if it is her voluntary act. Although on the evidence we may have found the act involuntary, we must accept the chancellor's findings because of his superior position to make this subtle distinction.
* * *

As we have indicated, the chancellor found on the merits that the appellant did not act under duress or undue influence. We have accepted his finding because there was evidence to support it. * * *

DECREE AFFIRMED.
APPELLANT TO PAY THE COSTS.

Assignment 10.3

(a) Assume that the facts of *Bell v. Bell* arose in your state. How would the case be decided? (If your state is *Maryland,* answer this question based on the law of any other state. See General Instructions for the Court-Opinion Assignment in chapter one.)

(b) Does a separation agreement have to be fair to both parties to be enforceable in your state? Check the statutes and the court opinions of your state. (See General Instructions for the State-Code Assignment in chapter one, and General Instructions for the Court-Opinion Assignment in chapter one.)

Consideration

All contracts must be supported by consideration in order to be valid. *Consideration* is something of value that is exchanged. The separation agreement is a set of promises by the parties of what they will do. The exchange of these promises (some of which may have already been performed, at least in part, at the time the agreement is signed) is the consideration for the separation agreement. A wife's promise to relinquish all claims that she may have against her husband's estate when he dies is an example of her consideration to him. A husband's promise to transfer to his wife full title to land that he solely owns is an example of his consideration to her.

We have already seen, however, that certain kinds of consideration are improper. A couple, for example, cannot exchange promises that one party will file for divorce and the other party will refrain from asserting any defenses he or she might have. Such consideration is illegal because it is conducive to

divorce, and may be collusive. Also, a few states may not allow a wife to promise in the separation agreement to release the husband from all support claims she may have against him. In most states, however, such a promise is valid consideration so long as the agreement is otherwise fair to the wife.

Perhaps the main consideration in the separation agreement involves the separation itself. A husband and wife have the right to live with each other, as husband and wife, i.e., the right of cohabitation. By reason of the separation agreement, the parties promise each other that they will never again claim this cohabitation right.

Section F. Alimony Payments and Property Division: Introduction

Alimony

The amount of money or other property paid in fulfillment of a duty to support one's spouse after a separation or divorce. (Sometimes referred to as *maintenance*.)

Property division

The distribution of property accumulated by the parties as a result of their joint efforts during the marriage. (Sometimes referred to as a property *settlement*.)

While the above definitions are generally accepted as accurate, there is often an unfortunate amount of confusion concerning alimony and property division. A separation agreement (or a court opinion) may refer to a property division but mean *both* support and property division. In part, the confusion may be due to the fact that in the minds of the husband and wife, there is not always a clear distinction between these two concepts.

Listed below are some major consequences of the distinction between alimony and property division. These consequences must be understood before examining the options available to the parties in drafting those clauses of the separation agreement that cover alimony and property division.

☐ **Effect of Bankruptcy**
☐ **Effect of Remarriage and Death**
☐ **Availability of Contempt**
☐ **The Court's Power to Modify Terms**
☐ **Federal Income Tax Treatment**

Alimony and Property Division Terms of a Separation Agreement

Effect of Bankruptcy

Alimony	Property Division
If the husband goes into bankruptcy, his obligation to pay alimony is not discharged. All unpaid or delinquent alimony is still owed. (Same for wife if she has the alimony obligation to her husband.)	If either party goes into bankruptcy, the remaining property division obligations are discharged.

Effect of Remarriage and Death

Alimony	Property Division
If the person receiving alimony obtains a divorce and remarries, the alimony payments stop unless the separation agreement specifically provides otherwise. If the person paying alimony remarries, the alimony payments to first spouse must continue unless a court provides otherwise. If the husband or wife dies, alimony payments cease unless the separation agreement specifically provides otherwise.	Remarriage or death of either party does not affect the terms of the property division. All remaining obligations under the property division must be fulfilled regardless of remarriage or death.

Availability of Contempt

Alimony	Property Division
If a party fails to fulfill an alimony obligation and falls into arrears, the contempt power of the court can be used as an enforcement device if the separation agreement has been incorporated and merged into a later divorce decree.	If either party fails to fulfill the obligations under the property division, the contempt power of the court usually cannot be used as an enforcement device.

The Court's Power to Modify Terms

Alimony	Property Division
If the alimony terms of the separation agreement later prove to be seriously inadequate, the court often has the power to modify those terms in order to require more alimony to be paid.	If either party later becomes dissatisfied with the terms of an otherwise valid property division, the court will rarely, if ever, modify those terms.

Federal Income Tax Treatment

Alimony	Property Division
When tax regulations are followed, alimony payments are includible in the gross income of the wife and are deductible for the husband. (Vice versa if the wife is paying alimony.)	Transfers of property incident to a divorce are not reportable as income by the transferee nor deductible by the transferor. The basis of the property in the hands of the transferee is the same as the transferor's basis.

☐ **Effect of Bankruptcy**

Bankruptcy is a system that allows a person to eliminate all or most of his or her debts in order to make a fresh start. If a husband has fallen behind on his obligation under a separation agreement and/or a divorce decree, all arrears constitute a debt to his wife. Each time an alimony payment becomes due, a new debt is created. Also, all outstanding (i.e., unpaid) obligations

under a property division agreement are debts. To have a debt *discharged* in bankruptcy means that the debt does not have to be paid; it is eliminated. As indicated, however, not all debts are discharged in bankruptcy. The Bankruptcy Act of Congress provides as follows:

> A discharge . . . does not discharge an individual debtor from any debt . . . to a spouse, former spouse, or child of the debtor, for alimony to, maintenance for, or support of such spouse or child, in connection with a separation agreement, divorce decree or other order of a court of record. . . . 11 U.S.C.A. § 523(a)(5).

On the other hand, debts stemming from a property division *are* dischargeable.

There are a number of practical consequences of this. If there is the slightest suspicion that the husband is in serious financial difficulties and that bankruptcy is a possibility (a fact that must be carefully investigated by the lawyer and paralegal representing the wife), then the wife may be advised in the negotiation stage of the separation agreement to accept a small property division in exchange for a high amount of alimony. In the event that a bankruptcy does occur, she could lose everything still owed her under the property division, whereas the alimony debt survives the bankruptcy.

□ Effect of Remarriage and Death

Normally a spouse will want to stop paying alimony in the event that the receiving spouse remarries. But if alimony ends upon the receiving spouse's remarriage, it can be argued that this operates as an incentive *not* to remarry. To offset this, at least to some extent, the separation agreement might provide that the alimony payments will continue after the remarriage of the receiving spouse, but at a much lower rate.

If the paying spouse remarries, his or her alimony obligation continues unless modified by a court.

If either party dies, alimony payments cease, unless the separation agreement specifically provides otherwise. It is possible, for example, that the separation agreement could provide that the alimony payments continue after the death of the husband, in which event the wife would collect the alimony from his estate or from a trust fund set up by him. Furthermore, the husband might take out a life insurance policy payable on his death to his wife. This, in effect, continues some measure of support for the wife after he dies. Absent such provisions, the death of the paying spouse terminates the alimony obligation in most states.

The situation is entirely different with respect to property division commitments; they continue no matter who dies or remarries. As part of a property division (having nothing to do with support), John agrees to pay Mary $25,000. After John has paid Mary $1,000 of this amount, he dies. Mary can make a claim against John's estate for $24,000. If Mary died after John paid the $1,000, her estate could require John to pay the remaining $24,000 to it (i.e., Mary's estate) for distribution according to Mary's will or according to the laws of intestacy. The same is true if either party remarries. The funds or other property due and owing under the property division clauses of the separation agreement remain due and owing no matter who remarries.

□ Availability of Contempt

When one of the parties breaches a term of the separation agreement, ensuing legal action may depend upon whether the agreement is incorporated and merged into a subsequent divorce decree. If it is not, the regular breach-of-contract remedies are available, e.g., suit for damages, suit to rescind the contract. The *contempt* sanction (e.g., fine, prison) is *not* available. To some extent, the picture changes if the divorce decree incorporates and merges with the separation agreement. Alimony provisions *can* be enforced by the contempt powers of the court when there is *incorporation and merger*. The property-division terms of the agreement, however, cannot be enforced by contempt even if incorporation and merger has occurred—with the possible exception of a term that requires a party to transfer (convey) property. If the party does not transfer the property, he or she can be held in contempt of court for noncompliance.

In summary, when the separation agreement is incorporated and merged into the divorce decree, alimony terms are enforceable by contempt, but property terms are not (except in connection with a property transfer order).

□ Court's Power to Modify Terms

A court will modify an alimony term only if the consequences of not doing so would be that the wife would become a public charge or would otherwise face serious financial difficulties due to a change of circumstances since the time she signed the separation agreement containing the original alimony term. A property-division term, on the other hand, is rarely, if ever, modifiable by a court.

□ Federal Income Tax Treatment

The federal tax implications of alimony and property division in a separation agreement will be treated in detail in Chapter 15, page 428.

Distinguishing between Alimony and Property Division

As you can see, it can make a great deal of difference whether a term of a separation agreement is classified as alimony or as property division. The classification hinges on the intent of the parties at the time they entered the separation agreement. For example, did the parties intend a five-year annual payment of $50,000 to be alimony or property division? Unfortunately, it is often difficult to answer this question. As indicated earlier, the parties may either be confused about the distinction or pay no attention to it. At a later date, however, when the parties realize the importance of the distinction (e.g., at tax time or when bankruptcy occurs), they will probably make conflicting claims about what their intentions were. It is the court's job to turn the clock back to when they were negotiating the separation agreement and determine what their intent was at that time. In making this determination, the court will consider a number of factors:

- Labels used in the agreement
- Contingencies
- Method of payment
- The nature of what is transferred

Usually none of these factors is conclusive by itself. All of them must be considered. One factor, for example, may clearly indicate an intent that a term is alimony. If, however, the other factors clearly suggest that the term is part of the property division, the court may conclude that it is the latter. Unhappily, the factors often point in opposite directions.

Labels Used in the Agreement

Sometimes the separation agreement will explicitly label a provision as "alimony" or as a "property settlement" or "property division." These labels, however, do not always control. For example, suppose that an annual payment of $10,000 given to the wife is labeled "Property Division." If it is otherwise clear to the court that this money was in the nature of support, the court will classify it as alimony in spite of the label.

Contingencies

Terms that are *contingent* on the occurrences of certain events are often interpreted as alimony rather than as a property division, e.g., $10,000 a year to the wife until she remarries or dies. The presence of such contingencies suggests an intent to provide support while needed rather than an intent to divide property.

Method of Payment

A term may provide a single *lump-sum payment* (e.g., $10,000), *periodic payment* (e.g., $10,000 a year), or a *fluctuating payment* (e.g., $10,000 a year to be increased or decreased depending upon the earnings in a particular year). Single lump sum payments often suggest a property division. Periodic and fluctuating payments often suggest alimony.

The Nature of What is Transferred

A conveyance of property other than cash (e.g., a house, a one-half interest in a business) often suggests a property division. Cash alone, however, usually suggests alimony.

Again, these are only guides. All of the circumstances must be examined in order to determine the intent of the parties. It may be that a court will conclude that a transfer of a house was intended as alimony or support. The court might also conclude that a single lump-sum payment was intended as alimony. While a court will be inclined to rule otherwise in these examples, specific proof that alimony was intended will control.

Section G. Alimony

We will now examine individual clauses in the separation agreement, starting with alimony. Keep in mind, however, that no individual clause of a separation agreement can be fully understood in isolation. As pointed out earlier, the negotiation process involves a large variety of factors. A party may agree to a term in the agreement not so much because that term in and of itself gives the party what he or she wants, but rather because the party decided to concede that term in order to gain another term, e.g., a wife may accept a lower alimony provision in exchange for the husband's agreement to the term giving her custody of their child. This is the nature of the bargaining process.

Alimony, as we have seen, is the amount of money or other property paid in fulfillment of a duty to support one's spouse after a separation or divorce. Later, in the chapter on taxation, we will discover that the Internal Revenue Service uses a much broader definition of alimony to determine when it is deductible page 433. Traditionally, it was the husband's duty to support the wife. Today, however, the duty is mutual in the sense that it will be imposed on the party who has the resources. To impose the duty only on a man would amount to unconstitutional sex discrimination in violation of the Equal Protection Clause of the U.S. Constitution. In the vast majority of situations, however, it is the woman who is the recipient of support through a separation agreement and/or through a court order.

First we will examine some of the major negotiating options that must be considered in drafting the support provisions of the separation agreement. Then we turn to how a court will handle spousal support if the parties have not been able to negotiate an agreement.

Support Provisions in a Separation Agreement

Periodic Payments or Lump-Sum?

In a few states, it is illegal for a husband and wife to agree on a lump-sum payment in satisfaction of the support duty. In most states, however, it is permissible. From the perspective of recipient, collectibility is an important factor in deciding whether to seek a single lump-sum alimony payment. The wife may find it safer to take the single lump-sum payment now rather than have to hassle with installment or periodic payments if there is any likelihood that the husband will fall behind in his payments. It can be expensive and psychologically draining to have to go after a delinquent husband.

Fixed or Fluctuating Periodic Payments?

If periodic payments are decided upon, a number of questions need to be considered and resolved. Should the payments have a fixed dollar amount, e.g., $300 per month or per week? On what day of the month or week is each payment due? Another major option is the flexible periodic payment. The amount of the payment may fluctuate up or down depending upon the income of the husband, of the wife, or of both. An alimony payment of 25 percent of the husband's earnings, for example, provides an automatic fluctuating standard.

Medical and Dental Expenses

Does the alimony payment cover medical, dental, or mental health expenses (e.g., psychiatrist)? If not, do the parties want to include a term in the separation agreement on how these expenses are to be covered? They must also consider the tax consequences of paying these expenses.

Life Insurance

Even though the husband's duty to support his wife usually ends at his death or the death of his wife, the parties might agree that the support payments will continue after he dies. (If the wife is the one with the duty to provide support, then the question is whether the parties want to continue payment after she dies.) If so, one way to do this is through a life insurance policy on the life of the party with the support duty. The beneficiary would be the other spouse and/or the children. If a life insurance policy already exists, the parties may decide to include a term in the separation agreement that requires a spouse to continue paying the premiums, to increase the amount of the policy, to name the other spouse as the irrevocable beneficiary, etc. The agreement should also specify whether an existing policy remains in force if either side remarries. If no life insurance policy exists, the parties need to decide whether to take one out.

Relationship to Child Support

A husband may urge his wife to agree to a lower child-support payment in exchange for a higher alimony payment. He cannot deduct child-support payments, but he can deduct alimony. One reason the wife may resist this is that alimony payments are taxable to her, whereas child-support payments are not.

Modification

The separation agreement may contain a clause that the terms of the agreement shall not be modified unless both parties agree in writing to do so. Will a court honor such a clause? The answer is no where children are involved. As we shall see later, judges will change custody and child-support clauses when they feel the best interest of the children warrants it. This is so whether or not the separation agreement is later incorporated and merged into the divorce decree.

What about the alimony term of the separation agreement? Will a court modify this term if the separation agreement has been incorporated and merged into the divorce decree even though the agreement has a no-modification clause? States differ on their answer to this question. Some state courts *will* modify the alimony term if a change of circumstances since the divorce decree justifies it, e.g., the woman is about to become destitute. We will return to the subject of modification in Section N of this chapter (page 267).

Termination of Support Payments

The circumstances that will terminate the support obligation should be explicitly spelled out in the separation agreement. To be silent on these circumstances would be unwise. The separation agreement may provide that the support or alimony payments to the wife will end when:

- The wife dies.
- The husband dies. (In some states, however, it is possible to force a husband's estate to continue supporting his wife even after he dies.)
- The wife remarries. (If the second marriage is later annulled, states differ on whether the original support obligations of the first husband revive, page 200.)
- The wife commits adultery. (Many courts will honor a separation agreement term providing that the wife's support payments end if she commits adultery.)

- The wife fails to abide by the custody terms of the separation agreement. (This is usually upheld.)

- The wife competes with her husband in business. (Such a term will *not* be enforced since a wife's support payments cannot be conditioned on something that is not reasonably related to the marriage relationship.)

Of course, the separation agreement can provide the opposite. It may state, for example, that the wife's support payments will *continue* when:

- The husband dies. (The husband's estate would then have the obligation to continue the support payments. Life insurance is often used as a method of continuing support payments after the husband's death.)

- The wife remarries. (Rather than continue the support payments in full after the wife remarries, the separation agreement usually provides for a reduced support payment in the event that the wife remarries. As indicated earlier, some husbands fear that if the total support payment ends upon remarriage, the wife will have little incentive to remarry. It should be pointed out, however, that there are a few states that forbid support payments to continue after the wife remarries.)

The termination of alimony payments does not affect *arrears,* i.e., unpaid back payments. All delinquent payments that accrued before the support obligation terminated must be paid. If they terminated upon the death of the husband, for example, all payments he failed to make before he died can be enforced against his estate.

Security

When a husband fails to make a support payment, the wife can sue him, but this is hardly an adequate remedy. Litigation can be expensive, lengthy, and emotionally draining. Preferable would be a term in the separation agreement that provides *security* to the wife for the performance of the husband's support obligation. This security can be provided in a number of forms:

1. *Escrow.* The husband deposits a sum of money with an escrow agent, e.g., a bank, with instructions to pay the wife a designated amount of money in the event that the husband falls behind in a payment.

2. *Surety bond.* The husband gives his wife a surety bond. The husband pays premiums to the surety company. The surety company guarantees the wife that if the husband fails to fulfill his support obligation, the company will fulfill it up to the amount of the bond.

3. *Annuity.* The husband purchases an annuity contract that provides a fixed income to the wife (annuitant) in the amount of the support obligation.

4. *Trust.* The husband transfers property (e.g., cash) to a trustee (e.g., a bank) with instructions to pay a fixed income to the wife (the beneficiary) in the amount of the support obligation.

The last two forms of security do not depend upon a breach by the husband of his support obligation under the separation agreement in order to come into effect.

Court-ordered Alimony in the Absence of a Separation Agreement

How will a court decide the question of support if the parties have not been able to reach agreement on the matter? The major factors considered by the court are outlined in the following chart. The chart assumes that the wife is the party seeking alimony, although the husband can be a potential recipient if he is the one with the need and she has the resources. Once a court decides to grant alimony, it will consider many of the same options discussed above, e.g., whether the amount should fluctuate, whether security should be provided.

Factors a Court Will Consider in the Alimony Decision

1. The Needs of the Wife
- The traditional general guideline is that alimony should enable the wife to maintain substantially the same standard of living she enjoyed during the marriage.
- Her needs may vary according to her age and health.
- Most courts will provide a lower alimony award, or none at all, if she has independent income and property sufficient for her needs. They will consider any resources she has, e.g., retirement benefits accumulated on her own, the expectation of inheritances. Also relevant is whether she was responsible for bringing assets into the marriage.
- Most courts consider her current employability. The presence of young children, of course, substantially limits the employment prospects of many women.
- Many states authorize a court to grant *rehabilitative alimony* which is alimony for a *limited* period until the wife can "get back on her feet" to become self-sufficient. In other states, however, the alimony award is granted for an indefinite period until modified by court order.

2. The Length of the Marriage
- Courts are very reluctant to grant significant alimony for a marriage of a short duration, e.g., under two years.

3. The Ability of the Husband to Pay
- The age and heatlh of the husband.
- His standard of living.
- His present and anticipated debts and other financial obligations.
- The voluntariness of his financial condition. A husband, for example, cannot voluntarily enter a state of poverty by quitting a high-paying job in order to avoid alimony. The focus is not simply on his present resources. The court will want to know what the husband is reasonably *capable* of earning.

4. Marital Fault
- In most states, marital fault of the wife will *not* disqualify her from receiving alimony, although it may be taken into consideration in determining the amount of the alimony award.
- In some states, however, only if the wife was granted the divorce based on her husband's fault will she be entitled to alimony. If the husband was granted the divorce and she was found at fault, she would not receive any alimony in such states.
- In a few states, if the husband is found at fault, his alimony obligation may be increased.

5. Other Factors

- Some courts say that a factor in the award of alimony is the contribution (financial or otherwise) of the wife in helping the husband generate assets during the marriage. This factor, however, is more relevant to property division. Yet, as indicated, there are courts that tend to blur the distinction between alimony and property division.
- The court's decision on property division is sometimes a factor in awarding alimony. A court may be inclined to give a lower alimony award to a wife if it feels that she has been given "a good deal" in the property division. Some courts take the position that the adequacy of a support award can be determined only after the marital assets have been divided—again supporting the view that no single item in a separation agreement or court decree should be examined in isolation.

Assignment 10.4

Answer the following questions after examining your state code. (See General Instructions for the State-Code Assignment in chapter one.)

(a) What standards will a court use in awarding alimony, e.g., is marital fault relevant?

(b) When can alimony be awarded to a man?

(c) Are there any limitations on the form that alimony can take, e.g., periodic payments, lump-sum, etc.?

(d) When alimony is awarded, is it always for an indefinite period?

(e) If the court denies the divorce to both parties, can alimony still be awarded?

Assignment 10.5

Find an opinion decided within the last ten years by a court in your state that awarded alimony. List all the considerations that the court used in making its alimony decision. Try to find an opinion in which the court mentioned a specific dollar amount as alimony. If you cannot find such an opinion written by a court sitting in your state, select a neighboring state. (See General Instructions for the Court-Opinion Assignment in chapter one.)

Section H. Property Division: General Principles

Categorizing Property

A property division should be based on a fair allocation of the property accumulated by the spouses during the marriage due to their joint efforts. Whether the property division is agreed to by the parties or imposed by a court in the absence of agreement, the following preliminary questions must be examined:

1. What kind of property do the parties have? Real or personal?
2. With what resources was the property acquired?
3. How is the property held, i.e., who has title?

Real vs. Personal

There are two kinds of property: *real property* and *personal property*. Real property is land and those things attached or affixed to the land. Real property may consist of a main home, a vacation home, land and/or buildings used in a business, a condominium, etc. Personal property consists of movable items, e.g., cars, boats, cash, stocks, bonds, royalties, furniture, jewelry, art objects, books, records, clothes, photographic equipment, sports equipment, pets, business supplies (inventory), credits, accounts receivable, exclusive options to buy, insurance policies.

Later we will examine three categories of assets that have generated considerable controversy in recent years: future pensions, professional degrees, and the goodwill of a business or profession (page 252).

Note on Embryos as "Property"

Assume that a woman is unable to conceive because damaged tubes prevent her eggs from reaching the womb. The eggs can be removed surgically, fertilized with her husband's sperm in the laboratory *(in vitro fertilization),* and reimplanted in the uterus at a later time during a normal ovulation cycle, hopefully to mature to a healthy fetus. Billig, *High Tech Earth Mothering,* 9 DISTRICT LAWYER 57 (July/August 1985). The procedure is known as an embryo transplant. In Chapter 20 we will examine the question of what happens when the implantation is made in a "rented womb" of a surrogate mother (page 524). Here our concern is the woman from whom the eggs were removed.

What happens if she and her husband separate and file for divorce *before* the reimplantation occurs in her? An embryo can be frozen between fertilization and implantation. What is the status of the *frozen embryo?* Who "owns" it? Is the embryo "property" to be divided upon divorce? Does the court have to decide its "custody?" Should the embryo be treated as potential life? When does life begin? Is the embryo a potential child?

The problem arises when the parties disagree about what should be done with the embryo. Suppose that husband wants it destroyed because he does not want to become the father of a child with his soon-to-be ex-wife, but she wants the embryo kept alive so that a reimplantation can be attempted in her at a later time. Can he be forced to be a father against his will? Is this question any different from whether a man can force the woman he impregnants to have an abortion because he does not want to become a father? The courts have answered the latter question in the negative; he cannot force the woman to have an abortion. Is this any different from whether he can force a doctor to destroy a frozen embryo?

Clear answers to such questions do not exist. What is clear is that medical technology is moving much faster than the development of law and ethics in our society. The experts are at loggerheads:

> "We're talking about four-celled embryos—they haven't developed into organs or anything. They are too rudimentary; . . . therefore, they can't really be harmed, and there should be no requirement that unwanted embryos be saved."

> "Obviously, embryos are not property. These entities should not be defined as being property in terms of being able to be bought and sold. They are potential beings and declaring the embryos as property comes up to the threshold of crossing the barrier of assaulting the value of a potential person." Curriden, *Frozen Embryos,* American Bar Association Journal 69–70 (August 1980).

Thousands of embryos are currently in frozen storage in laboratories across the United States. The few trial court decisions that exist seem to favor the woman's right to keep the embryos alive for later implantation, but until appellate courts and legislatures address the problem, this is an area of uncertainty that many call the new frontier.

Assignment 10.6

What is the status of a frozen embryo in your state? (See General Instructions for the State-Code Assignment in chapter one, and for the Court-Opinion Assignment in chapter one).

Resources Used to Acquire Property

There are a variety of ways that real and personal property could have been obtained:

- As a gift to one of the spouses
- As a gift to both of the spouses
- As a *bequest* (personal property given by will) to one or both spouses
- As a *devise* (real property given by will) to one or both spouses
- Through intestate succession (an inheritance given to an heir of a person who died without leaving a valid will)
- Through funds from the salary of one of the spouses
- Through funds from the salaries of both of the spouses

Etc.

Timing is important. When did the party or parties receive the property? Was it brought into the marriage or was it acquired during the marriage? If the property was separately owned before the marriage, was its value increased due to mutual efforts during the marriage?

Way in Which Property Is Held (Who has title?)

There are a number of ways that property can be held:

1. *Legal title in name of one spouse only.* The title to the property is in the name of only one of the parties. This could be due to the fact that the property was purchased with the funds of that one spouse. Or, it may be that the property was purchased with the funds of one spouse but placed in the name of the other spouse (perhaps in the hope of insulating the property from the claims of the creditors of the spouse who purchased the property). Finally, title may be in the name of one spouse even though both contributed funds for its purchase.

2. *Joint tenancy.* The entire property is equally owned by two or more individuals. Each joint tenant has an equal right to possess the entire property. They do not each own a piece of the property; each joint tenant owns it all. When one joint tenant dies, his or her interest passes to the surviving joint tenants (by the right of survivorship).

3. *Tenancy by the entireties.* In most states, a joint tenancy held by a husband and wife is called a tenancy by the entireties. Each spouse has a right of survivorship as with any joint tenancy.

4. *Tenancy in common.* All parties have a right to possession of the property, but their share in the property may not be equal. There is no right of survivorship. When one tenant in common dies, the property does not automatically pass to the surviving tenants in common. The property goes to whomever the deceased designated by will, or to the heirs of the deceased by intestate succession if the deceased died without leaving a valid will. Hence, a major distinction between (1) a joint tenancy and a tenancy by the entireties and (2) a tenancy in common is that the property of a deceased tenant passes through the estate of that tenant only in the case of a tenancy in common. In the other tenancies, the property passes immediately to the surviving tenant(s) by operation of law.

5. *Community property.* This information on community property is taken from Clark, *The Law of Domestic Relations in the United States,* 512–515 (2d ed., Practitioner's edition 1987):

> Eight states have adopted community property as a means of providing equitably for the property interests of married persons.[1] [Most of the other states in the country are generally classified as *common-law property* states.] The principle underlying community property is that the efforts of both spouses are instrumental in contributing to the welfare of the family, and that therefore property acquired by either spouse during the marriage, with certain exceptions, should belong to both spouses. Community property was originally a Spanish institution and was enacted first in those states whose law was influenced by Spanish law, spreading later to other states. It has also had an influence on common law property states which did not directly adopt it but which for divorce purposes have classified the property of the spouses as either separate or marital property and have authorized the marital property to be divided on divorce.
>
> Although a full account of the law of community property cannot be included in this work, especially since there are many variations among the eight states which have adopted it, a word or two concerning its main outlines is essential. It arises when the spouses are married[2] and includes property acquired by either spouse during the marriage, except property acquired by gift, devise or inheritance.[3] Property which does not fall within the definition of community property is characterized as separate property of the spouse who has acquired it. The difficulty of

---

[1] These are Arizona, California, Idaho, Louisiana, Nevada, New Mexico, Texas and Washington. 4A R. Powell, Real Property § 625[2] (Rev.ed.1982). At one time Wisconsin was considering the adoption of a community property system.

[2] 4A R. Powell, Real Property § 625.1 (Rev.ed.Rohan 1982). In states such as Texas and Idaho which recognize common law marriage, such a marriage may be a sufficient basis for acquiring community property.

[3] Id. at § 625.2[1]. The Uniform Marital Property Act § 4, 9A Unif.L.Ann. 29 (Supp.1985) defines marital property in substantially the same way. Under that Act the parties may by agreement vary the manner in which property is held. Uniform Marital Property Act § 3, 9A Unif.L.Ann. 28 (Supp.1985) Community property states permit this also.

applying this ostensibly simple definition to the many forms in which
property is acquired has led to the development of a rebuttable presumption that property acquired by either spouse during the marriage,
whether title is taken in the name of either spouse or of both, is community property.[4] The presumption may be rebutted if it can be proved
that the funds with which the property was acquired were the separate
funds of one of the spouses.

In most community property states the parties may by agreement
vary the usual rules. They may agree that all property acquired by either
of them is separate property, or that it is all community property, or
they may agree on the characterization of particular items of property.

Some examples indicate the difficulties of determining whether particular property is community or separate property. Thus veterans' education benefits have been held to be separate property when they were
earned before marriage, but paid after marriage, even though the statute
provided for increased benefits for dependents, including spouses. There
is a conflict in the decisions concerning damages for personal injury. The
Texas authorities classify such damages as separate property, but they
hold that the medical expenses and loss of earnings recovered in such a
suit are community property. Other courts hold that the entire recovery
is community property. Where property is purchased before marriage
but paid for in part after marriage out of community funds, its classification as community or separate varies among the community property
states. Some would characterize it as separate property, some as separate
or community depending upon when title vested, and some would apply
complex calculations to establish the proportion of separate to community funds going into the purchase.

The diversity in characterization of property as community or separate, and the differences between the community property states and
the common law states, have created difficult questions of the conflict
of laws. An early case, *Saul v. His Creditors,*[5] established the rule that
when the marriage occurred in a common law state, where the parties
were then domiciled, but they later became domiciled in the community
property state, property acquired after the change in domicile had the
status of community property. California has carried this a step further
by enacting a statute creating the institution of "quasi-community property." This is defined as real or personal property, wherever situated,
which was acquired by either spouse while domiciled outside California,
and which would have been community property if the spouse who
acquired it had been domiciled in California at the time of acquisition.
Quasi-community property is divisible on divorce in the same fashion
as community property.

The right to manage and control community property is a subject
for differing statutory provisions among the various community property
states. Traditionally the husband alone had this power. The United States

[4]There may be other presumptions, such as the statutory presumption in California
that where a single family residence is acquired by husband and wife as joint tenants,
it is community property.
[5] Mart. (N.S.) 569, 16 Am.Dec. 212 (La.1827).

Supreme Court, in *Kirchberg v. Feenstra,*[6] was presented with an Equal Protection Clause challenge to the former Louisiana statute which made the husband the "head and master" of the community and gave him the power to convey community property without the wife's consent. The Court held that such gender-based classifications cannot stand in the absence of proof that they further some important governmental interest. Finding no such interest in this case, the Court held that the statute violated the [Equal Protection Clause of the] Fourteenth Amendment. Within the constitutional limit so laid down, the states have provided for management and control by each spouse, have required the consent of both spouses for certain transfers of community property, and have authorized joint management of at least some forms of community property. The obvious analogy here is to the law of partnership, since the spouses owe each other fiduciary duties of good faith and fair treatment in dealing with community property, as do partners with respect to partnership property.

What Property is Divided and Who Gets What?

The general rule in community-property states and in common-law property states is that property acquired by a party *before the marriage* is deemed to be the separate property of that party and therefore not divisible upon divorce. The same is usually true of property obtained solely by one spouse through gift, devise (by a will), or inheritance during the marriage, e.g., from a relative of that spouse. During the marriage, however, such property will undoubtedly increase in value. This *appreciation* may be deemed to be divisible property regardless of the manner in which the property was acquired or when it was acquired.

All other property obtained during the marriage is potentially divisible upon divorce, depending upon the special laws of individual states.

After identifying which property is divisible, the next question is how the division is made. In community property states like California, the division is usually 50/50 unless the parties agree otherwise in a separation agreement. In common-law property states, courts have considerably more discretion in determining what division would be *equitable* in the absence of a separation agreement that lays out a division to the mutual satisfaction of the parties. Even in common-law property states, however, many courts strive for an equal distribution of property, particularly in view of the fact that there is a trend against awarding permanent alimony for relatively young spouses who have not been married for a long time. In such cases, the major opportunity for the court to achieve equity is through the property division. Courts often act on the following assumption: whether a spouse worked at home or "out in the world," any property accumulated during the marriage (with the exceptions mentioned above) was due to their joint efforts. For example, a husband would not be able to earn $100,000 a year, and buy two cars and two homes out of his salary if he also had to stay home to care for the three kids and worry about why the washing machine was not working!

---

[6]450 U.S. 455, 101 S.Ct. 1195, 67 L.Ed.2d 428 (1981).

In a property division, the parties rarely sell all their assets to others and then divide the proceeds of the sales according to an allocation formula. In the separation agreement, the parties bargain. For example,

- The wife will keep the house, and the husband will keep the car and bank account.

- The wife will live in the house, but the husband will retain a designated amount of the equity in the house, which must be paid to him if the house is sold.

- The wife receives $60,000 as a lump-sum payment, and the husband receives everything else.

(etc.)

Other bargaining options also enter the negotiations. The wife may agree to a lower property division in exchange for the husband's agreement to let her have custody of the children. She may agree to a higher alimony award in exchange for a relatively lower property division out of fear that he is on the brink of bankruptcy (in which the property division debts, but not the alimony debts, will be discharged). He may be able to convince her to take more alimony and less property so that he can take advantage of the alimony tax deduction (page 429). She may agree to this even though she must pay taxes on the alimony received since they both know that his higher income would cause the same money to be taxed at a higher rate. He may find ways to compensate her for this in other terms of the separation agreement.

If the parties are not able to agree on the property division, then the court must do it for them. The goal is to achieve equity and avoid undue hardship on either party. Neither side will receive everything it wants. Courts have a great deal of discretion in this aspect of the divorce. Next to the custody decision, it is often the most painful task that the court has.

Assignment 10.7

When parties are not able to agree on a property division, what standards will a court use in your state to do it for them? (See General Instructions for the State-Code Assignment in chapter one.)

Pensions, Degrees, and Goodwill

As indicated earlier, three recent areas of contention involving property division are pensions, professional degrees (or occupational licenses), and the goodwill of a business. Traditionally, parties negotiating a separation agreement did *not* include these items in their bargaining. They were either considered too intangible or were simply assumed to belong to one of the parties separately, usually the husband. Litigation and legislation, however, have forced drastic changes in these views. As a result, the negotiations for a separation agreement now regularly take account of these items in one way or another.

Dividing a Pension

Many workers are covered by private *pension plans* at work.[7] Employer-sponsored plans may be financed entirely by the employer or by the employer with employee contributions. There are two main kinds of pension plans, the *defined-benefit* and the *defined-contribution* plan.

Defined-Benefit Plan

The amount of the benefit is fixed, but not the amount of contribution. Such plans usually gear the benefits to years of service and earnings (e.g., a benefit of $10 a month for each year of employment) or a stated dollar amount. Whatever the formula, the benefit is spelled out in the plan.

Defined-Contribution Plan

In this kind of plan, each employee has his or her own individual account. The amount of contribution is generally fixed, but the amount of the benefit is not. These plans usually involve profit-sharing, stock-bonus, or money-purchase arrangements where the employer's contribution, usually a percentage of profits, is divided among the participants based on the individual's wages and/or years of service and accumulations in the individual's pension account. The eventual benefit is determined by the amount of total contributions and investment earnings in the years during which the employee is covered.

Accumulated benefits in these plans are not *vested* until the employee has a nonforfeitable right to receive the benefits, whether or not the employee leaves the job before retirement.

Can pension benefits be divided upon divorce? Assume that a wife stayed home to care for the children while her husband worked. Is she entitled to any of his pension benefits? The question is important because retirement benefits may be the largest portion of the marital estate in many marriages.

Yes, it is possible for a spouse, an ex-spouse, or a child to receive some or all of these pension benefits if the court so directs in a special order called a *Qualified Domestic Relations Order* (QDRO). Any one of these individuals can become an *alternate payee* under the plan. A judge will issue a QDRO to enforce an obligation of child support (page 366), alimony, or other marital property right of the alternate payee. Before this dramatic change in the law became effective in 1984, individuals other than the employee could not demand that pension benefits be paid directly to them. QDROs have now made this practice commonplace. Exhibit 10–2 provides an example of a typical QDRO provided by an employer as guidance to its employees in drafting proposed QDROs to be signed by a judge. The example assumes that the alternate payee will receive one-half of the employee's pension benefits. It is certainly possible, however, for a different allocation to be ordered.

How much does the nonemployee receive from the employee's pension fund? What amount or percentage will be ordered in the QDRO? The answer depends on what the parties negotiate in their separation agreement. If they

---

[7]Almost all government workers, of course, are covered by public pension plans as part of a civil service retirement program.

☐ **EXHIBIT 10–2** Qualified Domestic Relations Order (QDRO)

This sample QDRO is provided by Apex Company, Inc. as an example of an order the company will treat as a QDRO. You may include the language in a separate order or as part of the divorce decree itself. The company does not give individual tax advice or advice about the marital property rights of either party.

    1. Pursuant to Section 414(p) of the Internal Revenue Code, this qualified domestic relations order (''Order'') assigns a portion of the benefits payable in the Apex Company, Inc. Annuity Plan (''the Plan'') from _____ [Member's Name]_____ (Member No. _____) to _____ [Spouse's Name]_____ in recognition of the existence of his/her marital rights in _ _____[Member's Name]_____ retirement benefits.

    2. The Member in the Plan is _____[Member's Name]_____, whose last known mailing address is _____ , Social Security No. _____ .

    3. The Alternate Payee is _____[Spouse's Name]_____ , whose last known mailing address is _____ , Social Security No. _____ .

[Use the following paragraph if the Member is <u>not</u> already receiving retirement benefits:]

    4. Apex Company, Inc. is hereby ORDERED to assign a portion of the accumulations so that each party as of the date of the assignment has a retirement account of approximately the same value. The date of assignment is _____ .

[Use the following paragraph if the Member <u>is</u> already receiving retirement benefits:]

    4. Apex Company Inc. is hereby ORDERED to make monthly payments equal to one-half of the amount payable to _____[Member's Name]_____ directly to _____[Spouse's Name]_____ . These direct payments to _____[Spouse's Name]_____

cannot reach an agreement on this issue, the court will decide. It is possible for an alternate payee to receive up to 100 percent of the employee's pension benefits.

Employees and employers do not like QDROs—the former because they had thought their pension could never be touched by anyone, and the latter because of the extra administrative burden imposed. During negotiations, the employee will usually try to get the other side to accept some other benefit in lieu of asking the court for a QDRO. If, however, there is nothing else available of comparable value, the "division" of the pension benefits through a QDRO is unavoidable.

A great deal depends on the *value* of the employee's pension plan. Without knowing this value, the negotiations are meaningless. Yet determining value can be a complex undertaking, often requiring the services of actuarial and accounting specialists. Value will depend on factors such as:

■ Type of pension plan

■ Amount contributed to the plan by the employee and by the employer

□ **EXHIBIT 10–2** Qualified Domestic Relations Order (QDRO) continued

---

shall be made beginning after the date of this Order and ending at
_____[Member's Name]_____'s death.

   5. This qualified domestic relations order is not intended to require
the Plan to provide any type or form of benefits or any option not otherwise provided by the Plan, nor shall this Order require the Plan to provide
for increased benefits not required by the Plan. This Order does not require the Plan to provide benefits to the Alternate Payee that are required
to be paid to another alternate payee under another order previously determined to be a qualified domestic relations order.

   6. All benefits payable under the Apex Company, Inc. Annuity Plan other
than those payable to _____[Spouse's Name]_____ shall be payable to _____
[Member's Name]_____ in such manner and form as he/she may elect in his/
her sole and undivided discretion, subject only to plan requirements.

   7. _____[Spouse's Name]_____ is ORDERED AND DECREED to report any re-
tirement payments received on any applicable income tax return. The Plan
Administrator of Apex Company, Inc. is authorized to issue the appropriate
Internal Revenue Form for any direct payment made to _____[Spouse's Name]_____

   8. While it is anticipated that the Plan Administrator will pay directly
to _____[Spouse's Name]_____ the benefit awarded to her, _____[Member's
Name]_____ is designated a constructive trustee to the extent he receives
any retirement benefits under the Plan that are due to _____[Spouse's
Name]_____ but paid to _____[Member's Name]_____. _____[Member's Name]_____
is ORDERED AND DECREED to pay the benefit defined above directly to _____
[Spouse's Name]_____ within three days after receipt by him.

_____   _____
[NAME OF COURT]   [NAME OF JUDGE]

- How benefits are determined, e.g., when they accrue or are vested
- Age of employee
- Employee's earliest retirement date
- Employee's life expectancy
- Present values of the benefits

(etc.)

   Often the parties must calculate the *present value* of a benefit, meaning
the amount of money an individual would have to be given now in order to
produce a certain amount of money in a designated period of time. Assume
that at the beginning of the year you become entitled to $1,000 by the end of
the year. On January 1, you are *not* given $1,000; you are given the present
value of $1,000. The present value of $1,000 is $900 if we assume that you
could invest $900 in a local bank (or in some other investment entity) at 10
percent interest. When a benefit is distributed, what is actually received may
be the present value of the benefit, calculated in this way. If a 10 percent rate
of interest is too high in today's market, the parties will have to assume a

lower interest percentage and a higher present value. At 5 percent interest, for example, the present value of $1,000 is $950. (If you brought $950 to a bank offering 5 percent interest, at the end of the year you would have $1,000 in your account.)

A number of companies have been formed that assist parties in valuing pensions involved in property divisions. One such company is Legal Economic Evaluations, Inc., whose application is presented in Exhibit 10–3.

Assignment 10.8

Find a friend or relative who works at a place where he or she is covered by a pension. Assume that you work at an office where your friend or relative is a client who is seeking a divorce in which one of the issues is the division of pension benefits. (If you are covered by an employee pension plan, use yourself as the client in this assignment.)

Your supervisor asks you to do two things. First, obtain as much information as you can about the client's pension, e.g., the kind of plan it is, when benefits become available. Second, obtain an employer-approved copy of a sample QDRO. Ask the client to call the personnel office at work in order to speak to the "plan administrator" (the person in charge of administering the pension plan) and request these items.

Prepare a report, using these items but changing the name of your friend or relative. Summarize the plan's features, pointing out whatever you think will be relevant to later negotiations on dividing the pension benefits. Attach the copy of the sample QDRO to your report.

Dividing a Degree

Bill and Pat are married in 1973. While Bill attends college, medical school, and internship to become a doctor, Pat works full time to support the two of them. On the day he obtains his license to practice medicine, they decide to divorce. During the long years of Bill's education, they have accumulated almost no property. Pat earns $15,000 a year at her job. Since she is fully capable of supporting herself, the court decides that she should receive no alimony. They have no children.

Many would consider it an outrage that Pat walks away from the marriage with nothing. *She* is not eligible for alimony, and there is no tangible property to divide. *He* walks away with a professional degree and a doctor's license ready to embark on a lucrative career. Courts are slowly coming to the realization that the supporting spouse should be given a remedy in such a situation.

In the example above, what financial factors are involved?

1. The amount that Pat and/or her family contributed to Bill's support while he was in school

2. The amount that Pat and/or her family contributed to pay Bill's education expenses

3. The amount that Bill would have contributed to the marriage if he had worked during these years rather than gone to school

□ EXHIBIT 10—3 Pension Valuation Form

LEGAL _____
ECONOMIC _____
EVALUATIONS, INC. _____
1000 Elwell Court   #203   Palo Alto   CA 94303   [415] 969-7682

PENSION VALUATION

ATTORNEY INFORMATION

Name _____   Today's Date ____ / ____ / ____

Name of Firm _____   Representing: □ Pensioner's Spouse

Street _____   □ Pensioner

City, State & Zip Code _____   □ Both

Telephone Number [   ] _____ How Did you Hear of Us? _____

CASE INFORMATION

(For Faster Service, please collect the information below and call one of our Economists at (800) 221–6826 or (800) 648–9900 inside California.)

Pensioner Name _____ Gender   M   F   Birthdate ____ / ____ / ____

Employer _____ Occupation _____

Date of Employment ____ / ____ / ____   Date Entered Plan ____ / ____ / ____   Termination Date ____ / ____ / ____

Spouse Name _____   Birthdate ____ / ____ / ____

Date of Marriage ____ / ____ / ____   Date Spouse's Interest in Pension Ends ____ / ____ / ____

If the pensioner is already receiving benefits, how much are they ($ _____) and when did they begin (____ / ____ / ____)?

Have you enclosed a copy of the pension plan booklet? □ Yes

Have you enclosed the pensioner's most recent benefits statement? □ Yes

Is there any other recent correspondence regarding pension benefits? □ Yes □ No   If so, please enclose a copy.

If no information regarding benefit amounts is available, please list the pensioner's salary for the last five years below:

Please state any other relevant information below:

_____
_____
_____
_____

In addition to the present value of the pension, do you wish us to show the spouse's net interest based on the ratio of service during marriage to total plan service (also known as the "Time Rule" or "Coverture Percentage")? □ Yes □ No

BILLING
□ Enclosed is a check for $100 payable to Legal Economic Evaluations, Inc.
   Please mail remittance and this completed form to the above address.

M3

4. Any increased earnings that Pat would have had if she had taken a different job, e.g., by moving to a different location

5. Any increased earnings that Pat would have had if she had continued her education rather than working to support Bill through his education

6. The increased standard of living that Pat would have enjoyed due to Bill's expected high earnings if they had stayed married.

7. The share of his increased earnings to which Pat would have been entitled if they had stayed married.

Some courts will consider only items (1) and (2) above in providing Pat with a remedy. As a matter of equity, she is entitled only to restitution—a return of what she and/or her family contributed while Bill was acquiring his degree and license. A degree and license are not considered divisible property by such courts. They are personal to the holder. Under this view, it logically follows that she is not entitled to a share of his increased earnings as a result of the degree and license. All of the above items (1–7) are taken into consideration in deciding the question of *spousal support*. Increased earnings as a result of the degree and license are taken into consideration because one of the factors in an alimony or maintenance decree is the spouse's ability to pay. The problem, however, is that the wife may not be eligible for alimony because of her own employability. Nor can equity be done by giving the wife a generous share of tangible property since no such property may have been accumulated due to the fact that the husband had high educational expenses and little or no income of his own. In such situations, one minimal remedy is a direct award for items (1) and (2) above, which again amounts to little more than restitution. A few courts, however, will deny even this remedy, taking the position that the wife, in effect, was making a gift of her resources to the husband during his education.

A small number of cases have ruled that the degree and license *do* constitute divisible marital property and that more than restitution is called for. The *Woodworth* case is one example:

Woodworth v. Woodworth

Court of Appeals of Michigan
126 Mich. App. 258, 337 N.W.2d 332 (1983)

T. M. Burns, Presiding Judge

On January 6, 1982, the parties' divorce was finalized. Both parties appeal as of right.

The parties were married on June 27, 1970, after plaintiff had graduated from Central Michigan University with a bachelor's degree in secondary education and defendant had graduated from Lansing Community College with an associates degree. They then moved to Jonesville, where plaintiff worked as a teacher and coach for the high school and defendant worked as a nursery school teacher in Hillsdale. In the Fall of 1973, they sold their house, quit their jobs,* and moved to Detroit, where plaintiff attended Wayne State Law School. Three years later, they moved to Lansing where plaintiff took and passed the bar exam and accepted a job as a research attorney with the Court of Appeals. Plaintiff is now a partner in a Lansing law firm.

---

*Defendant had already quit her job the year before after the parties' first child was born.

For all intents and purposes, the marriage ended on August 25, 1980, when the parties separated. The following summarizes each party's earnings during the marriage:

Year	Plaintiff		Defendant	
1970	$ 2,591	Jonesville HS teacher/coach	$ 1,422	Nursery School Teacher
			$ 2,549	Grant Company (clerk)
1971	$ 7,989	Teacher	$ 4,236	Teacher
	$ 410	St. Anthony Ch. (instructor)	$ 280	St. Anthony Ch. (instructor)
1972	$ 9,691	Teacher	$ 2,525	Teacher
1973	$ 6,557	Teacher	$ 986	Bank Teller
1974	$ 2,483	Legal Aid (student lawyer)	$ 6,572	Bank Teller
1975	$ 2,588	Legal Aid (student lawyer)	$ 1,050	Bank Teller
			$ 8,191	Dept/Social Services (case worker)
1976	$ 6,342	Court of Appeals (attorney)	$10,276	Dept/Social Services (case worker)
1977	$12,493	Court of Appeals (attorney)	$ 1,586	Dept/Social Services (case worker)†
	$ 5,595	Assistant Prosecuting Attorney		
1978	$21,085	Assistant Prosecuting Attorney	$—0—	
1979	$27,247	Assistant Prosecuting Attorney	$—0—	
1980	$ 2,057	Assistant Prosecuting Attorney	$—0—	
	$30,000	Private Practice		

†Defendant quit this job in January after the parties' third child was born.

The basic issue in this case is whether or not plaintiff's law degree is marital property subject to distribution. The trial court held that it was, valued it at $20,000, and awarded this amount to defendant in payments of $2,000 over ten years. Plaintiff contends that his law degree is not such a marital asset. We disagree.

The facts reveal that plaintiff's law degree was the end product of a concerted family effort. Both parties planned their family life around the effort to attain plaintiff's degree. Toward this end, the family divided the daily tasks encountered in living. While the law degree did not preempt all other facets of their lives, it did become the main focus and goal of their activities. Plaintiff left his job in Jonesville and the family relocated to Detroit so that plaintiff could attend law school. In Detroit, defendant sought and obtained full time employment to support the family.

We conclude, therefore, that plaintiff's law degree was the result of mutual sacrifice and effort by both plaintiff and defendant. While plaintiff studied and attended classes, defendant carried her share of the burden as well as sharing vicariously in the stress of the [law school] experience known as the "paper chase."

We believe that fairness dictates that the spouse who did not earn an advanced degree be compensated whenever the advanced degree is the product of such concerted family investment. The degree holder has expended great effort to obtain the degree not only for him or herself, but also to benefit the family as a whole. The other spouse has shared in this effort and contributed in other ways as well, not merely as a gift to the student spouse nor merely to share individually in the benefits but to help the marital unit as a whole. . . .

We are aware that numerous other cases have held that an advanced degree is not a marital asset and may be considered only (if at all) in determining alimony.

However, we reject the reasons given in these cases to support their conclusions. The cases first contend that an advanced degree is simply not "property":

"An educational degree, such as an M.B.A., is simply not encompassed by the broad views of the concept of 'property'. It does not have an exchange value or any objective transferable value on an open market. It is personal to the holder. It terminates on death of the holder and is not inheritable. It cannot be assigned, sold, transferred, conveyed, or pledged. An advanced degree is a cumulative product of many years of previous education, combined with diligence and hard work. It may not be acquired by the mere expenditure of money. It is simply an intellectual achievement that may potentially assist in the future acquisition of property. In our view, it has none of the attributes of property in the usual sense of that term." *Graham v. Graham,* 194 Colo. 432, 374 P.2d 75 (1978).

Yet whether or not an advanced degree can physically or metaphysically be defined as "property" is beside the point. Courts must instead focus on the most equitable solution to dissolving the marriage and dividing among the respective parties what they have.

"[T]he student spouse will walk away with a degree and the supporting spouse will depart with little more than the knowledge that he or she has substantially contributed toward the attainment of that degree." Comment, *The Interest of the Community in a Professional Education,* 10 Cal.West L.Rev. 590 (1974).

In *DeLa Rosa v. DeLa Rosa,* 309 N.W.2d 758, (1981), the Minnesota Supreme Court added:

"[O]ne spouse has foregone the immediate enjoyment of earned income to enable the other to pursue an advanced education on a full time basis. Typically, this sacrifice is made with the expectation that the parties will enjoy a higher standard of living in the future."

Where, as in this case, the family goal of obtaining the law degree was the purpose of the substantial contribution and sacrifice, both the degree holder and his or her spouse are entitled to share in the fruits of the degree. The trial judge recognized as much:

"Here the plaintiff quit his job and entered law school. The defendant secured employment so plaintiff could become a professional with far greater earning capacity than he had, which would benefit him and their children. To permit this, upon divorce, to benefit only the party who secured the professional degree is unconscionable."

The next argument is that a marriage is not a commercial enterprise and that neither spouse's expectations are necessarily going to be met after the divorce:

"I do not believe that a spouse who works and contributes to the education of the other spouse during marriage normally does so in the expectation of compensation." *Sullivan v. Sullivan,* 184 Cal.Rptr. 801 (1982) (Kaufman, P.J., concurring). Furthermore:

"They do not nor do they expect to pay each other for their respective contributions in any commercial sense. Rather, they work together, in

both income and nonincome producing ways, in their joint, mutual and individual interests.

"The termination of the marriage represents, if nothing else, the disappointment of expectations, financial and nonfinancial, which were hoped to be achieved by and during the continuation of the relationship. It does not, however, in our view, represent a commercial investment loss. Recompense for the disappointed expectations resulting from the failure of the marital entity to survive cannot, therefore, be made to the spouses on a strictly commercial basis which, after the fact seeks to assign monetary values to the contributions consensually made by each of the spouses during the marriage.

*   *   *   *   *   *

"If the plan fails by reason of the termination of the marriage, we do not regard the supporting spouse's consequent loss of expectation by itself as any more compensable or demanding of solicitude than the loss of expectations of any other spouse who, in the hope and anticipation of the endurance of the relationship in its commitments, has invested a portion of his or her life, youth, energy and labor in a failed marriage." *Mahoney v. Mahoney,* 182 N.J.Super. 612–614, 442 A.2d 1062 (1982).

We agree that a marriage is not intrinsically a commercial enterprise. Instead, it is a relationship sanctioned by law governed as its essence by fidelity and troth. Neither partner usually expects to be compensated for his or her efforts. But that consideration does not end the discussion. We are not presently concerned with how best to characterize a marriage while it endures. Instead, we are concerned with how best to distribute between the parties what they have once the marriage has for all intents and purposes dissolved. In other words:

"To allow a student spouse * * * to leave a marriage with all the benefits of additonal education and a professional license without compensation to the spouse who bore much of the burdens incident to procurring these would be unfair * * *." *O'Brien v. O'Brien,* 4452 N.Y.S.2d 805 (1982).

Furthermore, we also agree that divorce courts cannot recompense expectations. However, we are not talking about an expectation here. Defendant is not asking us to compensate for a failed expectation that her husband would become a wealthy lawyer and subsequently support her for the rest of her life. Instead, she is merely seeking her share of the fruits of a degree which she helped him earn. We fail to see the difference between compensating her for a degree which she helped him earn and compensating her for a house in his name which her earnings helped him buy.

The third argument against including an advanced degree as marital property is that its valuation is too speculative. In *Lesman v. Lesman*, 452 N.Y.S.2d 938–939 (1982), the Court stated:

> "Gross inequities may result from predicating distribution awards upon the speculative expectations of enhanced future earnings, since distributive awards, unlike maintenance, once fixed may not be modified to meet future realities. It is almost impossible to predict what amount of enhanced earnings, if any, will result from a professional education. The degree of financial success attained by those holding a professional degree varies greatly. Some, even, may earn less from their professional practices than they could have earned from non-professional work. Moreover, others, due to choice or factors beyond their control, may never practice their professions."

Michigan has already recognized that:

> "Interests which are contingent upon the happening of an event which may or may not occur are not distributable. The party seeking to include the interest in the marital estate bears the burdens of proving a reasonably ascertainable value; if the burden is not met, the interest should not be considered an asset subject to distribution." *Miller v. Miller*, 83 Mich.App. 672, 677, 269 N.W.2d 264 (1978).

However, future earnings due to an advanced degree are not "too speculative." While a degree holder spouse might change professions, earn less than projected at trial, or even die, courts have proved adept at measuring future earnings in such contexts as personal injury, wrongful death, and workers' compensation actions. In fact, pain and suffering, professional goodwill and mental distress, within these general legal issues, have similar valuation "problems". . . . We, therefore, do not believe that the *Miller* contingency caveat applies to future earnings.

The last argument is that these matters are best considered when awarding alimony rather than when distributing the property. . . . A trial judge is given wide discretion in awarding alimony. . . . However, alimony is basically for the other spouse's support. The considerations for whether or not a spouse is entitled to support are different than for dividing the marital property. *McLain v. McLain*, 108 Mich.App. 166, 310 N.W.2d 316 (1981), listed eleven factors that the trial judge is to consider in determining whether or not to award alimony. Some of these deal with the parties' financial condition and their ability to support themselves. If the spouse has already supported the other spouse through graduate school, he or she is quite possibly already presently capable of supporting him or herself. Futhermore, M.C.L.A. § 552.13; M.S.A. § 25.93 give the trial court discretion to end alimony if the spouse receiving it remarries. We do not believe that the trial judge should be allowed to deprive the spouse who does not have an advanced degree of the fruits of the marriage and award it all to the other spouse merely because he or she has remarried. Such a situation would necessarily cause that spouse to think twice about remarrying.

Having determined that the defendant is entitled to compensation in this case, we must next determine how she is to be compensated. Two basic methods have been proposed—a percentage share of the present value of the future earnings attributable to the degree or restitution.

[Some Courts limit] the recovery to restitution for any money given to the student spouse to earn the degree. While this solution may be equitable in some circumstances, we do not believe that restitution is an adequate remedy in this case. Limiting the recovery to restitution "would provide [the supporting spouse] no realization of [his or] her expectation of economic benefit from the career for which the education laid the foundation." Pinnel, *Divorce After Professional School: Education and Furture Earning Capacity May Be Marital Property*, 44 Mo.L.Rev. 329, 335 (1979). Clearly, in this case, the degree was a family investment, rather than a gift or a benefit to the degree holder alone. Treating the degree as such a gift would unjustly enrich the degree holder to the extent that the degree's value exceeds its cost. . . . We note that this case does not involve the situation where both parties simultaneously earned substantially similar advanced degrees during the marriage. In such a situation, equity suggests that the parties have already amply compensated each other.

The trial court in this case valued plaintiff's law degree at $20,000 and ruled that plaintiff must pay defendant $2,000 per year for ten years. We are unable to determine how this value was reached and therefore, remand to the trial court to permit that court to revalue the degree in light of the following factors: the length of the marriage after the degree was obtained, the sources and extent of financial support given plaintiff during his years in law school, and the overall division of the parties' marital property. In determining the degree's present value, the trial court should estimate what the person holding the degree is likely to make in that particular job market and subtract from that what he or she would probably have earned without the degree. . . . The ultimate objective in a property distribution is to be fair. . . . Both parties may present new evidence on these matters and the degree's valuation.

One of the tragedies of this divorce, as in so many others, is that what used to be financially adequate is no longer enough. As the trial court aptly stated: "The tablecloths * * * will not cover both tables." We, therefore, note that the trial court has discretion to order that the payments be made on an installment basis. . . . If the trial court should order such a payment schedule, the trial court should also consider the possibility of insuring these payments by a life insurance policy on plaintiff's life benefitting defendant.

Plaintiff has also appealed the overall property division while defendant has cross-appealed from the alimony determination. If the trial court alters the value placed on plaintiff's law degree, the property division and alimony award must also be reassessed. We, therefore, refrain from addressing these issues at this time.

Pursuant to GCR 1963, 726.1, we order plaintiff to pay defendant reasonable attorney fees for this appeal. Costs to defendant.

Remanded with instructions to proceed in a manner consistent with this opinion. We do not retain jurisdiction.

Assignment 10.9

Was *Woodworth* v. *Woodworth* correctly decided? Why or why not?

Assignment 10.10

Frank and Elaine are married in your state. Both work at low paying jobs at a fast-food restaurant. Elaine wishes to become a paralegal, and Frank would like to become an electrician. A local institute has a one-year paralegal training program, and a nine-month electrician training program. Frank and Elaine decide that only one of them can go to school at a time. Frank volunteers to let Elaine go first, keeping his job at the restaurant to support them both while she is at the institute. A month before Elaine is scheduled to graduate, Frank has a serious accident at the restaurant. He will not be able to go to school for at least five years in order to recover fully from his injury. When Elaine is graduated, she obtains a good job as a paralegal. The parties seek a divorce a month after graduation. There are no children from the marriage, and no tangible property to divide. In the divorce proceeding, Frank tells the court that the only asset that can be divided is Elaine's paralegal certificate. He asks the court to award him a percentage of the earnings that Elaine will have during the next five years as a paralegal.

(a) How would *Woodworth v. Woodworth* apply to this case? (See General Instructions for the Legal-Analysis Assignment in chapter one.)

(b) How would your state resolve the case of Elaine and Frank? (See General Instructions for the Court-Opinion Assignment in chapter one.)

Dividing a Business

When a divorce occurs, one of the assets to be divided may be a business acquired during the marriage or at least developed during this time even if one of the parties had the business before the marriage. The business could be a large corporation, a small sole proprietorship, a partnership, a law practice, a medical practice, etc. Business appraisers are often hired to place a value on the business. In addition to plant and equipment, a number of intangible items must be valued, e.g., patents, trademarks, employment agreements, copyrights, securities, and goodwill.

Many standard business documents[8] must be collected in valuating a business. For example:

- Federal, state, and local income tax returns for the last five years
- Annual financial statements
- Interim financial statements
- Bank statements
- Depreciation schedules
- Articles of incorporation and bylaws or partnership agreements, including amendments
- Minutes of meetings of shareholders and directors
- Buy/sell agreements of shareholders or partners, including amendments
- Loan applications
- W-2 statements (or the equivalent) for the highest paid employees
- Leases
- Production schedules
- Inventory reports
- Management reports
- Billing records

(etc.)

One aspect of a business that is sometimes particularly difficult to evaluate is its *goodwill*. Goodwill is the favorable reputation of a company that generates additional customers. Because of goodwill, the company is expected to have earnings beyond what is considered normal for the type of business involved. Individuals providing services, such as accountants and lawyers, may also have goodwill:

> If you are a lawyer facing divorce, it is open season on your practice. . . . Like it or not, law practices and lawyer's goodwill are assets. That you can't sell your practice doesn't mean it has no value. And there are almost no legal limits on the methods an appraiser may use in assigning a value to a law practice. . . . One approach is called the excess earnings method. An appraiser looks at published surveys to find the average income for a lawyer of your experience and type of practice, then compares your earnings with the average. If your earnings are higher than the average, the increment is said to be attributable to goodwill. If your ability to attract clients and collect substantial fees from them brings you more income than you would earn working for an average salary, you have built real goodwill. Gabrielson & Walker, *Surviving Your Own Divorce*, 76, 77 Calif. Lawyer (June 1987).

If goodwill was developed during the marriage, the spouse who stayed at home may be deemed to have contributed to it (as well as to the rest of the business). In community-property states, spouses have a 50/50 interest in the portion of the business (including goodwill) that materialized during the marriage. In other states, the court might reach a different equitable allocation.

---

[8]Part of the following list comes from Business Valuation Research, Inc. of Seattle, Washington.

The fact that a business (with or without goodwill) is a divisible part of the marital estate does not necessarily mean that upon divorce the business must be sold so that the proceeds can be physically divided. The separation agreement may provide, for example, that the husband gives the wife $250,000 in exchange for the release of any interest that the wife may have in his business. Or vice versa, if she is the one primarily responsible for the business. Similarly, a court may order such an exchange if the parties have not been able to come to terms on their own in a separation agreement.

Assignment 10.11

Are there any statutes in your state on the division of a business or profession following a divorce? If so, briefly summarize their terms. (See General Instructions for the State-Code Assignment in chapter one).

Section I. Insurance

A number of questions must be considered by the parties:

- What kinds of insurance do the parties now have?
- How have the insurance premiums been paid?
- Following the separation, what will happen to the policies?
- Is there a need for additional insurance?

There are several different kinds of insurance policies that could be in effect at the time the parties draft the separation agreement:

- Life insurance
- Homeowner's insurance
- Hospitalization or other medical insurance
- Liability insurance (for business)
- Car insurance

(etc.)

Each kind of policy should be carefully identified with notations as to how much the premiums are, who has paid them, who the beneficiaries are, whether the beneficiaries can be changed and, if so, by whom, etc. Unfortunately, parties often neglect such important details. Insurance policies can be as crucial as other "property" items that must be divided or otherwise negotiated as part of the separation agreement. The parties may opt to leave the policies as they are with no changes. This is fine if it is a conscious decision of *both* parties after *all* the facts are known about each policy, the tax consequences are explained, and the economic advantages and disadvantages of the various ways of handling each policy are discussed.

As we have seen, a husband usually has no obligation to support his wife or children after he dies. There is nothing, however, to prevent him from voluntarily assuming this obligation. Life insurance on his life, with the beneficiaries being his wife and/or his children, is a common way of doing this. If such a life insurance policy already exists, then the husband may agree to keep it effective (e.g., pay the premiums) after the separation. The wife and children, however, may not gain much protection from such an agreement if the husband can change the beneficiaries at his pleasure. Hence, as part of the bargaining process, the wife may ask that the designation of herself and the children as beneficiaries be made irrevocable (page 243).

Section J. Debts

The parties must discuss how to handle:

- Debts outstanding (i.e., unpaid) at the time the separation agreement is signed
- Debts incurred after the separation agreement is signed

A great variety of debts may be outstanding:

- Debts between the spouses (e.g., a loan made by one spouse to the other during the marriage)
- Business debts incurred by the husband
- Family debts incurred by the husband
- Business debts incurred by the wife
- Family debts incurred by the wife
- Business or family debts incurred by both the husband and wife (i.e., the debts are in both names so that they are jointly and severally liable on the debts, meaning that a creditor could sue the husband and wife *together* on the debt, or could sue *either* the husband or the wife).

The parties must decide who is going to pay what debts, and the separation agreement should specifically reflect what they have decided.

The extent to which the parties are in debt is relevant to (1) the necessity of using present cash and other resources to pay these debts, (2) the availability of resources to support spouse and children, and (3) the possibility of bankruptcy now or in the immediate future. As for the husband's personal or business debts, for example, the wife should not take the attitude that such debts are "his problem" since his bankruptcy could cause her to lose whatever he still owes her under the property-division arrangement. (As we have seen, however, a bankruptcy would not discharge alimony and child support obligations, page 238.)

As to future debts (i.e., those incurred after the separation agreement is signed), the normal expectation of the parties is that they will pay their own debts. Except for the obligations that arise out of the separation agreement itself, the parties are on their own, e.g., a wife will not make a purchase of necessaries (page 367) on the credit of her husband. A clause should be inserted in the agreement providing that each party promises not to attempt to use the credit of the other.

Section K. Taxes

In Chapter 15, the tax consequences of separation agreements are discussed (page 428). Our focus here is on the question of who pays the taxes and who will be able to take advantage of certain tax benefits. The following are the kinds of situations that need to be anticipated:

- If the Internal Revenue Service assesses a tax deficiency and penalty for a prior year during which the parties had filed a joint return, who pays the deficiency and penalty?

- If, for the current tax year, the parties file their last joint return, and then, many months later, the Internal Revenue Service assesses a tax deficiency and penalty on that last tax return, who pays this deficiency and penalty?

- In the year in which the separation agreement is signed, if the wife files a separate return, with whose resources are her taxes paid?

- In the current and in future years, who takes the tax deduction for the payment of interest on the mortgage and for the payment of property taxes?

- In the current and in future years, who takes the tax exemption for each of the dependent children?

- What happens to any tax refunds for the current tax year and for any prior year?

Often, the husband will agree to a clause in the separation agreement that indemnifies the wife against any tax deficiencies and penalties that may arise out of the last joint return filed and out of the joint returns filed in any prior year during their marriage. Under such a clause, he will have to pay the entire deficiency and penalty for which they both may be jointly and severally liable. Similarly, the parties must also agree on how tax refunds, if any, are to be divided. Such refunds are usually payable by government check to both of the parties.

There are laws on who can receive the tax benefits of exemptions and deductions from alimony, interest payments, and property-tax payments. The parties do not have total freedom in deciding who can use these tax benefits. The point, however, is that one of the parties will be entitled to the benefits. This is an economic advantage that should be taken into consideration in the overall evaluation of who is getting what from the separation agreement. The parties make a big mistake when they fail to take account of such matters. The separation agreement may specify a dollar amount to be transferred pursuant to a support clause and/or a property division clause. If, however, all the tax factors have not been considered, the parties may later be surprised by the discrepancy between such stated dollar figures and the *real* amounts that they receive and pay out.

Section L. Wills

There are a number of questions involving wills and estates that the parties must consider:

- Do the spouses already have wills naming each other as beneficiaries? If so, are these wills to be changed?

- Have they named each other as executor of their estates? If so, is this to be changed?
- Is the husband going to agree to leave his wife and/or children something in his will? If so, and this requires a change in his will, when is this change to be made?
- Is either spouse mentioned as a beneficiary in the will of a relative of the other spouse? If so, is this likely to be changed?

When a spouse dies, the surviving spouse has important rights in the property of the deceased spouse, sometimes in spite of what the latter intended or provided for in a will. To understand these rights, the following distinction should be kept in mind:

- To die *testate* means to die leaving a valid will.
- To die *intestate* means to die without leaving a valid will.

Assume that a spouse dies testate in which nothing is left to the surviving spouse. In most states, a surviving spouse who is dissatisfied with a will can *elect against the will* and receive a *forced share* of the deceased's property. This share is often the same share that the surviving spouse would have received if the deceased had died intestate.

The separation agreement should specify what happens to the right to elect against a will and similar rights such as dower and curtesy (page 453). The normal provision is that each side *releases* all such rights in the other's property.

Section M. Miscellaneous Provisions

A number of other items need to be considered:

Counsel Fees

The husband is often ordered by the court to pay the attorney fees of the wife in a divorce action. The parties may decide to specify this in the separation agreement itself. They should consider not only the legal costs (counsel fees, filing fees, etc.) of a potential divorce, but also the legal costs incurred in connection with the preparation of the separation agreement itself. Of course, if the wife has her own resources, the parties may agree that she will pay her own legal bills.

Nonmolestation Clause

Most separation agreements contain a *nonmolestation clause,* in which both parties agree, in effect, to leave each other alone. Specifically, they will not try to live with the other person, interfere with each other's lifestyle, or bother each other in any way.

Section N. Modification of the Separation Agreement

Generally, a court has no power to alter the terms of a contract unless it was procured by fraud or duress. A separation agreement is a contract. Can its terms be modified? Clearly, the parties to any contract can mutually agree to modify its terms. But can the court *force* a modification on the parties when only one party wants it?

The answer may depend on which terms of the separation agreement are in question. *Property division* terms, as indicated earlier, are rarely modifiable (page 240). *Child-custody* and *child-support* terms, however, are almost always modifiable according to the court's perception of the best interest of the child (page 300). The area of greatest controversy concerns *alimony* or *spousal-support* terms.

First, consider two extreme and relatively rare circumstances where the court can modify spousal-support terms:

1. The separation agreement itself includes a provision allowing a court to modify its terms.

2. The needy spouse has become so destitute that he or she will become a public charge unless a modification is ordered.

If neither of these situations exists, can the court order a modification of the spousal terms of the separation agreement? This involves two separate questions. Does the court have the power to modify, and if so, when will it exercise this power?

The Power to Modify

In a few states a court has no power to modify a spousal support term unless the parties have agreed in the separation agreement to allow the court to do so. Most states, however, will allow their courts to modify a separation agreement even if it expressly says that modification is not allowed. A number of theories have been advanced to support this view. Some states hold that the separation agreement is merely advisory to the court and that as a matter of public policy, the court cannot allow the question of support to be determined solely by the parties. The state as a whole has an interest in seeing to it that this sensitive question is properly resolved. What the parties have agreed upon will be a factor in the court's determination, but it will not be the controlling factor. Other states advance the theory of merger. When a court accepts the terms of a separation agreement, it can *incorporate* and *merge* them into the divorce decree. The agreement loses its separate identity. The question is not whether the separation agreement can be modified, but whether the decree can be modified. Courts are much less reluctant to modify their own decrees than they are to modify the private contracts of parties. Under the merger doctrine, the contract no longer exists.

The Exercise of the Power to Modify

Assuming the court has the power to modify spousal support orders, when will the court use it? The general rule is that a modification will be ordered only when there has been a substantial change of circumstances of a continuing nature that is not due to voluntary action or inaction of the parties. Furthermore, some courts limit the exercise of their modification power to periodic or ongoing alimony payments; they will not modify a *lump-sum* support award.

Tom and Mary enter a separation agreement that is approved, incorporated, and merged by the court in its divorce decree. Tom is required to pay Mary $750 a month alimony. Assume that Tom comes to the court a year later seeking a decrease, and/or Mary comes seeking an increase.

Unfortunately, courts are not always consistent as to when they will allow a modification in such a case. Consider the following circumstances:

1. *The ex-husband becomes sick and earns substantially less.* Most courts would modify the decree to lessen the amount he must pay—at least during the period when his earning capacity is affected by the illness.

2. *The ex-husband suddenly starts earning a great deal more.* The ex-wife will usually not be able to increase her alimony award simply because her ex-husband becomes more wealthy than he was at the time of the divorce decree. The result might be different if she can show that the *original* alimony award was inadequate due to his weaker earning capacity at that time.

3. *The ex-wife violates the terms of the separation agreement relating to the visitation rights of the ex-husband/father.* Some courts feel that alimony payments and visitation rights are interdependent. If the ex-wife interferes with the father's visitation rights with the children, these courts will reduce or terminate her alimony. For such a result, however, the interference must be substantial.

4. *The ex-wife engages in "immoral" conduct, e.g., has a live-in lover.* When the ex-husband finds out about the lover, his concern is that his alimony payments are being used to support his ex-wife's lover. Most states will not reduce the alimony payments for this reason. In the states that will, the ex-wife's affair usually must be flagrant and ongoing.

5. *The ex-husband wants to retire, change jobs, or go back to school.* When his income is reduced in this way, the courts will consider a downward modification of the alimony obligation only if the proposed change in lifestyle is made in good faith and not simply as a way to avoid paying the original amount of alimony. A rich executive, for example, cannot "drop out" and become a poor farmer. Such an executive, however, may be able to take a lower paying job if this is required for his health.

6. *The ex-husband remarries.* In most states, his alimony obligation to his first wife is not affected by his remarriage. There are a few states, however, that will consider a reduction if it is clear that he cannot meet the burden of supporting two families, particularly when there are children from the second marriage.

7. *The ex-wife remarries.* If the ex-wife remarries, most courts will terminate his alimony obligation unless the parties agreed in the separation agreement that alimony would continue in some form after she remarried.

8. *The ex-husband dies.* Alimony ends on the death of the ex-husband unless the separation agreement provides for its continuance and/or the divorce decree imposes his obligation on the ex-husband's estate.

Assignment 10.12

Find authority (e.g., a statute or a court opinion) in your state for the court's power to modify an alimony award. When will such a modification be made? (See also General

Instructions for the State Code Assignment in chapter one and the Court-Opinion Assignment in chapter one.)

Assignment 10.13

Karen and Jim obtain a divorce decree that awards Karen $500 a month in alimony "until she dies or remarries." A year after the divorce decree becomes final, Karen marries Paul. Jim stops the alimony payments. A year later, this marriage to Paul is annulled. Karen now wants Jim to resume paying her $500 a month alimony and to pay her $6,000 to cover the period when she was "married" to Paul ($500 × 12). What result? (See General Instructions for the Legal-Analysis Assignment in chapter one.)

Section O. Arbitration and Mediation

Many separation agreements contain a clause providing that disputes arising in the future about the agreement shall be subject to *arbitration*. Normally, a professional arbitration organization, such as the American Arbitration Association, is specified as the arbitrator who will resolve the dispute. A professional group, however, is not necessary. The parties may select a mutually trusted friend or associate as the arbitrator. The agreement should specify who the arbitrator will be and who will pay the arbitration expenses, if any.

An alternative to arbitration is *mediation*. In arbitration, the parties agree in advance to abide by the decision rendered by the arbitrator. A mediator, however, does not make a decision. He or she tries to guide the parties to reach a decision *on their own* in much the same manner as a labor mediator tries to assist union and management to reach a settlement. If mediation does not work, the parties either agree to submit the dispute to an arbitrator or are forced to litigate it in court.

Section P. Reconciliation

What happens if the parties become reconciled to each other after they execute the separation agreement? They certainly have the power to cancel or rescind their contract so long as both do so voluntarily. If it is clear that they want to cancel, no problem exists. Legally, the separation agreement goes out of existence. The problem arises when the parties say nothing about the separation agreement after they reconcile and resume cohabitation. Courts handle the problem in different ways:

- The *reconciliation* will cancel the alimony or spousal-support terms of the separation agreement, but will not cancel the property-division terms.

- The reconciliation will cancel the *executory* (unperformed as yet) terms of the separation agreement, but will not cancel the executed (already performed) terms.

Reconciliation usually means the full resumption of the marital relationship; occasional or casual contact will not suffice. The intent must be to abandon the separation agreement and to resume the marital relationship permanently.

 ## Interviewing and Investigation Checklist

Have the Parties Reconciled?

Legal Interviewing Questions

1. When did the two of you sign the separation agreement?

2. When did you stop living together?

3. Where did you both live when you were separated?

4. Was your separation bitter?

5. After you signed the separation agreement, when did the two of you have your first contact? Describe the circumstances.

6. Have the two of you had sexual intercourse with each other since the separation agreement was signed? How often?

7. Did you ever discuss getting back together again? If so, describe the circumstances, e.g., who initiated the discussion, was there any reluctance?

8. During this period, did the two of you abide by the terms of the separation agreement? Explain.

9. Did you move in together? If so, where did you both stay? Did one of you give up a house or apartment?

10. Did you discuss what to do with the separation agreement?

11. Did the two of you assume that it was no longer effective?

12. After you came together again, did either of you continue abiding by any of the terms of the separation agreement?

13. Did either of you give back whatever you received under the terms of the separation agreement?

14. When you resumed the relationship, did you feel that the reunion was going to be permanent? What do you think your spouse felt about it?

15. Did either of you attach any conditions to resuming the relationship again?

16. What have the two of you done since you came together again to indicate that you both considered each other to be husband and wife, e.g., both sign joint tax returns, make joint purchases, spend a lot of time together in public, etc.?

17. Have you separated again? If so, describe the circumstances.

Possible Investigation Tasks

- Obtain a copy of the separation agreement in order to verify its date of execution.

- Interview people who know the plaintiff (P) and defendant (D) well to find out what they know about the alleged reconciliation.

- Obtain any documents executed after the separation agreement was signed which may indicate the extent to which P and D did things together during this time, e.g., rent receipts with both of their names on them, opening or continuing joint checking or savings accounts.

Assignment 10.14

Tom and Mary execute a separation agreement on February 17, 1978, in which they mutually release all rights (dower, curtesy, right of election, etc.) in each other's estate. They ceased living together on February 2, 1978. On March 13, 1978, Tom moves out of the city. On the next day, he makes a long distance call to Mary in which he says, "This is ridiculous; why don't you come live with me. You know I still love you." Mary answers, "I guess you're right, but if we are going to live together again, I want you to come back here." Tom then says, "I'm sure we can work that out." They agree to meet next week to discuss it further. Before they meet, Tom dies. Tom's will makes no provision for Mary. Mary now seeks a share of his estate through the exercise of a *right of election* (page 267). What result? At the time of Tom's death, he was still married to Mary. (See General Instructions for the Legal-Analysis Assignment in chapter one.)

Section Q. Computer Help

Computer companies have designed software to assist the law office in managing the large volume of data involved in the negotiation of a separation agreement. One such company is California Family Law Report, Inc. (CFLR). It describes its software, called PROPertizer™, as follows:

> PRO*Pertizer*™ is a software program designed to help the family law professional divide the client's marital assets.
>
> You enter a list of up to 500 marital assets for possible division during the dissolution of a marriage, along with the present fair market value and any encumbrances [See Exhibit 10–4]. The program automatically calculates each item's equity (fair market value (FMV) less debt). With only a keystroke, you can see the result of assigning an item's full value to either party, or of assigning the item to each in equal or unequal parts. The constant, instantaneous recalculations keep totals accurate and save hours of running and rerunning calculator tapes when formulating and considering proposals.
>
> When each party's combined marginal bracket (CMB) is entered, each item's tax basis may be entered to view the after-tax effect for both parties as a result of the way in which assets have been assigned.
>
> Items can be temporarily blanked out to remove them from consideration and to see how they affect a possible settlement. Rows can be inserted or deleted anywhere, and at any time, within the list of items. To arrive at an equalizing payment of $0, or as close to $0 as possible, any item can be considered separately in order to redistribute equity. With one key, you can redistribute an asset to minimize or zero out the before-tax equalizing payment. A *Moore/Marsden* calculation for separating joint and separate interests in real property can be performed for any or all items.
>
> The program also allows *optional* entry of losses. Because losses are not always allowed under tax laws, how individual losses will be viewed by the court or accepted by the IRS will be a matter decided on a case-by-case basis; however, the option to address losses is available.

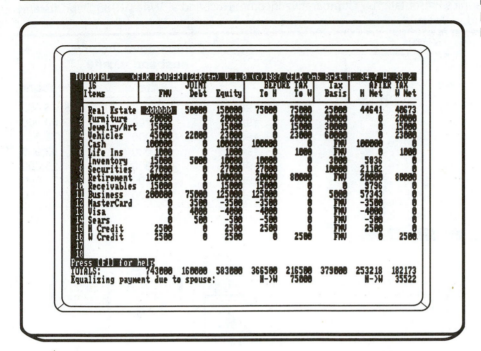

The legal calls are left to the discretion of the practitioner. PROP*ertizer*™ is a tool to make the practitioner's work load lighter and more productive; it relieves you of the drudgery of calculating and recalculating each time you make a change.

For more information on computer software used in the calculations of child-support payments, see page 350. Many software programs have the ability to turn financial data into interesting and effective graphic presentations. For example, the first charts in Exhibit 10–5 compare the income of a husband and wife over a seven-year period. The second chart in Exhibit 10–5 depicts bank deposits and withdrawals over a twelve-month period. A dry listing of numbers can come alive when used in conjunction with such charts.

Assignment 10.15

Contact a lawyer or paralegal who works in a law office that practices family law in whole or part, and find out what computer software programs are used on family law cases other than basic word-processing programs that can be used in any kind of case. Write a report about one such program, including its author, use, cost, level of difficulty, and strengths and weaknesses. Try to obtain the address and phone number of the company that wrote the program. (Perhaps you can write the company and ask for promotional literature on the product. Use its 800 number, if available.)

☐ **EXHIBIT 10–5** Graphics Presentations: Comparative Income, Husband v. Wife; 1988 Deposits and Withdrawals, Husband v. Wife

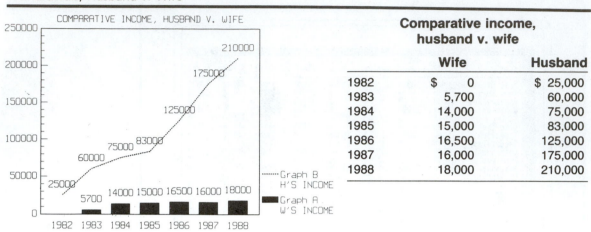

Comparative income, husband v. wife

	Wife	Husband
1982	$ 0	$ 25,000
1983	5,700	60,000
1984	14,000	75,000
1985	15,000	83,000
1986	16,500	125,000
1987	16,000	175,000
1988	18,000	210,000

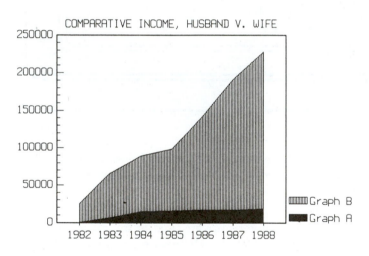

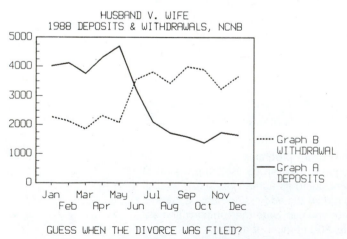

Bank Account

1988	Deposit	W/D
Jan	$4,010	$2,270
Feb	4,120	2,120
Mar	3,755	1,850
Apr	4,305	2,310
May	4,700	2,080
Jun	3,210	3,550
Jul	2,102	3,810
Aug	1,721	3,420
Sep	1,595	3,985
Oct	1,380	3,880
Nov	1,750	3,225
Dec	1,660	3,660

Source: Raggio, "Lawyer-Proof Presentation Graphics," 12 *Family Advocate* 41 (Summer, 1989).

Section R. Sample Separation-Agreement Clauses

Following are the examples of some typical separation-agreement clauses.

Stone B., Modern Legal Forms
§ 4515ff., p. 274ff. (West Publishing Co. (1977)

(I)
Separation Agreement—Significant Clauses*

Agreement made this 19th day of November, 19 ___ , between John Jones, presently residing at 10 South Street, _____ , hereinafter sometimes referred to as "the Husband," and Mary Jones, presently residing at 25 North Street, _____ , hereinafter sometimes referred to as "the Wife."

Witnesseth:

Whereas, the parties are husband and wife and were married in _____ , on June 15, 19 ___ , and

Whereas, there are two children of the marriage, namely a daughter, Elizabeth Ann Jones, hereinafter referred as "Elizabeth," born on April 1, 19 ___ , and a son, William Roe Jones, hereinafter referred to as "William," born on August 15, 19 ___ and

Whereas, in consequence of disputes and irreconcilable differences, the parties have separated, and are now living separate and apart, and intend to continue to live separate and apart for the rest of their natural lives; and

Whereas the parties desire to confirm their separation and make arrangements in connection therewith, including the settlement of all questions relating to their property rights, the custody of their children (which the parties recognize as paramount), and other rights and obligations growing out of the marriage relation;

Now, Therefore, in consideration of the premises and of the mutual convenants and undertakings herein set forth, the parties covenant and agree as follows:

Separation

1. The parties may and shall at all times hereafter live and continue to live separate and apart for the rest of their natural lives. Each shall be free from interference, authority and control, direct or indirect, by the other as fully as if he or she were single and unmarried. Subject to the provisions of this agreement, each may reside at such place or places as he or she may select. The parties shall not molest each other or compel or endeavor to compel the other to cohabit or dwell with him or her, by any legal or other proceedings for restitution of conjugal rights or otherwise.

Wife's Debts.

2. The Wife convenants and represents that she has not heretofore incurred or contracted, nor will she at any time in the future incur or contract, any debt, charge or liability whatsoever for which the Husband, his legal representatives, or his property or estate is now or may become liable, and the Wife further convenants at all times to keep the Husband free, harmless and indemnified of and from any and all debts, charges and liabilities heretofore and hereafter contracted by her.

---

*From a lecture by John Scully, Jr., on *Significant Clauses in a Separation Agreement*, published in 7 Record of the Bar Association of the City of New York 236–250.

Mutual Release.

3. Subject to the provisions of this agreement, each party has remised, released and forever discharged and by these presents does for himself or herself, and his or her heirs, legal representatives, executors, administrators and assigns remise, release and forever discharge the other of and from all cause or causes of action, claims, rights or demands whatsoever, in law or in equity, which either of the parties hereto ever had or now has against the other, except any or all cause or causes of action for divorce.

Waivers of Claims Against Estates.

4. Subject to the provisions of this agreement, each of the parties may in any way dispose of his or her property of whatsoever nature, real or personal, and each of the parties hereto, for himself or herself, and for his or her heirs, legal representatives, executors, administrators and assigns, hereby waive any right of election which he or she may have or hereafter acquire regarding the estate of the other, or to take against any last will and testament of the other, whether heretofore or hereafter executed, . . . and renounces and releases all interest, right or claim of right to dower, or otherwise, that he or she now has or might otherwise have against the other, on the property of whatsoever nature, real or personal, of the other, under or by virtue of the laws of any State or country, and each will at the request of the other, or his or her legal representatives, executors, administrators and assigns execute, acknowledge and deliver any and all deeds, releases, or any other instruments necessary to bar, release or extinguish such interests, rights and claims, or which may be needful for the proper carrying into effect of any of the provisions of this agreement. Each of the parties renounces and relinquishes any and all claims and rights that he or she may have or may hereafter acquire to act as executor or administrator of the other party's estate.

Division of Personal Property.

5. The parties have heretofore divided their personal property to their mutual satisfaction. Henceforth, each of the parties shall own, have and enjoy, independently of any claim or right of the other party, all items of personal property of every kind, nature and description and wheresoever situate, which are now owned or held by or which may hereafter belong or come to the Husband or the Wife, with the full power to the Husband or the Wife to dispose of same as fully and effectually, in all respects and for all purposes, as if he or she were unmarried.

Custody of Children.

6. (a) The Wife shall have custody of Elizabeth and shall have custody of William, except that the Husband may at his option have the custody of either child or both, concurrently or at different or overlapping periods, as follows:

(1) between the 1st day of June and the 30th day of September in each year for a continuous period not to exceed three months; and
(2) during the Christmas holidays each year, for a period of not more than 5 days; and
(3) during the Easter school vacations, for a period of not more than 5 days; and
(4) for one week end, consisting of Saturday and Sunday, in each calendar month.

(b) The Husband shall exercise his option by notifying the Wife in writing of his intention so to do at least 30 days before the beginning of any such period referred to in subparagraph (1) of paragraph 6(a) hereof and at least 10 days before the beginning of any such period referred to in subparagraphs (2), (3) or (4) of paragraph 6(a) hereof.

(c) It is the Husband's intent to exercise the right of partial custody each year and from time to time, but the Husband's partial custody as provided in subparagraph 6(a) hereof shall be entirely optional with him and his waiver thereof on any occasion, and for any reason, shall not constitute a waiver of his right to insist thereafter upon compliance with the provision thereof.

(d) The Husband shall have the right to meet with the children at any time on reasonable notice, and the Wife shall afford the Husband the opportunity to do so.

(e) Neither the Husband nor the Wife shall have the right to take or send the children or either of them outside of the continental territorial limits of the United States of America without obtaining the prior written consent of the other.

(f) Each of the parties agrees to keep the other informed at all times of the whereabouts of the children while the children or either of them are with the Husband or Wife respectively, and they mutually agree that if either of them has knowledge of any illness or accident or other circumstances seriously affecting the health or welfare of either of the children, the Husband or the Wife, as the case may be, will promptly notify the other of such circumstances.

(g) The parties shall consult with each other with respect to the education and religious training of the children, their illnesses and operations (except in emergencies), their welfare and other matters of similar importance affecting the children, whose well-being, education and development shall at all times be the paramount consideration of the Husband and the Wife.

(h) The parties shall exert every reasonable effort to maintain free access and unhampered contact between the children and each of the parties, and to foster a feeling of affection between the children and the other party. Neither party shall do anything which may estrange either child from the other party, or injure the opinion of the children as to their mother or father, or which may hamper the free and natural development of either child's love and respect for the other party.

Support of Wife and Children.

7. If the Wife has not remarried (should the parties be divorced), the Husband shall make the following payments to the Wife for her life and for the support and maintenance of the Wife and for the support, maintenance and education of the children:

Wife's Counsel Fees.

8. The Husband will pay the reasonable counsel fees and legal expenses of the Wife in connection with negotiation and preparation of this agreement.

Acceptance and Release by Wife.

The Wife recognizes and acknowledges that the foregoing provisions for her benefit are satisfactory and that they are reasonable and adequate for her support and maintenance, past, present and future, and in keeping with her accustomed mode of living, reasonable requirements and station in life. The Wife accordingly releases and discharges the Husband, absolutely and forever, for the rest of her life from any and all claims and demands, past, present and future for alimony or for any provision for maintenance and support except as contained in this agreement.

Subsequent Divorce.

10. In the event that an action for divorce is instituted at any time hereafter by either party against the other in this or any other state or country, the parties hereto agree that they shall be bound by all the terms of this agreement and this agreement shall not be merged in any decree or judgment that may be granted in such action but shall survive the same and shall be forever binding and conclusive on the parties and nothing herein contained shall be construed to prevent the decree of judgment in any such action from incorporating in full or in substance the terms of this agreement.

Entire Agreement.

11. Both the legal and practical effect of this agreement in each and every respect and the financial status of the parties has been fully explained to both parties by their

respective counsel and they both acknowledge that it is a fair agreement and is not the result of any fraud, duress or undue influence exercised by either party upon the other or by any other person or persons upon either, and they further agree that this agreement contains the entire understanding of the parties. There are no representations, promises, warranties, convenants or undertakings other than those expressly set forth herein.

Additional Instruments.

12. Each of the parties hereto agrees further at any time and from time to time to make, execute and deliver all instruments necessary to effectuate the provisions of this agreement.

Notices.

13. For the purpose of this agreement, all notices or other communications given or made hereunder shall, until written notice to the contrary, be given or mailed to the Wife at 25 North Street, _____ , and to the Husband at 10 South Street, ____ .

Each party shall at all times keep the other party informed of his or her place of residence and business and shall promptly notify the other party of any change, giving the address of any new place of residence or business.

Situs.

14. All matters affecting the interpretation of this agreement and the rights of the parties hereto shall be governed by the laws of the State of _____ .

Binding Effect.

15. All the provisions of this agreement shall be binding upon the respective heirs, next of kin, executors, administrators and assigns of the parties hereto.

Counterparts.

16. This agreement shall be executed in triplicate, each of which so executed shall be deemed an original and shall constitute one and the same agreement.

In Witness Whereof, the parties hereto have hereunto set their respective hands and seals and initialed each page of this agreement the day and year first above written.

Witnesses:

_____ .   _____ . [L.S.]

_____ .   _____ . [L.S.]

[Add acknowledgments]
_____

(II)
Separation Agreement—Fixed Monthly Payments—Custody and Support of Children

This Agreement is made the _____ day of _____ , 19 __ , between _____ , herein called the Husband, and _____ , his wife, herein called the Wife.

Whereas the Husband and Wife were married on the _____ day of _____ , 19 __ , and have two children, _____ and _____ ;

Whereas differences have arisen between the Husband and Wife as the result of which they are now living separate and apart;

Whereas the Husband and Wife have entered into this Agreement freely, with the advice of counsel, and acknowledge that its provisions are fair.

The parties agree as follows:

Separation.

1. The Husband and Wife may live apart from each other as if they were unmarried. Each shall be free from the control of the other and may reside at such place as he or she shall think fit.

No Interference.

2. The Husband and Wife will not in any manner annoy, molest or disturb the other, or compel or endeavor to compel the other to cobahit or dwell with him or her.

Wife's Debts.

3. The Wife will at all times keep the Husband indemnified against all debts and liabilities which she may hereafter contract and from all actions, claims, demands, costs, damages and expenses on account thereof. In case the Husband shall at any time be called on to and shall pay any debt or debts which she may hereafter contract, then it shall be lawful for the Husband to retain out of the next amount payable to the Wife hereunder the amount of such debt or debts with all costs and expenses which he may incur on account thereof.

Division of Household Goods.

4. The Husband and Wife have divided between them to their mutual satisfaction the personal effects, household furniture and furnishings, and all other articles of personal property which have been used by them in common, in accordance with the Schedule attached hereto.

Transfer of Home.

5. The Husband has conveyed to the Wife by deed, executed, acknowledged and delivered simultaneously with the execution of this Agreement, the property which was the former home of the parties and in which the Wife now resides.

Support of Wife.

6. The Husband shall during the life of the Wife and until she remarries pay to the Wife, or to such person as she shall from time to time appoint in writing, the yearly sum of _____ dollars by equal monthly payments beginning on the _____ day of _____ , 19 __ , for the support and maintenance of herself.

Custody of the Children in Wife.

7. The Wife shall have the sole custody and control of the children, _____ and _____ , without any interferance on the part of the Husband except as herein provided.

Right of Husband to Visit Children.

8. The Husband shall have the right to visit the children or either of them one day every two weeks if he so desires at reasonable times and places. Further, the Husband shall at his option have the custody of the children or either of them during the summer school holidays for a continuous period of one month.

Duty to the Wife to Care for Children.

9. The Wife shall properly care for, educate and maintain the children until they respectively reach the age of 21 years.

Support of Children.

10. The Husband shall pay to the Wife as long as she shall have custody of the children or either of them the sum of _____ dollars each month beginning on the _____ day of _____ , 19 __ , for the support and education of each child so in the custody of the Wife until such child reaches the age of 21 years.

Mutual Release.

11. Except as herein otherwise provided the Husband and Wife release and forever discharge the other of and from all causes of action, claims, rights or demands whatsoever in law or in equity which either of the parties hereto ever had or now has against the other except all causes of action for divorce.

Subsequent Divorce.

12. If the Husband or Wife shall hereafter apply for a divorce and the court shall grant the same, this Agreement shall be submitted to the court for approval. If it is approved by the court, the terms thereof shall be carried into the decree of divorce and operate as a final determination of the property rights of the parties.

Wife's Attorney's Fees.

13. The Husband shall pay to _____ the sum of _____ dollars for his services as attorney to the Wife in connection with the negotiation and preparation of this Agreement.

Additional Instruments.

14. The Husband and Wife shall at the request of the other execute, acknowledge and deliver to the other party any and all further instruments that may be reasonably required to give full force and effect to the provisions of this Agreement.

Binding Effect.

15. This Agreement shall be binding on the heirs, executors, administrators and assigns of the parties hereto.

In witness whereof the parties have signed and sealed this Agreement.

_____ [Seal]

_____ [Seal]

[Add acknowledgments]

_____

(III)
Separation Agreement—Dismissal of Pending Action for Separation—Lump Sum Cash and Property Settlement—No Children

This agreement, made this _____ day of _____ , 19 __ , between _____ , the Husband, and _____ , the Wife.

Whereas, the parties were married on _____ day of _____ , 19 __ , and thereafter, on or about the _____ day of _____ , 19 __ , separated and have since lived apart;

Whereas, an action was instituted by the Wife against the Husband in the _____ Court of _____ , for a separation and provision for the maintenance of the Wife;

Whereas, the parties have agreed upon what is a reasonable provision for the support and maintenance of the Wife, past, present and for the remainder of her natural life; and

Whereas, the parties have agreed on a reasonable and just disposal of all of the property of the Husband, free and discharged of any and all past, present and future claims, demands, charges, dower estate rights, interests, liens, or other property rights of any kind whatsoever of the Wife.

Now, therefore, the parties agree as follows:

Separation

1. The parties agree to continue to live separate and apart from each other the same as if unmarried. Each may reside from time to time at such place or places, and,

conduct, carry on and engage in any employment, business or trade which he or she shall deem fit, free from any control, restraint, or interference direct or indirect by the other.

Dismissal of Action

2. The parties agree that the said action for separation and maintenance now pending in the _____ Court shall be immediately dismissed without costs to either party.

Wife's Support

3. Simultaneously with the signing of this agreement the Husband agrees to pay to the Wife the sum of _____ dollars, and to pay her attorney's bills and court disbursements in said action, amounting to _____ dollars, and further to convey to her by warranty deed the following described property: [*Description*]. It is understood that said money and property is given to the Wife for her support and maintenance. The Wife agrees that such provision is ample and will in fact provide her with a support and maintenance befitting her station in life, and she accepts said money and property in full satisfaction and in lieu of support and maintenance by the Husband during her life.

No Future Liability

4. Neither party shall contract any debts in the name of the other, or in any way attempt to charge the other with liability therefor, nor will either party claim or demand maintenance or support from the other.

Each Spouse Releases Right in Property of Deceased Spouse

5. The Wife agrees that the estate of the Husband, after the payment of the consideration herein mentioned to the Wife, shall belong to the person or persons who would have become entitled thereto if the Wife had died during the lifetime of the Husband; and the Wife further agrees that she will permit any will of the Husband to be probated, and allow administration upon his personal estate to be taken out by the person or persons who would have been entitled so to do, had the Wife died during the lifetime of the Husband. The Husband agrees that the estate of the Wife, including the consideration herein mentioned, shall belong to the person or persons who would have become entitled thereto if the Husband had died during the lifetime of the Wife; and the Husband further agrees that he will permit any will of the Wife to be probated, and allow administration upon her personal estate to be taken out by the person or persons who would have been entitled so to do, had the Husband died during the lifetime of the Wife.

Further Assurance

6. The parties shall make, execute and deliver any and all such further assurances as the other of the parties shall reasonably require, for the purpose of giving full effect to the provisions of this agreement.

Effect of Divorce

7. The Wife agrees that in case the marriage between the parties should be dissolved by order of court, then the consideration passing to the Wife under this agreement shall stand as full satisfaction and discharge of alimony, counsel fees and other claims and demands which might be made by the Wife against the Husband for any cause whatever.

In Witness Whereof, *etc.*

_____

(IV)
Separation Agreement Incident
to Divorce Action—Lump Sump Cash
Settlement—No Children

This agreement made _____ , 19__ , between _____ , the Husband, and _____ , the Wife.

Whereas on _____ , 19__ , the parties were married in _____ County, _____ , and lived together as husband and wife until _____ , 19__ , and have reached the conclusion that it will be impossible for them to continue to live together;

Whereas a bill for divorce has been prepared and the parties are desirous of settling any and all claims for alimony that the Wife might have against the Husband; and

Whereas each party acknowledges that this agreement has been entered into freely with full knowledge of the facts, and each party believes that under the circumstances the sum of $_____ is a fair and adequate settlement of all alimony;

Now, therefore, in consideration of the payment to the Wife of the sum of $_____ , the receipt of which is hereby acknowledged, the Wife does hereby release the Husband from any and all claims, now and hereafter, that might arise by way of alimony. The said settlement of alimony is hereby accepted as a full release of any and all liability, present and future, in so far as any alimony or property adjustment between the Husband and the Wife is concerned.

The foregoing settlement is approved by the undersigned _____ as attorney for the Wife.

[*Signatures*]

(V)
Separation Agreement—Divorce Action Pending—Fixed
Monthly Payments—Deposit of Property to Secure Such
Payments—Release of Wife's Interest in Community
Property—No Children*

This agreement made this _____ day of _____ , 19__ , between _____ , herein called the Husband, and _____ , herein called the Wife.

Whereas, the parties were united in marriage at _____ , on or about the _____ day of _____ , 19__ , and lived together as husband and wife until about the ___ day of _____ , 19__ ; and

---

*Adapted from the record in Farrell v. Commissioner of Internal Revenue, 134 F.2d 193 (C.C.A.Tex.1943) certiorari denied 64 S.Ct. 47, 320 U.S. 745, 88 L.Ed. 442; a proceeding to collect a deficiency in income taxes from one of the parties to this agreement.

The community property released in this contract consisted in part of oil leases that subsequently turned out to be very valuable. Shortly after this agreement was executed, Mrs. Farrell secured a divorce from her husband and the decree embodied the terms of the contract with respect to the monthly payments and the transfer of the community interest to the husband. Four days later she married again.

About two years later she brought suit in the Texas courts to have the property provisions of the divorce decree set aside on the ground that she was induced to enter into this agreement by fraud. The Court of Civil Appeals in Burguieres v. Farrell, 85 S.W.2d 952 (Tex.Civ.App.1935), upheld the agreement, holding that the entire transaction was fair, that the wife was fully informed and there was no fraud.

Whereas, during the time the parties lived together as husband and wife they acquired certain real and personal property which comprises their community estate and which is not susceptible of partition; and

Whereas, on the _____ day of _____ , 19__ , the Wife filed her petition in the _____ Court of _____ County, _____ , praying that the marriage relation between herself and the Husband be dissolved, and the parties have agreed that in the event said marriage relation is dissolved by judgment of said Court as prayed for in said petition, in lieu of a partition of said community estate the Husband shall pay to the Wife the sum of _____ dollars per month so long as she shall live, and the Wife shall transfer, assign and convey to the Husband all her right, title, and interest in and to said community estate;

Now, therefore, it is agreed as follows:

1. The Husband agrees to pay to the Wife the sum of _____ dollars on the first day of _____ , 19__ , and the sum of _____ dollars on the first day of each and every month thereafter so long as she shall live, said payments to be made by the Husband to the _____ National Bank of _____ , with instructions to said bank to promptly pay the same to the Wife. For the purpose of guaranteeing such payments the Husband shall deposit with said bank the sum of _____ dollars in cash and _____ shares of the capital stock of _____ Corporation, of the approximate present value of _____ dollars; provided that the Husband shall have the right at any time to withdraw such shares of stock upon depositing with said bank the further sum of _____ dollars in cash in lieu thereof; and provided further that in the event the Husband shall fail to make any of the payments herein provided for, said _____ bank shall have the right to sell said shares of stock for cash and make such payments to the Wife out of such fund and in such event the Wife shall have the right to require the Husband to deposit the amount of such payment or payments with said bank in order that such fund shall at all times be maintained at the sum of _____ dollars or at the sum of _____ dollars and said _____ shares of the capital stock of _____ Corporation.

2. The Wife agrees that all property, belonging to the community estate of the parties, shall be and become the separate property of the Husband, and any and all rights, title and interest in and to said property now belonging to the Wife, or which might be claimed by her, shall be, and the same hereby is, transferred, assigned, and conveyed to the Husband, free from any and all liens or claims on the part of the Wife, and the Wife further agrees that she will, upon demand, execute and deliver to the Husband proper deeds, assignments or conveyances for any and all of such property conveying the title therein to the Husband.

In Witness Whereof, *etc.*

(VI)

Separation Agreement—Divorce Action Pending—Lump Sum and Fixed Monthly Payments to Wife—Transfer of Community Property to Husband—Custody and Support of Children

This agreement made the _____ day of _____ , 19__ , between _____ , herein called the Husband, and _____ , herein called the Wife.

Whereas, disputes have arisen between the parties, and by reason thereof they have agreed to live separate and apart from each other during their natural lives; and

Whereas, the Husband as plaintiff filed a suit for divorce in the _____ Court of _____ County, _____ , numbered _____ on the docket of said Court, which suit is now pending, and the Wife has filed her cross-action for divorce in said suit, and regardless of the outcome of the trial thereof, the parties recognize that their differences are so great that a reconciliation is impossible; and

Whereas, the Husband has furnished to the Wife a list of all principal assets and liabilities as of _____ , 19__ , and has also furnished additional information as to change of assets and liabilities as of this date, and the Wife has investigated and appraised these assets and liabilities with the aid of her legal counsel and is thoroughly conversant with all facts; and

Whereas, the parties desire to completely and forever settle their property rights in and to their community property, which is all of the property that either of them possesses.

The parties agree as follows:

Separation

1. They shall live separate and apart from each other the remainder of their natural lives, and neither shall have any right in any way to control the personal actions or conduct of the other, or to complain about such actions or conduct except in so far as the same may affect the right of custody of their children, and neither shall in any way molest, disturb or trouble the other.

Alimony to Wife

2. In full, final and complete settlement of all the rights of the Wife in and to the community property of the parties, as well as any and all other claims which she may now or hereafter have against the Husband arising out of the marriage relationship, the Husband has paid and promises to pay to the Wife the following amounts:

(a) *Lump Sum Payment*. The Husband has this day paid to the Wife the sum of $_____ , receipt of which is hereby acknowledged.

(b) *Fixed Monthly Payments*. The Husband promises to pay to the Wife at _____ , the sum of $_____ per month for _____ years, the first payment being due _____ and one payment being due on the _____ day of each month thereafter for _____ full years. Such payments may be made by check mailed to the Wife on or before the due dates, addressed to the last address that the Wife may have given in writing to the Husband.

(c) *Insurance Policies to Secure Monthly Payments*. The Husband shall at all times carry life insurance in solvent companies, payable to the Wife as beneficiary, for the amount of the then unpaid installments hereinabove provided, discounted at _____ per cent per year compounded for the period of prepayment; and upon the Husband's death, the Wife shall accept payment of said insurance money in full payment and satisfaction of all of the then unpaid monthly payments provided for in paragraph (b) hereof. The Husband shall have the right to discharge his obligations under said paragraph (b) at any time after the expiration of _____ years from date by paying the value of unmatured installments discounted at _____ per cent per year compounded for the period of prepayment.

(d) *Upon Death of Wife, Wife's Monthly Payments to be Made to Children*. Should the Wife die before the monthly installments are all paid, the then remaining installments shall be paid as they mature to the _____ children of the parties in equal parts, or to their guardian if they are then minors.

(e) *Transfer to Wife of Personal Belongings*. The Wife shall have as her property all of the silverware, dishes, glass-ware, linens, rugs, drapes, furniture, pictures and furnishings now in the home at _____ , except _____ , which excepted articles shall belong to the Husband. The Wife shall vacate the home on or before _____ , 19__ , but agrees that the Husband may keep all of her said personal property in the home until _____ , 19__ , at which time she shall remove the same, provided however that if the home is sold at an earlier date she shall upon demand remove her personal property.

Transfer of Community Property to Husband

3. All other property, rights, claims and choses in action belonging to the Husband or to their community estate, whether or not herein specifically mentioned, shall belong

absolutely to the Husband, as his separate property, and the Wife agrees to execute to the Husband upon demand general warranty deeds covering her interest in all real property owned by them and bills of sale or other conveyances of title to such personal property. The principal items of property to be conveyed are as follows: [*Here list*].

Wife's Debts

4. The Wife agrees to pay promptly all bills incurred by her since _____ , 19___ . Should the Wife fail to pay any of such bills, and demand for payment is made on the Husband, he may pay same and deduct the amount so paid from the monthly payments owing by him to the Wife.

Community Debts

5. The Husband agrees to pay all of the community indebtedness of the parties not herein assumed by the Wife.

Custody of Children

6. The two children, _____ and _____ , shall remain with the Wife, subject to the orders of the Court as is provided by law in such cases. The Husband shall have the right to visit his children and to have their company and companionship at reasonable times to be arranged.

Support of Children

7. The Husband shall pay to the Wife the sum of $_____ per month for each child on the first day of each month for the support and maintenance of the two children, which payments shall continue until the Husband's legal obligation to support them ends, or until changed as to amount by agreement of the parties or by order of the Court. Such payments shall cover all living expenses of the children that could be chargeable to the Husband, except tuition to schools to be selected by agreement of the parties which the Husband shall also pay, and such medical expenses as the Husband may first approve in writing. If one or both of the children shall at any time, by agreement of the parties, be sent to boarding schools or to summer camps, the Husband shall pay their reasonable expenses while there, but during such times he shall not be required to make the monthly payments otherwise required to be made to the Wife for their support and maintenance.

Mutual Release

8. In consideration of the payments now made and agreed to be hereafter made, the parties do each declare this to be a full, final and complete settlement of all of their property rights, and each party does hereby release and relinquish to the other all of his or her rights, title, claim, interest and demand, accrued or accruing in and to the property of the other whether now in being or hereafter acquired; and this shall be a full and complete settlement of the controversy over the property rights of the parties, involved in cause No. _____ in the _____ Court of _____ County, and, except for the right of either party to prosecute his or her suit for complete divorce, this settlement shall be a bar to any suit at law or otherwise for anything growing out of the marriage relation of the parties as well as the property rights of the one against the other.

Witness our hands, in triplicate, at _____ , this _____ day of _____ , 19___ .

_____

_____

Witnesses:

_____

_____

[Add acknowledgments]

_____

(VII)
Separation Agreement—Divorce
Action Pending—Alimony Based on
Oil Royalties—Custody and Support of Child

This agreement, made this _____ day of _____ , 19___ , between _____ , of _____ , herein called the Husband, and _____ , of _____ , herein called the Wife, witnesseth:

Whereas, the parties are husband and wife, but are now living separate and apart from each other, and it is their intention to continue to live separate and apart; and,

Whereas, the Wife has this day instituted suit for divorce against the Husband in the _____ Court of _____ County, _____ , under cause numbered _____ in said Court, and has asked that she be awarded the custody, care, control and education of _____ , minor child of the parties and for the ratification and approval of this property settlement and agreement concerning the support and maintenance of said child; and,

Whereas, the parties have this day reached a satisfactory agreement between themselves out of Court concerning the custody, support and maintenance of said child, and the support, maintenance and alimony of the Wife, as well as for a division of and settlement of property rights, claims or demands of any nature, either past, present or future, as hereinafter set out.

Now, therefore, the parties agree as follows:

Custody of Child

1. The Wife is to have the care, custody and control of _____ , minor child of the parties, subject to the approval of the _____ Court of _____ County, _____ , subject to any future orders of said Court concerning the custody of said child and subject to the right of the Husband to visit said child at any and all reasonable times and occasions; and the Wife, subject to the conditions hereinafter stated, accepts the custody of said child and agrees to properly care for, support, rear, train and educate said child to the best of her ability, it being understood that the Wife shall have the right to select the residence for said child at whatsoever place within the State of _____ she may desire, but that she will inform the Husband of any change in said place of residence.

Support of Wife and Child

2. The Husband shall turn over to the Wife for the support of and maintenance of herself and _____ , minor child of the parties, until such time as the Wife may remarry, all of the proceeds arising from his interest in oil and gas royalties from wells now producing, and one half of all of the proceeds arising from his interest in oil and gas royalties from any wells which may be hereafter drilled upon any and all land now owned by the Husband, or in which he may own any interest, either legal or equitable, said land being particularly described as follows: [*Here describe*].

Remarriage or Death of Wife

3. It is further agreed that in the event of the remarriage of the Wife to any person other than the Husband during the lifetime of _____ , minor child of the parties, then all of said oil and gas royalties, oil and gas runs, or proceeds from same arising from said lands shall be paid to said child, or to her duly appointed guardian. In the event the Husband and the Wife remarry each other, or in the event the Wife marries someone other than the Husband during the lifetime of said child, and said child thereafter dies, or in the event of the remarriage of the Wife after the death of said child, or in the event of the death of the Wife at any time, then immediately upon the happening thereof, the Husband shall be entitled to, and shall have and receive all such oil and gas royalties, oil and gas runs, or other proceeds arising from the same not already paid over to the Wife or to said child under this agreement; and the Wife

agrees that in the event of any such remarriage she will promptly make, execute and deliver any necessary and proper transfer orders, division orders, or other instruments necessary to enable such person as is entitled thereto under this agreement to collect and receive same, and that in the event she should refuse or neglect to do so, then this instrument shall be treated and construed as a compliance and assignment of said interests, runs and royalties.

Sale of Royalty Interest

4. It is further agreed that the Husband shall have the full and unrestricted use of all of the lands in any manner acquired by him and the rents and profits thereof, except the royalties and oil and gas runs above mentioned, but that in the event of the sale by the Husband of any of said real estate herein described during the lifetime of _____ , minor child of the parties, the Husband shall pay over to said child, or to her duly appointed guardian, for her use, support, maintenance and education, one third of any and all sums realized from the sale of any or all of said property and that the Wife will, upon request, join with the Husband, or will execute, acknowledge and deliver any and all necessary and proper instruments in writing to effectuate the sale and conveyance of any such property; it being understood, however, that nothing in this paragraph shall be construed as conferring the right upon the Husband to make any sale or conveyance of any oil or gas royalty in, to or under any of the land above described, but that said oil and gas royalty interests in said land shall be held for the use, support and maintenance of the Wife and said child, as herein provided.

Release by Wife

5. The Wife agrees that she will not at any time undertake to hold the Husband liable for, or undertake to collect from him any sums for alimony, court costs, attorneys' fees, support and maintenance for herself or said child, and that this agreement may be pleaded in any suit as a defense to any action for alimony, court costs, attorneys' fees, support and maintenance.

Witness our signatures in duplicate the day and year above written.

_____
Husband

_____
Wife

[*Add acknowledgments*]

Assignment 10.16

Two members of the class will role-play in front of the rest of the class a negotiation session involving a husband and wife who want to enter a separation agreement. The spouses are representing themselves. They have two children, ages two and three. Each member of the class (including the two role-players) will draft a separation agreement based upon the understandings reached at the negotiation session. The role-players can make up the facts as they go along, e.g., names of the parties, addresses, kinds of assets involved. Use the checklist on page 211 as an overview of the topics to be negotiated. In the negotiation session, the role-players should not act hostile toward each other. They should be courteous but anxious to protect their own rights. Finally, they should not leave any matters hanging—everything discussed should result in some form of agreement through the process of bargaining and compromise. (See General Instructions for the Agreement-Drafting Assignment in chapter one.)

☐ **EXHIBIT 10—6** Sample Property Agreement

Sample Property Agreement

California Judicial Council Form Manual
3-99 to 3-82 (Jan. 1988)

I.   We are Waldo P. Smedlap, hereafter called Husband,[1] and Lydia T. Smedlap, hereafter called Wife. We were married on October 7, 1978 and separated on December 5, 1979. Because irreconcilable differences have caused the permanent breakdown of our marriage,[2] we have made this agreement together to settle once and for all what we owe to each other and what we can expect from each other. Each of us states here that nothing has been held back, that we have honestly included everything we could think of in listing the money and goods that we own; and each of us states here that we believe the other one has been open and honest in writing up this agreement. And each of us agrees to sign and exchange any papers that might be needed to complete this assignment.

Each of us also understands that even after a Joint Petition for Summary Dissolution is filed, this entire agreement will be cancelled if either of us revokes the Dissolution Proceeding.[3]

II. Division of Community Property[4]
We divided our community property as follows:

1. Husband transfers to Wife as her sole and separate property:
   A. All household furniture and furnishings located at her apartment at 180 Needlepoint Way, San Francisco.[5]
   B. All rights to cash in savings account #08-73412-085 at Home Savings.
   C. All cash value in life insurance policy #798567 Sun Valley Life Insurance, insuring life of Wife.
   D. All retirement and pension plan benefits earned by Wife during marriage.
   E. 2 U.S. Savings Bond Series E.
   F. Wife's jewelry.
   G. 1972 Chevrolet 4-door sedan, License No. EXL 129.

2. Wife transfers to Husband as his sole and separate property:
   A. All household furniture and furnishings located at his apartment on 222 Bond Street, San Francisco.
   B. All retirement and pension plan benefits earned by Husband during the marriage.
   C. Season tickets to Golden State Terriers Basketball games.
   D. 1 stereo set.
   E. 1 set of Jock Nicklaus golf clubs.
   F. 1 RAC color television.
   G. 1973 Ford station wagon License No. EPX 758.
   H. 1 pet parrot named Arthur, plus cage and parrot food.
   I. All rights to cash in Checking Account #1721-319748-07, Bank of America.

[1] *Wherever the word Husband appears in this agreement, it will stand for Waldo P. Smedlap; wherever the word Wife appears, it will stand for Lydia T. Smedlap.*

[2] *This means that there are problems in your marriage which you think can never be solved. Irreconcilable differences are the only legal grounds for getting a Summary Dissolution.*

[3] *This means that the property agreement is a part of the divorce proceedings. If either of you decides to stop the Dissolution proceedings by turning in a Notice of Revocation of Summary Dissolution, this entire agreement will be cancelled.*

[4] *Community property is property which you own as a couple.*
If you have no community property, replace part II with the simple statement, "We have no community property."

[5] *If the furniture and household goods in one apartment are to be divided, then they may have to be listed item by item.*

☐ **EXHIBIT 10–6** Sample Property Agreement—Continued

III. **Division of Community Property (Debts)**[6]

    1. Husband shall pay the following debts and will not at any time hold wife responsible for them:
      A. Mister Charge account #417-38159 208-094.
      B. Debt to Dr. R. C. Himple.
      C. Debt to Sam's Drugs.
      D. Debt to U.C. Berkeley for college education loan to Husband.[7]

    2. Wife shall pay the following debts and will not at any time hold Husband responsible for them:
      A. Cogwell's charge account #808921.
      B. Debt to Wife's parents, Mr. and Mrs. Joseph Smith.
      C. Debt to Green's Furniture.
      D. Debt to Dr. Irving Roberts.

IV. **Waiver of Spousal Support**[8]
Each of us waives any claim for spousal support now and for all time.

V. Dated: _____ Dated: _____

       Waldo P. Smedlap   Lydia T. Smedlap

[6]*If you have no unpaid debts, replace part III with the simple statement, "We have no unpaid community obligations."*

[7]*A general rule for dividing debts is to give the debt over to the person who benefited most from the item. In the sample agreement, since the Husband received the education, he should pay off the loan.*

[8]*You give up the right to have your spouse support you.*

Key Chapter Terminology

Separation Agreement	Security
Post-Nuptial Contract	Arrears
Financial Assets	Escrow
Interrogatories	Surety Bond
Public Policy	Annuity
Collusion	Trust
Inducement to Divorce	Rehabilitative Alimony
Facilitate Divorce	Real Property
Migratory Divorce	Personal Property
Capacity to Contract	Frozen Embryos
Duress	In Vitro Fertilization
Fraud	Bequest
Consideration	Devise
Alimony	Joint Tenancy
Maintenance	Tenancy by Entireties
Property Division	Tenancy in Common
Discharge in Bankruptcy	Community Property
Contempt of Court	Common Law Property
Incorporation and Merger	Quasi-Community Property
Contingencies	Appreciation
Lump-Sum vs. Periodic Payment	Pensions
Fluctuating Payment	Defined Benefit Plan

Defined Contribution Plan
Vested
Qualified Domestic Relations Order
     (QDRO)
Alternate Payee
Present Value
Goodwill
Testate
Intestate

Elect against Will
Forced Share
Nonmolestation Clause
Modification
Arbitration
Mediation
Reconciliation
Executory

Child Custody

■ Chapter Outline

L egal custody and physical custody can be given to one parent (sole cus-tody), or to both parents (joint custody). Variations include "bird's nest" custody and split custody.

In negotiating custody and visitation terms of a separation agreement, many factors need to be considered, such as the age and health of the parents and child, the emotional attachments of the child, the work schedules of the parents, etc. If negotiations fail and the parties cannot agree, litigation is necessary. This can be a bitter experience, not only for the parents, but also for the person caught in the middle—the child.

The court has considerable discretion in resolving a custody battle between two biological parents according to the standard of the best interest of the child. It will consider a number of relevant factors such as availability to respond to the child's day-to-day needs, and emotional ties that have already developed. At one time, courts applied evidentiary guidelines such as the presumption that a child of tender years is better off with his or her mother. Today, such controversial presumptions are rejected by many courts, although fathers continue to complain that the mother is still given an undue preference.

The moral values and lifestyles of the parent seeking custody are generally not considered by the court unless they affect the welfare of the child. If the parents practice different religions, the court cannot prefer one religion over another, but can consider what effect the practice of a particular religion will have on the child. To the extend possible, the court will try to maintain continuity in the child's cultural development. If the child is old enough to express a preference, it will be considered. Often the court will also consider the testimony of expert witnesses.

Using the same best-interest-of-the-child standard, the court will generally favor liberal visitation rights for the noncustodial parent. Occasionally, such rights will be granted to individuals other than biological parents, e.g., grandparents. One of the most distressing issues in this area is the charge by the custodial parent that the child has been sexually molested during visitation.

When the custody battle is between a biological parent and a nonparent (often called a psychological parent), the biological parent usually wins unless he or she can be shown to be unfit.

Occasionally it is in the best interest of the child for a court to modify an earlier custody decision because of changed circumstances. Frantic parents will sometimes engage in forum shopping and child snatching in order to find a court that will make a modification order. To cut down on this practice, two important laws have been enacted: the state Uniform Child Custody Jurisdiction Act, and the federal Parental Kidnapping Prevention Act. When the child has been taken to a foreign country, the aid of the Hague Convention on Child Abduction might be enlisted.

Section A. Kinds of Custody

Legal Custody

Legal custody is the right and the duty to make the decisions about raising a child, e.g., decisions on the child's health, education, religion, and discipline. While married and living together, both parents have legal custody of their children. Upon divorce or separation, if both parents continue to make the major decisions together about the health, education, religion, and discipline of the child, they are sharing legal custody, a situation known as joint custody, or joint legal custody.

Physical custody

Physical custody simply refers to the parent with whom the child lives. If a court awards custody to one parent only, that parent is called the *custodial* parent. The other is the *noncustodial* parent, who usually has visitation rights.

Sole custody

Sole custody exists when one parent has both legal custody and physical custody. The other parent has visitation rights. About 70 percent of all custody decisions today are sole-custody arrangements.

Joint custody

Joint custody means that each parent shares legal custody (joint legal custody) and/or shares physical custody (joint physical custody) over alternating but not necessarily equal, periods of time. These arrangements are sometimes referred to as shared parenting or *co-parenting*.

Shared custody

Shared custody has the same meaning as joint custody.

Bird's-nest custody

Bird's-nest custody is joint custody where the child remains in a single home and each parent moves in and out during alternate periods of time.

Split custody

Split custody has two meanings. First, it refers to an arrangement in which one parent has legal custody, with physical custody going to each parent in alternating periods when the child lives with him or her. Second, it refers to a situation involving more than one child. Each parent receives sole custody of at least one child with visitation rights to the other children. This second definition is also referred to as *divided custody*.

None of these categories is static. One kind of custody arrangement may eventually evolve into another kind, either by formal agreement or by informal mutual understanding. For example, one side may have sole custody, but because of circumstances, (e.g., illness or job change), visitation becomes so extensive that the parents end up with the equivalent of a joint-custody arrangement.

Section B. Separation Agreement

Custody

In negotiating the custody term of a separation agreement, many circumstances must be considered by the parties:

- The kind of custody they want (see options in Section A).
- The age and health of the child.
- The age and health of the parents. (Which parent is physically and mentally more able to care for the child on a day-to-day basis?)
- The parent with whom the child has spent the most time up to now. (With whom are the emotional attachments the strongest?)
- Which parent(s) must work on a full-time basis?
- The availability of backup assistance, e.g., from grandparents or close friends, who can help in emergencies.
- How are the major decisions on the child's welfare made, e.g., whether to transfer schools, whether to have an operation? Must one parent consult the other on such matters? Is joint consent ever needed?
- The religious upbringing of the child.

- The child's surname. (Can the name be changed if the mother remarries?)
- Can the child be moved from the area?
- Who would receive custody if both parents died?
- If disputes arise between the parents concerning custody, how are they to be resolved? (Arbitration? Mediation?)
- What happens if one parent violates the agreement on custody, e.g., moves out of the state contrary to the agreement? Can the other parent stop paying alimony?
- Mutual respect. (Do the parties specifically agree to encourage the child to love both parents?)

In recent years, joint custody has received a good deal of attention. Advocates of this option claim that it is psychologically the most healthy alternative for the child. It arguably produces less hostility between parents, less hostility between child and individual parent, less confusion in values for the child, less sexual stereotyping of parental roles (one parent "works," the other cares for children), less manipulation of the child by one or both parents, less manipulation by the child of one or both parents, etc. Others, however, argue that the decision on joint custody should be approached with great caution since it will work only in exceptional circumstances. The parents have just separated. By definition, therefore, they are not able to cooperate in the manner called for by a joint-custody arrangement.

The following factors are relevant to a decision on whether joint custody will work. Any one of these factors might tip the scale *against* its feasibility.

1. Is each parent fit and suitable as a custodial parent?
2. Do both parents agree to joint custody, or is one or both opposed?
3. Have the parents demonstrated that they are able to communicate at least to the extent necessary to reach shared decisions in the child's best interest?
4. Is there geographical proximity so that there will be no substantial disruption of the child's schooling, association with friends, religious training, etc.?
5. Is there similarity in the environment of each parent's home, or will the child be confronted with vastly different or potentially disruptive environmental changes?
6. Is there any indication that the psychological and emotional needs and development of the child will suffer due to a particular joint custodial arrangement?
7. Does each parent have a work schedule and home routine that is compatible with the child's needs so that either can assume full parental duties when he or she has the child?
8. Is joint custody in accord with the child's wishes or does the child have strong opposition to such an arrangement?

Visitation

In negotiating visitation rights in a separation agreement, a number of details must be worked out:

- When can the noncustodial parent have the child visit? Alternating weekends? School vacations? Holidays? Which ones? How much advance notice is needed if additional time is desired?
- At what time is the child to be picked up and returned?
- Can the noncustodial parent take the child on long trips? Is the consent of custodial parent needed?
- Can the custodial parent move out of the area even though this makes visitation more burdensome and costly?
- Who pays the transportation costs, if any, when the child visits the noncustodial parent?
- Is the noncustodial parent required to be available for visits? Will it be a violation of the separation agreement if he or she does not visit? Or, is visitation at the sole discretion of the noncustodial parent?
- When the noncustodial parent decides not to visit at a given time, must he or she notify the custodial parent in advance, or attempt to?
- Do any third parties have visitation rights, e.g., grandparents?
- If disputes arise between the parents on visitation, how are they resolved? (Arbitration? Mediation?)
- What happens if one of the parties violates the agreement on visitation? Does this breach justify nonperformance by the other party or another term of the separation agreement, e.g., alimony payments?

The following article addresses some implications of child custody and provides a sample visitation schedule.

"Fixing Definite Schedules" by Fain

The Matrimonial Strategist 2 (May 1983)

The traumatic and emotional issues that often dominate determination of custody and visitation . . . rights of parents of minor children continues to provoke much litigation. This has perhaps been measurably improved by constructive mediation efforts that have now been initiated by many courts of this country,

As much as it would be preferable to maintain a degree of flexibility in allowing parents to agree on reasonable visitation rights, it is the opinion of most family-law practitioners that it is more important to fix visitation or shared physical custody rights as specifically as possible . . . . This will minimize friction and ensuing disputes between parents who are frequently in a hostile posture to begin with. When visitation rights are set down with particularity, it is more likely that arguments will be discouraged, and less likely that the custodial parent will attempt to limit or defeat the noncustodial parent's visitation rights.

Problems Can Arise

In certain situations, though, specifying visitation rights . . . can lead to problems for parents and child. For example, if a non-custodial parent has an occupation or job with defined hours during the week and regular vacations every year, specificity is fine. But, if the non-custodial parent has an occupation or profession which frequently requires travel, or in which the work requirements do not permit vacations to be planned in advance, specifying rigid visitation rights can often lead to conflict. Such situations should be resolved by tailor-made provisions.

It is clear that regularity and consistency of visits, . . . is better for children because it promotes stability and security of the children's lives, as well as for the parents. However, as with all theories of custody and visitation, even these theories are now being challenged, as exemplified by the continued stress on joint legal and physical custody arrangements. . . .

In a typical traditional visitation arrangement the following schedule has been found reasonably effective in agreements. As with all example clauses, it should be varied or modified by the attorneys and parties to comport with the facts and circumstances of a given case.

SAMPLE VISITATION SCHEDULE: CUSTODY AND VISITATION RIGHTS

Custody of the minor children, Jane X and Joe X, is awarded **Wife.**

I. **Husband** shall have the children with him at the following times:

A. Regular Visitation:

1. On alternate weekends from seven (7:00) p.m. Friday to seven (7:00) p.m. Sunday, commencing Friday, ___ , 19XX.

2. The entire month of **July,** 19XX, the entire month of **August,** the following year, and alternating July and August in subsequent years.

B. Holidays and Special Days:

1. Lincoln's Birthday, 19XX, from seven (7:00) p.m. the day before said holiday to seven (7:00) p.m. the day of said holiday, and thereafter on alternate years.

2. Washington's Birthday, 19XX, from seven (7:00) p.m. the day before said holiday to seven (7:00) p.m. the day of said holiday, and thereafter on alternate years.

3. Memorial Day, 19XX, from seven (7:00) p.m. the day before said holiday to seven (7:00) p.m. the day of said holiday, and thereafter on alternate years.

4. Independence Day, 19XX, from seven (7:00) p.m. the day before said holiday to seven (7:00) p.m. the day of said holiday, and thereafter on alternate years.

5. Labor Day, 19XX, from seven (7:00) p.m. the day before said holiday to seven (7:00) p.m. the day of said holiday, and thereafter on alternate years.

6. Columbus Day, 19XX, from seven (7:00) p.m. the day before said holiday to seven (7:00) p.m. the day of said holiday, and thereafter on alternate years.

7. Veteran's Day, 19XX, from seven (7:00) p.m. the day before said holiday to seven (7:00) p.m. the day of said holiday, and thereafter on alternate years.

8. Thanksgiving Day, 19XX, from seven (7:00) p.m. the day before said holiday to seven (7:00) p.m. the day of said holiday, and thereafter on alternate years.

9. Christmas 19XX, the first week of the Christmas school vacation, commencing seven (7:00) p.m. the last day of school before the vacation and ending at eleven (11:00) a.m. Christmas Day to five (5:00) p.m. New Year's Day, and thereafter on alternate years.

10. Christmas Day, 19XX, the second week of Christmas school vacation, commencing eleven (11:00) a.m. Christmas Day to five (5:00) p.m. New Year's Day, and thereafter on alternate years.

11. The entire Easter school vacation in the year 19XX, including Easter Sunday, commencing seven (7:00) p.m. the last day of school before the vacation and ending at seven (7:00) p.m. the day before school resumes, and thereafter during the Easter vacation on alternate years.

[Editor's Note: If it does not occur automatically from the rest of your visitation schedule, consider providing that the noncustodial parent have custody on one of the two weekends surrounding the child's birthday irrespective of the rest of the visitation schedule. In [the above] example, since visitation is on alternate weekends, this would occur automatically.]

12. On the children's birthdays in the year 19XX, and thereafter on alternate years.

13. Every Father's Day.

14. On Husband's birthday.

15. Religious Holidays (where applicable):

a. Good Friday of 19XX, from noon (12:00) p.m. to six (6:00) p.m. of said day, and thereafter on alternate years, or

b. The first day of the Jewish Holidays of Yom Kippur, Rosh Hashannah and Passover during 19XX, commencing at five (5:00) p.m. on the eve of each such day and terminating at seven (7:00) p.m. on such day, and thereafter on alternate years.

II. **Wife** shall have the children with her on the holiday and special days listed in Clause I-B in the years alternate to the years in which Husband has the children with him pursuant to Clause I-B; Wife shall also have the children on every Mother's Day and on Wife's birthday.

[Editor's Note: A common variation would be to split the holidays between Husband and Wife and have them switch halves in alternate years. Another suggested addition if the children are young is Halloween, with the parents alternating years.]

III. **Priorities:**

The rights of Wife under Clause II shall override the regular visitation rights of Husband set forth in Clause I-A, in the event of conflict between Clause I-A and Clause II, except that Husband shall not be limited in his right to take the children out of the Home-City area during the period set forth in Clause I-A2 above, even though Wife shall thereby be deprived of the right she would otherwise have under Clause II to have the children with her during said period. In the event of conflict between Clause I-B and Clause II, the rights of Husband under Clause I-B shall override the rights of Wife under Clause II.

[Editor's Note: The significance of Clause III cannot be overrated. A key function of any drafter is to avoid argument over meaning and intention. A provision establishing a hierarchy of clauses will avoid a host of problems.]

Assignment 11.1

Richard and Helen Dowd have been married for six years. They are both computer consultants who work out of their home. They have one child, Kevin, aged four. Recently, they decided to separate. Draft a joint-custody agreement for them. Assume that on a rotating basis only one of the parents will live in the home for a six-month period. While a parent is living in the home, he or she will support Kevin. The other parent will have visitation rights. As you draft the agreement, think of possible problems that might arise and that need to be resolved in the agreement. Make up whatever reasonable resolution you think appropriate. (See General Instructions for the Agreement-Drafting Assignment in chapter one.)

Section C. Court-Ordered Custody: The Child's Perspective

When they brought the sword before him, he said, "Cut the living child in two, and give half to one woman and half to the other." 1 Kings 3:24–25 (NAB)

When the parties are unable to agree on how custody is to be handled, the courts must resolve the matter. Judges, forced into the role of King Solomon, often say that child custody is one of the most painful issues that they face. In a contested custody battle, it is sometimes difficult for a court to force the parents to focus on the best interests of the child rather than on their own hostility toward each other.

In the debate between mothers and fathers or between parent and a third party seeking custody, the concentration is often on rights and on the technicalities of the law. The child can easily get lost in the shuffle. Before examining how a court makes the custody decision, we should try to appreciate the perspective of the child. In the following guidelines from Wisconsin (written on the assumption that the mother is granted custody), an effort is made to get the parents to understand the child's perspective.

Guidelines

Dade County Family Court Counseling Service Staff, Madison, Wisconsin (Oct. 1974)

Relation Toward Children

Although the court does have the power to dissolve the bonds of matrimony, the court does not have the power to dissolve the bonds that exist between you as parents and your children. Both of you, therefore, are to continue your responsibility to emotionally support your children. You are to cooperate in the duty and right of each other to love those children. By love, the court means the training, the education, the disciplining and motivation of those children. Cooperation means to present the other party to the children with an attitude of respect either for the mother or for the father. Neither of you should in any way downplay, belittle or criticize the other in the presence of those children because you may emotionally damage your children and/or you may develop a disappointment or hatred in the minds of those children for the party that attempts to belittle or demean the other in the presence of those children. It is of utmost importance you both recognize your children's right to love both parents without fear of being disloyal to either one of you.

In support of this admonition, the courts have drafted written guidelines on your future conduct relating to the best interest of your children. I sincerely urge that you preserve them, periodically read them and always be guided by them.

Guidelines for Separated Parents

As you know, your children are usually the losers when their parents separate. They are deprived of full-time, proper guidance that two parents can give—guidance and direction essential to their moral and spiritual growth.

It is highly desirable that you abstain from making unkind remarks about each other. Recognize that such remarks are not about a former spouse but are about a parent of your children. Such comments reflect adversely upon the children.

It is urged that both parties cooperate to the end that mutual decisions concerning the interest of the children can be made objectively. Parents should remember that the mother who has custody should urge the children to find time to be with the father and encourage them to realize that their father has affection for them and contributes to their support. The father should recognize that his plans for visitation must be adjusted from time to time in order to accommodate the planned activities of the child. Visitation should be a pleasant experience rather than a duty. Cooperation in giving notice and promptness in maintaining hours of visitation are important to avoid ruffled feelings.

Although there is probably some bitterness between you, it should not be inflicted upon your children. In every child's mind there must and should be an image of two good parents. Your future conduct with your children will be helpful to them if you will follow these suggestions.

i. Do Not's

a. Do not poison your child's mind against either the mother or father by discussing their shortcomings.

b. Do not use your visitation as an excuse to continue the arguments with your spouse.

c. Do not visit your children if you have been drinking.

ii. Do's

a. Be discreet when you expose your children to [anyone] with whom you may be emotionally involved.

b. Visit your children only at reasonable hours.

c. Notify your spouse as soon as possible if you are unable to keep your visitation. It's unfair to keep your children waiting—and worse to disappoint them by not coming at all.

d. Make your visitation as pleasant as possible for your children by not questioning them regarding the activities of your spouse and by not making extravagant promises which you know you cannot or will not keep.

e. Minimize the amount of time the children are in the care of strangers and relatives.

f. Always work for the spiritual well-being, health, happiness and safety of your children.

iii. General

a. The parent with whom the children live must prepare them both physically and mentally for the visitation. The children should be available at the time mutually agreed upon.

b. If one parent has plans for the children that conflict with the visitation and these plans are in the best interests of the children, be adults and work out the problem together.

c. Arrangements should be made through visitation to provide the mother with some time "away" from the family. She needs the time for relaxation and recreation. Upon her return, she will be refreshed and better prepared to resume her role as mother and head of the household. Therefore, provide for extended periods of visitation such as weekends and vacations.

Bill of Rights for Children in Divorce Action

1. The right to be treated as important human beings, with unique feelings, ideas and desires and not as a source of argument between parents.

2. The right to a continuing relationship with both parents and the freedom to receive love from and express love for both.

3. The right to express love and affection for each parent without having to stifle that love because of fear of disapproval by the other parent.

4. The right to know that their parent's decision to divorce is not their responsibility and that they will live with one parent and will visit the other parent.

5. The right to continuing care and guidance from both parents.

6. The right to honest answers to questions about the changing family relationships.

7. The right to know and appreciate what is good in each parent without one parent degrading the other.

8. The right to have a relaxed, secure relationship with both parents without being placed in a position to manipulate one parent against the other.

9. The right to have the custodial parent not undermine visitation by suggesting tempting alternatives or by threatening to withhold visitation as a punishment for the children's wrongdoing.

10. The right to be able to experience regular and consistent visitation and the right to know the reason for a cancelled visit.

Section D. Parent vs. Parent: Considerations in the Custody Decision

First, we consider the custody decision when the dispute is between the two *biological parents*. The standard used by the court is the *best interest of the child*. In the vast majority of cases, the court will award sole custody to *one* of the parents and give visitation rights to the other. Earlier, we examined other kinds of custody, e.g., joint custody (page 293). Most courts have the power to grant any of these other options if they are deemed to be in the best interest of the child. As indicated, there is considerable debate on the feasibility of a joint-custody decree. The factors listed on page 294 will be given careful consideration by the court. Unless the parties mutually agree to try joint custody, however, it is unlikely that a court will order it. The primary focus of the following discussion, therefore, will be on the kind of custody that is most commonly awarded: sole custody.

In a contested custody case of this kind, the main participants are the mother and her lawyer against the father and his lawyer. If one parent has all or most of the financial resources, he or she will be ordered to pay reasonable attorney fees for the other parent. In some states, the court has the power to appoint *separate* counsel for the child. A *guardian ad litem* is an individual (often a lawyer) who is appointed to represent the interests of a third party—here, the child. This lawyer is to act independently of the other lawyers in the case.

How does the court decide who receives custody? What factors go into the decision? Earlier in this chapter you found a list of factors that parties negotiating a separation agreement must consider in arriving at a mutually acceptable custody arrangement (page 293). A court will usually consider many of these same factors in rendering a custody decision when the parties have not been able to reach agreement, or in deciding whether to approve a custody arrangement that they have agreed upon.

- ☐ **Court discretion**
- ☐ **Availability**
- ☐ **Emotional ties**
- ☐ **Legal preferences**
- ☐ **Morality and lifestyle**
- ☐ **Religion**
- ☐ **Cultural continuity**
- ☐ **Wishes of the child**
- ☐ **Expert witnesses**

☐ The Court's Discretion

Of necessity, trial judges are given great discretion in making the custody decision. There are no rigid formulas that can be followed. The standard is very broad: the best interest of the child. Inevitably, the judge's personal views and philosophy of life help shape his or her concept of what is in the best interest of a child, e.g., views on the traditional family, alternate lifestyles, working women, child discipline. Of course, a judge would never admit that he or she is following his or her own personal views and philosophy; judges are supposed to be guided by "the law" and not by their individual biases. In reality, however, they are guided by both.

☐ Availability

One of the major considerations is availability. Which parent will be available to spend the time necessary to respond to the day-to-day needs of the child? There is a danger that the child will feel abandoned and responsible for the divorce. To offset this danger, it is important that at least one of the parents be available to the child to provide reassurance and comfort. The court will want to know which parent in the past:

- Took the child to doctor's appointments
- Met with teachers
- Took the child to church
- Helped with homework
- Attended school plays with the child
- Involved the child in athletic activities
- Arranged and attended birthday parties
(etc.)

Then the court will want to know what *plan* each parent has for the future as to these needs. The health, age, and employment responsibilities of each parent are obviously relevant to this plan.

Immediately after the separation, it is common for one of the parents to have temporary custody, since one of them usually moves out of the family home. Upon filing for divorce, the court may formally order a temporary-custody arrangement (with visitation rights) pending the final court proceeding which may take place months later. During this interval, the court will inquire into the amount and kind of contract each parent had with the child. Again, the above list of questions becomes important, particularly with respect to the parent who moved out. How much time has this parent spent with the child? Have letters and gifts been sent? What about visits and telephone calls? To what extent has this parent gone out of his or her way to be with the child?

☐ Emotional Ties

Closely related to time availability is the emotional relationship that has developed in the past between a parent and child, and the future prospects for this development. Which parent has been sensitive or insensitive to the psychological crisis that the child has experienced and will probably continue to experience? Of particular importance is the extent to which one parent has tried and succeeded in fostering the child's love for the *other* parent. A qualification to become a custodial parent is the ability and inclination to cooperate in arranging visitations by the other parent. Hence, a major issue will be which parent can separate his or her own needs and lingering bitterness from the need of the child to maintain emotional ties with both parents. (Children who have been pressured by one parent to be hostile toward the other suffer from what is called the *parental alienation syndrome*.)

A number of other factors are relevant to the emotional needs of the child:

- The level of education of the parent
- The psychological health of the parent: Has the parent been in therapy? Has it been helpful? What is the parent's attitude about seeking such help? Positive? Realistic? Does the parent think that the *other* parent is the only one who needs help?
- The stability of the parent's prior work history
- Views on discipline, TV watching, studying, religious activities, cleaning the child's room, etc.
- How siblings get along in the home
- General home and neighborhood environment: Cramped apartment conditions? Residential area? Easy accessibility to school and recreational facilities?

Also, does the parent seeking sole custody plan to move from the area? If so, into what kind of environment? How will the proposed move affect the other parent's ability to visit the child? Depending upon the circumstances of the case, a court might award custody to a parent on condition that he or she not move out of a designated area without the consent of the other parent.

☑ Legal Preferences

Until the 1850s, fathers had a near-absolute right to the custody of their children. Following this period, most states adopted the *tender years presumption:* a child of tender years would be better off with its mother than with its father. The court presumed that a young child's best interest was to be with its mother. This presumption was justified on the basis of biological dependence, socialization patterns, and tradition. "There is but a twilight zone between a mother's love and the atmosphere of heaven, and all things being equal, no child should be deprived of that maternal influence." *Tuter v. Tuter*, 120 S.W.2d 203, 205 (Mo.App.1938). A very strong case had to be made against the mother in order to overcome the presumption, e.g., proof that the mother was unfit.

Within the last twenty years, more and more fathers have been seeking sole custody. They have argued that it is unconstitutional for a court to give preference to one parent over the other solely on the basis of sex. Recent courts have tended to agree and have been granting custody to fathers in increasing numbers. (Eleven percent of single-parent families in America are headed by men, a fair number of whom have achieved this status by court order.) Yet most courts *continue to grant custody to mothers in the vast majority of cases.* Such courts would deny that they are making their decisions on the basis of sex alone. Their opinions are always careful to state that they reached the conclusion that the child "needs its mother" after considering *all* of the circumstances.

In place of the tender-years presumption, many courts have substituted a *primary-caretaker presumption* by which the court presumes that custody should go to the parent who has been the primary person taking care of the child over the years. This, of course, usually means that the mother continues to receive sole custody in most cases since she is usually the one who stays home to care for the child. Even when both the mother and father work outside the home, the mother is more likely to be awarded custody as the primary caretaker. Some, therefore, have argued that the primary caretaker presumption is simply the tender-years presumption in disguise.

Frustrated fathers have been forming organizations throughout the country to fight what they perceive as the legal system's prejudice against them. They have succeeded in forcing lawmakers to say that no preferences shall be given on the basis of sex. Yet, according to many fathers, the tradition of awarding custody to the mother is so ingrained that judges continue to give her what amounts to a controlling preference without explicitly saying so.

One preference favored the father: it was presumed to be in the best interest of older boys to be placed with their fathers. Today, very few courts even mention this presumption. Although it has not been as controversial as the tender-years presumption, when it is explicitly or implicitly relied upon by a court, it is subject to the same criticisms.

A less controversial presumption is that brothers and sisters are best kept together with the same parent whenever possible. Finally, courts widely accept the idea that the preference of older, more mature children as to their own custody should be given great, though not necessarily controlling, weight.

☐ Morality and Lifestyle

"A judge should not base his decision upon [a] disapproval of the morals or other personal characteristics of a parent that do not harm the child. . . . We do not mean to suggest that a person's associational or even sexual conduct may not be relevant in deciding a custody dispute where there is compelling evidence that such conduct has a significant bearing upon the welfare of the children." *Wellman v. Wellman*, 104 Cal.App.3d 992, 998, 164 Cal.Rptr. 148, 151–52 (1980).

Is it possible to separate the private morality (particularly sexual morality) of a parent from the welfare of his or her children? If a parent engages in what the community considers immoral conduct, can we presume (conclusively presume?) that this parent is unfit and that it is in the best interest of the child to be placed with the other parent? In *Stanley v. Illinois*, 405 U.S. 645, 92 S.Ct. 1208, 31 L.Ed.2d 551 (1972), the United States Supreme Court held that a state cannot presume that a father is unfit simply because he never married the mother of his illegitimate child. The father must be given a hearing to determine his *actual* fitness or unfitness. Examine the following highly publicized opinion of *Jarrett v. Jarrett*. Do you think that the majority opinion violates *Stanley?*

Jarrett v. Jarrett

Supreme Court of Illinois, 1980.
78 Ill.2d 337, 36 Ill.Dec. 1, 400 N.E.2d 421.

UNDERWOOD, Justice:

On December 6, 1976, Jacqueline Jarrett received a divorce from Walter Jarrett in the circuit court of Cook County on grounds of extreme and repeated mental cruelty. The divorce decree, by agreement, also awarded Jacqueline custody of the three Jarrett children subject to the father's right of visitation at reasonable times. Seven months later, alleging changed conditions, Walter petitioned the circuit court to modify the divorce decree and award him custody of the children. The circuit court granted his petition subject to the mother's right of visitation at reasonable times, but a majority of the appellate court reversed * * * and we granted leave to appeal.

During their marriage, Walter and Jacqueline had three daughters, who, at the time of the divorce, were 12, 10 and 7 years old. In addition to custody of the children, the divorce decree also awarded Jacqueline the use of the family home, and child support; Walter received visitation rights at all reasonable times and usually had the children from Saturday evening to Sunday evening. In April 1977, five months after the divorce, Jacqueline informed Walter that she planned to have her boyfriend, Wayne Hammon, move into the family home with her. Walter protested, but Hammon moved in on May 1, 1977. Jacqueline and Hammon thereafter cohabited in the Jarrett home but did not marry.

The children, who were not "overly enthused" when they first learned that Hammon would move into the family home with them, asked Jacqueline if she intended to marry Hammon, but Jacqueline responded that she did not know. At the modification hearing Jacqueline testified that she did not want to remarry because it was too soon after her divorce; because she did not believe that a marriage license makes a relationship; and because the divorce decree required her to sell the family home within six months after remarriage. She did not want to sell the house because the children did not want to move and she could not afford to do so. Jacqueline explained to the children that some people thought it was wrong for an unmarried man and woman to live together but she thought that what mattered was that they loved each other. Jacqueline testified that she told some neighbors that Hammon would move in with her but that she had not received any adverse comments. Jacqueline further testified that the children seemed to develop an affectionate relationship with Hammon, who played with them, helped them with their homework, and verbally disciplined them. Both Jacqueline and Hammon testified at the hearing that they did not at that time have any plans to marry. In oral argument before this court Jacqueline's counsel conceded that she and Hammon were still living together unmarried.

Walter Jarrett testified that he thought Jacqueline's living arrangements created a moral environment which was not a proper one in which to raise three young girls. He also testified that the children were always clean, healthy, well dressed and well nourished when he picked them up, and that when he talked with his oldest daughter, Kathleen, she did not object to Jacqueline's living arrangement.

The circuit court found that it was "necessary for the moral and spiritual well-being and development" of the children that Walter receive custody. In reversing, the appellate court reasoned that the record did not reveal any negative effects on the children caused by Jacqueline's cohabitation with Hammon, and that the circuit court had not found Jacqueline unfit. It declined to consider potential future harmful effects of the cohabitation on the children. . . .

Both parties to this litigation have relied on sections 602 and 610 of the new Illinois Marriage and Dissolution of Marriage Act (Ill.Rev.Stat.1977, ch. 40, pars. 602, 610), which provide:

"Sec. 602. Best interest of child.

(a) The court shall determine custody in accordance with the best interest of the child. The court shall consider all relevant factors including:

   (1) the wishes of the child's parent or parents as to his custody;

   (2) the wishes of the child as to his custodian;

   (3) the interaction and interrelationship of the child with his parent or parents, his siblings and any other person who may significantly affect the child's best interest;

   (4) the child's adjustment to his home, school and community; and

   (5) the mental and physical health of all individuals involved.

(b) The court shall not consider conduct of a present or proposed custodian that does not affect his relationship to the child."

"Sec. 610. Modification.

(a) No motion to modify a custody judgment may be made earlier than 2 years after its date, unless the court permits it to be made on the basis of affidavits that there is reason to believe the child's present environment may endanger seriously his physical, mental, moral or emotional health.

(b) The court shall not modify a prior custody judgment unless it finds, upon the basis of facts that have arisen since the prior judgment or that were unknown to the court at the time of entry of the prior judgment, that a change has occurred in the circumstances of the child or his custodian and that the modification is necessary to serve the best interest of the child. In applying these standards the court shall retain the custodian appointed pursuant to the prior judgment unless:
* * *

(3) the child's present environment endangers seriously his physical, mental, moral or emotional health and the harm likely to be caused by a change of environment is outweighed by its advantages to him. . . .

The chief issue in this case is whether a change of custody predicated upon the open and continuing cohabitation of the custodial parent with a member of the opposite sex is contrary to the manifest weight of the evidence in the absence of any tangible evidence of contemporaneous adverse effect upon the minor children. * * * [W]e conclude that under the facts in this case the trial court properly transferred custody of the Jarrett children from Jacqueline to Walter Jarrett.

The relevant standards of conduct are expressed in the statutes of this State: Section 11–8 of the Criminal Code of 1961 (Ill.Rev.Stat.1977, ch. 38, par. 11–8) provides that "[a]ny person who cohabits or has sexual intercourse with another not his spouse commits fornication if the behavior is open and notorious." In *Hewitt v. Hewitt* (1979), * * * we emphasized the refusal of the General Assembly in enacting the new Illinois Marriage and Dissolution of Marriage Act * * * to sanction any nonmarital relationships and its declaration of the purpose to "strengthen and preserve the integrity of marriage and safeguard family relationships". * * *

Jacqueline argues, however, that her conduct does not affront public morality because such conduct is now widely accepted, and cites 1978 Census Bureau statistics that show 1.1 million households composed of an unmarried man and woman, close to a quarter of which also include at least one child. This is essentially the same argument we rejected last term in *Hewitt v. Hewitt* (1979), * * * and it is equally unpersuasive here. The number of people living in such households forms only a small percentage of the adult population, but more to the point, the statutory interpretation urged upon us by Jacqueline simply nullifies the fornication statute. The logical conclusion of her argument is that the statutory prohibitions are void as to those who believe the proscribed acts are not immoral, or, for one reason or another, need not be heeded. So stated, of course, the argument defeats itself. The rules which our society enacts for the governance of its members are not limited to those who agree with those rules—they are equally binding on the dissenters. The fornication statute and the Illinois Marriage and Dissolution of Marriage Act evidence the relevant moral standards of this State, as declared by our legislature. The open and notorious limitation on the former's prohibitions reflects both a disinclination to criminalize purely private relationships and a recognition that open fornication represents a graver threat to public morality than private violations. Conduct of that nature, when it is open, not only violates the statutorily expressed moral standards of the State, but also encourages others to violate those standards, and debases public morality. While we agree that the statute does not penalize conduct which is essentially private and discreet, * * * Jacqueline's conduct has been neither, for she has discussed this relationship and her rationalization of it with at least her children, her former husband and her neighbors. It is, in our judgment, clear that her conduct offends prevailing public policy. * * *

Jacqueline's disregard for existing standards of conduct instructs her children, by example, that they, too, may ignore them, * * * and could well encourage the children to engage in similar activity in the future. That factor, of course, supports the trial court's conclusion that their daily presence in that environment was injurious to the moral well-being and development of the children.

It is true that, as Jacqueline argues, the courts have not denied custody to every parent who has violated the community's moral standards, nor do we now intimate a different rule. Rather than mechanically denying custody in every such instance, the courts of this State appraise the moral example currently provided and the example which may be expected by the parent in the future. We held in *Nye v. Nye* (1952), * * * that past moral indiscretions of a parent are not sufficient grounds for denying custody if the parent's present conduct establishes the improbability of such lapses in the future. This rule focuses the trial court's attention on the moral values which the parent is actually demonstrating to the children.

Since the decision in *Nye,* the appellate courts of this State have repeatedly emphasized this principle, particularly when the children were unaware of their parent's moral indiscretion. * * * At the time of this hearing, however, and even when this case was argued orally to this court, Jacqueline continued to cohabit with Wayne Hammon and had done nothing to indicate that this relationship would not continue in the future. Thus the moral values which Jacqueline currently represents to her children, and those which she may be expected to portray to them in the future, contravene statutorily declared standards of conduct and endanger the children's moral development.

Jacqueline argues, however, that *Rippon v. Rippon* * * * (1978) indicate[s] that the moral indiscretion of a parent is not sufficient ground for denial of custody. In *Rippon* the mother who had committed the indiscretion planned to marry her paramour and there was no indication of future misconduct. *Rippon* therefore falls within the rule set out in *Nye.* * * *

Jacqueline also argues, and the appellate court agreed * * * that the trial court's decision to grant custody of the children to Walter Jarrett was an improper assertion by the trial judge of his own personal moral beliefs. She further argues that the assertion of moral values in this case, as in *Hewitt v. Hewitt* (1979), * * * is a task more appropriately carried out by the legislature. As pointed out earlier, however, it is the legislature which has established the standards she has chosen to ignore, and the action of the trial court merely implemented principles which have long been followed in this State.

The mother argues, too, that * * * the Illinois Marriage and Dissolution of Marriage Act * * * requires the trial court to refrain from modifying a prior custody decree unless it finds that the children have suffered actual tangible harm. The statute, however, directs the trial court to determine whether "the child's present environment *endangers* seriously his physical, mental, moral or emotional health." [Emphasis added.] * * * In some cases, particularly those involving physical harm, it may be appropriate for the trial court to determine whether the child is endangered by considering evidence of actual harm. In cases such as this one, however, such a narrow interpretation of the statute would defeat its purpose. At the time of the hearing the three Jarrett children, who were then 12, 10 and 7 years old, were obviously incapable of emulating their mother's moral indiscretions. To wait until later years to determine whether Jacqueline had inculcated her moral values in the children would be to await a demonstration that the very harm which the statute seeks to avoid had occurred. Measures to safeguard the moral well-being of children, whose lives have already been disrupted by the divorce of their parents, cannot have been intended to be delayed until there are tangible manifestations of damage to their character.

While our comments have focused upon the moral hazards, we are not convinced that open cohabitation does not also affect the mental and emotional health of the children. Jacqueline's testimony at the hearing indicated that when her children originally learned that Wayne Hammon would move in with them, they initially expected that she would marry him. It is difficult to predict what psychological effects or problems may later develop from their efforts to overcome the disparity between their concepts of propriety and their mother's conduct. * * * Nor will their attempts to adjust to this new environment occur in a vacuum. Jacqueline's domestic arrangements are known to her neighbors and their children; testimony at the hearing indicated that Wayne Hammon played with the Jarrett children and their friends at the Jarrett home and also engaged in other activities with them. If the Jarrett children remained in that situation, they might well be compelled to try to explain Hammon's presence to their friends and, perhaps, to endure their taunts and

jibes. In a case such as this the trial judge must also weigh these imponderables, and he is not limited to examining the children for current physical manifestations of emotional or mental difficulties.

Finally, we do not believe that the United States Supreme Court's opinion in *Stanley v. Illinois* (1972), 405 U.S. 645, 92 S.Ct. 1208, 31 L.Ed.2d 551, requires a different result. In *Stanley* the Supreme Court found that Illinois statutes created a presumption that an unwed father is unfit to exercise custody over his children. The court held that depriving an unwed father of his illegitimate children without a prior hearing to determine his actual rather than presumptive unfitness, when the State accords that protection to other parents, deprives him of equal protection of the law.

The case before us is fundamentally different. The trial court did not presume that Jacqueline was not an adequate parent, as the juvenile court in effect did in *Stanley*. Rather the trial court recognized that the affection and care of a parent do not alone assure the welfare of the child if other conduct of the parent threatens the child's moral development. Since the evidence indicated that Jacqueline had not terminated the troublesome relationship and would probably continue it in the future, the trial court transferred custody to Walter Jarrett, an equally caring and affectionate parent whose conduct did not contravene the standards established by the General Assembly and earlier judicial decisions. Its action in doing so was not contrary to the manifest weight of the evidence.

Accordingly, we reverse the judgment of the appellate court and affirm the judgment of the circuit court of Cook County.

Appellate court reversed; circuit court affirmed.

GOLDENHERSCH, Chief Justice, with whom THOMAS J. MORAN, Justice, joins, dissenting:

The majority states, "The chief issue in this case is whether a change of custody predicated upon the open and continuing cohabitation of the custodial parent with a member of the opposite sex is contrary to the manifest weight of the evidence in the absence of any tangible evidence of contemporaneous adverse effect upon the minor children." * * * An examination of the opinion fails to reveal any other issue, and the effect of the decision is that the plaintiff's cohabitation with Hammon *per se* was sufficient grounds for changing the custody order previously entered. This record shows clearly that the children were healthy, well adjusted, and well cared for, and it should be noted that both the circuit and appellate courts made no finding that plaintiff was an unfit mother. The majority, too, makes no such finding and based its decision on a nebulous concept of injury to the children's "moral well-being and development." * * * I question that any competent sociologist would attribute the increase of "live in" unmarried couples to parental example.

* * *

As the appellate court pointed out, the courts should not impose the personal preferences and standards of the judiciary in the decision of this case. Courts are uniquely equipped to decide legal issues and are well advised to leave to the theologians the question of the morality of the living arrangement into which the plaintiff had entered.

As a legal matter, simply stated, the majority has held that on the basis of her presumptive guilt of fornication, a Class B misdemeanor, plaintiff, although not declared to be an unfit mother, has forfeited the right to have the custody of her children. This finding flies in the face of the established rule that, in order to modify or amend an award of custody, the evidence must show that the parent to whom custody of the children was originally awarded is unfit to retain custody, or that a change of conditions makes a change of custody in their best interests. This record fails to show either. Mr. Justice Moran and I dissent and would affirm the decision of the appellate court.

MORAN, Justice, with whom GOLDEN-HERSCH, Chief Justice, joins, dissenting:

I join in the dissent of the chief justice, but also dissent separately. My primary disagreement with the majority lies with its countenancing a change of custody based solely on a *conclusive presumption* that harm to the Jarrett children stemmed from Jacqueline's living arrangements. The majority purports to follow the Illinois Marriage and Dissolution of Marriage Act. Yet, under that act, only on the basis of fact can there be a finding that a change in circumstances has oc-

curred and that modification of the prior custody judgment is necessary to serve the best interest of the children. * * * The court is not to consider conduct of a custodian if that conduct does not affect his relationship to the child. * * * In this case, not one scintilla of actual or statistical evidence of harm or danger to the children has been presented. To the contrary, all of the evidence of record, as related by the majority, indicates that under Jacqueline's custodianship the children's welfare and needs were met. Also, the trial court expressly declined to find Jacqueline unfit. Nevertheless, the majority's finding of a violation of the seldom-enforced fornication statute effectively foreclosed any further consideration of the custody issue. Instead of focusing solely on the best interest of the children—the "guiding star" * * *—the majority has utilized child custody as a vehicle to punish Jacqueline for her "misconduct." Such selective enforcement of a statute is inappropriate and, especially in the child-custody context, unfortunate.

The majority decision also is at odds with the principle of *Stanley v. Illinois* (1972), 405 U.S. 645, 92 S.Ct. 1208, 31 L.Ed.2d 551. The constitutional infirmity of the statutory presumption in *Stanley* casts doubt on the validity of the judicially created conclusive presumption in this case. After *Stanley,* an unwed father may not be deprived of his illegitimate children without a prior hearing to determine his actual fitness. Similarly, Jacqueline should not be deprived of the children in the absence of evidence that a change is necessary to serve the best interest of the children. A hearing at which custody is determined on the basis of the conclusive presumption sanctioned by the majority amounts to no hearing at all.

Assignment 11.2

(a) What did the dissenting opinion of Chief Justice Goldenhersh mean when he charged that the majority opinion of Justice Underwood was applying theology rather than law? Do you agree with the Chief Justice? Explain.

(b) Is the majority opinion inconsistent with *Stanley v. Illinois?* Explain.

What happens if one of the parents seeking custody is homosexual? There are some courts that would never grant custody to a gay parent, especially if the other parent follows a more traditional lifestyle. Other courts, however, take a different view. They will want to know whether:

■ The gay parent has a live-in lover
■ The parent's sexual activities are open and obvious to the child

- The child has been or is likely to become homosexual because of the parent's homosexuality (some studies, however, show that a child's sexual preferences are established during infancy)
- The child is psychologically able to handle the parent's homosexuality
- The child will be put in a position of having to explain or defend his or her parent, e.g., to classmates who are aware of the parent's homosexuality.

These courts will award custody of the child to a gay parent if all of the factors point to a healthy home environment for the child and there is no evidence that the homosexuality will have an adverse impact on the child. It must be acknowledged, however, that a gay parent has a substantial uphill battle in gaining custody (or in keeping custody if the homosexuality is revealed only after the parent has been awarded custody). Gay parents have been most successful in winning custody when the heterosexual parent is either no longer available or is demonstrably unfit. In such cases, the homosexual parent wins by default unless his or her conduct is so offensive that the court will grant custody to neither biological parent.

Religion

Under our Constitution, a court cannot favor one religion over another or prefer organized religion over less orthodox forms of religion beliefs. To do so could amount to an unconstitutional "establishment" of religion. The state must remain neutral. In the law of custody, the question is what effect the practice of religion is likely to have on the child, not which religion is preferable or correct according to the judge's personal standards, or according to the standards of the majority in the community, or according to "respectable" minorities in the community. The court will want to know what religion, if any, the child has practiced to date. Continuity is desirable. Also, will the practice of religion tend to take the child away from other activities? For example, will the child be asked to spend long hours in door-to-door selling of religious literature, and hence be unable to attend regular school? If so, the court will be reluctant to award custody to the parent who would require this of the child.

Assignment 11.3

When Helen married John, she converted from Catholicism to his religion, Judaism. Neither Helen nor John, however, were very religious persons. To a moderate extent, their two children were raised in the Jewish faith. The couple divorced when the children were ages four and five. Because of John's job, he could not be the sole custodian of the children. Hence he agreed that Helen receive sole custody. But he asked the court to order Helen to continue raising the children in the Jewish faith.

(a) Under what circumstances do you think a court can grant this request so that, in effect, John will be granted *spiritual custody* of the children even though physical custody and legal custody (in all matters except religion) will be granted to Helen? (See General Instructions for the Legal-Analysis Assignment in chapter one.)

(b) Suppose that Helen returns to her original religion, and starts taking the children to Catholic Mass. What options does John have in your state? (See General Instructions for the State-Code Assignment in chapter one.)

☐ **Cultural Continuity**

The following assignment and case address the role of cultural continuity in the custody decision.

Assignment 11.4

Richard and Lisa have been married three years. Richard is black; Lisa is white. They have one child, Donald, who is twenty months old. In a divorce proceeding, both parents are seeking custody of Donald.

(a) What facts do you think are needed to represent Richard or Lisa? (See General Instructions for the Investigation-Strategy Assignment in chapter one.)

(b) Assume that Richard and Lisa are equally competent and able to care for Donald. When the divorce is final, Richard plans to marry Mary (who is also black), and Lisa plans to marry Ted (who is also white). How should the custody decision be made?

(c) If all the parties lived in Alaska, how do you think the court would apply *Carle v. Carle* which follows?

Carle v. Carle

Supreme Court of Alaska, 1972.
503 P.2d 1050.

Rabinowitz, Chief Justice

This appeal concerns the superior court's determination of child custody in a divorce proceeding between George Carle, appellant, and Charlotte Carle, appellee. As part of its decree of divorce, the trial court awarded custody of George Carle, Jr., the parties' 7 year old son, to his mother Charlotte Carle. George Carle has appealed from the superior court's custody determination.

George Carle and Charlotte Carle were married in 1963, when George was 21 and Charlotte 16. George is a Haida Indian whose family is from Hydaburg. Charlotte is a Tlinget Indian with family ties at Klawock.[1] George's primary source of income is employ-

ment on commercial fishing boats, although he has worked at other jobs. During the fishing off-season, he leads the traditional subsistence existence of village Alaska, hunting, trapping, fishing, and picking berries. Since the marriage of the parties, Charlotte has held many different jobs and has also attended school. At the time the custody hearing was held in this case, she had been employed in Juneau for some 6 months.

When the matter was before the trial court, Charlotte was living in Juneau with Tom Hughes, a non-native, with whom she had been living since shortly after she separated from George in 1965. Charlotte and Hughes expressed their intent to marry after her divorce. They also indicated that they hoped to be able to bring Hughes' three children from an earlier marriage into their home in addition to George Jr. and two children of their own union. Hughes and Charlotte work alternate shifts at their respective employments and have outside help for the brief period when their shifts overlap and neither can be home.

George Jr. was born at Mt. Edgecumbe, Alaska, December 20, 1964. He first lived with Charlotte's grandmother in Klawock when Charlotte was working in a cannery for a short time in the summer of 1965. He returned to this home when his father brought him back from San Diego where Charlotte had taken him in 1965, and remained there until 1968. In October, 1968, Charlotte's grandmother became ill, so one of her daughters took the boy to Charlotte in Juneau. He stayed with Charlotte about 9 months until her finan-

---

[1] From the time of their marriage in 1963 through the summer of 1965, George and Charlotte lived in Klawock off and on with Charlotte's grandmother. From 1966 to 1968, when the grandmother was taking care of his son, George spent the off-seasons in her home also. In September 1970, George took his son with him to Hydaburg where the boy lived with two of George's sisters—with one during the fall fishing season and with the other from the end of the season through the time of the custody hearing. The custody decree left the child with the latter married sister temporarily so that the boy could finish the year in the Headstart program he had been attending.

cial situation became so bad that she could not adequately care for her two children.[2] To see that they were properly cared for, she sent them to her grandmother who was at home again in Klawock.[3] George Jr. remained in Klawock until after the 1970 fishing season. His father then came to get him because the grandmother was too old and sick to be able to care for the child any longer. After visiting various relatives, George Sr. took his son to Hydaburg to live with one of the boy's paternal aunts briefly during the fishing season. At the end of the season, George Sr. made more permanent living arrangements for the boy; placing him with another aunt and her family where he could live next door and participate in the boy's upbringing. Had custody been awarded to the father, the boy would have continued to live with this married aunt indefinitely.

In our jurisdiction it is well established that the trial court is possessed of broad discretion to determine where custody should be placed. We will disturb the trial court's resolution of custody issues only if convinced that the record shows an abuse of discretion, or if controlling findings of fact are clearly erroneous.

* * * In the case at bar, the trial court recognized that the paramount consideration in any custody determination is what appears to be for the best interests of the child.[4]

The facts have been set forth in some detail because of appellant George Carle's contentions that the trial court erred in its evaluation of the relevant facts for the purpose of deciding what custody disposition would be in the best interests of the minor child, George Jr. George Carle's argument before this court is two-pronged: first, the trial court failed to give adequate consideration to the "actual interests" of the child, defined essentially as his psychological well-being; and second, that the trial judge's custody decision was the

result of his cultural bias against the Native village way of life. In regard to this latter argument, appellant contends that the trial judge erroneously employed a presumption that the Native village culture is "inevitably succumbing" to the caucasian, urban culture.

We turn first to the asserted failure of the trial court to consider the actual interest or psychological well-being of the child. George Carle contends that the interests of the child in a custody dispute merit constitutional protection and that due process requires courts to "determine custody according to criteria which assure full and meaningful consideration of the child's actual interest."[5] According to the father, this would mean focusing primarily on "the actual psychological interests of the child," and more particularly, on "the existence and quality of . . . emotional relationships between the child and his possible custodian." We agree that the nature of the child's existing relationships should be a significant factor in choosing his custodian. Nevertheless, we believe that the "best interests" criterion adequately encompasses this factor.

Even were we to adopt the father's position and focus primarily on the actual psychological interests of the child the evidence does not clearly require a different result as to the choice of custody. The child's most stable, continuous, and long-lasting relationship was with his great-grandmother who can no longer care for him. He has spent relatively little time in 7 years with his mother, but his contacts with his father have been transitory also.[6] The child has related well to both parents and to the respective living situations they offered him. Moreover, the trial court's decision frequently touched on elements of the child's relationship with others—with his aunt and her family, with Hughes, with his school in Hydaburg. In fact, it was precisely his concern for the child's psychological development that led the judge to place him with his mother in Juneau. In his decision the trial judge found that the child's mother had obtained stable employ-

---

[2]By that time she and Hughes had had one baby. Hughes had gone to Hawaii to work in the summer of 1969, but did not stay much more than a month because of Charlotte's financial status.
[3]When Charlotte sought the return of the two children two weeks later, her grandmother would only send back the baby. The grandmother refused to give up George Jr. to Charlotte once before in 1967. Recognizing her grandmother's great attachment to the boy, Charlotte did not insist on recovering custody either time.
[4]AS 09.55.205 provides that in deciding custody, the trial court should be guided by the following considerations:
"(1) by what appears to be for the best interests of the child and if the child is of a sufficient age and intelligence to form a preference, the court may consider that preference in determining the question;
(2) as between parents adversely claiming the custody neither parent is entitled to it as of right."
* * *

---

[5]Whether or not a constitutional right of the child is involved, parents have standing to challenge on appeal a determination of what is in the best interests of the child. * * * We deem this an appropriate occasion to reiterate the point we made in *Sheridan v. Sheridan*, 436 P.2d 821, 825 n. 16 (Alaska 1970) to the effect that in contested custody cases the trial court, in its discretion, is empowered to appoint a guardian ad litem to represent the interests of the minor child. * * *
[6]While there might be some preference for leaving the child in the custody of the person with whom he has most recently and continuously resided, we decline to establish such a presumption lest it lead to pre-hearing maneuvering for possession of the child. In any event such a rule would have been no help in the instant case where neither party actually has lived with George Jr. for long or continuous periods.

ment and possessed the means of providing good care for the child; that the mother and Hughes provided a sense of family and home for the child, "a settled place of security and safety"; that the paternal aunt could not fulfill the necessary filial relationship; that placing the child in the mother's custody provided greater assurance of a settled, stable, family environment for the child; and that the mother was in a position to materially aid the child's development of a sense of identity, worth, and self confidence. The trial court was also of the view that the transition from the village to urban way of life could be more easily accomplished while the child was still young than if delayed until his character and personality were more rigidly formed.[7] In short the trial court concluded that the child would be emotionally and economically more secure in an urban setting.

The father asserts that the trial court failed "to give sufficient recognition to the traditional manner of care and upbringing of Native children" in weighing the custody alternatives available to the minor child of the parties. This assertion is not borne out by the record. Throughout the custody hearing the trial judge allowed evidence bearing on the nature and quality of village life. Before hearing final argument, the trial judge indicated what he thought was the most important question for counsel to discuss. In doing so, he said that the custody alternatives offered were perhaps somewhat unique, and that

> "I'm most fundamentally faced with a decision whether this child is to be reared in a Native culture in a village or in the Anglo-Saxon culture in a developed community. And I'm concerned about the basic differences between the environmental circumstances of the village life on the one hand, where his family associations are offered, apart from the specific capabilities of the [father], and on the other hand, the advantages and disadvantages of a different way of life."

Finally, in his oral decision the trial judge explicitly recognized that it is common in villages for members of the extended family to assist the natural parents of a child in his rearing, and that the village offered certain advantages to children raised there.[8] More particularly, the trial court recognized that George Jr. was then being well and lovingly cared for in his aunt's home.

From an overall appraisal of the record, it appears that the trial court's decision to award custody to the mother was influenced by the view that there existed a great probability of a more stable home, emotionally and economically, if the mother was awarded custody.

This brings us to appellant's second argument to the effect that the trial court's custody decision was dictated by the court's cultural bias against the Native village way of life and denied the child the "right of cultural survival." This contention arises out of the trial judge's statement made in the course of his decision that

> "Inevitably, the village way of life is succumbing to the predominate [sic] caucasian, urban society of the land, and of necessity the youth of the villages must confront and adjust to this new life style. That transition can more easily be accomplished in the case of this child at his young age than if delayed until this character and personality are more rigidly formed."

In light of these comments, the closeness of the custody questions and the fact that the child's best interests were not independently protected by the appointment of a guardian ad litem,[9] we have concluded

---

[7] As to the quality of emotional relationships between the child and his possible custodian, in his decision the trial judge alluded to the fact that the father's hearing loss and speech difficulties hampered his ability to readily communicate; that the father's occupation as a commercial fisherman requires that he be absent for several months during fishing season; that the father did not have a home of his own in which to care for the child; that the father's capacity to provide the necessities of life for himself and his son was limited; and that the father's married sister cared for and loved the child and that it was not an unusual facet of Native village culture to provide care and a home when the child's natural parents are unable to do so.

[8] The trial court's findings of fact, where pertinent, read as follows:

"The evidence indicated that it is not unusual in the village culture for the relatives of a child, such as the paternal aunt here, to provide a home and care for a child where for some reason the natural parents are not suitably situated to do so. In this case, the boy does appear to be loved and accepted in his aunt's home and family in Hydaburg. The evidence also indicated that he is currently doing well in a so-called 'Headstart' program in the village school. . . .

From the evidence it may be said there are indeed, some significant and praiseworthy values in the Native village cultural environment in which the boy would be reared under defendant's custody. These include a rapport with nature and with a community of people which is perhaps less characteristic of urban life. The village environment may well nurture a sense of pride and self-worth in this Native child which a community such as Juneau could tend to suppress in his status as a member of a minority race."

[9] See n. 5, supra. During the course of the trial the trial judge remarked that the issue before him "really concerns a party who is in a sense not represented in this suit." Although counsel was not appointed to represent the child, the trial judge alluded to the fact that in the past he contemplated such appointments.

that the case should be remanded for futher proceedings. We are reluctant to finalize the decree in this case, given the possibility that an improper criterion was employed by the court in its resolution of the custody issue. Admittedly, the precise meaning of the trial judge's assertion that "the village way of life is succumbing to the predominate [sic] caucasian, urban society" is not free of ambiguity. Similarly, it is not clear whether the trial judge was suggesting that the Native youth must necessarily adopt urban life-styles. Yet, on the basis of the trial judge's questioned remarks, we think a cogent argument can be advanced that the custody issue here was decided in part through the utilization of an impermissible criteria.

Both judicial decision and statutory provision mandate that the paramount consideration in any custody determination is "what appears to be for the best interests of the child." We think it is not permissible, in a bicultural context, to decide a child's custody on the hypothesis that it is necessary to facilitate the child's adjustment to what is believed to be the dominant culture. Such judgments are, in our view, not relevant to the determination of custody issues. Rather, the focus should be on the fitness of the parent and the parent's ability to accord the child the most meaningful parent-child relationship. It is not the function of our courts to homogenize Alaskan society. Recently we had occasion to observe that, "The United States of America, and Alaska in particular, reflect a pluralistic society, grounded upon such basic values as the preservation of maximum individual choice, protection of minority sentiments, and appreciation for divergent lifestyles." *Breese v. Smith,* 501 P.2d 159, 169 (Alaska 1972). Since we are unable to conclude with any degree of certainty that custody was decided without taking into consideration impermissible factors, we hold that the case must be remanded for further proceedings.

We think it necessary to comment on one other facet of the proceedings below. Here the differing life-styles flowing from the two cultures have significance in determining which parent could provide the best possible parent-child relationship. In such circumstances, we deem it inappropriate to decide the custody issue on the basis of cultural assumptions which are not borne out by the record. Rational decision-making requires, as a necessary prerequisite, a solid evidentiary base upon which evaluation can be made of these factors as they relate to the primary question of what custody disposition is in the best interests of the child.

We therefore reverse and remand to the superior court for further proceedings not inconsistent with the foregoing. Upon remand, the superior court is empowered to appoint a guardian ad litem for the child, and to take such other steps as are deemded appropriate, including the taking of additonal evidence in the event any party raises issues as to changed circumstances arising since trial that bear on the custody issue.

□ Wishes of the Child

Courts are understandably reluctant to ask children to take sides in custody disputes. If this becomes common practice, there would be an incentive for both parents to pressure the child to express preferences. If, however, the court is convinced that the child is mature enough to state a rational preference and that doing so would not harm the child, evidence of such a preference will be admissible. Great caution must be used in questioning the child. The judge may decide to speak to the child outside the formal courtroom (with the lawyers but not the parents present), or the judge may allow a professional (e.g., child psychologist, social worker) to interview the child at home.

□ Expert Witnesses

Psychologists, psychiatrists, social workers, and other experts can be called as expert witnesses by either parent to testify on the child's home environment and emotional development, the mental stability of the parents, the suitability of various custody plans, etc. An example of a custody-evaluation report by such an expert witness is provided in Exhibit 11–1.

Psychiatric Custody Evaluation

August 25, 1981

Honorable James K. O'Brien
Supreme Court of New York
New York County
60 Centre Street
New York, New York 10007

Re: Johnson v. Johnson
Docket No. M–3784–81

Dear Judge O'Brien:

This report is submitted in compliance with your court order dated June 9, 1981, requesting that I conduct an evaluation of the Johnson family in order to provide the court with information that would be useful to it in deciding which of the Johnson parents should have custody of their children Tara, Elaine, and Charles.

My findings and recommendations are based on interviews conducted as itemized below:

July 6, 1981 —Mrs. Carol Johnson and	
Mr. Frank Johnson, seen jointly	2 hours
July 7, 1981 —Mr. Frank Johnson	1 hour
July 11, 1981—Mrs. Carol Johnson	1 hour
July 13, 1981—Tara Johnson	1½ hours
July 14, 1981—Mr. Frank Johnson	1 hour
July 20, 1981—Mrs. Carol Johnson	1 hour
July 21, 1981—Charles Johnson	¾ hour
Elaine Johnson	¾ hour
July 22, 1981—Tara Johnson	½ hour
Mrs. Carol Johnson and	
Tara Johnson, seen jointly	½ hour
July 24, 1981—Mrs. Carol Johnson	1 hour
July 27, 1981—Mrs. Carol Johnson and	
Mr. Frank Johnson, seen jointly	1 hour
Aug. 3, 1981 —Elaine Johnson	¾ hour
Aug. 4. 1981 —Tara Johnson	¼ hour
Mr. Frank Johnson and	
Tara Johnson, seen jointly	½ hour
Aug. 10, 1981—Tara Johnson	
Mr. Frank Johnson and	
Mrs. Carol Johnson, seen jointly	¾ hour
Aug. 11, 1981—Tara Johnson	
Elaine Johnson	
Charles Johnson	
Mrs. Carol Johnson and	
Mr. Frank Johnson, seen jointly	¾ hour

Aug. 14, 1981—Tara Johnson
            Elaine Johnson
            Charles Johnson
            Mrs. Carol Johnson and
            Mr. Frank Johnson, seen jointly   1 hour
                                                16 hours

In addition, on Aug. 16, 1981, Mr. and Mrs. Johnson were seen together for the purpose of my presenting these findings and recommendations to them. This interview lasted two hours, bringing to 18 the total number of hours spent with the Johnson family in association with this evaluation.

Mr. Frank Johnson, an airline pilot, is 43 years old. His first wife died soon after the delivery of Tara, who is now 16 years of age. He married Mrs. Carol Johnson when Tara was 2 years old. Mrs. Johnson, a housewife, who was formerly an elementary school teacher, is now 40. Her first marriage ended in divorce. A child of this relationship died soon after birth. There are two children of the Johnson marriage: Elaine, 11 and Charles, 7. Mrs. Johnson adopted her stepdaughter Tara in July 1980. In October 1980, Mr. Johnson initiated divorce proceedings because he felt that his wife no longer respected him and that she was a poor mother for the children, especially his daughter Tara. However, Mr. and Mrs. Johnson are still occupying the same domicile.

Both parents are requesting custody of all three children. It is this examiner's recommendation that Mr. Frank Johnson be granted custody of Tara and that Mrs. Carol Johnson be granted custody of Elaine and Charles. The observations that have led me to these conclusions will be divided into four categories: 1) Mr. Frank Johnson's assets as a parent, 2) Mr. Frank Johnson's liabilities as a parent, 3) Mrs. Carol Johnson's assets as a parent, and 4) Mrs. Carol Johnson's liabilities as a parent. Following these four presentations I will comment further on the way in which my observations brought about the aforementioned recommendations. Although much information was obtained in the course of the evaluation, only those items specifically pertinent to the custody consideration will be included in this report.

Mr. Frank Johnson's Assets as a Parent

Mr. Frank Johnson is Tara's biological father. The special psychological tie that this engenders is not enjoyed by Mrs. Carol Johnson and Tara. It is not the genetic bond per se that is crucial here; rather, it is the psychological attachment that such a bond elicits. Mr. Johnson had already started to develop a psychological tie with Tara while his first wife was pregnant with her. He was actually present at her birth and assumed an active role in her rearing—almost from birth because of the illness and early death of his first wife. This situation prevailed until the time of his marriage to Mrs. Johnson when Tara was 2 years of age. Although Mrs. Johnson has been Tara's primary caretaker since then, Mr. Johnson's early involvement with Tara during these crucial years of her development contributes to a very strong psychological tie between them that has continued up to the present time.

My observations have convinced me, and both parents agree, that at this time, Tara has a closer relationship with her father than her mother. Her relationship with Mrs. Johnson at this time is characteristically a difficult one in that there are frequent battles and power struggles. Although Tara is not completely free of such involvement with her father, such hostile interaction is far less common. In my interviews with Mr. Johnson and Tara I found her to be far more friendly with him than I observed her to be with Mrs. Johnson in my joint interviews with them.

In every interview, both alone and in joint sessions with various members of the family, Tara openly and unswervingly stated that she wished to live with her father: ''I want to live with my father. I am closer to him.'' ''When I was younger, my mother did more things; but since I'm older, my father does more things.'' ''My father listens to what I say; my mother doesn't.''

Mr. Johnson and Tara both utilize a similar method of communication. Neither feels a strong need to give confirmation or examples to general statements that they make, and they are therefore comfortable with one another. Mrs. Johnson, on the other hand, is much more specific in her communications and this is a source of difficulty, not only in her relationship with Tara, but in her relationship with her husband as well.

All five family members agree that Mr. Johnson spends significant time with Charles, involved in typical father-son activities, sports, games, etc. It is also apparent that Charles has a strong masculine identification and this arose, in part, from his modeling himself after his father.

Mr. Frank Johnson's Liabilities as a Parent

Mr. Johnson states that he would not have involved himself in the custody evaluation conducted by this examiner if he had to contribute to its financing. Accordingly, Mrs. Johnson assumed the total financial obligation for this evaluation. I conclude from this that with regard to this particular criterion for comparing the parents Mr. Johnson's position is less strong than Mrs. Johnson's.

On many occasions Mr. Johnson made general comments about his superiority over his wife with regard to parental capacity. For example, ''She's a very poor mother,'' ''She neglects the children,'' and ''If you had all the information you would see that I'm a better parent.'' However, it was extremely difficult to elicit from Mr. Johnson specific examples of incidents that would substantiate these statements. I not only considered this to be a manifestation of Mr. Johnson's problem in accurately communicating, but also considered it to be a deficiency in his position. One cannot be convinced of the strength of such statements if no examples can be provided to substantiate them.

In the hope that I might get more specific information from Mr. Johnson I asked him, on at least three occasions, to write a list of specifics that might help corroborate some of his allegations. He came to three subsequent interviews without having written anything in response to my invitation. I

consider such failure to reflect a compromise in his motivation for gaining custody of the three children. When he did
finally submit such a list it was far less comprehensive than
that which was submitted by Mrs. Johnson and in addition, the
issues raised had far less significance, e.g., ''She's late
once in a while,'' ''She's sometimes forgetful,'' and ''She
doesn't like playing baseball with Charles.''

Although I described Mr. Johnson's communication problem
as a factor supporting his gaining custody of Tara, I would
consider it a liability with regard to his gaining custody of
Elaine and Charles. Tara (possibly on a genetic basis) commu-
nicates in a similar way and so, as mentioned, is comfortable
with her father when they communicate. Elaine and Charles,
however, appear to be identifying with their mother with regard to communication accuracy. Accordingly, intensive exposure to Mr. Johnson might compromise what I consider a
healthier communicative pattern.

Mr. Johnson's profession as an airline pilot has not enabled him to have predictable hours. Not only is his schedule
variable, but there are times when he is required to work on
an emergency basis. All three children agree that Mrs. Johnson is more predictably present. Mr. Johnson's irregular
schedule is not a significant problem for Tara who, at 16, is
fairly independent and would not suffer significantly from
her father's schedule. The younger children, however, are
still in need of predictability of parental presence and Mr.
Johnson has not demonstrated his capacity to provide such
predictability. In my final interview with Mr. Johnson he
stated that he would change his work pattern to be available
to his children during non-school hours. Mrs. Johnson was
very dubious that this could be arranged because his job does
not allow such flexibility. Both parents agreed, however,
that it had not occurred in the past and that such predictability was not taking place at the time of this evaluation.

Both Charles and Elaine stated that they wanted to live
with their mother and not live with their father. Charles
stated, ''I want to be with my mother. I'd be alone when my
father goes to work.'' Elaine stated, ''I want to live with
my mother. I'm closer to my mother. I'm not as close to my
father.''

In a session in which I was discussing his future plans
with Mr. Johnson, he stated that he was considering moving to
California because he could earn more money there by supple-
menting his income with certain business ventures that he had
been invited to participate in. He stated also that he would
still move even if he were only to be granted custody of
Tara. Although I appreciate that a higher income could provide Mr. Johnson's children with greater financial flexibility, I believe that the disadvantages of such a move would
far outweigh its advantages from their point of view. Specifically, the extra advantages they might enjoy from such a
move would be more than offset by the even greater absence of
their father who, his liabilities notwithstanding, is still
an important figure for them.

In an interview in which I discussed with Mr. Johnson how
he would react to the various custodial decisions, he was far

more upset about the prospect of losing Tara than he was about the possibility of losing Charles and Elaine. In fact, he appeared to be accepting of the fact that Elaine would go to her mother. Although somewhat distressed about the possibility of Charles' living with his mother, he did not show the same degree of distress as his wife over the prospect of losing the younger two children.

Mrs. Carol Johnson's Assets as a Parent

Mrs. Carol Johnson was far more committed to the custody evaluation than her husband. As mentioned, she was willing to make the financial sacrifices involved in the evaluation. I consider this to be a factor reflecting greater motivation than her husband for gaining custody of the children. Mrs. Johnson is more available to the children during non-school hours than her husband and this is one element in her favor regarding gaining custody, especially of the younger children. Mrs. Johnson is a more accurate and clearer communicator than her husband and this is an asset. As mentioned, the younger children do not seem to have been affected by their father's communication difficulty. Having them live with him might result in their acquiring this maladaptive trait.

During her pregnancy with Elaine, Mrs. Johnson suffered with toxemia and associated high blood pressure and convulsions. Most physicians generally discourage women with this disorder from becoming pregnant again because it is genuinely life endangering. However, Mrs. Johnson did wish to have a third child, primarily because her husband, she states, was so desirous of having a son. Her pregnancy with Charles was complicated by the exacerbation of a preexisting asthmatic condition from which she states that she almost died. A less maternal woman would not have become pregnant again.

Elaine stated on many occasions, and in every interview, both alone and with other family members, that she wished to live with her mother: ''I'm closer to my mother,'' ''She's home more than my father,'' ''They call my father to do things at work all the time,'' and ''My mother has more feelings for me than my father.''

Charles also, both in individual session and in joint interviews, emphatically stated that he wished to live with his mother: ''I want to stay with my mother because she doesn't work as much as my father.'' ''If you get sick the father might not know what to do, but the mother does.'' ''My mother knows how to take care of me.'' ''She doesn't work that much.'' ''She reads me books more than my father.''

On one occasion Mr. Johnson stated: ''Carol is closer to Elaine than I am. They are similar. They're both sore losers. Both get emotional if they don't have their way.'' Mrs. Carol Johnson agrees that she and her daughter Elaine have these traits, but not to the degree described by her husband. Although there are certainly negative elements regarding the reasons why Mr. Johnson sees Elaine to be closer to his wife, this statement is an admission of his recognition of this preference of Elaine for her mother. The situation is analogous to Mr. Johnson's involvement with Tara. They are closer to one another, yet maladaptive and undesirable factors are contributing to the closeness.

Mrs. Carol Johnson's Liabilities as a Parent

Tara is not Mrs. Johnson's biological daughter. Although she has raised Tara from her infancy, as if she were her own biological child, and although she has adopted her, Mrs. Johnson is at a certain disadvantage regarding the development of a strong psychological parent-child tie. As mentioned, I believe that a biological relationship increases the strength of the psychological bond. Accordingly, Mrs. Johnson is at a disadvantage when compared to Mr. Johnson regarding this aspect of the custody consideration.

Mrs. Johnson and Tara have a poor relationship at this point. In my interviews with Mrs. Johnson and Tara I found the latter to view her mother scornfully and to be openly resentful of her authority. On one occasion Tara said: ''She has a lot of nerve telling me what to do.'' Were this an isolated statement, it would probably not have much significance. However, all agreed that it epitomized her general attitude toward her mother. Although some of the scornful attitude Tara exhibits toward her mother can be viewed as age-appropriate, I believe the extent goes beyond what is to be expected for teen-agers.

Mrs. Johnson cannot provide Charles with the same kind of father model and father-type involvement that her husband can. Although she claims an interest in sports and a greater degree of facility than the average woman, it is still clear that her husband has been far more involved in this type of activity with his son than has Mrs. Johnson.

Mr. Johnson accuses Mrs. Johnson of being excessively punitive and too strong a disciplinarian. Mrs. Johnson claims that her husband is too lax with the children and does not implement proper disciplinary measures. I believe that it is most likely that Mrs. Johnson is a little too punitive and that Mr. Johnson is a little too lenient. However, neither parent exhibits these difficulties to a degree that would be significantly injurious to the children, nor would I consider this to be a factor compromising either of their capacities as parents. It is probable, however, that these differences are playing a role in Tara's antagonism to her mother and her gravitating toward her father.

In every interview, both individual and joint, Tara openly stated that she wished to live with her father. ''I would be very unhappy if the judge made me go with my mother.'' ''He can't make me live with my mother. I'd run away to my father if he did.''

Conclusions and Recommendations

Weighing the above factors as best I can, I believe that the evidence is strongly in favor of Mr. Johnson being given custody of Tara. I believe, also, that the above evidence strongly supports the conclusion that Elaine should be given to Mrs. Johnson. Although there are certain arguments supporting Mr. Johnson's gaining custody of Charles, I believe

that these are greatly outweighed by arguments in favor of
Mrs. Johnson's gaining custody. Were the court to conclude
that Tara would be better off living with Mrs. Johnson, I believe that there would be a continuation of the present hos-
tilities, and this could be disruptive to the healthy psychological development of the younger children—if they were
exposed to such hostile interactions over a long period. I
believe that if Mr. Johnson were to be granted custody of
Elaine and Charles it is most likely that they would suffer
psychological damage. All things considered, I believe he is
the less preferable parent for the younger children and, if
they had to live with him, they would suffer emotional depri-
vations that could contribute to the development of psychiatric disorders.

Richard A. Gardner, M.D.

Source: R. Gardner, M.D., *Family Evaluation in Child Custody Litigation,* 318–25 (1982)

Assignment 11.5

(a) What standards exist in your state code to guide the judge on the decision to grant custody when the dispute is between the two biological parents? (See General Instructions for the State-Code Assignment in chapter one.)

(b) Find an opinion written by a court in your state in which the court granted custody to one of the parents following a divorce or legal separation. State the factors that the court used in making this decision. Why did the judge decide not to give custody to the other parent? Do you agree with the judge's decision on the custody issue? Are there other facts about the case that you would like to know, but were not provided in the opinion? Do you think the investigators for each side did a good job of gathering all the facts? (See General Instructions for the Court-Opinion Assignment in chapter one.)

Note on Frozen Embryos

A husband and wife participate in *in vitro* fertilization resulting in an embryo that is frozen for later implantation. Before this can occur, the parties file for divorce. What is the status of the frozen embryo? Is it "property" to be divided between the parties? Does the court have to make a "custody" decision? See the discussion on page 247.

Section E. Court Decisions on Visitation

As indicated, courts want to preserve as much of the child's relationship with both parents as possible. Hence, visitation rights are almost always granted to the noncustodial parent. Failing to grant such rights so would be a step in the direction of terminating the parental rights of that parent (page 511). Moreover, as indicated earlier, one of the criteria that a court will use in awarding sole custody to a parent is whether the latter will cooperate in the exercise of visitation rights by the other parent. Custodial parents who fail to provide such cooperation are sometimes dealt with harshly by the court, e.g., terminating spousal support, transferring custody to the other parent, contempt orders. It is never permissible, however, for the noncustodial parent to terminate child-support payments in retaliation for the custodial parent's violation of visitation rights.

Whenever possible, the court will favor frequent and regular visitation by the noncustodial parent, e.g., every other weekend, alternating holidays, substantial summer vacation time. When the custody battle is between two relatively fit parents, the court is even more inclined to grant greater visitation rights to the loser so long as the court is convinced that the losing parent had the proper motivation in seeking custody.

In addition to an inclination to cooperate, another essential component of successful visitation in most cases is physical proximity between the child and the noncustodial parent. A great deal of litigation has centered on the right of the custodial parent to move the child substantial distances away. Some courts flatly forbid such moving. In a few states, there are statutes that cover this problem. For example:

> **Minn.Stat.Ann. § 518.175(3) (1969).**   The custodial parent shall not move the residence of the child to another state except upon the order of the Court or with the consent of the non-custodial parent, when the non-custodial parent has been given visitation rights by the decree.

In extreme cases, the court might order the custodial parent to post a bond to secure compliance with the visitation rights of the noncustodial parent.

Another issue that is occasionally litigated is whether *third parties* can be given rights of visitation, e.g., grandparents, stepparents. Factors considered by the court in deciding this question include:

- The language of the statute in the state, if any, that governs who can visit. A court will want to know if it has statutory power to grant visitation rights to third parties.

- Whether the custodial parent objects to granting the visitation rights. And if so, why.

- Whether the child has lived with the third party for a substantial period of time in the past or has otherwise formed close emotional ties with the third party.

The best interest of the child is again the standard that the court will use if it has the power to grant visitation rights to anyone other than biological parents. Even when the power exists, however, it is rarely used except in situations such as the following:

> The father dies soon after the divorce in which the mother was given sole custody of the child. The paternal grandparents are granted visitation rights. The child had a warm relationship with these grandparents in the past. If visitation is not allowed, the child may lose all contact with the father's side of the family.
>
> A stepparent has been supporting his wife's child by a prior marriage. When the stepparent and mother divorce, he seeks visitation rights, even though he

never adopted the child (page 498). Visitation rights are granted if the stepparent had a close relationship with the child while together, and it would be very disruptive to end the relationship abruptly.

Section F. The New "Terror Weapon"

"I had to face the fact that for one year [during the exercise of unsupervised visitation rights by the father], I sent my child off to her rapist."*

"For many parents engaged in seriously contested child custody disputes, false allegations of child abuse have become an effective weapon for achieving an advantage in court."**

In alarming numbers, parents are being accused of *sexually abusing* their children, usually during visitation. The issue can also arise during an initial custody proceeding where one parent claims that the other committed sex abuse during the marriage, and hence should not be granted custody, or should not be granted visitation rights in unsupervised settings.

The level of bitterness generated by this accusation is incredibly high. It is the equivalent of a declaration of total war between the parties. The chances of reaching a settlement or of mediating the custody dispute—or anything else that is contested—often vanishes the moment the accusation is made. Protracted and costly litigation is all but inevitable.

Nor does litigation always resolve the matter. Assume that a mother with sole custody is turned down when she asks a court to terminate the father's right to visit the child because of an allegation of child abuse. The court finds the evidence of abuse to be insufficient and orders a continuation of visitation. Unable to accept this result, the mother goes underground out of desperation and a total loss of faith in the legal system. She either flees with the child, or she turns the child over to sympathetic third parties who agree to keep the child hidden from the authorities. The child might be moved from one "safe house" to another to avoid detection. This underground network consists of a core of dedicated women who at one time were in a similar predicament or who are former child-abuse victims themselves.

If the mother remains behind, she is hauled back into court. If she refuses to obey an order to produce the child, she faces an array of possible sanctions, including imprisonment for civil contempt or even prosecution for criminal kidnapping. Unfortunately, the media has an excessive interest in cases of this kind. Once reporters and cameras become involved, a circus atmosphere prevails.

Attorneys can find themselves in delicate situations. The first question they face is whether to take the case. When an alleged child abuser—usually the father—seeks representation, the attorney of course understands the father's need for a vigorous defense. What if he didn't do it? Yet cases of this kind tend to be placed in a different category by attorneys. Many need to believe in his innocence before they will take the case. According to a prominent matrimonial attorney, "I have a higher duty to make sure some wacko doesn't

*Szegedy-Maszak, WHO'S TO JUDGE, New York Times Magazine, 28 (May 21, 1989).
**Gordon, FALSE ALLEGATIONS OF ABUSE IN CHILD CUSTODY DISPUTES, 2 Minn. Fam. L. J. 225 (1985).

get custody of his child." Before proceeding, therefore, the attorney might ask him to:

- Take a lie detector test
- Take the *Minnesota Multiphasic Personality Index (MMPI) test,* which may be able to reveal whether someone has a propensity to lie, and is the kind of person who statistically is likely to be a child abuser
- Be evaluated by a knowledgeable psychologist or psychiatrist.

Some attorneys have even insisted that the father undergo hypnosis as a further aid in trying to assess the truth of the allegation.

Attorneys representing the mother face similar concerns. Is she telling the truth? Is she exaggerating, knowingly or otherwise? Is she trying to seek some other strategic advantage from the father, e.g., more financial support? (Custody blackmail?) What advice should the attorney give her when she first reveals the charge of sexual abuse, particularly when the evidence of abuse is not overwhelming? Should she be advised to go public with the charge? As indicated, the consequences of doing so—and of not doing so can be enormous. Bitter litigation is almost assured. What if the attorney talks her out of going public with the charge in order to settle the case through negotiation, "and a month or two later something terrible happens?" Faced, therefore, with a need to know if the accusation is true, the attorney may ask *her* to go take a polygraph test or an MMPI test, or to undergo an independent evaluation by a psychologist or psychiatrist.

Other attorneys disagree with this approach. They do not think that clients should be subject to such mistrust by their own attorney. And they fail to see much value in some of the devices used to assess the truth. Some typical comments from such attorneys are that: professionals "trained in sexual abuse are wrong very often;" "Frankly I trust my horse sense more than I trust psychiatrists;" and "There is no research that says the polygraph or MMPI is of any use."[1]

Of course, attorneys for both sides will have to interview the child involved. This can be a very delicate task. There is a danger of emotional damage every time the child is forced to focus on the events in question. Even though children are generally truthful, many are susceptible to suggestion and manipulation. Very often, the charge is made that the child has been "brainwashed" into believing that abuse did or did not occur. Clearly, the child needs protection. A separate attorney is usually appointed by the court to represent the child in the litigation. (As indicated earlier, this individual is often called a *guardian ad litem.*) Guidelines may exist in the state on who can interview the child and in what setting. Trained child counselors are commonly used. Using special, anatomically correct dolls, the counselor will ask the child to describe what happened. These interviews are usually videotaped. When the time comes for a court hearing, the judge will often interview the child outside the courtroom, e.g., in the judge's chambers without either parent being present.

---

[1]Fisk, *Abuse: The New Weapon,* The National Law Journal, 20 (July 17, 1989).

Assignment 11.6

Diane and George are the parents of Mary. When the child is two years old, the parents divorce. The decree awards Diane sole custody with visitation rights to George (on alternating weekends). Diane soon suspects that George is sexually abusing Mary during the visits. Answer the following questions for your state. (See General Instructions for the State-Code Assignment and General Instructions for the Court-Opinion Assignment in chapter one).

(a) What options does Diane have?

(b) Under what circumstances can the child be interviewed about the alleged molestation? Are there any restrictions on such interviews?

(c) Can Diane be jailed for contempt of court if she refuses to obey an order to disclose the location of Mary following a court determination that there was no sexual abuse by George? If so, for how long? Indefinitely?

Section G. Biological Parent vs. Psychological Parent

Thus far our main focus has been the custody dispute where the main combatants are the two biological parents. Suppose, however, that the dispute is between one biological parent an a third party such as a:

- Grandparent
- Other relative
- Stepparent (who never adopted the child)
- Foster parent (someone whom the state has asked to care for the child)
- Neighbor
- Friend

Assume that the other biological parent is out of the picture because he or she has died, has disappeared, or does not care. The third party is usually someone with whom the child has established close emotional ties. Frequently, the child has lived with the third party for a substantial period of time. This may have occurred for a number of reasons:

- The biological parent was ill, out of the state, out of work, etc.
- The biological parent was in prison.
- The state was asked the third party to care for the child temporarily.
- The child could not stay at home because of marital difficulties between the biological parents.
- The biological parent was in school for substantial periods of time.
- The biological parent once considered giving the child up for adoption.

Third parties who have formed such emotional ties with a child are referred to as *psychological parents*. See Goldstein, Freud, and Solnit, *Beyond the Best Interests of the Child* (1979).

There are two main schools of thought among courts when the custody dispute is between a biological parent and a psychological parent:

1. It is in the best interest of the child to be placed with its biological parent (this is a strong presumption).

2. It is in the best interest of the child to be placed with the adult who will provide the most wholesome, stable environment.

The emphasis of the first approach is on parental rights: unless you can show that the biological parent is *unfit*, he or she has the right to custody. The emphasis of the second approach is on the child's needs. A majority of states follow the first approach. In these states, the question is not whether the biological parent or the psychological parent can provide the best home for the child. The question is whether it is clear that placement with the biological parent would he harmful to the child. While the child may suffer some damage if his or her relationship with the psychological parent is severed, this does not necessarily overcome the biological parent's overriding right to have the child. The law is very reluctant to start taking children away from their natural parents because of a determination that someone else could do a better job raising them.

In practice, courts sometimes tend to blur the two approaches listed above. While maintaining allegiance to the doctrine of parental rights, the court might still undertake a comparison between the benefits to the child of living with the biological parent, as opposed to the benefits of living with the psychological parent. When the benefits to be derived from the latter are overwhelming, the court might be more inclined to find unfitness in the biological parent or to conclude that giving custody to the biological parent would be detrimental to the child. The interpretation of the evidence can be very subjective. There is often enough data to support any conclusion the court wants to reach. A person's mistakes in raising children can be viewed both as a detrimental inability to cope, or as an inevitable component of the nearly impossible job of parenting in today's society.

Assignment 11.7

(a) Are there any statutes in your state on how the court is to resolve a custody dispute between a biological parent and a psychological parent? If so, what do they say? (See General Instructions for the State-Code Assignment in chapter one.)

(b) Find an opinion written by a court in your state in which the dispute was between a biological parent and psychological parent. Who won? Why? What standards did the judge apply? Were there other facts about the case that you wish the court had provided? If so, what facts and why would you want them? (See General Instructions for the Court-Opinion Assignment in chapter one.)

(c) Make up a fact situation involving a custody dispute between a biological parent and psychological parent. Make it a close case. Include facts that would strongly favor each side. Now write a memorandum in which you discuss the law that would apply in your state to your case. Assume that you are working for the office that represents the psychological parent. (See General Instructions for the Legal-Analysis Assignment in chapter one.)

Section H. Modification of the Custody Order by the State That Issued the Order

In this section we consider the *modification* of a custody order by the same state that issued the order. Later we will examine the special jurisdiction problems that arise when a party faced with a custody order from one state tries to have it modified in another state (page 330). While our discussion will focus on the two biological parents, the same principles apply no matter who is given custody by the original order.

Two reasons justify a court in modifying its own custody order:

- There has been a change in circumstances since the original order, or
- Relevant facts were not made available to the court at the time of its original order.

In either situation, new facts are now before the court. The question becomes whether it is in the best interest of the child for the court to change its mind and award custody to the other parent. Given the disruption of such a change, the answer is no, unless the new facts *substantially* alter the court's perception of the child's welfare. For example:

- The custodial parent has been neglecting or abusing the child.
- The custodial parent has moved from the area, contrary to the court's order, thus making visitation extremely difficult or impossible.
- The custodial parent has adopted an unorthodox lifestyle which has negatively affected the child's physical or moral development (or there is a danger that this lifestyle will have this effect). See, for example, the *Jarrett* case presented earlier in which the mother began an open relationship with a live-in lover (page 303).

It is not enough that the custodial parent has experienced hard times such as sickness or loss of a part-time job since the original order. To justify a modification of this order, the adverse circumstances must be (1) ongoing, (2) relatively permanent, (3) serious, and (4) detrimental to the children. The same is true of misconduct by the custodial parent or mistakes that he or she has made in raising the children.

Assignment 11.8

(a) Are there any statutes in your state specifying the conditions for modifying a custody order that was issued within your state? If so, what are they? (See General Instructions for the State-Code Assignment in chapter one.)

(b) Find an option in which a custody order issued by your state was modified by a court in your state. Why was the modification ordered? What standards did the court use? Were there other facts about the case that you would have liked to have had? If so, what facts and why would you want to know about them? (See General Instructions for the Court-Opinion Assignment in chapter one.)

(c) Make up a fact situation involving a case in which sole custody was granted to one parent and the other parent is now seeking a modification. Make it a close case. Include facts that support a modification and facts that support a continuance of the status quo. Now write a memorandum in which you discuss the law that would apply in your state to your case. Assume that you are working for the office that represents the party who wants to prevent the other side from modifying the order. (See General Instructions for the Legal-Analysis Assignment in chapter one.)

(d) Read the following affidavit in support of a motion to modify a custody decree. Do you think the court should reconsider the custody order as requested? What further facts, if any, would you like to have? (See General Instructions for the Investigation-Strategy Assignment in chapter one.)

The following document is an affidavit used by a party seeking custody modification.

Affidavit in Support of a Motion to Modify the Custody Decree

Marino, J., McKinney's Forms, Form 14:24B and Form 14:33A
West Publishing Co. (1976).

AFFIDAVIT IN SUPPORT
Index No. 3

STATE OF NEW YORK }
COUNTY OF _____ } ss.

_____ , being duly sworn, deposes and says:

1. I am defendant herein. This affidavit is submitted in support of an application for reconsideration of the decision of the court made in this action on ____ , 19 __ , insofar as custody of my children is concerned.

2. Custody of the children has been awarded to my ex-wife, plaintiff. I did not contest her claim in the divorce. When I reported this to the children, they became extremely upset. My son told me that he did not want to live with his mother and that he felt it was unfair for a boy of his age to be forced to live with a parent contrary to his desires. My daughter had a similar reaction.

3. I tried to convey the situation to the Court by an informal application of reconsideration, on the strength of simple notes written to the Court by my children. My attorney advised me that the Court would not alter its determination.

4. I love my children very much. A history of prior proceedings between my wife and myself indicates that she had been awarded custody of the children under a Family Court order several years ago. At that time, she lived with the children in our house in [*Peekskill*]. I paid support, as directed for the children and my wife, and for the upkeep of the house. About two years ago my wife ousted my son from the house and sent him to live with me. At that time, I occupied a small apartment in [*Peekskill*] so that I could be near the children. I would see them quite often and would take them to school on many mornings. When my son came to me, I made room for him and we lived together until my daughter came to live with us about a year ago. We made room for her. My wife made no objections to the children living with me and made no attempts to get them to come back to her. While we all lived in my small apartment, my wife continued to live in the [*Peekskill*] house all by herself. I continued paying the upkeep on the house, although my wife permitted it to fall into a state of deteriorating disrepair. I contributed to her support.

5. I took care of my children as best I could. They were grown and attended school most of the day. In the evening we enjoyed a family life. We were together on week-ends. There were many week-ends when their mother would not attempt to spend any time with them. My son stayed away from the [*Peekskill*] house. My daughter

visited there with her mother on occasion. I know that on many occasions my wife stayed away from the [*Peekskill*] house for days at a time.

6. I have devoted my non-working hours to my children. I altered my schedule so that I would see them off to school each morning when I was not away from the City. If I was to be away, I would arrange adult supervision. I worked with my children on their homework and on anything else where they sought my participation. We shopped together and played together. My children were encouraged to maintain their friendships and to bring their friends to our home. Because of cramped quarters, my children would often visit with their friends and I encouraged them to maintain relationships with companions of their respective ages. I shared their problems and their joys. I tried to set responsible examples for them. My son had demonstrated to me that he is growing into a responsible young man who aspires to attend *Massachusetts Institute of Technology*. I am proud of his seriousness and of his healthy outlook in times like this. I have tried to maintain a closely knit family between my children and myself so that they should know the advantages of love, companionship, and security. I know that they did not find any such relationship at their mother's bosom.

7. My children have revealed to me that they were wrong in not having made a definite choice during this interview with the court on the matter of their preference of a home. I understand that they will still love their mother and I have not attempted to sway them from that plateau. They told me that they wanted the court to decide the problem for them and that they had hoped that they could be the force which could solve the rift between plaintiff and myself. They were unaware that at the time of the interview my wife's prayer for divorce had already been granted. My son told me that he indicated to the court that he preferred to live with me although he did not state, unequivocally, that he did not desire to live with his mother.

8. I gather from my children's reaction and from what they have told me that they misunderstood what was required of them during their interview with the court. I submit that another interview should be granted if the court feels that my children's affidavits are insufficient to establish their desires. Had I not seen the effect of the custody decision on my children and had they not indicated their grief over it, I would sit back and abide by the will of the court.

9. I seriously question my wife's fitness as our children's custodian. She voluntarily relinquished their custody, as aforesaid. Under adverse living conditions (cramped quarters), my children have thrived and demonstrated a progression toward adulthood. I believe that my wife's having been competitive instead of being cooperative with the children operated to compromise their welfare. I believe that using the children as a pawn against my wife has lost our children's respect. I feel that my pleasures must be subservient to the welfare of my children. They deserve as real a home as can be possible under the circumstances. They are entitled to eat a meal in peace and one which shows concern in its preparation. I believe that the children deserve some security in the knowledge that they have the genuine care and love of a parent. I believe that they cannot get this from their mother.

10. WHEREFORE, I respectfully pray that this application be granted and that upon reconsideration I be awarded custody of my children.

[*Signature*]

Section I. Jursidictional Problems and Child Snatching

Earlier we discussed the modification of a child custody order by the state that issued the order (page 325). Suppose, however, that a party tries to have the order modified by *another* state. Consider the following sequence:

> Dan and Ellen are divorced in New York where they live. Ellen receives custody of their child. Dan moves to New Jersey. During a visit of the child in New Jersey, Dan petitions a New Jersey court for a modification of the New York custody order. Ellen does not appear in the New Jersey proceeding. Dan tells the New Jersey court a horror story about the child's life with Ellen in New York. The New Jersey court modifies the New York order on the basis of changed circumstances, awarding custody to Dan.

Or worse:

> While their child is in a New York school yard, Dan takes the child out of the state without telling Ellen. Dan petitions the New Jersey court for a modification of the custody order. If he loses, he tries again in Florida. If he loses, he tries again in another state until he finds a court that will grant him custody.

The latter situation involves what has been commonly called *child snatching*. The parent "grabs" the child and then "shops" for a favorable forum (*forum shopping*). For years the problem reached epidemic proportions.

Courts are caught in a dilemma. When a custody order is made, it is not a final determination by the court. Custody orders are always modifiable on the basis of changed circumstances that affect the welfare of the child. This rule is designed to help the child by making the court always available to protect the child. But if an order is not final, it is not entitled to *full faith and credit* by another state, i.e., another state is not required to abide by it. Hence, other states are free to reexamine the case to determine whether new circumstances warrant a modification. In order to maintain flexibility, states require very little to trigger its jurisdiction to hear a custody case, e.g., the domicile or mere presence of the child in the state along with that of one of the parents. The result is chaos: scandalous child snatching and unseemly forum shopping.

The question, therefore, is how to cut down or eliminate child snatching and forum shopping without taking away the flexibility that courts need to act in the best interest of the child. Two major statutes need to be discussed:

- The *Uniform Child Custody Jurisdiction Act* (See Appendix B, page 561)
- The *Parental Kidnaping Prevention Act* (See Appendix C, page 567)

Uniform Child Custody Jurisdiction Act (UCCJA)

In 1968 the UCCJA was issued by the National Conference of Commissioners on Uniform Laws. This conference proposes laws for adoption by the various state legislatures (page 58). When first proposed, only a small number of states adopted the UCCJA. When, however, a top-rated television program (*60 Minutes*) gave national exposure to the problem, almost all of the states fell in line.

Two important questions are covered in the UCCJA:

- When does a court in the state have the power or jurisdiction to make the *initial* decision on child custody?
- When will a court modify a custody order of another state?

A goal of the UCCJA is to "avoid jurisdictional competition and conflict with courts of other states in matters of child custody which have in the past resulted in the shifting of children from state to state with harmful effects on their well-being" (§ 1).

Jurisdiction to Make the Initial Child-Custody Decision

The foundation of the UCCJA is § 3, which specifies the conditions that must exist for a court to hear a child-custody case. Without one of these conditions being present, the court will have no jurisdiction to decide the case. Any *one* of the following four conditions will be sufficient to confer such jurisdiction:

1. *Home state.*
   - This is the home state of the child at the time the case is brought. A home state is where the child has lived for at least six consecutive months (or since birth if the child is less than six months old). These time periods can include temporary absence from the state. *Or*
   - This state was the home state of the child (as defined above) within six months of the commencement of the custody suit, but the child is now being kept out of state and at least one parent or person claiming the right to custody still lives in this state.

2. *Significant connection/substantial evidence.* Even though this is not the home state of the child, it is in the best interest of the child for this state to take jurisdiction because:
   - The child and parents, or the child and at least one person claiming custody, have a significant connection with this state, and
   - There is substantial evidence in this state concerning the child's present or future care, protection, training, and personal relationships.

3. *Physical presence/abandonment/emergency.* Even though this is not the home state of the child and even though there is not significant connection with or substantial evidence in this state, the state can still take jurisdiction if:
   - The child is physically present in the state and has been abandoned, or
   - The child is physically present in the state and an emergency exists because the child has been subjected to or threatened with mistreatment, abuse, neglect, etc.

4. *No other state has jurisdiction.* Even though this is not the home state of the child, even though there is no significant connection with or substantial evidence in this state, and even though there is no abandonment or emergency, this state can still take jurisdiction if:
   - It is in the best interest of the child for this state to take jurisdiction, and no other state would have jurisdiction under any of the conditions substantially similar to those listed above. No other state is the home state (1). There is no significant connection with or substantial evidence in another state (2). And the child is not physically present in another state faced with abandonment or an emergency (3). *Or*
   - It is in the best interest of the child for this state to take jurisdiction, and another state has declined to accept jurisdiction because this state is the more appropriate forum to determine custody.

Section 8(a) of the UCCJA also has a *"clean hands"* provision. A court can decline to exercise jurisdiction if the petitioner for custody has "wrongfully taken the child from another state or has engaged in similar reprehensible conduct" and it is "just and proper" for the court to decline jurisdiction under the circumstances.

Thus, simply because a court has jurisdiction to take a custody case, it will not necessarily use that jurisdiction. In addition to refusing jurisdiction in a case where the petitioner has "dirty hands," a court can also decline to use its jurisdiction if it is clear under the circumstances that another state would be a more convenient forum to resolve the custody dispute (§ 7). For example, it may be possible for two states to have a significant connection with the parties. Substantial evidence on the child's welfare may exist in both states. One of these states, however, could decline to exercise its jurisdiction because the other state has a *more* significant connection and *more* substantial evidence. The UCCJA, therefore, encourages states to defer to the most convenient and appropriate state available.

Assignment 11.9

Fred and Jane were married in Ohio on Jan. 1, 1980. On March 13, 1980, they had a child, Bob. From the first day of their marriage, however, they began having marital difficulties. On July 4, 1980, Fred moved to Kentucky. Bob continued to live with his mother in Ohio. By mutual agreement, Fred can occasionally take the child to Kentucky for visits. After a scheduled one-day visit on November 5, 1980, Fred decides not to return the child. He keeps Bob until November 1, 1981 when he returns him to Jane. Fred then joins the Army. When he returns on October 6, 1985, he discovers that Jane has been beating Bob.

Assume that both Ohio and Kentucky have adopted the UCCJA. Under § 3 and § 8(a) of the UCCJA, which state would have jurisdiction to determine the custody of Bob on the following dates:

April 4, 1980

November 6, 1980

January 1, 1981

September 1, 1981

October 6, 1985

See General Instructions for the Legal-Analysis Assignment in chapter one.

Assignment 11.10

Interview Fred on the basis of the fact situation outlined in Assignment 11.9. See General Instructions for the Interviewing Assignment in chapter one.

Jurisdiction to Modify a Custody Order of Another State

Thus far we have examined the jurisdiction of a state to make an *initial* custody order. We have addressed the question of when does a court have jurisdiction to decide the custody question for the first time, and if more than one state has jurisdiction, which is the most convenient forum? We now turn to the question of modification: when does one state have jurisdiction to modify a custody order to another state? Section 14 of the UCCJA governs:

§ 14. A court in this state (where a modification is being sought) can modify the custody order of another state only if:

   (i) The state that issued the custody order no longer appears to have jurisdiction under conditions substantially similar to § 3 (i.e., it is no longer the home state, or it no longer has significant connection/substantial evidence, or the child is not physically present in the state faced with abandonment or an emergency), *or,* the state has declined to assume jurisdiction to modify its own custody order. And,

   (ii) This state (where a modification is being sought) has jursidiction under § 3 (i.e., it is the home state, or it has significant connection/substantial evidence, or the child is physically present in the state faced with abandonment or an emergency).

For example, before a California court can modify a New York custody order, the California court must first determine whether New York would now have jurisdiction under § 3 (or under provisions substantially similar thereto), *and* whether California now has jurisdiction under § 3.

   Again, however, even though a state has jurisdiction to modify the order of another state, the state may decline to exercise this jurisdiction. Section 8(b) is the dirty-hands provision for modification cases:

§ 8(b). Unless required in the interest of the child, the court shall not exercise its jurisdiction to modify a custody decree of another state if the petitioner, without consent of the person entitled to custody, has improperly removed the child from the physical custody of the person entitled to custody or has improperly retained the child after a visit or other temporary relinquishment of physical custody. If the petitioner has violated any other provision of a custody decree of another state the court may decline to exercise its jurisdiction if this is just and proper under the circumstances.

Assignment 11.11

Reread the facts in Assignment 11.9, page 330. Assume that in 1981, an Ohio court awarded custody of Bob to Jane. On October 10, 1985, Fred asks a Kentucky court to grant him custody. Assume further that both Ohio and Kentucky have adopted the UCCJA. Can Kentucky modify? (See General Instructions for Legal-Analysis Assignment in chapter one.)

Assignment 11.12

(a) Find the most recent court opinion in your state in which your state refused to modify the custody order of another state. Why did it refuse?

(b) Find the most recent opinion of your state in which your state modified the custody order of another state. Why did it do so? (See General Instructions for the Court-Opinion Assignment in chapter one.)

(c) Is the opinion you discussed in part "a" consistent with the opinion you discussed in part "b"?

Exhibit 11–2 shows the form used to file a declaration under the UCCJA.

☐ **EXHIBIT 11–2** Declaration under Uniform Child Custody Jurisdiction Act (UCCJA)

ATTORNEY OR PARTY WITHOUT ATTORNEY *(Name and Address)*:	TELEPHONE NO.:	*FOR COURT USE ONLY*

ATTORNEY FOR *(Name)*:

SUPERIOR COURT OF CALIFORNIA, COUNTY OF

STREET ADDRESS:

MAILING ADDRESS:

CITY AND ZIP CODE:

BRANCH NAME:

CASE NAME:

DECLARATION UNDER **UNIFORM CHILD CUSTODY JURISDICTION ACT (UCCJA)**	CASE NUMBER:

1. **I am a party** to this proceeding to determine custody of a child.
2. *(Number)*: _____ minor children are subject to this proceeding as follows:
   (Insert the information requested below. The residence information must be given for the last FIVE years.)

a. Child's name	Place of birth	Date of birth	Sex

Period of residence	Address	Person child lived with *(name and present adress)*	Relationship
to present			
to			
to			
to			

b. Child's name	Place of birth	Date of birth	Sex
☐ Residence information is the same as given above for child a. *(If NOT the same, provide the information below.)*			

Period of residence	Address	Person child lived with *(name and present address)*	Relationship
to present			
to			
to			
to			

c. ☐ Additional children are listed on Attachment 2c. *(Provide requested information for additional children on an attachment.)*

(Continued on reverse)

Form Approved by the
Judicial Council of California
MC-150 [Rev. January 1, 1987] [Cor. 1/2/87]

DECLARATION UNDER
UNIFORM CHILD CUSTODY JURISDICTION ACT (UCCJA)

Civil Code, § 5158
Probate Code, §§ 1510(f), 1512

☐ **EXHIBIT 11–2** continued

SHORT TITLE:	CASE NUMBER:

3. Have you participated as a party or a witness or in some other capacity in another litigation or custody proceeding, in California or elsewhere, concerning custody of a child subject to this proceeding?
   ☐ No ☐ Yes *(If yes, provide the following information:)*

   a. Name of each child:

   b. Capacity of declarant: ☐ party ☐ witness ☐ other *(specify)*:
   c. Court *(specify name, state, location)*:

   d. Court order or judgment *(date)*:

4. Do you have information about a custody proceeding pending in a California court or any other court concerning a child subject to this proceeding, other than that stated in item 3?
   ☐ No ☐ Yes *(If yes, provide the following information:)*

   a. Name of each child:

   b. Nature of proceeding: ☐ dissolution or divorce ☐ guardianship ☐ adoption ☐ other *(specify)*:

   c. Court *(specify name, state, location)*:

   d. Status of proceeding:

5. Do you know of any person who is not a party to this proceeding who has physical custody or claims to have custody of or visitation rights with any child subject to this proceeding?
   ☐ No ☐ Yes *(If yes, provide the following information:)*

a. Name and address of person	b. Name and address of person	c. Name and address of person
☐ Has physical custody ☐ Claims custody rights ☐ Claims visitation rights	☐ Has physical custody ☐ Claims custody rights ☐ Claims visitation rights	☐ Has physical custody ☐ Claims custody rights ☐ Claims visitation rights
Name of each child	Name of each child	Name of each child

I declare under penalty of perjury under the laws of the State of California that the foregoing is true and correct.
Date:

▶

....
(TYPE OR PRINT NAME)   (SIGNATURE OF DECLARANT)

6. ☐ Number of pages attached after this page:

NOTICE TO DECLARANT: You have a continuing duty to inform this court if you obtain any information about a custody proceeding in a California court or any other court concerning a child subject to this proceeding.

MC-150 [Rev. January 1, 1987]   **DECLARATION UNDER**   Page two
   [Cor. 1/2/87]   **UNIFORM CHILD CUSTODY JURISDICTION ACT (UCCJA)**

Parental Kidnaping Prevention Act (PKPA)

In 1980 Congress passed the PKPA which gave added clout to the anti-child snatching movement. Congress was concerned about the lack of nation-wide consistency in state custody laws contributing to a tendency of parties "to frequently resort to the seizure, restraint, concealment, and interstate transportation of children, the disregard of court orders, excessive relitigation of cases, obtaining of conflicting orders by the courts, . . . and interstate travel and communication that is so expensive and time consuming . . . ." To remedy this problem, Congress enacted the PKPA, the essential terms of which are reprinted in Appendix C, page 567.

The PKPA addresses the question of when one state *must* enforce (without modification) the custody decree (or visitation order) of another state. Phrased another way, when must one state give *full faith and credit* to the custody decree of another state? In answering this question, the PKPA adopts many of the principles of the UCCJA. The essential question is whether the state that rendered the custody decree had jurisdiction to do so based on provisions very similar to § 3 of the UCCJA, discussed earlier. First, this state must have had jurisdiction according to its own laws. Additionally, one of the following conditions must be met as of the time the state rendered its custody decree:

"(A) such State (i) is the home State of the child on the date of the commencement of the proceeding, or (ii) had been the child's home State within six months before the date of the commencement of the proceeding and the child is absent from such State because of his removal or retention by a contestant or for other reasons, and a contestant continues to live in such State;

(B)(i) it appears that no other State would have jurisdiction under subparagraph (A), and (ii) it is in the best interest of the child that a court of such State assume jurisdiction because (I) the child and his parents, or the child and at least one contestant, have a significant connection with such State other than mere physical presence in such State, and (II) there is available in such State substantial evidence concerning the child's present or future care, protection, training, and personal relationships;

(C) the child is physically present in such State and (i) the child has been abandoned, or (ii) it is necessary in an emergency to protect the child because he has been subjected to or threatened with mistreatment or abuse;

(D)(i) it appears that no other State would have jurisdiction under subparagraph (A), (B), (C), or (E), or another State has declined to exercise jurisdiction on the ground that the State whose jurisdiction is in issue is the more appropriate forum to determine the custody of the child, and (ii) it is in the best interest of the child that such court assume jurisdiction; or

(E) the court has continuing jurisdiction . . . ."

In these circumstances, the custody order shall be given full faith and credit by another state. Another state "shall not modify" it. Once a court has proper jurisdiction to render a custody decree, this jurisdiction continues so long as this state remains the residence of the child *or* of any party claiming a right to custody.

Congress also made available to the states the Federal Parent Locator Service which will help to locate an absent parent or child for the purpose of enforcing laws on the unlawful taking or restraint of a child or for the purpose of making or enforcing a child custody determination. Previously, this service has been used mainly in child-support cases (page 359).

Assignment 11.13

(a) Is it a crime for a parent in your state to take his or her child from the other parent without the consent of the latter? Check the statutes and cases of your state. See General Instructions for the State-Code Assignment in chapter one and General Instructions for the Court-Opinion Assignment in chapter one.

(b) Is it a tort? Check the case law of your state. (See General Instructions for the Court-Opinion Assignment in chapter one.)

Section J. Children Abroad: Special Problems

The following material deals with child abduction over international borders. As we have seen, parental kidnaping within the United States can lead to complex jurisdictional problems. These problems multiply when the child is taken out of the country.

Locating a Missing Child Abroad

United States Department of State,
Office of Citizens Consular Services, Washington, D.C.

The resolution of child custody disputes is a private legal matter in which the Department of State may not properly intervene. Our role is limited to questions concerning the welfare and whereabouts of the American citizen children abducted by one parent and transported to a foreign jurisdiction and the issuance of passports to children who are the subject of custody disputes.

Consular Welfare/Whereabouts Search

When a child has been abducted by a parent, the American embassy or consulate can conduct a welfare/whereabouts check for the child. Under this procedure, the consular officer attempts to locate the child and ascertain the child's state of health. The consular officer will endeavor to either personally interview the child or enlist the services of local authorities to determine the child's health and welfare. The consular officer may begin by contacting local authorities to verify the child's entry and/or residence in the country. When the child is located, the consular officer may telephone the parent/guardian abroad or speak directly to the child. A personal visit to the child by the consular officer may be requested by the parent in the United States. If difficulty ensues when the parent/guardian refuses the consular officer access to the child, local officials, family services agencies or police authorities may be requested to determine the child's well-being. A report of the child's condition is then relayed to the requesting parent. If the welfare/whereabouts check convinces the consular officer that the child may have been abused or if evidence provided by the parent in the U.S. such as police reports, medical records or school records supports allegations of child abuse, the consular officer will make strong representations to the local authorities for a thorough investigation and, if necessary, request the removal of the child into the protective custody of the local courts or child welfare service. Consular officers cannot, however, take custody or force the return of the child to the deprived parent in the United States.

After an Abduction—A Checklist for Parents

International Parental Child Abduction, 3d ed.,
United States Department of State, Bureau of Consular Affairs (1989)

This list assumes that you know, or strongly suspect, that your child has been abducted abroad.

1. Emergency Action—What to do Right Away

☐ If you do not know where your child is, have you filed a missing person report with your local police department?

☐ Have you reported the abduction to the National Center for Missing and Exploited Children?

☐ Have you obtained a decree of sole custody or one that prohibits your child from traveling without your permission? In most states you can obtain such a decree even after a child is abducted. A custody decree in your favor is necessary for any legal action.

☐ Has your child's name been entered in the U.S. passport namecheck system?

☐ If your child is a dual national, have the embassy and consulates of the foreign country been informed of your custody decree and asked not to issue a foreign passport to your child?

☐ If your child is a U.S. citizen only but the other parent has close ties to a particular country, have the embassy and consulates of that country been informed of your custody decree and asked not to issue a visa to your child?

☐ Have you asked the Department of State's Office of Citizens Consular Services (CCS) to initiate a welfare and whereabouts search for your child overseas?

2. The Search

☐ Have you obtained certified copies of your custody decree from the court that issued it? You may need to furnish proof of your custody rights at various stages in your search and recovery effort.

☐ Have you obtained a copy of the National Center for Missing and Exploited Children's publication, *Parental Kidnapping: How to Prevent an Abduction and What to Do If Your Child Is Abducted?*

☐ Have you tried to establish contact with relatives or friends of the abducting parent?

☐ Has the Federal Parent Locator Service been contacted?

☐ Have you contacted the principal of your child's school and asked to be informed of requests for transfer of your child's school records?

☐ Have you prepared a poster of your child?

☐ Have you asked local law enforcement authorities to ask the U.S. Postal Inspection service to put a "mail cover" on addresses in the U.S. to which the abductor might write?

☐ Have you asked local law enforcement authorities to help you obtain information from telephone and credit card companies on the whereabouts of the abductor?

3. After Your Child has been Located Abroad

☐ Have you retained the services of a foreign attorney?

☐ Have you sent certified copies of the custody decree, court orders, state and Federal warrants, copies of state custody and parental child abduction laws, and the Federal Parental Kidnapping Prevention Act to the foreign attorney?

4. Legal Proceedings: Possible Criminal Remedies

☐   Is parental child abduction a crime in the state where your child resides or was abducted?

☐   Has a state warrant been issued for the arrest of the abductor?

☐   Has a Federal Unlawful Flight to Avoid Prosecution (UFAP) warrant been issued for the arrest of the abductor?

☐   If a warrant has been issued, has the abductor's name been entered in the wanted persons section of the National Crime Information Center (NCIC) computer?

☐   Is it possible or useful to take legal action against agents or accomplices to the abduction?

☐   If the abductor is a U.S. citizen, have you considered seeking to have his or her passport revoked?

☐   Would extradition of the abductor, if possible, be effective in your case?

One Possible Solution: The Hague Convention

International Parental Child Abduction, 3d ed.,
United States Department of State, Bureau of Consular Affairs (1989)

The most difficult and frustrating element for most parents whose child has been abducted abroad is that U.S. laws and court orders are not directly enforceable abroad. Each sovereign country has jurisdiction within its own territory and over persons present within its border, and no country can force another to decide cases or enforce laws within its confines in a particular way. Issues that have to be resolved between sovereign nations can only be handled by persuasion, or by international agreement.

The increase in international marriages since World War II increased international child custody cases to the point where 23 nations, meeting at the Hague Conference on Private International Law in 1976, agreed to seek a treaty to deter international child abduction. Between 1976 and 1980, the United States was a major force in preparing and negotiating the Hague Convention on the Civil Aspects of International Child Abduction. The Convention came into force for the United States on July 1, 1988, and applies to abductions or wrongful retentions that occurred on or after that date.

As of March 1989, the convention is in force in Australia, Austria, Canada, France, Hungary, Luxembourg, Portugal, Spain, Switzerland, and the United Kingdom. Norway will become a party on April 1, 1989, and other countries are working toward ratification. Call or write Citizens Consular Service to learn which countries have joined.

What is Covered by the Convention

The countries that are parties to the Convention have agreed with each other that, subject to certain limited exceptions, a child wrongfully removed or retained in one of these countries shall promptly be returned to the other member country where the child habitually resided before the abduction or wrongful retention. The Convention also provides a means for helping parents to exercise visitation rights abroad.

There is a treaty obligation to return an abducted child below the age of 16 if application is made less than one year from the date of wrongful removal or retention. After one year, the court is still obligated to order the child returned unless the person resisting return demonstrates that the child is settled in the new environment. A court may refuse to order a child returned if there is a grave risk that the child would be exposed to physical or psychological harm or otherwise placed in an intolerable situation. A court may also decline to return the child if the child objects to being returned and has reached an age and degree of maturity at which the court can take account of the child's views. Finally, the return of the child may be refused if the return would violate the fundamental principles of human rights and freedoms of the country where the child is being held.

How to Invoke the Hague Convention

You do not need to have a custody decree to invoke the Convention. However, to apply for the return of your child, you must have been actually exercising custody at the time of the abduction and you must not have consented to the removal or retention of the child. You may apply for the return of your child or the ability to exercise your visitation rights. You can also ask for assistance in locating your child and for information on your child's welfare.

Each country that is a party to the Convention has designated a Central Authority to carry out specialized duties under the Convention. You may submit an application either to the U.S. Central Authority or directly to the Central Authority of the country where the child is believed to be held. The Central Authority for the United States is the Department of State's Office of Citizens Consular Services (CCS).

An application to invoke the Hague Convention must be written. Submit one copy of the application to CCS along with two copies of any supporting documents you have that are asked for in section IX of the form. The supporting documents may need to be translated into the official language of the requested country. Ask CCS about translation requirements.

The Role of the U.S. Central Authority (CCS)

CCS will review your application to see that it complies with the Convention and, if it does, will forward it to the foreign Central Authority and assist you, if necessary, in working with that authority. If the abducting parent does not voluntarily agree to the return of your child, you may need to choose an attorney abroad to pursue your case. Your attorney may have to present your case to the foreign court.

The Department of State is prohibited from acting as an agent or attorney in your case. We can, however, help in many other ways. We can give you information on the operating procedures of the Central Authority in the country where your child is believed to be located. We can help you obtain information on the laws of the state in which your child resided prior to the abduction and can transmit statements concerning the wrongfulness of the abduction under the laws of that state. Six weeks after court action commences, we can request a status report.

The Central Authority in the country where your child is located, however, has the primary responsibility of responding to your application. In the words of the Convention, those countries agree to "ensure that rights of custody and access under the law of one Contracting State are effectively respected in the other Contracting State."

☐ **EXHIBIT 11—3** Hague Convention Application

UNITED STATES DEPARTMENT OF STATE

APPLICATION FOR ASSISTANCE UNDER THE HAGUE CONVENTION ON CHILD ABDUCTION

SEE PRIVACY STATEMENT ON REVERSE

OMB NO. 1405-0076
EXPIRES: 6-91
Estimated Burden – 1 Hour

I. IDENTITY OF CHILD AND PARENTS

CHILD'S NAME (LAST, FIRST, MIDDLE)		DATE OF BIRTH	PLACE OF BIRTH	
ADDRESS (Before removal)		U.S. SOCIAL SECURITY NO.	PASSPORT/IDENTITY CARD COUNTRY: NO.:	NATIONALITY
HEIGHT	WEIGHT	COLOR OF HAIR		COLOR OF EYES

FATHER			MOTHER		
NAME (Last, First, Middle)			NAME (Last, First, Middle)		
DATE OF BIRTH	PLACE OF BIRTH		DATE OF BIRTH	PLACE OF BIRTH	
NATIONALITY	OCCUPATION	PASSPORT/IDENTITY CARD COUNTRY: NO.:	NATIONALITY	OCCUPATION	PASSPORT/IDENTITY CARD COUNTRY: NO.:
CURRENT ADDRESS AND TELEPHONE NUMBER			CURRENT ADDRESS AND TELEPHONE NUMBER		
U.S.SOCIAL SECURITY NO.			U.S.SOCIAL SECURITY NO.		
COUNTRY OF HABITUAL RESIDENCE			COUNTRY OF HABITUAL RESIDENCE		
DATE AND PLACE OF MARRIAGE AND DIVORCE, IF APPLICABLE					

II. REQUESTING INDIVIDUAL OR INSTITUTION

NAME (Last, First, Middle)		NATIONALITY	OCCUPATION	
CURRENT ADDRESS AND TELEPHONE NUMBER			PASSPORT/IDENTITY CARD COUNTRY: NO.:	
COUNTRY OF HABITUAL RESIDENCE				
RELATIONSHIP TO CHILD	NAME, ADDRESS, AND TELEPHONE NO. OF LEGAL ADVISER, IF ANY			

III. INFORMATION CONCERNING THE PERSON ALLEGED TO HAVE WRONGFULLY REMOVED OR RETAINED CHILD

NAME (Last, First, Middle)		KNOWN ALIASES	
DATE OF BIRTH	PLACE OF BIRTH	NATIONALITY	
OCCUPATION, NAME AND ADDRESS OF EMPLOYER	PASSPORT/IDENTITY CARD COUNTRY: NO.:	U.S. SOCIAL SECURITY NO.	
CURRENT LOCATION OR LAST KNOWN ADDRESS IN THE U.S.			
HEIGHT	WEIGHT	COLOR OF HAIR	COLOR OF EYES

FORM 6-88   DSP-105

☐ **EXHIBIT 11–3** Hague Convention Application (continued)

OTHER PERSONS WITH POSSIBLE ADDITIONAL INFORMATION RELATING TO THE WHEREABOUTS OF CHILD
(Name, address, telephone number)

IV. TIME, PLACE, DATE, AND CIRCUMSTANCES OF THE WRONGFUL REMOVAL OR RETENTION

V. FACTUAL OR LEGAL GROUNDS JUSTIFYING THE REQUEST

VI. CIVIL PROCEEDINGS IN PROGRESS, IF ANY

VII. CHILD IS TO BE RETURNED TO:

NAME *(Last, First, Middle)*	DATE OF BIRTH	PLACE OF BIRTH
ADDRESS		TELEPHONE NUMBER

PROPOSED ARRANGEMENTS FOR RETURN TRAVEL OF CHILD

VIII. OTHER REMARKS

IX. DOCUMENTS ATTACHED (PREFERABLY CERTIFIED)

☐ DIVORCE DECREE ☐ PHOTOGRAPH OF CHILD ☐ OTHER _____
☐ CUSTODY DECREE ☐ OTHER AGREEMENT CONCERNING CUSTODY _____

SIGNATURE OF APPLICANT AND/OR STAMP OF CENTRAL AUTHORITY	DATE	PLACE

PRIVACY ACT STATEMENT

THIS INFORMATION IS REQUESTED UNDER THE AUTHORITY OF THE INTERNATIONAL CHILD ABDUCTION REMEDIES ACT, PUBLIC LAW 100–300. THE INFORMATION WILL BE USED FOR THE PURPOSE OF EVALUATING APPLICANTS' CLAIMS UNDER THE HAGUE CONVENTION ON THE CIVIL ASPECTS OF INTERNATIONAL CHILD ABDUCTION, LOCATING ABDUCTED CHILDREN, AND ADVISING APPLICANTS ABOUT AVAILABLE LEGAL REMEDIES. WITHOUT THE REQUESTED INFORMATION, U.S. AUTHORITIES MAY BE UNABLE EFFECTIVELY TO ASSIST IN LOCATING ABDUCTED CHILDREN.

Comments concerning the accuracy of the burden hour estimate on page 1 may be directed to OMB, OIRA, State Department Desk Officer, Wash., D.C. 20503

Key Chapter Terminology

Legal Custody
Physical Custody
Custodial Parent
Sole Custody
Joint Custody
Shared Custody
Co-Parenting
Bird's-Nest Custody
Split Custody
Divided Custody
Visitation
Best Interest of the Child
Biological Parent
Guardian ad Litem
Parental Alienation Syndrome
Legal Preferences
Tender-Years Presumption
Primary-Caretaker Presumption

Homosexual Parent
Spiritual Custody
Sexual Abuse
MMPI
Psychological Parent
Parental Fitness
Modification
Child Snatching
Forum Shopping
Uniform Child Custody Jurisdiction Act
    (UCCJA)
Home State
Clean Hands
Parental Kidnapping Prevention Act
    (PKPA)
Full Faith and Credit
Abduction
Hague Convention

Child Support

■ Chapter Outline

In negotiating the child-support terms of a separation agreement, the parties must consider a number of factors, the most important of which are the new state guidelines on child support, the standard of living to which the child was accustomed during the marriage, and the financial resources that are available for support. A court will consider many of these same factors in deciding whether to approve what the parties have negotiated.

Before the court can make a child-support order, it must have personal jurisdiction over the defendant, which is acquired through in-person service of process or through the long-arm statute. The defendant can be the father, the mother, or anyone who has formally adopted the child. Child-support orders can be later modified if changed circumstances are serious enough to warrant it.

The major problem in this area is enforcement: a very large number of noncustodial parents are not making their child-support payments. Title IV-D agencies have been established to combat this problem by locating delinquent parents (called *obligors*) and by using new enforcement tools to make them pay what they owe.

In a civil contempt proceeding, an obligor with the present ability to pay can be jailed for nonpayment. A writ of execution can be levied against his property. Other options include criminal prosecution, income withholding, tax-refund intercept, unemployment-compensation intercept, qualified domestic relations orders, credit clouding, and posting security. If the obligor physically threatens the custodial parent, a protective order can be sought.

In some states, the custodial parent or child can make purchases of necessaries and charge them to the credit of the obligor.

Section A. Separation Agreement

When the parties are negotiating the child-support terms of a separation agreement, they need to consider a wide range of factors:

- According to state guidelines, what is the minimum amount of child support that must be paid?

- What standard of living was the child accustomed to during the marriage?

- Does the provider of support have the financial resources to maintain this standard of living?

- What are the tax considerations? Child-support payments are not deductible by the provider, unlike alimony. Consequently, the provider may try to convince the custodial parent to agree to a lower child-support payment in exchange for a higher alimony payment in order to take advantage of the deduction. Also, alimony payments, unlike child-support payments, are taxable to the recipient. Hence, the alimony recipient will usually want some other benefit to compensate for the increased taxes that will result from agreeing to the higher alimony and lower child-support payments, e.g., some extra benefit in the property division terms of the separation agreement. (See page 429.)

- On what day is each payment to be made?

- How many payments are to be made? One covering everyday expenses and a separate one covering large, emergency expenses, e.g., hospitalization?

- Will there be security for the payments, e.g., a trust account, an escrow account that can be used in the event of nonpayment?

- Is the child to be covered by medical insurance? If so, who pays the premiums?

- Is the child to be the beneficiary of a life insurance policy on the life of the provider? If so, how much, who pays the premiums, and can the beneficiaries be changed by the provider? Does the payment of premiums end when the child reaches the age of majority?

- Is there an escalation clause? Do the support payments fluctuate with the income of either of the parents?

- Do the support payments fluctuate with the income of the child, e.g., summer jobs, inheritance?

- Do they fluctuate in relationship to the Consumer Price Index?

- Do the payments end or change when the child reaches a certain age, marries, moves out of the house, or becomes disabled?

- When the provider dies, is his or her estate obligated to continue payments? If so, must the provider's will so state?

- What educational expenses will be covered by the provider? Tutors, preparatory school, college, graduate/professional school, room, board, books, transportation, entertainment expenses, etc.?

- When the child is away at school, does the provider have to continue sending child-support payments to the custodial parent?
- Do school payments go to the custodial parent or directly to a child away at school?
- If disputes arise between the parents concerning child-support payments, what happens? (Arbitration? Mediation?)

Section B. Initial Decision by a Court

The issue of child support, however, is not a matter that is left to the sole discretion of the parents. A court must make the final determination, whether or not the parties are able to reach agreement on who should pay or how much should be paid. We turn now to an examination of the court's role in this area.

Jurisdiction to Make Child Support Order

A court must have *personal jurisdiction* over the noncustodial parent from whom child support is being sought. This usually means that this parent must be served with process *(service of process)* while physically in the state. Normally, child support is sought in a divorce proceeding so that service of process occurs when the following documents are delivered to the defendant: a copy of the divorce complaint or petition, and a summons to appear in court at a designated time to answer the complaint. In the vast majority of cases, the defendant is a resident of the state, so it is relatively easy to obtain personal jurisdiction over him or her. If such a defendant is difficult to find within the state, alternative methods of service are usually available, e.g., publishing a notice in a newspaper.

Problems arise, however, if the defendant is a nonresident of the state. If personal jurisdiction (sometimes called *in personam jurisdiction*) is not obtained over such a defendant, then a child-support order rendered by the state is invalid and cannot be enforced. A different result is reached if the issue before the court is whether the parties should be divorced. Personal jurisdiction over a nonresident is not necessary in order for the court to grant a divorce so long as one of the spouses is domiciled in the state. Later, we will consider the enforceability of a decree that divorces the parties, page 396. Here our focus is the enforceability of a child-support decree in the absence of personal jurisdiction.

> Ted and Wilma are married in New York. They have one child. Wilma moves to California with the child where she files for divorce. Ted remains in New York. He has never been in California and therefore is not served in California. The California court grants the divorce and orders Ted to pay child support.

The support order in the California court is invalid since California never had personal jurisdiction over Ted. The divorce itself, however, is valid assuming Wilma was domiciled in California. Personal jurisdiction over the defendant is not necessary for a court to have the power to terminate the marriage. The divorce decree is *divisible* in the sense that only part of it is enforceable.

Earlier, we discussed alimony or spousal-support orders by a court, page 245. Such orders are equally invalid in the absence of personal jurisdiction over the defendant. As we shall see later, a court cannot order child support *or* spousal support unless personal jurisdiction exists (page 396).

How, then, does a court acquire pesonal jurisdiction over a nonresident defendant? The defendant, of course, can always consent to a court's assertion of personal jurisdiction by agreeing to appear in the court and fully litigate all the issues in the case. Can personal jurisdiction be obtained in the absence of such consent?

Most states have what are called *long-arm statutes* that enable states to acquire jurisdiction over nonresident defendants who have sufficient purposeful contact with the state so that it is fair and reasonable for the state to resolve (i.e., adjudicate) the disputes involved. Any contact, however, will not be sufficient to confer personal jurisdiction through the long-arm statute. For example, in the situation above involving Ted and Wilma, the fact that Ted may often call or write his child in California is not sufficient to confer personal jurisdiction on a New York state resident. Nor would it be sufficient if Ted originally had custody of the child and agreed to send the child to California to live with its mother. Suppose, however, that Ted often visited the child in California, arranged for the child to attend a certain school in California, and opened a bank account for the child in California. Of course, if Ted is personally served with process while physically in California, the latter state would acquire personal jurisdiction over him for purposes of rendering a child support order. The question is whether personal jurisdiction can be acquired in the absence of such service. Did he have enough contact with California to make it fair and reasonable for him to be forced to defend a child support action in California? The answer is *probably yes*. The courts are still developing standards for determining when a nonresident defendant has sufficiently minimal contacts with a state for the purpose of acquiring personal jurisdiction through a long-arm statute. Each case must be decided on its own facts. When Ted visited the child in California and arranged for a school and a bank account there, he in effect took advantage of the services of the state of California. He arguably became purposefully involved with the state. It therefore seems fair and reasonable to expect him to come to California and litigate the child-support issue.

It again must be emphasized, however, that the law does not inevitably point to this result. The United States Supreme Court has not yet given us clear guidelines on when a long-arm statute can validly confer personal jurisdiction over a nonresident in a family law case of this kind. See *Kulko v. Superior Court*, 436 U.S. 84, 98 S.Ct. 1690, 56 L.Ed.2d 132 (1978).

Who Pays Child Support?

The traditional rule was that only the father had the legal duty to support his children. Today, each parent has an equal duty of supporting the children regardless of who has custody and day-to-day control of them. The essential question is, who has the ability to pay? The mother, the father, or both? In practice, it is usually the father who is ordered to pay. He is the one who often has most of the financial resources. Furthermore, the prejudice of the traditional rule still lingers in the minds of many judges. While there has been some advancement toward the equality of the sexes in our society, the man is still often viewed as the one primarily responsible for supporting the family.

What about a stepparent (someone who has married one of the natural parents)? If the stepparent has adopted the child (formally or equitably, page 523), there is a duty to support the child even after the marriage ends in divorce. Without adoption, however, most states say that the stepparent has no duty of support unless an agreement was made for such.

Assignment 12.1

George and Helen are not married but are living together. George impregnates Helen. He asks her to have an abortion. She refuses. When the child is born, can she force George to support it? Would it make any difference if Helen became pregnant after lying to George about using contraceptives? (See General Instructions for the Legal-Analysis Agreement in chapter one.)

Standards to Determine Amount of Support

A child has many needs that must be paid for: shelter, food, clothing, education, medical care, transportation, recreation, etc. A court will consider a number of factors in determining the amount of child support. These factors are quite similar to what the parties must assess on this issue in their separation agreement:

- State guidelines (see discussion below).
- Child's age.
- Child's own financial resources, e.g., from a trust fund set up by a relative, from part-time employment.
- Financial resources of custodial parent.
- Financial resources of noncustodial parent.
- Earning potential of both parents.
- Standard of living enjoyed by child before the separation or divorce.
- Child's need and capacity for education, including higher education.
- Financial needs of noncustodial parent.
- Responsibility of noncustodial parent to support others, e.g., a second family from a second marriage.

Note that marital fault is not on the list. Which parent was at fault in "causing" the divorce is not relevant and should not be considered in assessing the need for child support.

Since 1987 every state has been under a federal mandate to adopt *guidelines* for the determination of child support by its courts.[1] The guidelines establish a rebuttable presumption on the amount of child support that should be awarded. A judge is required to use this amount unless to do so would be inequitable to the parties or the child.

---

[1]42 U.S.C.A. 667; 45 C.F.R. 302.52, 302.56.

While the guidelines are not the same in every state, many states have based their guidelines on the *Income Shares Model,* which operates on the principle that the children should receive the same proportion of parental income that they would have received had the parents lived together. Studies have shown that individuals tend to spend money on their children in proportion to their income, and not solely on need. Child support is calculated as a *share* of each parent's income that would have been spent on the children if the parents and children were living in the same household. The calculation of these shares is based on the best available economic data on the amount of money ordinarily spend on children by their families in the United States. This amount is then adjusted to the cost of living for a particular state.

Exhibits 12–1 and 12–2 provide further information on how this amount is calculated in one particular state, South Carolina.

Cost of College

A good deal of litigation has centered on the issue of educational expenses, particularly higher education. Does a divorced parent have a duty to send his or her child to college? Arguments against imposing this duty are as follows:

- A parent's support duty is limited to providing the necessities to the child. e.g., food, shelter, clothing. College is not a necessity; it is a luxury.

- A parent's support duty terminates when the child reaches the age of majority in the state, e.g., eighteen. A child in college will be over the age of majority during some or most of the college years.

- Children of parents who are still married have no right to force their parents to send them to college. Why should children of divorced parents have the right to be sent to college?

Many states, however, have rejected all of these arguments and have required the divorced parent to pay for a college education as part of the child-support payments if the parent has the ability to pay and the child has the capacity to go to college. Arguments supporting this position:

- In today's society, college is not a luxury. A college degree, at least the first one, is considered a necessity.

- A parent's duty to provide child support does not terminate in all cases when the child reaches majority. For example, a physically or mentally handicapped child may have to be supported indefinitely. Some courts take the position that the support duty continues so long as the child's need for support continues, i.e., so long as the child remains dependent. This certainly includes the period when the child is in college.

- It is true that married parents have no obligation to send their children to college. But there is a strong likelihood they will do so if they have the means and their children have the ability. When the Court requires a divorced parent to send his or her children to college, the same tests are applied: ability to pay and capacity to learn. Thus, the court, in effect, is trying simply to equalize the position of children of divorced parents with those of married parents.

☐ EXHIBIT 12–1 South Carolina Schedule of Basic Child Support Obligations

Important: These figures are *not* child-support payments to be made by either parent. They are the amounts of child support to be contributed by *both* parents. An individual parent's share of this amount must be computed by use of the formula found on the Child-Support Obligation Worksheet [Exhibit 12–2].

Monthly Combined Gross Income	One Child	Two Children	Three Children	Four Children	Five Children	Six Children
$ 600*	$ 82	$ 83	$ 84	$ 85	$ 86	$ 87
650	111	112	114	115	116	117
700	140	141	143	144	116	117
750	150	170	172	174	146	148
800	158	199	201	203	176	177
850	165	227	230	232	205	207
900	172	255	258	261	235	237
950	179	277	287	290	264	267
1,000	186	288	315	319	293	296
1,050	192	299	344	347	322	325
1,100	199	309	371	375	351	355
1,150	206	320	399	404	379	383
1,200	213	331	414	432	408	413
1,250	220	341	427	460	437	441
1,300	226	351	440	490	465	470
1,350	233	362	453	511	495	501
1,400	240	373	467	527	529	534
1,450	247	384	481	542	562	568
1,500	253	393	492	555	591	602
1,550	259	402	504	568	605	629
1,600	265	411	515	580	618	657
1,650	270	420	526	593	632	676
1,700	276	429	537	606	646	691
1,750	282	438	549	618	660	706
1,800	288	447	560	631	673	720
1,850	293	456	571	644	687	735
1,900	299	465	582	656	701	750
1,950	305	474	594	669	714	764
2,000	311	483	605	682	728	779
2,050	317	492	616	695	742	794
2,100	323	502	628	708	756	809
2,150	333	511	640	721	771	824
2,200	335	520	651	734	785	840
					799	855

*For combined monthly gross income less than this amount, child support to be paid by the noncustodial parent is left to judicial discretion. In no case, however, should support be set at less than $50 per month.

Computation of Child Support [see Exhibit 12–2]

The court can determine a total child-support obligation in line 9 of Worksheet A by adding the basic child-support obligation (line 6), net day-care costs (line 7), and extraordinary medical expenses (line 8).

The total child-support obligation is divided between the parents in proportion to their income. Line 10 calculates each parent's proportionate share of combined adjusted gross income. Line 11 computes the obligation of each

☐ **EXHIBIT 12–2** South Carolina Child Support Obligation Worksheet

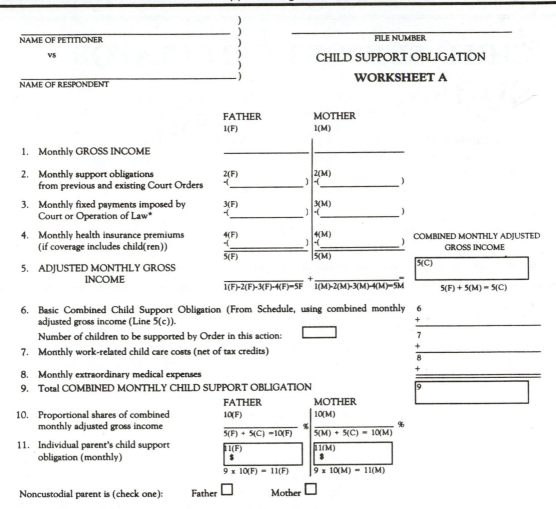

(See Item 3) Fixed payments are considered to be any ongoing obligations imposed by a Court or by Operation of Law to the extent the payor is actually paying. It is presumed there are no such obligations and the burden of proof is imposed on the person claiming such obligations. The following are examples of such obligations: bankruptcy payments; county and state assessments; state and federal tax assessments or liens or arrears (periodic income tax withholding payments are not included); and, etc. Therfore, these amounts will need to be deducted from gross income, to the extent the payor is actually paying, on line 3, Worksheet A.

parent by multiplying each parent's share of income by the total child support obligation.

Although a monetary obligation is computed for each parent, the guidelines presume that the custodial parent will spend that parent's share directly on the child in that parent's custody. In cases of joint custody or split custody where both parents have responsibility of the child for a substantial portion of the time, there are provisions for adjustments. Line 11 reflects that portion of the calculated total child support obligation to be paid by the parents.

A number of computer companies have devised software for lawyers who need to calculate child support under there state's guidelines. Exhibit 12–3).

□ **EXHIBIT 12–3** Advertisement for Software That Calculates Child Support Payments

The Second Family

Another area of controversy concerns the noncustodial parent's responsibility of supporting others. Should the amount of child support be less because this parent has since taken on the responsibility of supporting a second family? Suppose there is a remarriage with someone who already has children and/or they have additional children of their own. The old view was that the parent's primary responsibility was to the first family. No adjustment should be made because the parent has voluntarily taken on additional support obligations. Many courts, however, no longer take this hard line. While they will not permit the parent to leave the first family destitute, they will take into consideration the fact that a second family has substantially affected the parent's ability to support the first. Given this reality, an appropriate adjustment will be made. It must be emphasized, however, that not all courts are this understanding. Some continue to adhere to the old view.

Assignment 12.2

(a) How does a court determine the amount of child support in your state? Describe the main features of whatever guidelines exist and explain how they are used.

(b) Under what circumstances, if any, does a noncustodial parent have an obligation to pay for his or her child's college education in your state?

To answer these questions, check your state code and opinions of courts in your state. (See General Instructions for the State-Code Assignment in chapter one, and General Instructions for the Court-Opinion Assignment in chapter one.)

Assignment 12.3

Jim and Carla have one child, George, who is two years old at the time they seek a divorce. By mutual agreement, Carla will have custody of George. When the issue of child support arises in the divorce proceeding, Carla asks the court to take into consideration the fact that Jim has already announced his engagement to a rich widow. Carla feels that this should prompt the court to require Jim to make higher child-support payments. Should it? Would it make any difference if Carla were the one about to marry a wealthy new spouse? Would this affect the amount of child support that Jim should pay? (See General Instructions for the Legal-Analysis Assignment in chapter one.)

Section C. Modification of Child-Support Orders

The standard rule is that a child-support order can be *modified* on the basis of *changed circumstances* that have arisen since the court granted the order, assuming, of course, that the court has personal jurisdiction over the parent from whom a modification is sought, page 344. The changed circumstances must be serious enough to warrant the conclusion that the original award has become inequitable, e.g., the child's welfare will be jeopardized if the child support award is not increased due to an unexpected illness of the child, requiring costly medical care. Alternatively, the child support award can be decreased if it is clear that the need no longer exists at all or to the same degree—e.g., if the child has died, acquired independent resources, moved out on his or her own.

Frequently the claim of the custodial parent is that child support should be increased because the noncustodial parent has an increased ability to pay since the time of the original order, e.g., by obtaining a much better paying job. This is a ground to increase child support only when it is clear that the original decree was inadequate to meet the needs of the child. At the time of the original decree, a lesser amount may have been awarded because of an inability to pay more *at that time*. Hence, a later modification upward is simply a way for the court to correct an initially inadequate award. Since most initial awards *are* inadequate, courts are inclined to grant the modification.

What happens when the noncustodial parent seeks a modification downward because he or she can no longer afford the amount originally awarded? If the circumstances that caused this change are beyond the control of the parent, e.g., a long illness, the courts will be sympathetic. Suppose, however, that the change is voluntary. For example:

> At the time of a 1990 child-support order, Dan was a fifty-year-old sales manager earning $120,000 a year. The order required him to pay his ex-wife $3,000 a month in child support. In 1991, Dan decides to go to evening law school. He quits his job as a sales manager and takes a part-time job as an investigator earning $10,000 a year. He then petitions the court to modify his child-support payments to $250 a month.

In many courts, Dan's petition would be denied because he has not lost the *capacity* to earn a high salary. Self-imposed poverty is not a ground to reduce child support in such courts. Other courts are not this dogmatic. They will grant the modification petition, if:

- The child will not be left in a destitute condition, and,
- The petitioner is acting in good faith.

The court will want to know whether a legitimate change-of-career or change-of-lifestyle is involved. Is it the kind of change that the party would have probably made if the marriage had not ended? If so, the court will be inclined to grant a modification downward, so long as the child is not seriously harmed thereby. On the other hand, is the parent acting out of *bad faith*, or malice, e.g., to make life more miserable for the custodial parent? If so, the modification request will be denied.

On the subject of whether a downward modification will be allowed on the basis of the noncustodial parent's acquisition of a second family and additional support obligations, see page 350.

We have seen that separation agreements are often sloppily written in that they fail to distinguish between property division terms (which are not modifiable by a court) and support terms (which are), page 237. For example, suppose that the parties agree to give the "wife the exclusive use of the marital home until the youngest child reaches the age of twenty-one." Is this a division of property or a child support term? If it is the former, then the husband cannot modify it on the basis of changed circumstances (e.g., her remarriage). If it is a child support term, then a modification is possible. Most courts would interpret the above clause as a child support term since it is tied to a period of time when the child would most likely need support. Yet a court *could* rule the other way. Needless litigation often results from poor drafting.

Assignment 12.4

(a) What standards apply to a request to modify child-support payments in your state? (See General Instructions for the State-Code Assignment in chapter one.)

(b) Sara pays her ex-husband, Harry, $800 a month in child support under a 1990 court order that granted custody to Harry but gave liberal visitation rights to Sara. Due to continuing bitterness, Harry refuses to allow Sara to see their child. Sara then petitions the court to reduce her child-support payments. How would her request for a modification be handled in your state? (See General Instructions for the Court-Opinion Assignment in chapter one.)

(c) Reread the facts involving Dan, the sales manager who wants to go to law school, page 351. How would this request for a modification be handled in your state? (See General Instructions for the Court-Opinion Assignment in chapter one.)

Assignment 12.5

Assume the same facts as Assignment 12.3 on page 350 except that Jim does not announce his marriage to the rich widow until after the initial child-support order is made. Once the marriage occurs, Carla asks the court to modify the order by increasing the amount paid for child support. What result? Would it make any difference if Carla were the one to marry a wealthy new spouse? Can Jim ask the court to modify his child-support payments downward? (See General Instructions for the Legal-Analysis Assignment in chapter one.)

Assignment 12.6

In a 1989 divorce decree, Frank was ordered to pay $1,000 a month in child support to his former wife, Irene, who was granted custody of their child. He makes all of his payments in 1989. When he loses his job on January 1, 1990, however, he can only afford $500 a month, which he now pays every month. In June of 1990, he asks a court to modify the child support order to $500 a month. Assume that the court agrees that he can pay only $500 a month and modifies the order to this effect on July 1, 1990. By the end of 1990, what is the total amount of child support payments that he would be legally obligated to make in 1990? (See General Instructions for the Legal-Analysis Assignment in chapter one.)

Section D. Enforcement of Child Support Orders

Nonpayment of child support has reached epidemic proportions. Millions of children receive either partial or no child support payments from their noncustodial parents. In 1981 only 4 million of the 8.4 million women[1] raising children alone were awarded child support payments. For a variety of reasons, the remaining women were never given support orders: the fathers disappeared and hence evaded service of process; the states had weak or nonexistent systems of going after the fathers, particularly in the case of "out of wedlock" children; many mothers were simply unaware of rights that they had against the fathers.

Of the 4 million women who did receive child-support orders from the courts, 1.9 million collected the full amount ordered, 1 million collected less

[1]Throughout this discussion, we will refer to the delinquent absent parent as the father, although it is certainly possible for the mother to be the parent who has neglected financial responsibilities to the children. In fact, however, this is relatively rare. In the vast majority of cases, the custodial parent is the mother and the noncustodial parent who is not paying child support is the father.

than what they were due, and the rest collected no payment at all. Consequently, only about one-fourth of all the families entitled to and in need of child support collected it from noncustodial parents.[2] Statistics for later years are no less encouraging. In 1987, for example, only 23 percent of child support obligations were actually paid. (See Exhibit 12–4 for a California proclamation on the problem in that state.)

Predictably, there has been a dramatic increase in the number of families enrolled in the public-assistance program for families in such a predicament: Aid to Families with Dependent Children (AFDC). In response to the crisis, Congress added Title IV-D to the Social Security Act[3] in order to encourage the creation of *enforcement agencies,* remedies, and procedures throughout the country. In each state, an agency now exists whose function is to carry out the mandate of Title IV-D by providing new enforcement tools that will be employed along with the more traditional ones. The agencies have different names, e.g., Child Support Enforcement Branch, Office of Recovery Services, Child Support and Paternity Unit. Collectively, they are all known as *IV-D agencies* (see Appendix F, page 602). They assist AFDC recipients, as well as non-AFDC recipients, although the latter may be charged a nominal fee for the services provided. Exhibit 12–5 shows one state's application for child support enforcement services.

Assignment 12.7

What is the name of the IV-D agency in your state? Contact the closest branch. Ask for a copy of a brochure describing its services.

Assignment 12.8

Assume that a mother in your state applies for AFDC because the father of her children has abandoned the family. What steps must she take to obtain AFDC? What agencies are involved, etc.? (See General Instructions for the State-Code Assignment in chapter one.)

If a woman receives AFDC, she must "assign" or transfer her support rights to the state IV-D agency or other county welfare agency that collects support from the father. This simply means that she gives the agency the right to keep any support money that it collects on her behalf. This money is then used to offset the AFDC money she receives on an ongoing basis for herself and her children. If she fails to cooperate in assigning these rights, her share of the AFDC benefits can be terminated, and the AFDC benefits of her children can be sent to some other responsible adult who will agree to make them available for the children.

---

[2]United States Department of Commerce, Bureau of the Census, *Child Support and Alimony: 1981 Advance Report,* 1 CURRENT POPULATION REPORTS 1, Special Studies Series, P-23, no. 124, (May 1983).
[3]42 U.S.C.A. §§ 651–665.

☐ **EXHIBIT 12–4** Proclamation on Child Support

EXECUTIVE DEPARTMENT
STATE OF CALIFORNIA

A PROCLAMATION
by the Governor of the State of California

WHEREAS, all children deserve to be supported emotionally, physically and financially by their parents; and

WHEREAS, California's 6.8 million children are our most precious resource and represent the future of California; and

WHEREAS, more than one million custodial parents receive child support services through county district attorneys; and

WHEREAS, more than 300,000 of those absent parents are behind in paying their court-ordered child support, representing over $1.5 billion in unpaid support; and

WHEREAS, the children not receiving support from their absent parents are not receiving every opportunity to become productive, successful members of our society; and

WHEREAS, public awareness of the importance of paying child support is vital to the future of California's children and of our great state;

NOW, THEREFORE, I, GEORGE DUEKMEJIAN, Governor of the State of California, do hereby proclaim December 11–17, 1988 as Child Support Awareness Week in California.

IN WITNESS WHEREOF I have hereunto set my hand and caused the Great Seal of the State of California to be affixed this 22nd day of November 1988.

George Deukmejian
GOVERNOR OF CALIFORNIA

ATTEST:

March Fong Eu
SECRETARY OF STATE

□ **EXHIBIT 12–5** Massachusetts Application for Child Support Enforcement Services

Massachusetts Department of Revenue
Child Support Enforcement Division

Application for Child Support Enforcement Services

• • • •

Absent Parent Background and Financial Information:

a. Is the absent parent currently married? Yes □ No □ Don't Know □
(If no or don't know, skip to question #b.)

What is his or her spouse's name? _____

Does his or her spouse work? Yes □ No □ Don't Know □

If yes, where does she or he work, if you know? _____

What is her or his income $ _____ per _____ Don't Know □
                                                                    (Week, Month or Year)

b. If not married, does the absent parent share his or her household with another adult?
Yes □ No □ Don't Know □

c. Does the absent parent have any children who are not also your children?
Yes □ No □ Don't Know □

If yes, please list their names and ages here, along with the name of the adult with whom they live.

Name	Age	Living With:
_____	_____	_____
_____	_____	_____

d. Is the absent parent providing support for children who are not also your children?
Yes □ No □ Don't Know □

If yes, how much is he/she paying? $ _____ per _____ Don't Know □
                                                                        (Week, Month or Year)

e. To your knowledge, does the absent parent have any of the following sources of income?

Type of Income	Amount (if known)	Week/Month/Year
Worker's compensation	$ _____ per	_____
Unemployment compensation	_____	_____
Social Security retirement (over 62, green check)	_____	_____
Other pension	_____	_____
Social Security disability (green check)	_____	_____
Supplemental Security Income (SSI) (gold check)	_____	_____
Other disability	_____	_____
Welfare	_____	_____
Veteran's benefits	_____	_____
Commissions	_____	_____
Trust income	_____	_____
Rental income (from houses/apartments he or she owns)	_____	_____
Annuities	_____	_____
Interest income	_____	_____
Dividend income	_____	_____

f. To your knowledge, does he or she have — or has he or she ever had in the last three years:

	Yes	No	When	Amount
Royalties	☐	☐	19 ____	$ _____
Severance pay	☐	☐	19 ____	_____
Capital gains	☐	☐	19 ____	_____
Prizes and awards	☐	☐	19 ____	_____
Lottery winnings	☐	☐	19 ____	_____
Gambling winnings	☐	☐	19 ____	_____
Bonuses	☐	☐	19 ____	_____

g. Does the absent parent:

Own any houses or other real estate? Yes ☐ No ☐ Don't Know ☐

If yes, please describe and indicate location if you can. _____

_____

Own any motor vehicles? Yes ☐ No ☐ Don't Know ☐

If yes, for each vehicle, please identify the model, color, state where it is registered, and license plate number, if you can.

_____

_____

Own a boat? Yes ☐ No ☐ Don't Know ☐

If yes, please indicate the registration number, if you can. _____

Where is it moored? _____

   City or Town   State

Own any stocks or bonds? Yes ☐ No ☐ Don't Know ☐

If yes, please use a separate sheet of paper to identify the name and address of the absent parent's stock broker and list any stocks and/or bonds owned by the absent parent if that information is available to you. Indicate the name of the company, the number of shares, and the date the stock was purchased, if possible.

Have any bank accounts? Yes ☐ No ☐ Don't Know ☐

List the name(s) of the bank(s), location(s), and type(s) of account(s) if that information is available to you.

Bank Name	Location	Type of Account
_____	_____	_____
_____	_____	_____

If you need additional space, please continue on a separate piece of paper.

Have any credit cards? Yes ☐ No ☐ Don't Know ☐

If yes, please list the names of the companies and account numbers if that information is available to you.

Credit Company	Account Number
_____	_____
_____	_____
_____	_____

Have any outstanding loans? Yes ☐ No ☐ Don't Know ☐

If yes, please identify the name of the bank(s) or financial institution(s), location(s) and account number(s).

Lending Institution	Location	Account Number
_____	_____	_____
	City/Town State	
_____	_____	_____
	City/Town State	

h. Have you ever filed a joint income tax return with the absent parent? Yes ☐ No ☐

If yes, for which state(s) and for what year(s)?

    State   Tax Years
    _____   19 ___ to 19 ___
    _____   19 ___ to 19 ___ If you filed a joint federal tax return, for what years? 19 ___ to 19 ___

i. Does the absent parent have any disabilities or handicaps? Yes ☐ No ☐ Don't Know ☐

j. Does the absent parent have a driver's license? Yes ☐ No ☐ Don't Know ☐

If yes, from what state? _____ What is the license number? _____ Don't Know ☐

k. Does the absent parent have any trade or commercial licenses? Yes ☐ No ☐ Don't Know ☐

If yes, what sort of license is it? _____

From what state was it issued? _____

l. Has the absent parent ever belonged to any labor unions? Yes ☐ No ☐ Don't Know ☐

If yes, enter the name of the union, local number, city and state.

_____

m. Does the absent parent go by any other names or aliases? Yes ☐ No ☐ Don't Know ☐

If yes, please identify. _____

n. Has the absent parent ever been a member of the armed forces? Yes ☐ No ☐ Don't Know ☐

If yes, what branch of service? _____

    ___/___/___   ___/___/___   _____   _____
    Date Entered   Date Discharged   Service Number   Last Duty Station

o. What high school, trade school and/or college did the absent parent attend? Please indicate the name and address of each school, the dates attended and the degree earned.

Name	Address	Dates of Attendance	Degree
_____	_____	_____	_____
_____	_____	_____	_____

Please attach an additional piece of paper if you need more space.

p. Does the absent parent have a criminal record?
Yes ☐ No ☐ Don't Know ☐ If yes, in which state? _____

q. Please identify the names and addresses of as many of the absent parent's past employers as you can. (Do not include the most recent employer which you have already identified on earlier.)

Name	Address
_____	_____
_____	_____

Please attach an additional piece of paper if you need more space.

r. What are the names of the absent parent's parents? (Please indicate their names even if they are deceased.)

Father's Name	Mother's Maiden Name
_____	_____
Street or P.O. Box	Street or P.O. Box
_____	_____
City State Zip	City State Zip
( ) _____	( ) _____
Telephone	Telephone

s. Please provide the names and addresses of others who might know the whereabouts of the absent parent.

Name	Relationship		Phone
Street or P.O. Box	City	State	Zip
Name	Relationship		Phone
Street or P.O. Box	City	State	Zip

Source: Massachusetts Department of Revenue Child Support Enforcement Division

One of the valuable services provided by the state IV-D agency is its careful record keeping on when the noncustodial parent pays and fails to pay child support. The availability of this data helps to keep the pressure on. Furthermore, many IV-D agencies can be quite persistent in going after the noncustodial parent through automatic billing, telephone reminders, delinquency notices, etc. Other enforcement tools are also available through the IV-D agency as outlined below.

A new *federal* agency was created to coordinate, evaluate, and provide support for the state IV-D agencies—the Office of Child Support Enforcement within the U.S. Department of Health and Human Services.

But, first things first. A very large number of noncustodial parents simply disappear. Problem number one is to *find* the noncustodial parent in order to obtain a child-support order, and/or in order to enforce it. Another service provided by the IV-D agency is its *State Parent Locator Service*. At the national level, there is a comparable Federal Parent Locator Service that operates through the Office of Child Support Enforcement.

The starting point in the search is the custodial parent who is asked to provide the following leads to the state IV-D agency on the whereabouts of the noncustodial parent:

- Social security number (check old state and federal tax returns, hospital records, police records, bank accounts, insurance policies, credit cards, loan applications, pay slips, union records)
- Last known residential address
- Current employer's name and address
- Prior employers' names and addresses
- Place of birth
- Addresses of relatives and friends
- Local clubs and organizations to which he once belonged
- Local banks, public utilities, and other creditors he may have had or now has

(etc.)

The State Parent Locator Service of the IV-D agency will use the leads provided by the custodial parent to try to locate the noncustodial parent. It will check the records of other state agencies for a current address, e.g., the

Department of Motor Vehicle Registration, the Unemployment Compensation Commission, the Tax Department, and the prisons. If the noncustodial parent has moved to another state, the IV-D agency in that state can be asked to provide comparable search services. Finally, the Federal Parent Locator Service can also be asked to search the records of federal agencies for leads, e.g., the Internal Revenue Service, the Department of Defense, the Selective Service Commission, the National Personnel Records Center, the Veterans Administration, and the Social Security Administration.

Assignment 12.9

How does the Parent Locator Service of the IV-D agency in your state operate? Describe how the service functions. (See General Instructions for the State-Code Assignment in chapter one.)

Once the noncustodial parent is located, the next step is to secure a child-support order against him. A paternity proceeding may be needed in order to establish the obligation of support. Paternity is discussed in Chapter 17. If the parent has moved to another state, the Uniform Reciprocal Enforcement of Support Act (URESA) can be used by a custodial parent in one state to obtain and enforce a child-support (or alimony) order in another state without ever having to travel to the latter state. URESA is discussed in Chapter 14.

The court has the following enforcement options available to it:[4]

☐ **Civil contempt proceeding**

☐ **Execution**

☐ **Prosecution for criminal nonsupport**

☐ **Income withholding**

☐ **Tax Refund Intercept Program (TRIP)**

☐ **Unemployment compensation intercept**

☐ **Qualified Domestic Relations Order (QDRO)**

☐ **Credit bureau referral ("credit clouding")**

☐ **Posting security**

☐ **Protective order**

In our discussion of these options the person obligated to make child-support payments will be referred to as the *obligor*.

☐ Civil Contempt Proceeding

Contempt of court exists when the authority or dignity of the court is obstructed or assailed. The most glaring example is an intentional violation of a court order. There are two kinds of contempt proceedings, civil and criminal, both of which can lead to the jailing of the offender. The purpose of a *civil contempt* proceeding is to compel future compliance with the court

---

[4]Some of these options—including URESA—also apply to the enforcement of alimony obligations, page 419.

order, whereas the purpose of a *criminal contempt* proceeding is to punish the offender. H. Clark, The Law of Domestic Relations in the United States, § 18.3, p. 390 (Practitioner's ed. 2 ed. 1987). Criminal contempt in child support cases in rare because of the cumbersome nature of any criminal proceeding.

When civil contempt occurs in child support cases, the offender is jailed until he agrees to comply with the court order. Suppose, however, that the offender has no resources and thus cannot comply. In effect, such a person would be imprisoned because of his poverty. This is illegal. Imprisonment for debt is unconstitutional because it amounts to a sentence for an indefinite period beyond the control of the offender. To bypass this constitutional prohibition, a court must determine that the offender has the *present ability* to pay the child support debt but simply refuses to do so. Such an individual is in control of how long the sentence will be; the keys to jail are in his own pocket. Release occurs when he pays the child support debt.

In addition to jailing the obligor, most courts have the power to order the less drastic sanction of imposing a fine when the obligor is found to be in civil contempt.

Assignment 12.10

What steps must be taken in your state to use a civil contempt proceeding to enforce a child support order? (See General Instruction for the Flowchart Assignment in chapter one.)

☐ Execution

Once an obligor fails to pay a judgment ordering child support, the sheriff can be ordered to seize the personal or real property of the obligor in the state. All of this occurs through a *writ of execution*. Its initial effect is to create a *lien* on the property that prevents the obligor from disposing of it. The property seized can then be sold by the sheriff. The proceeds from this *forced sale* are used to pay the judgment and the expenses of the execution. Not all property of the obligor, however, is subject to execution in every state. Certain property, e.g., clothes and cars, may be exempt from execution.

Assignment 12.11

Describe the steps that are taken in your state when a plaintiff seeks execution of a judgment ordering child-support payments that are not paid. What property of the obligor, if any, is exempt from execution? (See General Instructions for the State-Code Assignment in chapter one.)

Suppose that the obligor moves to another state after failing to pay a child-support order. To answer the question of whether the mother can go to the obligor's new state and seek execution or other enforcement remedies against him there, see page 415, where there is a discussion of when one state must give full faith and credit (i.e., enforce) the court order of another state.

☐ **Prosecution for Criminal Nonsupport**

In most states, the willful failure to support the child is a crime for which the obligor can be fully prosecuted. There must be an ability to provide support before he or she can be tried and convicted of *criminal nonsupport* or desertion. The range of punishment includes probation, fine, and imprisonment. Except for relatively wealthy offenders, imprisonment is seldom an effective method of enforcing child support. Most obligors are wage earners, and once they are jailed, their primary source of income obviously dries up. One way out of this dilemma is for the judge to agree to suspend the imposition of the jail sentence on condition that the obligor fulfill the support obligation. The obligor would be placed on probation under this condition.

The threat of prosecution has encouraged some delinquent obligors to come forward. Several states have launched highly publicized amnesty programs (see Exhibit 12–6).

☐ **EXHIBIT 12–6** Ad placed in Sports Section of Local Paper

---

Do You Owe Child Support?
—Has your luck run out?—

Beginning Monday morning, December 5, 1988, a substantial number of Kansas City area parents who have failed to make their court-ordered child support payments will be arrested, jailed, and prosecuted. Could you be one of those parents?

Rather than gamble, you can receive amnesty from criminal prosecution by coming in person to the child support enforcement office at 1805 Grand Avenue in Kansas City and making immediate payment arrangements. You only have until this Friday at 5 p.m. Next Monday, you may be in jail, and then it will be too late.

Come in—let's talk.
MO Division of Child Support Enforcement
1805 Grand Ave., Suite 300
Kansas City, MO

Assignment 12.12

(a) Is it a crime in your state to fail to pay child support? If so, quote the essential elements of the crime. (See General Instructions for the State-Code Assignment in chapter one.)

(b) Prepare a checklist of questions you would ask in order to help determine whether this crime was committed. (See General Instructions for the Investigation-Strategy Assignment in chapter one.)

(c) What steps must be taken in your state to prosecute someone for violating this crime? (See General Instructions for the Flowchart Assignment in chapter one.)

☐ **Income Withholding**

Income withholding is a mandatory, automatic deduction from the obligor's income when he falls behind in child-support payments. Wages of an employee are the most common example of income that is subject to withholding, although other kinds may qualify as well, e.g., commissions, retirement payments. The original child-support order of the court will include a provision authorizing income withholding to go into effect as soon as the obligor is in default for a designated amount, e.g., an amount equal to thirty days' support. A notice is sent to the obligor stating that withholding in a designated amount is about to occur because of an *arrearage* (amount past due). If he disputes the arrearage, a hearing can be requested at the state IV-D agency.

Once the matter is settled against the obligor, the withholding begins automatically and continues on an ongoing basis; the parties do not have to keep going back to court. The amounts withheld are applied to arrearages as well as to current support obligations. Some employers are irritated by the record keeping involved in income withholding even though they are usually entitled to a small fee for this service. But employers do not have a choice on whether to participate. Furthermore, they can be fined or otherwise sanctioned by the state for subjecting an obligor-employee to any discipline because of income withholding. Exhibit 12–7 outlines government guidelines to employers regarding this matter.

Income withholding is similar to the more traditional *garnishment* process under which third party, e.g., a bank or employer, who owes the obligor money or other property is ordered by a court to turn it over to a debtor of the obligor, such as the custodial parent. Garnishment, however, is usually less effective than income withholding because of the more cumbersome procedures for instituting garnishment and the restrictions that exist on how long it can be in effect.

Assignment 12.13

(a) Who can use income withholding in your state through the state IV-D agency? How does this enforcement mechanism operate?

(b) Compare income withholding to the garnishment process in your state.

(See General Instructions for the State-Code Assignment in chapter one.)

Assignment 12.14

Jim is subject to a child-support order in your state to pay his ex-wife, Wanda, $900 a month for their fifteen-year-old daughter, Paula. Jim fails to make payments for three months. Wanda then goes to the state IV-D agency to seek help. Income withholding is commenced through Jim's employer, the ABC Truck Company. Six months later, Paula gets married. Jim goes to his supervisor and asks that income withholding terminate because he no longer has a duty to support his daughter. Assume he is correct that a parent does not have to support a child who has been emancipated through marriage. Can the company stop the withholding? (See General Instructions for the State-Code Assignment in chapter one.)

☐ Tax Refund Intercept Program (TRIP)

Income tax refunds that are owed by state and federal tax authorities to obligors can be intercepted and used to fulfill past-due child support obligations. During the first four years of the Tax Refund Intercept Program (TRIP), 1.5 million such tax refunds were thus intercepted.

Employer's Guide for Wage Withholding

The following is a brief summary of your legal responsibilities as an employer:

1. If you refuse to hire or you discipline or discharge an employee due to wage withholding for child support you will be subjected to a fine under your State law.
2. A notice from the State CSE [Child Support Enforcement] agency will tell you when to begin, how much to deduct and where to send the money as well as when to stop deductions.
3. If you fail to withhold wages as specified in the notice, you will be liable for the full amount you should have withheld from the parent's wages.
4. Withholding is to begin no later than the first pay period that occurs 14 days after the mailing date of the notice. Then, withholding payments must be sent to the State within 10 days after the employee is paid.
5. If your State's law allows, you may collect a fee to cover costs of withholding. The fee, if any, which the State permits you to deduct, will be shown on the notice and can be deducted at the same time the payment is withheld. The fee is to be deducted from wages only, not from the support payment.
6. The employee will have been notified of the action by the CSE agency and given a chance to contest it in advance. If the employee states that he didn't receive the notice or the amount withheld is wrong, he should be instructed to contact the agency to resolve the matter. You should withhold as directed until otherwise notified by the CSE agency.
7. For each withholding agency you send payments to, you can combine all deductions made per pay period into one check as long as you include an itemization of the amount and the date withheld for each person.
8. The total amount which may be withheld from any paycheck is limited to that specified by the Consumer Credit Protection Act (CCPA) unless otherwise specified by State law. CCPA limits are 50% of disposable earnings when the absent parent has a second family, 60% with no second family. Each limit is increased by 5% if payments are in arrears for a period equal to 12 weeks or more. Under Federal wage withholding provisions, child support debts take precedence over any other consumer debts.
9. Federal law requires only that child support be withheld from wages. States have the option of requiring withholding from other forms of income such as commissions, dividends, retirement benefits, etc. Your State CSE agency can assist you, if necessary.
10. Do not stop or make any changes to the withholding until you are so notified by the withholding agency.
11. If the employee wishes to voluntarily initiate the withholding after receiving notice, the request should be made to the CSE agency.
12. When an employee leaves your firm, you must promptly notify the CSE agency and provide the employee's last know address and new employer's name and address, if known.

U.S. Department of Health and Human Services, Family Support Administration, GPO:1989–626–169/10232

The collection occurs through the state IV-D agency. It is not possible for a woman with four hungry children to call the Internal Revenue Service and ask that it send her the father's refund check. She must first apply to the IV-D agency in the state. A notice (Exhibit 12–8) is then sent to the taxpayer that his tax refund is about to be intercepted to meet the child-support debt. If the taxpayer contests the interception, a hearing is held.

☐ **EXHIBIT 12—8** Notice of Collection of Income Tax Refund

Department of the Treasury
Internal Revenue Service

If you have any questions, refer to this information:

Date of This Notice: January 4, 1984
Social Security Number: 215-32-2726
Document Locator Number:
Form   Tax Year Ended:

Call:

or

Write: Chief, Taxpayer Assistance Section
                Internal Revenue Service Center

Sam & Sarah Peach
999 Peachtree Street
Doraville, Ga 99999

If you write, be sure to attach this notice.

    THIS IS TO INFORM YOU THAT THE AGENCY NAMED BELOW HAS CONTACTED US REGARDING AN OUTSTANDING DEBT YOU HAVE WITH THEM.

    UNDER AUTHORITY OF SECTION 6402(c) OF THE INTERNAL REVENUE CODE, ANY OVERPAYMENT OF YOUR FEDERAL INCOME TAX WILL BE APPLIED TO THAT OBLIGATION BEFORE ANY AMOUNT CAN BE REFUNDED OR APPLIED TO ESTIMATED TAX. IF YOU HAVE ANY QUESTIONS ABOUT THE OBLIGATION OR BELIEVE IT IS IN ERROR, YOU SHOULD CONTACT THAT AGENCY IMMEDIATELY.

NAME OF AGENCY

DEPT. OF SOCIAL SERVICES
DIV. OF INCOME AND SUPPORT
CHILD SUPPORT ENFORCEMENT
1575 OBLIGATION STREET
TIMBUKTU, CO 92037

CONTACT: CHILD SUPPORT
PHONE: 619-456-9103

If you have any questions, you may call or write—see the information in the upper right corner of this notice. To make sure that IRS employees give courteous responses and correct information to taxpayers, a second employee sometimes listens in on telephone calls.

Assignment 12.15

How are *state* income tax refunds intercepted to meet child support needs in your state? Describe the steps involved. (See General Instructions for the State-Code Assignment in chapter one.)

☐ Unemployment Compensation Intercept

The unemployment compensation benefits of the obligor can be intercepted to meet ongoing (not just past-due) child support payments. This method of withholding enables the state IV-D agency to collect at least some support from an unemployed obligor. Nothing is left to chance. Computers at the unemployment compensation agency and at the state IV-D agency communicate with each other to identify delinquent parents who have applied for or who are eligible for unemployment compensation. An investigator from the IV-D agency will then contact the surprised obligor. It may even be possible to intercept benefits across state lines pursuant to reciprocal agreements among cooperating states.

Assignment 12.16

Can unemployment compensation benefits be intercepted to meet child support needs in your state? If so, describe the steps involved. (See General Instructions for the State-Code Assignment in chapter one.)

☐ Qualified Domestic Relations Order (QDRO)

Very often an obligor will have pension and other retirement benefit plans through his employer. A special court order, called a *Qualified Domestic Relations Order (QDRO),* allows someone other than the obligor to reach some or all of these benefits in order to meet a support obligation of the obligor such as child support. The child becomes an *alternate payee* under these plans.[5] This person cannot receive benefits under the plan that the obligor himself would not have been able to receive. For example, if the obligor is not entitled to a lump-sum payment, the child as alternate payee is also subject to this limitation.

☐ Credit Bureau Referral ("Credit Clouding")

An obligor may be warned that the credit bureau will be notified of his delinquency in making child-support payments unless the delinquency is eliminated by payment or unless satisfactory arrangements are made to pay the debt. Once the computers of a credit bureau have information on such payment problems, a "cloud" on the obligor's credit rating is created (*credit clouding*) which notifies potential creditors that the obligor may be a bad credit risk.

---

[5]For an example of a Qualified Domestic Relations Order in which the ex-spouse is the alternate payee seeking support through alimony, see page 254.

☐ **Posting Security**

In some cases, a noncustodial parent may be asked to post security in the form of a bond or other guarantee that that will cover future support obligations.

☐ **Protective Order**

Some men do not react kindly to requests from the mothers of their children that they meet their child-support obligations. In some instances, they may even physically assault the mother or threaten to do so. The police may be called in, although some have complained that the police do not take so-called "domestic disputes" seriously. Usually the woman can obtain through the local prosecutor or district attorney a *protective order* which threatens the man with arrest and jail unless he stays away from the children and their mother.

Assignment 12.17

Under what circumstances can a woman obtain a protective order against her husband in your state? Describe the steps involved. (See General Instructions for the State-Code Assignment in chapter one.)

Assignment 12.18

An unmarried couple lives together. The woman promises the man that she will use birth control, but has no intention of keeping this promise. When a child is born, can the father refuse to support it because of the "fraud" of the mother?

Section E. Necessaries

A seldom used but still available method for a wife and child to obtain support is to go to merchants, make purchases of *necessaries,* and charge them to the credit of the nonsupporting husband/father.[6] The latter must pay the bills, whether or not he knows about them or authorizes them so long as:

- They are in fact for necessaries, and,
- The husband/father has not already provided them for his family

Since the definition of necessaries is not precise, and since a merchant has difficulty knowing whether a husband/father has already made provision for the necessaries of his family, few merchants are willing to extend credit in these circumstances without express authorization from the husband/father. Some states, however, have eliminated the requirement that there be evidence of a failure of the husband/father to provide necessaries before his credit can be charged.

---

[6]If the wife is the primary source of support, the husband can purchase necessaries for himself and the children, and charge them to her.

What are necessaries? Generally, they encompass what is needed and appropriate to maintain the family at the standard of living to which it has been accustomed, e.g., home, food, clothing, furniture, medical care. The educational expenses of minor children are necessaries. A college education, on the other hand, is not in some states.

Assignment 12.19

(a) Find two opinions written by courts in your state that address the doctrine of necessaries. Try to find one opinion that reached the conclusion that the husband or father was liable, and one that reached the opposite conclusion. (If you cannot find such opinions written by courts in your state, try neighboring states.)

(b) Would a college education be considered necessary in your state so that a father would be required to pay the expenses of the education?

(c) Suppose that a wife wishes to complete her undergraduate degree. Would a husband in your state have to pay for it?

(See General Instructions for the Court-Opinion Assignment in chapter one.)

Note

Some states have tried to enforce the support obligation through their marriage-formulation statutes. The statute may provide, for example, that no individual will be allowed to enter a marriage if that person has failed to support his or her child in the custody of someone else. The United States Supreme Court has held, however, that such statutes are an unconstitutional interference with the fundamental right to marry. *Zablocki v. Redhail,* 434 U.S. 374, 98 S.Ct. 673, 54 L.Ed.2d 618 (1978). (See page 159).

Key Chapter Terminology

Personal Jurisdiction	Lien
In Personam Jurisdiction	Criminal Nonsupport
Service of Process	Suspend Sentence
Divisible Divorce	Criminal Nonsupport
Long Arm Jurisdiction	Income Withholding
Child Support Guidelines	Arrearage
Income Shares Model	Garnishment
Modification	Tax Refund Intercept Program
Changed Circumstances	Unemployment Compensation
Enforcement	Intercept
IV-D Agencies,	Qualified Domestic Relations Order
Parent Locator Service	(QDRO)
Obligor	Alternate Payee
Civil Contempt	Credit Clouding
Criminal Contempt	Post Security
Writ of Execution	Protective Order
Forced Sale	Necessaries

CHAPTER THIRTEEN

Divorce, Judicial Separation, and Separate Maintenance

■ Chapter Outline

This chapter will provide an overview of the three major court proceedings that can be used when a marriage is in deep trouble: divorce, judicial separation, and separate maintenance. Our main focus will be on the *grounds* that must exist before parties can use these three actions.

After identifying some of the historical reasons for reform in the law of divorce, we will examine the three major no-fault grounds for divorce: living apart, incompatibility, and irreconcilable differences that cause the irremediable breakdown of the marriage. The fault grounds for divorce, such as adultery, cruelty, and desertion are then covered. These grounds, and the defenses to them, will be given less attention, however, because they are less commonly used today.

Next, we turn to a brief discussion of judicial separation and separate maintenance. Both of these actions are primarily designed to secure spousal support in the marriage that will continue to exist, at least for the time being.

Section A. Divorce: Historical Background

In order to obtain a divorce that dissolves the marital relationship, specified reasons must exist. These reasons, called *grounds,* are spelled out in statutes. The two major categories of grounds are no-fault and fault. *No-fault grounds* are as follows:

- Living apart
- Incompatibility
- Irretrievable breakdown

Fault grounds are as follows:

- Adultery
- Cruelty
- Desertion and abandonment

While these are the main three, a number of other fault grounds also exist in some states.

For many years, fault grounds were the only grounds for divorce, the premise being that a marriage could not and should not be terminated unless there was evidence of serious wrongdoing by one of the spouses—blame had to be established. Many believed that such stringent divorce laws would help prevent the failure of marriages. In colonial America, it was common to deny the guilty spouse the right of remarriage if a divorce was granted. The payment of alimony was sometimes used to punish the guilty spouse rather than as a way to help the other become reestablished. In short, guilt, wrongdoing, and punishment were predominant themes of our divorce laws.

During the period of this fault system of divorce, numerous criticisms surfaced that the system was irrelevant and encouraged fraud. Over 90 percent

of the divorces were *uncontested*, meaning that there was no dispute between the parties. Since both spouses wanted the divorce, they rarely spent much time fighting each other about whether adultery, cruelty, or other fault grounds existed. In fact, parties often flagrantly lied to the courts about the facts of their case in order to quickly establish that fault did exist. While such *collusion* (i.e., an agreement to lie or mislead, in this case in order to facilitate obtaining a divorce) was obviously illegal, the parties were seldom caught. Since both sides wanted the divorce, there was little incentive to reveal the truth. The system also encouraged *migratory divorces*, where one of the parties would "migrate," or travel, to another state solely to take advantage of its more lenient divorce laws. Some of these states gained the reputation of being *divorce mills*.

Judges were aware of what was going on, but simply looked the other way unless one of the parties forced the court to look at what was really happening. In a sense, the system provided something for everyone. The conservatives had strict divorce laws on the books, and the liberals had permissive courts. F. Cox, Human Intimacy: Marriage, the Family and Its Meaning 517 (4th ed. 1987).

Reform was obviously needed. In 1969 California enacted the first no-fault divorce law in the country. Soon other states followed. Today, no-fault grounds exist in every state. Some states have eliminated the word *divorce* and replaced it with the word *dissolution* as a symbolic gesture that a new day has arrived. This does not mean, however, that fault grounds have been abolished. Most states have retained them, and oddly enough, there are times when fault becomes relevant to a court's discussion of a no-fault ground. Yet in the main, fault is largely ignored in current practice.[1]

---

[1]Except with respect to the issue of child custody where marital fault, insofar as it relates to parental fitness, is still very much alive, page 303.

Assignment 13.1

(a) In your state code, find the statute that lists the grounds for divorce. Give the citation to this statute and list all the grounds for divorce provided therein. See also Assignment 1.3(d), page 11. (See General Instructions for the State-Code Assignment in chapter one.)

(b) For each ground of divorce identified in part "a," draft a checklist of questions to help determine whether those grounds exist. (See General Instructions for the Checklist-Formulation Assignment in chapter one.)

Section B. No-Fault Grounds for Divorce

Living Apart

Living "separate and apart" is a ground for divorce in many states. The statutes authorizing this ground of *living apart* must be carefully read since slight differences in wording may account for major differences in meaning. The simplest statute authorizes the divorce if the parties have lived separate and apart for a designated period of consecutive time, as outlined below. While this requirement exists in all the statutes, some states impose additional and more restrictive requirements. For example, living separate and apart may have to be pursuant to a court order or a separation agreement, or it may have to be consensual or "voluntary."

Time

All the statutes require that the parties live apart for a designated period of time, ranging from six months to three years. The purpose of the time limitation is, in effect, to force the parties to think seriously about whether a reconciliation is possible.

Consecutiveness

If the parties have separated off and on over a period of time, the living-apart ground is not established, even if the sum total of time the parties were actually separated exceeds the designated time required for separation under the statute. The separated time must be consecutive, and it must continue right up to the time one of the spouses brings the divorce action on the ground of living apart. Hence, if the parties reconcile and resume cohabitation, even if only temporarily, the period of separation will not be considered consecutive. If, following cohabitation, the parties separate again, the requisite consecutiveness of the period of living apart will be calculated as of the time when the most recent cohabitation ended.

Consent

Several states require that the period of separation be consensual or voluntary on the part of *both* spouses. Thus, if one spouse is drafted into the service or is hospitalized for an extended period of time the separation is surely not by consent.

Sometimes the *cause* of the separation might be relevant to its voluntariness. Suppose, for example, that Bob deserts his wife Linda and they live apart for a period in excess of that required by the statute. Arguably, the parties did not separate voluntarily; they separated as a result of the *fault* of Bob. Some states will deny the divorce on the ground of living apart because the separation was not voluntary. Others will deny the divorce on this ground only when the plaintiff seeking the divorce is the "guilty" party. Most states, however, will grant the divorce to either party on the basis that voluntariness and marital fault are irrelevant so long as there was a living apart for the requisite period of time.

 ## Interviewing and Investigation Checklist

Divorce on the Ground of Living Apart

Legal Interviewing Questions

1. How long have you lived apart?
2. On what date did you separate?
3. Since that date, what contact have you had with D (defendant)?
4. Have you ever asked D to live with you again? Has D ever asked you?
5. Have you had sexual intercourse with D since you separated?
6. Describe the circumstances of your separation with D.
7. When you separated, did you intend a permanent separation? If so, what indications of this did you give?
8. Did D intend a permanent separation? If so, what indications did D give?
9. What was the condition of your marriage at the time of the separation?
10. Did you leave D? Did D leave you? Did you both leave at the same time by mutual agreement?
11. When the separation occurred, did either of you protest? Were either of you dissatisfied with the separation?
12. Since you separated, have either of you asked or suggested that the two of you get back together again? If so, what was the response of the other?
13. Have either of you ever obtained a judicial separation or a decree of separate maintenance? If so, when? Have you been living separate since that time? Have both of you abided by the terms of the judicial separation or of the maintenance decree?
14. Are you now living separate from D?
15. Since you separated, at what address have you lived? (Same question about D.)
16. Have you and D entered into a separation agreement?

Possible Investigation Tasks

- Collect evidence that the parties have lived separate and apart, e.g., rent receipts from the apartments of the client and of D, statements from landlords, separate utility bills.
- Obtain copy of separation decree, or separate maintenance decree (if any).

Assignment 13.2

Assume that a statute provides that one of the grounds for divorce is voluntary separation for a period of two consecutive years. This living-apart ground is the only one authorized in the state. Could a divorce be granted on the ground of living-apart in the following three situations? (See General Instructions for the Legal-Analysis Assignment in chapter one.)

(a) Fred and Gail are married. On June 10, 1985, they agree to separate. Fred moves out. On May 15, 1987, he learns that she is thinking about filing for divorce. Fred calls Gail and pleads with her to let him come back. She refuses. On July 25, 1987, she files for divorce on the ground of living apart.

(b) Tom and Diane are married. On November 1, 1985, Diane deserts Tom. Tom did not want her to go. On March 13, 1986, Tom meets Karen. They begin seeing each other regularly. On June 14, 1986, Tom tells Karen that he hopes he never sees Diane again. On December 28, 1987, Tom files for divorce on the ground of living apart.

(c) Bill and Susan are married. For over three years they have been living separate lives due to marital difficulties, although they have continued to live in the same house. They have separate bedrooms and rarely have anything to do with each other. One of them files an action for divorce on the ground of living apart.

Assignment 13.3

In your answer to Assignment 13.1, page 371, you made a list of the grounds for divorce in your state. If one of the grounds for divorce in your state is living apart, determine whether the divorce actions sought above in Assignment 13.2(a), (b), and (c) would be granted in your state. (See the General Instructions for the Legal-Analysis Assignment in chapter one.) In doing this, you should try to find opinions written by courts in your state that have interpreted the law governing the same facts, or facts similar to those involving Fred and Gail, Tom and Diane, Bill and Susan. (See General Instructions for the State Code Assignment and the General Instructions for the Court-Opinion Assignment in chapter one.)

Assignment 13.4

Pick one of the three fact situations involved in Assignment 13.2, above: (a), (b), or (c). Draft a complaint for the party seeking the divorce. (See General Instructions for the Complaint-Drafting Assignment in chapter one.)

As we shall see, many states allow parties to seek a *judicial separation*, which is a court authorization that the parties can live separate lives under specified terms, e.g., alimony, custody order (page 383). In some states, this judicial separation can be *converted* into a divorce after a designated period of time. Similarly, a decree of *separate maintenance* (page 385) can often be converted into a divorce after this period of time.

Note on Enoch Arden

When a spouse has disappeared for a certain period of time, *Enoch Arden* statutes presume that the missing spouse is dead, and in some states, this enables the spouse left behind to remarry without being charged with bigamy or having the second marriage annulled if the missing spouse returns after the statutory period (page 180).

Summary of Ground for Divorce: Living Apart

Definition: Living separate and apart for a designated, consecutive period of time. (In some states, the separation must be voluntary.)

Who Can Sue: In most states, either party. In a few states, the party at fault cannot bring the divorce action, i.e., the party who wrongfully caused the separation.

Major Defenses: 1. The parties have never separated.

2. The parties have not been separated for the period designated in the statute.

3. The parties reconciled and cohabited before the statutory period was over, i.e., the separation was not consecutive.

4. The separation was not voluntary (this defense is available in only a few states).

5. The agreement to separate was obtained by fraud or duress.

6. The court lacks jurisdiction, page 396.

7. *Res judicata* applies, page 394.

8. The statute of limitations or laches apply.

Is this also a ground for annulment? No.

Is this also a ground for judicial separation? Yes, in many states.

Is this also a ground for separate maintenance? Yes, in many states.

Incompatibility

Some states list *incompatibility* as a ground for divorce. It is often pointed out that "petty quarrels and minor bickerings" are not enough to grant the divorce on this ground. There must be such rift or discord that it is impossible to live together in a normal marital relationship. For most of the states that have this ground, fault is not an issue; the plaintiff does not have to show that the defendant was at fault in causing the incompatibility, and the defendant cannot defend the action by introducing evidence that the plaintiff committed marital wrongs. In other states, however, the courts *are* concerned about the fault of the defendant and the plaintiff.

Suppose that the plaintiff alleges that the parties are incompatible. Can the defendant defend by disagreeing? Do *both* husband and wife have to feel that it is impossible to live together? Assuming that the plaintiff is able to establish that more than "petty quarrels" are involved, most courts will grant the divorce to the plaintiff even though the defendant insists that they can still work it out. Each state's statute, however, must be carefully examined to determine whether this is a proper interpretation.

There appears to be a good deal of similarity between the ground of incompatibility and the ground of cruelty. Even though cruelty is a fault ground while incompatibility is not, the same or similar kind of evidence is used to establish both grounds. The major difference in most states is that for cruelty, unlike incompatibility, the plaintiff must show that the acts of the defendant endangered the plaintiff's physical health.

Interviewing and Investigation Checklist

Divorce on the Ground of Incompatibility

(This checklist is also relevant to the breakdown ground, page 377.)

Legal Interviewing Questions

1. Are you and D (defendant) now living together? If not, how long have you been separated?

2. Have you ever sued D or been sued by D for separate maintenance or for a judicial separation? If so, what was the result?

3. Describe your relationship with D at its worst.

4. How often did you argue? Were the arguments intense or bitter? Explain.

5. Did you ever have to call the police?

6. Did you ever receive medical attention as a result of arguments or fights with D?

7. Did D have a drinking or drug problem?

8. How did D act toward the children?

9. Have you and D had any sexual problems?

10. Do you feel that there is any possibility that you and D could reconcile your differences?

11. Do you think D feels that the two of you can solve your problems?

12. Have you or D, individually or together, ever sought counseling or therapy of any kind?

13. Are you now interested in any such help in order to try to save the marriage? Do you feel it would work? How do you think D feels about this?

Possible Investigation Tasks

■ Obtain copy of separation judgment, separate maintenance decree, police report, hospital records, if any.

Assignment 13.5

Is incompatibility a ground for divorce in your state? If so, what is the exact language of this ground in the statute? (See General Instructions for the State-Code Assignment in chapter one.)

Assignment 13.6

One married partner says to the other, "I no longer love you." By definition, are they incompatible for purposes of this ground for divorce? (See General Instructions for the Legal-Analysis Assignment in chapter one.)

Summary of Ground for Divorce: Incompatibility

Definition: The impossibility of two parties being able to continue to live together in a normal marital relationship because of severe conflicts and personality differences.

Who Can Sue: Either party in most states.

Major Defenses: 1. Differences between the parties are only minor.

2. The defendant was not at fault in causing the incompatibility (this defense is *not* available in most states).

3. The court lacks jurisdiction, page 396.

4. *Res judicata* applies, page 394.

5. The statute of limitations or laches apply.

Is this also a ground for annulment? No.

Is this also a ground for judicial separation? Yes, in many states.

Is this also a ground for separate maintenance? Yes, in many states.

Irreconcilable Differences, Irremediable Breakdown

The newest and most popular version of the no-fault ground for divorce adopted in many states provides that the marriage can be dissolved for *irreconcilable differences* that have caused the *irremediable breakdown* of the marriage. The goal of the legislatures that have enacted this ground has been to focus on the central question of whether it makes any sense to continue the marriage. The statutes often have similar language and content. For example:

- Discord or conflict of personalities that destroys the legitimate ends of marriage and prevents any reasonable expectation of reconciliation
- Irretrievable breakdown of the marriage
- Breakdown of marriage to such an extent that the legitimate objects of marriage have been destroyed and there remains no reasonable likelihood that the marriage can be preserved
- Substantial reasons for not continuing the marriage which make it appear that the marriage can be dissolved.

This ground for divorce is obviously quite similar to the incompatibility ground just considered.

What happens if the defendant denies that the breakdown of the marriage is irremediable and feels that marriage counseling would help? In most states, this is simply one item of evidence that the court must consider in deciding whether remediation is possible. It is likely, however, that if one party absolutely refuses to participate in any reconciliation efforts, the court will conclude that the breakdown of the marriage is total even if the other party expresses a conciliatory attitude. Again, the language of individual statutes would have to be examined on this issue.

Interviewing and Investigation Checklist

Divorce on the Ground of Irremediable Breakdown

Legal Interviewing Questions

1. How long have you been married to D (defendant)? How many children do you have?

2. How does D get along with the children?

3. How often do you and D communicate meaningfully?

4. Does D insult you? If so, how?

5. Does D ridicule your religion, your political views, your family?

6. Does D do this in front of anyone? Who else knows that D does this? How do they know?

7. Has D ever ridiculed or criticized you to your friends, relatives, or other associates?

8. Do you think that D has ever tried to turn the children against you? If so, how do you know? What specifically have the children or others said or done to make you think so?

9. Does D drink? If so, how much, how often, and how has it affected your marriage?

10. Does D take any drugs? If so, what kind, how often, and how has it affected your marriage?

11. Has D ever hit you? If so, describe the circumstances. How often has D done this? Did the children see it? Has anyone else ever seen it?

12. Were there any other major events or scenes that were unpleasant for you? If so, describe them.

13. How would you describe your sexual relationship with D?

14. Has D ever refused your request for sex? Has D ever made any unreasonable sexual demands on you?

15. Has D ever accused you of infidelity?

16. Does D stay away from home often? Does D ever not come home at night?

17. Have you ever had to call the police because of what D did? Explain.

18. Has D ever sued you, or have you ever sued D?

19. How often do you fight or argue with D?

20. Is D now living with you? If not, explain the circumstances of the separation.

21. Has D's behavior affected your health in any way?

22. Have you had to see a doctor?

23. Have you seen or have you considered seeing a psychiatrist or some other person in the field of mental health?

24. How old are you? What is your prior education?

25. Have you ever experienced any behavior like this before?

26. How was your health before D started behaving this way?

27. Do you have any difficulty sleeping?

28. Do you have any difficulty doing your regular work because of D?

29. What is D's opinion of you as a spouse?

30. Do you think that you will ever be able to live in harmony with D? Explain why or why not.

31. Does D think the two of you will ever be able to get back together again? Explain why or why not.

Possible Investigation Tasks

■ Obtain all of C's (client's) medical records, if any, from doctors, hospitals, etc., that have treated her as a result of what D has done.

■ If the children are old enough and it is determined that it would not be harmful to them, they should be interviewed to see how they viewed D's relationship with C and, specifically, how D treated them.

■ Obtain police records, if any, resulting from any fights or disturbances.

Assignment 13.7

(a) Is irremediable breakdown a ground for divorce in your state? If so, what is the exact language of this ground in the statute? (See General Instructions for the State-Code Assignment in chapter one.)

(b) Dan and Helen were married in your state. Helen does not want to be married anymore. She loves Dan and enjoys being his wife, but simply wants to live alone indefinitely. Dan does not want a divorce. In the divorce papers filed by Helen, she lies when she says that there is no hope for their marriage. Can she obtain a divorce in your state? (See General Instructions for the State-Code Assignment in chapter one, and the Court-Opinion Assignment in chapter one.)

Summary of Ground for Divorce: Irremediable Breakdown

Definition: The breakdown of the marriage to the point where the many differences and conflicts between the spouses are beyond any reasonable hope of conciliation.

Who Can Sue: Either party.

Major Defenses: 1. The breakdown is remediable.

2. The court lacks jurisdiction, page 396.

3. *Res judicata* applies, page 394.

4. The statute of limitations or laches apply.

Is this also a ground for annulment? No.

Is this also a ground for judicial separation? Yes, in many states.

Is this also a ground for separate maintenance? Yes, in many states.

Section C. Fault Grounds for Divorce

Although fault grounds are less often considered in today's courts, they remain in force. They include:

- Adultery
- Cruelty
- Desertion and abandonment
- Others

Adultery

Adultery is voluntary sexual intercourse between a married person and someone to whom he or she is not married. This person is called the *co-respondent*. The intercourse is not voluntary, of course, if the defendant is raped or if the defendant is insane at the time. Since direct evidence of adultery is seldom available, circumstantial evidence must be relied upon. Specifically, the plaintiff must prove that the defendant had the *opportunity* and the *inclination* to commit adultery. *Corroboration* is often required. Corroboration is the introduction of evidence (other than the testimony of the plaintiff) that supports the plaintiff's testimony.

Notes on Sexual Relations as a Crime and as a Tort

1. In most states adultery (as defined above), fornication, and illicit cohabitation are crimes. *Fornication* is sexual intercourse between unmarried persons. *Illicit cohabitation* is fornication between two individuals who live together. It is rare, however, for the state to prosecute anyone for these crimes.

2. Criminal conversation is a tort brought against a third party who has had sexual intercourse (adultery) with the plaintiff's wife (page 551).

▐ Assignment 13.8

Is adultery, fornication, or illicit cohabitation a crime in your state? If so, what are their elements? (See General Instructions for the State-Code Assignment in chapter one.)

Cruelty

In most marriage ceremonies, the parties take each other "for better or worse." This concept was viewed quite literally early in our history, particularly when the woman was the one claiming to have received too much of the "worse." It was to be expected that a good deal of fighting, nagging, and mutual abuse would occur within the institution of marriage. The concept of permitting the marriage to be dissolved because of "mere" cruelty or indignities was alien to our legal system for a long time. The change in the law came slowly. When *cruelty* was allowed as a ground for divorce, the statute would often require that it be "extreme" or "inhuman" before the divorce could be granted. Furthermore, some states limited the ground to actual or threatened *physical* violence. Later, *mental anguish* came to be recognized as a form of cruelty and indignity, but there was often a requirement that the psychological cruelty must result in some impairment of the plaintiff's health. Some courts will accept a minimal health impairment, e.g., a loss of sleep. Other courts require more serious impairment. Whether a court will accept a minimal impairment or will require something close to hospitalization, the fact is that most courts have insisted on at least some physical effect from the cruelty. Only a few states will authorize a divorce on the ground of cruelty or indignity where the mental suffering does not produce physical symptoms.

Desertion and Abandonment

Desertion and abandonment occurs when (1) one spouse voluntarily leaves another, (2) for an uninterrupted statutory period of time, e.g., two years, (3) with the intent not to return to resume cohabitation, and when (4) the separation occurred without the consent of the other spouse and (5) there was no justification or reasonable cause for the separation. *Constructive desertion* exists when the conduct of the spouse who stayed home justified the other spouse's departure, or when the spouse who stayed home refuses a sincere offer of reconciliation (within the statutory period) from the other spouse who initially left without justification. In effect, the spouse who stayed home becomes the deserter! The spouse who left would be allowed to sue the other spouse for divorce on the ground of desertion.

Others

A number of closely related and sometimes overlapping grounds exist in some states, including:

- Bigamy
- Impotence
- Nonage
- Fraud
- Duress
- Incest
- Conviction of a serious crime
- Insanity
- Habitual drunkenness
- Drug addiction
- Nonsupport
- Unexplained absence
- Neglect of duty
- Obtaining an out-of-state divorce which is invalid
- Venereal disease
- Unchastity
- Pregnancy by someone else at the time of the marriage

- Treatment injurious to health
- Deviate sexual conduct
- Any other cause deemed by the court sufficient, if satisfied that the parties can no longer live together.

Section D. Defenses to the Fault Grounds for Divorce

The basic defenses to the fault grounds for divorce may be defined as follows:

Collusion

Fraud was committed on the court by parties to a divorce by agreeing on a story to be told to the court even though both parties know that the story is untrue.

Connivance

There was a willingness or a consent by one spouse that the marital wrong be done by the other spouse.

Condonation

There was an express or implied forgiveness by the innocent spouse of the marital fault committed by the other spouse.

Recrimination

The party seeking the divorce (the plaintiff) has also committed a serious marital wrong.

Provocation

The plaintiff incited the acts constituting the marital wrong by the other spouse.

These defenses are rarely used today, however, since the fault grounds are themselves seldom used.

Note on Religious Divorces

> When a man hath taken a wife, and married her, and it come to pass that she find no favor in his eyes, because he hath found some uncleanliness in her: then let him write her a bill of divorcement, and give it in her hand, and send her out of his house. Deuteronomy 24:1, (KJV)

A Jewish couple that wants a religious divorce can go to a special court called a *Beth Din* presided over by a rabbi who is aided by scribes and authorized witnesses. There the husband delivers a *get*, or bill of divorcement, to his wife. Fault does not have to be shown. Both the husband and wife must consent to the divorce, but it is the husband who gives the get, and the wife who receives it. In New York, a religious divorce is allowed only if a secular (i.e., civil) divorce or annulment is underway or has already been granted. If a Jewish man does not have a religious divorce, he is still free to take another wife, but a Jewish woman without a get—even if divorced in a civil court—is called an *agunah*, or abandoned wife, and cannot be remarried by a rabbi. Markoff, *How Couples "Get" a Religious Divorce*, 8 National Law J. (August 15, 1988).

A Moslem divorce is traditionally performed by a husband pronouncing the word *Talak* (I divorce you) three times. The wife need not be present. In some countries, however, the process is more public. In Pakistan, for example, the husband must notify the chairman of an arbitration council that he has pronounced the *Talak*. The council will then attempt to reconcile the parties. If this fails, the divorce becomes absolute 90 days after the husband pronounced the *Talak*. In Egypt, the husband must pronounce the *Talak* in the presence of two witnesses who are usually officers of a special court. *The Religious Effect of Religious Divorces*, 37 Modern Law Review, 611–613 (1974).

Section E. Judicial Separation

A *judicial separation* is a decree by a court that two people can live separately—from bed and board—while still remaining husband and wife. The decree also establishes the rights and obligations of the parties while they are separated. A judicial separation is also known as a:

- Legal separation
- Limited divorce
- Divorce a mensa et thoro
- Separation from bed and board
- Divorce from bed and board

Parties subject to a judicial separation are *not* free to remarry. The marriage relationship remains until it is dissolved by the death of one of the parties, by annulment, or by an absolute divorce, or a *divorce a vinculo matrimonii*, as the "full" divorce is called.[2]

Perhaps the main function of a judicial separation is to secure *support* from the other spouse. In this sense, an action for judicial separation is very similar to an action for separate maintenance, to be discussed in the next section. For religious or family reasons, the parties may not wish to end the marriage by obtaining a divorce. If support is needed, a judicial separation is an alternative in many states.

We should distinguish a judicial separation from a *separation agreement*. The latter is a private contract between a husband and wife. The agreement may or may not become part of (i.e., be incorporated or merged in) the judicial-separation decree or become part of the absolute divorce decree if one is later sought. Also, it is important that the word "separated" or "separation" be used carefully. The words mean a *physical* separation between the husband and wife without involving a judicial decree. If, however, a court-sanctioned or court-ordered separation is involved, then the reference should be to a *legal* or *judicial* separation.

---

[2]In some community-property states (see page 249), the "community estate" is dissolved by a separation from bed and board. See Internal Revenue Service, *Community Property and the Federal Income Tax*, page 2 (1988 Edition).

Assignment 13.9

Answer the following questions by examining your state code. (See General Instructions for the State-Code Assignment in chapter one.)

(a) Does your state have an action for a judicial separation?

(b) If so, what is the action called?

(c) What is the citation of the statute authorizing this action?

To obtain a judicial separation, *grounds* must be established in the same manner as grounds must be established to obtain an absolute divorce. In fact, the grounds for judicial separation are often very similar if not identical to the grounds for an absolute divorce, e.g., no-fault grounds such as incompatibility or irretrievable breakdown, and fault grounds such as adultery or cruelty.

Assignment 13.10

(a) What are the grounds in your state for a judicial separation?

(b) Are there any grounds for judicial separation that are *not* grounds for divorce?

(c) What defenses exist for an action for judicial separation?

(See General Instructions for the State-Code Assignment and General Instructions for the Court-Opinion Assignment in chapter one.)

In a judicial-separation decree, the court can award alimony, and can issue custody and child-support orders, all of which are enforceable through traditional execution and contempt remedies. If the parties have drafted a separation agreement, the court will consider incorporating the terms of this agreement into the judicial-separation decree. The separation agreement, of course, will reflect the wishes of the parties on the critical issues of alimony, property division, child custody, and child support.

After a judicial separation decree has been rendered, the fact that the parties reconcile and resume cohabitation does not mean that the decree becomes inoperative. It remains effective until a court declares otherwise. Hence, a husband who is under an order to pay alimony to his wife pursuant to a judicial separation decree must continue to pay alimony even though the parties have subsequently reconciled and are living together again. To be relieved of this obligation, a petition must be made to the court to change the decree.

The major consequence of a judicial separation decree in many states is its *conversion* feature. The decree can be converted into a divorce—an absolute divorce. In effect, the existence of the judicial-separation decree for a designated period of time can become a ground for a divorce (page 374).

Assignment 13.11

Prepare a flowchart of the procedural steps that are necessary for a judicial separation in your state. (See General Instructions for the Flowchart Assignment in chapter one.)

Section F. Separate Maintenance

An action for *separate maintenance* (sometimes called an action for *support*) is a proceeding brought by a spouse (usually the wife) to secure support. Like the judicial-separation decree, a separate-maintenance decree does not alter the marital status of the parties; they remain married to each other while living separately. To the extent that both decrees resolve the problem of support, there is very little practical difference between them.

Since the main objective of the separate maintenance action is to reach the property (e.g., cash, land) of the defendant for purposes of support, the court must have personal jurisdiction over the defendant (page 396).

The major ground for a separate-maintenance decree is the refusal of one spouse to support the other without just cause. In addition, most states provide that all grounds of divorce (page 370) will also be grounds for a separate maintenance award. Futhermore, in a divorce action, if the court refuses to grant either party a divorce, it usually can still enter an order for separate maintenance.

If the plaintiff refuses a good-faith offer by the defendant to reconcile, the plaintiff becomes a wrongdoer, which may justify the defendant in refusing to provide support. If the separate-maintenance action is still pending, the plaintiff will lose it. If a separate-maintenance decree has already been awarded, the defendant may be able to discontinue making payments under it.

The court determines the amount and form of a separate-maintenance award in the same way that it makes the alimony determinations in a divorce (page 245). If needed, the court can also make the child-support and child-custody decisions in the separate-maintenance action.

Separate-maintenance decrees can be enforced in the same manner as alimony awards in divorce decrees, e.g., contempt, execution (page 415).

Assignment 13.12

(a) Does your state have an action for separate maintenance or its equivalent? If so, on what grounds will the action be granted?

(b) Prepare a flowchart of all the procedural steps required in a proceeding for separate maintenance or its equivalent.

(See General Instructions for the State-Code Assignment, for the Court-Opinion Assignment, and for the Flowchart Assignment in chapter one.)

Key Chapter Terminology

Grounds
No-Fault Grounds
Fault Grounds
Uncontested
Collusion
Divorce Mill States
Dissolution

Living Apart
Conversion into Divorce
Enoch Arden
Incompatibility
Irreconcilable Differences
Irremediable Breakdown
Reconciliation

Illicit Cohabitation
Cruelty
Desertion and Abandonment
Constructive Desertion
Collusion
Connivance
Condonation
Adultery
Co-respondent
Corroboration
Fornication

Recrimination
Provocation
Get
Talak
Judicial Separation
Legal Separation
Limited Divorce
Divorce a Mensa et Thoro
Separation from Bed and Board
Separate Maintenance

Divorce Procedure

■ Chapter Outline

The word *divorce* is found in a number of frequently used phrases, such as *uncontested divorce* and *divisible divorce*. These phrases, as well as the critical concepts of domicile and residence, will be defined before we begin examining the specifics of procedure.

Jurisdiction is the power of a court to act. When a jurisdictional attack is made on a divorce decree, we must ask ourselves four questions. First, which of the three kinds of jurisdiction is alleged to be defective (subject-matter jurisdiction, in rem jurisdiction, or personal jurisdiction)? Second, which part of the divorce decree is being attacked (the part that dissolved the marriage; or the part that awarded alimony, child support, and property division)? Third, who is bringing the attack (the person who obtained the divorce decree or the person who obtained the benefits of the decree)? Fourth, in what court is the divorce decree being attacked (in the state where the divorce decree was obtained or in another state)?

Once these questions are addressed, we will cover the mechanics of divorce as we walk through the pretrial, trial, appeal, and enforcement stages of litigation. Among the topics treated are venue, pleading, discovery devices, preliminary orders, voir dire, evidence, and judgments. Special attention is given to the problems of enforcing divorce decrees, particularly the enforcement of spousal-support or alimony orders.

Section A. Kinds of Divorce

Over 90 percent of divorce cases are uncontested, i.e., the parties are in agreement on the termination of the marital relationship, alimony, property division, child custody, and child support. In such cases, the actual steps of divorce procedure are frequently a matter of ritual. If, however, the bitterness of the past has not subsided and agreements have not been reached, the technicalities of procedure can occupy center stage in costly and complicated proceedings.

The following terms are often used in connection with divorce procedure:

Migratory Divorce

The husband and/or wife travels (migrates) to another state in order to obtain a divorce—usually because it is procedurally easier to divorce there. He or she establishes domicile in the state, obtains the divorce, and then returns to the "home" state, where at some point there will be an attempt to enforce the "foreign" divorce judgment. If the domicile was valid, this divorce is entitled to full faith and credit (i.e., it must be enforced) by the home state or any other state.

Transitory Divorce

A divorce is granted in a state where neither spouse was domiciled at the time of the divorce. For example, while temporarily stationed in a state, a member of the armed forces files for and obtains a divorce against a spouse who has never been in the state. Since the state is not the domicile of either party, the divorce judgment may not be entitled to full faith and credit in other states.

Foreign Divorce

A divorce decree obtained in a state other than the state where an attempt is made to enforce that decree. For example, a divorce decree that is granted in Iowa or in France would be a foreign divorce when an attempt is made to enforce it in New York.

"Quickie" Divorce

A migratory divorce obtained in what are often called *divorce mill states,* i.e., a state where the procedural requirements for divorce are very slight in order to encourage out-of-state citizens to come in for a divorce and while there, to spend some tourist dollars.

Collusive Divorce

A divorce that results from an agreement or "conspiracy" between a husband and wife to commit fraud on the court by falsely letting it appear that they qualify procedurally or substantively for a divorce.

Default Divorce

A divorce granted to the plaintiff because the defendant failed to appear to answer the complaint of the plaintiff. (In most states, the divorce is not granted automatically; the plaintiff must still establish grounds for the divorce.)

Divisible Divorce

A divorce decree does two things: (1) dissolves the marital relationship, and (2) resolves the questions of alimony, property division, child custody, and child support. The divorce decree is thus *divisible*, or "divideable" into these two objectives. A *divisible divorce* is a divorce decree granted in one state but enforceable in another state only as to the dissolution of the marriage, not as to support, property division, etc. The other state does not have to give full faith and credit to other parts of the divorce decree. The divorce is divisible because only part of it must be recognized in another state.

Bilateral Divorce

One rendered by a court when both parties were present before the court. The opposite of a bilateral divorce is an *ex parte divorce*.

Ex Parte Divorce

One rendered by a court when only one party was present before the court. The court did not have personal jurisdiction over the defendant.

Dual Divorce

The divorce is granted to both husband and wife. A court might award the divorce decree to one party only—to the plaintiff or to the defendant, if the latter has filed a counterclaim for divorce against the plaintiff. A dual divorce, however, is granted to *both* parties.

Uncontested Divorce

The defendant does not appear at the divorce proceeding (see *default divorce* above) or appears without disputing any of the plaintiff's claims.

Contested Divorce

The defendant appears and disputes some or all of the claims made by the plaintiff at the divorce proceeding.

Divorce a Mensa et Thoro

A *judicial separation* (page 383); a *limited divorce*. The parties are not free to remarry since they are still married after receiving this kind of "divorce."

Limited Divorce

A *judicial separation;* a *divorce a mensa et thoro*.

Divorce a Vinculo Matrimonii

An *absolute divorce*. The parties are no longer married. They are free to remarry.

One of our objectives in this chapter is to have you prepare a flowchart of divorce procedure for your state. There will be a number of individual assignments to be answered mainly by reference to the state code and court rules of your state, and, to a lesser degree, by reference to court opinions of your state. The answers to these assignments on pieces of the procedural picture will also be used to complete Assignment 14.23 on the divorce flowchart, page 421.

Section B. Domicile

The word *domicile* is often confused with the word *residence*. In many divorce statutes the word *residence* is used even though the meaning intended is *domicile*. Except for such oddities, there are distinct differences between the two words:

Residence
Where someone is living at a particular time. A person can have many residences, e.g., a home in the city, plus a beach house, plus an apartment in another state or country.

Domicile
The place (1) where someone has physically been (2) with the intention to make that place his or her permanent home, or with no intention to make any other place a permanent home. It is the place to which one would intend to return when away. With rare exceptions, a person can have only one domicile.

It is important to be able to determine where one's domicile is, particularly in such a mobile society. Two specific reasons why this is important are:

- In most states, a court does not have jurisdiction to divorce parties unless one or both spouses are domiciled in the state where that court sits.
- Liability for inheritance taxes may depend upon the domicile of the decedent at the time of death.

Generally, a child cannot acquire a domicile of his or her own until reaching majority (e.g., eighteen years of age) or becoming otherwise emancipated (page 491). In effect, a child acquires a domicile by *operation of law* rather than by *choice*. The law operates to impose a domicile on the child regardless of what the child may want (if the child is old enough to form any opinion at all). The domicile of a child is the domicile of its parents. If they are separated, the child's domicile is that of the parent who has legal custody.

An emancipated child and an adult can pick any domicile they want (*domicile by choice*) so long as they are physically present in a place (even if only momentarily) and have the intention to make it their permanent home at the time of their presence there. This intention can sometimes be very difficult to prove. *Intention* is a state of the mind, and the only way to determine a state of mind is by interpreting external acts.

Verbal statements are not necessarily conclusive evidence as to the state of mind of the person making those statements. Suppose, for example, that Bill is domiciled in Ohio and, while visiting California, becomes violently ill. He knows that if he dies domiciled in California, his beneficiaries will pay a lower inheritance tax than if he had died domiciled in Ohio. While lying in a

California sick bed just before he dies, Bill openly says, "I hereby declare that I intend California to be my permanent home." This statement in itself fails to prove that Bill was domiciled in California at the time of his death. Other evidence may show that he made the statement simply to give the *appearance* of changing his domicile and that, if he had regained his health, he would have returned to Ohio. If this is so, then his domicile at death is Ohio in spite of his declaration, since he never actually intended to make California his permanent home.

In the following chart, you will gain an insight into some of the factors that courts will consider in determining whether the requisite state of mind on intention existed.

Interviewing and Investigation Checklist

How to Determine When a Person Has Established a Domicile

Legal Interviewing Questions

1. When did you move to the state?

2. How often have you been in the state in the past? (Describe the details of your contacts with the state.)

3. Why did you move to the state?

4. Was it your intention to stay there for a short period of time? A long period of time? Indefinitely? Forever?

5. While you were in the state, did you also have homes elsewhere in the state, and/or in another state and/or in another country? If so, give details, e.g., addresses, how long you spent at each home, etc.

6. Where do you consider your permanent home to be?

7. Have you ever changed your permanent home in the past? (If so, give details.)

8. Do you own a home in the state? Do you rent a home or apartment?

9. How long have you had the home or apartment?

10. Where are you registered to vote?

11. Did you inform the board of elections in your old state that you had moved?

12. Where is your job or business?

13. In what state is your car registered?

14. What state issued your driver's license?

15. In what states do you have bank accounts?

16. In what states do you have club memberships?

17. In what state do you attend church or synogogue?

18. Did you change your will to mention your new state?

19. When you stay at hotels, what address do you give?

20. What is your address according to the credit card companies you use?

21. In what states do you own land?

22. Where do your relatives live?

Possible Investigation Tasks

- Interview persons with whom the client may have discussed the move to the state, e.g., relatives, neighbors, business associates.
- Obtain copies of records that would indicate the extent of contact with the state, e.g., state tax returns, bank statements, land ownership papers, leases, hotel receipts, voting records, library cards.

In some states—Florida, for example—it is possible to make a formal *declaration*, or affidavit, *of domicile*, which is filed with an official governmental body (Exhibit 14–1).

Assignment 14.1

(a) For purposes of obtaining a divorce, how is domicile determined in your state? (See General Instructions for the State-Code Assignment and General Instructions for the Court-Opinion Assignment in chapter one.)

(b) Using the index volume(s) of your state code, find as many references as you can to *domicile* (up to a maximum of ten). Briefly state the context in which the word is used in each of the statutes to which you were referred by the index.

Assignment 14.2

Try to find an individual (e.g., relative, friend, classmate) who now lives, or who in the past lived, in more than one state at the same time, e.g., for business purposes, for school purposes, for vacation purposes, etc. Interview this individual with the objective of determining where his or her domicile is (or was). List all the facts that would tend to show that the person's domicile was in one state, and then list all the facts that would tend to show that his or her domicile was in another state.

Assignment 14.3

In each of the following situations, determine in what state the person was domiciled at the time of death. (See General Instructions for the Legal-Analysis Assignment in chapter one.)

(a) While living in Illinois, Fred hears about a high paying job in Alaska. He decides to move to Alaska, since he is tired of Illinois. He sells everything he owns in Illinois and rents an apartment in Alaska. While there he discovers that jobs are not easy to find. He decides to leave if he cannot find a job in three months. If this happens, he arranges to move in with his sister in New Mexico. Before the three months are over, Fred dies jobless in Alaska.

(b) Gloria lives in New York because she attends New York University. Her husband lives in Montana. Gloria finishes school in six months, at which time she plans to rejoin her husband in Montana. Two months before graduation, her husband decides to move to Oregon. Gloria is opposed to the move and tells him that she will not rejoin him if he does not return to Montana. Her husband refuses to move back to Montana. One month before graduation, Gloria dies in New York.

□ **EXHIBIT 14–1** Florida Declaration of Domicile

DECLARATION OF DOMICILE

TO THE STATE OF FLORIDA AND COUNTY OF LEON:

    This is my Declaration of Domicile in the State of Florida that I am filing this day in accordance, and in conformity with Section 222.17, Florida Statutes.

I, _____, was formerly a legal resident of
     PLEASE PRINT NAME

_____, and I resided at _____
    City   State   Street and Number

_____,

however, I have changed my domicile to and am and have been a bona fide resident of the State of

Florida since the _____ day of _____, 19_____. I now reside at

_____, Leon County, Florida, and this statement is to be
taken as my declaration of actual legal residence and permanent domicile in this State and County to
the exclusion of all others, and I will comply with all requirements of legal residents of Florida.

    I understand that as a legal resident of Florida: I am subject to intangible taxes; I must purchase
Florida license plates for motor vehicles, if any, owned by me and/or my spouse; I must vote in the
precinct of my legal domicile (if I vote), and that my estate will be probated in the Florida Courts.

I was born in the U.S.A.: Yes_____ No_____ Place of Birth:_____

Naturalized citizen — Where: _____ Date_____ No._____

Permanent Visa: Yes_____ No_____ Date_____ No._____

Sworn and subscribed before me this _____ day

of _____, A.D. 19_____.

PAUL F. HARTSFIELD, Clerk of Circuit Court

By_____
           Deputy Clerk

_____
            Signature

_____
        (Mailing Address)
    (To be executed and filed with
       Clerk of Circuit Court)

Penalty for perjury — up to 20 years in state prison — (Section 837.01, Florida Statutes)

Section C. Jurisdiction

Before discussing the nature of jurisdiction, some definitions that apply to this area of the law must be examined:

Full Adversarial Proceeding

Both the plaintiff and the defendant appear at the hearing to contest all the issues.

Ex Parte Proceeding

Only one party appears at the hearing; the defendant is not present.

Direct Attack

A challenge to the validity of a judgment made in a proceeding brought specifically for that purpose, such as an appeal of that judgment brought immediately after it was rendered by the trial court. R. Casad, *Res Judicata in a Nutshell,* 271 (1976).

Collateral Attack

A nondirect attack or challenge to the validity of a judgment. X obtains a judgment against Y. A year later, X brings a *separate* action against Y to enforce the judgment. In this action, Y claims that the judgment was invalid because the court had no jurisdiction to render it. This is a collateral attack by Y against the judgment. A collateral attack is an attempt to challenge a judgment in a proceeding other than the proceeding that issued the judgment.

Res Judicata

When a judgment on its merits has been rendered, the parties cannot relitigate the same dispute (i.e., the same cause of action); the parties have already had their day in court.

Estop or Estoppel

Stop or prevent.

Equitable Estoppel

An attack by a party on the validity of a judgment (e.g., on jurisdictional grounds), even a clearly invalid judgment, will be considered unfair and thus not permitted if:

■ The party obtained the judgment or participated in obtaining it *or*
■ The party relied on the judgment by accepting benefits based on it, *or*
■ The party caused another person to rely on the judgment to the detriment of the other person.

Foreign

Another state or country. A foreign divorce decree, for example, is one rendered by a state other than the state where one of the parties is now seeking to enforce the decree.

Forum State

The state in which the parties are now litigating a case.

Full Faith and Credit

Under the U.S. Constitution, a valid public act of one state must be recognized by other states. Hence a divorce granted by a state with proper jurisdiction must be recognized by every other state.

Service of Process

Providing formal notice to a defendant that orders him or her to appear in court to answer allegations in claims made by a plaintiff. The notice must be delivered in a manner prescribed by law.

Substituted Service

Service of process other than by handing the process documents to the defendant in person, e.g., service by mail, service by publication in a local newspaper.

The word *jurisdiction* has two main meanings: a *geographic* meaning and a *power* meaning. A specific geographic area of the country is referred to as the jurisdiction. A Nevada state court, for example, will often refer to its entire state as "this jurisdiction." The more significant definition of the word, which we will examine below, relates to power—the power of a court to resolve a particular controversy. If a citizen of Maine wrote to a California court and asked for a divorce through the mail, the California court would be without jurisdiction (without power) to enter a divorce decree if the husband and wife never had any contact with that state. The issue of how a court acquires the power—the jurisdiction—to hear a divorce case can sometimes be a complicated one.

To understand jurisdiction, we need to examine the following themes:

- Kinds of jurisdiction
- What part of the divorce decree is being attacked
- Who is attacking the divorce decree
- In what court is the divorce decree being attacked
- How jurisdiction is acquired

To a very large extent, the success of a jurisdictional attack on a divorce decree depends on the kind of jurisdiction involved, the part of the divorce decree being attacked, the identity of the person bringing the attack, etc. We will now turn to a discussion of these critical factors.

Kinds of Jurisdiction

1. *Subject-matter jurisdiction.* The power of the court to hear cases of this kind. A criminal law court would not have subject-matter jurisdiction to hear a divorce case. A divorce decree rendered by a court without subject-matter jurisdiction over divorces is void.

2. *In rem jurisdiction.* The power of the court to make a decision affecting the *res,* or thing. In divorce actions, the *res* is the marriage status, which is "located" in any state where one or both of the spouses are domiciled. A state with in rem jurisdiction because of this domicile has the power to terminate the marriage. (Without *personal* jurisdiction over the defendant, however— see below—a court will not have the power to grant alimony, child support,

or a property division; it can only dissolve the marriage.) A court that renders a divorce judgment even though neither party is domiciled in that state is not entitled to full faith and credit (see discussion below); therefore, another state is not required to enforce the divorce.

3. *Personal jurisdiction* (also called *in personam jurisdiction*). The power of the court over the person of the defendant. If a court has personal jurisdiction over a defendant, it can order him or her to pay alimony and child support and divide the marital property. If a court makes such an order without personal jurisdiction, the order can be attacked on jurisdictional grounds; it is not entitled to full faith and credit.

Part of Divorce Decree Being Attacked

A divorce decree usually accomplishes three objectives:

1. *Dissolves the marriage.* For a court to have jurisdiction to dissolve a marriage, one or both of the spouses must be domiciled in the state. When this is so, the court has in rem jurisdiction, which is all that is needed to dissolve the marriage. Personal jurisdiction of both parties is not needed.

2. *Alimony, child support, and property division.* Alimony, child support, and property division cannot be ordered by the court unless it has personal jurisdiction over the defendant. Hence, it is possible for the court to have jurisdiction to dissolve the marriage (because of domicile) but not have jurisdiction to make alimony, child-support, and property-division awards (because the plaintiff was not able to take the steps necessary to give the court personal jurisdiction over the defendant). This is the concept of the *divisible divorce*—a divorce that is effective for some purposes but not for others.

3. *Child Custody.* On the jurisdictional requirements to make a child custody award, see page 327.

Person Attacking Divorce Decree

1. *The person who obtained the divorce.* A person should not be allowed to attack a divorce decree on jurisdictional grounds if that person was the plaintiff in the action that resulted in the divorce. This person will be estopped in any action to deny the validity of a divorce. The same result will occur if this person helped his or her spouse obtain the divorce or received benefits because of the divorce. (The effect of this rule, sometimes known as *equitable estoppel*, is to prevent a person from attacking a divorce decree that is clearly invalid, because, for example, someone lied to the court about being domiciled in the state. Note, however, that there are a few courts that do not follow this rule and *will* allow a person to attack a divorce he or she participated in obtaining earlier.)

2. *The person against whom the divorce was obtained.* If the person now attacking the divorce on jurisdictional grounds was the defendant in the action that led to the divorce and made a personal appearance in that divorce action, he or she will not be allowed to attack the divorce. He or she should have raised the jurisdictional attack in the original divorce action.

If the original divorce was obtained *ex parte* (i.e., no appearance by the defendant), the defendant *will* be able to attack the divorce on jurisdictional grounds, such as the fact that the plaintiff was not domiciled in the state that granted the divorce, or the court that granted the divorce had no subject-matter jurisdiction.

If the person against whom the divorce was obtained has accepted the benefits of the divorce, e.g., alimony payments, many courts will estop that person from now attacking the divorce on jurisdictional grounds.

If the person against whom the divorce was obtained has remarried, he or she will be estopped from claiming that the second marriage is invalid because of jurisdictional defects in the divorce decree on the first marriage. (There are some states, however, that will allow the jurisdictional attack on the divorce if the person making this attack did not know about the jurisdictional defect, e.g., no domicile, at the time.)

3. *A person who was not a party to the divorce action.* A second spouse who was not a party to the prior divorce action cannot challenge the validity of that divorce on jurisdictional grounds. This second spouse relied on the validity of that divorce when he or she entered the marriage and should not now be allowed to upset the validity of that marriage by challenging the validity of the divorce.

A child of the parties of the prior divorce action cannot challenge the validity of the divorce on jurisdictional grounds if that child's parent would have been estopped from bringing the challenge.

Court in Which Divorce Decree Is Being Attacked

Many of the disputes in this area arise when a divorce decree is obtained in one state and brought to another state for enforcement. Whether the *forum state* (where enforcement of the divorce decree is being sought) must give *full faith and credit* to the foreign divorce may depend on which of the three aspects of the divorce decree a party is attempting to enforce:

1. *The dissolution of the marriage.* If either the plaintiff or the defendant was domiciled in the state where the divorce was granted, every other state must give full faith and credit to the part of the divorce decree that dissolved the marriage. The forum state must decide for itself whether there was a valid domicile in the foreign state. The person attacking the foreign divorce decree has the burden of proving the jurisdictional defect, i.e., the absence of domicile in the foreign state.

2. *Alimony, child-support, and property-division awards.* If the state where the divorce was obtained did not have personal jurisdiction over the defendant, then that state's award of alimony, child support, and property division is *not* entitled to full faith and credit in another state. Again we see the divisible-divorce concept: only part of the divorce decree is recognized in another state if the court had jurisdiction to dissolve the marriage because of domicile but had no jurisdiction to grant alimony, child support, and a property division due to the absence of personal jurisdiction over the defendant.

3. *Custody award.* See page 327.

How Jurisdiction Is Acquired

1. *Subject-matter jurisdiction.* The only way a court can acquire subject-matter jurisdiction over a divorce is by a special statute or constitutional provision

giving the court the power to hear this kind of case. A divorce decree rendered by a court without subject-matter jurisdiction over divorces is void.

2. *In rem jurisdiction.* All that is needed for a court to acquire in rem jurisdiction is the domicile of at least one of the spouses in the state. The case can proceed so long as reasonable notice of the action is given to the defendant. If the defendant is not domiciled in the state, notice can be by substituted service, e.g., mail, publication of notice in a newspaper.

3. *Personal jurisdiction.* There are several ways that a court can acquire personal jurisdiction over the defendant:

   a. Personal service of process on the defendant in the state. This is effective whether or not the defendant is domiciled in the state.

   b. Consent. The defendant can always consent to personal jurisdiction simply by appearing in the action and defending the entire case. But if the defendant is a nondomiciliary, he or she can appear solely to contest the jurisdictional issue without being subjected to full personal jurisdiction. *Any* appearance by a *domiciliary,* however, will confer full personal jurisdiction on the court.

   c. Substituted service, e.g., mail, publication in a newspaper. Substituted service of process will confer personal jurisdiction only if the defendant is domiciled in the state. See, however, the discussion on long-arm jurisdiction below.

   d. Long-arm statute. This is used to acquire personal jurisdiction over a defendant who is not domiciled in the state. This defendant must have sufficient minimum contacts with the state so that it is reasonable and fair to require the defendant to appear and be subjected to full personal jurisdiction in the state. What constitutes sufficient minimum contacts to meet this standard has not been answered clearly by the courts. Here are some of the factors that will be considered by a court, no one of which is necessarily conclusive: the defendant was domiciled in the state at one time before he or she left, the defendant cohabited with his or her spouse in the state before the defendant left the state, the defendant visits the state, the defendant arranges for schooling for his or her children in the state, etc. In addition to these minimum contacts, the defendant must be given reasonable notice of the action.

   e. URESA (Uniform Reciprocal Enforcement of Support Act). For a discussion on how URESA can be used to acquire personal jurisdiction over a defendant, see p. 419.

Jurisdictional-Analysis: Examples

Some examples of how divorce jurisdiction is determined follow:

   1. Tom and Mary are married. Both are domiciled in Massachusetts. Mary moves to Ohio, which is now her state of domicile. She obtains a divorce decree from an Ohio state court. Tom is notified of the action by mail but does not appear. He has no contacts with Ohio. The decree awards Mary $500 a month alimony. Mary travels to Massachusetts and brings an action against Tom to enforce the alimony award of the Ohio court.

Jurisdictional Analysis

   ■ The Ohio court had jurisdiction to dissolve the marriage because of the domicile of Mary in Ohio. This part of the divorce decree is entitled to full faith and credit in Massachusetts, i.e., Massachusetts *must* recognize this aspect of the Ohio divorce decree if Massachusetts determines that Mary was in fact domiciled in Ohio at the time of the divorce decree.

- The Ohio court did not have jurisdiction to render an alimony award since it did not have personal jurisdiction over Tom. This part of the divorce decree is not entitled to full faith and credit in Massachusetts, i.e., the Massachusetts court does not have to enforce the Ohio alimony award.

- Suppose that Tom had procured an out-of-state divorce in a state where he alone was domiciled. Suppose further that the divorce decree provided that Mary was *not* entitled to alimony. If this court did not have personal jurisdiction over Mary, she would not be bound by the no-alimony decision even though she would be bound by the decision dissolving the marriage.

2. Bill and Pat are married in New Jersey. Bill brings a successful divorce action against Pat in a New Jersey state court. Bill is awarded the divorce. Pat was not served with process or notified in any way of this divorce action. Bill then marries Linda. Linda and Bill begin having marital difficulties. They separate. Linda brings a support action (separate-maintenance action) against Bill. Bill's defense is that he is not married to Linda because his divorce with Pat was invalid due to the fact that Pat had no notice of the divorce.

Jurisdictional Analysis

- Bill is raising a collateral attack against the divorce decree. He is attacking the jurisdiction of the court to award the divorce because Pat had no notice of the divorce action.

- Bill is the person who obtained the divorce decree. In most states, he will be estopped from attacking the decree on jurisdictional grounds. Whether or not the court in fact had jurisdiction to render the divorce decree, Bill will not be allowed to challenge it. He relied on the divorce and took the benefits of the divorce when he married Linda. He should not be allowed to attack the very thing he helped accomplish.

3. Joe and Helen are married in Texas. Helen goes to New Mexico and obtains a divorce decree against Joe. Joe knows about the action but does not appear. Helen has never been domiciled in New Mexico. Joe marries Paulene. When Helen dies, Joe claims part of her estate. His position is that he is her surviving husband because the New Mexico court had no jurisdiction to divorce them since neither was ever domiciled there.

Jurisdictional Analysis

- Joe was not the party who sought the New Mexico divorce. The divorce proceeding was ex parte. Normally, he would be allowed to attack the divorce decree on the ground that no one was domiciled in New Mexico at the time of the divorce.

- But Joe relied upon the divorce and accepted its benefits by marrying Paulene. It would be inconsistent to allow him to change his mind now, and it could be unfair to Paulene. Hence, Joe will be estopped from attacking the divorce on jurisdictional grounds.

Assignment 14.4

John and Sandra were married in Florida but live in Georgia. Sandra returns to Florida with their two children. John never goes back to Florida. He often calls his children on the phone, and they come to visit him pursuant to arrangements he makes with Sandra. Once he asked his mother to go to Florida to look after the children while Sandra was sick. Sandra files for a divorce in Florida. John does not appear, although he is given notice of the action. Sandra is granted the divorce and $840 a month in child support. No alimony is awarded. She later travels to Georgia and asks a Georgia court to enforce the child-support order which John has been ignoring. What result? (See General Instructions for the Legal-Analysis Assignment in chapter one.) What would the result be in your state? Check your state code and court opinions. (See General Instructions for the State-Code Assignment in chapter one and General Instructions for the Court-Opinion Assignment in chapter one.)

The remaining assignments in this section focus on the mechanics of jurisdiction—specifically, what courts have subject-matter jurisdiction over divorce, and what the residency requirements and service of process rules are for your state. (Exhibit 14–2 shows a summons used in service of process.)

You cannot go into a United States District Court or any federal court to obtain a divorce. Federal courts do not have subject-matter jurisdiction over divorces. Parties who want to dissolve their marriage must use their local state courts.

Most states require that the plaintiff be a resident of the forum state for a designated period of time before a divorce can be granted, e.g., six weeks, a year. In a few states, it is sufficient that the defendant is a resident even if the plaintiff is not. While the word "residence" is frequently used in the state statutes, the meaning intended by most of the statutes is domicile: one's permanent home where one intends to stay indefinitely. As we saw in the preceding pages, for a court to have jurisdiction to divorce a couple, domicile must exist. The statutes on residency (domicile) state the length of time during which there must be residence (domicile) in the state.

Assignment 14.5

Identify each court in your state with subject-matter jurisdiction over divorces. See Assignment 2.2, page 61. Write your answer in step 1 of the Divorce Litigation Flowchart in Assignment 14.23 at the end of the chapter. (See General Instructions for the State-Code Assignment in chapter one.)

Assignment 14.6

(a) What is the residency requirement for a divorce action in your state? Write your answer in step 2 at the end of the chapter. (See General Instructions for the State-Code Assignment in chapter one.)

(b) If your state code uses the word *residence* in its divorce statute without defining it, find a court opinion in your state that does define it. (See General Instructions for the Court-Opinion Assignment in chapter one.)

Assignment 14.7

Tara, a member of the armed services is temporarily stationed in your state. She and her husband George are domiciled in another state. Under what circumstances, if

☐ **EXHIBIT 14–2** Summons with Certification of Service

SUPERIOR COURT OF THE DISTRICT OF COLUMBIA
FAMILY DIVISION
DOMESTIC RELATIONS BRANCH
451 Indiana Avenue, N.W., Washington, D.C. 20001

SUMMONS

TO:

Jacket Number: ....
.... : Plaintiff
vs.
.... :Defendant

You are hereby SUMMONED and required to file an answer to the complaint, which is herewith served upon you, at the office of the Clerk of this Court in Room 220, 451 Indiana Avenue, N.W., within twenty (20) days after service of this summons upon you, exclusive of the day of service, and to serve a copy of said answer upon the plaintiff's attorney, indicated below. If you fail to do so, action may be taken against you for the relief demanded in the complaint. It is recommended that you seek the advice of an attorney to assist you in this case.

PLAINTIFF'S ATTORNEY:

Name:	Address:

Witness, the Honorable Chief Judge of the Superior Court of the District of Columbia and seal of said Court.

Clerk of the Superior Court
of the District of Columbia

SEAL

Date: ....   By: ....

Deputy Clerk

FOR USE OF U.S. MARSHAL OR PROCESS SERVER

I hereby certify and return that I served the within Summons and Complaint upon

Name: ....

Address: ....

on the ..... day of ...., 19.... at .....AM/PM

☐ Personally.
☐ Individual served is a person of suitable age and discretion then abiding in the defendant's usual place of abode.
☐ I further certify that defendant is not a resident of the District of Columbia.
☐ I hereby certify and return that after diligent investigation I am unable to serve the individual, company, corporation, etc., named above.

Dates of Endeavor and/or Remarks:	Time: AM/PM

OFFICE OF THE U.S. MARSHAL   By: ....
DISTRICT OF COLUMBIA
Signature of Marshal Representative

PROCESS SERVER'S CERTIFICATION

I hereby certify that I am a competent person over eighteen years of age residing or maintaining a regular place of business in the District of Columbia with no interest in the subject matter of this suit nor am I party thereto and that I have served this SUMMONS and COMPLAINT as indicated above.

Signature of Process Server: .... Age:......

Business Address: ....

Residence: ....

Subscribed and sworn to before me this ..... day of ...., 19....

....
Notary Public   (Deputy Clerk)
District of Columbia

any, can Tara obtain a divorce in your state? Assume that George has never been in your state. (See General Instructions for the State-Code Assignment in chapter one.)

Assignment 14.8

Answer the following questions by examining your statutory code. Your answers will also become part of the Divorce-Litigation Flowchart, page 421. (See General Instructions for the State-Code Assignment in chapter one.)

(a) What is the fee for filing a divorce complaint in your state? Write your answer in step 3 at the end of the chapter.

(b) What happens if a party is seeking a divorce cannot afford the filing fee or any court costs? Can he or she proceed as a poor person (i.e., *in forma pauperis*) and thereby have these fees and costs waived?

(c) Who may serve process in your state? Write your answer in step 4 at the end of the chapter.

(d) How is personal service made on an individual? Write your answer in step 5 at the end of the chapter.

(e) In a divorce action, when can substituted service be used?

(f) How is substituted service made? By publication of a notice? By posting a notice? Other methods? Summarize your answer in step 6 at the end of the chapter.

(g) How is proof of service made? Write your answer in step 7 at the end of the chapter.

(h) Does your state have a long-arm statute for divorce actions? If so, when can it be used?

In some states it is possible to obtain a divorce primarily through the mail without going through elaborate court procedures. Such a divorce is often referred to as a *summary dissolution* (see Exhibit 14–3). The requirements for taking advantage of this option are quite strict. In California, for example, the couple must be childless, married for five years or less, have no interest in real property (other than a lease on a residence), waive any rights to spousal support, etc. Cal. Civil Code § 4550 (1983). In short, there must be very little need for courts, lawyers, and the protection of the legal system. The less conflict between parties over children, property, and support, the easier it is to obtain a divorce.

A party who represents him or herself in a divorce action (summary or traditional) is proceeding *pro se*.

Section D. Miscellaneous Pretrial Matters

Proctor

At one time, many states appointed a government official, sometimes called a *proctor,* to protect the interests of the children, to watch for collusion between the husband and wife, and in a general sense to play the role of a "party" in the divorce litigation.

Assignment 14.9

Is a government official appointed in divorce cases in your state? If so, what is the function of this individual? (See General Instructions for the State-Code Assignment in chapter one.)

Guardian Ad Litem

If the husband or wife is a minor or if the defendant is insane at the time of the divorce action, the court may require that the individual be represented by a *guardian ad litem* or *conservator* in order to ensure that the interests of the individual are protected during the proceeding. In a disputed child-custody case, the state might appoint a guardian ad litem to represent the child.

Assignment 14.10

Under what circumstance can a guardian ad litem be appointed in a divorce action in your state? Write your answer in step 8 at the end of the chapter. (See General Instructions for the State-Code Assignment in chapter one.)

Venue

Venue refers to the place of the trial. Within a state, it may be that the divorce action could be brought in a number of different counties or districts because each one of them has or could acquire the necessary jurisdiction. The *choice of venue* is the choice of one county or district among several where the trial could be held. The state's statutory code will usually specify the requirements for the selection of venue. The requirements often relate to the residence (usually meaning domicile) of the plaintiff or defendant.

Assignment 14.11

In a divorce action in your state, how is venue determined? Write your answer in step 9 at the end of the chapter. (see General Instructions for the State-Code Assignment in chapter one.)

Pleading

The *complaint* (often called the *petition*) must concisely state the nature of the action, the fact that the parties are married, the basis of the court's jurisdiction, the grounds for the divorce, the relief sought, etc. See the sample divorce complaint, page 27. If there is an *affirmative defense* (i.e., a defense that raises new facts other than those raised by the plaintiff in the complaint) it usually must be specifically pleaded in the defendant's answer (often called the *response*). In most states, the defendant can counterclaim for divorce in his or her answer. This is so when the defendant is being sued for annulment

☐ **EXHIBIT 14–3** Joint Petition for Summary Dissolution of Marriage

3-57

ATTORNEY OR PARTY WITHOUT ATTORNEY *(Name and Address)*:	TELEPHONE NO.:	FOR COURT USE ONLY

ATTORNEY FOR *(Name)*:

SUPERIOR COURT OF CALIFORNIA, COUNTY OF

STREET ADDRESS:

MAILING ADDRESS:

CITY AND ZIP CODE:

BRANCH NAME:

MARRIAGE OF

    HUSBAND:

    WIFE:

JOINT PETITION FOR SUMMARY DISSOLUTION OF MARRIAGE	CASE NUMBER:

We petition for a summary dissolution of marriage and declare that all the following conditions exist on the date this petition is filed with the court:

1. We have read and understand the Summary Dissolution Information booklet.

2. We were married on *(date)*:
   [A SUMMARY DISSOLUTION OF YOUR MARRIAGE WILL NOT BE GRANTED IF YOU FILE THIS PETITION MORE THAN FIVE YEARS AFTER THE DATE OF YOUR MARRIAGE.]

3. One of us has lived in California for at least six months and in the county of filing for at least three months preceding the date of filing.

4. There are no minor children born of our relationship before or during our marriage or adopted by us during our marriage and the wife, to her knowledge, is not pregnant.

5. Neither of us has an interest in any real property anywhere. *(You may have a lease for a residence in which one of you lives. It must terminate within a year from the date of filing this petition. The lease must not include an option to purchase.)*

6. Except for obligations with respect to automobiles, on obligations either or both of us incurred during our marriage, we owe no more than $4,000.

7. The total fair market value of community property assets, excluding all encumbrances and automobiles, is less than $14,000.

8. Neither of us has separate property assets, excluding all encumbrances and automobiles, in excess of $14,000.

9. *(Check whichever statement is true)*
   a. ☐ We have no community assets or liabilities.

   b. ☐ We have signed an agreement listing and dividing all our community assets and liabilities and have signed all papers necessary to carry out our agreement. A copy of our agreement is attached to this petition.

10. Irreconcilable differences have caused the irremediable breakdown of our marriage and each of us wishes to have the court dissolve our marriage without our appearing before a judge.

11. ☐ Wife desires to have her former name restored. Her former name is *(specify name)*:

12. Upon entry of final judgment of summary dissolution of marriage, we each give up our rights as follows:
    a. to appeal, and
    b. to move for a new trial.

(Continued on reverse)

Form Adopted by Rule 1295.10
Judicial Council of California
1295.10 [Rev. January 1, 1987]

**JOINT PETITION FOR SUMMARY
DISSOLUTION OF MARRIAGE**
(Family Law — Summary Dissolution)

Civil Code, §§ 4550–4556

☐ **EXHIBIT 14–3** continued

3-58

HUSBAND:	CASE NUMBER:
WIFE:	

JOINT PETITION FOR SUMMARY DISSOLUTION OF MARRIAGE

13. EACH OF US FOREVER GIVES UP ANY RIGHT TO SPOUSAL SUPPORT FROM THE OTHER.

14. We stipulate that this matter may be determined by a commissioner sitting as a temporary judge.

15. **Mailing Address of Husband**
Name:
Address:

City:
State:
Zip Code:

16. **Mailing Address of Wife**
Name:
Address:

City:
State:
Zip Code:

I declare under penalty of perjury under the laws of the State of California that the foregoing is true and correct.

Date:

▶ _____
(SIGNATURE—HUSBAND)

I declare under penalty of perjury under the laws of the State of California that the foregoing is true and correct.

Date:

▶ _____
(SIGNATURE—WIFE)

YOU HAVE A RIGHT TO REVOKE THIS PETITION ANY TIME BEFORE A REQUEST FOR FINAL JUDGMENT IS FILED. YOU WILL REMAIN MARRIED UNTIL ONE OF YOU FILES FOR AND OBTAINS A FINAL JUDGMENT OF DISSOLUTION. YOU MAY NOT REQUEST A FINAL JUDGMENT OF DISSOLUTION SOONER THAN SIX MONTHS FROM THE DATE THIS PETITION IS FILED.

(page 176) or legal separation (page 383) as well as for a divorce. (A counterclaim is simply a cause of action by the defendant against the plaintiff.)

Assignment 14.12

Answer the following questions on pleading after examining your state code and your court rules. (See General Instructions for the State-Code Assignment in chapter one.)

(a) What must a complaint for divorce contain? Write your response in step 10 at the end of the chapter.

(b) Must the complaint be subscribed and/or verified? If so, by whom? Write your response in step 11 at the end of the chapter.

(c) Where is the complaint filed and served? Write your response in step 12 at the end of the chapter.

(d) How many days does the defendant have to answer the complaint? Write your response in step 13 at the end of the chapter.

(e) Where and how is the answer filed and served? Write your response in step 14 at the end of the chapter.

(f) Must the defendant specifically plead all available affirmative defenses in the answer? Write your responses in step 15 at the end of the chapter.

(g) Must the defendant's answer be subscribed and/or verified? If so, by whom? Write your response in step 16 at the end of the chapter.

(h) How many days does the plaintiff have to reply to the defendant's counterclaim? Write your response in step 17 at the end of the chapter.

(i) Where and how is the reply of the plaintiff to be filed and served? Write your response in step 18 at the end of the chapter.

Waiting Period

In some states, there is a compulsory *waiting period* or "cooling-off" period (e.g., sixty days) that usually begins to run from the time the divorce complaint is filed. During this period of time, no further proceedings are held in the hope that tempers might calm down, producing an atmosphere of reconciliation.

Assignment 14.13

Is there a waiting period in your state? If so, how long is it and when does it begin to run? Write your answer in step 19 at the end of the chapter. (See General Instructions for the State-Code Assignment in chapter one.)

Section E. Discovery

Discovery refers to a series of devices designated to assist the parties prepare for trial, particularly in reference to the financial status of the parties.

For example, when the plaintiff is the wife who needs alimony, she might use some of the discovery devises to identify her defendant-husband's assets. The standard devices are as follows:

Interrogatories (see page 213)

A series of written questions to be answered in writing on matters relevant to the litigation.

Deposition

A deposition is an in-person, question-and-answer session conducted outside the courtroom, e.g., in one of the attorney's offices.

Request for Admissions

If a party believes that there will be no dispute over a certain fact at trial, it can request that the other party admit (i.e., stipulate) the fact to avoid the expense and delay of proving the fact at trial. The other party, of course, need not make the admission if it feels that there is some dispute over the fact.

Mental and Physical Examination

If the mental and physical condition of a party is relevant to the litigation, many courts can order him or her to undergo an examination. If paternity, for example, is at issue, the court might order the husband to undergo a blood-grouping test.

Assignment 14.14

Answer the following questions for a divorce action after examining your statutory code and your court rules. (See General Instructions for the State-Code Assignment in chapter one.)

(a) Who can be deposed? When must a deposition be requested? How must the request be made? Write your response in step 20 at the end of the chapter.

(b) Are there any restrictions on the use of depositions in divorce actions? Write your response in step 21 at the end of the chapter.

(c) When and on whom can interrogatories be filed? Write your response in step 22 at the end of the chapter.

(d) When must interrogatories be answered? Write your response in step 23 at the end of the chapter.

(e) When can a request for admission be made? Write your response in step 24 at the end of the chapter.

(f) When will a court order a physical or mental examination? Write your response in step 25 at the end of the chapter.

(g) What sanctions can be imposed if a party improperly refuses to comply with valid discovery requests? Summarize your response in step 26 at the end of the chapter.

Assignment 14.15

Pick any well-known married couple. Assume that they are getting a divorce and that you work for the law firm that is representing the wife. You are asked to draft a set of interrogatories meant to elicit as much relevant information as possible about the husband's personal and business finances. Information will be used in the firm's representation of the wife on alimony and property-division issues. Draft the interrogatories. (See General Instructions for the Interrogatories Assignment in chapter one.)

Section F. Preliminary Orders

Obtaining a divorce can be time-consuming even when the matter is uncontested. The court's calendar may be so crowded that it may take months to have the case heard. If the case is contested and some bitterness exists between the parties, the litigation can be seemingly endless. While the litigation is going on (or to use the latin phrase, *pendente lite*), the court may be asked to make a number of *preliminary* rulings that remain in effect only until final determinations are made later:

- Granting custody of the children
- Granting a child-support order
- Granting alimony
- Granting attorney's fees and related court costs in the divorce action
- Enjoining (preventing) the husband from bothering or molesting the wife and children
- Enjoining the husband from transferring any of his property which might make it unavailable for the support of the wife and children
- Appointing a receiver over the husband's property until the court decides what his obligations to his wife and children are
- Enjoining the defendant from leaving the state
- Enjoining the defendant from obtaining a foreign divorce

(etc)

Assignment 14.16

In a divorce action in your state, what preliminary orders can be granted by the court pendente lite? Summarize your response in step 27 at the end of the chapter. (See General Instructions for the State-Code Assignment in chapter one.)

For an example of a request for preliminary or temporary orders, see Exhibit 14–4.

Section G. Trial

Some states do not permit jury trials in divorce cases. If there is no jury, the judge decides both the questions of fact as well as the questions of law. If a jury trial is allowed, the jurors are selected through a procedure known as *voir dire*. During this procedure, the lawyers and/or judge ask questions of prospective jurors in order to assess their eligibility. Prospective jurors may

☐ **EXHIBIT 14—4** Motion and affidavit for Temporary Alimony, Maintenance of Support, or Custody of Minor Children.

SUPERIOR COURT OF THE DISTRICT OF COLUMBIA
FAMILY DIVISION
DOMESTIC RELATIONS BRANCH

-- *Plaintiff*

v.   Jacket No. ----------------------

-- *Defendant*

MOTION AND AFFIDAVIT

NOTE:
FINANCIAL STATEMENT REQUIRED FILL OUT AND ATTACH HERETO.

For ☐ TEMPORARY ALIMONY, MAINTENANCE OR SUPPORT
    ☐ CUSTODY OF MINOR CHILDREN

Now comes ☐ Plaintiff and moves the Court that ------------------------------------
         ☐ Defendant   (name)

be required to pay such amount as seems just and reasonable for the support and maintenance of

the ☐ Plaintiff (and ------ minor children) pending the final disposition of this cause (and to
    ☐ Defendant

award ☐ her the temporary custody of said minor children). Note: *Strike out portions of the pre-*
      ☐ him

ceding that do not apply.

The following facts are submitted in support of the above motion:

1. Marriage:	Date:	Place:	2. Are you agreeable to a reconciliation:	☐ Yes ☐ No

3. Children by this marriage:		Living with			Amounts Contributed to family
Name	Age	Name	Address	Relation	

4. WIFE		5. HUSBAND	
Age:	Married before: ☐ Yes—How terminated? ☐ No	Age:	Married before: ☐ Yes—How terminated? ☐ No
Occupation:	Employer:	Occupation:	Employer:
Living with	Name: / Relation: / Address:	Living with	Name: / Relation: / Address:

6. Wife asks for support of self (and -------- minor children):	Amount: $ / Per: ☐ Week ☐ Month	7. Husband willing to contribute as such support:	Amount: $ / Per: ☐ Week ☐ Month
8. Husband's support to family:	Before Separation: $ / After Separation: $	9. Previous divorce proceedings between parties. ☐ Yes ☐ No / Alimony awarded: ☐ Yes ☐ No	
10. Juvenile Court proceedings: ☐ Yes ☐ No / Explain:		11. Remarks	

☐ **EXHIBIT 14–4** continued

DISTRICT OF COLUMBIA, ss:

--------------------------------, being first duly sworn, deposes and says that he/she has read the
foregoing statement and subscribed to the same and that it is a true and correct statement of fact.

                                                                        Plaintiff (Defendant)

Subscribed and sworn to before me this ------------- day of ----------------------, 19----

----
                                                                        Notary Public, D.C.

------------------------------------   My commission expires ----------------------
                            Attorney

                            Address

FORM DR–4/SEPT. 71   IM–484

be eliminated from consideration for various reasons, e.g., they might be biased
for or against one of the parties because of a prior association with that party.
Such jurors are *challenged for cause*. Each party also has a limited number of
peremptory challenges (usually three) through which it can eliminate certain
prospective jurors without having to give any reason or cause.

The lawyers begin the trial by making opening statements outlining the
evidence they intend to try to prove during the trial.

The plaintiff's side will usually present its case first. The lawyer will call
the plaintiff's witnesses and directly examine them. The other side can cross-
examine these witnesses. Physical evidence such as documents are introduced
as exhibits. Some evidence may have to be *corroborated*, meaning that additional evidence must be introduced to support the position taken by the
party. The plaintiff's side will "rest" its case after presenting all of its witnesses
and evidence. The defendant's lawyer then begins his or her case through direct
examination of witnesses, introduction of exhibits, etc.

When a party has the burden of proving a fact, the standard of proof is
usually a *preponderance of the evidence:* the fact finder must be able to say
from the evidence introduced and found admissible that it is *more likely than
not* that the fact has been established as claimed. Occasionally, however, the
law requires a fact to meet a higher standard of proof, e.g., clear and convincing
evidence.

Within the marriage, there is a *privilege for marital communications*,
which means that one spouse cannot disclose in court any confidential communications that occurred between the spouses during the marriage. This
privilege does not apply to

- Criminal proceedings in which one spouse is alleged to have committed a
  crime against the other or against the children
- Civil cases between the spouses such as a divorce action

The privilege is limited to cases in which a third party is suing one or both of
the spouses and attempts to introduce into evidence what one spouse may
have said to another. Such evidence is inadmissible.

A default judgment can be entered against a defendant who fails to appear.
The plaintiff, however, is still required to introduce evidence to establish his
or her case. Unlike other civil proceedings, the default judgment is not automatic.

Assignment 14.17

Answer the following questions after examining your state code and court rules. (See General Instructions for the State Code Assignment in chapter one.)

(a) In a divorce action, what evidence, if any, must be corroborated? Write your response in step 28 at the end of the chapter.

(b) In a divorce action, are there any limitations on testimony that one spouse can give against the other? Write your answer in step 29 at the end of the chapter.

(c) Can there be a jury trial in a divorce case? If so, when must the request for one be made? Write your response in step 30 at the end of the chapter.

(d) What happens if the defendant fails to appear? Can there be a default judgment? Write your response in step 31 at the end of the chapter.

Assignment 14.18

In your state, can one spouse use wiretap evidence against the other spouse at the divorce hearing, e.g., the wife taps her husband's phone and wants to introduce into evidence the conversation he had with his business partner about large assets that he has previously denied he owned. Check the code of your state as well as the federal code: the *United States Code* or the *United States Code Annotated* or the *United States Code Service*. (See General Instructions for the State-Code Assignment in chapter one.)

Assignment 14.19

Go to a court hearing in your state on divorce. In Assignment 14.5, page 400 you identified what court(s) in your state have the power to grant divorce. Attend a divorce hearing in one of these courts and answer the following questions concerning what you observe:

(a) What court heard the case?

(b) What was the name of the case?

(c) Were both sides represented by counsel?

(d) Were both parties present?

(e) What kind of evidence, if any, was introduced?

Note on Alternative Dispute Resolution (ADR)

The following are alternatives to traditional litigation of a family law dispute in court, or at least alternatives that can be tried before resorting to traditional litigation.

Arbitration

Both sides agree to submit their dispute to a neutral third person who will listen to the evidence and make a decision. This individual is usually a professional arbitrator hired through an organization such as the American Arbitration Association. An arbitration proceeding is not as formal as a court trial. Generally, the decision of an arbitrator is not appealable to a court. If a party is dissatisfied, he or she must go to court and start all over again.

Rent-a-Judge

This is actually another form of arbitration. A retired judge is hired by both sides to listen to the evidence and to make a decision that has no more or less validity than any other arbitrator's decision.

Mediation

Both sides agree to submit their dispute to a neutral third person who will try to help the disputants reach a resolution on their own. The mediator does not render a decision, although occasionally he or she may make suggestions or recommendations.

Med-Arb

First mediation is tried. Those issues that could not be mediated are then resolved through arbitration. Often, the same person serves as mediator and arbitrator in a Med-Arb proceeding.

Section H. Divorce Judgment

An *interlocutory decree* (or a *decree nisi*) is one that will not become final until the passage of a specified period of time. In some states, after the court has reached its decision to grant a divorce, an interlocutory decree of divorce will be issued. During the period that this decree is in force, the parties are still married. The divorce decree could be set aside if the parties reconcile.

In many states, the parties may not remarry while the trial court's divorce judgment is being appealed. Finally, in a few states, even a final divorce judgment will not automatically enable a party to remarry. The court may have the power to prohibit one or both of the parties from remarrying for a period of time.

An absolute, or final, judgment (as opposed to an interlocutory judgment) will determine whether the marriage is dissolved. If it is, the divorce may be granted to the plaintiff, or to both parties if both initially filed for the divorce. The judgment will also resolve the questions of alimony, child custody, child support, and property division. (All of this, of course, assumes that the court had proper jurisdiction to make these determinations as outlined in Section C of this chapter, page 394.) In addition, the judgment will often restore the woman's maiden name, if that is her wish, and determine what the surname of the children will be as part of the custody decision.

Exhibit 14–5 shows a notice of entry of judgment, and Exhibit 14–6 shows a record of dissolution of marriage.

Assignment 14.20

Answer the following questions after examining your state code. (See General Instructions for the State-Code Assignment in chapter one.)

(a) Is there an interlocutory decree or a decree nisi in your state? If so, how long is it effective and how does the divorce become final? Write your answer in step 32 at the end of the chapter.

(b) After the divorce becomes final, can the court forbid either party to remarry?

(c) While the divorce decree is being appealed, can the parties remarry?

(d) To what court can the divorce decree be appealed? Write your answer in step 33 at the end of the chapter.

(e) How many days does a party have to appeal? Write your answer in step 34 at the end of the chapter.

(f) Where and how is the notice of appeal filed and served? Write your answer in step 35 at the end of the chapter.

☐ **EXHIBIT 14—5** Notice of Entry of Judgment

3-41

ATTORNEY OR PARTY WITHOUT ATTORNEY *(Name and Address)*:	TELEPHONE NO.:	FOR COURT USE ONLY

ATTORNEY FOR *(Name)*:

SUPERIOR COURT OF CALIFORNIA, COUNTY OF

STREET ADDRESS:

MAILING ADDRESS:

CITY AND ZIP CODE:

BRANCH NAME:

MARRIAGE OF

PETITIONER:

RESPONDENT:

NOTICE OF ENTRY OF JUDGMENT

CASE NUMBER:

You are notified that the following judgment was entered on *(date)*:

1. ☐ Dissolution of Marriage

2. ☐ Dissolution of Marriage — Status Only

3. ☐ Dissolution of Marriage — Reserving Jurisdiction over Termination of Marital Status

4. ☐ Legal Separation

5. ☐ Nullity

6. ☐ Other *(specify)*:

Date: _____ Clerk, by _____ , Deputy

— NOTICE TO ATTORNEY OF RECORD OR PARTY WITHOUT ATTORNEY —

Pursuant to the provisions of Code of Civil Procedure section 1952, if no appeal is filed the court may order the exhibits destroyed or otherwise disposed of after 60 days from the expiration of the appeal time.

Effective date of termination of marital status *(specify)*:

WARNING: NEITHER PARTY MAY REMARRY UNTIL THE EFFECTIVE DATE OF THE TERMINATION OF MARITAL STATUS AS SHOWN IN THIS BOX.

CLERK'S CERTIFICATE OF MAILING

I certify that I am not a party to this cause and that a true copy of the Notice of Entry of Judgment was mailed first class, postage fully prepaid, in a sealed envelope addressed as shown below, and that the notice was mailed

at *(place)*: _____ California,

on *(date)*:

Date: _____ Clerk, by _____ , Deputy

Form Adopted by Rule 1290
Judicial Council of California
1290 (Rev. July 1, 1985)

NOTICE OF ENTRY OF JUDGMENT
(Family Law)

☐ **EXHIBIT 14—6** Record of Dissolution of Marriage

OREGON DEPARTMENT OF HUMAN RESOURCES
HEALTH DIVISION
Vital Records Unit

SAMPLE

CO. FILE NO. _____

**RECORD OF DISSOLUTION
OF MARRIAGE, OR ANNULMENT**

136-

State File Number

TYPE OR PRINT PLAINLY IN BLACK INK

HUSBAND

1. HUSBAND'S NAME *(First, Middle, Last)*

2. RESIDENCE OR LEGAL ADDRESS | STREET AND NUMBER | CITY OR TOWN | COUNTY | STATE

3. SOCIAL SECURITY NUMBER *(Optional)* | 4. BIRTHPLACE *(State or Foreign Country)* | 5. DATE OF BIRTH *(Month, Day, Year)*

6a. WIFE'S NAME *(First, Middle, Last)* | 6b. MAIDEN SURNAME

WIFE

7. FORMER LEGAL NAMES (IF ANY) | (1) | (2) | (3)

8. RESIDENCE OR LEGAL ADDRESS | STREET AND NUMBER | CITY OR TOWN | COUNTY | STATE

9. SOCIAL SECURITY NUMBER *(Optional)* | 10. BIRTHPLACE *(State or Foreign Country)* | 13. DATE OF BIRTH *(Month, Day, Year)*

MARRIAGE

12a. PLACE OF THIS MARRIAGE - CITY, TOWN OR LOCATION | 12b. COUNTY | 12c. STATE OR FOREIGN COUNTRY | 13. DATE OF THIS MARRIAGE *(Month, Day, Year)*

14. DATE COUPLE LAST RESIDED IN SAME HOUSEHOLD *(Month, Day, Year)* | 15. NUMBER OF CHILDREN UNDER 18 IN THIS HOUSEHOLD AS OF THE DATE IN ITEM 14. Number _____ ☐ None | 16. PETITIONER ☐ Husband ☐ Wife ☐ Both

ATTORNEY

17a. NAME OF PETITIONER'S ATTORNEY *(Type/Print)* | 17b. ADDRESS *(Street and Number or Rural Route Number, City or Town, State, Zip Code)*

18a. NAME OF RESPONDENT'S ATTORNEY *(Type/Print)* | 18b. ADDRESS *(Street and Number or Rural Route Number, City or Town, State, Zip Code)*

DECREE

19. MARRIAGE OF THE ABOVE NAMED PERSONS WAS DISSOLVED ON: *(Month, Day, Year)* | 20. TYPE OF DECREE DISSOLUTION OF MARRIAGE ☐ ANNULMENT ☐ | 21. DATE DECREE BECOMES EFFECTIVE *(Month, Day, Year)*

22. NUMBER OF CHILDREN UNDER 18 WHOSE PHYSICAL CUSTODY WAS AWARDED TO: Husband _____ Wife _____ Joint (Husband/Wife) _____ Other _____ ☐ No children | 23. COUNTY OF DECREE | 24. TITLE OF COURT

25. SIGNATURE OF COURT OFFICIAL ➤ | 26. TITLE OF COURT OFFICIAL | 27. DATE SIGNED *(Month, Day, Year)*

ORS 432.010 REQUIRED STATISTICAL INFORMATION. THE INFORMATION BELOW WILL NOT APPEAR ON CERTIFIED COPIES OF THE RECORD.

	28. NUMBER OF THIS MARRIAGE — First, Second, etc. *(Specify below)*	29. IF PREVIOUSLY MARRIED, LAST MARRIAGE ENDED		30. RACE - *American Indian, Black, White, etc. (Specify below)*	31. EDUCATION *(Specify only highest grade completed)*	
		By Death, Divorce, Dissolution, or Annulment *(Specify below)*	Date *(Month, Day, Year)*		Elementary/Secondary (0-12)	College (1-4 or 5+)
HUSBAND	28a.	29a.	29b.	30a.	31a.	
WIFE	28b.	29c.	29d.	30b.	31b.	

THE PETITIONER OR LEGAL REPRESENTATIVE OF THE PETITIONER IS RESPONSIBLE FOR COMPLETING THE PERSONAL INFORMATION ON THIS FORM AND SHALL PRESENT THIS FORM TO THE CLERK OF THE COURT WITH THE PETITION.
IN ALL CASES THE COMPLETED RECORD SHALL BE A PREREQUISITE TO THE GRANTING OF THE FINAL DECREE.

45-5 (2-89)

ORIGINAL   VITAL RECORDS COPY

Section I. Enforcement of Divorce Judgment

In Chapter 12, we covered the enforcement of child support, page 353. Here, our main focus is the enforcement of the alimony portion of a divorce judgment and, to some extend, the property-division portion as well.[1] A good deal of this section, however, will also be relevant to child-support enforcement.

A number of enforcement options can be used against a delinquent party:

- Civil contempt
- Execution
- Garnishment
- Attachment
- Posting security
- Receivership
- Constructive trust
- Criminal nonsupport
- Qualified Domestic Relations Order (QDRO)
- Uniform Reciprocal Enforcement of Support Act (URESA)

Civil Contempt

A delinquent party who has failed to satisfy a money judgment, e.g., an alimony order, is called the *judgment debtor*. The person in whose favor the judgment is rendered is the *judgment creditor*. For disobeying the order, the judgment debtor can be held in *civil contempt,* for which he will be jailed until he complies with the order. This remedy, however, is not used if the judgment debtor does not have the present financial ability to pay the alimony obligation. Inability to pay does not mean burdensome or inconvenient to pay. Using all resources currently available or those which could become available with reasonable effort, he must be able to comply with the alimony order. (Exhibit 14–7 shows an affidavit in support of a motion to punish for contempt.)

Contempt is generally not available to enforce property-division orders. The latter are more often enforced by execution, attachment, posting security, receivership, and constructive trust which are discussed below.

Execution

A judgment is *executed* when the court orders the sheriff to carry it out by seizing the property of the judgment debtor, selling it, and turning the proceeds over to the judgment creditor.

Execution is usually possible only with respect to support orders that are *final* and *nonmodifiable*. There are two ways in which such orders can become final and nonmodifiable, as outlined at the top of page 418.

---

[1]While either party can be challenged for failure to abide by alimony and property division orders, it is usually the ex-husband who is in this position. The examples used herein reflect this.

☐ **EXHIBIT 14—7** Affidavit in Contempt Proceeding

SUPREME COURT OF THE STATE OF NEW YORK
COUNTY OF _____

_____ ,   Plaintiff,
              -against-   AFFIDAVIT IN SUPPORT OF MOTION
_____ ,   Defendant,   TO PUNISH FOR CONTEMPT

                                                          Index No. _____

STATE OF NEW YORK   }
COUNTY OF _____ } ss.:

_____ , being duly sworn, deposes and says:

That I am the plaintiff in the above entitled action and make this application to punish the defendant for contempt of Court for willfully neglecting and refusing to comply with the Judgment of this Court dated _____ , 19 ____ , directing the defendant, among other things, to pay to the plaintiff the sum of _____ ($ _____) Dollars per week as alimony, plus the sum of _____ ($ _____) Dollars per week per child for the maintenance and support of the infant children _____ , _____ , and _____ , for a total sum of _____ ($ _____) Dollars per week by check or money order at the residence of the plaintiff.

That hereto annexed is a copy of the Judgment of Divorce herein. That the defendant was duly personally served with a copy of said Judgment on the _____ day of _____ , 19 ____ .

That defendant has failed, neglected, and refused to pay me the amounts of money set forth in said Judgment of Divorce during the period commencing _____ , 19 ____ to date.

That the above named defendant has willfully neglected and failed to comply with said Judgment of this Court and he is now in arrears in the sum of _____ ($ _____) Dollars, and no part of which has been paid although duly demanded. That the neglect and refusal of the above named defendant to comply with said Judgment of the Court was calculated to and did defeat, impair, impede, and prejudice the rights and remedies of the above named plaintiff.

That the arrears are computed as follows:

☐ **EXHIBIT 14–7** Continued

DATE	AMOUNT DUE	AMOUNT PAID	ARREARS
_____	$ _____	$ _____	$ _____
_____	$ _____	none	$ _____
_____	$ _____	$ _____	$ _____
_____	$ _____	none	$ _____
_____	$ _____	none	$ _____
_____	$ _____	$ _____	$ _____
_____	$ _____	none	$ _____
_____	$ _____	$ _____	$ _____
_____	$ _____	none	$ _____
_____	$ _____	$ _____	$ _____
_____	$ _____	none	$ _____

TOTAL ARREARS

$ _____

That total arrears are therefore due me in the sum of _____($ _____) Dollars.

That it is respectfully submitted that the defendant deliberately does this to defeat and prejudice the rights and remedies of myself and my infant children.

That defendant is employed as a school teacher with the same position that he held at the time of the trial on _____ , 19 ____ , which was only _____ months ago. His income is at least as much as he was earning them, if not more. The defendant is also engaged in private tutoring.

That no order of sequestration has been made herein for the reason that there is no property to sequestrate.

That no bond or security has been given for the payment of said alimony.

That your deponent has been unable to obtain steady employment and is in dire financial straits by reason of the defendant's willful refusal to comply with said Judgment of Divorce.

That no previous application for the relief herein prayed for has been made.

That the reason that an order to show cause herein is requested is that the same is required on an application of this matter by virtue of section 245 of the Domestic Relations Law.

WHEREFORE, an order to show cause is respectfully prayed requiring the defendant to show cause why he should not be punished for contempt for willfully disobeying the Judgment of this Court.

[Signature] _____

[Signature] _____

[Type Name of Deponent]

Source: J. Marvins, *McKinney's Forms,* 13:131A (1976).

- In some states, each unpaid installment automatically becomes a final and nonmodifiable judgment of nonpayment as to which execution will be available.

- In other states, each unpaid installment does not become a final and non-modifiable judgment of nonsupport until the wife makes a specific application for such a judgment and one is entered. Execution is available only after the judgment is so entered or docketed.

As we shall see below, this distinction is also relevant to the application of the full-faith-and-credit-clause.

Garnishment

When *garnishment* is used, the court authorizes the judgment creditor to reach money or other property of the judgment debtor that is in the hands of the third party, e.g., the employer or bank of the judgment debtor.

Attachment

Property of the judgment debtor is *attached* when the court authorizes its seizure to bring it under the control of the court so that it can be used to satisfy a judgment.

Posting Security

The court may require the judgment debtor to post a bond, i.e., *post security,* which will be forfeited if he fails to obey the judgment.

Receivership

The court can appoint a *receiver* over all the judgment debtor's property to prevent him from squandering it or otherwise making it unavailable to satisfy the judgment.

Constructive Trust

The court could impose a trust on property that the judgment debtor conveys to a "friendly" third party, e.g., the judgment debtor's mother, in an effort to make it appear that he no longer owns the property. A *constructive trust* is a trust created by the law, rather than by the parties, in order to prevent a serious inequity or injustice.

Criminal Nonsupport

The state can criminally prosecute the judgment debtor for the willful failure to meet his support obligation—*criminal nonsupport.*

Qualified Domestic Relations Order (QDRO)

Under a (*QDRO*), the court authorizes the judgment creditor to receive all or a portion of the pension or other retirement benefits that the judgment debtor has available through his employer (page 366). The ex-spouse, as judgment creditor, becomes an *alternate payee* under these plans. She cannot, however, receive benefits under the plan that the obligor himself would not have been able to receive. For example, if the obligor is not entitled to a lump-sum payment, the ex-spouse as alternate payee is also subject to this limitation. A child in need of support can also be an alternate payee through a QDRO. For an example of a QDRO, see page 254.

Uniform Reciprocal Enforcement of Support Act (URESA)

What happens when the defendant leaves the state? As we have seen, a court must have personal jurisdiction over a defendant in order to obtain and enforce an alimony or child-support order against him (page 344). When the parties no longer live in the same state, the state of the wife or ex-wife may not be able to obtain personal jurisdiction over the husband/father if the latter is not domiciled in the state, or is not physically present in the state (and hence cannot be served with process in the state), or does not have sufficient minimal contacts with the state for the long-arm statute to apply. Furthermore, it may be quite impractical for her to travel to the new state of the husband/father to try to find him and obtain a support order against him there.

One remedy in that situation is the *Uniform Reciprocal Enforcement of Support Act* (URESA).[2] (See Appendix E, page 573.) It authorizes a two-state lawsuit without requiring the aggrieved party to leave her own state. The two states involved are the initiating state and the responding state. The *initiating state* is the state of the *obligee,* the party claiming child support and/or spousal support. The obligee can also be a government agency that wants to be reimbursed for the public assistance it has already paid the obligee(s). The *responding state* is the state of the obligor, the party allegedly owing support.

The obligee starts the process by filing a petition or complaint in a court in the initiating state. The petition identifies the obligor, provides facts that will help locate the obligor, and alleges a support obligation that is currently owed to the obligee.

If the court in the initiating state determines that further proceedings are warranted, it will send the petition to a court in the responding state. Up to this point, the obligor is not involved. There has been no notice sent to the obligor, and there has been no hearing at which the obligor has denied or admitted the support duty.

The responding state now acts to acquire personal jurisdiction over the obligor, e.g., by the service of process on the obligor within the state. The obligee does *not* have to travel to the responding state. The beauty of URESA is that a state official acts on the obligee's behalf in the responding state.

The case against the obligor now proceeds in the court of the responding state. The obligor raises any defenses he may have to the claim that he owes a duty of support to the obligee. Under URESA, the responding state can litigate the question of paternity if it is an issue. Once the court concludes that the duty does exist, it enters a support order against the obligor. The traditional enforcement mechanisms discussed earlier are used where appropriate, e.g., civil contempt, execution, garnishment.

---

[2]The latest version of the Act is the Revised Uniform Reciprocal Enforcement of Support Act.

Support payments made by the obligor are sent to the court that issued the order in the responding state. The latter then forwards them to the court in the initiating state, which in turn gives them to the obligee(s).

Assignment 14.21

Answer the following questions after examining your state code. (See General Instructions for the State-Code Assignment in chapter one).

(a) What remedies (enforcement devices) exist to collect unpaid alimony payments?

(b) What procedures must be followed to seek enforcement of an alimony order by contempt? Write your answer in step 36 at the end of the chapter.

(c) Has your state enacted the Uniform Reciprocal Enforcement of Support Act? If so, give the citation of the act and describe how it works.

(d) What is the statute of limitations for bringing an action to enforce an alimony award? Write your answer in step 37 at the end of the chapter.

(e) What procedures must be followed to set aside a divorce judgment on the ground that it was obtained by fraud? Write your answer in step 38 of the Divorce Litigation Flowchart in Assignment 14.23 at the end of the chapter.

Section J. Full Faith and Credit

Assume that an obligee obtains a support judgment in one state and then travels to another state where the obligor now lives (rather than use URESA) to try to enforce the judgment. Can the obligor relitigate the support issue in his state, or is his state required to enforce the earlier judgment against him?

Under the full-faith-and-credit-clause of the United States Constitution, one state must give effect to the public acts, e.g., the court judgments, of another state (page 397).

> Phyllis obtains a divorce from Bob in Ohio. Bob falls behind in the alimony and child support payments he is obligated to make under the terms of the Ohio divorce judgment. Bob then moves to Kentucky. Phyllis goes to Kentucky to bring a suit against Bob to collect all unpaid installments.

The question is whether Kentucky can relitigate the alimony and child-support issues, or whether it must give *full faith and credit* to the Ohio judgment by allowing Phyllis to sue on the Ohio judgment? The answer depends upon the status of the Ohio divorce judgment:

- Did the Ohio court have subject-matter jurisdiction over divorce actions?
- Did the Ohio court have personal jurisdiction over Bob?
- In Ohio, would each unpaid installment (of alimony and child support) be automatically considered a final and nonmodifiable judgment?

If the answer to each of these questions is yes, then the Kentucky court *must* give full faith and credit to the Ohio judgment and permit Phyllis to enforce it against Bob without allowing him to relitigate the alimony and child-support obligation. Suppose, however, that no Ohio final judgment exists on unpaid installments until Phyllis makes specific application to an Ohio court for such a judgment and that at the time she brought her Kentucky action, she had not obtained such a judgment. Under these circumstances, a Kentucky court would not be *obliged*, under the full-faith-and-credit clause, to force Bob to pay all unpaid installments.

Under the doctrine of *comity*, however, a state can decide to give full faith and credit to foreign judgment even though it is not obliged to do so. It may decide to do so to reduce the burden on an ex-wife seeking back alimony and child support payments. Another example of the application of the comity doctrine involves foreign land decrees. Suppose that as part of the Ohio divorce decree, the Ohio court ordered Bob to transfer title to land he owned in Kentucky to Phyllis. Phyllis then brings an action in Kentucky to force Bob to convey his Kentucky land to her. Generally, a forum state (here, Kentucky) does not have to give full faith and credit to the judgment of a foreign state (Ohio) that affects the title to land in the forum state. The latter state, however, many nevertheless decide to enforce that foreign judgment affecting its land as a matter of comity.

Assignment 14.22

Interview a paralegal, a lawyer, or legal secretary who has been involved in divorce actions in your state. (See General Instructions for the Systems Assignment in chapter one.) Obtain answers to the following questions:

(a) Approximately how many divorce cases have you worked out?

(b) How many of them have been uncontested?

(c) Approximately how long does it take to process an uncomplicated, uncontested divorce?

(d) Is there a difference between working on a divorce case and working on another kind of case in the law office? If so, what is the difference?

(e) What are the major steps for processing a divorce action in this state? What documents have to be filed? What court appearances must be made? Etc.

(f) What formbook or other treatise do you use, if any, that is helpful?

(g) Does your office have its own internal manual that covers any aspect of divorce practice?

(h) In a divorce action, what is the division of labor among the attorney, the paralegal, and the legal secretary?

(i) What computer software, if any, is used? What is its function and how useful is it? What would the office have to do if such software did not exist?

Assignment 14.23

Divorce Litigation Flowchart for Your State

(Fill in each step after checking the law of your state, particularly your state statutory code. You may also need to refer to court rules and judicial opinions. See General Instructions for the Flowchart Assignment in chapter one. For each step, cite the statute, court rule, or other law that you are relying upon as authority for your answer.)

■ **Step 1** _____
Name the court or courts that have subject-matter jurisdiction over divorces:

Citation:

■ **Step 2** _____
What is the residency requirement for a divorce action?

Citation:

■ **Step 3** _____
Filing fee for a divorce.

Citation:

■ **Step 4** _____
Who may serve process?

Citation:

■ **Step 5** _____
How is personal service made on an individual?

Citation:

■ **Step 6** _____
In divorce actions, how is substituted service made?

Citation:

■ **Step 7** _____
How is proof of service made?

Citation:

■ **Step 8** _____
When can a guardian ad litem be appointed in a divorce action?

Citation:

■ **Step 9** _____
In a divorce action, how is venue determined?

Citation:

■ **Step 10** _____
What must a complaint for divorce contain?

Citation:

■ **Step 11** _____
Must the complaint be subscribed and/or verified? If so, by whom?

Citation:

■ **Step 12** _____
Where is the complaint filed and served?

Citation:

■ **Step 13** _____
How many days does the defendant have to answer the complaint?

Citation:

■ **Step 14** _____
Where and how is the answer filed and served?

Citation:

■ **Step 15** _____
Must the defendant specifically plead all available affirmative defenses in the answer?

Citation:

■ **Step 16** _____
Must the defendant's answer be subscribed and/or verified? If so, by whom?

Citation:

■ **Step 17** _____
How many days does the plaintiff have to reply to the counterclaim of the defendant?

Citation:

■ **Step 18** _____
Where and how is the reply to the plaintiff filed and served?

Citation:

■ **Step 19** _____
Is there a waiting period? If so, how long is it and when does it begin to run?

Citation:

■ **Step 20** _____
Who can be deposed? When must a deposition be requested? How is the request made?

Citation:

■ **Step 21** _____
Are there any restrictions on the use of depositions in divorce actions?

Citation:

■ **Step 22** _____
When and on whom can interrogatories be filed?

Citation:

■ **Step 23** _____
When must interrogatories be answered?

Citation:

■ **Step 24** _____
When can a request for admissions be made?

Citation:

■ **Step 25** _____
When will a court order a physical or mental examination?

Citation:

■ **Step 26** _____
Summarize the sanctions that can be imposed if a party improperly refuses to comply with valid discovery requests:

Citation:

■ **Step 27** _____
In a divorce action, summarize the preliminary orders that can be granted by the court pendente lite:

Citation:

■ **Step 28** _____
In a divorce action, what evidence, if any, must be corroborated?

Citation:

■ **Step 29** _____
Are there any limitations on testimony that one spouse can give against the other?

Citation:

■ **Step 30** _____
Can there be a jury trial in a divorce case? If so, when must the request for one be made?

Citation:

■ **Step 31** _____
What happens if the defendant fails to appear? Can there be a default judgment?

Citation:

■ **Step 32** _____

Is there an interlocutory decree or decree nisi? If so, how long is it effective, and how does the divorce become final?

Citation:

■ **Step 33** _____

To what court can the divorce decree be appealed?

Citation:

■ **Step 34** _____

How many days does a party have to appeal?

Citation:

■ **Step 35** _____

Where and how is the notice of appeal filed and served?

Citation:

■ **Step 36** _____

Summarize the procedures that must be followed to seek enforcement of an alimony or child support order by contempt:

Citation:

■ **Step 37** _____

What is the statute of limitations for bringing an action to enforce an alimony award?

Citation:

■ **Step 38** _____

Summarize the procedures that must be followed to set aside a divorce judgment on the ground of fraud:

Citation:

Key Chapter Terminology

Migratory Divorce
Transitory Divorce
Foreign Divorce
Collusive Divorce
Default Divorce
Divisible Divorce
Bilateral Divorce
Ex Parte Divorce
Dual Divorce
Uncontested Divorce
Contested Divorce
Divorce a Mensa et Thoro
Judicial Separation
Limited Divorce
Divorce a Vinculo Matrimonii
Absolute Divorce
Domicile
Residence
Operation of Law
Domicile of Choice
Declaration of Domicile
Jurisdiction
Adversarial Proceeding
Ex Parte Hearing
Direct Attack
Collateral Attack
Res Judicata
Estoppel
Equitable Estoppel
Foreign
Forum State
Full Faith and Credit
Service of Process
Substituted Service
Subject-Matter Jurisdiction
In Rem Jurisdiction
Personal Jurisdiction
In Personam Jurisdiction
Long Arm Statute
Summons
In Forma Pauperis
Summary Dissolution
Pro Se Divorce
Proctor

Guardian ad Litem
Venue
Pleadings
Complaint
Affirmative Defense
Counterclaim
Waiting Period
Discovery
Interrogatories
Deposition
Request for Admissions
Mental and Physical Examination
Preliminary Orders
Pendente Lite
Voir Dire
Peremptory Challenges
Challenge for Cause
Corroboration
Preponderance of Evidence
Privilege for Marital Communications
Interlocutory Decree
Decree Nisi
Civil Contempt
Judgment Debtor
Judgment Creditor
Execution of Judgment
Nonmodifiable Order
Garnishment
Attachment
Posting Security
Receivership
Constructive Trust
Criminal Nonsupport
Qualified Domestic Relations Order (QDRO)
Uniform Reciprocal Enforcement of Support Act (URESA)
Initiating State
Responding State
Full Faith and Credit
Comity

CHAPTER FIFTEEN

Tax Consequences of Separation and Divorce

▪ Chapter Outline

Since a husband and wife are often in different tax brackets, the issue of who receives a tax deduction for a certain payment can be extremely important. Tax consequences, therefore, should be a part of the negotiation process in a separation and divorce.

If certain tests are met, alimony can be deducted by the payor but then must be declared as income by the recipient. The tests differ for alimony payments made after 1984 and those made before 1985.

For alimony payments after 1984, there are eight tests:

1. The payment must be to a spouse or former spouse and must be required by a divorce decree or separation agreement.

2. The parties must be filing separate returns, not a joint return.

3. The parties must not be members of the same household if they are separated under a decree of divorce.

4. The payment must be in cash.

5. The payor must be under no obligation to make payments after the death of the recipient.

6. The payment must not be improperly disguised as child support.

7. The minimum term rule must be met for 1985 and 1986 decrees or agreements.

8. The parties must not elect to treat qualifying alimony payments as nonalimony.

If substantial payments are made shortly after a divorce or separation, the IRS will suspect that the parties are trying to disguise nondeductible, property-division payments as deductible alimony payments. Such excessive *front loading* may result in a recalculation of taxes paid in prior years in order to recapture improper deductions for alimony.

Earlier, we outlined the eight tests that must be met to have deductible alimony after 1984. For alimony payments made before 1985, there are also eight tests that must be met:

1. The payment must be made pursuant to a court order or a separation agreement.
2. The payment must fulfill an obligation of support.
3. The parties must not file a joint return.
4. The parties must be separated and living apart.
5. The payment must not be for child support.
6. The payment must be periodic.
7. If installment payments are to be made over a period of ten years or less, the installments must be subject to one of three specified contingencies (described in the text).
8. If the installment payments are to be made over a period of more than ten years and if the installments are not subject to contingencies, a ten percent limitation applies.

In a property-division incident to a divorce, property is transferred from one ex-spouse to the other. The property can be cash (e.g., $50,000), or noncash (e.g., a house). When there is a transfer of cash, none of it is deducted by the transferor and none of it is included in the income of the transferee. When there is a transfer of noncash property that has appreciated in value, the following rules apply:

1. The transferor does not deduct anything.
2. The transferee does not include anything in income.
3. The transferor does not have to pay taxes on the amount of the appreciation.
4. The basis of the property in the hands of the transferee is the same basis that the property had in the hands of the transferor.

A fee paid to your own attorney, accountant, or other professional is deductible if for tax advice in connection with a divorce, or if paid to help you obtain alimony that is included in gross income.

Section A. The Role of Tax Law in the Bargaining Process

Tax law should play a major role in the representation of divorce clients. Clauses in a separation agreement, for example, may have little relationship to the real world of dollars and cents if their tax consequences are not assessed (and to the extent possible, *bargained for*) before the agreement is signed. Income that once supported one household must now support two households. Careful tax planning can be of some help in accomplishing this objective.

We need to examine three major categories of payments: alimony, child support, and property division. In general, the tax law governing these categories is as follows:

- The person who pays alimony (the payor) can deduct it.
- The person who receives alimony (the recipient) must report it as income.
- Child-support payments are not deductible to the payor nor reportable as income by the recipient.
- Payments pursuant to a property division are not deductible to the payor nor reportable as income by the recipient.

In this chapter, we will be spending a good deal of time studying the conditions that must be met before these four tax rules can apply.

Since alimony is deductible, but child-support and property-division payments are not, attempts are often made to disguise child-support or property-division payments as alimony. A major theme of this chapter is to determine when such attempts are legal and when they will be challenged by the Internal Revenue Service (IRS).

Under our *progressive tax system,* every taxpayer does not pay the same tax *rate.* A high-income taxpayer will pay a higher percentage of income as tax than a low-income taxpayer. We refer to these individuals as being in different *tax brackets.* Even though Congress recently reduced the number of tax brackets, it is still generally true that a deduction is worth more to someone in a high-income bracket than to someone in a lower bracket. The question at the bargaining table is whether the latter will cooperate in allowing such a deduction to be taken by the former. Since a tax advantage to one side may be a distinct tax *dis*advantage to the other side, cooperation will probably be withheld unless something else is offered to offset the disadvantage.

To understand the scope of what is negotiable between the parties, we need to understand the fundamentals of tax law and practice in this area.

Since the mid-1980s, dramatic changes have occurred in the tax law governing divorce and separation. Since all of these changes were not retroactive, many taxpayers are still making payments under the old rules. Hence, in the following discussion, we will occasionally be referring to the law that applies before and after the changes.

Section B. Alimony

When certain conditions or tests are met, alimony (or separate-maintenance) payments are deductible to the payor and taxable to the recipient. The payments are:

- Reported as taxable income on line 11 of the recipient's 1040 return (see Exhibit 15–1), and
- Deducted from gross income on line 29 of the payor's 1040 return to obtain the latter's adjusted gross income (AGI) (refer again to Exhibit 15–1)

☐ **EXHIBIT 15–1** 1040 Income Tax Form

Form **1040** Department of the Treasury—Internal Revenue Service
U.S. Individual Income Tax Return **1989** , 19 | OMB No. 1545-0074

For the year Jan.–Dec. 31, 1989, or other tax year beginning , 1989, ending

Label

Use IRS label.
Otherwise,
please print
or type.

Your first name and initial	Last name	Your social security number
If a joint return, spouse's first name and initial	Last name	Spouse's social security number
Home address (number and street). (If a P.O. box, see page 7 of Instructions.)	Apt. no.	**For Privacy Act and Paperwork Reduction Act Notice, see Instructions.**
City, town or post office, state and ZIP code. (If a foreign address, see page 7.)		

Presidential Election Campaign ▶
Do you want $1 to go to this fund? . . . . Yes | No | **Note:** Checking ''Yes'' will not change your tax or reduce your refund.
If joint return, does your spouse want $1 to go to this fund? . Yes | No

Filing Status

Check only
one box.

1 ☐ Single
2 ☐ Married filing joint return (even if only one had income)
3 ☐ Married filing separate return. Enter spouse's social security no. above and full name here. _____
4 ☐ Head of household (with qualifying person). (See page 7 of Instructions.) If the qualifying person is your child but not your dependent, enter child's name here. _____
5 ☐ Qualifying widow(er) with dependent child (year spouse died ▶ 19). (See page 7 of Instructions.)

Exemptions

(See
Instructions
on page 8.)

If more than 6
dependents, see
Instructions on
page 8.

6a ☐ **Yourself** If someone (such as your parent) can claim you as a dependent on his or her tax return, do not check box 6a. But be sure to check the box on line 33b on page 2 . .

| No. of boxes checked on 6a and 6b |

b ☐ **Spouse** . . . .

| No. of your children on 6c who: |

c **Dependents:**

(1) Name (first, initial, and last name)	(2) Check if under age 2	(3) If age 2 or older, dependent's social security number	(4) Relationship	(5) No. of months lived in your home in 1989
	:	:		
	:	:		
	:	:		
	:	:		
	:	:		

● lived with you _____
● didn't live with you due to divorce or separation (see page 9) _____

No. of other dependents on 6c

d If your child didn't live with you but is claimed as your dependent under a pre-1985 agreement, check here ▶☐
e Total number of exemptions claimed . . . .

Add numbers entered on lines above ▶ ☐

Income

Please attach
Copy B of your
Forms W-2, W-2G,
and W-2P here.

If you do not have
a W-2, see
page 6 of
Instructions.

Please
attach check
or money
order here.

7	Wages, salaries, tips, etc. (attach Form(s) W-2)	7	
8a	**Taxable** interest income (also attach Schedule B if over $400) . .	8a	
b	Tax-exempt interest income (see page 10). DON'T include on line 8a	8b	
9	Dividend income (also attach Schedule B if over $400)	9	
10	Taxable refunds of state and local income taxes, if any, from worksheet on page 11 of Instructions . .		
11	Alimony received		
12	Business income or (loss) (attach Schedule C)		
13	Capital gain or (loss) (attach Schedule D)	13	
14	Capital gain distributions not reported on line 13 (see page 11) . .	14	
15	Other gains or (losses) (attach Form 4797)	15	
16a	Total IRA distributions . . 16a	16b Taxable amount (see page 11)	16b	
17a	Total pensions and annuities 17a	17b Taxable amount (see page 12)	17b	
18	Rents, royalties, partnerships, estates, trusts, etc. (attach Schedule E)	18	
19	Farm income or (loss) (attach Schedule F)	19	
20	Unemployment compensation (insurance) (see page 13)	20	
21a	Social security benefits. 21a	21b Taxable amount (see page 13)	21	
22	Other income (list type and amount—see page 13) _____		
23	Add the amounts shown in the far right column for lines 7 through 22. This is your **total income** ▶		

Recipient reports alimony as income.

Adjustments to Income

(See
Instructions
on page 14.)

24	Your IRA deduction, from applicable worksheet on page 14 or 15	24	
25	Spouse's IRA deduction, from applicable worksheet on page 14 or 15	25	
26	Self-employed health insurance deduction, from worksheet on page 15	26	
27	Keogh retirement plan and self-employed SEP deduction . .	27	
28	Penalty on early withdrawal of savings	28	
29	Alimony paid. **a** Recipient's last name _____ and **b** social security number . . :	29	
30	Add lines 24 through 29. These are your **total adjustments** . . . . ▶	30	

Payor of alimony reports payments as adjustment to income. You deduct alimony from gross income to obtain your adjusted gross income.

Adjusted Gross Income

| 31 | Subtract line 30 from line 23. This is your **adjusted gross income**. If this line is less than $19,340 and a child lived with you, see "Earned Income Credit" (line 58) on page 20 of the Instructions. If you want IRS to figure your tax, see page 16 of the Instructions . . . ▶ | 31 | |

Since the deduction comes through the determination of *adjusted gross income (AGI)*, there is no need to itemize deductions in order to take advantage of it.

Note that line 29 requires the payor to give the name and social security number of the recipient. Failure to do so can result in a fine and in a disallowance of the deduction. Giving this information will facilitate internal checking of the returns of both parties by the IRS, e.g., to make sure that the recipient is reporting as income what the payor is deducting as alimony.

Unfortunately, defining alimony can be a complex undertaking. The IRS has its definition *for tax purposes,* and as we shall see, this definition—at least after 1984—is broader than the traditional notion of alimony as spousal support.

Deductible Alimony After 1984: The Eight Tests

The requirements for alimony differ for divorces[1] and separation agreements executed *after* 1984, and those that cover the period *before* 1985.[2] First, we look at the eight post-1984 rules.

Requirements for Alimony after 1984

A payment qualifies as alimony when:

1. The payment is to a spouse or former spouse under a divorce decree or separation agreement.

2. The parties do not file a joint return.

3. The parties are not members of the same household when the payment is made. (This third requirement applies only if the parties are separated under a decree of divorce or separate maintenance.)

4. The payment is in cash.

5. There is no obligation to make any payment (in cash or other property) after the death of the recipient.

6. The payment is not treated as child support.

7. The minimum-term rule is met for 1985 and 1986 decrees or agreements.

8. The parties have not exercised the option of treating qualifying alimony payments as nonalimony.

For tax purposes after 1984, alimony exists when the eight requirements given above are met. A more thorough discussion of each requirement follows:

☐ **Divorce or Separation Agreement**
☐ **No Joint Return**
☐ **Parties Are Not Members of the Same Household**

---

[1]The rules discussed here on the tax treatment of alimony payments pursuant to a decree of divorce also apply to payments pursuant to a decree of separate maintenance, page 385, and a decree of annulment, page 176.
[2]It should be noted, however, that the post-1984 rules can also apply to payments made under a pre-1985 divorce decree or separation agreement if the decree or agreement is changed to specify that the post-1984 rules apply.

☐ **Payment in Cash**

☐ **No Payment After Death of Recipient**

☐ **Payment Is Not Treated as Child Support**

☐ **Minimum-term Rule Is Met for 1985 and 1986 Decrees or Agreements**

☐ **Parties Have Not Exercised Nonalimony Option**

☐ Divorce or Separation Agreement

The payment must be to a spouse or former spouse pursuant to and required by a divorce decree or a separation agreement. The decree does not have to be final. A payment ordered by an *interlocutory* (interim or nonfinal) decree, or a decree *pendente lite* (while awaiting the court's final decree) can also qualify.

Note that there is no specific requirement that the payment of alimony be for the *support* of the recipient, although this is what we normally think of as the purpose of alimony. This is a major change in the tax law. *To qualify as alimony after 1984, a payment does not have to discharge an obligation of support.* (As we shall see, another post-1984 change is that the payments no longer have to be periodic.) The great attraction of alimony to the payor is its deductibility. The fact that alimony, for tax purposes, is not limited to spousal support is an open invitation to payors to try to fit different kinds of payments under the rubric of alimony in order to take advantage of this deductibility feature. Later we will examine the extent to which such efforts can succeed.

Finally, if a spouse makes an *additional* payment beyond what is required by the divorce or separation agreement, the additional payment is not alimony for tax purposes.

Example 1

A 1990 separation agreement requires Linda to pay her ex-husband, Fred, a total of $1,000 per month in alimony. Assume that this amount fulfills all the requirements of deductible alimony. Hence, Linda can deduct each $1,000 payment and Fred must report it as income. During the last seven months of the year, Linda decides to increase her alimony payments to $3,000 each month in order to cover some extra expenses Fred was incurring.

Linda may *not* deduct the extra $14,000 ($2,000 × 7 months) she voluntarily added, and Fred does not have to report this $14,000 as income on his return. This is so even if state law considers the entire $3,000 payment each month to be alimony. Under *federal tax* law, voluntary alimony payments are not deductible.

☐ No Joint Return

Parties must be filing separate returns at the time the attempt is made to deduct the alimony.

☐ Parties Are Not Members of the Same Household

This *same-household* requirement applies when the parties have been separated under a decree of divorce.[3] (Note that two people living in physically

---

[3]As indicated earlier, references to a divorce decree include decrees of separate maintenance. See footnote 1.

separate rooms are still considered part of the same household.) If there is no divorce decree, alimony payments can be deductible even if the parties are still living in the same household, so long as the other requirements for *deductible alimony* are met.

There is a one-month grace period for those separated by divorce. A payment made while the parties are together in the same household can be deductible if one party moves out within one month after the payment.

Example 2

Jack and Tara live at 100 Elm Street. They are divorced on January 1, 1990. Jack is obligated to pay Tara $500 a month in alimony on the first of each month. He makes his first payment January 1, 1990. He moves out of the Elm Street house on February 15, 1990.

The January 1, 1990, payment is *not* deductible. Since the parties have a divorce decree, they must not be living in the same household at the time of the alimony payment. Jack and Tara were both living at 100 Elm Street—the same household—at the time of that payment. The one-month grace period does not apply since Jack did not move out within a month of this payment. If he had left earlier (e.g., January 29, 1990), the payment would have been deductible. Of course, all payments after February 15, 1990 (when they opened separate households) are deductible, if the other requirements for deductible alimony are met.

☐ Payment in Cash

Only *cash* payments, including checks and money orders, qualify.

Example 3

Under the terms of a separation agreement, Bob:
- Gives Mary, his ex-wife, a car
- Paints her house
- Lets her use his mother's house
- Gives her stocks, bonds, or an annuity contract

The value of these items cannot be deducted as alimony since they are not in cash.

Can cash payments made by the payor to a third party be deducted as alimony?

Example 4

Bob sends $1,000 to Mary's landlord to pay her rent. He also sends $800 to Mary's college to cover part of her tuition costs, and $750 to Mary's bank to pay the mortgage on the house she owns.

Can Bob deduct any of these payments as alimony, and does Mary have to report them as income? The answer is yes, if the cash payment to the third party is required by the divorce decree or by the separation agreement, or, when not so required, if Mary sends Bob a written request to make the cash payment to the third party. The written request must state that Bob and Mary both intend the payments to the third party to be treated as alimony. If all the other tests for alimony are met, the payment to the third party is deductible to the payor and includible in the income of the recipient on whose behalf the payment is made.

Suppose that the third party is an insurance company.

Example 5

Bob pays an annual premium of $1,700 on a life insurance policy on his life with Mary as the beneficiary.

Can he deduct these premiums as alimony? The answer is yes, but only if two conditions are met:

- The payor (Bob) is obligated to make these premium payments by the divorce decree or separation agreement.

- The beneficiary (Mary) *owns* the policy so that the payor cannot change the beneficiary.

☐ No Payment after Death of Recipient

If the payor is obligated (under the divorce decree or separation agreement) to make payments after the death of the recipient, none of the payments made after *or before* the death of the recipient qualify as alimony. Here the IRS is trying to catch a blatant and improper attempt to disguise property division as alimony in order to take advantage of a deduction.

Example 6

Under the terms of a separation agreement, Bob agrees to pay Mary $20,000 a year "in alimony" for ten years. If Mary dies within the ten years, Bob will make the remaining annual payments to Mary's estate. In the sixth year of the agreement, after Bob has paid Mary $120,000 (6 years × $20,000), Mary dies. For the next four years, Bob makes the remaining annual payments totaling $80,000 (4 years × $20,000) to Mary's estate.

All of the payments made by Bob will be disallowed as alimony—the entire $200,000 covering the periods before and after Mary's death. It makes no difference that the separation agreement called the payments alimony. To qualify as deductible alimony, one of the tests is that the payor must have no liability for payments after the death of the recipient.

This condition does not have to be explicitly stated in the decree or agreement, so long as it is clear under state law that there is no obligation to pay alimony after the death of the payor.

Whenever the payor must make payments beyond the death of the recipient, there is a strong suspicion that the payments are really part of a property-division arrangement. Most normal debts continue in effect after the death of either party. If, for example, I pay you $3,500 to buy your car, and you die before delivering the car to me, it is clear that your obligation to give me the car survives your death. Your estate would have to give me the car. The same is true of a property-division debt. Assume that Bob is obligated under a property-division agreement to transfer a house to Mary, his ex-wife. If Bob dies before making this transfer, his estate can be forced to complete the transfer to Mary. Property-division debts survive the death of either party. On the other hand, it is very rare for a "real" alimony debt to continue after the death of the recipient. After the recipient dies, he or she does not need alimony!

Example 7

At the time of their separation, Mary had a separate career in which she earned a high salary. Bob owned a going business valued at $400,000, which he started when he married Mary. Bob and Mary agreed that she should have a substantial share of this business as part of the property division between them. But Bob does not want to sell the business in order to give Mary her share. In the negotiations, Mary asks for $150,000, payable immediately. Bob agrees that $150,000 is a fair amount, but he doesn't have it. Hence, he counters by offering her $200,000 payable over ten years in $20,000 annual payments to be labeled as "alimony" in their separation agreement. If Mary dies within the ten years, Bob will make the annual payments to Mary's estate. The extra $50,000 is added to offset the fact that Mary will have to wait in order to receive all her money and will have to pay income tax on whatever Bob declares as deductible alimony.

Again, this arrangement will not work. There are ways to disguise property division as alimony, but this is not one of them. The $200,000 can never be deductible alimony since the parties planned to continue the payments after the death of the recipient.

The IRS will reach the same conclusion if the payor agrees to make a *substitute payment* to a third party on the death of the recipient, or a lump-sum payment to the estate of the recipient after his or her death.

□ Payment Is Not Treated as Child Support

Child support is neither deductible by the payor nor includible in the income of the recipient. But what is child support? This question is easy to answer if the divorce decree or separation agreement specifically designates or fixes a payment (or part of a payment) as child support.

Example 8

Under the terms of a divorce order, Jane must pay Harry $2,000 a month, of which $1,600 is designated for the support of their child in the custody of Harry.

The $1,600 has been fixed as child support. Hence it is not deductible by Jane nor includible in the income of Harry. This remains true even if the amount so designated varies from time to time.

Suppose, however, payments are made to the parent with custody of the children, but the parties say nothing about child support in their separation agreement, and the divorce decree is equally silent. The payments may even be labeled "alimony." In such a case the IRS will suspect that the parties are trying to disguise child-support payments as alimony in order to trigger a deduction for the payor. The suspicion will be even stronger if the separation agreement or divorce decree states that the payments are to be *reduced* upon the happening of certain events or contingencies that relate to the child's need for support.

Example 9

Under the terms of a separation agreement, Bill will pay Grace $2,000 a month, "in alimony," which will be reduced to $800 a month when their child leaves the household and gets a job.

The parties are trying to disguise $1,200 a month as alimony, although it is fairly obvious that this amount is child support. Otherwise, why would the parties reduce the payment at a time when the child would no longer need support? What other reason would the parties have to add such a contingency? The device will not work.

Child Support Improperly Disguised as Alimony

The IRS will fix a payment as child support rather than as alimony when the amount of the payment is to be reduced:

1. On the happening of a contingency relating to the child, or
2. At a time that can be clearly associated with a contingency relating to the child.

A contingency relates to a child when the contingency depends on an event that relates to that child.

Example 10

A payment required by a divorce decree or a separation agreement is to be reduced if the child does any of the following:

- Reaches a specified age (see discussion below on when the reduction is to occur at the age of majority)
- Attains a specified income level
- Dies
- Marries
- Leaves school
- Leaves home (temporarily or permanently)
- Gains employment

Since each of these contingencies depends on an event that obviously relates to the child, no alimony deduction is allowed.

A payor will often want to reduce a payment when the child reaches the age of majority, which is usually 18 or 21 under state law. Will the IRS treat this reduction as an indication that alimony is being improperly disguised as child support? From what we have said thus far, one would expect the answer to be an unqualified "yes." But this is not necessarily so. The rule is as follows:

Reduction Upon Age of Majority: Presumption of Child Support

The IRS will *presume* that a reduction is child support if the reduction is to occur not more than six months before or after the child reaches the age of majority in the state.

Thus, if the reduction is to occur *more* than six months before or after the child reaches the age of majority, it will be treated as an alimony reduction.

Example 11

Leo, Elaine, and their son Fred live in a state where the age of majority is 18. Fred was born on March 13, 1972. Leo and Elaine are divorced on January 12, 1980. Under the terms of the divorce decree, Elaine gets custody of Fred, and Leo must pay Elaine $2,000 a month in "alimony" until July 1, 1990, when the monthly payments are reduced to $1,200.

On these facts, the IRS will presume that the amount of the reduction is child support. Fred reaches the age of majority on March 13, 1990, when he turns 18. The reduction occurs on July 1, 1990, four months afterward. Since this reduction occurs "not more than six months . . . after the child reaches the age of majority," the presumption of child support applies.[4] The IRS will presume that the amount of the reduction ($800) is child support.

---

[4]This presumption can be rebutted by showing that the time at which the payments are to be reduced was determined independently of any contingencies relating to the children. For example, the payment period might be one customarily provided in the state, such as a period equal to one-half the duration of the marriage.

Example 12

Same facts as in Example 11 except that the reduction is to occur on March 13, 1991.

On these facts, the presumption of child support does not apply. The reduction occurs one year after Fred reaches the age of majority, which of course is more than six months. The entire $2,000 can be deductible alimony.[5]

☐ The Minimum-Term Rule Is Met for 1985 and 1986 Decrees or Agreements

This test applies *only* to payments that are still being made under separation agreements that were executed in 1985 and 1986, or under decrees covering these years. Payments over $10,000 under such agreements or decrees must meet the *minimum-term rule:*

Minimum Term Rule (1985 & 1986 only)

Alimony payments over $10,000 are not deductible unless the separation agreement or divorce decree requires that payments continue for at least six years.[6]

Example 13

A 1986 divorce decree provides that Frank is to make alimony payments to his ex-wife, Jill, of $20,000 in each of the five calendar years from 1986 through 1990. Frank will not have to make a payment in 1991.

Under the minimum-term rule, only $10,000 can qualify as an alimony payment in each calendar year from 1986 through 1990. The payments do not continue for at least six years.

Example 14

Same facts as in Example 13 except that the divorce decree also requires Frank of make a $1 payment in 1991.

Since the minimum-term rule is satisfied, $20,000 will be treated as an alimony payment in *each* of the calendar years 1986 through 1990.

☐ Parties Have Not Exercised Nonalimony Option

Assume that all of the preceding tests (1–7) for alimony are met by the parties. As a result, the payor can deduct the payments and the recipient must include them in income. But suppose the parties do *not* want the payments to be deductible/includible. It may be, for example, that both parties are in the same tax bracket and hence neither would benefit significantly more than the other by having the tax alimony rules apply. They can decide to treat otherwise

---

[5]Another problem area involves reductions pertaining to more than one child. Here the concern of the IRS is the taxpayer who is trying to time the reductions according to the successive emancipation of the children. The IRS will presume that a reduction is child support if the payments are to be reduced on two or more occasions that occur not more than one year before or after a different child attains a certain age from 18 to 24. This certain age must be the same for each child, but need not be a whole number of years.

[6]To determine whether alimony payments are to be made in any year, the possible termination of the payments by a contingency (other than by the passage of time) which has not yet occurred is ignored, unless the contingency may cause part of the payment to be treated as a child support payment.

qualifying alimony payments as *nonalimony*. This is done by including a provision in the separation agreement or by asking the court to include a provision in the divorce decree that the payments will *not* be deductible to the payor and will be excludible from the income of the recipient. If the parties want to exercise this option after the separation agreement is executed, they can simply sign a statement that they both designate otherwise qualifying alimony as nondeductible and nonincludible. The statement should refer to the already existing separation agreement.

This designation of nondeductibility/nonincludibility must be attached to the recipient's tax return for every year in which it is effective.

Recapture Rule after 1986: Front Loading of Payments

A common tactic of a party who wants to try to disguise property-division payments as alimony is to make substantial payments shortly after the divorce or separation, i.e., to *front load* the payments.

Example 15

> Jim runs a cleaning business, which he developed during his marriage to Pat. The value of the business is $180,000 on the date of their divorce. During their negotiations for the separation agreement, they both agree that each should receive an equal share of the business, which Jim wants to continue to run after the divorce. They are clearly thinking about a property division. Of course, any payments pursuant to a property division are not deductible. Jim suggests a different route: he will pay Pat $30,000 a year in "alimony" for the first three years after their separation in return for a release of all her interest in the business. To secure this arrangement, Jim gives Pat a lien on the business until he pays the $90,000. For each of the three years, the payor (Jim) takes a $30,000 deduction, and the recipient (Pat) includes $30,000 in her income.

Recall that there is no requirement that alimony be for the support of the recipient (page 433). Accordingly, in theory it is not improper to try to disguise property-division payments as deductible alimony. But the parties must not go too far. The *recapture rule* is designed to catch parties who have gone too far through excessive front loading. To this end, the rule limits the extent to which large payments made over a relatively short period can qualify as deductible alimony. The effect of the rule is to change the tax treatment of past payments by:

- Requiring the payor to remove the deduction previously taken for payments, and hence to include such payments in the calculation of the payor's income, and

- Allowing the recipient who previously included the alimony in income and paid taxes on it, to deduct it from income so that taxes do not have to be paid on it

The recapture rule applies to payments made under separation agreements that were entered into after 1986, or under decrees covering any such year.[7]

---

[7]It also applies to payments made under instruments (e.g., separation agreements) entered into before 1987 if the instrument has been modified since 1986 to specify that the 1986 Tax Reform Act changes are to apply. A different recapture rule applies to instruments entered into before 1987 and *not* modified to have the 1986 Tax Reform Act changes apply.

To apply the rule, let us look at a three-year period, beginning with the first calendar year that a payment qualifies as alimony. (This first year is sometimes referred to as the first *post-separation year,* which is not necessarily the year the parties separated.) The second and third years are the next two calendar years whether or not payments are made during these years.

Example 16

Al and Jane were divorced on February 3, 1987. Under the terms of the divorce decree, Jane pays Al the following amounts of "alimony:"

Year	Amount
1987	$60,000
1988	40,000
1989	20,000

To figure the amounts that must be recaptured, if any, use the worksheet in Exhibit 15–2. In our example, $22,500 must be recaptured by Jane, the payor. She must show this amount as income on line 11 of her 1989 return. (Line 11 now says "Alimony received." She must cross out the word "received" and write in the word "recapture," so that 11 will read "Alimony recapture.") Al, the payee, can deduct $22,500 on line 29 of his 1989 return. (Line 29 now says "Alimony paid." He must cross out the word "paid" and write in the word "recapture" so that line 29 will read "Alimony recapture.")[8]

Recapture Rule in 1985 or 1986: Front Loading of Payments

Special recapture rules, not covered here, apply to separation agreements (and/or divorce decrees) in 1985 or 1986.[9] In general, the danger sign that may trigger these special recapture rules for such years is a drop in the amount of alimony of more than $10,000. If the amount of alimony paid in the computation year is over $10,000 less than alimony paid in any prior calendar year, an amount must be recaptured for the computation year.

Deductible Alimony before 1985

For divorces or separation agreements in effect before 1985, different rules apply on the deductibility of alimony, unless the agreement is changed to specify that the *post*-1984 rules (discussed above) will apply instead. A summary of the pre-1985 rules is found at the bottom of the next page.[10]

---

[8]There are a number of important exceptions to the recapture rule. Regardless of the amount of the payment, the recapture rule does not apply (a) to payments under a temporary support order before the divorce or separation, (b) to payments required over a period of at least three calendar years of a fixed part of the payor's income from a business or property, or from compensation for employment or self-employment, or (c) to payments that end because the payor or recipient dies or the recipient remarries within the first three calendar years of payments.

[9]Note, however, that the post-1986 recapture rules discussed earlier *can* apply to separation agreements and divorce decrees in 1985 or 1986 if such agreements or decrees have been modified to specify that the 1986 Tax Reform changes are to apply.

[10]See WEST'S FEDERAL TAXATION: INDIVIDUAL INCOME TAXES, W. Hoffman, ed., 4–24 (1989).

☐ **EXHIBIT 15–2** Recapture Worksheet

Worksheet for Recapture of Alimony
(For instruments executed after 1986)

Note: Do not enter less than zero on any line.

1.	Alimony paid in **2nd year**		$40,000
2.	Alimony paid in **3rd year**	$20,000	
3.	Floor	$15,000	
4.	Add lines 2 and 3		35,000
5.	Subtract line 4 from line 1		$ 5,000
6.	Alimony paid in **1st year**		60,000
7.	Adjusted alimony paid in **2nd year** (line 1 less line 5)	35,000	
8.	Alimony paid in **3rd year**	20,000	
9.	Add lines 7 and 8	55,000	
10.	Divide line 9 by 2	27,500	
11.	Floor	$15,000	
12.	Add lines 10 and 11		42,500
13.	Subtract line 12 from line 6		*17,500
14.	**Recapture alimony.** Add lines 5 and 13		$22,500

***If you deducted alimony paid**, report this amount as income on line 11, Form 1040.
If you reported alimony received, deduct this amount on line 29, Form 1040.

Requirements for Alimony before 1985

1. The payment must be made pursuant to a court order or a separation agreement (i.e., the payment cannot be voluntary).

2. The payment must be in discharge of a legal obligation arising from marital or family obligations, which generally means that the payment must fulfill an obligation of support.

3. The parties must not file a joint return.

4. The parties must be separated and living apart.

5. The payment must not be for child support.

6. The payment must be periodic. There are three kinds of *periodic payments:*

   a. A payment of a fixed amount for an indefinite period; e.g., Bill pays Mary $50.00 per week until she remarries.

   b. A payment of an indefinite amount for a fixed period; e.g., Bill pays Mary 10 percent of his earnings for six years.

   c. A payment of an indefinite amount for an indefinite period, e.g., Bill pays Mary 10 percent of his earnings until she remarries.

7. If the decree or separation agreement lists a principal sum payable in installments over a period of ten years or less, the *installment payments* are not periodic payments unless the installment payments are subject to one of three contingencies. The first contingency is that the payments end or change upon the death of either spouse. The second is that the payments end or change upon the remarriage of the recipient. The third is that the payments end or change upon a change in the economic status of either spouse.

8. If the decree or separation agreement lists a principal sum payable in installments over a period of more than ten years, and if the installment payments are not subject to contingencies, the installment payments will be considered periodic payments, but only to the extent of 10 percent of the principal sum per taxable year of the recipient.

Example 17

A 1982 separation agreement obligates Harry to pay Jane, his former spouse, $200 a month for life.

Example 18

A 1981 divorce decree obligates Susan to pay Fred, her former spouse, now an invalid, one-fourth of her net income (she works on sales commissions) for a total of six years or until Fred dies, whichever occurs sooner.

In Example 17, Harry is making periodic payments—a fixed amount for an indefinite period. In Example 18, Susan is making periodic payments—an indefinite amount for an indefinite period.

Example 19

A 1984 divorce decree states that Fred must pay his ex-wife, Lee, $150,000 in installments of $20,000 per year for six years, and $5,000 per year for the following six years. The payments are not subject to any contingencies.

A principal sum is listed in the decree ($150,000) payable in installments over a period of more than ten years (twelve). Fred can deduct only 10 percent of the $150,000 (or $15,000) during each of the first six years. During the last six years, he can deduct the entire $5,000 he pays each year since this amount is within the 10 percent limit, assuming the other pre-1985 requirements for deductibility are met.

Failure To Fix and Allocate Child Support (before 1985)

Very often a payment will be intended by the parties to cover both alimony and child support. If, however, the decree or separation agreement does not *fix and allocate* a portion of the payment as child support, the entire payment is treated as deductible alimony, so long as it is a periodic payment. This is true even if:

- The amount of the payment is reduced by a stated dollar amount when a child dies, stops living with the parent, marries, joins the armed forces, or reaches the age of majority.
- The custodial parent in fact uses some of the payment as child support. ·
- The decree or agreement says that some of the payment can be used for child support, but fails to fix and allocate the amount for this purpose.

Again, this rule applies only to pre-1985 decrees and separation agreements. After 1984, totally different child-support/alimony rules apply, as we have seen.

Example 20

Under a 1982 divorce decree, Tom must pay Elaine, his ex-wife, $700 a month to support her and their child David. When David dies, marries, or reaches majority (whichever occurs first), the payments are reduced to $300 a month.

Since the divorce decree fails to fix and allocate how much of the $700 is for Elaine's support and how much is for David's, the entire $700 payment is treated as alimony that is deductible by Tom and includible in the income of Elaine. The fact that the $700 is reduced to $300 when David dies, marries, or reaches majority strongly suggests that $400 was for child support. This, however, is not significant. The failure to fix and allocate renders the entire payment as alimony that is deductible to the payor and includible in the income of the recipient. This result, of course, favors the payor, and is quite detrimental to the recipient, who must now pay taxes on what is being used for child support. (Again, if all of this occurred under a decree or separation agreement executed after 1984, very different tax rules would apply. See the earlier discussion of the sixth test or requirement for the deductibility of alimony after 1984).

Section C. Property Divisions

In this section our focus will be the division of property between spouses that fairly accounts for their mutual efforts in obtaining and/or improving the property during the marriage. Before discussing the tax consequences of such a property division, we need to review some basic terminology. The following example will be used to help explain this terminology.

Example 21
Tom buys a house in 1970 for $60,000. He spends $10,000 to add a new room. In 1981, he sells the house to a stranger for $100,000.

Transferor
The person who transfers property. Tom is the transferor.

Transferee
The person to whom property is transferred. The stranger is the transferee.

Appreciation
An increase in value. Tom's house appreciated by $40,000 (from $60,000 to $100,000). He has made a profit, called a *gain*. The gain, however, is *not* $40,000. See the definition for *basis* below.

Depreciation
A decrease in value. If the highest price Tom could have obtained for his house had been $55,000, the house would have depreciated by $5,000.

Realize
To benefit from or receive. Normally, *income, gain,* or *loss* are realized when they are received. If Tom could sell his house for $100,000, but he decides not to do so, he has not realized any income. He has a "paper" gain only. He does not have to pay taxes on a gain until he has realized a gain, e.g., by actually selling the house.

Fair Market Value

The price that could be obtained in an open market between a willing buyer and a willing seller dealing *at arm's length*. A sale between a parent and a child will usually not be at fair market value since the fact that they are related will probably affect the price paid. It is possible for a happily married husband and wife to sell something to each other at fair market value, but the likelihood is that they will not. In our example, Tom sold his house for $100,000 to a stranger. There is no indication that the buyer or seller was pressured into the transaction or that either had any special relationship with each other that might have affected the price or the terms of the deal. The price paid, therefore, was the fair market value.

Basis

The initial capital investment, usually the cost of the property. Tom's basis in his house is $60,000.

Adjusted Basis

The basis of the property after adjustments are made. The basis is either adjusted upward (increased) by the amount of *capital improvements* (i.e., structural improvements on the property) or adjusted downward. Tom added a room to his house—a structural improvement. His basis ($60,000) is increased by the amount of the capital expenditure ($10,000), giving him an adjusted basis of $70,000.

When Tom sold his house for $100,000, he *realized* income. When we factor in the adjusted basis, he has realized a gain or profit. The amount of gain for tax purposes is determined as follows:

$$\text{SALE PRICE} - \text{ADJUSTED BASIS} = \text{TAXABLE GAIN}$$
$$(\$100,000) \qquad (\$70,000) \qquad (\$30,000)$$

Tom must declare this gain of $30,000 on his tax return. Of course, if the sale price had been *less* than the adjusted basis, he would have realized a loss. If, for example, he had sold the house for $65,000, his loss would have been $5,000 ($70,000 − $65,000).

Tax Consequences of a Property Division

A property division can be in cash or in other property. To illustrate:

Cash:

> Ex-wife receives a lump sum of $50,000 (or five yearly payments of $10,000) in exchange for the release of any rights she may have in property acquired during the marriage.

Other-Property:

> Ex-wife receives the marital home, and the ex-husband receives stocks and the family business. They both release any rights they may have in property acquired during the marriage.

Cash property divisions rarely pose difficulties unless the parties are trying to disguise property division as alimony in order to take advantage of the deductibility of alimony. We already discussed when such attempts will be unsuccessful (page 434). A property division in cash is a nontaxable event;

nothing is deducted and nothing is included in the income of either party. The IRS will assume that what was exchanged was of equal value.

Suppose, however, that property other than cash is transferred in a property division and that the property so transferred had *appreciated* in value since the time it had been acquired by the transferor. Our problem is twofold:

- When *appreciated* property is transferred as part of a property division, is any gain or loss realized?
- What is the basis of such property in the hands of the transferee?

To examine these questions in concrete terms, let us return to Tom and his house. Suppose that instead of selling the house to a stranger, he transfers it to his wife.

Example 22

> Tom buys a house in 1970 for $60,000. He spends $10,000 to add a new room. In 1981, on the date of his divorce, he transfers the house to his wife, Tara, as part of a property division that they negotiated. Tara releases any rights, e.g., dower, (page 453). that she may have in his property. On the date of the transfer, the fair market value of the house is $100,000.

Note that all of this occurred before 1984. The law changed in 1984, but in order to understand the change, we need to understand the old law. The first question in Example 22 is whether Tom realized a gain of $30,000 at the time of the transfer to his ex-wife. Prior to 1984, the answer was yes. The United States Supreme Court so held in *United States v. Davis* 370 U.S. 65, 82 S.Ct. 1190, 8 L.Ed.2d 335 (1962). Hence, when Tom transferred a $100,000 home to his ex-wife as part of a property division, he received no deduction, since the transfer did not qualify as alimony, and he had to pay tax on his realized gain of $30,000. In answer to the second question, the basis of the property in the hands of Tara, the transferee, was the fair market value of the property at the time of the transfer, here $100,000. What Tara gave Tom (i.e., a release of her rights in his property) was assumed to be equal in value to what she received.

Example 23

> Same facts as in Example 22. In 1983 Tara sells the home to a stranger for $105,000. Assume that she made no capital improvements in the land since she acquired it from her ex-husband, Tom, in 1981.

Tara has realized a gain of $5,000. When she received the property, her basis was its fair market value, $100,000. Since she did not improve the property, this was her adjusted basis when she sold it in 1983:

$$\text{SALE PRICE} - \text{ADJUSTED BASIS} = \text{TAXABLE GAIN}$$
$$(\$105,000) \quad (\$100,000) \quad (\$5,000)$$

Everybody was unhappy about these tax rules—except the transferee, who was delighted to have fair market value as the basis. Transferors complained about being hit twice. "It's bad enough having to turn over property to my ex-wife that I can't deduct. On top of it all, I owe tax to the IRS on the appreciation." The IRS was also unhappy, because many transferors were neglecting to report the gain that resulted from the appreciation. Furthermore, the high basis of the property in the hands of the transferee (i.e., fair market value) meant that the IRS often collected very little tax when the transferee sold the property to someone else. See Example 23.

In 1984 Congress made a radical change in the law, which had the effect of overruling *United States v. Davis*. Under the new law, no gain or loss is recognized upon the transfer of appreciated property, and the adjusted basis in the property of the transferor is carried over to become the transferee's basis.

Example 24

Use the same facts as in Examples 22 and 23 except that the date of the divorce, when Tom transferred the house to Tara, is 1985 (rather than in 1981), and the date Tara sold the house to a stranger is 1986 (rather than in 1983).

The new rules apply. Tom does not pay a tax on the appreciation at the time of the transfer to Tara. And the tax picture at the time Tara sells the property is substantially different:

$$\text{SALE PRICE} - \text{ADJUSTED BASIS} = \text{TAXABLE GAIN}$$
$$(\$105,000) \quad\quad (\$70,000) \quad\quad\quad (\$35,000)$$

Tara takes over Tom's adjusted basis at the time she receives the property from him—$70,000. This becomes her basis when she sells it to someone else.

Needless to say, it is essential that a spouse know the adjusted basis of the property in the hands of the other spouse before accepting that property as part of a property division. It is meaningless, for example, to be told that property is "worth $150,000" on the market unless you are also told what the adjusted basis of that property is.

The 1984 (anti-*Davis*) rules do not apply to every transfer of property between spouses or ex-spouses. We turn now to those that are covered.

Property Transfers Covered

In general, the new tax rules governing a property division apply to property transfers that are *incident to a divorce,* that is, property transfers that:

- Occur within one year after the date on which the marriage ends, *or*
- Are related to the ending of the marriage

A property transfer is related to the ending of the marriage *if* it occurs within six years after the date on which the marriage ends *and* is made under a divorce or separation instrument *or* a modification of such an instrument.

A property transfer that is not made under a divorce or separation instrument, or that does not occur within six years after the end of the marriage is *presumed* to be unrelated to the ending of the marriage, unless the parties can show that some business or legal factors prevented an earlier transfer of the property.

Example 25

Gabe solely owns a garage and a residence. Pursuant to a property division with his wife, Janet, that is spelled out in their separation agreement, Gabe will keep the residence but will transfer the garage to Janet on March 13, 1992. They are divorced on January 10, 1985.

Was the property transfer incident to a divorce? It did not occur within a year of the ending of the marriage. But was it related to the ending of the marriage?

It did not occur within six years of the ending of the marriage. The transfer was made just over seven years after the divorce. We are not told why the parties waited this long after the divorce, but there is no evidence of business or legal factors that prevented an earlier transfer. Hence the IRS will *presume* that the transfer was not related to the ending of the marriage, and the new tax rules discussed above will *not* apply to the transfer.

Tax Treatment of Payments and Transfers Pursuant to Post-1984 Divorce Agreements and Decrees

	Payor	Recipient
Alimony	Deduction from gross income	Included in gross income.
Alimony recapture	Included in gross income of the third year.	Deducted from gross income of the third year.
Child support	Not deductible.	Not includible in income.
Property settlement	No income or deduction.	No income or deduction; basis for the property is the same as the transfer-or's basis.

Source: WEST'S FEDERAL TAXATION: INDIVIDUAL INCOME TAXES, 4–26 (1989).

Section D. Legal and Related Fees in Obtaining a Divorce

Obtaining a divorce can be expensive. In addition to attorney fees, one or both parties may have to hire an accountant, actuary, and appraiser. Only two types of such fees are deductible:[11]

- Fees paid for *tax* advice in connection with a divorce
- Fees paid to obtain *alimony* included in gross income

Other fees are not deductible. For example, you cannot deduct legal fees paid to negotiate the most advantageous or financially beneficial property division.[12]

Bills from professionals received by a taxpayer should include a breakdown showing the amount charged for each service performed.

Example 26

For representation in divorce case	$9,000
For tax advice in connection with the divorce	800
Total bill	$9,800

Only $800 is deductible.

---

[11]If you itemize deductions, you may claim such deductible charges on Schedule A (for Form 1040) as a miscellaneous deduction. Such deductions, however, are subject to the 2 percent of adjusted gross income limit.

[12]You can, however, add certain legal fees paid specifically for a property division to the *basis* of the property you receive, for purposes of figuring depreciation and gain or loss on its later sale. For example, the cost of preparing and filing a deed to put title to your house in your sole name may be added to its basis.

Example 27

For representation in divorce case	$6,500
For services in obtaining alimony	1,200
Total bill	$7,700

Only $1,200 is deductible.

As indicated, both sides usually incur separate expenses in connection with the divorce. The above rules apply to the fees incurred by the professionals hired by one party. If that party also pays the fees of his or her spouse or ex-spouse, those fees cannot be deducted, even though they are for tax advice only.

Assignment 15.1

John and Carol are divorced on September 1, 1991. Their separation agreement requires John to pay Carol $500 a week for her support until she dies. Use the guidelines of this chapter to answer the following questions that present a number of variations in the case of John and Carol. (See General Instructions for the Legal-Analysis Assignment in chapter one.)

(a) Carol has an automobile accident. To help her with medical bills, John sends her a check for $900 with the following note: "Here's my monthly $500 payment plus an extra $400 alimony to help you with your medical bills." Can John deduct the entire $900 as alimony?

(b) A year after the divorce, Carol has trouble paying her state income tax bill of $1,200. John wants to give her a gift of $1,200 in addition to his regular $500 monthly alimony. He sends $1,200 to the state tax department on her behalf. Can John deduct the $1,200 as alimony?

(c) Assume that in the September 1, 1991 divorce, Carol is awarded $1,500 a month in alimony, effective immediately and payable on the first of each month. John makes a payment on September 1, 1991. (He also paid her $1,000 for her support on August 1, 1991 before they went to court.) During all this time, John lived in the basement of their home, which has a separate entrance. He moves into his own apartment in another town on October 25, 1991. Which of the following 1991 payments, if any, are deductible: $1,000 (on August 1), $1,500 (on September 1), and $1,500 (on October 1)?

(d) Assume that under the divorce decree, John must make annual alimony payments to Carol of $30,000, ending on the earlier of the expiration of fifteen years or the death of Carol. If Carol dies before the expiration of the fifteen-year period, John must pay Carol's estate the difference between the total amount he would have paid her if she survived, minus the amount actually paid. Carol dies after the tenth year in which payments are made. John now pays her estate $150,000 ($450,000 − $300,000). How much of the $300,000 paid before her death is deductible alimony? How much of the $150,000 lump sum is deductible alimony?

(e) Assume that under the terms of the separation agreement, John will pay Carol $200 a month in child support for their only child, Nancy, and $900 a month as alimony. If Nancy marries, however, the $900 payment will be reduced to $400 a month. What is deductible?

(f) Assume that under the terms of the separation agreement, John will pay Carol $200 a month as child support for their only child, Nancy, and $900 a month as alimony. While Nancy is away at boarding school, however, the $900 payment will be reduced to $400 a month. What is deductible?

Assignment 15.2

(a) Greg was born on July 31, 1980. He is the only child of Bill and Karen. Under the terms of their separation agreement, which becomes effective on December 5, 1995, Bill is to have custody of Greg, and Karen is to pay him $4,000 a month in alimony. The agreement specifies that "none of the alimony is to be used for child support." On April 15, 1998, the alimony payment is to be reduced to $2,200 a month. What will be deductible?

(b) Millie pays Paul the following amounts of alimony under the terms of her 1987 divorce decree:

Year	Amount
1987	$25,000
1988	4,000
1989	4,000

What amounts, if any, must be recaptured?

(c) Reread the facts of Example 20. How would the IRS treat the case if the divorce decree were issued in 1988? What would be deductible? What would be nondeductible child support?

(d) Under a 1989 separation agreement and divorce decree, Helen transfers a building she solely owns to her ex-husband, Ken, in exchange for his release of any rights he has in other property that Helen acquired during the marriage. The transfer is made on the day of the divorce. Helen had bought the building in 1986 for $1,000,000. In 1987 she made $200,000 worth of capital improvements in the building. Its fair market value on the date she transfers it to Ken is $1,500,000. A week later, however, the market crashes and Ken is forced to sell the building for $800,000. What are the tax consequences of these transactions?

(e) Same facts as "d" except assume that all of these transactions occurred before 1984. What are the tax consequences of the transactions?

(f) Dan and Karen are negotiating a separation agreement in contemplation of a divorce that they expect to occur within six months of today's date. Karen wants $1,000 a month in alimony, and she wants Dan to pay all of her legal fees. Dan agrees to do so. Assume that there will be no difficulty deducting the $1,000 a month under the post-1984 alimony rules. Dan would also like to deduct what he pays for her legal fees which are anticipated to be $12,000, of which $3,000 will be for obtaining alimony from Dan. What options exist for Dan?

Key Chapter Terminology

Progressive Tax System
Tax Brackets
Adjusted Gross Income (AGI)
Deductible Alimony
Same Household
Substitute Payment
Contingency Relating to Child
Minimum-Term Rule
Front Loading
Recapture Rule
Post-separation Year
Periodic Payments

Installment Payments
Transferor
Transferee
Appreciation
Depreciation
Realize Income, Gain, Loss
Fair Market Value
At Arm's Length
Tax Basis
Adjusted Basis
Capital Improvements
Incident to Divorce

The Legal Rights of Women

■ Chapter Outline

Man is, or should be, woman's protector and defender. The natural and proper timidity and delicacy which belongs to the female sex evidently unfits it for many of the occupations of civil life. The constitution of the family organization, which is founded in the divine ordinance, as well as in the nature of things, indicates the domestic sphere as that which properly belongs to the domain and function of womanhood . . . The paramount destiny and mission of woman are to fulfill the noble and benign offices of wife and mother. This is the law of the Creator.
Bradwell v. Illinois, 83 U.S. (16 Wall.) 130, 140–41, 21 L. Ed. 442 (1872)

No longer is the female destined solely for the home and the rearing of the family, and only the male for the marketplace, and the world of ideas.
Stanton v. Stanton, 412 U.S. 7, 15, 95 S.Ct. 1373, 1378, 43 L.Ed.2d 688 (1975).

Historically, a married woman had very few rights independent of her husband. Today her situation is very different. For example, her right to own and dispose of property, and to enter contracts is now equal to that of her husband. True, there are some restrictions on contracts and conveyances between *spouses*, e.g., they cannot enter a contract to provide services and support if they are still living together, and they cannot transfer property to each other in order to defraud creditors. However, these restrictions apply equally to husband and wife.

When a husband dies, his wife has a right of dower in his property. Many states have replaced this with a right to elect a forced share of his estate. In most states the wife is not required to take her husband's surname upon marriage, nor is she required to keep it upon divorce if she used it when married.

An applicant for credit cannot be discriminated against on the basis of sex or marital status. Sex discrimination in employment is illegal unless sex is a bona fide occupational qualification. Certain forms of pregnancy-related discrimination and sexual harassment are also prohibited. These laws are enforced by the federal Equal Employment Opportunity Commission and by state agencies that administer rules on fair employment practices.

In the area of sexuality and reproductive rights, neither men nor women can be denied access to contraceptives. But they can be subjected to forced sterilization if they are mentally retarded or insane. And recent Supreme Court opinions have permitted state legislatures to increase restrictions on the right of a woman to choose an abortion.

Wife beating is a major problem in our society in spite of the laws against it and the availability of restraining orders and protective orders to keep the offending husband away. A few wives have taken the drastic step of killing their husbands. In such cases, the defense of the battered-wife syndrome has not been successful.

Finally, marital rape is not a crime in every state, although most states allow prosecution if a petition has been filed for divorce or separate maintenance.

Section A. The Status of Women at Common Law

Today, a married woman would probably consider it condescending to be told that she has the right to:

- Make her own will
- Own her own property
- Make a contract in her own name
- Be a juror
- Vote
- Bring a suit, and to be sued
- Execute a deed

The fact is, however, that there was a time in our history when a married woman could engage in none of these activities, or could not engage in them without the consent of her husband. For example, she could not bring a suit against a third party unless her husband agreed to join in it. Upon marriage, any personal property that she owned automatically became her husband's. If she committed a crime in the presence of her husband, the law assumed that he forced her to commit it. If she worked outside the home, her husband was entitled to her earnings. In short, at common law, the husband and wife were considered one person, and the one person was the husband![1]

While a great deal has happened to change the status of married women, not all *sex discrimination* has been eliminated.

Section B. Owning and Disposing of Property

Most states have enacted *Married Women's Property Acts* that remove the disabilities married women suffered at common law. Under the terms of most of these statutes, women are given the right to own and dispose of property in the same manner as men.

Assignment 16.1

Mary and Thad are married. Mary is a doctor and Thad is an architect. Before the marriage, Thad incurred a $35,000 debt at a local bank for his own education expenses. He is now in default on the loan. To collect this debt in your state, can the bank reach a vacation home that is solely owned by Mary? (See General Instructions for the State-Code Assignment and for the Court-Opinion Assignment in chapter one). Answer this question based on the following assumptions:

(a) Mary acquired title to the vacation home as an inheritance from her uncle before she married Thad.

(b) Mary acquired title to the vacation home as an inheritance from her uncle during her marriage to Thad.

(c) Mary acquired title to the vacation home by buying it from a stranger solely from her own earnings as a doctor during her marriage to Thad.

(d) Mary acquired title to the vacation home by buying it from Thad for $1 during the marriage. Thad inherited it from his mother before he married Mary. The sale to Mary was made just before Thad discovered that he was going to default on the bank loan. (See the next section on "Contracts and Conveyances.")

Section C. Contracts and Conveyances

Today women have the power to enter into all forms of *contracts and conveyances* (i.e., transfers of land) in their own names, independent of their husbands. If, however, both spouses own property together, the wife normally must have the consent of her husband—and vice versa—to convey the property to someone else.

What about contracts and conveyances between the spouses? Are there any restrictions on the ability of one spouse to enter into agreements with the

---

[1]An unmarried woman at common law was not as handicapped, since she could own property and enter into contracts in her own name. But she could not vote or serve on juries, and her inheritance rights were limited. H. Clark, *The Law of Domestic Relations in the United States*, § 8.1, p. 498 (Practitioner's ed. 2d ed. 1987).

other? If they are still living together, they cannot enter a contract concerning one spouse's duty to support the other (although such a contract will be valid after the parties have separated, page 230).

Courts tend to be very suspicious of conveyances of property between husband and wife. Suppose, for example, that a husband transfers all his property into his wife's name, for which she pays nothing, so that when he is sued by his creditors, he technically does not own any assets from which they can satisfy their claims. The transfers would be considered fraudulent and would be invalidated by a court.

Two other situations can cause difficulty:

- The husband buys property with his own funds but places the title in his wife's name. (Assume this is not a fraudulent transfer—he is not trying to defraud his creditors.)
- The wife buys property with her own funds but places the title in her husband's name. (Again, assume no intent to defraud her creditors.)

Some courts treat the above two situations differently. In the first, most courts presume that the husband intended to make a gift of the property to his wife. In the second circumstance, however, a few courts do *not* presume a gift of the wife to her husband. Rather, the presumption is that the husband is holding the property in trust for his wife. Arguably, however, this is an unconstitutional discrimination based on sex, and some courts have so held. In these courts, whatever one spouse contributes to the purchase price is considered a gift to the other spouse unless it is clear that they had a different intention.

Assignment 16.2

For the following questions, you will need to consult the statutory code of your state and/or the opinions of the courts sitting in your state. (See General Instructions for he State-Code Assignment and for the Court-Opinion Assignment in chapter one.)

(a) In your state, is there a Married Women's Property Act or an equivalent statute? If so, what is the citation?

(b) Is the consent of the husband required when his wife wishes to convey her separately owned property to a third person?

(c) What restrictions, if any, exist in your state on the capacity of one spouse to enter into a contract with the other?

(d) Suppose that a wife worked for her husband in the latter's business in your state. Does the husband have to pay her or would such work be considered part of the "services" that she owes him?

Section D. Death of the Husband

Dower

At common law, when a husband died, the surviving wife was given the protection of *dower,* although not all states defined dower in the same way. In many states, it was the right of a surviving wife to use one-third of all the real estate her deceased husband owned or acquired during the marriage which her issue, if any, could have inherited.[2] The practical impact of this law was that the husband could not give his property to others without accounting for her dower right. Very often she was paid to "waive her dower rights" in order to allow others to obtain clear title to this property.

Right of Election

Dower has been abolished in many states. In its place, the wife is given a share of her deceased husband's estate, often called a *forced share* because she can elect to take it in place of, and in spite of, what he gives her in his will. In exercising this right of election, she usually receives whatever the state would have provided for her if her husband had died intestate, i.e., without leaving a valid will.

Assignment 16.3

For the following questions, examine the statutory code of your state. (See General Instructions for the State-Code Assignment in chapter one.)

(a) Has dower been abolished in your state? If so, give the citation to the statute that abolished it.

(b) If a widow is not satisfied with the property left her in the will of her deceased husband, what can she do in your state? Can she elect against the will?

(c) If her husband dies intestate (i.e., without leaving a valid will), what proportion of his estate will his widow receive in your state?

(d) Does curtesy still exist in your state? If so, what is it? If not, what has replaced it, if anything?

Section E. Name

Most women change their surname to that of their husband at the time of marriage. This is done for one of two reasons:

- The law of the state gives her a choice on keeping her maiden name or taking her husband's name, and she chooses the latter.

- The law of the state gives her a choice that she does not know about; she uses her husband's name simply because that is the custom of her environment.

At one time, the law of some states *required* her to use her husband's name. Such laws have either been repealed or are clearly subject to constitutional attack since husbands are not required to take the name of their wife and no rational reason exists for the distinction. If she decides not to use her husband's name, she does not have to go through any special steps to exercise this choice.

---

[2]Some states imposed the requirement that she die leaving issue capable of inheriting the estate. If the wife died, the surviving husband was protected by *curtesy* which was the portion of his wife's estate, which he was entitled to use for the rest of his life.

Once she is married, she simply continues using her maiden name, or she starts using a totally new name (other than her husband's). In such states, her legal name is whatever name she uses after her marriage so long as she is not trying to defraud anyone (e.g., to make it difficult for her creditors to locate her), and so long as her use of the name is exclusive and consistent.

Once there has been a divorce, most states permit the woman to request that the court allow her to resume using her maiden name or another name. Some states, however, place restrictions on resuming a maiden name, or selecting a new name if there are children of the marriage.

Suppose that she makes the request that her child's name be changed to her maiden name or to the name of her new husband. Many courts are reluctant to authorize this change unless it can be shown to be in the best interest of the child.

Independent of marriage or divorce, there is a statutory procedure in every state that must be used when citizens (male or female) wish to change their name. This *change-of-name* procedure involves several steps, e.g., filing a petition to change one's name in the appropriate state court, stating the reasons for the change, paying a fee to the court, publishing a notice of the court proceeding in a local newspaper. The process is usually not complicated so long as the court is convinced that the name change will not mislead anyone who may need to contact the individual, e.g., police officials, a former spouse, creditors.

Assignment 16.4

For most of the following assignments, you will need to examine your state statutory code. You may also need to check opinions written by your state courts. (See General Instructions for the State-Code Assignment in chapter one, and for the Court-Opinion Assignment in chapter one.)

(a) When a woman marries in your state, does she have to take her husband's name?

(b) Following a divorce, how can a woman have her name changed back to her maiden name?

(c) Make a list of three different administrative agencies situated in your state that require the filling out of some kind of application e.g., for a driver's license, for state employment, for food stamps, for worker's compensation, etc. Assume that a recently married woman is filling out all of these applications, and she wants to use her maiden name, not her husband's name, on the application. She has not been through a change-of-name statutory procedure. Contact each agency and ask if a woman can use her maiden name on the application.

(d) Prepare a flowchart of all the steps that an individual must go through to change his or her name in your state through the appropriate statutory procedure. (See General Instructions for the Flowchart Assignment in chapter one.)

(e) Assume that you want to change your name. Pick a new name. Draft all the necessary court papers to acquire your new name via the statutory procedure outlined in the flowchart prepared in part "d."

(f) Mary Jones married Tom Smith in your state. Her name then became Mary Smith. They had one child, Paul Smith. Tom abandons Mary. Can Mary have Paul's name changed to Paul Jones in your state? Assume that Paul is five years old and that Mary does not want to bring a divorce proceeding against Tom.

Section F. Credit

In a *credit application*, federal law prohibits discrimination on the basis of sex or marital status.[3] Creditors such as banks or department stores that violate this prohibition can be sued and subject to punitive damages. In addition, a successful plaintiff can force the defendant to pay her court costs and reasonable attorney's fees in bringing the suit. Some of the specific prohibitions are as follows:

- A creditor cannot refuse to grant a woman an individual account because of her sex or marital status. For example, a woman cannot be required to open a joint account with her husband if she wants her own account and otherwise qualifies for one.
- A creditor cannot refuse a woman's request to open an account in her maiden name or in her hyphenated surname with her husband.
- A creditor cannot ask a woman for information about her husband or ex-husband unless she is relying on his income in seeking the credit.
- A creditor cannot ask about a woman's plans to have children. (In order to estimate her expenses, however, the creditor may ask how many children she has, their ages, and the cost of caring for them.)
- A creditor cannot require that a woman disclose income from alimony, child support, or separate maintenance in her application for credit. If, however, she decides to disclose such items, the creditor cannot refuse to consider them. Furthermore, she can be asked how regularly she receives them in order to determine whether they are dependable sources of income.
- A creditor cannot require that a woman use a courtesy title (Miss, Ms., or Mrs.) on the application form.
- A creditor cannot request a woman's marital status on an application for an individual, unsecured account (such as a bank credit card or an overdraft checking account) where no community property is involved. A creditor cannot discriminate against a woman because of her marital status, but may consider her marital status in deciding whether to extend credit to her if she lives in a state where differences in her marital status may affect the creditor's ability to collect if she defaults, e.g., in a community property state.
- A creditor cannot consider a woman's sex as a factor in deciding whether she is a good risk.

Section G. Employment

Job Discrimination

There are a good many laws that in theory have eliminated job discrimination against women. The Equal Protection Clause of the United States Constitution provides that:

---

[3]Or on the basis of race, color, religion, national origin, or age. 15 U.S.C.A. §§ 1691-1691f.

☐ **EXHIBIT 16–1** Charge of Discrimination

CHARGE OF DISCRIMINATION	ENTER CHARGE NUMBER
This form is affected by the Privacy Act of 1974; see Privacy Act Statement on reverse before completing this form.	☐ FEPA ☐ EEOC

_____ and EEOC
(State or local Agency, if any)

NAME *(Indicate Mr., Ms., or Mrs.)*	HOME TELEPHONE NO. *(Include Area Code)*
STREET ADDRESS CITY, STATE AND ZIP CODE	COUNTY

NAMED IS THE EMPLOYER, LABOR ORGANIZATION, EMPLOYMENT AGENCY, APPRENTICESHIP COMMITTEE, STATE OR LOCAL GOVERNMENT AGENCY WHO DISCRIMINATED AGAINST ME *(If more than one list below.)*

NAME	NO. OF EMPLOYEES/ MEMBERS	TELEPHONE NUMBER *(Include Area Code)*
STREET ADDRESS	CITY, STATE AND ZIP CODE	
NAME		TELEPHONE NUMBER *(Include Area Code)*
STREET ADDRESS	CITY, STATE AND ZIP CODE	

CAUSE OF DISCRIMINATION BASED ON *(Check appropriate box(es))* ☐ RACE ☐ COLOR ☐ SEX ☐ RELIGION ☐ NATIONAL ORIGIN ☐ AGE ☐ RETALIATION ☐ OTHER *(Specify)*	DATE MOST RECENT OR CONTINUING DISCRIMINATION TOOK PLACE *(Month, day, year)*

THE PARTICULARS ARE *(If additional space is needed, attached extra sheet(s))*:

☐ I also want this charge filed with the EEOC. I will advise the agencies if I change my address or telephone number and I will cooperate fully with them in the processing of my charge in accordance with their procedures.	NOTARY—(When necessary to meet State and Local Requirements)
	I swear or affirm that I have read the above charge and that it is true to the best of my knowledge, information and belief.
I declare under penalty of perjury that the foregoing is true and correct.	SIGNATURE OF COMPLAINANT SUBSCRIBED AND SWORN TO BEFORE ME THIS DATE *(Day, month, and year)*
Date Charging Party *(Signature)*	

EEOC FORM 5   PREVIOUS EDITIONS OF THIS FORM ARE OBSOLETE AND MUST NOT BE USED
     MAR 84

FILE COPY

> No State shall . . . deny to any person within its jurisdiction the equal protection of the laws.

If a state passes a law that treats women differently from men, it will be invalidated unless there is a reasonable purpose for the differentiation. Only *unreasonable* discrimination violates the constitution. *Title VII* of the 1964 *Civil Rights Act* provides that:

> It shall be an unlawful employment practice for an employer . . . to fail or refuse to hire or to discharge any individual, or otherwise to discriminate against any individual with respect to his compensation, terms, conditions, or privileges of employment, because of such individual's . . . sex; . . . 42 U.S.C.A. § 2000e-2(a)(1)(1974).

Again, this does not mean that all sex discrimination in employment is illegal. If men and women are doing the same job in a company but are being paid differently, the practice would be invalid, since they are both performing the same job. *Job-related* sex discrimination is permitted, however, if sex is a *Bona Fide Occupational Qualification (BFOQ)*, meaning that sex discrimination is reasonably necessary to the operation of a particular business or enterprise. For example, it would be proper for a state prison to exclude women from being guards in all-male prisons where a significant number of the inmates are convicted sex offenders. It is reasonable to anticipate that some of the inmates would attack the female guards, creating a security problem. In this instance, the discrimination based on sex (i.e., being a male) in an all-male prison would be a BFOQ. An even clearer example of a BFOQ would be an acting job that required someone to play a mother. On the other hand, a BFOQ does *not* exist simply because customers or co-workers prefer a person of a particular sex to fill a position.

Finally, an employer cannot refuse to hire a woman because of her pregnancy-related condition so long as she is able to perform the major functions necessary to the job. Also, an employer may not terminate workers because of pregnancy, force them to go on leave at an arbitrary point during pregnancy if they are still able to work, or penalize them in reinstatement rights, including credit for previous service, accrued retirement benefits, and accumulated seniority.

Sexual Harassment

Sexual harassment is also an unlawful employment practice under Title VII of the Civil Rights Act. Unwelcome sexual advances, requests for sexual favors, and other verbal or physical conduct of a sexual nature constitute sexual harassment when:

- Submission to such conduct is either explicitly or implicitly made a term or condition of an individual's employment; or
- Submission to or rejection of such conduct by an individual is used as the basis for employment decisions affecting that person; or
- Such conduct has the purpose or effect of unreasonably interfering with an individual's work performance or creating an intimidating, hostile, or offensive working environment.

It is not a defense for an employer to say that it did not know that one of its employees engaged in sexual harassment of another employee, or that the harassment took place in spite of an explicit company policy forbidding it. If it *should have known of the harassing conduct,* the employer must take immediate and appropriate corrective action, which usually entails more than merely announcing to all employees not to engage in sexual harassment.

Enforcement

The *Equal Employment Opportunity Commission* (EEOC) is a federal agency with the primary responsibility of enforcing Title VII of the Civil Rights Act. A charge of employment discrimination (see Exhibit 16–1) can be made to the EEOC through its offices throughout the country.

Most states have a *fair employment practices* (FEP) law that also provides protection against sex discrimination in employment. A complaint can be initiated at an EEOC office or at the state or city agency that administers the local FEP law.

The major complaint leveled against the laws outlawing sex discrimination in employment is that they have been very inadequately enforced. The law of discrimination can be complex and confusing. Bringing a discrimination case is usually time-consuming and expensive. Many feel we have a long way to go before the problem is solved.

Section H. Sexuality and Reproductive Rights

Topics relevant to a discussion of sexuality and reproductive rights:

- Contraception
- Sterilization
- Abortion
- New routes to motherhood
- Lesbianism

The first three topics are discussed below. New routes to motherhood, covering surrogate motherhood, in vitro fertilization, and similar themes are examined in chapter 20 (page 524). Legal problems involving homosexuality and lesbianism are covered in the chapters on marriage (page 170) and adoption (page 498).

Contraception

Married and unmarried individuals cannot be denied access to contraceptives. "If the right of privacy means anything, it is the right of the *individual,* married or single, to be free from unwarranted governmental intrusion into matters so fundamentally affecting a person as the decision whether to bear or beget a child." *Eisenstadt v. Baird,* 405 U.S. 438, 453, 92 S.Ct. 1029, 1038, 31 L.Ed.2d 349 (1972).

☐ NOW President Molly Yard addresses a gathering of abortion-rights activists in Washington D.C.

Sterilization

There are state laws that authorize the forced sterilization of persons legally considered mentally retarded or insane to prevent them from reproducing. To date this practice has *not* been declared unconstitutional. If, however, the United States Supreme Court were asked to rule on the practice today, it would probably conclude that there are constitutional problems with the practice. The most definitive pronouncement of the Supreme Court was made over sixty years ago. The Court decided that the state could sterilize a person it termed "feeble-minded," an institutionalized eighteen-year-old who was the daughter of a feeble-minded woman in the same institution, and who had already had a baby that was feeble-minded. In a well-known passage, Justice Oliver Wen-

□ A woman marches with her children to protest legalized abortion.

dell Holmes said, "Three generations of imbeciles are enough." *Buck v. Bell,* 274 U.S. 200, 208, 47 S.Ct. 584, 585, 71 L.Ed. 1000 (1927).

Abortion

To understand the recent law of abortion, we need to look at three periods of history: the time before *Roe v. Wade,* the time between *Roe* and *Webster* v. *Reproductive Health Services,* and the time since *Webster.*

Before Roe

In the early 1970s, abortion was a crime in every state. It was permitted only when the health of the woman necessitated it (usually to preserve her life) or when special circumstances warranted it, e.g., when the pregnancy was caused by rape or incest.

Roe

In 1973 the law was dramatically changed by the landmark case of *Roe v. Wade,* 410 U.S. 113, 93 S.Ct. 705, 35 L.Ed.2d 147 (1973), in which the United States Supreme Court held that a pregnant woman's right to privacy included her right to terminate the pregnancy. The right, however, was not absolute:

1. For the stage prior to approximately the end of the first trimester, the abortion decision and its effectuation must be left to the medical judgment of the pregnant woman's attending physician.

2. For the stage subsequent to approximately the end of the first trimester, the state, in promoting its interests in the health of the mother, may, if it chooses, regulate the abortion procedure in ways that are reasonably related to maternal health.

3. For the stage subsequent to viability, the state in promoting its interest in the potentiality of human life may, if it chooses, regulate, and even proscribe, abortion except where it is necessary, in appropriate medical judgment, for the preservation of the life or health of the mother.

A major theme of *Roe* was that the state should not be regulating abortions until *viability,*[3] unless the regulations were clearly necessary to protect the health of the mother. Otherwise, during the first trimester when a fetus is not viable, the state should not prohibit a woman from obtaining an abortion from a doctor. *Roe* held that to deny her this right would infringe upon her constitutional right to privacy. Different considerations applied during the next twelve weeks—the second trimester. Between the end of the first trimester and the beginning of the child's viability (a child is usually considered viable after about six months), the state could regulate medical procedures to make sure that abortions are performed safely but could not prohibit abortions altogether. Once the child is viable—during the third trimester—abortions could be prohibited unless they were necessary to preserve the life or health of the mother.

The Court later reinforced *Roe* by holding that a wife may have an abortion without the consent of her husband.

Some limits, however, were upheld. For example, if a poor woman wanted an abortion for nonhealth reasons (a nontherapeutic abortion), the state was *not required* to pay for it, although a number of states decided to set aside funds for such abortions. Also, if a pregnant minor was living with and dependent on her parents, it was permissible for a state to require that the parents be notified of, and give their consent to, the child's desire to have an abortion—so long as the girl had the opportunity to go to court to try to convince a judge that she was a mature minor and that therefore parental notice and consent was not needed in her particular case.

---

[3]Viability is a medical term that usually refers to that stage of fetal development when the life of the unborn child may be continued indefinitely outside the womb by natural or artificial life-support systems.

These restrictions in *Roe*, however, did not significantly limit the large number of abortions performed in America—approximately 1.5 million a year.

Webster

In the 1989 case of *Webster v. Reproductive Health Services*, 492 U.S. 490, 109 S.Ct. 3040, 106 L.Ed.2d 410 (1989), the Supreme Court again examined abortion, "the most politically divisive domestic legal issue of our time." *Roe* was not overturned by *Webster*, but many felt that *Webster* signaled the coming of major new roadblocks to abortion, and perhaps an eventual return to the days when a state could make abortion a crime.

Webster moved away from the trimester analysis of *Roe*. Justice Rehnquist said that the "rigid trimester" framework of *Roe* was "unsound in principle and unworkable in practice." He also said that the state had an interest in protecting potential human life before viability as well as after viability.

Among other things, *Webster* held that a state could ban the use of public employees and public facilities for the performance of nontherapeutic abortions, and could require physicians to test for fetal viability after twenty weeks. The Court did not hold that every state had to ban abortions at public facilities, nor that every state had to order this kind of viability testing. It simply said that such restrictions would not be unconstitutional *if* a state decided to impose them. The impact of *Webster* was to thrust the abortion issue back to the legislatures of every state. What about other restrictions on the right to an abortion? Chief Justice Rehnquist said, "There is no doubt that our holding today will allow some governmental regulation of abortion that would have been prohibited [in the past]." Arguably, this was an open invitation to anti-abortion states to create new restrictions or to resurrect some of the old ones that had been struck down under *Roe*.

Many questions, therefore, remained unanswered after *Webster*. Suppose, for example, that a state passed a law requiring all abortions to be conducted at full-service hospitals, or a law requiring women seeking abortions to wait forty-eight hours before proceeding, or to view photographs of developing fetuses before consenting to the abortion. In the past, similar laws were struck down as being inconsistent with *Roe*. The signal from *Webster*, however, was that such restrictions might be upheld in the future. In short, after *Webster*, the law of abortion was left in a state of turmoil.

Section I. The Battered Wife

Consider the following facts:

- Spousal violence occurs in close to one of every three marriages. Trent, *Wife Beating: A Psycho-Legal Analysis,* Case and Comment 14 (November–December 1979).

- Almost 2 million women are beaten by their husbands each year. Over half of these husbands beat their wives at least three times a year.

- One-third of murdered women are killed by their husbands or lovers.

- According to a recent poll, 20 percent of all Americans (and 25 percent of college-educated Americans) condone the use of physical violence in marriage. Strong and DeVault, The Marriage and Family Experience, 427 (4th ed. 1989).

These alarming figures are actually considered low, since wife beating is one of the most underreported crimes in the country.

Historically, the wife was considered the property of her husband in many respects. Hence it is not surprising to find religious and legal approval of his use of physical force against her. Around 1475, for example, Friar Cherubino of Siena compiled the following *Rules of Marriage:*

> When you see your wife commit an offense, don't rush at her with insults and violent blows. . . . Scold her sharply and terrify her. And if this still doesn't work . . . take up a stick and beat her soundly, for it is better to punish the body and correct the soul than to damage the soul and spare the body. . . . Then readily beat her, not in rage but out of charity and concern for her soul, so that the beating will redound to your merit and her good. Quoted in T. Davidson, *Conjugal Crime,* 99 (1978).

Hence, wife beating was acceptable and indeed was considered a duty of the husband. Society even condoned a particular weapon for the deed: a "rod not thicker than his thumb," or a stick that was not too thick to pass through a wedding ring! United States Commission on Civil Rights, Under the Rule of Thumb: Battered Women and the Administration of Justice 2 (January 1982).

In 1864, a North Carolina court upheld a man's use of force against his wife.

State v. Black

Supreme Court of North Carolina
60 N.C. 274 (1 Winst. 266) (1864)

Summary:

A husband cannot be convicted of battery on his wife, unless he inflicts a permanent injury, or uses such excessive violence or cruelty, as indicates malignity or vindictiveness: and it makes no difference that the husband and wife are living separate by agreement.

This was an indictment of assault and battery, tried before BAILEY, Judge, at—Term of Ashe Superior Court, 1864.

The defendant was indicted for an assault on Tamsey Black, his wife. The evidence showed, that the defendant and his wife lived separate from one another. The defendant was passing by the house of one Koonce, where his wife then resided, when she called to him in an angry manner and asked him, if he had patched Sal Daly's bonnet, (Sal Daly being a woman of ill-fame.)

She then went into the house, and defendant followed her and asked her what she wanted, when she repeated her question about the bonnet. Angry words then passed between them. He accused her of connection with a negro man, and she called him a hog thief, whereupon the defendant seized her by her hair, and pulled her down upon the floor, and held her there for sometime. He gave her no blows, but she stated on the trial, that her head was considerably hurt, and that her throat was injured, and continued sore for several months, but that he did not choke her, nor attempt to do so. At the trial she was entirely recovered. After she got up from the floor, she continued her abuse of him. A verdict of guilty was entered, subject to the opinion of the Court. The Judge, being of opinion with the State, gave judgment accordingly.

Winston, Sr., for the State
No counsel for the defendant in this Court.

PEARSON, C. J. A husband is responsible for the acts of his wife, and he is required to govern his household, and for that purpose, the law permits him to use towards his wife such a degree of force, as is necessary to control an unruly temper, and make her behave herself; and unless some permanent injury is inflicted, or there be an excess of violence, or such a degree of cruelty as shows that it is inflicted to gratify his own bad passions, the law will not invade the domestic forum, or go behind the curtain. It prefers to leave the parties to themselves, as the best mode of inducing them to make the matter up and live together as man and wife should.

Certainly, the exposure of a scene like that set out in this case, can do no good. In respect to the parties, a public exhibition in the Court House of such quarrels and fights between man and wife, widens the breach, makes a reconciliation almost impossible, and encourages insubordination; and in respect to the public, it has a pernicious tendency: so, *pro bono publico,* such matters are excluded from the Courts, unless there is a permanent injury or excessive violence or cruelty indicating malignity and vindictiveness.

In this case the wife commenced the quarrel. The husband, in a passion provoked by excessive abuse, pulled her upon the floor by the hair, but restrained himself, did not strike a blow, and she admits he did not choke her, and she continued to abuse him after she got up. Upon this state of facts the jury ought to have been charged in favor of the defendant. *State v. Pendergrass,* 18 N. C., 365; *Joyner v. Joyner,* 59 N. C., 322.

It was insisted by Mr. Winston that, admitting such to be the law when the husband and wife lived together, it did not apply when, as in the case, they were living apart. That may be so when there is a divorce "from bed and board," because the law then recognizes and allows the separation, but it can take no notice of a private agreement to live separate. The husband is still responsible for her acts, and the marriage relation and its incidents remain unaffected.

This decision must be certified to the Superior Court of law for Ashe County, that it may proceed according to law.

Eventually, laws were passed outlawing wife beating. Yet the crime continues at an alarming rate today. As indicated, women frequently do not report such violence, particularly when they are still living with their abuser/husband. Furthermore, when a women does report the incident to the authorities, she often is not taken seriously. Many complain that the police handle violence in a "domestic quarrel" differently, that is, less seriously, from an assault on the street between strangers. Politically active women's groups have campaigned for a change in the attitude and policies of courts, legislatures, and law enforcement agencies. In addition, they have fought for the creation of shelters to which battered women can flee.

If a woman is persistent and desperate enough, her main remedy is to go to court to ask for an injunction (see Exhibit 16–2), which is a court order to do or to refrain from doing something. In this situation, the injunction is to stop abusing the plaintiff and/or her children. Depending on the state, the injunction is called a *restraining order* or a *protective order.*

For purposes of obtaining the injunction, abuse is often defined in language such as the following:

Abuse
Attempting to cause bodily injury or intentionally, knowingly, or recklessly causing bodily injury, or by threat of force placing another person in fear of imminent serious physical harm.

In addition to the civil remedy of an injunction, a woman can ask the state to prosecute the defendant for a crime, e.g., assault, aggravated assault, battery, aggravated battery, reckless conduct, disorderly conduct, harassment. Some states have special crimes that are limited to acts committed against a spouse.

Unfortunately, these civil and criminal remedies have not been effective in substantially decreasing the incidence of domestic violence. In fact, many argue that the violence is on the rise.

Some women have taken the extreme step of killing the husband who has been abusing them. Does this killing constitute the crime of murder or man-

☐ **EXHIBIT 16–2** Protective Order

3-116.3

SUPERIOR COURT OF CALIFORNIA, COUNTY OF
STREET ADDRESS:
MAILING ADDRESS:
CITY AND ZIP CODE:
BRANCH NAME:

FOR COURT USE ONLY

PROTECTED PERSON (NAME):

RESTRAINED PERSON (NAME):

EMERGENCY PROTECTIVE ORDER

COURT CASE NUMBER:

1. **THIS EMERGENCY PROTECTIVE ORDER WILL EXPIRE AT 5 P.M. ON :**
   (INSERT DATE OF NEXT COURT DAY)

2. Reasonable grounds appear that an immediate danger of domestic violence exists and this order should be issued

   a. AGAINST RESTRAINED PERSON *(name)* : _____

   b. WHO must not contact, molest, attack, strike, threaten, sexually assault, batter, telephone, or otherwise harass or disturb the peace of the protected person

   (1) ☐ or the peace of the following family or household members *(names)* : _____
   _____
   _____

   c. ☐ WHO must stay away from the protected person at least *(yards)* : _____

   d. ☐ WHO must move out and not return to the residence at *(address)* : _____

3. ☐ Temporary custody of the following minor children is given to the protected person:

   Children *(names and ages)* : _____
   _____

4. ☐ The protected person has been given a copy of this order, the application, and instructions about how to get a more permanent order.

5. Date: _____

6. **Law Enforcement Officer:** . . . . ▶ _____
   (PRINT NAME)   (SIGNATURE)

   a. Badge No.: _____   b. Incident Case No.: _____

   c. Agency: _____   d. Telephone No.: _____

7. **Service of this order and application on the restrained person was completed as follows:**

	Date	Time	Signature
a. ☐ I orally advised person of contents:	_____	_____	_____
b. ☐ I personally gave person copies:	_____	_____	_____

   DESCRIPTION OF RESTRAINED PERSON (fill out what you know)

   (1) approximate age: _____   (4) weight: _____   (7) vehicle make: _____

   (2) race: _____   (5) hair color: _____   (8) vehicle model: _____

   (3) height: _____   (6) eye color: _____   (9) vehicle license No.: _____

   (10) other distinguishing features: _____

   VIOLATION OF THIS ORDER IS A MISDEMEANOR PUNISHABLE BY A $1000 FINE, SIX MONTHS IN JAIL, OR BOTH.
   THIS ORDER SHALL BE ENFORCED BY ALL LAW ENFORCEMENT OFFICERS IN THE STATE OF CALIFORNIA.

   (See reverse for important notices)

Form Adopted by Rule 1295.95
Judicial Council of California
1295.95 (New July 1, 1988)

EMERGENCY PROTECTIVE ORDER
(Domestic Violence Prevention)

Code of Civil Procedure, § 546(b)

WHITE copy to court, CANARY to restrained person, PINK to protected person slaughter? In part, the answer depends on when the killing occurs. Compare the predicament of the women in the following two situations. Assume that both women had been physically abused by their husband for years:

> Carol is being physically attacked by her husband, who is coming at her with a knife. As he approaches, Carol shoots him.

> Hours after being beaten by her husband, Helen takes a gun to his bedroom and shoots him while he is asleep.

It is highly unlikely that Carol has committed a crime. She is protected by the traditional defense of self-defense. Citizens can use deadly force that they reasonably believe is necessary to protect themselves from imminent death or serious bodily injury.

What about Helen? Unless she can prove temporary insanity, she must establish the elements of self-defense to avoid conviction. But she apparently was not in *imminent* danger at the time she shot her husband. Arguably, for example, she could have left the home while he was sleeping if she felt that he might kill or maim her once he awoke. Women in Helen's situation have been prosecuted for crimes such as manslaughter and murder.

In these prosecutions, a novel argument that is often raised by the woman is the *battered wife syndrome*. She claims that she acted out of a *psychological paralysis*. A variety of circumstances combined to block all apparent avenues of escape: financial dependence, loneliness, guilt, shame, and fear of reprisal from her husband. Buda & Bulter, *The Battered Wife Syndrome*, 23 Journal of Family Law 359 (1984–85). From this state of helplessness, she kills her husband. This argument is not an independent defense, it is an argument designed to bolster the self-defense argument. More accurately, it is an attempt to broaden the definition of *imminent danger* in self-defense. To a woman subjected to the psychological terror and paralysis of long-term abuse, the danger from her husband is real and close at hand. At any moment his behavior might trigger a flashback in her mind to an earlier beating, causing her to honestly believe that she is in immediate danger.

Prosecutors are not sympathetic to the battered-wife-syndrome argument. They say it is too easy to exaggerate the extent of the abuse, and more importantly, the extent to which the abuse resulted in such a state of paralysis that the wife felt her only way to protect herself—immediately—was to kill her husband. Some courts, however, are at least willing to listen to testimony on the syndrome. This has been very helpful for the defendant because when jurors hear this testimony, they are often reluctant to return guilty verdicts even if the traditional elements of self-defense that the judge instructs them to apply does not warrant such a verdict.

Assignment 16.5

For the following questions, see General Instructions for the State-Code Assignment in chapter one.

(a) In your state, if a wife is threatened with violence, what remedies does she have?

(b) When, if ever, can an injunction or protective order be issued *ex parte*, meaning that the defendant is not present in court when the order is issued?

(c) Without justification, a husband stabs his wife, but does not kill her. What are the possible crimes the husband can be charged with in your state?

Assignment 16.6

Prepare a flowchart on obtaining an injunction (or restraining order) against violence threatened by a husband against his wife in your state. (See General Instructions for the Flowchart Assignment in chapter one.)

Assignment 16.7

(a) Do you think that a court encourages killing when it allows evidence of the battered wife syndrome to be introduced in trials of women who kill their spouses? Explain why or why not.

(b) Do you think it is possible for a battered *husband* syndrome to exist? Explain why or why not?

Section J. Marital Rape

The common-law rule was that a husband cannot rape his wife. "The husband cannot be guilty of rape committed by himself upon his lawful wife, for by their mutual matrimonial consent and contract, the wife hath given up herself in this kind unto her husband which she cannot retract." 1 M. Hale, *The History of the Pleas of the Crown* 629 (1736). This view is still the law in some states. Most states, however, allow prosecution if the couple is living apart and a petition has been filed for divorce or separate maintenance. The reluctance of courts and legislatures to allow the criminal law of rape to apply to married couples is in part based on a fear that evidence of nonconsent to sexual intercourse will be fabricated.

Assignment 16.8

Under what circumstances, if any, can a husband be guilty of raping his wife in your state? (See General Instructions for the State-Code Assignment and for the Court-Opinion Assignment in chapter one.)

Key Chapter Terminology

Sex Discrimination	Fair Employment Practices
Married Women's Property Acts	Reproductive Rights
Contracts and Conveyances	Contraception
Credit Application	Sterilization
Dower	Abortion
Curtesy	*Roe v. Wade*
Right of Election	Viability
Forced Share	*Webster v. Reproductive Health Services*

Change of Name
Civil Rights Act
Title VII
Bona Fide Occupational Qualification
    (BFOQ)
Sexual Harassment
Equal Employment Opportunity
    Commission

Battered Wife Syndrome
Restraining Order
Protective Order
Imminent Danger
Marital Rape

CHAPTER SEVENTEEN

Illegitimacy and Paternity Proceedings

■ Chapter Outline

At one time, an illegitimate child had very few rights. This situation has changed, although the discrimination has not been entirely eliminated. An illegitimate child can now fully inherit from his or her father who dies intestate. Some states insist, however, that paternity be established before the parent dies. If the parent dies testate, leaving property "to my children," or "to my heirs," the answer to the question of whether illegitimate children were included in these phrases depends on the intent of the parent.

Legitimate and illegitimate children have the same right to be supported, to bring wrongful-death actions because of the death of a parent, and to receive worker's compensation benefits if the parent dies on the job. To obtain social security benefits, however, an illegitimate child must prove he or she was dependent on a deceased father, whereas the law presumes the dependence of a legitimate child.

In most states, when a child is born through artificial insemination with the semen of a man other than the husband, the latter has a duty to support the child, and the child is considered legitimate if the husband consented to the insemination.

Legitimation can occur in a number of ways: acknowledgment of paternity, marriage of the mother and father, legitimation proceeding, paternity proceeding, etc. In some states, all children are legitimate regardless of whether the mother and father ever married.

A major function of a paternity proceeding is to establish a father's duty of support. For this purpose, the court must have personal jurisdiction over him. The child should be joined as a party in the proceeding to ensure that the judgment will be binding on the child. If the defendant is married to the mother, he faces a number of evidentiary obstacles at the trial, e.g., the presumption of legitimacy and Lord Mansfield's rule. Traditional blood-group testing can help establish the nonpaternity, though not the paternity, of a particular defendant. More modern scientific techniques, however, claim the ability to establish the high probability of paternity.

Some states allow fathers who do not wish to contest paternity to file a formal document acknowledging paternity.

Section A. Illegitimacy

"The status of illegitimacy has expressed through the ages society's condemnation of irresponsible liaisons beyond the bonds of marriage. But visiting this condemnation on the head of an infant is illogical and unjust. Moreover, imposing disabilities on the illegitimate child is contrary to the basic concept of our system that legal burdens should bear some relationship to individual responsibility or wrongdoing. Obviously, no child is responsible for his birth and penalizing the illegitimate child is an ineffectual—as well as an unjust—way of deterring the parent. Courts are powerless to prevent the social opprobrium suffered by these hapless children, but the Equal Protection Clause does enable us to strike down discriminatory laws relating to status of birth where . . . the classification is justified by no legitimate state interest, . . ." *Weber* v. *Aetna Casualty & Surety Co.,* 406 U.S. 164, 175, 92 S.Ct. 1400, 1406, 31 L.Ed.2d 768 (1972).

At common law, the illegitimate child (still referred to as a *bastard* in many legal texts) was *filius nullius,* the child of nobody. The central disability imposed by this status was that the child born out of wedlock had no right to inherit from either parent. In addition, the child had no right to be supported by the father. Fortunately, the pronounced discrimination that has existed for centuries between the legitimate and the illegitimate child is eroding. This is not to say, however, that the discrimination has ended.

Inheritance

Statutes have been passed in most states permitting an illegitimate child to inherit from its mother when the latter dies *intestate,* i.e., without leaving a valid will. Some states have tried to prevent the child from inheriting from its father who dies intestate, but such laws have been declared unconstitutional. *Trimble* v. *Gordon,* 430 U.S. 762, 97 S.Ct. 1459, 52 L.Ed.2d 31 (1977). Cf. *Labine* v. *Vincent,* 401 U.S. 532, 91 S.Ct. 1017, 28 L.Ed.2d 288 (1971). Yet restrictions on inheritance do exist. For example, assume that an illegitimate child waits until after his or her father dies before declaring that a parent-child relationship existed. Some states would not allow such a child to inherit, insisting that paternity would have to be determined by a court *before* death as a condition of inheriting from an intestate parent.

Testate Distribution

Assume that the father of an illegitimate child dies testate (i.e., leaving a valid will), and that a clause in the will gives property "to my children" or "to my heirs." If the father has legitimate and illegitimate children living when he dies, the question sometimes arises as to whether he intended to include his illegitimate children in the word "children" or "heirs." In order to resolve this question of intent, the court must look at all of the circumstances, e.g., how much contact the illegitimate child had with the father at the time the latter wrote the will and at the time he died. A surprisingly large number of cases exist in which the court concluded that the illegitimate child was *not* included in the words "children" or "heirs."

Support

There was a time when many state laws did not obligate a father to support his illegitimate children. Such laws have been invalidated as an improper discrimination between legitimate and illegitimate children. Hence, so long as paternity can be established, a father has an equal duty to support all his children.

Wrongful Death

When a parent dies due to the wrongful act of another, who can sue? Legitimate and illegitimate children have an equal right to bring wrongful-death actions against defendants who have caused the death of one or both parents.

Workers' Compensation

When a father dies from an injury on the job, the workers' compensation laws of the state permit the children of the deceased to recover benefits. If the state gives a preference to legitimate children over illegitimate children in claiming these benefits, the state is unconstitutionally denying equal protection of the law to the illegitimate children.

Social Security

Social security laws discriminate against illegitimate children in various phases of the social security system. Some of these discriminatory provisions have been declared unconstitutional, yet others have been allowed to stand. While it is unconstitutional to deny social security survivorship benefits to a child solely because that child is illegitimate, it may be permissible to impose greater procedural burdens on illegitimate children than on legitimate children in applying for benefits. For example, if the law requires that a child be "dependent" on the deceased father as a condition of receiving survivorship benefits, an illegitimate child can be forced to *prove* that he or she was dependent on the father, whereas no such requirement will be imposed on the legitimate child—the law will *presume* that the legitimate child was dependent on the father without requiring specific proof of it.

Artificial Insemination

Artificial insemination occurs when a woman is impregnated with the semen of a donor without sexual intercourse (page 527). Three main kinds are possible:

1. Artificial insemination with the semen of the husband (AIH)

2. Artificial insemination with the semen of a third-party donor (AID)

3. Artificial insemination in which the semen of the husband is mixed (confused) with that of a third-party donor (AIC or CIA)

Children born through AIH are clearly legitimate; the natural father is the mother's husband. States differ as to the legitimacy of the children born through AID and AIC. In some states, such children are illegitimate. Most states, however, provide that the child is legitimate only if the insemination was with the consent of the husband of the mother. This consent also obligates the husband to support the child no matter how the insemination occurred.

Assignment 17.1

Answer the following questions by examining your state code. (See General Instructions for the State-Code Assignment in chapter one.)

(a) What are the inheritance rights of an illegitimate child in your state? From whom can an illegitimate child inherit?

(b) Who can inherit from an illegitimate child?

(c) Make a list of every mention of legitimacy/illegitimacy in your state code. Explain each reference, e.g., in what context and for what purpose is legitimacy/illegitimacy mentioned? (Do not include references to how an illegitimate child is legitimated, how paternity is proved, or what inheritance laws apply in this area.)

(d) Is a child born through artificial insemination legitimate?

Section B. Legitimation and Paternity

Legitimation is the process by which an illegitimate child becomes a legitimate child. A *paternity proceeding* is a process by which the fatherhood of a child is determined. In most states, a finding of paternity does not necessarily lead to the legitimation of the child.

Legitimation

States have different methods by which illegitimate children can be legitimated:

- *Acknowledgment.* The father publicly recognizes or acknowledges the illegitimate child as his. States differ on how this acknowledgment must take place. In some states, it must be in writing and witnessed. In others, no writing is necessary if the man's activities strongly indicate that he is the father of the child, e.g., the father treats the child the same as the children who were born legitimate.

- *Marriage.* If the mother and father of the illegitimate child marry, the child is usually automatically legitimated.

- *Combination of acknowledgment and marriage.* Some states require marriage of the parents and some form of acknowledgment by the father.

- *Legitimation proceeding.* A few states have special proceedings by which illegitimate children can be legitimated.

- *Paternity proceedings*. Although most paternity proceedings deal with fatherhood only, in a few states a finding of paternity also legitimates the child.
- *Legitimation by birth*. In a very few states, all children are legitimate whether or not their parents were married at the time of birth.

As indicated earlier, children of annulled marriages are considered legitimate according to special statutes, even though technically the parents were not validly married at the time the children were born (page 198).

Assignment 17.2

In what way(s) can an illegitimate child be legitimated in your state? (See General Instructions for the State-Code Assignment in chapter one.)

Paternity

A major method by which a father is forced to support his illegitimate child is through a *paternity proceeding,* sometimes called a *filiation proceeding* or a *bastardy proceeding*. Once fatherhood is determined, the support obligation is imposed.

The starting point in establishing paternity is to obtain detailed facts from the mother. A questionnaire with this objective is shown in Exhibit 17–1.

The paternity proceeding itself looks a good deal like a criminal proceeding in some states. A warrant is issued for the arrest of the putative (i.e., alleged) father, the jury renders a guilty or not guilty verdict, etc. In most states, however, the proceeding is civil rather than criminal.

The mother of the child is the one who usually initiates the paternity proceeding, although the child is often also given standing to sue through a specially appointed representative, e.g., a *guardian ad litem*. (Exhibit 17–2 shows a paternity petition.) When the mother brings the action, it is important to know whether the child was made a party to the proceeding and was represented. If not, then in some states, the child will not be bound by the judgment. For example:

> Mary, the mother of Sam, brings a paternity proceeding against Kevin, alleging he is the father of Sam. Sam is not made a party to the proceeding. A guardian ad litem is not appointed for him, and he is not otherwise represented in court. The court finds that Kevin is not the father of Sam. Ten years later, Sam brings his own action against Kevin for support, alleging that he is the son of Kevin.

Is Sam's support action ten years later barred by the defense of *res judicata*? That is, was the fatherhood issue already resolved in the paternity proceeding? States differ in their answer to this question. Many will bar the later suit of the child only if the latter was a party to the earlier case that decided the fatherhood issue. In such states, Sam *would* be able to relitigate the paternity issue against Kevin since he was not represented in the proceeding ten years earlier.

A related question is whether the mother can enter a settlement with the putative father under which she agrees to drop the paternity proceeding in

□ **EXHIBIT 17-1** Paternity Questionnaire

1. Your full name _____

   Your Social Security number _____

   Your address _____

   Your home phone _____ Your work phone _____

   Your date of birth _____

   With whom are you living: _____

2. List two people who will always know where you live:

   Name _____ Name _____

   Address _____ Address _____

   _____ _____

   Phone _____ Phone _____

3. Give the following information regarding the father of your child:

   Full name _____

   Address _____

   Date of birth _____ Social Security Number _____

   Home phone _____ Work phone _____

   Do you have a picture of the father? _____

4. Child's name _____ Child's date of birth _____ Child's sex _____

5. Do you have a picture of the child? _____

6. Does the child look like the father: _____

7. Does the child have the same coloring: _____

8. When and where did you meet the father: _____

9. When did you begin dating the father: _____

10. Did you ever live with the father: _____ If so, where and when: _____

    Landlord _____ Phone Number _____

    Address _____

11. Others that knew you were living together:

    Name _____ Name _____

    Relationship to you _____ Relationship to you _____

    Address _____ Address _____

    Phone _____ Phone _____

12. When did you first have sexual relations with the father: _____

13. When did you last have sexual relations with him? _____

☐ **EXHIBIT 17—1** Paternity Questionnaire—Continued

14. Where was the child conceived? (Where did you get pregnant):

    City _____ County _____ State _____

15. Date father was told that you were pregnant _____

16. Who told the father that you were pregnant: _____

17. What did he say when he was told you were pregnant: _____

    _____

18. Was a father listed on your child's birth certificate: _____ Did he sign

    it? _____

19. If no father was listed, explain why the father was not named on the birth

    certificate: _____

20. Write anything the father said suggesting to you that he is the child's
    father such as ''Isn't our baby cute.'' or ''I am glad you had my baby.''

    _____

    _____

21. Did the father sign any papers or write any letters suggesting he is your
    baby's father:

    _____

22. What did he sign: _____ Where: _____

23. Did the father offer to help pay for an abortion? If so briefly explain

    what he said, when, where, and if anyone else was present: _____

    _____

24. Did the father ever give or offer to give you money for the child? If so

    how much and when: _____

25. Did the father ever buy the child gifts: If so list the gifts and dates

    given: _____

    _____

26. Did you ever tell anyone that the father of your child is someone other

    than the man you are naming on this form: _____ If so, whom did

    you tell: _____

27. What was said (include name of other man named): _____

28. Give the names, addresses, phone numbers of all witnesses who may be called
    to testify who have:
    a. Seen you and the father together during time of conception (8—10 months
       prior to birth).

□ **EXHIBIT 17—1** Paternity Questionnaire—Continued

    b. Seen you and the father kissing, necking, petting, or aware of or have knowledge of any intimate relations you had with the alleged father.

    c. Heard the father make a statement to anyone about you getting an abortion or helping pay for an abortion.

    d. Heard the father make a statement to anyone suggesting or admitting he was the father of the child? (Indicate for each witness briefly what his or her testimony would be.)

    Name: _____ Phone #: _____

    Address: _____

    Testimony: _____

    Name: _____ Phone #: _____

    Address: _____

    Testimony: _____

29. Answer these questions for the 8th month before the birth (one month pregnant):

    a. Month _____ Year _____

    b. Were you having sex with the father: _____

    c. How frequently did you have intercourse: _____

    d. Did you use birth control on any occasion: _____

    e. Did the father use birth control on any occasion: _____

    f. Did you have sex with any other men during that month: _____ .
      If so, list their names, addresses or other information which may be helpful in locating them.

    Name _____ Address _____

    Phone # _____

    Name _____ Address _____

    Phone # _____

30. Answer these questions for the 7th month before the birth (two months pregnant):

    a. Month _____ Year _____

    b. Were you having sex with the father: _____

    c. How frequently did you have intercourse: _____

    d. Did you use birth control on any occasion: _____

    e. Did the father use birth control on any occasion: _____

    f. Did you have sex with any other men during that month: _____ .
      If so, list their names, addresses or other information which may be helpful in locating them.

□ **EXHIBIT 17–1** Paternity Questionnaire—Continued

Name _____ Address _____

Phone # _____

Name _____ Address _____

Phone # _____

31. Answer these questions for the 11th month before the birth (2 months before you became pregnant):

    a. Month _____ Year _____

    b. Were you having sex with the father: _____

    c. How frequently did you have intercourse: _____

    d. Did you use birth control on any occasion: _____

    e. Did the father use birth control on any occasion: _____

    f. Did you have sex with any other men during that month: _____ .
       If so, list their names, addresses or other information which may be helpful in locating them.

    Name _____ Address _____

    Phone # _____

    Name _____ Address _____

    Phone # _____

32. Answer these questions for the 10th month before the birth (1 month before you became pregnant):

    a. Month _____ Year _____

    b. Were you having sex with the father: _____

    c. How frequently did you have intercourse: _____

    d. Did you use birth control on any occasion: _____

    e. Did the father use birth control on any occasion: _____

    f. Did you have sex with any other men during that month: _____ .
       If so, list their names, addresses or other information which may be helpful in locating them.

    Name _____ Address _____

    Phone # _____

    Name _____ Address _____

    Phone # _____

33. Answer these questions for the 9th month before the birth (the month you became pregnant):

    a. Month _____ Year _____

    b. Were you having sex with the father: _____

☐ **EXHIBIT 17–1** Paternity Questionnaire—Continued

    c. How frequently did you have intercourse: _____

    d. Did you use birth control on any occasion: _____

    e. Did the father use birth control on any occasion: _____

    f. Did you have sex with any other men during that month: _____ .
       If so, list their names, addresses or other information which may be
       helpful in locating them.

       Name _____   Address _____

       Phone # _____

       Name _____   Address _____

       Phone # _____

34. Are you presently married _____ If so, give name of husband, _____

35. Date of Marriage _____ , Place of Marriage _____

36. Were you married at any time between one year before and one year after the
    birth of the child? _____ If so, give name of each husband, date, and
    place of marriage, and, if applicable, the date and place of divorce or
    annulment:

    Name _____   Date of marriage _____

    Place _____   Date of divorce/annulment _____

    Name _____   Date of marriage _____

    Place _____   Date of divorce/annulment _____

37. On what date did your last menstrual flow begin before the birth of your

    child: _____

38. On what date did your last menstrual flow end before the birth of your

    child: _____

39. Do you have a calendar or other records showing these dates: _____

40. Do you have a diary or other written records of the dates you had inter-

    course with your child's father: _____

41. Name of doctor who cared for you before the child was born: _____

42. Name of doctor who cared for child after birth: _____

43. Address: _____

44. Circle one: Child premature, overdue, or normal term.

45. Exact due date _____ Birth Weight _____

46. Who paid for the birth of the child

    FHP _____ Medicaid _____ Other (Please Name) ____

☐ **EXHIBIT 17—1** Paternity Questionnaire—Continued

47. Name of hospital in which child was born: _____

State of   )
) ss.
County of   )

_____ , being duly sworn states that she has read the above document and that the statements contained therein are true to the best of her knowledge.

_____

Signature

_____

Date

Subscribed and sworn to before me this _____ day of _____ , 19_____ .

_____

Notary Public

Resides at: _____

My Commission Expires: _____

exchange for defendant's agreement to pay a certain amount for the support of the child and for the mother's expenses in giving birth to the child. In some states, it is illegal to enter into such an agreement. In states where this type of settlement is permitted, the child must be represented and/or the settlement must be approved by the court.

The paternity proceeding is considered an *in personam* action requiring *personal jurisdiction* over the defendant-putative father (page 396). This generally means that service of process must be made on the defendant in person within the forum state, i.e., the state where the paternity proceeding is being brought. If the defendant is not a resident of the forum state, personal jurisdiction over him may be obtainable under the state's long-arm statute on the basis of his not having supported his alleged child in the forum state, or on the basis that his in-state acts of intercourse caused the mother's pregnancy.

Once the trial on the paternity issue begins, the defendant may be faced with a *presumption of legitimacy*. A child born to a married woman is presumed to be legitimate unless conclusively proven otherwise. This means that if the defendant is the husband of the mother and denies paternity, he must introduce very strong evidence that he is not the father, e.g., evidence that he is sterile. At one time, neither spouse could introduce evidence that he or she had no sexual intercourse around the time of conception (i.e., evidence of nonaccess) if such evidence would tend to *bastardize* the child. This was known

☐ **EXHIBIT 17—2** Paternity Petition

FAMILY COURT OF THE STATE OF
COUNTY OF

....

In the Matter of a Paternity Proceeding   Docket No.

_____ Petitioner,   PATERNITY PETITION
                                                          (Parent)
              -against-

_____ Respondent,

....

TO THE FAMILY COURT:

       The undersigned Petitioner respectfully shows that:

       1. Petitioner resides at _____

       2. Petitioner had sexual intercourse with the abovenamed Respon-
dent (on several occasions covering a period of time beginning on or about the
day of _____ , 19 ____ , and ending on or about the _____ day of _____
, 19 ____ , and as a result thereof (Petitioner) became pregnant.

       3. *(a) (Petitioner) gave birth to a (male) (female) child out of
wedlock on the _____ day of _____ , 19 ____ , at

         *(b) (Petitioner) is now pregnant with a child who is likely to
be born out of wedlock.

       4. (Respondent) who resides at _____ is the father of the child.

       5. (Respondent) (has acknowledged) (acknowledges) paternity of the
child (in writing) (and) (by furnishing support).

       6. No previous application has been made to any court or judge for
the relief sought herein (except _____

_____ .)

WHEREFORE, Petitioner prays that this Court issue a summons or warrant requiring the Respondent to show cause why the Court should not enter a declaration of paternity, an order of support and such other and further relief as may be appropriate under the circumstances.

                             _____

                                       Petitioner

Dated: _____ , 19 ____ .

*Alternative allegations.

as *Lord Mansfield's rule*. Hence, if a defendant had not had sexual intercourse with his wife in years, he could not introduce evidence to this effect if it would tend to bastardize the mother's recently born child.

The United States Supreme Court recently traced the origin of these rules in its opinion, *Michael H. v. Gerald D.*

Michael H. v. Gerald D.
United States Supreme Court
109 S.Ct. 2333, 2342–43 (1989)

The presumption of legitimacy was a fundamental principle of the common law. H. Nicholas, Adulturine Bastardy 1 (1836). Traditionally, that presumption could be rebutted only by proof that a husband was incapable of procreation or had had no access to his wife during the relevant period. *Id.*, at 9–10 (citing Bracton, De Legibus et Consuetudinibus Angliae, bk. i, ch. 9, p. 6; bk. ii, ch. 29, p. 63, ch. 32, p. 70 (1569)). As explained by Blackstone, nonaccess could only be proved "if the husband be out of the kingdom of England (or, as the law somewhat loosely phrases it, *extra quatuor maria* [beyond the four seas]) for above nine months. . . ." 1 Blackstone's Commentaries 456 (Chitty ed. 1826). And, under the common law both in England and here, "neither husband nor wife [could] be a witness to prove access or nonaccess." J. Schouler, Law of the Domestic Relations § 225, p. 306 (3d ed. 1882); R. Graveson & F. Crane, A Century of Family Law: 1857–1957, p. 158 (1957). The primary policy rationale underlying the common law's severe restrictions on rebuttal of the presumption appears to have been an aversion to declaring children illegitimate, see Schouler, *supra*, § 225, at 306–307; M. Grossberg, Governing the Hearth 201 (1985), thereby depriving them of rights of inheritance and succession, 2 Kent's Commentaries 175 (1827), and likely making them wards of the state. A secondary policy concern was the interest in promoting the "peace and tranquillity of States and families," Schouler, *supra*, § 225, at 304, quoting Boullenois, Traité des Status, bk. 1, p. 62, a goal that is obviously impaired by facilitating suits against husband and wife asserting that their children are illegitimate. Even though, as bastardy laws became less harsh, "[j]udges in both [England and the United States] gradually widened the acceptable range of evidence that could be offered by spouses, and placed restraints on the 'four seas rule' . . . [,] the law retained a strong bias against ruling the children of married women illegitimate." Grossberg, *supra*, at 202.

It is obviously very difficult for a husband to deny that he is the father of his wife's child. The harshness of this rule has been criticized. A number of states have either eliminated or substantially limited Lord Mansfield's rule.

The discovery of human *blood groups* and types has been of great assistance in paternity cases because they:

1. Can be determined at birth or shortly thereafter
2. Remain constant throughout an individual's life
3. Are inherited

In 1981, the United States Supreme Court commented on the operation and effectiveness of blood group tests as follows:

> If the blood groups and types of the mother and child are known, the possible and *impossible* blood groups and types of the true father can be determined under the rules of inheritance. For example, a group AB child cannot have a group O parent, but can have a group A, B, or AB parent. Similarly, a child cannot be type M unless one or both parents are type M, and the factor rh' cannot appear in the blood of a child unless present in the blood of one or both parents. . . .

Since millions of men belong to the possible groups and types, a blood grouping test cannot conclusively establish paternity. However, it can demonstrate *non-paternity,* such as where the alleged father belongs to group O and the child is group AB. It is a negative rather than an affirmative test with the potential to scientifically exclude the paternity of a falsely accused putative father.

The ability of blood grouping tests to exonerate innocent putative fathers was confirmed by a 1976 report developed jointly by the American Bar Association and the American Medical Association. Miale, Jennings, Rettberg, Sell & Krause, Joint AMA–ABA Guidelines: Present Status of Serologic Testing in Problems of Disputed Parentage, 10 Family L. Q. 247 (Fall 1976). The joint report recommended the use of seven blood test "systems"—ABO, Rh, MNS, Kell, Duffy, Kidd, and HLA—when investigating questions of paternity. . . . These systems were found to . . . provide a 91% cumulative probability of negating paternity for erroneously accused Negro men and 93% for white men. . . .

The effectiveness of the seven systems attests the probative value of blood test evidence in paternity cases. The importance of that scientific evidence is heightened because "[t]here are seldom accurate or reliable eye witnesses since the sexual activities usually take place in intimate and private surroundings, and the self-serving testimony of a party is of questionable reliability." Larson, *Blood Test Exclusion Procedures in Paternity Litigation: The Uniform Acts and Beyond,* 13 J. Family L. 713 [1974].

Little v. Streater, 452 U.S. 1, 101 S.Ct. 2202, 68 L.Ed.2d 627 (1981).

Since the preceding commentary was written in 1981, the effectiveness of scientific testing has significantly increased. Today newly discovered serologic and statistical methods have made major changes in the law of evidence in this area. A "wider range of genetic tests have come to be admissible, and not merely to demonstrate that it is biologically impossible for a particular man to be the father, but also to show that it is highly probable that a specific man *is* the father." Kay & Kanwischer, *Admissibility of Genetic Testing in Paternity Litigation,* 22 Family L. Quarterly 109, 109–10 (1988). The tests are used to indicate the likelihood or *probability of paternity* of a man who is not excluded by the tests:

The test results will establish whether your client is excluded as being the father of the child; or if not, what is the probability or likelihood of his being the actual father. If the client is excluded by the blood test, then the case has ended and the mother will have to accuse some other man as being the father. If your client is not excluded, the probability or likelihood of his paternity will be mathematically determined. The likelihood that he is the actual father is then compared statistically to that of a fictional man who is assumed to have had sexual intercourse with the mother and who is assumed not to be excluded by the test. These results are expressed in the form of a "paternity index" and in the form of a "probability of paternity". For example, the paternity index would be expressed as (53 to 1) fifty-three to one; that is, the putative father is fifty-three times more likely to have fathered the child than some other man who could have had intercourse with the mother and who would not be excluded by the blood test. The "probability of paternity" is generally expressed in a percentage figure; for example, 98.15%. Neubaum, *Defense of Paternity Cases,* Case & Comment, 38–39 (July–August, 1987).

Special testing laboratories have been established to conduct these tests. An example of how one such laboratory operates follows in Exhibit 17–3.

☐ **EXHIBIT 17–3** Paternity Testing Procedures

PATERNITY TESTING
Parker Laboratories

Parker Laboratories, provides paternity testing for disputed paternity cases. The tests performed at Parker are ABO, HLA, Rh, MNSs, Duffy, Kidd and Kell. ABO, Rh, MNSs and HLA typing will be performed on all non-excluded cases. The cumulative probability of exclusion (CPE) for these four systems is 97% for Caucasians and 96% for Blacks. Duffy, Kidd and Kell typings are reserved for the non-excluded cases with low likelihoods of paternity. The addition of these three systems provides a CPE of 98% for Caucasians and 97% for Blacks.

If more markers are required, the blood will be sent to a reference laboratory for serum protein and red cell enzyme testing. When combined with the testing performed at the Parker Laboratories, this further testing yields a CPE greater than 99%.

Paternity cannot be proven with 100% certainty. Non-paternity can be proven by obtaining exclusions..

The charge is $170.00 per person regardless of which tests are required for conclusive results. The amount must be paid by money order, certified check, cashier's check or attorney's check at the time the blood is drawn or mailed to us prior to the appointment. Cash or personal checks will not be accepted. Payment will be waived only if prior arrangements for billing have been made with county or state agencies. Free depositions by the medical director and/or a medical technologist are available, if taken at the Parker Laboratories. Court testimony is available at a fee of $75.00 per hour for the medical director or $25.00 per hour for a medical technologist. These rates, plus travel expenses, are charged for each hour the witness is absent from the laboratory in connection with providing court testimony. NOTE: Because of medical responsibilities to the Parker Laboratories, the medical director is not to be more than two (2) hours away from the laboratory for an extended period of time for court testimony.

Testing will be performed in duplicate by separate technologists and reviewed by the medical director before mailing. A copy of the final results will be sent to the alleged father's attorney, the mother's attorney and the child's attorney, if any. An explanation of the results will accompany the final reports.

We recommend that the mother, alleged father and child's blood specimens be drawn at the same time and place, preferably at the Parker laboratory, in order that each can serve as witness to the event. At the time an appointment for paternity testing is made, the following information is required:

1. Name of alleged father
2. Name of mother
3. Name and age of child
4. Names, addresses and phone numbers of all attorneys involved

If it is not possible for the parties to come to the laboratory to have specimens drawn, a kit will be sent to the laboratory that will be drawing the blood. However, the Parker Laboratories does not take responsibility for any errors in identification of the blood samples if they are not drawn at our laboratory. The kit will contain all information necessary for the drawing and sending of the blood; e.g., instructions for drawing, identification and consent forms, tubes and labels. A witness must sign the identi-

☐ **EXHIBIT 17–3** Paternity Testing Procedures—Continued

fication and consent forms, check the driver's license of each party and ensure that the tubes are properly labelled. Photographs and fingerprints are required to be taken on all parties.

Specimens must reach Parker Laboratories within 24 hours after being drawn. Federal Express or some other similar air carrier service which delivers within 24 hours is recommended. Blood should arrive at our laboratory before 10:30 a.m. on the day of the scheduled appointment.

If testing is required from a reference laboratory, letters will be sent immediately to all involved attorneys concerning the further testing.

A written report of final test results will be mailed within a two week period in most cases. Phone reports will not be given.

In criminal law, a major controversy exists on the admissibility of genetic fingerprinting through *DNA testing,* depicted in Exhibit 17–4. From a specimen of blood, semen, or hair, scientists identify a biological or *genetic code.* The likelihood of two people having the same DNA pattern (except for identical twins) is astronomically low. In family law, companies such as Cellmark Diagnostics have used such tests to establish paternity. Parents are identified by matching their genetic material to that of the child. The odds against two unrelated people having the same genetic fingerprinting are said to be about 50 billion to one!

In a recent case, the probability of paternity of a particular man who had undergone DNA testing was said to be 99.98000 percent, as compared to an untested North American Caucasian. In the case of *In re Paternity of J.L.K.,* 445 N.W.2d 673, 674 (Wis. Ct. App. 1989), the court gave the following description of the test:

> DNA probe, also known as "DNA fingerprinting," is a term given to a genetic and molecular biological process that is based on the fact that each individual has an entirely unique genetic "signature," except in the case of identical twins, derived from the overall configuration of DNA (deoxyribonucleic acid) found in every cell containing a nucleus. In molecular biology, the techniques used in this process are known as "Restriction Fragment Length Polymorphism," abbreviated as "RFLP." Under RFLP technology, DNA can be extracted, fragmented and analyzed at the molecular level, then compared with DNA from a known biological specimen for identification purposes.

One consequence of the effectiveness of all of these tests is that most disputed paternity cases today are resolved on the basis of the tests rather than by trial. Yet this may change. Critics have charged that the legal community has been too quick to accept the new technology. Recently, a number of criminal convictions were thrown out because they were based on faulty DNA evidence. It is anticipated that the use of such evidence in paternity cases in the future will come under continuing scrutiny.

Testing can be expensive. If the putative father is indigent, the state must pay for the tests. If he refuses to undergo the tests, many states will either force him to be tested or allow the trial court to take his refusal into consideration in making the paternity decision. The strong implication of such a refusal is that he has something to hide. Many states provide state-appointed counsel for the putative father in these proceedings.

☐ **EXHIBIT 17–4** The DNA Fingerprinting Process

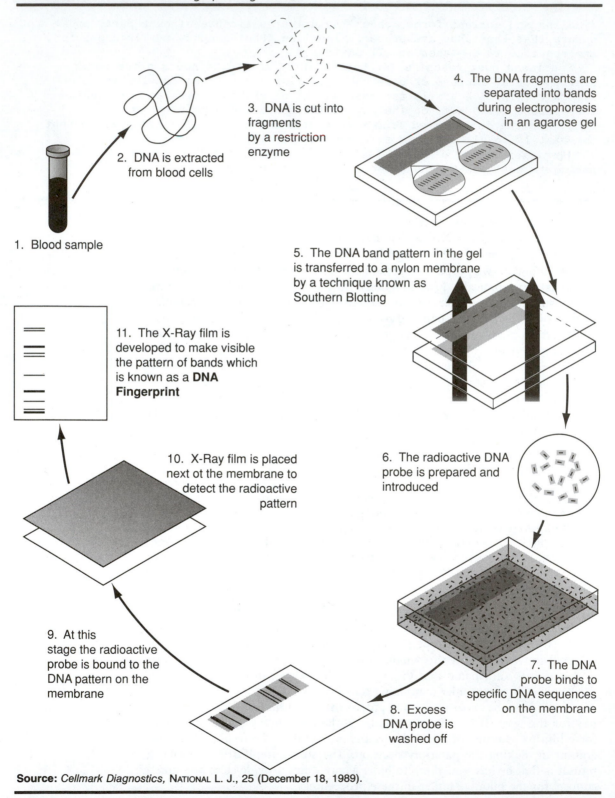

1. Blood sample

2. DNA is extracted from blood cells

3. DNA is cut into fragments by a restriction enzyme

4. The DNA fragments are separated into bands during electrophoresis in an agarose gel

5. The DNA band pattern in the gel is transferred to a nylon membrane by a technique known as Southern Blotting

6. The radioactive DNA probe is prepared and introduced

7. The DNA probe binds to specific DNA sequences on the membrane

8. Excess DNA probe is washed off

9. At this stage the radioactive probe is bound to the DNA pattern on the membrane

10. X-Ray film is placed next ot the membrane to detect the radioactive pattern

11. The X-Ray film is developed to make visible the pattern of bands which is known as a **DNA Fingerprint**

Source: *Cellmark Diagnostics*, NATIONAL L. J., 25 (December 18, 1989).

Assignment 17.3

(a) In what way(s) can the fatherhood of a child be determined by a court in your state?

(b) Select the main way that fatherhood is established in your state, e.g., a paternity proceeding, and prepare a flowchart of all the procedural steps of the process.

(c) What is the statute of limitations for paternity actions in your state?

(d) What is the standard of proof in paternity cases in your state? Does paternity have to be proven by a "preponderance of the evidence," by "clear and convincing evidence," "beyond a reasonable doubt," or by some other standard?

(e) How, if at all, can blood grouping or similar tests be used in your state?

(f) Can a polygraph test be used?

(g) Does Lord Mansfield's rule apply in your state?

(See General Instructions for the State-Code Assignment, General Instructions for the Flowchart Assignment, and General Instructions for the Court-Opinion Assignment in Chapter one.)

Assignment 17.4

In a paternity action against a putative mother, she is asked to state with whom she has had sexual intercourse during the period of possible conception. Can she refuse to answer?

Assignment 17.5

In a divorce action, the court concludes that Tom is the father of two children born during the marriage and is ordered to pay child support for them. Five years later, a criminal nonsupport case is brought against Tom who admits that he made only two of the child-support payments in the five years. During the criminal trial, he contests paternity and asks the court to order blood tests for himself, his ex-wife, and the two children. Assume these tests were not available at the time of the divorce action. What result? (See General Instructions for the Legal-Analysis Assignment in chapter one.)

Of course, not every father must be dragged into court in order to establish paternity. Some openly declare paternity even though they do not wish to marry the mother, or may not be able to because she is already married to someone else (or because he is already married). In some states, a father in such cases can file a document declaring paternity. In New York, for example, there is a special office within the Department of Social Services where a father can "register" himself as the father by filing an *Instrument to Acknowledge Paternity of an Out of Wedlock Child* (see Exhibit 17–5). This document will ensure that he will receive legal notice of an attempt to adopt the child. Additionally, it will make clear that the child has a right to inherit from the father in the event that the latter dies without leaving a valid will.

☐ **EXHIBIT 17–5** Form to Register Paternity

The **Putative Father Registry** is a confidential file maintained in Albany to register fathers of children born out of wedlock.

PURPOSE

The Putative Father Registry was developed to ensure that, if an individual has registered (or has been registered by a court) as the father of a particular child, he will receive legal notice if that child is to be adopted. Additionally, registration provides such a child the right of inheritance in the event of the death of an out of wedlock father. A father may be registered for both purposes provided he follows the instructions in this leaflet.

REGISTRATION

The attached form, called "An Instrument to Acknowledge Paternity of An Out of Wedlock Child," must be filled out in the presence of a witness and signed and notarized before it is returned to the address indicated. Once it is received it will be filed in the Putative Father Registry. The New York State Department of Social Services shall, upon request from any court or authorized agency, provide the names and addresses of persons listed with the registry. The department will not divulge this information to any other party.

The mother and other legal guardian of the child, (if any) will be contacted by registered mail to notify her (them) that a registration has been received.

- -

INSTRUMENT TO ACKNOWLEDGE PATERNITY OF AN OUT OF WEDLOCK CHILD

(pursuant to Section 4-1.2 of New York Estates, Powers and Trust Law)

I _____, residing at _____
   NAME OF FATHER   ADDRESS

_____ hereby acknowledge that I am
   TOWN   STATE   ZIP CODE

the natural father of _____ born on _____ in
                           NAME OF CHILD   DATE OF BIRTH

_____. The natural mother of the child
   TOWN   STATE   ZIP CODE

_____ is _____ who resides
   CHILD'S NAME   NAME OF NATURAL MOTHER

at _____
   ADDRESS   TOWN   STATE   ZIP CODE

Witness_____   _____
              ,SIGNATURE   NATURAL FATHER (SIGNATURE)

       _____
                ADDRESS

   _____
   TOWN   STATE   ZIP CODE

STATE OF NEW YORK

COUNTY OF _____

On the _____ day of _____ _____, before
          DAY   MONTH   YEAR

me came _____ to me known to be the individual described
           NATURAL FATHER

herein and who executed the foregoing instrument, and acknowledges to me that he executed same.

                              _____
                                     NOTARY PUBLIC

STATE OF NEW YORK

COUNTY OF _____

This instrument must be filed with the New York State Department of Social Services, Putative Father Register, 40 North Pearl Street, Albany, New York 12243, within sixty days after it is completed. The natural mother indicated on this instrument will be sent notification of this acknowledgement within seven days after its filing.

COMPLETE THIS SECTION

Key Chapter Terminology

Legitimacy of Children
Filius Nullius
Inheritance
Intestate
Testate
Heirs
Artificial Insemination
Legitimation
Paternity
Acknowledgment
Guardian Ad Litem

In Personam
Personal Jurisdiction
Presumption of Legitimacy
Bastardize
Lord Mansfield's Rule
Blood Group Tests
Paternity Index
Probability of Paternity
DNA Testing
Genetic Code

The Legal Status of Children

■ Chapter Outline

The age of majority is eighteen, but a state may impose different age requirements for performing different activities. Emancipation before the age of majority can make a minor eligible for some of these activities.

A number of special laws apply to minors. For example, they have the right to disaffirm contracts they have entered. They can own real and personal property in their own name, but unless they have been emancipated, their parents have a right to keep their earnings. Also, minors cannot acquire their own domicile without parental consent, and in most states, an unemancipated minor is ineligible to make a will. If the parents of a minor die, the court will appoint a guardian to oversee his or her affairs.

School is compulsory until a designated age. Teachers stand in the place of parents and, as such, can impose reasonable corporal punishment. However, students are entitled to certain procedural rights, e.g., a hearing, if the school wants to expel or suspend them long-term.

When a parent neglects or abuses a child, the state has a number of options, e.g., criminal prosecution, foster home placement, and termination of parental rights. A child below the age of seven cannot commit a crime, but one between seven and fourteen can be prosecuted if the state can overcome the presumption that such a child is not old enough to form the necessary criminal intent. A modern tendency is to treat misbehaving children as juvenile delinquents or as persons in need of supervision rather than as defendants in criminal courts.

Section A. Age of Majority and Emancipation

In most states and for most purposes, an adult is an individual who is eighteen years of age or older. A minor (i.e., a child) is anyone under eighteen.

(Note: a person reaches eighteen on the day *before* his or her eighteen birthday.) At this age, *majority* is achieved. There was a time, however, when the age of majority was twenty-one, and in some states it still is. Furthermore, a person may be a minor for one purpose, but not for another. Hence, one cannot always rely on eighteen as the critical age to determine rights and obligations. Three questions must always be asked:

1. What is the individual trying to do, e.g., vote, enter a contract, avoid a contract?
2. Does the state set a specific age that is relevant to that task or objective?
3. Has the individual been emancipated? If so, does the emancipation mean that the person is no longer a minor for purposes of that particular task or objective?

Emancipation is the relinquishment of parental control over the child. Children can be emancipated before the age of majority if certain events take place that clearly indicate they are living independently of their parents with the consent of the latter. Such events include marriage, entering the military service, abandonment by the parents, an explicit agreement between the parents and the child that the latter can live independently, etc. In some states, a child can apply to a court for an order of emancipation when the consent of the parents cannot be obtained. As we discuss the various rights and obligations of "minors," we will see that it is sometimes important to know whether emancipation has occurred.

Assignment 18.1

How does emancipation occur in your state? Find one opinion written by a court in your state in which the court held that emancipation had occurred. (If you cannot find an opinion written by a court of your state, try the courts of a neighboring state.) State the facts of the opinion. What specific events led the court to conclude that emancipation had occurred? (See General Instructions for the Court-Opinion Assignment in chapter one.)

Section B. Contracts

As a general rule (to which there are exceptions), a minor does not have legal capacity to enter a binding contract. Consequently, a minor has no legal obligation to perform a contract if he or she repudiates or disaffirms it at any time before reaching majority or within a reasonable time after reaching majority. In effect, such contracts are voidable.

> Tom is fifteen years of age—clearly a minor. He goes to the ABC Truck Co. and purchases a truck. The sales contract calls for a small down payment (which Tom pays) with the remainder to be paid in installments—on credit. Six months later, Tom changes his mind about the truck and decides to take it back to the dealer. The truck is still in good working order.

If Tom were an adult, he would be bound by his contract. Once the contract is entered by an adult and a merchant, they both are bound by it. Neither party can rescind a contract simply because of a change of mind. The difference in our example is that Tom is a minor. Most states give minors the right to *disaffirm* their contracts so long as they do so while they are still minors or within a reasonable time (e.g., several months) after they have reached majority. In Tom's case, this would mean that he is not bound by the contract to buy the truck. He can take it back, and perhaps even force the company to return whatever money he paid on it. In some states, however, the merchant may be able to keep all or part of the purchase price paid thus far to cover depreciation resulting from the minor's use of the item.

Why are minors given this right to disaffirm? The objective of the law is to protect young people from their immaturity. Merchants are on notice that if they deal with minors, they do so at their own risk.

This does not mean that every contract of a minor is invalid. If the minor does not disaffirm, the contract is valid and can be enforced against the minor. Similarily, if a minor tries to disaffirm too late, the contract will be enforced. Suppose that Tom tried to disaffirm the truck contract when he was twenty years old (and that the age of majority in his state is eighteen). He must disaffirm *before* he reaches majority or within a *reasonable* time thereafter.

What happens if the minor commits fraud in order to induce the merchant to enter a contract, e.g., lies about his or her age through a forged birth certificate? Some courts take the position that such wrongdoing by the minor prevents (i.e., estops) him or her from being able to disaffirm. Other courts, however, argue that the policy of protecting minors against their own immaturity is so strong that even their own fraud will not destroy their right to disaffirm.

Special statutes have been passed in many states to limit the minor's right to disaffirm, particularly with respect to certain kinds of contracts. In several states, for example, some contracts of employment are binding on minors, such as sports and show business contracts. Similarly, contractural arrangements with banks and other lending institutions cannot be disaffirmed in many states. Finally, when a minor makes a contract with a merchant for necessaries such as food or clothing (page 367), the contract can rarely be disaffirmed.

When a guardian has been appointed over a minor and the guardian enters a contract on behalf of that minor, the contract generally cannot be disaffirmed by the minor. Suppose, for example, that a minor is involved in litigation and an offer of settlement is made. A settlement is a contract. If a court appoints a guardian over the minor and the guardian negotiates a settlement contract on behalf of the minor, which the court finds is fair, the minor cannot later disaffirm the settlement.

Most states have enacted the Uniform Gifts to Minors Act pursuant to which gifts of certain kinds of property, e.g., securities, can be made to minors through custodians of the property. The custodian can sell the property on behalf of the minor. Contracts made by the custodian for this purpose cannot be disaffirmed by the minor.

Suppose that a minor has become emancipated before reaching the age of majority, e.g., by marrying or by being abandoned by the parents. Does this end the child's power to disaffirm? There is no absolute answer to this question. A minor so emancipated may be denied the power to disaffirm in some states, while in others, it will not affect the power.

Assignment 18.2

Answer the following questions by examining the statutory code of your state and/or the opinions of the courts in your state. (See General Instructions for the State-Code Assignment and for the Court-Opinion Assignment in chapter one.)

(a) What is the minimum age to enter a contract that cannot be disaffirmed in your state?

(b) Are there specific kinds of contracts a minor cannot disaffirm in your state? If so, what are they?

(c) Does lying about his or her age in entering a contract affect the minor's power to disaffirm the contract in your state? If so, how?

(d) If the minor in your state still has the item purchased through the contract, must he or she return the item to the merchant as a condition of the exercise of the power to disaffirm?

(e) Does your state have the Uniform Gifts to Minors Act? If so, give the citation and briefly explain how it works.

Assignment 18.3

George is a wealthy thirteen-year-old who owns an expensive painting. He signs a contract to exchange the painting for a valuable horse owned by Helen, an equally wealthy twelve-year-old. Both George and Helen are represented by their separate attorneys during the negotiations on the contract. Once the contract is signed and the items are exchanged, what rights do George and Helen have? Assume that there are no problems with the quality and condition of the painting and horse. (See General Instructions for the Legal-Analysis Assignment in chapter one.)

Section C. Property and Earnings

A minor can own real property and most personal property in his or her own name. The parents of a minor do not own and cannot dispose of the minor's property. Earnings are an exception. A minor does *not* have a right to keep his or her own earnings. The parent with the duty to support the child has a right to keep the earnings of the child. If, however, the child has not yet reached the age of majority but has been emancipated (e.g., by express agreement with the parents, by marriage, by abandonment by the parents), the parents would not be entitled to the earnings of the child.

Section D. Domicile

The domicile of a minor is the domicile of the parents—even in some instances when the minor lives in a different state from the parents. With parental consent, however, a minor can acquire his or her own separate domicile. Similarly, if a minor who has not yet reached the age of majority is emancipated, most states give that individual the power to acquire his or her own domicile.

Section E. Estates

States have specified certain minimum ages for the disposition of property by a will. Some states have different minimum ages for the disposition of personal property (e.g., clothes, cash) and of real property (e.g., land). In a few states, the emancipation of the minor by his or her marriage will enable the minor to make a valid will before reaching the minimum age.

If the parent of a minor dies, the court will appoint a guardian over the person and/or estate of the minor. This person may be called a *general guardian,* a *guardian of the estate,* or a *guardian ad litem.* It is this guardian's duty to:

- Manage the minor's property
- Collect funds due the minor
- Sell, lease, or mortgage the minor's property (with the approval of the court)
- Invest the minor's funds
- Pay the minor's debts
- Support the minor (and the family of the minor, if any) from the minor's funds
- Represent the minor in court when needed

For such services, the minor must pay the guardian a fee, which might be a percentage of the minor's estate. If the guardian is not an attorney and legal services are required, the guardian will hire an attorney on behalf of the minor.

Assignment 18.4

Answer the following questions by examining the statutory code of your state and/ or the opinions of the courts of your state. (See General Instructions for the State-Code Assignment and for the Court-Opinion Assignment in chapter one.)

(a) What is the minimum age for an individual to execute the valid will in your state?

(b) When a minor dies without leaving a valid will (i.e., dies intestate), what happens to his or her property?

(c) What happens to the estate of a minor when his or her parents die? Is a guardian appointed? What are the duties of this person?

Section F. Education

School attendance is compulsory for children up to designated age, usually sixteen. The school does not have to be public if an alternate private school meets minimum educational standards.

Children at home can be subject to *corporal* (i.e., physical) *punishment* by their parents so long as the punishment does not constitute abuse. Teachers are *in loco parentis,* which means that they stand in the place of parents. As such, teachers can also impose corporal punishment on children if reasonably necessary for proper education and discipline. Subjecting children to such punishment is *not* considered cruel and unusual punishment under the Constitution.

A student cannot be expelled or given a long-term suspension from school without being accorded certain procedural rights. For example:

- The right to receive written notice of the charges against the student
- The right to a hearing on the charges to determine whether they are valid
- The right to an impartial hearing officer. (The latter cannot be directly involved in the matter. For example, the teacher who brought the charges against the student cannot be the hearing officer.)
- The right to be represented by counsel at the hearing
- The right to present evidence and to confront the accuser at the hearing

If the student is faced with a less severe punishment, such as a short-term suspension, all of these procedural rights are not provided. The student has a right to know the basis of the charges and the right to have an opportunity to respond to them, but not necessarily to a hearing with legal representation.

Section G. Neglect and Abuse

Statutes exist to protect children who have been neglected or abused by their parents. *Neglect* is often defined as failing to give support, education, medical care, or other care necessary for the child's welfare, e.g., the refusal of a parent to give a child a needed operation, leaving a young child unattended at home for a long period of time. *Abuse* often involves physical harm inflicted by the parent on the child. (See Exhibit 18–1 for relevant statistics on maltreatment by parents and by others.)

If a court finds that a child has been neglected or abused, a number of options are usually available. Criminal penalties might be imposed. The court may have the power to terminate the parent's parental rights (page 511), or

☐ **EXHIBIT 18–1** Child Maltreatment Cases Reported—Summary: 1976 to 1985

ITEM (In percent, except as indicated.)	1976	1977	1978	1979	1980	1981	1982	1983	1984	1985
Number of children reported (1,000)	669	838	836	988	1,154	1,225	1,262	1,477	1,727	1,928
Rate per 10,000 children ...	101.0	128.0	129.0	154.0	181.0	194.0	201.0	236.0	273.0	306.0
Type of maltreatment:										
Deprivation of necessities...	70.7	64.0	62.9	63.1	60.7	59.4	62.5	58.4	54.6	55.7
Minor physical injury	18.9	20.8	21.2	15.4	19.8	20.4	16.8	18.5	17.7	15.4
Sexual maltreatment	3.2	6.1	6.6	5.8	6.8	7.5	6.9	8.5	13.3	11.7
Emotional maltreatment	21.6	25.4	23.8	14.9	13.5	11.9	10.0	10.1	11.2	8.9
Unspecified physical injury ..	.5	.4	.4	2.5	3.1	3.2	4.7	5.2	3.6	4.1
Major physical injury	3.1	3.7	3.5	4.4	3.9	4.1	2.4	3.2	3.3	2.2
Other maltreatment	7.6	7.5	7.4	8.9	7.7	11.7	9.2	8.3	9.6	10.2

Source: Statistical Abstract of the United States, 1989, 172.

the child may be placed in the custody of the state's child welfare agency for foster care placement.

Assignment 18.5

Answer the following questions after examining your state statutory code. (See General Instructions for the State-Code Assignment in chapter one.)

(a) What is the state code definition of a neglected, abandoned, dependent, or abused child in your state?

(b) What court has jurisdiction to determine whether a child is neglected, abandoned, dependent, or abused?

(c) What can the court do once it determines that such a child exists?

Assignment 18.6

Prepare a checklist of questions you could use to help determine whether a child has been neglected, abandoned, etc. (See General Instructions for the Checklist-Formulation Assignment in chapter one.)

Assignment 18.7

Draft a flowchart of the procedural steps that are necessary in your state to determine whether a child has been neglected, abandoned, etc. (See General Instructions for the Flowchart Assignment in chapter one.)

Section H. Delinquency

At common law, a minor below the age of seven was incapable of committing a crime—or so the law conclusively presumed. Evidence that such a child was in fact capable of committing a crime was inadmissible. A minor between the ages of seven and fourteen could be guilty of a crime if the prosecutor could show that the minor was mature enough to have formed the criminal intent necessary for the particular crime. A rebuttable presumption existed that a minor between these ages could not possess the requisite criminal intent. This simply meant that the court would assume the absence of this intent unless the prosecutor affirmatively proved otherwise. Minors over fourteen were treated and tried the same as adults.

In the early part of this century, a trend developed to remove the stigma of criminality from the misconduct of minors. Juvenile courts were created. Terms such as *juvenile delinquent, PINS* (Person In Need of Supervision), *MINS* (Minor In Need of Supervision), and *CHIPS* (Child In Need of Protection and Services) began to be widely used. A juvenile delinquent is a person under a certain age, e.g., sixteen, whose conduct would constitute a crime if performed by an adult. A PINS, MINS, or CHIPS is a person who has committed a so-called *status offense*, which is noncriminal misconduct by a person under a certain age. Examples of such offenses include habitual truancy from school and incorrigibility at home. When a juvenile court decided (i.e., adjudicated) that a child fit into one of these special categories, it had a number of options, including sending the child home with a warning, institutionalization in a juvenile facility, probation under the supervision of a youth counselor, and foster home placement.

While this system of special treatment is now widely used, it has been criticized as too lenient, particularly when the child commits a serious act such as homicide or sexual assault. Experts say that "about 250 children under age twelve commit homicides each year." Anderson, *Grown-up Crime, Boy Defendant,* 75 Amer. Bar Assoc. J. 26, 27 (November 1989). When a child of a specified age is accused of particularly heinous conduct of this kind, most states give a judge discretion in deciding whether the case should be handled in a juvenile court, or whether the regular criminal adult courts should take over.

Assignment 18.8

Most of the following questions can be answered by examining your state statutory code. (See General Instructions for the State-Code Assignment in chapter one.)

(a) What is a juvenile delinquent in your state?

(b) What court has jurisdiction to determine juvenile delinquency?

(c) Is any classification other than juvenile delinquent used in your state to describe a minor who has misbehaved, e.g., the classification of PINS? If so, define the classification.

(d) Draft a flowchart of the procedural steps required in your state for the processing of a juvenile delinquency case. (See General Instructions for the Flowchart Assignment in chapter one.)

(e) Once a minor has been found to be a juvenile delinquent, what disposition options are available to the court in your state?

(f) Under what circumstances, if any, can a child be prosecuted in an adult criminal court?

Notes on the Legal Status of Children

1. Twenty-one has been the traditional minimum voting age, although most states have recently lowered this to eighteen.

2. On the tort liability of a minor, see page 552.

3. On the abortion rights of minors, see page 461.

Key Chapter Terminology

Age of Majority	Corporal Punishment
Minor	In Loco Parentis
Emancipation	Neglect and Abuse
Disaffirm Contracts	Juvenile Delinquency
Fraud	Criminal Intent
Uniform Gifts to Minors Act	PINS
Earnings	MINS
Domicile	CHIPS
Guardian ad Litem	Status Offense

Adoption

■ Chapter Outline

After covering some introductory definitions, this chapter examines the three main kinds of adoptions. First is an agency adoption, where a child is placed for adoption by a private or public agency. Second is an independent/private adoption, where a natural parent places a child for adoption with the adoptive parents, often through an intermediary such as an attorney and after an investigation by an adoption agency. In such an arrangement, any payment to the natural mother beyond covering her expenses constitutes illegal baby buying. Third is a black-market adoption, where illegal payments are made to the natural mother beyond her expenses.

A court will allow an adoption if it is in the best interest of the child. In making this determination, a number of factors are considered: the petitioner's age, marital status, health, religion, economic status, home environment, and lifestyle. Race cannot be the sole reason an adoption is granted or denied. If the child is old enough, his or her preference will usually be considered.

An adoption must follow strict procedures. The court must have subject-matter jurisdiction. Proper venue must be selected. The petition must contain the required information. The natural parents must be notified of the proceeding and must consent to the adoption unless their parental rights have been terminated because of conduct that clearly demonstrates an intention to relinquish parental duties. Under certain circumstances, a parent will be given the right to revoke an earlier consent to the adoption. An agency investigates the prospective adoptive parents and reports back to the court. An interlocutory decree of adoption is then made by the court, which becomes final within a designated period of time.

Once the adoption becomes final, the adopted child is treated the same as a natural child with respect to inheritance rights, support rights, etc. In a traditional adoption, the records are sealed, and matters such as the identity of the natural parents are kept confidential except in relatively rare circumstances. In an open adoption, there may be varying degrees of contact between a natural parent and the child after the adoption becomes final.

An equitable adoption occurs when a person dies before fulfilling a contract to adopt a child, and when unfairness can be avoided only by treating the child as having been adopted.

A number of important terms should be defined and distinguished before discussing the subject of adoption.

Custody

The control and care of an individual.

Guardianship

The legal right to the custody of an individual.

Ward

An individual who is under guardianship.

Termination of Parental Rights

A judicial declaration that a parent shall no longer have any right to participate in decisions affecting the welfare of the child.

Adoption of a Child

The legal process by which an adoptive parent assumes all the rights and duties of the natural (i.e., biological) parents.

Paternity

The fatherhood of a child.

Foster Care

A child welfare service that provides shelter and substitute family care when a child's own family cannot care for it. Foster care is designed to last for a temporary period during which adoption is neither desirable nor possible, or during the period when adoption is under consideration.

Stepparent

A person who marries the natural mother or father of a child, but is not one of the child's natural parents.

Assignment 19.1

(a) Find statutes or court opinions that define the words *custody* and *guardianship* in your state. For each word, try to find at least one statute or opinion that defines the word. If either or both words have more than one meaning in your state, give each meaning. (See General Instructions for the State-Code Assignment and General Instructions for the Court-Opinion Assignment in chapter one.)

(b) Prepare a flowchart of guardianship procedures in your state involving a minor child. If there is more than one kind of such guardianship in your state, select any one. (See General Instructions for the Flowchart Assignment in chapter one.)

(c) Draft a custody agreement under which your best friend agrees to care for your child while you are in the hospital for six months. (See General Instructions for the Agreement-Drafting Assignment in chapter one.)

Adoption establishes a permanent, legal, parent-child relationship between the child and a person who is not the natural parent of the child. (Between 2 to 4 percent of Americans in the country today are adopted.) The new parent is called the *adoptive* or *adopting parent*. In many states, the child's birth certificate is reissued, listing the adoptive parents as the "mother" or "father" of the child. The relationship is permanent in that only the court can end the relationship by terminating the parental rights of the adoptive parent. Even the divorce or death of the adoptive parent does not end the relationship. Assume, for example, that Tom marries Linda and then adopts her son, Dave, by a previous marriage. If Tom subsequently divorces Linda, he does not cease to be Dave's parent. His obligation to support Dave, for example, continues after the divorce. Similarly, when Tom dies, Dave can inherit from Tom as if he were a natural child of Tom. In this sense, the parent-child relationship continues even after the death of the adoptive parent.

Section A. Kinds of Adoption

The three main kinds of adoption are agency adoption, independent adoption, and black-market adoption. A fourth, equitable adoption, will be considered later in the chapter.

Agency Adoption

In an *agency adoption*, the child is placed for adoption by a licensed private or public agency. The mother transfers the child to the agency by executing a formal surrender document relinquishing all of her rights in the child. Agency adoptions are most common when the child is not related to, and is not a stepchild of, the adoptive parents.

Independent/Private Adoption

In an *independent* or *private adoption,* a natural parent places the child for adoption with the adoptive parents, often with the help of an attorney, a doctor, or both. (See Exhibit 19–1 for sample adoption ads.) As with agency adoptions, a court must give its approval to the independent adoption. Furthermore, the state may require an agency to investigate the prospective adoption and file a report, which is considered by the court. It should be noted, however, that in an independent adoption, the level of involvement by the

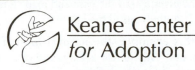
□ **EXHIBIT 19–1**
Sample ads used in
adoption.

agency is far less extensive and intrusive than in a traditional agency adoption, where the agency supervises the entire process.

Most, but not all, independent adoptions are initiated by a stepparent or by someone who is otherwise already related to the child. Yet many independent adoptions occur when no such relationship exists.

Here is an example of how an independent adoption might occur:

When Ralph and Nancy Smith discovered that they were infertile, they decided to adopt. Several visits to adoption agencies, however, were quite discouraging. One agency had such a long waiting list of couples seeking to adopt healthy, white infants that it refused to take any new applications. Another accepted their application, but warned that the process might take up to five years, with no guarantee that a child would eventually become available. Nationally, only about 100,000 infants are likely to be adopted per year—with over 2,000,000 infertile couples seeking to adopt them! The small number of available children is due to the widespread use of abortion and the declining social stigma attached to the single-parent motherhood.

Acting on the advice of a friend, the Smiths then tried the alternative of an independent adoption. They placed personal ads in newspapers and magazines seeking to contact an unwed pregnant woman who would be willing to relinquish her child for adoption. They also sent their résumé and letters of inquiry to doctors, members of the clergy, and lawyers specializing in independent adoptions. In some cities, the yellow pages had listings for attorneys with such a specialty. Their efforts were finally successful when an attorney led them to Diane Kline, a seventeen-year-old pregnant girl. The Smiths prepared a scrapbook on their life which Diane reviewed. She then interviewed the Smiths and decided to allow them to adopt her child. The Smiths paid the attorney's fees, Diane's medical bills, the cost of her psychological counseling, travel expenses, and living expenses related to the delivery of the baby. Diane signed a consent form relinquishing her rights in the baby and agreeing to the adoption by the Smiths, who formally applied to the court for the adoption. A social worker at a local agency investigated the case and made a report to the court, which then issued an order authorizing the adoption.

In this example, the natural mother had personal contact with the adoptive parents. This is not always the case. Independent adoptions can also resemble agency adoptions, where anonymity is more common.

Note that the money paid by the Smiths covered medical, legal, and related expenses. Other payments would be illegal. Assume, for example, that Diane had hesitated about going through with the adoption and the Smiths had offered her $10,000 above expenses. This could constitute illegal *baby buying*, turning an independent adoption into a *black-market adoption*. Such a payment to a birth parent, to an attorney, or to anyone is illegal. A person may pay those expenses that are naturally and reasonably connected with the adoption, so long as no consideration is given to induce someone to participate in the adoption. (The separate but related problems of surrogate motherhood will be considered in the next chapter.)

In some states, independent adoptions are more common than agency adoptions. Critics argue that illegal payments are frequent, and that the lack of safeguards in independent adoptions can lead to disastrous consequences. A dramatic example occurred in 1988 when a New York City attorney was convicted in the battery death of a six-year-old girl who had been placed in his care so that he might arrange an independent adoption. The attorney had kept the child—and then abused her—when prospective adoptive parents failed to pay his fee for the adoption. Proponents of independent adoptions view this case as an aberration and maintain that the vast majority of independent adoptions are legal and are adequately supervised.

Black-Market Adoptions

Frustration with agency adoptions leads to the alternative of independent adoptions. And frustration with both kinds of legal adoptions leads to *black-market adoptions,* which involve a payment beyond reasonable expenses.

An adoption becomes *baby buying* when the payment is for the placement of the child rather than for reasonable expenses. The most blatant example is the *baby broker* who financially entices women to give up their children and then charges adoptive parents a large "fee" for arranging the adoption. In 1984, a typical black-market adoption cost up to $50,000.

It is difficult to know how many independent adoptions turn into black-market adoptions, since the participants have an interest in keeping quiet about the illegal payment. To discourage such payments, some states require the adoptive parent to file with the court a list of all expenditures pertaining to the adoption. This, however, has not stopped black-market adoptions, and critics argue that the only way to do so is to eliminate independent adoptions so that all adoptions will be closely supervised by traditional public and private agencies.

Assignment 19.2

Answer the following questions based on your state code. (See General Instructions for the State-Code Assignment in chapter one.)

(a) Are independent or private adoptions allowed in your state? If so, how do they differ from agency adoptions? In what ways does the state try to prevent "baby buying"?

(b) Is it a crime to "buy" a baby? If so, how is this crime committed?

Section B. Who May Be Adopted?

In the vast majority of cases, the person adopted is a child, usually an infant. Yet in most states it is possible for one adult to adopt another adult as well. The most common reason for this practice is that the adoptive parent wants to give the adopted adult rights of inheritance from the adoptive parent. In effect, the latter is designating an heir.

Suppose, however, that a homosexual wants to adopt his or her homosexual lover. While there have been a few courts that have allowed it, most courts agree with New York in disallowing it. The "sexual intimacy" between such individuals "is utterly repugnant to the relationship between child and parent in our society, and . . . a patently incongruous application of our adoptive laws." *In the Matter of Robert Paul P.*, 63 N.Y.2d 233, 481 N.Y.S.2d 652, 653 (1984).

Assignment 19.3

Can one adult adopt another adult in your state? If so, can one homosexual adult adopt another? (Check your state code and cases, interpreting its relevant provisions. See General Instructions for the State-Code Assignment and General Instructions for the Court-Opinion Assignment in chapter one.)

Section C. Who May Adopt?

The petitioners (i.e., the persons seeking to become the adoptive parents) will be granted the adoption if it is in "the best interest of the child." Such a broad standard gives the judge a good deal of discretion. In addition to relying on the child welfare agency's investigation report, the judge will consider a number of factors, no one of which is usually controlling:

1. *Age of petitioner.* Most states require the petitioner to be an adult. The preference is for someone who is not unusually older than the child. A court would be reluctant, for example, to allow a seventy-five-year old to adopt an infant, unless special circumstances warranted it.

2. *Marital status of petitioner.* While many states allow single persons to adopt, the preference is for someone who is married. His or her spouse is usually required to join in the petition.

3. *Health of petitioner.* Adoptive parents are not expected to be physically and emotionally perfect. If a particular handicap will not seriously interfere with the raising of the child, it will not by itself bar the adoption.

4. *Race.* The unspoken preference of most judges and agencies is for the race of the child and of the adoptive parents to be the same. It is impermissible, however, to allow race to be the *sole* reason why an adoption is granted or rejected. Indeed, there is some doubt about whether the United States Constitution permits race to be considered at all in the adoption decision.

5. *Religion.* "When possible" or "when practicable," the religion of the adoptive parents should be the same as the religion of the natural parents. Interfaith adoptions, though allowed, are generally not encouraged.

6. *Wishes of the child.* The court will consider the opinion of the prospective adoptee if he or she is old enough to communicate a preference.

7. *Economic status.* The adoptive parents must have the financial means to care for the child. The court will examine their current financial status and prospects for the future in the light of the support needs of the child.

8. *Home environment and morality.* Everyone's goal is for the child to be brought up in a wholesome, loving home where values are important and where the child will be nutured to his or her potential. Illegal or conspicuously unorthodox lifestyles are frowned upon.

Earlier we saw that most states do not allow the adoption of a homosexual adult by another homosexual. The hesitancy is even stronger against a homosexual adopting a child. Even in Denmark where same-sex marriages are now legal, the couple cannot adopt minor children. There are circumstances, however, when a gay *natural* parent will be given custody of his or her child following a divorce. This is usually because the child is old enough to have already established a healthy relationship with this parent, and because the heterosexual natural parent is either absent or unfit. Courts are more reluctant, however, to allow a homosexual to *initiate* a relationship with a child through adoption.

Assignment 19.4

(a) In your state, who is eligible to adopt children? Who is not eligible?

(b) What standards exist to guide a judge's decision in your state on whether to approve a particular adoption?

(c) Mary Jones is a Baptist. She wants to place her one-year-old child for adoption. Mr. and Mrs. Johnson want to adopt the child and file the appropriate petition to do so in your state. The Johnsons are Jewish. Mary Jones consents to the adoption. What effect, if any, will the religious differences between Mary Jones and the Johnsons have on the adoption? Assume that Mary has no objection to the child's being raised in the Jewish faith.

(d) Same facts as in part "c" above except that the Johnsons are professed athiests. Mary Jones does not care. (See General Instructions for the State-Code Assignment in chapter one. You may also need to check court opinions. See General Instructions for the Court-Opinion Assignment in chapter one.)

(e) Both Paul and Helen Smith are deaf and mute. They wish to adopt the infant daughter of Helen's best friend, a widow who just died. Prepare an investigation strategy to collect evidence relevant to whether the adoption will be permitted. (See General Instructions for the Investigation-Strategy Assignment in chapter one.)

Assignment 19.5

(a) Contact a *private* child welfare agency in your state involved in adoption placement. Ask the agency what criteria it uses in recommending an adoption. Also, ask the agency to send you any available literature that lists such standards, e.g., pamphlets, applications. Compare these standards with your answers to the questions in the preceding assignment (19.4). Does the agency's practice conform with the standards of the law of your state?

(b) Same question as in part "a" above except that this time a *public* child welfare agency should be contacted.

(Note: Let your teacher know in advance which private and public agency you propose to contact. The teacher may want to coordinate the contacts so that no single agency receives more than its share of contacts from the class.)

Section D. Adoption Procedure

A rather elaborate set of procedures exists for adoption; it is not easy to adopt a child. Courts are very concerned about protecting the interests of the child, the natural parents, and the adoptive parents. When the most sought-after babies (i.e., healthy white infants) are in short supply, the temptation to "buy" a baby on the black market is heightened.

Jurisdiction and Venue

Subject-matter jurisdiction refers to the power of the court to hear a particular kind of case. Not every court in a state has subject-matter jurisdiction to issue adoption decrees. The state constitution or state statutes will designate one or perhaps two courts that have authority to hear adoption cases, e.g., the state family court or the state juvenile court. There are also specifications for selecting the county or district in which the adoption proceeding must be brought. The selection is referred to as the *choice of venue*. It will usually depend on the residence (or occasionally on the domicile) of one or more of the participants, usually the natural parents, the adoptive parents, or the child.

Assignment 19.6

(a) What court or courts in your state have the power to hear adoption cases?

(b) In what county or section of your state must the adoption proceeding be initiated? Does your answer depend upon the residence or domicile of any of the participants? If so, what is the definition of residence or domicile?

(To answer the above questions, you may have to check your state constitution, state statutory code, and perhaps opinions of your state courts. See General Instructions for the State-Code Assignment in chapter one.)

Petition

States differ on the form and content of the adoption petition that is filed by the adoptive parents to begin the adoption proceeding. The petition will contain data such as: the names of the petitioners; their ages; whether they are married and, if so, whether they are living together; the name, age, and religion of the child, etc. While the natural parents play a large role in the adoption proceeding, not all states require that they be mentioned in the petition itself. (For an example of the format of a petition, see Exhibit 19–2.)

Assignment 19.7

(a) What must a petition for adoption contain in your state? Must it name the natural parents? (See General Instructions for the State-Code Assignment in chapter one.)

(b) Draft an adoption petition. Assume that you are seeking to adopt the one-year-old baby of your friend who has recently been hospitalized. This friend has no other relatives. The natural father of the child is no longer alive. You can make up facts you need to draft the petition. (Although an adoption petition is not a complaint, you may find some of the suggestions on drafting complaints to be useful, page 25.)

Notice

For due process purposes, it is fundamental that the natural parents be given *notice* of the petition to adopt the child by the prospective adoptive parents. This usually does not mean that the natural parents must be personally served with process within the state where the adoption petition is brought. Substituted service, e.g., registered mail, is often adequate.

There was a time when the father of an illegitimate child was not entitled to notice of the adoption proceeding; only the mother of such a child was given notice. The situation has changed, however, due to recent decisions of the United States Supreme Court. While the full scope of the rights of the father of an illegitimate child have not yet been fully defined by the courts, it is clear that he can no longer be ignored in the adoption process. As we shall see, however, there is a difference between a parent's right to notice of the adoption proceeding and the parent's right to prevent the adoption by refusing to consent to it.

Assignment 19.8

(a) In your state, who must receive notice of an adoption proceeding?

(b) When can substituted service of process (e.g., mail, publication) be used in your state for persons who must receive notice of adoption proceedings?

(See General Instructions for the State-Code Assignment and General Instructions for the Court-Opinion Assignment in chapter one.)

Consent

Adoption occurs in essentially two ways: with or without the consent of the natural parents. When consent is necessary, the state's statute will usually

☐ **EXHIBIT 19–2** Adoption Petition

FAMILY COURT OF THE STATE OF _____
COUNTY OF _____

In the Matter of the Adoption by	Index No.
of a minor having the first name of	
	PETITION (Agency)
whose last name is contained in the Schedule annexed to the Petition herein.	

TO THE FAMILY COURT:

  1. (a) The name and place of residence of the petitioning adoptive mother is:

     Name:

     Address: (including county)

She is (of full age) (a minor), born on

She is (unmarried) (married to

and they are living together as husband and wife).

Her religious faith is

Her occupation is

and her approximate annual income is $

     (b) The name and place of residence of the petitioning adoptive father is:

     Name:

     Address:

He is (of full age) (a minor), born on

He is (umarried) (married to

and they are living together as husband and wife).

His religious faith is

His occupation is

and his approximate annual income is $

□ **EXHIBIT 19–2** Adoption Petition—Continued

2. As nearly as the same can be ascertained, the full name, date and place of birth of the (male) (female) adoptive child are set forth in the Schedule annexed to this Petition and verified by a duly constituted official of an authorized agency.

3. (a) As nearly as the same can be ascertained, the religious faith of the adoptive child is
(b) As nearly as the same can be ascertained, the religious faith of the natural parents of the adoptive child is

4. The manner in which the adoptive parents obtained the adoptive child is as follows:

5. The adoptive child has resided continuously with the adoptive parents since

6. The name by which the adoptive child is to be known is

7. The consent of the above-mentioned authorized agency has been duly executed and is filed herewith. The consent of the natural parents of the adoptive child is not required because

8. No previous application has been made to any court or judge for the relief sought herein, except

9. The adoptive child has not been previously adopted, except

10. To the best of petitioner's information and belief, there are no persons other than those hereinbefore mentioned interested in this proceeding except

11. WHEREFORE, your Petitioners pray for an order approving the adoption of the aforesaid adoptive child by the above named adoptive parents and directing that the said adoptive child shall be regarded and treated in all respects as the child of the said adoptive parents and directing that the name of the said adoptive child be changed as specified in paragraph 6 above and that henceforth (s)he shall be known by that name.

Source: 1 GUIDE TO AMERICAN LAW, 103 (1983).

specify the manner in which the consent must be given, e.g., whether it must be witnessed, whether it must be in writing, whether the formalities for consent differ for agency adoptions as opposed to independent adoptions, whether the consent form must mention the names of the parties seeking to adopt the child, etc. See Exhibit 19–3 for an example of a consent form.

Both natural parents must consent to the adoption unless the parental rights of one or both of them have been formally terminated because of *unfitness*. An unfit parent loses the power to veto the adoption. As indicated earlier, the father of an illegitimate child has a right to present his views on the propriety of the proposed adoption. He must be given notice of the adoption proceeding unless he has abandoned the child. If he has lived with his illegitimate child, supported him or her, or otherwise maintained close contacts with the child, a court will grant him the same rights as the mother, e.g., he *will* be allowed to veto the proposed adoption.

Often a child welfare agency will place the child in a foster home. Foster parents are not legal guardians and therefore cannot prevent the adoption of the child by someone else. The consent of foster parents to the adoption is not necessary. This does not mean that the foster parents can be ignored entirely. When an agency attempts to remove the child from the foster home, many states give the foster parents the right to object to the removal and to present their arguments against the removal. While foster parents may be given a right to be heard on the removal, they cannot veto the adoption of the child.

Assignment 19.9

(a) Give the citation to the statute that contains the formalities necessary for consent to adoption in your state.

(b) Who must give consent?

(c) Is it necessary to obtain the consent of a natural parent who is mentally ill?

(d) Is it necessary to obtain the consent of a natural parent who previously was *not* awarded custody of the child in a divorce proceeding?

(e) Is there a minimum age for giving consent? Can a minor parent consent to adoption?

(f) When, if ever, must the child consent to his or her own adoption?

(g) In what form or with what formalities must the consent be given? Does your answer differ for a public agency adoption is opposed to an independent adoption? If so, explain the difference.

(h) Does the consent form have to mention the names of the prospective adoptive parents?

(See General Instructions for the State-Code Assignment in chapter one. You may also need to check court opinions for some of the above questions. See General Instructions for the Court-Opinion Assignment in chapter one.)

Assignment 19.10

In Assignment 19.7, part "b", you drafted an adoption petition based primarily on facts that you invented yourself. Using those facts, draft a consent form (to be signed by the best friend) that complies with the statutory requirements for consent in your state.

☐ **EXHIBIT 19–3** Consent Form

CONSENT TO ADOPTION

We, the undersigned, being the father and mother, respectively, of _____
_____ , who was born on _____ , 19 __ , in _____ County, California, and being the persons entitled to the sole custody of said child,
do hereby give our full and free consent to the adoption of said child by
_____ and _____ _____ , his wife, and do hereby
relinquish to said persons forever all of our rights to the care, custody,
control, services, and earnings of said child.

Each of us hereby promises that, as soon as adoption proceedings are commenced in the state of _____ , we will properly execute any further instruments or papers necessary to effectuate the adoption of said
child by said persons.

Each of us hereby authorizes said persons, or either of them, to procure
and provide any and all medical, hospital, dental, and other care needed
for said child, it being understood by us that said persons have agreed to,
and will pay, such expenses without seeking reimbursement from us prior to
the adoption of said child.

Each of us fully understand that, upon the signing of this instrument, we
have irrevocably relinquished and waived all right to withdraw the consent
and authority herein given.

DATED: _____ , 19 __ .

Source: D. Adams, CALIFORNIA CODE FORM (1960).

Once a natural parent (or a guardian or an agency) consents to the adoption, can the consent be changed assuming that it was given according to the requisite formalities? When the adoptive decree has been entered, most states will *not* allow the consent to be revoked, but some states permit revocation beforehand if:

1. The court determines that the revocation would be in the best interest of the child.
2. The court determines that the consent was obtained by fraud, duress, or undue pressure.

See Exhibit 19-4 for an example of a notice of hearing on revocation.

Assignment 19.11

When, if ever, can consent to adoption be revoked in your state? (See General Instructions for the State-Code Assignment in chapter one. You may also have to check court opinions of your state if no statutes on revocation exist. See General Instructions for the Court-Opinion Assignment in chapter one.)

Involuntary Termination of Parental Rights

It would be illogical to permit a natural parent to prevent the adoption of his or her child by withholding consent if that parent has abandoned the child. Many statutes, therefore, provide that abandonment, extreme cruelty, conviction of certain crimes, willful neglect, etc., will mean that the consent of a parent engaged in such conduct is not necessary. The difficulty, however, is the absence of any clear definition of terms such as *abandonment* or *extreme cruelty*. Many courts have taken the position that a parent does not lose the right to withhold consent to an adoption unless the parent's conduct demonstrates *a clear intention to relinquish all parental duties*. Nonsupport in itself, for example, may not be enough if the parent has made some effort to see the child, at least occasionally.

As demonstrated in the following chart, many factors are relevant to the question of whether a parent had the *intention to abandon* or otherwise relinquish all rights in the child. A court will consider all of these factors in combination; no one factor is usually determinative.

Interviewing and Investigation Checklist

Factors Relevant to Whether an Intent to Abandon the Child Existed
Legal Interviewing Questions

1. How old are you now?
2. With whom is your child living?
3. Is the person who is caring for the child your relative, a friend, a stranger?
4. How did the child get there?
5. How long has the child been there?

6. When is the last time you saw the child?

7. How often do you see your child per month?

8. How often do you speak to your child on the phone per month?

9. How often do you write to your child?

10. Did you ever tell anyone that you did not want your child or that you wanted your child to find a home with someone else? If so, explain.

11. Did you ever tell anyone that you wanted your child to live with someone else temporarily until you got back on your feet again? If so, explain.

12. Have you ever placed your child in an adoption agency? Have you ever discussed adoption with anyone?

13. Have you ever been charged with neglecting, abandoning, or failing to support your child?

14. Has your child ever been taken from you for any period of time? If so, explain the circumstances.

15. Have you ever been found by a court to be mentally ill?

16. How much have you contributed to the support of your child while you were not living with the child?

17. Did you give the child any presents?

18. While your child was not with you, did you ever speak to the child's teachers or doctors?

19. Were you on public assistance while the child was not living with you? If so, what did you tell the public assistance workers about the child?

20. How well is the child being treated now?

21. Could anyone claim that the child lived under immoral or unhealthy circumstances while away from you and that you knew of these circumstances?

22. Has the child ever been charged with juvenile delinquency or been declared a person in need of supervision?

Possible Investigation Tasks

- Interview relatives, friends, and strangers who knew that the client visited the child.

- Interview anyone with whom the client may have discussed the reasons for leaving the child with someone else.

- Prepare an inventory of all the money and other property given by the client for the support of the child while the child was living with someone else.

- Collect receipts, e.g., cancelled check stubs, for all funds given by the client for such support.

- Locate all relevant court records, if any, e.g., custody order in divorce proceeding, neglect or juvenile delinquency petitions and orders.

- Interview state agencies that have been involved with the child. Determine how responsive the client has been to the efforts of the agency to help the client.

To take the drastic step of ordering an involuntary termination of parental rights, a court must be shown clear and convincing evidence that the parent is unfit. It is not enough to show that the parent has psychological or financial

☐ **EXHIBIT 19–4** Notice of Hearing on Issue of Revocation of Adoption

---

STATE OF NEW YORK

_____ COURT

COUNTY OF _____

ADDRESS _____

In the Matter of the Adoption of

_____

Adoptive Child

NOTICE OF HEARING ON ISSUE OF
REVOCATION AND DISPOSITION AS TO
CUSTODY, PRIVATE PLACEMENT ADOPTION

　　　PLEASE TAKE NOTICE that the _____Court, _____County, New York, on the ___
day of _____ , 19 ___ at _____ o'clock in the _____ noon of that day, or as
soon thereafter as counsel can be heard, will hear and determine whether
the revocation of consent of the parent in the above entitled matter shall
be permitted and, in any event, hear and determine what disposition should
be made with respect to the custody of said child.

　　　　　　　　　　　　　　　　　　　　_____
　　　　　　　　　　　　　　　　　　　　Chief Clerk of the _____ Court

To: _____
　　Adoptive Parents

　　_____
　　Parents

　　_____ , Esq.
　　Attorney for Adoptive Parent(s)

　　_____ , Esq.
　　Attorney for Parent(s)

　　_____
　　Law Guardian

Source: WEST'S MCKINNEY'S FORMS, NEW YORK § 22:24 (1986)

problems, or that there are potential adoptive parents waiting in the wings who can provide the child with a superior home environment. There must be a specific demonstration of unfitness through abandonment, willful neglect, etc.

The parent can be represented by counsel at the termination proceeding. There is, however, no automatic right to state-appointed counsel if the parent cannot afford to pay one. A court must decide on a case-by-case basis whether an indigent parent needs free counsel because of the complexity of the case.

If parental rights are terminated and there are adoptive parents available, a separate adoption procedure will take place. Of course, the parent whose rights have been terminated is not asked to consent to the adoption.

Assignment 19.12

(a) When is the consent of a natural parent *not* necessary in your state for the adoption of his or her child?

(b) Is there a proceeding to terminate the parental rights in your state that is separate from the adoption process? If so, explain.

(c) When will parental rights be terminated in your state? What are the grounds? What standard of proof must be met? Clear and convincing evidence?

(d) Who can initiate a petition to terminate parental rights in your state?

(See General Instructions for the State-Code Assignment in chapter one.)

(e) Prepare a flowchart of all the procedural steps necessary to terminate parental rights in your state. (See General Instructions for the Flowchart Assignment in chapter one.)

Assignment 19.13

Mary is the mother of two children. She is convicted of murdering her husband, their father. What facts do you think need to be investigated in order to determine whether Mary's parental rights will be terminated? (See General Instructions for the Investigation-Strategy Assignment in chapter one.)

Placement

Before ruling on a petition for adoption, the court will ask a public or private child welfare agency to investigate the case and make a recommendation to the court. The agency, in effect, assumes a role that is very similar to that of a social worker or a probation officer in many juvenile delinquency cases.

Assignment 19.14

(a) What is the role of child welfare agencies in your state after an adoption petition has been filed?

(b) Once an agency files a report in your state containing the results of its investigation and its recommendation on the proposed adoption, who has access to the report? Can the prospective adoptive parents have access to it? Can they (through their attorney) question the person who wrote the report?

(See General Instructions for the State-Code Assignment in chapter one. You may also need to check court opinions of your state. See General Instructions for the Court-Opinion Assignment in chapter one.)

Challenges to the Adoption Decree

In many states, an adoption decree does not become final immediately. An *interlocutory* (temporary) *decree* of adoption is first issued, which becomes final after a set period of time. During the interlocutory period, the child is placed with the adoptive parents. Since it would be very unhealthy for the child to be moved from place to place as legal battles continue to rage among any combination of adoptive parents, natural parents, and agencies, statutes place time limitations within which challenges to the adoption decree must be brought, e.g., two years.

Assignment 19.15

(a) Is there an interlocutory period in your state that must pass before the adoption can become final? If so, how long is it?

(b) After the trial court in your state issues a final adoption decree, to what court can the decree be appealed?

(c) If someone wants to challenge an adoption decree in your state, within what period of time must the challenge be brought? What happens if the challenge is not brought within this time?

(See General Instructions for the State-Code Assignment in chapter one. You may also need to check the court rules of your state courts, and perhaps court opinions as well. See General Instructions for the Court-Opinion Assignment in chapter one.)

Assignment 19.16

Rich and Paula Davis are the natural parents of John. Following a divorce, Rich is granted custody of John. Rich illegally takes John to another state, where his girlfriend adopts him. During the adoption proceeding, Rich falsely tells the court that John's mother, Paula, is dead. Paula therefore never receives notice of the adoption proceeding. Years later, after the passing of the statute of limitations, Paula learns about the adoption for the first time. Can she still challenge the adoption? (See General Instructions for the Legal-Analysis Assignment in chapter one.)

Assignment 19.17

Draft a flowchart of all the procedural steps involved in an adoption proceeding in your state. (See General Instructions for the Flowchart Assignment in chapter one.)

Assignment 19.18

Contact a paralegal, an attorney, or a legal secretary in your state who has worked on adoption cases in the past. Obtain answers to the following questions. (See General Instructions for the Systems Assignment in chapter one.)

1. How many adoption cases have you worked on?

2. How many of them have been uncontested?

3. Approximately how long does it take to process an uncomplicated, uncontested adoption?

4. Is there a difference between working on an adoption case and working on another kind of case in the law office? If so, what is the difference?

5. What are the major steps for processing an adoption in this state? What documents must be filed? What court appearances must be made? Etc.

6. What formbook or other treatise do you use, if any, that is helpful?

7. Does your office have its own internal manual that covers any aspect of adoption practice?

8. In an adoption case, what is the division of labor among the attorney, the paralegal, and the legal secretary?

Section E. Consequences of Adoption

Once the adoption becomes final, the adopted child and the adoptive parents have almost all the rights and obligations toward each other that natural parents and children have toward each other. The major exception involves the death of a relative of the adoptive parent.

Example

Kevin is the adopted child of Paul. Paul's brother, Bill, dies intestate (i.e., without leaving a valid will). Can Kevin inherit from Bill?

In some states, the answer would be no: an adopted child cannot take an intestate share of a relative of its adoptive parents. Other states do not impose this limitation.

In most other respects, an adopted child is treated the same as a natural child:

- Adopted children can take the name of their adoptive parents.

- The birth certificate can be changed to reflect the new parents.

- Adopted children can inherit from their adoptive parents (and in a few states, can continue to inherit from their natural parents).

- Adoptive parents have a right to the services and earnings of the adopted children.

- Adoptive parents must support adopted children.

- Adopted children are entitled to workers' compensation benefits due to the on-the-job injuries of their adoptive parent.

- If an adoptive parent dies with a will leaving property to "my heirs" or to "my children" or to "my issue," without mentioning any individuals by name, most (but not all) courts are inclined to conclude that the intention of the deceased adoptive parent was to include its adopted children as well as its natural children within the designation of "heirs," "children," or "issue."

Assignment 19.19

(a) What rights and obligations are assumed by adoptive parents and children in your state?

(b) In the hypothetical immediately above involving Kevin, Paul, and Bill, could Kevin inherit from Bill in your state?

(c) Suppose that Kevin's natural parent dies intestate. Can Kevin inherit from his natural parent in your state?

(d) Helen is the natural child of George and Sally; Bob is their adopted child. Can Helen and Bob (now a widower) marry in your state?

(Check statutory law and case on the above questions. See General Instructions for the State-Code Assignment in chapter one, and General Instructions for the Court-Opinion Assignment in chapter one.)

Section F. Confidentiality

In recent years there has been great controversy over whether adopted children have a right to discover the identity of their natural parents. The traditional answer has been no. Once the adoption becomes final, the record is sealed. The data within it is confidential. Some states, however, have created limited exceptions to this rule. If *good cause* can be shown, access to part of the adoption records may be allowed. For example, an adopted child may need medical information on its natural parents to help treat diseases that might be hereditary. Similarly, the adopted child may need some information about the identity of its natural parents to avoid unknowingly marrying a natural brother or sister. Access to any information in the records, however, is the exception. The need must be great. Many courts have held that it is not enough for the adopted child to prove that he or she is experiencing emotional distress due to not knowing the identity of his or her natural parents.

Some independent or private adoptions give the participants the option of maintaining limited contact between the natural parent and the child after the adoption. These are called *open adoptions,* involving face-to-face meetings or an exchange of identifying information. Some believe that such adoptions should be discouraged. Young women "are finding it harder to get on with their lives . . . ." "They start living for the photos that the adoptive parents send them every month." Adoptive parents sometimes "find themselves not only raising a new baby but providing counseling for the birth mother who often finds it difficult to break her bond with the child." The Council of State Governments, *Adoption,* State Government News 31 (September 1989). Not many adoptive parents, therefore, pursue open adoptions. A few states have established a register in which adopted children and natural parents can indicate a willingness to communicate with each other. If both do not register, however, the traditional rule of anonymity prevails.

☐ **EXHIBIT 19–5** Adoption in America

	Is independent adoption legal?	Can a profit-making organization be licensed to provide children?	What is the length of time between filing for and finalizing an adoption?	How soon after birth can a mother consent to adoption?	How long is she given to revoke her consent?*
Alabama	Yes‡	Yes	6 months	Anytime	Not specified
Alaska	Yes	Yes	Varies	Anytime	10 days
Arizona	Yes	Yes	6 months	72 hours	No time
Arkansas	Yes	Yes	6 months	24 hours	10 days
California	Yes‡	No	Usually 6–12 months	After hospital discharge‡	Until adoption is filed‡
Colorado	Yes‡	Yes	6 months	Anytime in court	Several days
Connecticut	No	No	1 year after placement	48 hours	20–30 days
Delaware	No	Yes	2–30 days	Anytime once drug-free	Until parental rights ended
D.C.	Yes	Yes	6–12 months	72 hours	10 days
Florida	Yes	No	At least 30 days	Anytime	Not specified
Georgia	Yes‡	No	At least 60 days	Anytime	10 days
Hawaii	Yes	No	Varies (131-day average)	3 days	Until placement
Idaho	Yes	Yes	30 days	Anytime	30 days
Illinois	Yes	Yes	6 months	72 hours	No time
Indiana	Yes	Yes	Varies	State policy: 48 hours	Until adoption is final
Iowa	Yes	Yes	6 months from placement	72 hours	Until parental rights ended
Kansas	Yes	Yes	At least 30 days	Anytime	Until adoption is final‡
Kentucky	Yes‡	Yes	Usually within 180 days	5 days, in court	No time
Louisiana	Yes	Yes	6–12 months	5 days	30 days
Maine	Yes	Yes	Varies, a week to several months	Anytime in probate court	Varies
Maryland	Yes	Yes	2–6 months	15 days	90 days
Massachusetts	No	No	Varies	4 days	No time
Michigan	No	Yes	1 year	Anytime	Until placement‡
Minnesota	No‡	No	At least 3 months	Anytime	10 working days
Mississippi	Yes	Yes	0–6 months	72 hours	No time
Missouri	Yes	Yes	9 months	48 hours	Until adoption hearing
Montana	Yes‡	No	No time set	Anytime	Until adoption is final

☐ **EXHIBIT 19—5** Adoption in America (continued)

	Is independent adoption legal?	Can a profit-making organization be licensed to provide children?	What is the length of time between filing for and finalizing an adoption?	How soon after birth can a mother consent to adoption?	How long is she given to revoke her consent?*
Nebraska	Yes‡	Yes	6 months	Varies	No time
Nevada	Yes	No	6 months	72 hours	No time
New Hampshire	Yes	No	At least 6 months	72 hours	Until adoption is final
New Jersey	Yes	No	At least 6 months	72 hours	Not specified
New Mexico	Yes	Yes	90–180 days from placement	72 hours	No time
New York	Yes	No	6 months	Anytime	0–45 days
North Carolina	Yes‡	Yes	1 year	Anytime	1–3 months
North Dakota	No	Yes	At least 6 months	72 hours	10 days
Ohio	Yes	Yes	6 months	72 hours	Until adoption is final
Oklahoma	Yes	No	6 months	Anytime	30 days
Oregon	Yes	Yes	About 90 days	Anytime	Until placement
Pennsylvania	Yes	Yes	No set time	72 hours	Until adoption is final
Rhode Island	Yes	No	At least 6 months	15 days	1 year
South Carolina	Yes	Yes	90–365 days	Anytime	No time
South Dakota	Yes	Yes	6 months, 10 days	5 days	30-day appeal period
Tennessee	Yes	No	6 months	Anytime	15 days
Texas	Yes	Yes‡	6 months	Anytime	0–60 days
Utah	Yes	Yes	At least 6 months	Anytime once drug-free	Until adoption is final
Vermont	Yes	No	6 months from placement	Anytime	10 days
Virginia	Yes‡	Yes	0–12 months	Anytime; effective in 10 days	Before placement or in court
Washington	Yes	Yes	No set time	Before birth‡	Until adoption is final‡
West Virginia	Yes	Yes	At least 6 months	72 hours	No time
Wisconsin	Yes‡	Yes	At least 6 months	Anytime in court	No time
Wyoming	Yes	Yes	6 months	Anytime	No time‡

Source: © 1989 by the National Committee for Adoption, Inc. From *Adoption Factbook*, available from the Committee at P.O. Box 33366, Wash., D.C. 20033. Note: Adoptions of American Indians are governed by the federal Indian Child Welfare Act, which prevents a mother from signing consent papers until 10 days after birth and allows her to revoke her consent until an adoption is final.

☐ **EXHIBIT 19–5** Adoption in America (continued)

	What expenses are prospective parents allowed to pay?**	What are the legal penalties for baby selling and for baby buying?	Are sealed records available to adult adoptees?
Alabama	Not defined by law	Maximum 3 months in jail and/or $100 fine	Yes†
Alaska	Not defined by law; must report all payments to court	No defined penalties; judge decides	Yes
Arizona	Birthmother's medical, legal and counseling costs; must report to court	6 months to 1.9 years in prison and/or $1,000 to $150,000 fine	No
Arkansas	Birthmother's medical, living and other costs; must report to court	Felony: 3–10 years in prison	No†
California	Not defined by law; all payments must be reported to court	Misdemeanor: local D.A. decides penalty	No
Colorado	Reasonable expenses approved by court	Felony: 4–16 years in prison and/or up to $750,000 fine	No†
Connecticut	Agency fees, birthmother's medical, living, counseling costs; must report to court	Felony: 1–5 years in prison and/or $5,000 fine	No†
Delaware	Agency fees, birthmother's legal costs; must report to court	No defined penalties; judge decides	No
D.C.	Not defined by law	90 days in jail and/or $300 fine	No
Florida	Not defined by law; must report all payments to court	Felony: maximum 5 years in prison	No
Georgia	Birthmother's medical costs; must report to court	Felony: maximum 10 years in prison and/or $1,000 fine	No
Hawaii	Not defined by law	No defined penalties; judge decides	No
Idaho	Not defined by law	Felony: maximum 14 years in prison and/or $5,000 fine	No†
Illinois	Birthmother's medical and legal costs; must report to court	Felony: 1–3 years in prison and/or $10,000 fine	No†
Indiana	Birthmother's medical, legal and other court-approved costs	Felony: maximum 2 years in prison and/or $10,000 fine	No†
Iowa	Birthmother's medical and other costs; must report to court	30 days in jail and/or $100 fine	No
Kansas	Not defined by law; must report all payments to court	No defined penalties; judge decides	Yes
Kentucky	Not defined by law; must report all payments to court	6 months in prison and/or $500 to $2,000 fine	No†
Louisiana	Birthmother's medical, legal and living costs‡; must report to court	Felony: maximum 5 years in prison and/or $5,000 fine	No†

☐ **EXHIBIT 19–5** Adoption in America (continued)

	What expenses are prospective parents allowed to pay?**	What are the legal penalties for baby selling and for baby buying?	Are sealed records available to adult adoptees?
Maine	Not defined by law	No defined penalties; judge decides	No[†]
Maryland	Birthmother's medical and legal costs	Maximum 3 months in jail and/or $100 fine	No[†]
Massachusetts	In identified adoption, all of birthparents' adoption-related costs	2½–5 years in jail and/or $5,000 to $30,000 fine	No
Michigan	Agency fees and other court-approved costs	Maximum 90 days in jail and/or $100 fine	No
Minnesota	Agency fees	Maximum 90 days in jail and/or $700 fine	No[†]
Mississippi	Birthmother's medical and legal costs	Maximum 5 years in prison and/or $5,000 fine	No
Missouri	Not defined by law	Felony: maximum 7 years in prison and/or $5,000 fine	No[†]
Montana	Not defined by law; must report all payments to court	Maximum fine: $1,000	No
Nebraska	Not defined by law	Maximum 3 months in jail and/or $500 fine	No[†]
Nevada	Birthmother's medical and necessary living costs; must report to court	1–6 years in prison and/or a maximum $5,000 fine	No[†]
New Hampshire	Not defined by law	No defined penalties; judge decides	No
New Jersey	Birthmother's medical and reasonable living costs; must report to court	3–5 years in prison and/or $7,500 fine	No[†]
New Mexico	Not defined by law; must report all payments to court	Maximum fine: $500	No
New York	Birthmother's medical, legal and other necessary costs	No defined penalties; judge decides	No[†]
North Carolina	Agency fees	Misdemeanor: court decides penalty	No
North Dakota	Not defined by law; must report all payments to court	Felony: maximum 5 years in prison and/or $5,000 fine	No[†]
Ohio	Birthmother's medical, legal and other costs; must report to court	Maximum 6 months in jail and/or $500 to $1,000 fine	No
Oklahoma	Birthmother's medical, legal and counseling costs; must be approved by court	Minimum 1 year in jail	No

☐ **EXHIBIT 19–5** Adoption in America (continued)

	What expenses are prospective parents allowed to pay?**	What are the legal penalties for baby selling and for baby buying?	Are sealed records available to adult adoptees?
Oregon	Not defined by law; must report all payments to court	No defined penalties; judge decides	No†
Pennsylvania	Birthmother's medical costs; must report to court	Maximum 5 years in prison and/or $10,000 fine	No†
Rhode Island	Not defined by law	No defined penalties; judge decides	No
South Carolina	Not defined by law; must report all payments to court	Felony: maximum 10 years in prison and/or $10,000 fine	No†
South Dakota	Not defined by law; must report all payments to court	Felony: maximum 2 years in prison and/or $2,000 fine	No†
Tennessee	Birthmother's medical and legal costs; must report to court	Felony: 1–10 years in prison	No†
Texas	Birthmother's medical and legal costs	Felony: 2–10 years in prison and/or $5,000 fine	No†
Utah	Birthmother's medical, legal and other adoption-related costs	Must forfeit payment and pay $10,000 maximum fine	No†
Vermont	Law specifies only those "directly related to mother's support"; must report to court	No defined penalties; judge decides	No
Virginia	Not defined by law	No defined penalties; judge decides	No
Washington	Birthmother's medical and legal costs	Felony: maximum 5 years in prison and/or $10,000 fine	No
West Virginia	Birthmother's medical and legal costs; must report to court	No defined penalties; judge decides	No
Wisconsin	Birthmother's medical, legal and counseling costs; must report to court	Felony: maximum 2 years in prison and/or $10,000 fine	No†
Wyoming	Not defined by law	No defined penalties; judge decides	No

*Assuming no fraud, duress or coercion is proved. **Living expenses usually include medical, housing, food, travel and clothing costs. †Information may be obtained through a voluntary state registry or adoption agency. ‡With restrictions or exceptions.

Assignment 19.20

Under what circumstances, if any, can an adopted child gain access to adoption records? (See General Instructions for the State-Code Assignment in chapter one. You may also have to check court opinions. See General Instructions for the Court-Opinion Assignment in chapter one.)

Section G. Equitable Adoption

What happens when a person breaks an adoption contract with a natural parent? Such contracts are occasionally in writing but more often are simply oral understandings between the parties. Assume that the person takes custody of the child, treats him or her as a member of the family, but never goes through formal adoption procedures. The person then dies intestate, i.e., without leaving a valid will. Technically, the child cannot inherit from the deceased because the adoption never took place. This argument may be used by the deceased's natural children to prevent the nonadopted children from sharing in the deceased's estate.

Many feel that it would be unfair to deny the child inheritance benefits simply because the deceased failed to abide by the agreement to adopt. To avoid the unfairness, some courts conclude that such a child was adopted under the doctrine of *equitable adoption* and hence is entitled to inheritance and all other rights of adopted children. The doctrine is also referred to as *adoption by estoppel;* challengers will be estopped (i.e., prevented) from denying that such a child has been adopted.

Some courts will reach the same result *even if there was no initial agreement to adopt.* If clear evidence exists that the deceased treated the child as his or her own in every way, a court might rule that a contract to adopt was *implied.* When the deceased dies intestate, equitable adoption status will be accorded the child so that he or she will have full inheritance rights from the deceased.

Assignment 19.21

To what extent, if at all, does your state recognize equitable adoption or adoption by estoppel? (See General Instructions for the Court-Opinion Assignment in chapter one.)

Key Chapter Terminology

Custody✓	Petition for Adoption
Guardianship✓	Notice
Ward	Consent
Termination of Parental Rights	Parental Unfitness
Foster Home	Revocation of Consent
Stepparent	Intent to Abandon
Adoption	Placement
Agency Adoption	Interlocutory Decree
Independent Adoption	Challenges to Decree
Baby Buying	Confidentiality
Black-Market Adoptions	Open Adoptions
Preferences	Sealed Records
Subject-Matter Jurisdiction	Equitable Adoption
Choice of Venue	

CHAPTER TWENTY

Surrogacy and the New Science of Motherhood

■ Chapter Outline

''Abram's wife Sarai had not borne him any children. But she had an Egyptian slave girl named Hagar, and so she said to Abram, 'The Lord has kept me from having children. Why don't you sleep with my slave girl? Perhaps she can have a child for me.' ''
Genesis 16:1–2 (TEV)

''The reproductive capabilities available to assist infertile couples today are astonishing. Pioneering doctors can now remove eggs from a woman, fertilize them in a laboratory, and reinsert them into that same woman or into another woman; regulate the woman's hormone balance to enhance implantation; monitor the gestation of embryo and fetus, and perform surgery on the fetus in some cases. We now have the ability to separate a child's genetic, gestational, and legal parents so that it is possible to have five different individuals contributing to the birth of a single child: egg donor, sperm donor, womb donor or gestator, and the social parents who will raise the child.''
Billig, *High Tech Earth Mothering,* 9 DISTRICT LAWYER, 57 (July/August 1985).

"Just as men have the right to sell their sperm and become surrogate fathers, so women should have the right to sell their reproductive services and become . . . surrogate mothers."

Gale, *The Right to Pregnancy by Contract*, NEW YORK TIMES BOOK REV. 12 (December 17, 1989).

O ne of the most dramatic family law issues to emerge in the last twenty years has been surrogate motherhood. An unpregnant woman enters a contract to become pregnant, to give birth to a child, and then to relinquish all parental rights upon birth through adoption. Due to spectacular scientific advances, a variety of methods of becoming pregnant are available. Unfortunately, traditional legal principles do not always fit results made available by the innovations of medicine and biology.

When something goes wrong in a surrogacy contract, e.g., the surrogate mother changes her mind about giving up the child, someone inevitably sues. The courts then enter the picture. But what law does a court apply to such a contract? The first instinct of the court is to look to the legislature to determine whether any statutes apply. Until recently, no such statutes existed. Hence the court is forced to write common law to resolve the controversy. (Common law is judge-made law created in the absence of other controlling law such as statutes.) This approach has not been satisfactory. The development of common law is painfully slow, and many feel that it is ill-suited to respond to the rapid developments of science in this area.

Consequently, state legislatures have been under pressure to do something. But the legislatures are not sure what to do. Are new statutes needed? If so, what kind? In Nevada, the state legislature asked Dana Bennett to prepare a report that identified the options the legislature should consider. Excerpts from the report, which draws heavily from a similar report in Wisconsin, are reprinted in this chapter.

The main methods of achieving surrogate motherhood are *artificial insemination* and *in vetro fertilization*. Married couples seek the services of surrogates because of female infertility and the relatively small number of babies available through adoption.

Those who argue that surrogate contracts should be legalized point out that since society cannot stop the practice of surrogacy, it would be better to regulate it in order to ensure competency and honesty in the process. Those who would ban surrogate contracts denounce the very notion of "buying and selling babies" in an atmosphere of exploitation.

Numerous questions arise as the topic of surrogacy comes before the legislatures of the country. For example, if a surrogate mother is paid as she goes through adoption, has there been a violation of the law that prohibits paying someone to consent to an adoption? Under current paternity laws, is the husband of the surrogate mother presumed to be the father of the child that she is under contract to allow another man to adopt? On the ultimate question of custody, what assurances exist that giving the child to the couple that hires the surrogate mother will always be in the best interest of the child? Also, numerous enforcement questions must be addressed when it becomes clear that one of the parties to the surrogate contract refuses to go along with its terms, or when something happens that is not covered in the terms of the contract, e.g., the surrogate mother gives birth to a baby with AIDS.

State legislatures have handled such questions in different ways, including the following: doing nothing; prohibiting surrogate contracts; permitting such contracts, but regulating them; studying the question further; and finally, giving serious consideration to a new model act called the *Uniform Status of Children of Assisted Conception Act* proposed by the National Conference of Commissioners on Uniform State Laws. This model act is printed at the end of the chapter.

Surrogate Parenting

D. Bennett, *Surrogate Parenting* (1988) (Background Paper 88-2
prepared for the Legislative Counsel Bureau of Nevada

I
Introduction

In March 1987, the nation's attention focused on a breach of contract battle underway in New Jersey. The contract in question was between Elizabeth and William Stern and Mary Beth Whitehead (now Mary Beth Whitehead-Gould). The Sterns had contracted with Ms. Whitehead in 1985 to act as a surrogate mother. [Under the terms of the contract, Ms. Whitehead was to be artificially inseminated with Mr. Stern's sperm, become pregnant, give birth to a baby, turn it over to the Sterns, and cooperate in the termination of her parental rights. Mrs. Stern would then adopt the baby.] Upon the birth of the baby—known as Baby M in the case—Ms. Whitehead reconsidered and refused to relinquish her parental rights. The Sterns then sued in an attempt to hold Ms. Whitehead to the terms of the contract.

On March 31, 1987, a New Jersey trial court upheld the contract, granted permanent custody to the Sterns, permitted Mrs. Stern to adopt the child, and denied any rights to Ms. Whitehead. On February 3, 1988, the New Jersey Supreme Court approved only the custody portion of the lower court's decision, ruling that surrogate parenting contracts fall under the New Jersey "baby-selling" statutes and are therefore illegal.[1]

The publicity surrounding this case led to a flurry of activity in legislative bodies around the country as pro- and anti-surrogacy groups attempted to sway policymaking bodies to one side or the other. . . .

II
Definitions

Although the term "surrogate parenting" has become widely used since the Baby M case, it can refer to more than one method of achieving parenthood. In addition, the parties involved in a surrogacy contract may not necessarily be limited to a married couple contracting with a single woman. The parties could involve a married surrogate mother, a single father, or single-sex couples. However, for ease of discussion, . . . the terms "married couple," "husband," and "wife" will be used, keeping in mind that a broader definition may apply to these words.

A. Methods

Four general methods of surrogate parenting are recognized. These methods are:

1. *Artificial Insemination by Husband (AIH).* The AIH method is an
   arrangement in which the surrogate, a woman other than the wife of the

---

[1] *In the Matter of Baby M,* 109 N.J. 396, 537 A.2d 1227 (1988).

sperm donor, is artificially inseminated with the sperm of the husband of a married couple.

2. *In-Vitro Fertilization (IVF).* The IVF method is a process by which a sperm and an egg are joined in a laboratory and the fertilized egg is implanted in the surrogate.

3. *Artificial Insemination by Donor (AID[1]).* The AID[1] method is a technique in which the surrogate is artificially inseminated with the sperm of a donor other than the contracting male. Such sperm is typically a specimen obtained from a sperm bank.*

4. *Natural Insemination (NI).* The NI method involves a situation where sexual intercourse occurs between the surrogate and the husband of a married couple.

Of the four methods, AIH is the most common and NI is the least. Sometimes, the IVF and AID[1] methods are chosen in surrogate parenting situations, but not as frequently as AIH. . . . Because AIH is the most common method chosen in surrogate parenting agreements, that definition will be applied to the term *surrogate parenting* in this [discussion].

B. Agreements

The agreement between the surrogate mother and the intended parents takes one of two forms: (1) commercial; or (2) noncommercial. Both agreements involve similar factors. A couple contracts with a woman to bear a child for them. The woman agrees to be artificially inseminated with the husband's sperm, carry the child to term and surrender her parental rights to the biological father upon the birth of the child.

Once the husband has full parental rights to the child [upon birth], the wife (technically the child's stepmother) begins adoption proceedings. Some . . . [states allow] the wife to forego formal adoption procedures and obtain a substitute birth certificate from a court of competent jurisdiction. In return, the couple agrees to pay all of the surrogate's medical expenses and other necessary expenses (such as maternity clothing).

The difference between a commercial and a noncommercial agreement centers on whether a fee is paid to the surrogate mother. If a fee—usually around $10,000—is paid, then the agreement is considered to be commercial. However, many surrogacy agreements are between family members or friends and do not involve the payment of a fee. These agreements are the noncommercial contracts.

A major argument in the courts and the legislatures involves the nature of this fee. Is it a fee for the surrogate mother's services or is it a fee in exchange for the surrender of her parental rights? . . .

Another factor in surrogacy contracts is the broker. Either a private agency or a lawyer, the broker is a third party who coordinates a surrogate parenting agreement. Although a broker receives a fee (again, in the $10,000 range), a broker could be used in both commercial and noncommercial arrangements. However, most arrangements made through a broker include a fee paid to the surrogate mother.

III
Reasons for Choosing Surrogate Parenting Agreements

According to a study of surrogacy recently completed in Wisconsin, the demand for surrogate mothers stems primarily from female infertility. The National Center for

---

*Artificial Insemination by Donor (AID[2]) is a technique in which the *wife* is artificially inseminated with the sperm of a donor other than her husband. Such sperm is typically a specimen obtained from a sperm bank.

Health Statistics estimates that 10 to 15 percent of all married couples are infertile (defined as partners who are sexually active, not using contraception, and unable to conceive after at least one year). The center excludes the surgically sterile from its statistics. The Wisconsin study also cites evidence that suggests the number of infertile women is on the increase due to the use of intrauterine birth control devices, greater incidence of sexually-transmitted diseases, previous abortions and the postponement of childbearing to establish careers. Studies indicate that women who delay having children have a greater risk of being infertile, bearing children with birth defects, and/or being physically impaired. The most common treatments for female infertility are drugs and surgery. Until recently, when these treatments failed, adoption was the only alternative available.

Couples who want children, but cannot conceive, usually consider adoption. The Wisconsin study noted that, despite a marked increase in the number of live births to single women, fewer unrelated individuals are adopted. Recorded births to all unmarried women increased by almost 30 percent from 1975 to 1984, while births to unmarried women 15 to 24 years of age increased by more than 50 percent. However, the National Committee for Adoption reports that only 50,720 healthy infants were adopted by parents who were not blood relatives in 1982, compared to 82,800 adoptions in 1971. At the same time, demand has steadily increased. In 1984, the national committee estimated that the 2 million couples seeking to adopt were competing for 58,000 babies, a 35 to 1 ratio.

Adoption experts believe that the increasing willingness of single mothers to keep their children is a significant factor in limiting the number of infants available for adoption. An American Bar Foundation researcher reported that 15 percent of unwed teenage mothers gave their children up for adoption in 1972, while 4 percent allowed adoptions in 1978. One explanation offered for this trend is that the stigma once attached to single mothers has diminished. Peers and relatives often encourage single mothers to keep their babies. Medical personnel and social workers are less likely to encourage women to give babies up for adoption.

Laws have changed in recent years to allow single mothers more time to make or revoke a decision to allow adoption. Consequently, couples often cite long waiting periods and other obstacles to adoption (such as the age limit placed on prospective parents) as reasons for seeking surrogate mothers. [R. Roe, *Childbearing by Contract*, 4 (Wisconsin Legislative Bureau, March, 1988).]

Not all couples who contract with a surrogate have failed at adoption. Some couples would rather be childless than adopt an unrelated child. For such families, a genetic link to their child is of primary importance. For example, William Stern lost most of his family in Adolf Hitler's holocaust and wanted a child biologically linked to him. Newspaper interviews of intended fathers confirm the importance of a biological link to some seeking surrogates. One father favored a surrogate birth because "that child will be biologically half-mine" while another father stated that "we believe strongly in heredity."

IV
Major Arguments for and Against Surrogate Parenting

A review of the literature on surrogate parenting reveals several common policy positions on each side of this issue.

A. Supporting Arguments

Those who support surrogacy contracts and the regulation of them generally cite the following:

- A limitation placed on the fees charged by brokers and the licensing and regulation of brokers will ensure competency, honesty and legitimacy in this process.
- Due to the ever-decreasing number of babies available for adoption and the ever-increasing technology in the area of human reproduction, couples who desperately

want children will continue to seek out surrogate mothers. Consequently, some form of protection must be provided for the couple, the surrogate mother, and the resulting child.

- Proper examination of both couple and surrogate as provided in state law would ensure:

  1. That the couple is emotionally and financially ready to bear the responsibility of parenthood.
  2. That the couple is truly in need of this service, such as when the wife is unable to carry a child to term.
  3. That the woman who will bear the child is emotionally, physically, and psychologically able to carry the child and to give up her rights to the child at birth.

The majority of previous surrogate contracts were completed without [controversy]. Only a small percentage of surrogate mothers have refused to surrender the resulting babies. . . .

B. Opposing Arguments

Those people who advocate a ban on surrogacy contracts argue that:

- Children will be psychologically damaged when they discover that they were "bought."
- Surrogate parenting arrangements are in violation of the Thirteenth Amendment of the United States Constitution, which applies to slavery and can be interpreted to forbid the buying and selling of people.
- Surrogate parenting will become another form of economic exploitation of rich people over poor. As exemplified by the Baby M affair, the adoptive couples tend to have an economic and educational advantage over the surrogate. [A] study of potential and existing surrogate mothers also indicates that most of the women are unemployed or on some form of public assistance and only have a high school diploma. Thus, surrogate parenting arrangements will serve to create a class of "womb-sellers."
- There are plenty of nonwhite babies, older children, and special needs children available for adoption.
- Women will be forced—not because they choose, but because the contract requires—to abort fetuses upon demand or to become pregnant again in the case of a miscarriage.

V
Legislative Background

Surrogate parenting was not invented by the Sterns or Ms. Whitehead. It has been an option exercised by many prospective parents ever since advances in technology made it possible. Estimates indicate that over 500 babies were born through this arrangement between 1976 and 1986. . . . Recently, the American Bar Foundation estimated that the rate has risen to 500 surrogate births annually.

The Baby M case was unique because its public format opened national debate on the ethical, legal and moral aspects of a practice not defined in federal or state law. Previously, most custody cases were resolved behind closed doors.

Before March 1987, most legal decisions regarding surrogacy were determined by the courts. Two brief, nonspecific state laws existed, and only five bills had been introduced in state legislatures across the country. Four of those bills supported the practice, and one opposed it.

In the United States Congress, three bills were introduced after the Baby M affair. One would have banned the practice, one would have forbid federal enforcement of the contracts, and the other would have prohibited the use of federal money for veterans who wished to create a family through surrogacy. None of these bills passed. Historically, Congress has left family issues to be regulated by the states, so the bulk of legislative activity has been located at the state level.

According to the National Conference of State Legislatures (NCSL), in legislative sessions held in 1987, 71 bills to ban, regulate, or study the practice were introduced in 26 states and the District of Columbia. . . . These bills indicated that the Baby M case affected not only the number of bills but also the attitude of legislators regarding surrogacy. Of these 71 bills, 25 sought to ban or severely restrict surrogate parenting. Twenty-two of them called for study commissions, and 24 would have been recognized and regulated the practice. Although the majority of these bills did not pass their respective legislatures, the issue did not die. . . .

VI
Issues in State Law

According to the Wisconsin study of surrogacy, court decisions and discussions of surrogacy indicated that four existing areas of law affect surrogate parenting agreements. These areas are (1) adoption and termination of parental rights; (2) artificial insemination and legal paternity; (3) child custody; and (4) contracts. . . .

A. Adoption Laws

Two aspects of many state adoption laws may restrict or prevent surrogate parenting agreements. One forbids compensation in exchange for the consent to an adoption, and the other forbids consent to an adoption to be given prior to the birth of the child.

At least 24 states . . . prohibit the payment of compensation for adoptions. Often called "baby-selling" laws, these statutes range from those prohibiting all payments to those allowing payment of certain expenses. Nevada for example, forbids the payment of a fee in return for the mother's agreement to terminate her parental rights of the child.

While surrogacy opponents favor the use of adoption statutes to control it, proponents maintain that modern anti-"baby-selling" laws predate surrogate parenting and were designed to protect unwed mothers. Under a surrogacy agreement, the intended father is also the biological father; therefore, how can he buy his own child? Also, proponents argue, surrogates have voluntarily agreed to surrender the child. She is not doing so under pregnancy related stress. Finally, the fees are paid primarily to replace lost work time or pain and suffering.

All 50 states . . . have laws that prohibit a mother from granting consent to adoption before a child's birth or for some period of time after birth. Waiting periods range up to as much as 20 days (Pennsylvania). A mother's consent to surrender a newborn for adoption is not valid in Nevada until at least 72 hours after birth.

However, as with "baby-selling" laws, consent laws were designed to protect unwed mothers. The decision facing an unwed mother are not like those facing the surrogate mother who has voluntarily chosen to bear children for another couple.

B. Paternity Laws

Paternity laws may also affect surrogate arrangements. Some states retain the common-law rule that the husband of a woman who gives birth to a child is presumed to be the father. Courts in many of these states will not admit evidence to the contrary. A majority of states now allow a rebuttal to the presumption of paternity, but place a strict burden of proof on the contending party. . . .

Surrogate supporters argue that paternity laws were designed to protect the child, particularly the rights to inheritance, and were not drafted in anticipation of surrogate parenting arrangements. Rights and duties outlined in surrogate agreements fall on the natural father and would secure the child's rights. Critics point out that paternity determinations are made by courts and do not necessarily give custody to one party or the other.

Paternity laws could also affect surrogate arrangements based on the reliance on artificial insemination. Since most surrogate mothers are artificially inseminated, laws on that subject might be relevant. At least 30 states, . . . have laws that presume that the husband of the woman being inseminated is the child's father and that relieves the sperm donor of any legal obligation.

Although some critics approve applying artificial insemination law to surrogate agreements, others find the analogy suspect and open to court challenge.

C. Custody Issues

The basis for custody decisions is a determination of the best interest of the child. The standards for judging the suitability of intended parents include marital and family status, mental and physical health, income and property, any history of child abuse or neglect and other relevant facts. In the case of Baby M, custody of the child was awarded to the Sterns because the court felt it was in the best interest of the child. Ms. Whitehead's divorce after 13 years of marriage and subsequent marriage to the father of her unborn child 2 weeks after the divorce were key factors in the court's decision.

A spokesperson for the National Committee for Adoption objects to surrogate contracts because they are not required to take into account the best interest of the child. Unlike normal adoption proceedings, no one screens intended parents. Currently, surrogacy agreements require nothing more than the financial ability to hire a lawyer and pay the surrogate mother.

Supporters of surrogate agreements argue that intended parents should receive the same treatment as ordinary parents, since the only qualification they lack is the physical ability to have children. Supporters also maintain that surrogate agreements are inherently in the best interest of the child because the intended parents have given much thought to their actions and decided that they truly want a child. Adoption proceedings, on the other hand, were devised to provide a permanent home for a child who otherwise would not have one. In a surrogate agreement, the child's home is provided by contract.

D. Contractual Duties

Existing federal and state contract laws do not address the issues of the surrogate's liability or acceptable remedies in case of breach of contract, nor do they address the responsibilities of the intended parents.

Contracts impose a number of duties on one or both of the intended parents. These duties include the payment of expenses and fees and the assumption of responsibility for the child at birth. If the birth mother performs as agreed, does she have recourse if the other party refuses to pay all or part of the expenses and fees? What happens if the intended parents refuse to take the child? Can the surrogate mother sue the natural father for child support?

Some of these issues are already facing state courts. For example, in Texas, a 24-year-old surrogate mother died of heart failure in her eighth month of pregnancy; and in Washington, D.C., a baby born through a surrogate agreement was diagnosed as having acquired immune deficiency syndrome (AIDS). Now, neither the surrogate mother nor contracting parents want the AIDS baby. These issues were not previously addressed in the contracts.

Enforcement of a surrogate mother's duties are even more difficult. She agrees to be inseminated, bear a child and surrender all parental rights. She is also to refrain from sexual intercourse during the insemination period and has the duty to refrain from activities that may harm the fetus. If medical clauses are included in the contract, what recourse do the intended parents have if the surrogate refuses to follow them? If she refuses the insemination, are any expenses refunded to the intended parents? If the surrogate chooses to have an abortion in the first trimester, which is legally her right, can the intended parents sue for expenses? Can they sue for damages if the surrogate decides to keep the child?

Even if the surrogate agreement clears all other legal hurdles, many questions remain about the responsibilities of each party to the contract.

VII
Existing Legislation

As of November 1988, nine states have laws which—in some way—govern paid surrogate contracts. Indiana, Kentucky, Louisiana, and Nebraska prohibit paid surrogacy agreements. These state laws also allow surrogates to choose not to give up their babies to the other couples. Michigan is the only state that makes involvement in a paid surrogate contract a criminal activity. Arkansas, Florida, Kansas, and Nevada have taken mixed approaches to the issue. The following discussion summarizes the laws in these states.

A. Arkansas

The Arkansas law states that any child born to an unmarried woman through artificial insemination is the child of that woman, except in surrogate parenting situations. The law further allows the intended mother in a surrogate parenting situation to obtain a substitute birth certificate from a court of competent jurisdiction.

B. Florida

The law in Florida prohibits the payment of a fee to a woman in return for agreement to surrender her parental rights. It allows for the payment of fees in connection with a preplanned pregnancy as long as the fees are not conditioned upon transfer of her parental rights.

The law further authorizes preplanned adoption arrangements, or surrogate parenting agreements, under certain conditions. For example, the birth mother has seven days to change her mind about surrendering the child; the intended parents can request appropriate tests on the child, if the father is presumed to be the biological parent of the child; and the intended parents and the surrogate mother must be represented by different legal counsel.

C. Indiana

Indiana . . . prohibits the state courts from enforcing surrogate mother contracts as contrary to public policy. The law declares that any surrogate agreements entered into after March 14, 1988, are void, and no custody decisions are to be based on the existence of such a contract. . . .

D. Kansas

Kansas . . . prohibits a person from advertising for adoption services, either as one wanting to adopt or as one wanting to give a child up for adoption. The law also prohibits advertisements from those acting as a third party in an adoption. However, the law specifically exempts three groups from these provisions: (1) a licensed child placement agency; (2) the department of social and rehabilitation services; and (3) those wishing to contract with or as a surrogate mother.

E. Kentucky

Kentucky . . . prohibits paid surrogacy agreements. It declares all such agreements void and unenforceable. However, no penalties are assigned to any parties found guilty of engaging in such contracts.

F. Louisiana

Louisiana was the first state to pass a law [banning] . . . paid surrogate contracts. However, no penalties are provided.

G. Michigan

Michigan was the first state to establish criminal penalties for involvement in surrogate contracts. Effective on September 1, 1988, [the law] bans paid surrogate parenting contracts. . . .

Parties who engage in such a contract are guilty of a misdemeanor and face a penalty of a fine up to $10,000 and/or up to one year in prison. Parties involved in arranging such a contract are guilty of a felony and face a fine up to $50,000 and/or up to five years in prison.

The law further states that such contracts are void and unenforceable. In the case of a custody dispute as a result of one of these contracts, custody would be decided in light of prevailing custody laws, and not the laws governing contracts.

Late in September 1988, Michigan's Wayne County Circuit Court Judge John Gillis ruled that the law is constitutional, but needs further interpretation. At the time, he . . . indicated that he would probably interpret the law to mean that it is unlawful to pay a woman to surrender her parental rights, but that it is not unlawful to pay a woman for her services. This interpretation would allow a woman to be paid for being artificially inseminated and the biological father to initiate a custody action for the resulting child. The Michigan Attorney General's Office, the American Civil Liberties Union, and the legislators involved in the passage of the bill all indicated agreement with the suggested compromise interpretation.

H. Nebraska

Nebraska . . . maintains that surrogate parenting agreements are void and unenforceable. No penalty is provided. However, the law states that the biological father of a child born under a surrogate agreement will have all the rights and responsibilities as allowed by law.

I. Nevada

As do many other states, Nevada . . . prohibits the payment of fees in exchange for parental rights. It also prohibits the acceptance of expense money by the birth mother with the intent of not completing a preplanned adoption, but it does not prohibit the birth mother from reconsidering her decision to relinquish custody of the child upon that child's birth.

However, subsection 5 of NRS 127.287 . . . distinctly exempts surrogate contracts from these provisions. Specifically, this subsection provides that:

> The provisions of this section do not apply if a woman enters into a lawful contract to act as a surrogate, be inseminated and give birth to the child of a man not her husband.

The legislation introduced in the 1987 session (which resulted in the above subsection) did not specifically address the issue of regulation of surrogacy contracts or make provisions for those contracts. But the reference to "lawful" surrogate contracts has led some analysts to interpret this statutes as permitting surrogacy arrangements. . . .

VIII
Legislative Alternatives

A number of options are available for states in dealing with surrogacy. The alternatives include:

1. No legislation, which would require the courts to rule under current law and/or force the private sector to regulate the practice
2. Outlaw all forms of arrangements or ban commercial contracts and third party profits
3. Regulate either all arrangements or purely commercial ones

4. Appoint study commissions to examine the issues in greater detail before deciding what legislation, if any, is needed

5. Use model legislation already drafted. . . .

A. No Legislation

The "no legislation" alternative argues that the courts rather than the legislatures are more flexible instruments for resolving surrogacy cases. Since few contracts end in dispute, those that do can be resolved by the courts. Although New Jersey's Superior Court originally ruled in favor of the contract terms in the Baby M matter, the state's supreme court found the authority in current law to overturn that decision and rule against surrogacy contracts. Kentucky's supreme court found grounds for allowing contracts. The circumstances of each case were different.

A Northwestern University law professor argues that the "heavy hand of the state" should be kept out of surrogate arrangements. He contends that the law has no business being involved in what are private and often painful family decisions. Legislation would set up regulations that would need continual revision. He further believes that courts should simply refuse to enforce surrogate contracts, treating them as illegal in the same manner as they treat gambling contracts. Couples wanting surrogate mothers would go to private agencies that provide the service. If everything works out, the intended parents receive a child and the agency and mother are paid. The "no contract" approach, the professor argues, would protect the weakest party, the natural mother. Agencies would have incentives to screen for reliable mothers or they would go out of business. Contracting parents would only lose time and could try again.

B. Prohibiting Surrogate Agreements

Three options relate to surrogate prohibition. The first would prohibit all arrangements whether or not they involved a fee. The second type would ban commercial contracts, which would allow women who conceive and bear someone else's child to be reimbursed for expenses. The first two options would also void any existing contracts. A third option would bar brokers from operating surrogate practices, but would not disturb relationships between individual parties.

Most state legislators seeking to outlaw surrogacy have made proposals based on the first two options. Although several bills proposed to bar surrogate brokers, none have used this method as an exclusive means to eliminate commercial contracts.

C. Permit but Regulate

Regulating surrogate parenting would mean that the state recognizes the practice and has a compelling interest that makes certain restrictions necessary.

In its January 1987 report, "Surrogate Parenting in New York: A Proposal for Legislative Reform," the judiciary committee of the New York Senate made four findings:

1. Surrogate parenting is a viable solution to female infertility.

2. Legislation should consider the implications for the contracting parties and society.

3. Surrogacy presents the legislature with the problems of adapting law to social change.

4. Legislation is appropriate because a compelling state interest exists in ensuring the status of the child.

The committee identified three types of regulatory proposals under consideration in a number of states:

1. Proposals based on a contract law model that would legalize contracts and guarantee the adoption of the child by the natural father and his wife.

2. Proposals that would regulate surrogate parenting in a highly structured manner, in close resemblance to adoption laws.

3. Proposals based on an informed consent model that would establish the legal status of the child, ensure informed consent of the parties and limit the potential abuses of the practice.

Assembly Bill 3038, considered in 1987 in the New Jersey Legislature, exemplifies a contract law approach. The bill declares that:

> * * * it is the intent of the Legislature to facilitate the ability of infertile married couples to become parents through the employment of the services of a surrogate mother.

The bill would require the surrogate to relinquish the child for adoption, and the married couple to adopt the child, regardless of condition. In a custody dispute, the terms of the contract would prevail and in the event of a breach of the contract, a court would be authorized to grant any legal and equitable relief, including specific performance [which would require the parties to carry out the contract]. . . .

Michigan House Bill No. 4753, introduced June 4, 1987, parallels adoption procedures by allowing a surrogate to revoke consent in writing within 20 days and initiate a custody action after the child is born. The bill would also require a statement signed by a licensed medical professional that the surrogate is capable of termination of parental rights and responsibilities. This bill was not reported out of committee. As noted previously, Michigan adopted a proposal to establish criminal penalties for involvement in surrogacy contracts.

New York Senate Bill No. 1429, introduced in February 1987, follows an informed consent model. One of the stated purposes of the bill was "to ensure informed and voluntary decisionmaking." To that end, the parties involved would have their own legal counsel and the agreement would not be binding until approved by a court. The procedure would have included advanced filing of petitions, an initial appearance and subsequent appearances until the contract was either approved or ended by the court. . . .

D. Study Committees

Because surrogate parenting raises novel issues of law, a number of states have appointed study commissions as an intervening step prior to the consideration of specific legislation. Legislatures in Delaware, Indiana, Louisiana, North Carolina, Rhode Island and Texas established study commissions. Proposals in six other states to appoint commissions were not enacted.

As of March 1988, only one state had completed a study and published its recommendations. The Maine Subcommittee to Study Surrogate Parenting (January 1988) offered two possible approaches to the issue: (1) ban surrogate parenting; or (2) ban commercial surrogate parenting and regulate noncommercial agreements. At the request of the chairman of the drafting committee of the National Conference of Commissioners on Uniform State Laws, the subcommittee decided to postpone proposing any legislation until the commissioners voted on their proposed legislation which is discussed in the next section.

E. Model Legislation

In August 1988, the National Conference of Commissioners on Uniform State Laws drafted and approved for use in all state legislatures the "Uniform Status of Children of Assisted Conception Acts." . . . The model act provides two alternatives—one to regulate surrogate parenting agreements and the other to ban the agreements.

Alternative A would allow surrogate parenting contracts and provides a regulatory framework. A court hearing would be held at which both parties would be required to submit medical evidence to prove that the would-be mother cannot bear her own child and that the surrogate mother is mentally and physically fit to bear the child. The proposal also would allow the surrogate mother to pull out of the agreement up to 180 days into her pregnancy.

The opposing language in the act (Alternative B) simply bans all surrogate parenting agreements. It does not make any distinction between commercial and noncommercial contracts; all such contracts are void.

IX
Conclusion

The legacy of Baby M to the states is a complex, confusing issue involving numerous ethical, legal and moral questions. Although some states have taken action on the issue, most states are still grappling with these questions. . . . Technology is advancing at an ever-increasing rate, especially in the area of human reproduction. These advances may force state legislatures to consider further proposals about reproduction practices. Choices made now about laws concerning surrogate parenting likely will lay a foundation for decisions to be made concerning further advances in procreation technology.

Uniform Status of Children of Assisted Conception Act

National Conference of Commissioners on Uniform States Laws (1988)

Section 1.
Definitions

In this [Act]:

(1) "Assisted conception" means a pregnancy resulting from (i) fertilizing an egg of a woman with sperm of a man by means other than sexual intercourse or (ii) implanting an embryo, but the term does not include the pregnancy of a wife resulting from fertilizing her egg with sperm of her husband.

(2) "Donor" means an individual [other than a surrogate] who produces egg or sperm used for assisted conception, whether or not payment is made for the egg or sperm used, but does not include a woman who gives birth to a resulting child.

[(3) "Intended parents" means a man and woman, married to each other, who enter into an agreement under this [Act] providing that they will be the parents of a child born to a surrogate through assisted conception using egg or sperm of one or both of the intended parents.]

(4) "Surrogate" means an adult woman who enters into an agreement to bear a child conceived through assisted conception for intended parents. . . .

Section 2.
Maternity

[Except as provided in Sections 5 through 9,] a woman who gives birth to a child is the child's mother. . . .

Section 3.
Assisted Conception by Married Woman

[Except as provided in Sections 5 through 9,] the husband of a woman who bears a child through assisted conception is the father of the child, notwithstanding a declaration of invalidity or annulment of the marriage obtained after the assisted conception, unless within two years after learning of the child's birth he commences an action in which the mother and child are parties and in which it is determined that he did not consent to the assisted conception.

Section 4.
Parental Status of Donors and Deceased Individuals

[Except as otherwise provided in Sections 5 through 9:]

(a) A donor is not a parent of a child conceived through assisted conception.

(b) An individual who dies before implantation of an embryo, or before a child is conceived other than through sexual intercourse, using the individual's egg or sperm, is not a parent of the resulting child. . . .

Alternative A
Comment

A state that chooses Alternative A should also consider Section 1(3) and the bracketed language in Sections 1(2), 2, 3, and 4.

Section 5.
Surrogacy Agreement

(a) A surrogate, her husband, if she is married, and intended parents may enter into a written agreement whereby the surrogate relinquishes all her rights and duties as a parent of a child to be conceived through assisted conception, and the intended parents may become the parents of the child pursuant to Section 8.

(b) If the agreement is not approved by the court under Section 6 before conception, the agreement is void and the surrogate is the mother of a resulting child and the surrogate's husband, if a party to the agreement, is the father of the child. If the surrogate's husband is not a party to the agreement or the surrogate is unmarried, paternity of the child is governed by [the Uniform Parentage Act]. . . .

Section 6.
Petition and Hearing
for Approval of Surrogacy Agreement

(a) The intended parents and the surrogate may file a petition in the [appropriate court] to approve a surrogacy agreement if one of them is a resident of this State. The surrogate's husband, if she is married, must join in the petition. A copy of the agreement must be attached to the petition. The court shall name a [guardian ad litem] to represent the interests of a child to be conceived by the surrogate through assisted conception and [shall] [may] appoint counsel to represent the surrogate.

(b) The court shall hold a hearing on the petition and shall enter an order approving the surrogacy agreement, authorizing assisted conception for a period of 12 months after the date of the order, declaring the intended parents to be the parents of a child to be conceived through assisted conception pursuant to the agreement and discharging the guardian ad litem and attorney for the surrogate, upon finding that:

  (1) the court has jurisdiction and all parties have submitted to its jurisdiction under subsection (e) and have agreed that the law of this State governs all matters arising under this [Act] and the agreement;

  (2) the intended mother is unable to bear a child or is unable to do so without unreasonable risk to an unborn child or to the physical or mental health of the intended mother or child, and the finding is supported by medical evidence;

(3) the [relevant child-welfare agency] has made a home study of the intended parents and the surrogate and a copy of the report of the home study has been filed with the court;

(4) the intended parents, the surrogate, and the surrogate's husband, if she is married, meet the standards of fitness applicable to adoptive parents in this State;

(5) all parties have voluntarily entered into the agreement and understand its terms, nature, and meaning, and the effect of the proceeding;

(6) the surrogate has had at least one pregnancy and delivery and bearing another child will not pose an unreasonable risk to the unborn child or to the physical or mental health of the surrogate or the child, and this finding is supported by medical evidence;

(7) all parties have received counseling concerning the effect of the surrogacy by [a qualified health-care professional or social worker] and a report containing conclusions about the capacity of the parties to enter into and fulfill the agreement has been filed with the court;

(8) a report of the results of any medical or psychological examination or genetic screening agreed to by the parties or required by law has been filed with the court and made available to the parties;

(9) adequate provision has been made for all reasonable health-care costs associated with the surrogacy until the child's birth including responsibility for those costs if the agreement is terminated pursuant to Section 7; and

(10) the agreement will not be substantially detrimental to the interest of any of the affected individuals.

(c) Unless otherwise provided in the surrogacy agreement, all court costs, attorney's fees, and other costs and expenses associated with the proceeding must be assessed against the intended parents.

(d) Notwithstanding any other law concerning judicial proceedings or vital statistics, the court shall conduct all hearings and proceedings under this section in camera. The court shall keep all records of the proceedings confidential and subject to inspection under the same standards applicable to adoptions. At the request of any party, the court shall take steps necessary to ensure that the identities of the parties are not disclosed.

(e) The court conducting the proceedings has exclusive and continuing jurisdiction of all matters arising out of the surrogacy until a child born after entry of an order under this section is 180 days old. . . .

Section 7.
Termination of Surrogacy Agreement

(a) After entry of an order under Section 6, but before the surrogate becomes pregnant through assisted conception, the court for cause, or the surrogate, her husband, or the intended parents may terminate the surrogacy agreement by giving written notice of termination to all other parties and filing notice of the termination with the court. Thereupon, the court shall vacate the order entered under Section 6.

(b) A surrogate who has provided an egg for the assisted conception pursuant to an agreement approved under Section 6 may terminate the agreement by filing written notice with the court within 180 days after the last insemination pursuant to the agreement. Upon finding, after notice to the parties to the agreement and hearing, that the surrogate has voluntarily terminated the agreement and understands the nature, meaning, and effect of the termination, the court shall vacate the order entered under Section 6.

(c) The surrogate is not liable to the intended parents for terminating the agreement pursuant to this section. . . .

Section 8.
Parentage under Approved Surrogacy Agreement

(a) The following rules of parentage apply to surrogacy agreements approved under Section 6:

(1) Upon birth of a child to the surrogate, the intended parents are the parents of the child and the surrogate and her husband, if she is married, are not parents of the child unless the court vacates the order pursuant to Section 7(b).

(2) If, after notice of termination by the surrogate, the court vacates the order under Section 7(b) the surrogate is the mother of a resulting child, and her husband, if a party to the agreement, is the father. If the surrogate's husband is not a party to the agreement or the surrogate is unmarried, paternity of the child is governed by [the Uniform Parentage Act].

(b) Upon birth of the child, the intended parents shall file a written notice with the court that a child has been born to the surrogate within 300 days after assisted conception. Thereupon, the court shall enter an order directing the [Department of Vital Statistics] to issue a new birth certificate naming the intended parents as parents and to seal the original birth certificate in the records of the [Department of Vital Statistics]. . . .

Section 9.
Surrogacy: Miscellaneous Provisions

(a) A surrogacy agreement that is the basis of an order under Section 6 may provide for the payment of consideration.

(b) A surrogacy agreement may not limit the right of the surrogate to make decisions regarding her health care or that of the embryo or fetus.

(c) After the entry of an order under Section 6, marriage of the surrogate does not affect the validity of the order, and her husband's consent to the surrogacy agreement is not required, nor is he the father of a resulting child.

(d) A child born to a surrogate within 300 days after assisted conception pursuant to an order under Section 6 is presumed to result from the assisted conception. The presumption is conclusive as to all persons who have notice of the birth and who do not commence within 180 days after notice, an action to assert the contrary in which the child and the parties to the agreement are named as parties. The action must be commenced in the court that issued the order under Section 6.

(e) A health-care provider is not liable for recognizing the surrogate as the mother before receipt of a copy of the order entered under Section 6 or for recognizing the intended parents as parents after receipt of an order entered under Section 6.]. . .

[End of Alternative A]

Alternative B
Comment

A state that chooses Alternative B shall consider Sections 10, 11, 12, 13, 14, 15, and 16, renumbered 6, 7, 8, 9, 10, 11, and 12, respectively.

Section 5.
Surrogate Agreements

An agreement in which a woman agrees to become a surrogate or to relinquish her rights and duties as parent of a child thereafter conceived through assisted conception is void. However, she is the mother of a resulting child, and her husband, if a party to the agreement, is the father of the child. If her husband is not a party to the agreement or the surrogate is unmarried, paternity of the child is governed by [the Uniform Parentage Act].]. . .

[End of Alternative B]

Section 10.
Parent and Child Relationship; Status of Child

(a) A child whose status as a child is declared or negated by this [Act] is the child only of his or her parents as determined under this [Act].

(b) Unless superseded by later events forming or terminating a parent and child relationship, the status of parent and child declared or negated by this [Act] as to a given individual and a child born alive controls for purposes of:

(1) intestate succession;

(2) probate law exemptions, allowances, or other protections for children in a parent's estate; and

(3) determining eligibility of the child or its descendants to share in a donative transfer from any person as a member of a class determined by reference to the relationship. . . .

Section 11.
Uniformity of Application and Construction

This [Act] shall be applied and construed to effectuate its general purpose to make uniform the law with respect to the subject of this [Act] among states enacting it.

Section 12.
Short Title

This [Act] may be cited as the Uniform Status of Children of Assisted Conception Act.

Section 13.
Severability

If any provision of this [Act] or its application to any person or circumstance is held invalid, the invalidity does not affect other provisions or applications of this [Act] which can be given effect without the invalid provision or application, and to this end the provisions of this [Act] are severable.

Section 14.
Effective Date

This [Act] shall take effect on _____ . Its provisions are to be applied prospectively.

Section 15.
Repeals

Acts or parts of acts inconsistent with this [Act] are repealed to the extent of the inconsistency.

Section 16.
Application to Existing Relationships

This [Act] applies to surrogacy agreements entered into after its effective date.

□ **EXHIBIT 20–1** New Ways to Make Babies

Artificial Insemination and Embryo Transfer

1. Father is infertile. Mother is inseminated by donor and carries child.

2. Mother is infertile but able to carry child. Donor of ovum is inseminated by father; then embryo is transferred and mother carries.

3. Mother is infertile and unable to carry child. Donor of ovum is inseminated by father and carries child.

4. Both parents are infertile, but mother is able to carry child. Donor of ovum is inseminated by sperm donor, then embryo is transferred and mother carries child.

Legend

Sperm from father

Ovum from mother

Baby born of mother

Sperm from donor

Ovum from donor

Baby born of donor (Surrogate)

In Vitro Fertilization

1. Mother is fertile but unable to conceive. Ovum from mother and sperm from father are combined in laboratory. Embryo is placed in mother's uterus.

2. Mother is infertile but able to carry child. Ovum from donor is combined with sperm from father.

3. Father is infertile and mother is fertile but unable to conceive. Ovum from mother is combined with sperm from donor.

4. Both parents are infertile, but mother is able to carry child. Ovum and sperm from donors are combined in laboratory (also see number 4, column at left).

5. Mother is infertile and unable to carry child. Ovum of donor is combined with sperm from father. Embryo is transferred to donor (also see number 2, column at left).

6. Bother parents are fertile, but mother is unable to carry child. Ovum from mother and sperm from father are combined. Embryo is transferred to donor.

7. Father is infertile; mother is fertile but unable to carry child.

Source: Strong & DeVault, THE MARRIAGE AND FAMILY EXPERIENCE, 234 (4th Ed. 1989).

Assignment 20.1

(a) Should surrogacy contracts be banned? If not, what kind of regulation is needed?

(b) Do you approve of an advertisement such as the following one placed in the want ad section of the newspaper along with ads for accountants and truck drivers:

"CASH AVAILABLE NOW. Married or single women needed as surrogate mothers for couples unable to have children. Conception to be by artificial insemination. We pay well! Contact the Infertility Clinic today."

(c) Do you favor Alternative A or B in the Uniform Status of Children of Assisted Conception Act? Why?

(d) What is the current state of law in your state on the validity of surrogacy contracts? (See General Instructions for the State-Code Assignment and General Instructions for the Court-Opinion Assignment in chapter one.)

Key Chapter Terminology

Baby Selling
Surrogate Parenting
Artificial Insemination
In Vitro Fertilization
Surrender of Parental Rights
Brokers
Termination of Parental Rights

Surrogacy Contracts
Uniform Status of Children of Assisted
    Conception Act
Assisted Conception
Donor
Intended Parents
Surrogate

Torts

■ Chapter Outline

Our first concern in this chapter is the *intrafamily tort* committed by one family member against another. Immunity is granted for some of these torts, which means that the injured party cannot sue. Courts traditionally have been reluctant to allow suits for intrafamily torts since the courtroom is hardly the best place to resolve family conflicts. But immunity is not the rule in every case. It depends on who the parties are and on what tort has been committed.

Intrafamily torts that damage property (e.g., trespass) are treated differently from torts that injure the person (e.g., battery). Generally, spouses can sue each other for negligent or intentional damage to property. The same is true for such damage caused by the parent to a child's property. There is no immunity for property torts. For torts against the person, however, one spouse cannot sue another, and a child cannot sue a parent; immunity does apply to such torts. There are some exceptions to these rules. For example, many states grant immunity only for negligent injury to the person; thus, any family member can sue another for intentional injury to the person.

Next we turn to torts committed primarily by individuals outside the family. If a doctor makes a negligent mistake that results in the birth of a deformed child when the parents had tried to avoid that birth by abortion or sterilization, the parents can bring a wrongful-birth action. If the child is born healthy, the parents may be able to bring a wrongful-pregnancy or wrongful-conception action, but the damages are limited. The courts, however, usually do not allow the child to bring his or own separate wrongful-life action.

Actions are *derivative* if they are dependent on an underlying wrongful act to someone else. Otherwise, they are nonderivative. The two main derivative actions are loss of consortium (covering injury to the companionship, love, affection, sexual relationship, and services that one spouse provides another) and loss of services (covering an interference with the right of parents to the services of their unemancipated child). The main nonderivative actions are alienation of affections, criminal conversation, enticement of a spouse, abduction or enticement of a child, and seduction.

Vicarious liability exists when one person is liable for someone else's tort. Vicarious liability cannot exist among family members, with two major exceptions. First, some states have statutes that impose limited vicarious liability on parents for the torts committed by their children. Second, under the family-purpose doctrine, the owner of a car can be liable for a tort committed by a family member driving the car for a "family purpose."

Section A. Classification of Torts

A tort is a private wrong for which the court will provide a remedy. Torts can be classified as follows:

Intentional Torts against Property

Trespass
A wrongful entry on the property of another.

Conversion
The exercise of dominion or control over someone's property without authorization.

Nuisance
The use of one's property in such a way as to interfere with someone else's enjoyment of his or her property.

Etc.

Intentional Torts against the Person

Assault
The attempt to inflict harmful or offensive contact on a person, placing that person in fear or apprehension of the contact.

False Imprisonment
The detention or restraint of a person without authorization (this tort does not necessarily involve prisons, jails, police, etc.; a person, for example, can falsely imprison his or her neighbor on the sidewalk).

Battery

Harmful or offensive contact with a person.

Malicious Prosecution

Bringing a civil or criminal action against someone for malicious reasons when no reasonable basis or probable cause exists for the action.

Slander

Oral statements that are false and that injure the reputation of another.

Libel

Written statements that are false and that injure the reputation of another.

Etc.

Unintentional Tort: Negligence

Negligence

Injury to person or property caused by a failure to act with reasonable care.

Section B. Intrafamily Torts

Here our concern is a tort committed by one family member against another. Courts have always been reluctant to permit tort actions among any combination of husband, wife and unemancipated child (a child is *emancipated* when a parent gives up his or her control over the child—usually when the child has married or is living independently). This reluctance is based on the theory that family harmony will be threatened if members know that they can sue each other in tort. If the family carries *liability insurance,* there is also a fear that family members will fraudulently try to collect under the policy by fabricating tort actions against each other. At common law, a more technical reason was given for why husbands and wives could not sue each other. The husband and wife were considered to be one person, and that one person was the husband! Hence, to allow a suit between spouses would theoretically amount to one person suing himself. With the passage of the Married Women's Property Acts (page 452) and the enforcement of the laws against sex discrimination, a wife now has her separate identity so that she can sue and be sued like anyone else.

Reform in the law, however, has not meant that intrafamily tort *immunity* no longer exists. A distinction must be made between suits against the person (such as battery) and a suit against property (such as conversion). For *torts against property,* most states allow suits between spouses and between parent and child. Most states, however, retain the immunity in some form when the suit involves a *tort against the person.* The state of the law is outlined in the following chart.

Intrafamily Torts

Husband and Wife

1. In most states, spouses can sue each other for negligent damage to their *property*, and for intentional damage to their *property*, e.g., trespass, conversion.

2. In many states, spouses cannot sue each other for negligent injury to their *person*, or for intentional injury to their *person*, e.g., assault, battery, false imprisonment.

3. Some states will permit actions for torts against the person if the man and woman are divorced or if the tort is covered by liability insurance.

4. Some states will permit intentional tort actions against the person to be brought by spouses against each other, but continue to forbid negligence actions for injury to the person.

Parent and Child

1. In all states, a child can sue a parent for negligent damage caused by the parent to the child's *property*, or for intentional damage caused by the parent to the child's *property*, e.g., trespass, conversion.

2. In many states, a child cannot sue a parent for negligent injury caused by the parent to the child's *person*, or for intentional injury caused by the parent to the child's *person*, e.g., assault, battery, false imprisonment.

3. If the child is emancipated (e.g., married, a member of the armed forces, self-supporting), the child in all states can sue its parent for intentional or negligent injury caused by the parent to the child's person.

4. Some states will permit any child (emancipated or not) to bring an intentional tort against its parent for injury to the person, but continue to forbid negligence actions for injury to the person.

5. A few states will permit any child (emancipated or not) to sue its parent for torts growing out of automobile accidents.

6. A few states allow the child to sue the parent for all intentional tort actions against the person except where the tort arises out of the parent's exercise of discipline over the child.

Other Related Persons

Brothers and sisters, aunts and uncles, grandparents and grandchildren, etc. can sue each other in tort. The restrictions imposed on husband-wife suits and on parent-child suits do not apply to tort actions involving other relatives.

Assignment 21.1

To answer the following questions, you may have to check both the state code and the opinions of courts sitting in your state. (See General Instructions for the State-Code Assignment and General Instructions for the Court-Opinion Assignment in chapter one.)

(a) Under what circumstances, if any, can one spouse bring a tort action against the other spouse in your state? Is it relevant that liability insurance exists?

(b) Can divorced spouses sue each other in tort?

(c) Under what circumstances, if any, can a child bring a tort action against its parent in your state?

(d) Pick any tort action that one family member *can* bring against another in your state. Draft a complaint in which the cause of action is this tort. (See General Instructions for the Complaint-Drafting Assignment in chapter one.)

Assignment 21.2

A husband in your state intentionally kills his wife and son. Can the estate of the wife bring a tort action against him for wrongful death? Can the estate of the son bring a tort action for wrongful death against his father? (See General Instructions for the State-Code Assignment and General Instructions for the Court-Opinion Assignment in chapter one.)

Assignment 21.3

(a) Dave knows that he has contagious genital herpes, but does not tell Alice, who contracts the disease from Dave. Can Alice sue Dave for battery? For intentional infliction of emotional distress? For deceit or fraud? Does it make any difference whether the disease was communicated before or after Dave and Alice were married? Does it make any difference that they are now divorced? (See General Instructions for the Legal-Analysis Assignment in chapter one.)

(b) Jim and Helen live together for a year before they are married. They separate two years after the marriage. While preparing to file for divorce, Helen discovers that she has contracted chlamydia trachomatis, a serious venereal disease that attacks the ovaries. Her reproductive system is permanently damaged. Assume that Jim gave her this disease through intercourse during the marriage. Jim carelessly thought that he was not capable of infecting Helen. Can she sue Jim for negligence in your state? (See General Instructions for the Court-Opinion Assignment in chapter one.)

Notes on Intrafamily Crimes and Contracts

1. The state can always *criminally* prosecute one family member for crimes committed against another family member's person or property. There is no intrafamily criminal immunity.

2. To a large extent, it is possible for family members to enter into contracts with each other, e.g., a husband and wife can enter a business partnership with each other, or a father who owns a department store can hire his daughter as president. Since such contracts are legal and enforceable, it follows that the parties can bring *breach-of-contract* actions against each other for alleged violations of these contracts. There is no intrafamily breach-of-contract immunity. Not all contracts among family members, however, are legal. In general, a party cannot enter into a contract to do what the law already requires that party to do. When two parties are happily married, for example, they cannot enter a contract to support each other. They already have this obligation under the law of marriage. Such a contract is said to be "without consideration," and hence unenforceable. On the other hand, business contracts among family members are treated differently. They are almost always enforceable in intrafamily contract actions.

Assignment 21.4

(a) Can one spouse rape another in your state? (See also Assignment 16.8, (page 468.)

(b) Can parents be prosecuted in your state for murder, manslaughter, or some other charge for the death of their child because they refuse to allow medical treatment on the basis of a religious belief that such treatment is against the will of God?

(See General Instructions for the State-Code Assignment and the General Instructions for the Court-Opinion Assignment in chapter one.)

Section C. Wrongful Life, Wrongful Birth, Wrongful Pregnancy

Doctors have been sued in three different kinds of cases for causing the birth of an unwanted child due to negligence, e.g., a mistake in sterilization or abortion procedures:

1. *Wrongful life.* An action by or on behalf of an unwanted deformed child for its own damages.

2. *Wrongful birth.* An action by parents of an unwanted deformed child for their own damages.

3. *Wrongful pregnancy.* An action by parents of a healthy child that they did not want

Most states deny a child the right to bring a *wrongful-life* case for the anguish of being born deformed. A major reason for this decision is the enormous difficulty of calculating the damages that should be awarded in such a case. According to one court, "The infant plaintiff would have us measure the difference between his life with defects against the utter void of nonexistence, but it is impossible to make such a determination." *Gleitman v. Cosgrove,* 49 N.J. 22, 25, 227 A.2d 689, 692 (1967). Another court was worried that allowing this infant to sue might encourage other infants to sue for being "born into the world under conditions they might regard as adverse. One might seek damages for inheriting unfortunate family conditions; one for being born into a large and destitute family, another because a parent has an unsavory reputation." *Zepeda v. Zepeda,* 190 N.E.2d 849, 858 (Ill. App. 1963).

Wrongful-birth cases by parents, on the other hand, have been more successful. Courts have not had the same problems in assessing the financial and emotional damages of the parents in giving birth to and in raising an impaired child.

When the unwanted child is born healthy, a *wrongful-pregnancy* action (also called a *wrongful-conception* action) by the parents is often allowed, but the damages are usually limited to the costs of the delivery and do not extend to the cost of raising the healthy child. The healthy child is usually not allowed to bring the same kind of action in his or her own right.

Assignment 21.5

(a) A pregnant woman in your state has a genetic disease that could lead to the birth of a deformed child. Her doctor negligently fails to diagnose this disease and inform the woman. The child is born deformed with this disease. If she had known of the disease, she would have aborted the pregnancy. Who can bring an action in your state against the doctor for negligence and for what damages? (See General Instructions for the Court-Opinion Assignment in chapter one.)

(b) A pharmacist in your state sells an unmarried couple birth control pills that are negligently defective. A healthy, illegitimate child is born to this couple. Who can bring an action in your state against the pharmacist for negligence and for what damages? (See General Instructions for the Court-Opinion Assignment in chapter one.)

Section D. Derivative Actions

Loss of Consortium

Consortium is the companionship, love, affection, sexual relationship, and services (e.g., cooking, making repairs around the house) that one spouse provides another. There can be a recovery for a wrongful injury to consortium. At one time, only the husband could recover for such a *loss of consortium*. In every state, this view has been changed by statute or has been ruled unconstitutional.

The loss-of-consortium action works as follows:

- Rich and Ann are married.
- Paul, a stranger, injures Ann, e.g., by negligently hitting her with his car (or by one of the intentional torts such as battery).
- Ann sues Paul for negligence. She receives damages to cover her medical bills, lost wages, if any, pain and suffering, punitive damages, if any.
- Rich then brings a separate suit against Paul for loss of his wife's consortium. He receives damages to compensate him for whatever loss or impairment he can prove to the companionship he had with Ann before the accident—to the love, affection, sexual intercourse, and services that she gave him as his wife before the accident.

In Rich's action against Paul, he cannot recover for injuries sustained by Ann. Ann must recover for such injuries in her own action against Paul. Paul's liability to Rich is limited to the specific injuries sustained by Rich—loss or impairment of his wife's consortium. If Ann loses her suit against Paul, e.g., because she was contributorily negligent, Rich will not be able to bring his consortium suit. To recover for loss of consortium, there must be an underlying tort.

Of course, parties do not have to be married for consortium to exist (in whole or in part) between them. For example:

- Jim and Rachel are engaged to be married. The defendant negligently injures Rachel before the wedding. Can Jim sue the defendant for loss of consortium?

- Barbara and Paul are living together; they are not married. The defendant negligently injures Paul. Can Barbara sue the defendant for loss of consortium?
- Gabe is the son of Bill. The defendant negligently injures Bill. Can Gabe sue the defendant for loss of parental society (*partial consortium*, sometimes called *parental consortium*.)?

In the vast majority of states, the answer is no to each of these questions. A marriage license is a precondition to a suit for loss of consortium. This conclusion has been criticized, however. Since the essence of consortium is the emotional commitment and devotion between two people and not the formality of the relationship, a serious interference with this commitment and devotion should be the basis of recovery, according to the critics. The loss suffered by Jim, Barbara, and Gabe is just as real as the loss suffered by a person whose spouse has been injured. Recovery is denied in most states, though.

Loss of Services

Suppose that it is the unemancipated child who is injured by the defendant. A parent has a *right to services* and earnings from the child. In most states, the parent can recover separate damages from the defendant for interference with this right. If, for example, a minor child is crippled by a battery committed by the defendant, the child will be able to recover for the injuries sustained as a result of the battery. The parent can receive *separate* damages due to the fact that the child is no longer able to provide the same services to the home that were possible prior to the accident, e.g., cutting the grass, running errands, etc.

The spouse's right to damages for loss of consortium rights in the other spouse is *derivative* in that it depends upon the existence of an underlying tort committed by the defendant. The same is true of the parent's right to damages for loss of services of the child. If the underlying injury was not tortious, the parent cannot recover.

Assignment 21.6

(a) Describe the loss of consortium action that can be brought in your state by a person whose spouse has been negligently injured.

(b) Under what circumstances, if any, can a loss of consortium action be brought in your state by an unmarried person whose lover was negligently injured? Assume that they lived together and held themselves out as husband and wife for twenty years, had children together, but never married.

(c) Can a child sue a third party for loss of parental consortium in your state?

(d) Can a parent bring an action for loss of child services and earnings in your state? (See General Instructions for the State-Code Assignment and General Instructions for the Court-Opinion Assignment in chapter one.)

Section E. Nonderivative Actions

In many states, a series of nonderivative actions can be brought by one family member because of what the defendant did with or to another family member. These actions consist of the following torts:

- Alienation of affections
- Criminal conversation
- Enticement (of spouse)
- Abduction or enticement of a child
- Seduction

To establish any of these causes of action, there is no need to prove an underlying tort; they are torts in their own right. They are nonderivative.

A number of states have passed statutes (sometimes called *heart-balm statutes*) that have abolished some or all of the above tort actions. The actions are not looked upon with favor and are seldom used today even where they have not been abolished.

Alienation of Affections

Elements of Alienation of Affections

1. Defendant (e.g., a lover, an in-law) intended to diminish the marital relationship between the plaintiff and the latter's spouse.
2. Affirmative conduct of the defendant.
3. Affections between plaintiff and spouse were in fact alienated.
4. Defendant caused the alienation ("but for" the defendant, the alienation would not have occurred, or defendant was a substantial factor in producing the alienation).

Criminal Conversation

Element of Criminal Conversation

Defendant had sex with the plaintiff's spouse (adultery).

Enticement (Of Spouse)

Elements of Enticement (of Spouse)

1. Defendant intended to diminish the marital relationship between the plaintiff and the latter's spouse.
2. Affirmative conduct by defendant:
   a. to entice or encourage the spouse to leave the plaintiff's home, *or*
   b. to harbor the spouse and encourage the latter to stay away from the plaintiff's home
3. Plaintiff's spouse left home.
4. Defendant caused the plaintiff to leave home or to stay away ("but for" what defendant did, the plaintiff would not have left or stayed away, or the defendant was a substantial factor in the spouse's leaving or staying away).

Abduction or Enticement of a Child

Elements of Abduction or Enticement of Child

1. Defendant intended to interfere with the parent's custody of the child.
2. Affirmative conduct by the defendant:
   a. to abduct or force the child from the parent's custody, *or*
   b. to entice or encourage the child to leave the parent, *or*

    c. to harbor the child and encourage the latter to stay away from the parent's custody.

3. The child left the custody of the parent.
4. Defendant caused the child to leave or to stay away ("but for" what the defendant did, the child would not have left or stayed away, or the defendant was a substantial factor in the child's leaving or staying away).

Seduction

Element of Seduction

The defendant has sex with the plaintiff's minor daughter by force or with the consent of the daughter.

Assignment 21.7

Can any of the above five causes of action be brought in your state? Check your state code and opinions written by courts in your state. If you find older cases that have permitted any of these actions, shepardize (page 46) these cases to be sure that they still represent good law in your state. (See General Instructions for the State-Code Assignment and General Instructions for the Court-Opinion Assignment in chapter one.)

Section F. Vicarious Liability of Family Members

Vicarious liability means that one person is liable solely because of what someone else does. For example, if a trucker negligently hits a pedestrian while making a delivery, the trucker's boss, the *employer*, is liable. The liability is vicarious since it is based on what someone else—the employee—has done.

The person injured could also sue the employee who is directly responsible for the injury. We are all personally liable for our own torts even if someone else is vicariously liable. Often, however, the one directly responsible has minimal resources out of which to satisfy a judgment. The person who is vicariously liable is usually the *deep pocket* who does have such resources.

In general, vicarious liability cannot exist among family members. While there are exceptions, the basic principle is that one family member is not liable for the torts of another family member. Thus, a spouse is not liable for the torts committed by the other spouse. Children are not liable for the torts of their parents, and vice versa. For example:

Mary is the ten-year-old daughter of Diane. Mary throws a brick through the window of Jim's hardware store.

Jim must sue *Mary* for the damage done to the store. Her mother is *not* vicariously liable for the tort of her daughter.

The first exception to this rule is fairly limited. A number of states have passed statutes that make parents vicariously liable for the torts of their children, but only up to a relatively modest amount, e.g., $1,000.

In the above example involving Diane and her daughter, note that there was no indication that Diane did anything wrong or improper herself. Suppose, however, that Diane knew that her daughter, Mary, had a habit of throwing bricks into windows. Or assume that Diane was with Mary when she threw the brick at Jim's window. If Diane failed to use reasonable care to control Mary in these circumstances, Diane *would* be liable to Jim. But this would not be a case of vicarious liability. When parents act unreasonably in failing to use available opportunities to control their children, the parents are *independently* liable for *negligence* in a suit brought by the person injured by the child. Since, however, parents are rarely with their children when the latter act mischieviously, and rarely know when their children are about to commit specific acts of mischief, it is usually very difficult to prove that the parents negligently failed to control and supervise their children.

Assignment 21.8

Jim is the thirteen-year-old son of Harry. Jim takes Harry's car on a joy ride and negligently injures George. Whom can George sue? (See General Instructions for the State-Code Assignment in chapter one, and General Instructions for the Court-Opinion Assignment in chapter one.)

The second exception to the rule of no intrafamily vicarious liability is the *family-purpose doctrine,* according to which a defendant will be liable for torts committed by a driver of the defendant's car who is a member of the defendant's family. Not all states have the doctrine, and those that have it do not all agree on its elements. Generally, the elements of the doctrine are as follows:

Elements of Family-Purpose Doctrine

1. Defendant must own the car, or have an ownership interest in it (e.g., co-owner), or control the use of the car.
2. Defendant must make the car available for family use rather than for the defendant's business (in some states, the defendant must make it available for general family use rather than for a particular occasion only).
3. The driver must be a member of the defendant's immediate household.
4. The driver must be using the car for a family purpose at the time of the accident.
5. The driver must have had the defendant's express or implied consent to be using the car at the time of the accident.

The defendant does not have to be the traditional head of the household and does not have to be in the car at the time of the accident. Again, individual states, by case law or by statute, may impose different elements to the doctrine or may reject it entirely.

Assignment 21.9

(a) Is there a family-purpose doctrine in your state? If so, what are its components or elements? (See General Instructions for the State-Code Assignment in chapter one, and General Instructions for the Court-Opinion Assignment in chapter one.)

(b) Fred has just bought a used car, but it will not be ready for a week. During the week he is waiting, he rents a car, paying a per-mile charge on it. He tells his family that the car is to be used only to drive to work. One day while the car is at home and Fred is at the supermarket, his child becomes sick. Fred's mother, who is staying with Fred until an opening comes up in a local nursing home, drives the child to the hospital. On the way, she has an accident, injuring the plaintiff. The plaintiff sues Fred for negligence. Apply the five elements of the family-purpose doctrine to determine whether it would apply. (See General Instructions for the Legal-Analysis Assignment in chapter one.) How would this case be handled in your state? (Refer to your answer to part "a" above.)

Key Chapter Terminology

Tort
Intrafamily Torts
Trespass
Conversion
Nuisance
Assault
False Imprisonment
Battery
Malicious Prosecution
Slander
Libel
Negligence
Immunity
Emancipation
Property Torts
Torts against the Person
Liability Insurance

Wrongful Life
Wrongful Birth
Wrongful Pregnancy
Wrongful Conception
Loss of Consortium
Loss of Services
Derivative Actions
Heart-Balm Statute
Alienation of Affections
Criminal Conversation
Enticement
Abduction
Seduction
Vicarious Liability
Deep Pocket
Parental Negligence
Family-Purpose Doctrine

Family Law Paralegal Job Descriptions

Legal Assistant Job Description Family Law

Source: *Attorneys' Guide to Practicing with Legal Assistants* (State Bar of Texas, 1986).

All job functions must be performed under the *direct supervision of a lawyer*. The words "draft" and "prepare" mean a preliminary writing to be approved by the attorney.

General Responsibilities:

Assist attorney through all phases of divorce and custody proceedings, including drafting pleadings, investigating financial affairs of the parties, assisting in discovery and at trial, and maintaining close relationship with client, all as illustrated by the following examples.

Specific Duties

Initial Client Interview (After attorney has talked with client)

1. Establish rapport with client and gather facts pertaining to preparation of initial pleadings.
2. Have client sign ancillary forms necessary for initial discovery, such as authorizations for medical records, income tax returns, employment records, etc.
3. Instruct client how to prepare the financial information statement and other forms to aid in discovery of the parties' assets and liabilities.
4. Prepare memorandum to the file.

Initial Pleadings

1. Draft pleadings.
2. After attorney approval, arrange for client's signature if applicable, see that pleadings are filed, get hearing set if necessary, and arrange for service if necessary.
3. Put hearing date on calendar and notify client of the date.

555

Preparation for Temporary Hearing and Post Hearing Procedure

1. Arrange for client to meet with attorney for briefing as to what to expect at the hearing and to discuss the client's financial information statement.
2. Draft temporary orders for attorney approval.
3. Transmit temporary orders to opposing counsel for approval, and upon receipt of executed orders, return to attorney for review and filing.
4. Keep in close contact with client to ensure compliance with temporary orders.
5. Set up child support payment account for client if he/she receives an award of child support.

Discovery

1. Monitor deadlines set by the court, such as filing of sworn inventory and appraisement, production of tax returns and other documents, appraisals, etc.
2. Work with client in obtaining all information necessary to prepare an inventory and appraisement, submit to attorney for approval, obtain client's signature, file with the court, and submit copy to opposing counsel.
3. Review inventory received from opposing counsel, compare with client's inventory, and prepare a memorandum for attorney evaluating both.
4. If separate property is involved, work with client on tracing.
5. Draft written interrogatories and requests for admissions.
6. Assist client in answering interrogatories and requests for admissions; then submit proposed answers to attorney.
7. Schedule, attend with attorney, and index depositions.
8. Act as intermediary between the attorney and accountants, appraisers, private investigators, and other agents.

Trial and Post-Trial

1. Prepare trial notebook.
2. Organize and index necessary exhibits.
3. Prepare, file, and follow up on service of subpoenas.
4. Schedule and notify witnesses as instructed by attorney.
5. Attend trial with attorney.
6. Draft decree.
7. Follow up on entry of decree or order, and draft all necessary closing documents, such as deeds, title transfers, stock transfers, etc.

Family Law Legal Assistant

Source: Colorado Bar Association Legal Assistant Committee[1]

Family law legal assistants may perform all or part of the following tasks:

A. *Screen Prospective Clients by Telephone Interviews*

B. *Commencement of Action*

1. Initial interview with client to obtain information for pleadings.
2. Prepare initial pleadings, including petition, summons and waiver of service, affidavit as to children, and response.
3. Draft correspondence with clients, courts and other attorneys.
4. Arrange for service of process.

C. *Temporary Orders*

1. Prepare motions for temporary orders or temporary injunctions.
2. Notice and set hearings.
3. Assist in settlement negotiations.
4. Draft stipulations for temporary orders after negotiations.

D. *Financial Affidavits*

1. Work with clients in gathering and compiling financial information.
2. Analyze income and expense information provided by client.
3. Work with accountants, financial advisors, brokers and other financial experts retained by client.
4. Retain appraisers for real estate, business and personal property.
5. Prepare financial affidavits.

E. *Discovery*

1. Prepare discovery requests.
2. Assist clients in gathering documents and data to respond to discovery requests.
3. Prepare responses to discovery requests.
4. Organize, index and summarize discovered materials.

F. *Settlement Negotiations*

1. Assist attorney in analysis of proposed settlements.

---

[1] This list of tasks has been approved by the Legal Assistant Committee of the Colorado Bar, not by the Board of Governors of the Bar.

2. Research legal questions and assist in drafting briefs and memoranda.

3. Assist in drafting separation agreements.

G. Hearings

1. Notice and set final orders hearings.

2. Research legal questions and assist in drafting briefs and memoranda.

3. Assist in preparation of trial exhibits and trial notebooks.

4. Arrange for expert witnesses and assist in preparing witnesses and clients for trial.

5. Attend hearings.

6. Prepare decree.

H. Post-Decree

1. Prepare documents for transfers of assets.

2. Arrange for filing and recording of transfer documents.

3. Review bills for tax deductible fees and prepare opinion letters to client.

4. Draft pleadings for withdrawal from case.

I. Special Projects

1. Develop forms for gathering information from client.

2. Maintain files on the following: separation-agreement provisions, current case law, resource materials for clients, and experts in various fields (i.e., custody, evaluation, business appraisals, etc.).

Family Law for Paralegals

Y. Spiegel, *Family Law for Paralegals* 6 THE JOURNAL 7 (Sacramento Association of Legal Assistants, June 1986).

The role of a legal assistant in a family law practice is exciting and varied. Whereas all areas of law can be interesting, the opportunities for client contact, full involvement and case responsibility in family law make it a truly satisfying area of specialty. Family law affords tremendous scope for helping people in a very basic change in their lives. With the divorce rate at roughly 50 percent, there are few families who haven't been touched in some way by the problems and trauma of a court action. Our job as legal assistants can be to smooth the way through this difficult time for the client, making the experience kinder, easier to understand, more efficient, and hopefully, less expensive. Divorce is not the only area covered in family law. Adoption, grandparent visitation issues, and emancipation of minors also come under this topic. . . .

The teamwork between attorney and legal assistant is crucial to the success of a paralegal working in the family law area. Your skills and interests, as well as the degree of trust and communication between you and your boss will determine the tasks that you will be assigned. If there is good communication and rapport between you as team members, the clients will come to rely on both of you as handling the case, and your participation will be invaluable.

In my office the attorney conducts the initial interview with the client. This is primarily done to establish the attorney/client bond, which is crucial to the successful processing of the case. Any general questions which the client has about the dissolution process, as well as discussing strategy, fees and expectations are all done at this stage. If there is an immediate need for temporary orders, such as restraining orders or temporary custody or support, the attorney will begin the information gathering process by taking detailed notes of the client's situation. The initial interview is usually concluded by inviting me into the office to be introduced as the "paralegal who will be assisting me with your case." This gives me the authority to contact the client on behalf of the attorney to gather more detailed information, and to answer the client's questions as to general procedure. I find that the clients are, for the most part, pleased to know that a paralegal will be working on their case. I am usually more accessible than the attorney to answer their questions, or to convey information, and they are billed at a lower rate for my time.

It is usually my responsibility to draft the opening documents. These include the summons, petition, and the income and expense forms. With the recent adoption of the Agnos income and expense forms, this job has become quite critical. The Agnos forms are complicated and in some instances intimidating, and clients often need a lot of assistance in filling them out. I find that often our women clients don't understand that the forms are meant to demonstrate "need" for support. They spend all their time trying to make their income on the form come out even with their expenses, and that is usually impossible. It is often my job to tell them that if they don't show the court any evidence of the need for support, the judge won't order any. I am also responsible for drafting mediation counseling stipulations, property declarations and even order to show cause and motions for pendente lite relief. I rely on notes from the attorney, as well as my own interviews with the client to obtain facts necessary to create the pleadings. The attorney then reviews the documents for accuracy and obtains the signature of the client. When the documents are filed, I see that the papers are served on the client's spouse and keep the client informed of subsequent developments.

Discovery plays an important role in family law. Over the years my office has developed a set of family law interrogatories on our word processor, which can be modified and used to flush out the details of the community, quasi-community, and separate property. Any real property or pension plans must be appraised for their value as community property, and this is also the responsibility of the legal assistant. Building a strong working relationship with the various legal support personnel, such as appraisers, actuaries, deposition reporters, mediation and rehabilitation counselors, process servers, and photocopy services is essential. These people trust and respect my role as professional and as a representative of my office, and often go out of their way to assist us in emergencies because of the relationship which we have built over the years.

Preparing and arranging the service of deposition notices is another important part of family law practice which falls within the scope of the paralegal's responsibility. After the transcript of the deposition has come back from the reporter, it is my job to index and summarize it for the attorney's use in trial preparation. Comparing the bank account dates, numbers, balances and other descriptions of property with the opposing party's previous descriptions is an important part of establishing the full extent of community or separate property interest and achieving an equal division.

Child custody and visitation is often the most traumatic aspect of a family law case. Parents who are separating are often terrified of what the affect will be on their children, and are frequently afraid that dividing their households will result in loss of closeness and opportunities for quality parenting time. Fortunately, California courts lean heavily in favor of joint custody whenever feasible. Mediation counseling programs have been set up in Sacramento, Yolo, and Solano counties and elsewhere to assist parents in working out arrangements for custody and visitation with the assistance of trained facilitators. The agreements they work out are then presented as stipulations to the court. Wherever possible, a judge will not hear a motion for custody or visitation until the parties have been to mediation. This is practical and beneficial, since the mediation session is often the first time that the parties have been able to sit down and actually *listen* to each other since their problems began. It also provides a beginning for the future cooperation that they will have to achieve to be separated parents with children in common. It is my job as legal assistant to prepare the mediation counseling stipulation, to see that it is signed by all parties and attorneys, to make sure that it is filed with the court, and then arrange contact between the mediator and the parties.

If the parties are unable to settle their disputes (and we try very hard to settle every family law case without the necessity of a trial) then I draft a trial brief setting out the facts, the history of the case, the contested and uncontested issues, our proposal for an equal division of property, and a memorandum setting forth the applicable law. Updated income and expense and property declarations must be filed along with the trial brief, and any appraisals or actuarial analyses of pension funds must also be updated as of the time of trial.

Before the day of the trial, I contact the client to make sure that he or she is psychologically prepared to go, and make arrangements with the client for last minute prepping by the attorney. I organize the file to make all exhibits and necessary documents fingertip-accessible to the attorney trying the case, and I subpoena any witnesses who may be needed. It is very hard to get a firm court date because of case congestion, and the client must be assisted in dealing with the resulting anxiety and inconvenience. If the case does go to trial, I often go along to help my boss keep organized with respect to the documents, take notes as to areas of inquiry to be explored, run emergency errands, and keep the witnesses organized.

When the judgment is prepared, either by stipulation in the form of a marital settlement agreement, or by reducing a decision by the trial court to judgment form, I often draft the first document for review by the attorney and client. Keeping track of dates, such as deadlines for appeal, and eligibility for final judgment is also my responsibility. Preparing transfer deeds and noticing pension plans of the divorced spouse's interest are some of the wrap-up details.

As the family law case progresses, a paralegal becomes intimately familiar with the client's life and affairs. You are in a unique position to offer comfort and guidance to people in deep transition. While the legal professional's role should never be confused with that of a therapist or psychiatrist, your positive attitude and sensitivity to the client's situation can make a big difference in how they experience the adjustment to what amounts to an entirely new life. Over the past six years in a practice which is predominantly devoted to family law, I have watched hundreds of clients pass through this difficult change in their lives, heal their wounds, and create more successful and satisfying lifestyles. This is a very rewarding part of my job.

While I have had to skip over many areas of a legal assistant's responsibilities in the area of family law, I have tried to give you a sense of some of the duties that a paralegal may have. Your particular tasks will be assigned by the attorney. Short of giving the client legal advice and appearing as their representative in court, there is tremendous scope for the utilization of paralegals in a family law practice.

Uniform Child Custody Jurisdiction Act

§ 1. Purposes of Act; Construction of Provisions.—

(a) The general purposes of this Act are to:

(1) avoid jurisdictional competition and conflict with courts of other states in matters of child custody which have in the past resulted in the shifting of children from state to state with harmful effects on their well-being;

(2) promote cooperation with the courts of other states to the end that a custody decree is rendered in that state which can best decide the case in the interest of the child;

(3) assure that litigation concerning the custody of a child take place ordinarily in the state with which the child and his family have the closest connection and where significant evidence concerning his care, protection, training, and personal relationships is most readily available, and that courts of this state decline the exercise of jurisdiction when the child and his family have a closer connection with another state;

(4) discourage continuing controversies over child custody in the interest of greater stability of home environment and of secure family relationships for the child;

(5) deter abductions and other unilateral removals of children undertaken to obtain custody awards;

(6) avoid re-litigation of custody decisions of other states in this state insofar as feasible;

(7) facilitate the enforcement of custody decrees of other states;

(8) promote and expand the exchange of information and other forms of mutual assistance between the courts of this state and those of other states concerned with the same child; and

(9) make uniform the law of those states which enact it.

(b) This Act shall be construed to promote the general purposes stated in this section.

§ 2. Definitions.—As used in this Act:

(1) "contestant" means a person, including a parent, who claims a right to custody or visitation rights with respect to a child;

(2) "custody determination" means a court decision and court orders and instructions providing for the custody of a child, including visitation rights; it does not include a decision relating to child support or any other monetary obligation of any person;

(3) "custody proceeding" includes proceedings in which a custody determination is one of several issues, such as an action for divorce or separation, and includes child neglect and dependency proceedings;

(4) "decree" or "custody decree" means a custody determination contained in a judicial decree or order made in a custody proceeding, and includes an initial decree and a modification decree;

(5) "home state" means the state in which the child immediately preceding the time involved lived with his parents, a parent, or a person acting as parent, for at least 6 consecutive months, and in the case of a child less than 6 months old the state in which the child lived from birth with any of the persons mentioned. Periods of temporary absence of any of the named persons are counted as part of the 6-month or other period;

(6) "initial decree" means the first custody decree concerning a particular child;

(7) "modification decree" means a custody decree which modifies or replaces a prior decree, whether made by the court which rendered the prior decree or by another court;

(8) "physical custody" means actual possession and control of a child;

(9) "person acting as parent" means a person, other

than a parent, who has physical custody of a child and who has either been awarded custody by a court or claims a right to custody; and

(10) "state" means any state, territory, or possession of the United States, the Commonwealth of Puerto Rico, and the District of Columbia.

§ 3.   Jurisdiction.—

(a) A court of this State which is competent to decide child custody matters has jurisdiction to make a child custody determination by initial or modification decree if:

(1) this State (i) is the home state of the child at the time of commencement of the proceeding, or (ii) had been the child's home state within 6 months before commencement of the proceeding and the child is absent from this State because of his removal or retention by a person claiming his custody or for other reasons, and a parent or person acting as parent continues to live in this State; or

(2) it is in the best interest of the child that a court of this State assume jurisdiction because (i) the child and his parents, or the child and at least one contestant, have a significant connection with this State, and (ii) there is available in this State substantial evidence concerning the child's present or future care, protection, training, and personal relationships; or

(3) the child is physically present in this State and (i) the child has been abandoned or (ii) it is necessary in an emergency to protect the child because he has been subjected to or threatened with mistreatment or abuse or is otherwise neglected [or dependent]; or

(4)(i) it appears that no other state would have jurisdiction under prerequisites substantially in accordance with paragraphs (1), (2), or (3), or another state has declined to exercise jurisdiction on the ground that this State is the more appropriate forum to determine the custody of the child, and (ii) it is in the best interest of the child that this court assume jurisdiction.

(b) Except under paragraphs (3) and (4) of subsection (a), physical presence in this State of the child, or of the child and one of the contestants, is not alone sufficient to confer jurisdiction on a court of this State to make a child custody determination.

(c) Physical presence of the child, while desirable, is not a prerequisite for jurisdiction to determine his custody.

§ 4.   Notice and Opportunity to be Heard.—Before making a decree under this Act, reasonable notice and opportunity to be heard shall be given to the con-

testants, any parent whose parental rights have not been previously terminated, and any person who has physical custody of the child. If any of these persons is outside this State, notice and opportunity to be heard shall be given pursuant to section 5.

§ 5.   Notice to Persons Outside this State; Submission to Jurisdiction.—

(a) Notice required for the exercise of jurisdiction over a person outside this State shall be given in a manner reasonably calculated to give actual notice, and may be:

(1) by personal delivery outside this State in the manner prescribed for service of process within this State;

(2) in the manner prescribed by the law of the place in which the service is made for service of process in that place in an action in any of its courts of general jurisdiction;

(3) by any form of mail addressed to the person to be served and requesting a receipt; or

(4) as directed by the court [including publication, if other means of notification are ineffective].

(b) Notice under this section shall be served, mailed, or delivered, [or last published] at least [10, 20] days before any hearing in this State.

(c) Proof of service outside this State may be made by affidavit of the individual who made the service, or in the manner prescribed by the law of this State, the order pursuant to which the service is made, or the law of the place in which the service is made. If service is made by mail, proof may be a receipt signed by the addressee or other evidence of delivery to the addressee.

(d) Notice is not required if a person submits to the jurisdiction of the court.

§ 6.   Simultaneous Proceedings in Other States.—

(a) A court of this State shall not exercise its jurisdiction under this Act if at the time of filing the petition a proceeding concerning the custody of the child was pending in a court of another state exercising jurisdiction substantially in conformity with this Act, unless the proceeding is stayed by the court of the other state because this State is a more appropriate forum or for other reasons.

(b) Before hearing the petition in a custody proceeding the court shall examine the pleadings and other information supplied by the parties under section 9 and shall consult the child custody registry established under section 16 concerning the pendency of proceedings with respect to the child in other states. If the court has reason to believe that proceedings may be pending in another state it shall direct an inquiry to the state court administrator or other appropriate official of the other state.

(c) If the court is informed during the course of the proceeding that a proceeding concerning the custody of the child was pending in another state before the court assumed jurisdiction it shall stay the proceeding and communicate with the court in which the other proceeding is pending to the end that the issue may be litigated in the more appropriate forum and that information be exchanged in accordance with sections 19 through 22. If a court of this State has made a custody decree before being informed of a pending proceeding in a court of another state it shall immediately inform that court of the fact. If the court is informed that a proceeding was commenced in another state after it assumed jurisdiction it shall likewise inform the other court to the end that the issues may be litigated in the more appropriate forum.

§ 7. Inconvenient Forum.—

(a) A court which has jurisdiction under this Act to make an initial or modification decree may decline to exercise its jurisdiction any time before making a decree if it finds that it is an inconvenient forum to make a custody determination under the circumstances of the case and that a court of another state is a more appropriate forum.

(b) A finding of inconvenient forum may be made upon the court's own motion or upon motion of a party or a guardian ad litem or other representative of the child.

(c) In determining if it is an inconvenient forum, the court shall consider if it is in the interest of the child that another state assume jurisdiction. For this purpose it may take into account the following factors, among others:

(1) if another state is or recently was the child's home state;

(2) if another state has a closer connection with the child and his family or with the child and one or more of the contestants;

(3) if substantial evidence concerning the child's present or future care, protection, training, and personal relationships is more readily available in another state;

(4) if the parties have agreed on another forum which is no less appropriate; and

(5) if the exercise of jurisdiction by a court of this State would contravene any of the purposes stated in section 1.

(d) Before determining whether to decline or retain jurisdiction the court may communicate with a court of another state and exchange information pertinent to the assumption of jurisdiction by either court with a view to assuring that jurisdiction will be exercised by the more appropriate court and that a forum will be available to the parties.

(e) If the court finds that it is an inconvenient forum and that a court of another state is a more appropriate forum, it may dismiss the proceedings, or it may stay the proceedings upon condition that a custody proceeding be promptly commenced in another named state or upon any other conditions which may be just and proper, including the condition that a moving party stipulate his consent and submission to the jurisdiction of the other forum.

(f) The court may decline to exercise its jurisdiction under this Act if a custody determination is incidental to an action for divorce or another proceeding while retaining jurisdiction over the divorce or other proceeding.

(g) If it appears to the court that it is clearly an inappropriate forum it may require the party who commenced the proceedings to pay, in addition to the costs of the proceedings in this State, necessary travel and other expenses, including attorneys' fees, incurred by other parties or their witnesses. Payment is to be made to the clerk of the court for remittance to the proper party.

(h) Upon dismissal or stay of proceedings under this section the court shall inform the court found to be the more appropriate forum of this fact, or if the court which would have jurisdiction in the other state is not certainly known, shall transmit the information to the court administrator or other appropriate official for forwarding to the appropriate court.

(i) Any communication received from another state informing this State of a finding of inconvenient forum because a court of this State is the more appropriate forum shall be filed in the custody registry of the appropriate court. Upon assuming jurisdiction the court of this State shall inform the original court of this fact.

§ 8. Jurisdiction Declined by Reason of Conduct.—

(a) If the petitioner for an initial decree has wrongfully taken the child from another state or has engaged in similar reprehensible conduct the court may decline to exercise jurisdiction if this is just and proper under the circumstances.

(b) Unless required in the interest of the child, the court shall not exercise its jurisdiction to modify a custody decree of another state if the petitioner, without consent of the person entitled to custody, has improperly removed the child from the physical custody of the person entitled to custody or has improperly retained the child after a visit or other temporary relinquishment of physical custody. If the petitioner has violated any other provision of a custody decree of another state the court may decline to exercise its jurisdiction if this is just and proper under the circumstances.

(c) In appropriate cases a court dismissing a petition under this section may charge the petitioner with necessary travel and other expenses, including attorneys' fees, incurred by other parties or their witnesses.

§ 9.   Information under Oath to be Submitted to the Court.—

(a) Every party in a custody proceeding in his first pleading or in an affidavit attached to that pleading shall give information under oath as to the child's present address, the places where the child has lived within the last 5 years, and the names and present addresses of the persons with whom the child has lived during that period. In this pleading or affidavit every party shall further declare under oath whether:

(1) he has participated (as a party, witness, or in any other capacity) in any other litigation concerning the custody of the same child in this or any other state;

(2) he has information of any custody proceeding concerning the child pending in a court of this or any other state; and

(3) he knows of any person not a party to the proceedings who has physical custody of the child or claims to have custody or visitation rights with respect to the child.

(b) If the declaration as to any of the above items is in the affirmative the declarant shall give additional information under oath as required by the court. The court may examine the parties under oath as to details of the information furnished and as to other matters pertinent to the court's jurisdiction and the disposition of the case.

(c) Each party has a continuing duty to inform the court of any custody proceeding concerning the child in this or any other state of which he obtained information during this proceeding.

§ 10.   Additional Parties.—If the court learns from information furnished by the parties pursuant to section 9 or from other sources that a person not a party to the custody proceeding has physical custody of the child or claims to have custody or visitation rights with respect to the child, it shall order that person to be joined as a party and to be duly notified of the pendency of the proceeding and of his joinder as a party. If the person joined as a party is outside this State he shall be served with process or otherwise notified in accordance with section 5.

§ 11.   Appearance of Parties and the Child.—

[(a) The court may order any party to the proceeding who is in this State to appear personally before the court. If that party has physical custody of the child the court may order that he appear personally with the child.]

(b) If a party to the proceeding whose presence is desired by the court is outside this State with or without the child the court may order that the notice given under section 5 include a statement directing that party to appear personally with or without the child and declaring that failure to appear may result in a decision adverse to that party.

(c) If a party to the proceeding who is outside this State is directed to appear under subsection (b) or desires to appear personally before the court with or without the child, the court may require another party to pay to the clerk of the court travel and other necessary expenses of the party so appearing and of the child if this is just and proper under the circumstances.

§ 12.   Binding Force and Res Judicata Effect of Custody Decree.—A custody decree rendered by a court of this State which had jurisdiction under section 3 binds all parties who have been served in this State or notified in accordance with section 5 or who have submitted to the jurisdiction of the court, and who have been given an opportunity to be heard. As to these parties the custody decree is conclusive as to all issues of law and fact decided and as to the custody determination made unless and until that determination is modified pursuant to law, including the provisions of this Act.

§ 13.   Recognition of Out-of-State Custody Decrees.—The courts of this State shall recognize and enforce an initial or modification decree of a court of another state which had assumed jurisdiction under statutory provisions substantially in accordance with this Act or which was made under factual circumstances meeting the jurisdictional standards of the Act, so long as this decree has not been modified in accordance with jurisdictional standards substantially similar to those of this Act.

§ 14.   Modification of Custody Decree of Another State.—

(a) If a court of another state has made a custody decree, a court of this State shall not modify that decree unless (1) it appears to the court of this State that the court which rendered the decree does not now have jurisdiction under jurisdictional prerequisites substantially in accordance with this Act or has declined to assume jurisdiction to modify the decree and (2) the court of this State has jurisdiction.

(b) If a court of this State is authorized under subsection (a) and section 8 to modify a custody decree of another state it shall give due consideration to the transcript of the record and other documents of all previous proceedings submitted to it in accordance with section 22.

§ 15.   Filing and Enforcement of Custody Decree of Another State.—

(a) A certified copy of a custody decree of another state may be filed in the office of the clerk of any [District Court, Family Court] of this State. The clerk shall treat the decree in the same manner as a custody decree of the [District Court, Family Court] of this State. A custody decree so filed has the same effect and shall be enforced in like manner as a custody decree rendered by a court of this State.

(b) A person violating a custody decree of another state which makes it necessary to enforce the decree in this State may be required to pay necessary travel and other expenses, including attorneys' fees, incurred by the party entitled to the custody or his witnesses.

§ 16.   Registry of Out-of-State Custody Decrees and Proceedings.—The clerk of each [District Court, Family Court] shall maintain a registry in which he shall enter the following:

(1) certified copies of custody decrees of other states received for filing;

(2) communications as to the pendency of custody proceedings in other states;

(3) communications concerning a finding of inconvenient forum by a court of another state; and

(4) other communications or documents concerning custody proceedings in another state which may affect the jurisdiction of a court of this State or the disposition to be made by it in a custody proceeding.

§ 17.   Certified Copies of Custody Decree.—The Clerk of the [District Court, Family Court] of this State, at the request of the court of another state or at the request of any person who is affected by or has a legitimate interest in a custody decree, shall certify and forward a copy of the decree to that court or person.

§ 18.   Taking Testimony in Another State.—In addition to other procedural devices available to a party, any party to the proceeding or a guardian ad litem or other representative of the child may adduce testimony of witnesses, including parties and the child, by deposition or otherwise in another state. The court on its own motion may direct that the testimony of a person be taken in another state and may prescribe the manner in which and the terms upon which the testimony shall be taken.

§ 19.   Hearings and Studies in Another State; Orders to Appear.—

(a) A court of this State may request the appropriate court of another state to hold a hearing to adduce evidence, to order a party to produce or give evidence under other procedures of that state, or to have social studies made with respect to the custody of a child involved in proceedings pending in the court of this State; and to forward to the court of this State certified copies of the transcript of the record of the hearing, the evidence otherwise adduced, or any social studies prepared in compliance with the request. The cost of the services may be assessed against the parties or, if necessary, ordered paid by the [County, State].

(b) A court of this State may request the appropriate court of another state to order a party to custody proceedings pending in the court of this State to appear in the proceedings, and if that party has physical custody of the child, to appear with the child. The request may state that travel and other necessary expenses of the party and of the child whose appearance is desired will be assessed against another party or will otherwise be paid.

§ 20.   Assistance to Courts of Other States.—

(a) Upon request of the court of another state the courts of this State which are competent to hear custody matters may order a person in this State to appear at a hearing to adduce evidence or to produce or give evidence under other procedures available in this State [or may order social studies to be made for use in a custody proceeding in another state]. A certified copy of the transcript of the record of the hearing or the evidence otherwise adduced [and any social studies prepared] shall be forwarded by the clerk of the court to the requesting court.

(b) A person within this State may voluntarily give his testimony or statement in this State for use in a custody proceeding outside this State.

(c) Upon request of the court of another state a competent court of this State may order a person in this State to appear alone or with the child in a custody proceeding in another state. The court may condition compliance with the request upon assurance by the other state that state travel and other necessary expenses will be advanced or reimbursed.

§ 21.   Preservation of Documents for Use in Other States.—In any custody proceeding in this State the

court shall preserve the pleadings, orders and decrees, any record that has been made of its hearings, social studies, and other pertinent documents until the child reaches [18, 21] years of age. Upon appropriate request of the court of another state the court shall forward to the other court certified copies of any or all such documents.

§ 22. Request for Court Records of Another State.

—If a custody decree has been rendered in another state concerning a child involved in a custody proceeding pending in a court of this State, the court of this State upon taking jurisdiction of the case shall request of the court of the other state a certified copy of the transcript of any court record and other documents mentioned in section 21.

§ 23. International Application.

—The general policies of this Act extend to the international area. The provisions of this Act relating to the recognition and enforcement of custody decrees of other states apply to custody decrees and decrees involving legal institutions similar in nature to custody institutions rendered by appropriate authorities of other nations if reasonable notice and opportunity to be heard were given to all affected persons.

[§ 24. Priority.

—Upon the request of a party to a custody proceeding which raises a question of existence or exercise of jurisdiction under this Act the case shall be given calendar priority and handled expeditiously.]

§ 25. Severability.

—If any provision of this Act or the application thereof to any person or circumstance is held invalid, its invalidity does not affect other provisions or applications of the Act which can be given effect without the invalid provision or application, and to this end the provisions of this Act are severable.

Parental Kidnaping Prevention Act of 1980
(28 U.S.C.A. 1738A)

§ 1738A. Full faith and credit given to child custody determinations

(a) The appropriate authorities of every State shall enforce according to its terms, and shall not modify except as provided in subsection (f) of this section, any child custody determination made consistently with the provisions of this section by a court of another State.

(b) As used in this section, the term—

(1) "child" means a person under the age of eighteen;

(2) "contestant" means a person, including a parent, who claims a right to custody or visitation of a child;

(3) "custody determination" means a judgment, decree, or other order of a court providing for the custody or visitation of a child, and includes permanent and temporary orders, and initial orders and modifications;

(4) "home State" means the State in which, immediately preceding the time involved, the child lived with his parents, a parent, or a person acting as parent, for at least six consecutive months, and in the case of a child less than six months old, the State in which the child lived from birth with any of such persons. Periods of temporary absence of any such person are counted as part of the six-month or other period;

(5) "modification" and "modify" refer to a custody determination which modifies, replaces, supersedes, or otherwise is made subsequent to, a prior custody determination concerning the same child, whether made by the same court or not;

(6) "person acting as a parent" means a person, other than a parent, who has physical custody of a child and who has either been awarded custody by a court or claims a right to custody;

(7) "physical custody" means actual possession and control of a child; and

(8) "State" means a State of the United States, the District of Columbia, the Commonwealth of Puerto Rico, or a territory or possession of the United States.

(c) A child custody determination made by a court of a State is consistent with the provisions of this section only if

(1) such court has jurisdiction under the law of such State; and

(2) one of the following conditions is met:

(A) such State (i) is the home State of the child on the date of the commencement of the proceeding, or (ii) had been the child's home State within six months before the date of the commencement of the proceeding and the child is absent from such State because of his removal or retention by a contestant or for other reasons, and a contestant continues to live in such State;

(B)(i) it appears that no other State would have jurisdiction under subparagraph (A), and (ii) it is in the best interest of the child that a court of such State assume jurisdiction because (I) the child and his parents, or the child and at least one contestant, have a significant connection with such State other than mere physical presence in such State, and (II) there is available in such State substantial evidence concerning the child's present or future care, protection, training, and personal relationships;

(C) the child is physically present in such State and (i) the child has been abandoned, or (ii) it is necessary in an emergency to protect the child because he has been subjected to or threatened with mistreatment or abuse;

(D)(i) it appears that no other State would have jurisdiction under subparagraph (A), (B), (C), or (E), or another State has declined to exercise jurisdiction on the ground that the State whose jurisdiction is in issue is the more appropriate forum to determine the custody of the child, and (ii) it is in the best interest of the child that such court assume jurisdiction; or

(E) the court has continuing jurisdiction pursuant to subsection (d) of this section.

(d) The jurisdiction of a court of a State which has made a child custody determination consistently with the provisions of this section continues as long as the requirement of subsection (c)(1) of this section continues to be met and such State remains the residence of the child or of any contestant.

(e) Before a child custody determination is made, reasonable notice and opportunity to be heard shall be given to the contestants, any parent whose parental rights have not been previously terminated and any person who has physical custody of a child.

(f) A court of a State may modify a determination of the custody of the same child made by a court of another State, if—

(1) it has jurisdiction to make such a child custody determination; and

(2) the court of the other State no longer has jurisdiction, or it has declined to exercise such jurisdiction to modify such determination.

(g) A court of a State shall not exercise jurisdiction in any proceeding for a custody determination commenced during the pendency of a proceeding in a court of another State where such court of that other State is exercising jurisdiction consistently with the provisions of this section to make a custody determination.

Federal International Child Abduction Act
(42 U.S.C.A. 11601)

§ 11601. Findings and declarations

(a) Findings. The Congress makes the following findings:

(1) The international abduction or wrongful retention of children is harmful to their well-being.

(2) Persons should not be permitted to obtain custody of children by virtue of their wrongful removal or retention.

(3) International abductions and retentions of children are increasing, and only concerted cooperation pursuant to an international agreement can effectively combat this problem.

(4) The Convention on the Civil Aspects of International Child Abduction, done at The Hague on October 25, 1980, establishes legal rights and procedures for the prompt return of children who have been wrongfully removed or retained, as well as for securing the exercise of visitation rights. Children who are wrongfully removed or retained within the meaning of the Convention are to be promptly returned unless one of the narrow exceptions set forth in the Convention applies. The Convention provides a sound treaty framework to help resolve the problem of international abduction and retention of children and will deter such wrongful removals and retentions.

(b) Declarations. The Congress makes the following declarations:

(1) It is the purpose of this Act to establish procedures for the implementation of the Convention in the United States.

(2) The provisions of this Act are in addition to and not in lieu of the provisions of the Convention.

(3) In enacting this Act the Congress recognizes—

(A) the international character of the Convention; and

(B) the need for uniform international interpretation of the Convention.

(4) The Convention and this Act empower courts in the United States to determine only rights under the Convention and not the merits of any underlying child custody claims.

§ 11602. Definitions.

For the purposes of this Act—

(1) the term "applicant" means any person who, pursuant to the Convention, files an application with the United States Central Authority or a Central Authority of any other party to the Convention for the return of a child alleged to have been wrongfully removed or retained or for arrangements for organizing or securing the effective exercise of rights of access pursuant to the Convention;

(2) the term "Convention" means the Convention on the Civil Aspects of International Child Abduction, done at The Hague on October 25, 1980;

(3) the term "Parent Locator Service" means the service established by the Secretary of Health and Human Services under section 453 of the Social Security Act (42 U.S.C. 653);

(4) the term "petitioner" means any person who, in accordance with this Act, files a petition in court seeking relief under the Convention;

(5) the term "person" includes any individual, institution, or other legal entity or body;

(6) the term "respondent" means any person against whose interests a petition is filed in court, in accordance with this Act, which seeks relief under the Convention;

(7) the term "rights of access" means visitation rights;

(8) the term "State" means any of the several States, the District of Columbia, and any commonwealth, territory, or possession of the United States; and

(9) the term "United States Central Authority" means the agency of the Federal Government designated by the President under section 7(a) [42 USCS § 11606(a)].

§ 11603. Judicial remedies

(a) Jurisdiction of the courts. The courts of the States and the United States district courts shall have concurrent original jurisdiction of actions arising under the Convention.

(b) Petitions. Any person seeking to initiate judicial proceedings under the Convention for the return of a child or for arrangements for organizing or securing the effective exercise of rights of access to a child may do so by commencing a civil action by filing a petition for the relief sought in any court which has jurisdiction of such action and which is authorized to exercise its jurisdiction in the place where the child is located at the time the petition is filed.

(c) Notice. Notice of an action brought under subsection (b) shall be given in accordance with the applicable law governing notice in interstate child custody proceedings.

(d) Determination of case. The court in which an action is brought under subsection (b) shall decide the case in accordance with the Convention.

(e) Burdens of proof. (1) A petitioner in an action brought under subsection (b) shall establish by a preponderance of the evidence—

(A) in the case of an action for the return of a child, that the child has been wrongfully removed or retained within the meaning of the Convention; and

(B) in the case of an action for arrangements for organizing or securing the effective exercise of rights of access, that the petitioner has such rights.

(2) In the case of an action for the return of a child, a respondent who opposes the return of the child has the burden of establishing—

(A) by clear and convincing evidence that one of the exceptions set forth in article 13b or 20 of the Convention applies; and

(B) by a preponderance of the evidence that any other exception set forth in article 12 or 13 of the Convention appleis.

(f) Application of the Convention. For purposes of any action brought under this Act—

(1) the term "authorities", as used in article 15 of the Convention to refer to the authorities of the state of the habitual residence of a child, includes courts and appropriate government agencies;

(2) the terms "wrongful removal or retention" and "wrongfully removed or retained", as used in the Convention, include a removal or retention of a child before the entry of a custody order regarding that child; and

(3) the term "commencement of proceedings", as used in article 12 of the Convention, means, with respect to the return of a child located in the United States, the filing of the petition in accordance with subsection (b) of this section.

(g) Full faith and credit. Full faith and credit shall be accorded by the courts of the States and the courts of the United States to the judgment of any other such court ordering or denying the return of the a child, pursuant to the Convention, in an action brought under this Act.

(h) Remedies under the Convention not exclusive. The remedies established by the Convention and this Act shall be in addition to remedies available under other laws or international agreements.

§ 11604. Provisional remedies

(a) Authority of courts. In furtherance of the objectives of article 7(b) and other provisions of the Convention, and subject to the provisions of subsection (b) of this section, any court exercising jurisdiction of an action brought under section 4(b) of this Act [42 USCS § 11630(b)] may take or cause to be taken measures under Federal or State law, as appropriate, to protect the well-being of the child involved or to prevent the child's further removal or concealment before the final disposition of the petition.

(b) Limitation on authority. No court exercising jurisdiction of an action brought under section 4(b) [42 USCS § 11603(b)] may, under subsection (a) of this section, order a child removed from a person having physical control of the child unless the applicable requirements of State law are satisfied.

§ 11605. Admissibility of documents

With respect to any application to the United States Central Authority, or any petition to a court under section 4 [42 USCS § 11603], which seeks relief under the Convention, or any other documents or information included with such application or petition or provided after such submission which relates to the application or petition, as the case may be, no authentication of such application, petition, document, or information shall be required in order for the application, petition, document, or information to be admissible in court.

§ 11606.　United States Central Authority

(a) Designation. The President shall designate a Federal agency to serve as the Central Authority for the United States under the Convention.

(b) Functions. The functions of the United States Central Authority are those ascribed to the Central Authority by the Convention and this Act.

(c) Regulatory authority. The United States Central Authority is authorized to issue such regulations as may be necessary to carry out its functions under the Convention and this Act.

(d) Obtaining information from Parent Locator Service. The United States Central Authority may, to the extent authorized by the Social Security Act [42 USCS §§ 301 et seq.], obtain information from the Parent Locator Service.

§ 11607.　Costs and fees

(a) Administrative costs. No department, agency, or instrumentality of the Federal Government or of any State or local government may impose on an applicant any fee in relation to the administrative processing of applications submitted under the Convention.

(b) Costs incurred in civil actions. (1) Petitioners may be required to bear the costs of legal counsel or advisors, court costs incurred in connection with their petitions, and travel costs for the return of the child involved and any accompanying persons, except as provided in paragraphs (2) and (3).

(2) Subject to paragraph (3), legal fees or court costs incurred in connection with an action brought under section 4 [42 USCS § 11603] shall be borne by the petitioner unless they are covered by payments from Federal, State, or local legal assistance or other programs.

(3) Any court ordering the return of a child pursuant to an action brought under section 4 [42 USCS § 11603] shall order the respondent to pay necessary expenses incurred by or on behalf of the petitioner, including court costs, legal fees, foster home or other care during the course of proceedings in the action, and transportation costs related to the return of the child, unless the respondent establishes that such order would be clearly inappropriate.

§ 11608.　Collection, maintenance, and dissemination of information

(a) In general. In performing its functions under the Convention, the United States Central Authority may, under such conditions as the Central Authority prescribes by regulation, but subject to subsection (c), receive from or transmit to any department, agency, or instrumentality of the Federal Government or of any State or foreign government, and receive from or transmit to any applicant, petitioner, or respondent, information necessary to locate a child or for the purpose of otherwise implementing the Convention with respect to a child, except that the United States Central Authority—

(1) may receive such information from a Federal or State department, agency, or instrumentality only pursuant to applicable Federal and State statutes; and

(2) may transmit any information received under this subsection notwithstanding any provisions of law other than this Act.

(b) Requests for information. Requests for information under this section shall be submitted in such manner and form as the United States Central Authority may prescribe by regulation and shall be accompanied or supported by such documents as the United States Central Authority may require.

(c) Responsibility of government entities. Whenever any department agency, or instrumentality of the United States or of any State receives a request from the United States Central Authority for information authorized to be provided to such Central Authority under subsection (a), the head of such department, agency, or instrumentality shall promptly cause a search to be made of the files and records maintained by such department, agency, or instrumentality in order to determine whether the information requested is contained in any such files or records. If such search discloses the information requested, the head of such department, agency, or instrumentality shall immediately transmit such information to the United States Central Authority, except that any such information the disclosure of which—

(1) would adversely affect the national security interests of the United States or the law enforcement interests of the United States or of any State; or

(2) would be prohibited by section 9 of title 13, United States Code;

shall not be transmitted to the Central Authority. The head of such department, agency, or instrumentality shall, immediately upon completion of the requested search, notify the Central Authority of the results of the search, and whether an exception set forth in the paragraph (1) or (2) applies. In the event that the United States Central Authority receives information and the appropriate Federal or State department, agency, or instrumentality thereafter notifies the Central Authority that an exception set forth in paragraph (1) or (2) applies to that information, the Central Authority may not disclose that information under subsection (a).

(d) Information available from Parent Locator Service. To the extent that information which the United States Central Authority is authorized to obtain under the provisions of subsection (c) can be obtained through the Parent Locator Service, the United States Central Authority shall first seek to obtain such information from the Parent Locator Service, before requesting such information directly under the provisions of subsection (c) of this section.

(e) Recordkeeping. The United States Central Authority shall maintain appropriate records concerning its activities and the disposition of cases brought to its attention.

§ 11609.   Interagency coordinating group.

The Secretary of State, the Secretary of Health and Human Services, and the Attorney General shall designate Federal employees and may, from time to time, designate private citizens to serve on an interagency coordinating group to monitor the operation of the Convention and to provide advice on its implementation to the United States Central Authority and other Federal agencies. This group shall meet from time to time at the request of the United States Central Authority. The agency in which the United States Central Authority is located is authorized to reimburse such private citizens for travel and other expenses incurred in participating at meetings of the interagency coordinating group at rates not to exceed those authorized under subchapter I of chapter 57 of title 5, United States Code [5 USCS §§ 5701 et seq.], for employees of agencies.

§ 11610.   Authorization of appropriations.

There are authorized to be appropriated for each fiscal year such sums as may be necessary to carry out the purposes of the Convention and this Act.

Revised Uniform Reciprocal Enforcement of Support Act

Part I: General Provisions

§ 1. Purposes

The purposes of this Act are to improve and extend by reciprocal legislation the enforcement of duties of support.

§ 2. Definitions

(a) "Court" means the [here insert name] court of this State and when the context requires means the court of any other state as defined in a substantially similar reciprocal law.

(b) "Duty of support" means a duty of support whether imposed or imposable by law or by order, decree, or judgment of any court, whether interlocutory or final or whether incidental to an action for divorce, separation, separate maintenance, or otherwise and includes the duty to pay arrearages of support past due and unpaid.

(c) "Governor" includes any person performing the functions of Governor or the executive authority of any state covered by this Act.

(d) "Initiating state" means a state in which a proceeding pursuant to this or a substantially similar reciprocal law is commenced. "Initiating court" means the court in which a proceeding is commenced.

(e) "Law" includes both common and statutory law.

(f) "Obligee" means a person including a state or political subdivision to whom a duty of support is owed or a person including a state or political subdivision that has commenced a proceeding for enforcement of an alleged duty of support or for registration of a support order. It is immaterial if the person to whom a duty of support is owed is a recipient of public assistance.

(g) "Obligor" means any person owing a duty of support or against whom a proceeding for the enforcement of a duty of support or registration of a support order is commenced.

(h) "Prosecuting attorney" means the public official in the appropriate place who has the duty to enforce criminal laws relating to the failure to provide for the support of any person.

(i) "Register" means to [record] [file] in the Registry of Foreign Support Orders.

(j) "Registering court" means any court of this State in which a support order of a rendering state is registered.

(k) "Rendering state" means a state in which the court has issued a support order for which registration is sought or granted in the court of another state.

(l) "Responding state" means a state in which any responsive proceeding pursuant to the proceeding in the initiating state is commenced. "Responding court" means the court in which the responsive proceeding is commenced.

(m) "State" includes a state, territory, or possession of the United States, the District of Columbia, the Commonwealth of Puerto Rico, and any foreign jurisdiction in which this or a substantially similar reciprocal law is in effect.

(n) "Support order" means any judgment, decree, or order of support in favor of an obligee whether temporary or final, or subject to modification, revocation, or remission, regardless of the kind of action or proceeding in which it is entered.

§ 3. Remedies Additional to Those Now Existing

The remedies herein provided are in addition to and not in substitution for any other remedies.

§ 4. Extent of Duties of Support

Duties of support arising under the law of this State, when applicable under section 7, bind the obligor present in this State regardless of the presence or residence of the obligee.

Part II: Criminal Enforcement

§ 5. Interstate Rendition

The Governor of this State may

(1) demand of the Governor of another state the surrender of a person found in that state who is charged criminally in this State with failing to provide for the support of any person; or

(2) surrender on demand by the Governor of another state a person found in this State who is charged criminally in that state with failing to provide for the support of any person. Provisions for extradition of criminals not inconsistent with this Act apply to the demand even if the person whose surrender is demanded was not in the demanding state at the time of the commission of the crime and has not fled therefrom. The demand, the oath, and any proceedings for extradition pursuant to this section need not state or show that the person whose surrender is demanded has fled from justice or at the time of the commission of the crime was in the demanding state.

§ 6. Conditions of Interstate Rendition

(a) Before making the demand upon the Governor of another state for the surrender of a person charged criminally in this State with failing to provide for the support of a person, the Governor of this State may require any prosecuting attorney of this State to satisfy him that at least [60] days prior thereto the obligee initiated proceedings for support under this Act or that any proceeding would be of no avail.

(b) If, under a substantially similar Act, the Governor of another state makes a demand upon the Governor of this State for the surrender of a person charged criminally in that state with failure to provide for the support of a person, the Governor may require any prosecuting attorney to investigate the demand and to report to him whether proceedings for support have been initiated or would be effective. If it appears to the Governor that a proceeding would be effective but has not been initiated he may delay honoring the demand for a reasonable time to permit the initiation of a proceeding.

(c) If proceedings have been initiated and the person demanded has prevailed therein the Governor may decline to honor the demand. If the obligee prevailed and the person demanded is subject to a support order, the Governor may decline to honor the demand if the person demanded is complying with the support order.

Part III: Civil Enforcement

§ 7. Choice of Law

Duties of support applicable under this Act are those imposed under the laws of any state where the obligor was present for the period during which support is sought. The obligor is presumed to have been present in the responding state during the period for which support is sought until otherwise shown.

§ 8. Remedies of State or Political Subdivision Furnishing Support

If a state or a political subdivision furnishes support to an individual obligee it has the same right to initiate a proceeding under this Act as the individual obligee for the purpose of securing reimbursement for support furnished and of obtaining continuing support.

§ 9. How Duties of Support Enforced

All duties of support, including the duty to pay arrearages, are enforceable by a proceeding under this Act including a proceeding for civil contempt. The defense that the parties are immune to suit because of their relationship as husband and wife or parent and child is not available to the obligor.

§ 10. Jurisdiction

Jurisdiction of any proceeding under this Act is vested in the [here insert title of court desired].

§ 11. Contents and Filing of [Petition] for Support; Venue

(a) The [petition] shall be verified and shall state the name and, so far as known to the obligee, the address and circumstances of the obligor and the persons for whom support is sought, and all other pertinent information. The obligee may include in or attach to the [petition] any information which may help in locating or identifying the obligor including a photograph of the obligor, a description of any distinguishing marks on his person, other names and aliases by which he has been or is known, the name of his employer, his fingerprints, and his Social Security number.

(b) The [petition] may be filed in the appropriate court of any state in which the obligee resides. The court shall not decline or refuse to accept and forward the [petition] on the ground that it should be filed with some other court of this or any other state where there is pending another action for divorce, separation, annulment, dissolution, habeas corpus, adoption, or custody between the same parties or where another court has already issued a support order in some other proceeding and has retained jurisdiction for its enforcement.

§ 12. Officials to Represent Obligee

If this State is acting as an initiating state the prosecuting attorney upon the request of the court [a state department of welfare, a county commissioner, an overseer of the poor, or other local welfare officer] shall represent the obligee in any proceeding under this Act. [If the prosecuting attorney neglects or refuses to represent the obligee the [Attorney General] may order him to comply with the request of the court or may undertake the representation.] [If the prosecuting attorney neglects or refuses to represent the obligee, the [Attorney General] [State Director of Public Welfare] may undertake the representation.]

§ 13. Petition for a Minor

A [petition] on behalf of a minor obligee may be executed and filed by a person having legal custody of the minor without appointment as guardian ad litem.

§ 14. Duty of Initiating Court

If the initiating court finds that the [petition] sets forth facts from which it may be determined that the obligor owes a duty of support and that a court of the responding state may obtain jurisdiction of the obligor or his property it shall so certify and cause 3 copies of the [petition] and its certificate and one copy of this Act to be sent to the responding court. Certification shall be in accordance with the requirements of the initiating state. If the name and address of the responding court is unknown and the responding state has an information agency comparable to that established in the initiating state it shall cause the copies to be sent to the state information agency or other proper official of the responding state, with a request that the agency or official forward them to the proper court and that the court of the responding state acknowledge their receipt to the initiating court.

§ 15. Costs and Fees

An initiating court shall not require payment of either a filing fee or other costs from the obligee but may request the responding court to collect fees and costs from the obligor. A responding court shall not require payment of a filing fee or other costs from the obligee but it may direct that all fees and costs requested by the initiating court and incurred in this State when acting as a responding state, including fees for filing of pleadings, service of process, seizure of property, stenographic or duplication service, or other service supplied to the obligor, be paid in whole or in part by the obligor or by the [state or political subdivision thereof]. These costs or fees do not have priority over amounts due to the obligee.

§ 16. Jurisdiction by Arrest

If the court of this State believes that the obligor may flee it may

(1) as an initiating court, request in its certificate that the responding court obtain the body of the obligor by appropriate process; or

(2) as a responding court, obtain the body of the obligor by appropriate process. Thereupon it may release him upon his own recognizance or upon his giving a bond in an amount set by the court to assure his appearance at the hearing.

§ 17. State Information Agency

(a) The [Attorney General's Office, State Attorney's Office, Welfare Department or other Information Agency] is designated as the state information agency under this Act, it shall

(1) compile a list of the courts and their addresses in this State having jurisdiction under this Act and transmit it to the state information agency of every other state which has adopted this or a substantially similar Act. Upon the adjournment of each session of the [legislature] the agency shall distribute copies of any amendments to the Act and a statement of their effective date to all other state information agencies;

(2) maintain a register of lists of courts received from other states and transmit copies thereof promptly to every court in this state having jurisdiction under this Act; and

(3) forward to the court in this State which has jurisdiction over the obligor or his property petitions, certificates, and copies of the Act it receives from courts or information agencies of other states.

(b) If the state information agency does not know the location of the obligor or his property in the state and no state location service is available it shall use all means at its disposal to obtain this information, including the examination of official records in the state and other sources such as telephone directories, real property records, vital statistics records, police records, requests for the name and address from employers who are able or willing to cooperate, records of motor vehicle license offices, requests made to the tax offices both state and federal where such offices are able to cooperate, and requests made to the Social Security Administration as permitted by the Social Security Act as amended.

(c) After the deposit of 3 copies of the [petition] and certificate and one copy of the Act of the initiating state with the clerk of the appropriate court, if the state information agency knows or believes that the prosecuting attorney is not prosecuting the case diligently it shall inform the [Attorney General] [State Director of Public Welfare] who may undertake the representation.

§ 18. Duty of the Court and Officials of This State as Responding State

(a) After the responding court receives copies of the [petition], certificate, and Act from the initiating court the clerk of the court shall docket the case and notify the prosecuting attorney of his action.

(b) The prosecuting attorney shall prosecute the case diligently. He shall take all action necessary in accordance with the laws of this State to enable the court to obtain jurisdiction over the obligor or his property and shall request the court [clerk of the court] to set a time and place for a hearing and give notice thereof to the obligor in accordance with law.

(c) [If the prosecuting attorney neglects or refuses to represent the obligee the [Attorney General] may order him to comply with the request of the court or may undertake the representation.] [If the prosecuting attorney neglects or refuses to represent the obligee, the [Attorney General] [State Director of Public Welfare] may undertake the representation.]

§ 19. Further Duties of Court and Officials in the Responding State

(a) The prosecuting attorney on his own initiative shall use all means at his disposal to locate the obligor or his property, and if because of inaccuracies in the [petition] or otherwise the court cannot obtain jurisdiction the prosecuting attorney shall inform the court of what he has done and request the court to continue the case pending receipt of more accurate information or an amended [petition] from the initiating court.

(b) If the obligor or his property is not found in the [county], and the prosecuting attorney discovers that the obligor or his property may be found in another [county] of this State or in another state he shall so inform the court. Thereupon the clerk of the court shall forward the documents received from the court in the initiating state to a court in the other [county] or to a court in the other state or to the information agency or other proper official of the other state with a request that the documents be forwarded to the proper court. All powers and duties provided by this Act apply to the recipient of the documents so forwarded. If the clerk of a court of this State forwards documents to another court he shall forthwith notify the initiating court.

(c) If the prosecuting attorney has no information as to the location of the obligor or his property he shall so inform the initiating court.

§ 20. Hearing and Continuance

If the obligee is not present at the hearing and the obligor denies owing the duty of support alleged in the petition or offers evidence constituting a defense the court, upon request of either party, shall continue the hearing to permit evidence relative to the duty to be adduced by either party by deposition or by appearing in person before the court. The court may designate the judge of the initiating court as a person before whom a deposition may be taken.

§ 21. Immunity from Criminal Prosecution

If at the hearing the obligor is called for examination as an adverse party and he declines to answer upon the ground that his testimony may tend to incriminate him, the court may require him to answer, in which event he is immune from criminal prosecution with respect to matters revealed by his testimony, except for perjury committed in this testimony.

§ 22. Evidence of Husband and Wife

Laws attaching a privilege against the disclosure of communications between husband and wife are inapplicable to proceedings under this Act. Husband and wife are competent witnesses [and may be compelled] to testify to any relevant matter, including marriage and parentage.

§ 23. Rules of Evidence

In any hearing for the civil enforcement of this Act the court is governed by the rules of evidence applicable in a civil court action in the _____ Court. If the action is based on a support order issued by another court a certified copy of the order shall be received as evidence of the duty of support, subject only to any defenses available to an obligor with respect to paternity (Section 27) or to a defendant in an action or a proceeding to enforce a foreign money judgment. The determination or enforcement of a duty of support owed to one obligee is unaffected by any interference by another obligee with rights of custody or visitation granted by a court.

§ 24. Order of Support

If the responding court finds a duty of support it may order the obligor to furnish support or reimbursement therefor and subject the property of the obligor to the order. Support orders made pursuant to this Act shall require that payments be made to the [clerk] [bureau] [probation department] of the court of the responding state. [The court and prosecuting attorney of any [county] in which the obligor is present or has property have the same powers and duties to enforce the order as have those of the [county] in which it was first issued. If enforcement is impossible or cannot be completed in the [county] in which the order was issued, the prosecuting attorney shall send a certified copy of the order to the prosecuting attorney of any [county] in which it appears that proceedings to enforce the order would be effective. The prosecuting attorney to whom the certified copy of the order is forwarded shall proceed with enforcement and report the results of the proceedings to the court first issuing the order.]

§ 25. Responding Court to Transmit Copies to Initiating Court

The responding court shall cause a copy of all support orders to be sent to the initiating court.

§ 26. Additional Powers of Responding Court

In addition to the foregoing powers a responding court may subject the obligor to any terms and conditions proper to assure compliance with its orders and in particular to:

(1) require the obligor to furnish a cash deposit or a bond of a character and amount to assure payment of any amount due;

(2) require the obligor to report personally and to make payments at specified intervals to the [clerk] [bureau] [probation department] of the court; and

(3) punish under the power of contempt the obligor who violates any order of the court.

§ 27. Paternity

If the obligor asserts as a defense that he is not the father of the child for whom support is sought and it appears to the court that the defense is not frivolous, and if both of the parties are present at the hearing or the proof required in the case indicates that the presence of either or both of the parties is not necessary, the court may adjudicate the paternity issue. Otherwise the court may adjourn the hearing until the paternity issue has been adjudicated.

§ 28. Additional Duties of Responding Court

A responding court has the following duties which may be carried out through the [clerk] [bureau] [probation department] of the court:

(1) to transmit to the initiating court any payment made by the obligor pursuant to any order of the court or otherwise; and

(2) to furnish to the initiating court upon request a certified statement of all payments made by the obligor.

§ 29. Additional Duty of Initiating Court

An initiating court shall receive and disburse forthwith all payments made by the obligor or sent by the responding court. This duty may be carried out through the [clerk] [bureau] [probation department] of the court.

§ 30. Proceedings Not to be Stayed

A responding court shall not stay the proceeding or refuse a hearing under this Act because of any pending or prior action or proceeding for divorce, separation, annulment, dissolution, habeas corpus, adoption, or custody in this or any other state. The court shall hold a hearing and may issue a support order pendente lite. In aid thereof it may require the obligor to give a bond for the prompt prosecution of the pending proceeding. If the other action or proceeding is concluded before the hearing in the instant proceeding and the judgment therein provides for the support demanded in the [petition] being heard the court must conform its support order to the amount allowed in the other action or proceeding. Thereafter the court shall not stay enforcement of its support order because of the retention of jurisdiction for enforcement purposes by the court in the other action or proceeding.

§ 31. Application of Payments

A support order made by a court of this State pursuant to this Act does not nullify and is not nullified by a support order made by a court of this State pursuant to any other law or by a support order made by a court of any other state pursuant to a substantially similar act or any other law, regardless of priority of issuance, unless otherwise specifically provided by the court. Amounts paid for a particular period pursuant to any support order made by the court of another state shall be credited against the amounts accruing or accrued for the same period under any support order made by the court of this State.

§ 32. Effect of Participation in Proceeding

Participation in any proceeding under this Act does not confer jurisdiction upon any court over any of the parties thereto in any other proceeding.

§ 33. Intrastate Application

This Act applies if both the obligee and the obligor are in this State but in different [counties]. If the court of the [county] in which the [petition] is filed finds that the [petition] sets forth facts from which it may be determined that the obligor owes a duty of support and finds that a court of another [county] in this State may obtain jurisdiction over the obligor or his property, the clerk of the court shall send the [petition] and a certification of the findings to the court of the [county] in which the obligor or his property is found. The clerk of the court of the [county] receiving these documents shall notify the prosecuting attorney of their receipt. The prosecuting attorney and the court in the [county] to which the copies are forwarded then shall have duties corresponding to those imposed upon them when acting for this State as a responding state.

§ 34.   Appeals

If the [Attorney General] [State Director of Public Welfare] is of the opinion that a support order is erroneous and presents a question of law warranting an appeal in the public interest, he may

(a) perfect an appeal to the proper appellate court if the support order was issued by a court of this State, or

(b) if the support order was issued in another state, cause the appeal to be taken in the other state. In either case expenses of appeal may be paid on his order from funds appropriated for his office.

Part IV: Registration of Foreign Support Orders

§ 35.   Additional Remedies

If the duty of support is based on a foreign support order, the obligee has the additional remedies provided in the following sections.

§ 36.   Registration

The obligee may register the foreign support order in a court of this State in the manner, with the effect, and for the purposes herein provided.

§ 37.   Registry of Foreign Support Orders

The clerk of the court shall maintain a Registry of Foreign Support Orders in which he shall [file] foreign support orders.

§ 38.   Official to Represent Obligee

If this State is acting either as a rendering or a registering state the prosecuting attorney upon the request of the court [a state department of welfare, a county commissioner, an overseer of the poor, or other local welfare official] shall represent the obligee in proceedings under this Part.

[If the prosecuting attorney neglects or refuses to represent the obligee, the [Attorney General] may order him to comply with the request of the court or may undertake the representation.] [If the prosecuting attorney neglects or refuses to represent the obligee, the [Attorney General] [State Director of Public Welfare] may undertake the representation.]

§ 39.   Registration Procedure; Notice

(a) An obligee seeking to register a foreign support order in a court of this State shall transmit to the clerk of the court (1) three certified copies of the order with all modifications thereof, (2) one copy of the reciprocal enforcement of support act of the state in which the order was made, and (3) a statement verified and signed by the obligee, showing the post office address of the obligee, the last known place of residence and post office address of the obligor, the amount of support remaining unpaid, a description and the location of any property of the obligor available upon execution, and a list of the states in which the order is registered. Upon receipt of these documents the clerk of the court, without payment of a filing fee or other cost to the obligee, shall file them in the Registry of Foreign Support Orders. The filing constitutes registration under this Act.

(b) Promptly upon registration the clerk of the court shall send by certified or registered mail to the obligor at the address given a notice of the registration with a copy of the registered support order and the post office address of the obligee. He shall also docket the case and notify the prosecuting attorney of his action. The prosecuting attorney shall proceed diligently to enforce the order.

§ 40.   Effect of Registration; Enforcement Procedure

(a) Upon registration the registered foreign support order shall be treated in the same manner as a support order issued by a court of this State. It has the same effect and is subject to the same procedures, defenses, and proceedings for reopening, vacating, or staying as a support order of this State and may be enforced and satisfied in like manner.

(b) The obligor has [20] days after the mailing of notice of the registration in which to petition the court to vacate the registration or for other relief. If he does not so petition the registered support order is confirmed.

(c) At the hearing to enforce the registered support order the obligor may present only matters that would be available to him as defenses in an action to enforce a foreign money judgment. If he shows to the court that an appeal from the order is pending or will be taken or that a stay of execution has been granted the court shall stay enforcement of the order until the appeal is concluded, the time for appeal has expired, or the order is vacated, upon satisfactory proof that the obligor has furnished security for payment of the support ordered as required by the rendering state. If he shows to the court any ground upon which enforcement of a support order of this State may be stayed the court shall stay enforcement of the order for an appropriate period if the obligor furnishes the same security for payment of the support ordered that is required for a support order of this State.

§ 41.   Uniformity of Interpretation

This Act shall be so construed as to effectuate its general purpose to make uniform the law of those states which enact it.

§ 42.   Short Title

This Act may be cited as the Revised Uniform Reciprocal Enforcement of Support Act (1968).

§ 43.   Severability

If any provision of this Act or the application thereof to any person or circumstance is held invalid, the invalidity does not affect other provisions or applications of the Act which can be given effect without the invalid provision or application, and to this end the provisions of this Act are severable.

The following pages contain sample URESA forms that are often used throughout the country.

COURT/ADMINISTRATIVE AGENCY IDENTIFICATION AND CASE NUMBER

PLAINTIFF/PETITIONER

ADDRESS

The Uniform Support Petition is a standard form for URESA cases. The petition is a legal pleading as opposed to an administrative form, and its purpose is to show how the court has jurisdiction, to show enough facts to notify the defendant/respondent of the claim being made, and to provide plaintiff/petitioner with a means to request specific court ordered action or relief. The Uniform Support Petition is simple and straightforward, yet provides some flexibility. Properly prepared it should be legally sufficient to initiate URESA cases and respond to URESA request in all states.

VS

DEFENDANT/RESPONDENT

☐ IV-D   ☐ NON IV-D

ADDRESS

OTHER REFERENCE NUMBER

UNIFORM SUPPORT PETITION

This petition of plaintiff/petitioner respectfully shows the court that:

1. This is a petition for:

   ☐ ESTABLISHMENT OF PATERNITY   ☐ SUPPORT   ☐ MEDICAL COVERAGE   ☐ ARREARAGE

   ☐ REIMBURSEMENT   ☐ OTHER _____

   ☐ The General Testimony for URESA is attached and incorporated by reference.   ☐ A Paternity Affidavit is attached and incorporated by reference.

2. _____ resides in

   CITY, COUNTY, STATE

   and has custody of the following dependents of defendant/respondent:

DEPENDENTS' NAMES (First MI Last)	DATE OF BIRTH (Month, Day, Year)

   ☐ Additional Names on attached sheet.

3. _____ and defendant/respondent were:

   ☐ Never married to each other

   ☐ Married on . . . .   DATE

   ☐ Divorce pending

   ☐ Divorced on . . . .   DATE   in   COUNTY AND STATE

UNIFORM SUPPORT PETITION

CASE NUMBER

4. Defendant/respondent resides in:

CITY, COUNTY, STATE

Defendant/respondent's last known employer is:

NAME, ADDRESS

5. The dependents are entitled to support and/or medical coverage from the defendant/respondent, who has a legal obligation to pay support pursuant to the laws of the initiating jurisdiction, which is enforceable under the reciprocal support statute which is:

REFERENCE

The responding state may obtain jurisdiction of defendant/respondent and/or his property.

6. Since on or about
DATE
defendant/respondent has refused or neglected to provide reasonable support for the above named dependents.

7. Defendant/respondent:

☐ a. is under a court order to provide support pursuant to:

☐ original Divorce decree . . . .
DATED

NOTE: A CERTIFIED COPY OF THE CURRENT ORDER IS ATTACHED AND INCORPORATED BY REFERENCE.

☐ other support order or agreement

☐ failure to comply with the support order has resulted in an arrearage of: . . . .
ARREARAGE AMOUNT
$
as of
DATE

☐ b. is not under a court order to provide support however
(name) _____
is entitled to reimbursement as stated in the testimony attached and incorporated by reference, in the amount of: . . . .

☐ PRINCIPAL ONLY   ☐ INCLUDES INTEREST

REIMBURSEMENT AMOUNT
$
as of
DATE

☐ c. should pay a reasonable amount of ongoing support for the dependents which is: . . . . or greater amount as permitted by the law of the responding state.

AMOUNT (CHILD SUPPORT)
$
per
MONTH, WEEK

AMOUNT (SPOUSAL)
$
per
MONTH, WEEK

☐ d. Other special pleading:

8. (name) _____

NAME & ADDRESS OF AGENCY

☐ has made an assignment of rights; and/or

☐ has given authority to the following agency to collect support for the above named dependents.

Form OS 550 (3/87)

RESPONDING JURISDICTION COURT/ADM. AGENCY COPY

UNIFORM SUPPORT PETITION
PAGE 2 OF 3 PAGES

UNIFORM SUPPORT PETITION

CASE NUMBER

Wherefore, plaintiff/petitioner requests an order for the following:

☐ Establishment of paternity

☐ Child support in the amount of: . . . .

AMOUNT (CHILD SUPPORT)		MONTH, WEEK
$	per	

☐ Spousal support in the amount of: . . . .

AMOUNT (SPOUSAL)		MONTH, WEEK
$	per	

☐ Registration and enforcement of the current support order

☐ Medical coverage

☐ Arrearage in the amount of: . . . .

ARREARAGE AMOUNT		DATE
$	as of	

☐ Reimbursement in the amount of: . . . .

REIMBURSEMENT AMOUNT		DATE
$	as of	

☐ Payment of costs and attorneys' fees by the defendant/respondent. (see instructions)

☐ Other:

Under penalties of perjury, all information and facts stated in this petition are true to the best of my knowledge and belief.

DATE	SIGNATURE OF PLAINTIFF/PETITIONER OR REPRESENTATIVE

SWORN TO AND SIGNED BEFORE ME THIS DATE	NOTARY PUBLIC	COMMISSION EXPIRES

Form OS 550 (3/87)

UNIFORM SUPPORT PETITION
PAGE 3 OF 3 PAGES

RESPONDING JURISDICTION COURT/ADM. AGENCY COPY

COURT/ADMINISTRATIVE AGENCY IDENTIFICATION AND CASE NUMBER

PLAINTIFF/PETITIONER

This document provides a framework for stating the detailed information necessary to support the action requested in the petition, as relevant to the particular case.

VS

DEFENDANT/RESPONDENT

☐ IV-D ☐ NON IV-D

OTHER REFERENCE NUMBER

GENERAL TESTIMONY FOR URESA

_____ being duly sworn, under penalties of perjury, testifies as follows:
(Name)

I. PERSONAL INFORMATION

1. NAME AND COMPLETE HOME ADDRESS	2. HOME/MESSAGE PHONE	3. WORK PHONE
	4. SOCIAL SEC. NO.	5. DATE OF BIRTH

6. RELATIONSHIP TO DEFENDANT/RESPONDENT:		
☐ NEVER MARRIED ☐ MARRIED	DATE OF MARRIAGE	PLACE OF MARRIAGE (STATE)
☐ COMMON LAW MARRIAGE ☐ DIVORCED	STATE (COMMON LAW MARRIAGE)	DATES (FROM - TO)
☐ OTHER: _____	DATE OF DIVORCE	DATE OF SUPPORT ORDER
☐ SUPPORT ORDER ENTERED ☐ NO SUPPORT ORDER	DATE OF SEPARATION	COURT AND LOCATION (DIVORCE AND SEPARATION)

NOTE: ATTACH A CERTIFIED COPY OF THE DIVORCE DECREE OR SEPARATION AGREEMENT AND THE CURRENT SUPPORT ORDER.

7. PRESENT MARITAL STATUS:	NAME OF NEW SPOUSE OR NON MARITAL PARTNER
☐ MARRIED TO DEFENDANT/RESPONDENT	
☐ MARRIED TO NEW SPOUSE	
☐ LIVING WITH NON-MARITAL PARTNER	
☐ SINGLE	

Form OS 548 (3/87)

RESPONDING JURISDICTION COURT/ADM. AGENCY COPY

GENERAL TESTIMONY FOR URESA
PAGE 1 OF 12 PAGES

GENERAL TESTIMONY FOR URESA   CASE NUMBER

II. DEPENDENTS' HOUSEHOLD INFORMATION

1. The following are the dependents for whom support is sought from the defendant/respondent:

FULL NAME	DATE OF BIRTH	IS PATERNITY AN ISSUE YES OR NO	SUPPORT ORDER ESTABLISHED YES OR NO	LIVING WITH PETITIONER? YES OR NO

NOTE; A PATERNITY AFFIDAVIT IS REQUIRED FOR EACH CHILD NOT OF THE MARRIAGE WHOSE PATERNITY IS AT ISSUE.

2. Did the dependents reside with the custodian during the entire period for which support is sought?   ☐ YES ☐ NO (if no, explain)

2. Does anyone else not of the marriage, live in custodian's household?   ☐ YES ☐ NO (if yes, provide information)

FULL NAME	DATE OF BIRTH	RELATIONSHIP	SOURCE OF INCOME OR SUPPORT	AMOUNT/MONTH GROSS	NET

III. DEFENDANT/RESPONDENT INFORMATION

1. FULL NAME (INCLUDE NICKNAME, ALIAS, ETC.)		
2. RESIDENCE ADDRESS	SOCIAL SECURITY NO.	DATE OF BIRTH
	HOME/MESSAGE PHONE	WORK PHONE
3. EMPLOYER NAME AND ADDRESS	OCCUPATION, TRADE OR PROFESSION	
	ESTIMATED GROSS MONTHLY INCOME	OTHER INCOME
4. REAL OR PERSONAL PROPERTY		

GENERAL TESTIMONY FOR URESA

CASE NUMBER

5. PHYSICAL DESCRIPTION OF DEFENDANT/RESPONDENT

RACE	HEIGHT	WEIGHT	HAIR COLOR	EYE COLOR

SCARS, MARKS OR OTHER DISTINGUISHING FEATURES

6. PRESENT MARITAL STATUS

☐ MARRIED

☐ LIVING WITH NON-MARITAL PARTNER

☐ SINGLE

☐ UNKNOWN

NAME OF NEW SPOUSE OR NON-MARITAL PARTNER

IS CURRENT SPOUSE/PARTNER EMPLOYED? ☐ YES ☐ NO

ESTIMATED GROSS MONTHLY EARNINGS

NAME AND ADDRESS OF CURRENT SPOUSE'S EMPLOYER

7. Is defendant/respondent responsible for dependents that are not living in the petitioner's household?

☐ YES ☐ NO ☐ UNKNOWN

FULL NAME (OF OTHER DEPENDENTS)	DATE OF BIRTH	RELATIONSHIP	LIVING WITH

This information is used to determine if medical coverage is currently provided for the dependents. If coverage is not provided additional information in this section is a basis for adding medical coverage to any new orders.

IV. MEDICAL INSURANCE

1. Are dependents for whom support is sought presently covered by medical insurance?

☐ YES ☐ NO

2. MEDICAL COVERAGE IS PROVIDED FOR DEPENDENT CHILDREN:

☐ CUSTODIAN

☐ STATE MEDICAID

☐ CUSTODIAN'S EMPLOYMENT

☐ RESPONDENT'S EMPLOYMENT

☐ _____

INSURANCE COMPANY OF CUSTODIAN'S EMPLOYER

POLICY NUMBER

INSURANCE COMPANY OF RESPONDENT'S EMPLOYER

POLICY NUMBER

THE MONTHLY COST PAID BY THE CUSTODIAN FOR MEDICAL INSURANCE FOR THE RESPONDENT'S CHILDREN ONLY IS:

$ _____

3. The petitioner can purchase needed medical insurance at a monthly cost of:

$ _____

4. Were the children ever covered by medical insurance provided by the defendant/respondent's current employer?

☐ YES ☐ NO

5. Do any of the respondent's children have special needs or extraordinary medical expenses not covered by insurance?

☐ YES ☐ NO (if yes, explain)

GENERAL TESTIMONY FOR URESA

CASE NUMBER

V. SUPPORT ORDER AND PAYMENT INFORMATION

1. Describe current ordered support:
   (Include the original order and all modifications)

NOTE: PLEASE ATTACH A CERTIFIED COPY OF ALL CURRENT ORDERS THAT RELATE TO SUPPORT

DATE OF ORDER	ORDERED SUPPORT AMOUNTS			
	CURRENT AMOUNT	PER MO, WK, ETC.	TOWARD ARREARAGE	PER MO, WK, ETC.
	NAME AND ADDRESS OF COURT OR ADMINISTRATIVE AGENCY			
	NAME AND ADDRESS OF COURT OR ADMINISTRATIVE AGENCY			

2. Summary of defendant/respondent arrearage

☐ Adjudicated arrearage . . . .

DATE OF ORDER | AMOUNT $ | FROM (DATE) TO (DATE) —

☐ By order

COURT OR ADMINISTRATIVE AGENCY

Issued by

☐ By operation of law . . . .

AMOUNT $ | FROM (DATE) TO (DATE) —

☐ Unadjudicated arrearage
(Amount not included in adjudicated arrearage)

AMOUNT $ | FROM (DATE) TO (DATE) —

Total Arrearage

☐ Principal only . . . .

AMOUNT $ | AS OF (DATE)

☐ Includes interest, explain:

3. Defendant/respondent made the last support payment of: . . . .

AMOUNT $ | DATE OF PAYMENT

4. Defendant/respondent's support payment history: ☐ A certified copy of Audit/Payment history is attached.

FROM (YEAR)	TO (YEAR)	AGENCY WHICH PREPARED AUDIT/PAYMENT HISTORY

GENERAL TESTIMONY FOR URESA (Payment History)

COURT CASE NUMBER

MONTH	YEAR			YEAR		
	AMOUNT DUE	AMOUNT PAID	BALANCE	AMOUNT DUE	AMOUNT PAID	BALANCE
JAN						
FEB						
MAR						
APR						
MAY						
JUN						
JUL						
AUG						
SEP						
OCT						
NOV						
DEC						
TOTAL						

MONTH	YEAR			YEAR		
	AMOUNT DUE	AMOUNT PAID	BALANCE	AMOUNT DUE	AMOUNT PAID	BALANCE
JAN						
FEB						
MAR						
APR						
MAY						
JUN						
JUL						
AUG						
SEP						
OCT						
NOV						
DEC						
TOTAL						

Form OS 548 (3/87)

RESPONDING JURISDICTION COURT/ADM. AGENCY COPY

GENERAL TESTIMONY FOR URESA
PAGE 5 OF 12 PAGES

GENERAL TESTIMONY FOR URESA

CASE NUMBER

VI. PUBLIC ASSISTANCE PAYMENT HISTORY

1. Agency from which grant/assistance was obtained.

AGENCY

2. The public assistance payment history is contained in a separate document which is attached.

☐ YES   ☐ NO   ☐ NA

(IF NO, COMPLETE SECTIONS 3 AND 4.)

3. Total amount of public assistance paid

TOTAL AMOUNT PAID	AS OF (DATE)
$	

This information is used to justify the amount requested by the state in the petition for reimbursement of public assistance paid to the family.

4. Payment history

MONTH	YEAR			YEAR		
	ASSISTANCE/ GRANT AMOUNT	TOTAL DEPENDENTS	RESPONDENT'S DEPENDENTS	ASSISTANCE/ GRANT AMOUNT	TOTAL DEPENDENTS	RESPONDENT'S DEPENDENTS
JAN						
FEB						
MAR						
APR						
MAY						
JUN						
JUL						
AUG						
SEP						
OCT						
NOV						
DEC						
TOTAL						

☐ CONTINUATION SHEETS ATTACHED

This section is used to determine the custodian/spouse's need for support. It is important to disclose all the information requested pertaining to income, expenses, assets and liabilities. Failure to disclose information may seriously affect the legal proceedings in the responding state and may unnecessarily delay the resolution of the child support issue.

GENERAL TESTIMONY FOR URESA   CASE NUMBER

VII. FINANCIAL STATEMENT

All of the following information relates to: **Name:** _____ .

A. MONTHLY INCOME

1. EMPLOYED? ☐ YES ☐ NO

IF YES - LIST OCCUPATION, IF NO - LIST USUAL OCCUPATION AND SOURCE OF SUPPORT.

2. PUBLIC ASSISTANCE	AMOUNT
MONTHLY AFDC PAYMENTS	
MONTHLY FOOD STAMP BENEFITS	
OTHER: EXPLAIN . . .	
3. **TOTAL** PUBLIC ASSISTANCE INCOME	

IF PUBLIC ASSISTANCE IS YOUR ONLY INCOME GO TO SECTION 7

4. EMPLOYMENT INCOME (ATTACH YOUR THREE MOST RECENT PAY STUBS FROM EACH CURRENT EMPLOYER)	
MONTHLY GROSS INCOME	
DEDUCTIONS INCOME TAX WITHHOLDING (FEDERAL, STATE & LOCAL)	
FICA (SOCIAL SECURITY)	
MANDATORY UNION DUES	
MANDATORY RETIREMENT	
MEDICAL INSURANCE PREMIUMS COVERING THE DEPENDENTS.	
OTHER:	
5. MONTHLY NET INCOME FROM EMPLOYMENT (GROSS INCOME MINUS DEDUCTIONS)	

6. OTHER INCOME	AMOUNT
MONTHLY BUSINESS INCOME (EXPLAIN)	
MONTHLY ALIMONY OR SPOUSAL SUPPORT INCOME	
GOVERNMENT PAYMENTS (EXPLAIN)	
MONTHLY PENSION BENEFITS (SOURCE)	
UNEMPLOYMENT COMPENSATION (SOURCE AND DURATION)	
OTHER MONTHLY INCOME (EXPLAIN)	
7. **TOTAL** NET OTHER INCOME	
8. **TOTAL** NET INCOME - SUM OF TOTALS IN SECTIONS 3, 5, AND 7.	
9. DEPENDENT'S INCOME	
10. CURRENT SPOUSE'S/PARTNER'S INCOME	
MONTHLY GROSS INCOME FROM EMPLOYMENT (ATTACH THE THREE MOST RECENT PAY STUBS)	
MONTHLY NET INCOME FROM EMPLOYMENT	

Form OS 548 (3/87)

RESPONDING JURISDICTION COURT/ADM. AGENCY COPY

GENERAL TESTIMONY FOR URESA

CASE NUMBER

B. MONTHLY EXPENSES

Indicate the basic monthly living expenses for the household and the respondent's children. Where expenses cannot be attributed directly to the respondent's children, prorate using the following formula:

$$\text{expense category} \quad \times \quad \frac{\text{number of respondent's children in household}}{\text{total individuals in the household}}$$

$$\$500.00 \quad \text{(Household rent)} \quad \times \quad \frac{2}{4} \quad = \quad \$250.00 \quad \text{(Respondent's dependents prorated share)}$$

EXPENSE ITEM OR CATEGORY	HOUSEHOLD	RESPONDENT'S DEPENDENTS
1. HOUSING AND UTILITIES		
RENT OR MORTGAGE PAYMENT		
TAXES		
HEATING FUEL (GAS, OIL, WOOD)		
ELECTRICITY		
WATER, SEWER, GARBAGE COLLECTION		
TELEPHONE		
CABLE TELEVISION		
OTHER HOUSING EXPENSES		
2. FOOD AND HOUSEHOLD SUPPLIES GROCERIES		
SCHOOL LUNCHES		
OTHER		
3. TRANSPORTATION (DO NOT INCLUDE ANY EXPENSES DEDUCTED AS BUSINESS EXPENSES) CAR LOAN PAYMENT		
OPERATING EXPENSES (GAS AND MAINTENANCE)		
PUBLIC TRANSPORTATION		
PARKING		
OTHER TRANSPORTATION EXPENSES		

GENERAL TESTIMONY FOR URESA

CASE NUMBER

B. MONTHLY EXPENSES (Continued)

EXPENSE ITEM OR CATEGORY	HOUSEHOLD	RESPONDENT'S DEPENDENTS
4. CLOTHING		
CLOTHING PURCHASE		
LAUNDRY		
DRY CLEANING		
OTHER CLOTHING EXPENSES		
5. HEALTH RELATED EXPENSES (NOT COVERED BY INSURANCE)		
DOCTORS		
DENTISTS		
MEDICATIONS AND DRUGSTORE ITEMS		
GLASSES, HEARING AIDS, ETC.		
6. PERSONAL EDUCATIONAL EXPENSES		
TUITION AND FEES		
BOOKS AND SUPPLIES		
7. EDUCATIONAL EXPENSES (RESPONDENT'S CHILDREN) TUITION AND FEES		
BOOKS AND SUPPLIES		
8. CHILD CARE WORK RELATED		
SCHOOL RELATED		
OTHER		
9. INSURANCE HOMEOWNERS OR RENTERS (IF SEPARATE FROM MORTGAGE)		
AUTO INSURANCE (IF SEPARATE FROM CAR PAYMENT)		
MEDICAL INSURANCE (IF NOT INCLUDED AS A PAYROLL DEDUCTION)		
LIFE INSURANCE		

Form OS 548 (3/87)

RESPONDING JURISDICTION COURT/ADM. AGENCY COPY

GENERAL TESTIMONY FOR URESA   CASE NUMBER

B. MONTHLY EXPENSES (Continued)

EXPENSE ITEM OR CATEGORY	HOUSEHOLD	RESPONDENT'S DEPENDENTS
10. MONTHLY PAYMENTS NOT INCLUDED ELSEWHERE (EXCEPT CAR & HOME)		
11. ENTERTAINMENT		
12. OTHER EXPENSES: SEE INSTRUCTIONS FOR SUGGESTED CATEGORIES AND LIST BELOW. List all other monthly expenses not covered in the specific expense categories. This category would include such items as: pets, sports equipment and supplies, work clothing or uniforms, union dues (if not deducted form pay), house repairs, hair care, cosmetics, stationer & postage, Christmas and birthday gifts, contributions to church and charities, organizational dues, newspapers, magazines and books, annual vacation, visitation expenses etc., as applicable.		
13. TOTAL MONTHLY EXPENSES		

C. ASSETS

Assets exceed a total value of $1500.00.   ☐ YES   ☐ NO
Complete this section if assets exceed a total value of $1500.00.

	AMOUNT OR VALUE
1. CASH AND CHECKING ACCOUNTS	
2. SAVINGS, CREDIT UNION, CERTIFICATES OF DEPOSIT	
3. VALUE OF INVESTMENTS: STOCKS	
BONDS	
MUTUAL FUNDS	
OTHER	

Form OS 548 (3/87)

GENERAL TESTIMONY FOR URESA
PAGE 10 OF 12 PAGES

RESPONDING JURISDICTION COURT/ADM. AGENCY COPY

GENERAL TESTIMONY FOR URESA

CASE NUMBER

C. ASSETS (Continued)	AMOUNT OR VALUE
4. INSURANCE - CASH VALUE	
5. REAL ESTATE - EQUITY: HOMESTEAD	
OTHER REAL PROPERTY	
6. MOTOR VEHICLES: AUTOMOBILES	
MOTOR HOMES	
BOATS	
OTHER VEHICLES	
7. OTHER PROPERTY - LIST:	
8. TOTAL ASSETS	

D. LIABILITIES

CREDITOR	TYPE OR PURPOSE OF LOAN (I.E. MORTGAGE, CHARGE ACCT., CAR LOAN)	MONTHLY PAYMENT	BALANCE OWED
TOTAL LIABILITIES:			

Form OS 548 (3/87)

GENERAL TESTIMONY FOR URESA
PAGE 11 OF 12 PAGES

RESPONDING JURISDICTION COURT/ADM. AGENCY COPY

GENERAL TESTIMONY FOR URESA

CASE NUMBER

VIII. OTHER PERTINENT INFORMATION

IX. WAIVER OF FEES

☐ _____ is indigent and unable to pay the costs of these proceedings.

All of the information and facts contained in this GENERAL TESTIMONY are true and correct to my best knowledge and belief.

DATE	PLAINTIFF/PETITIONER (NAME/TITLE)	SIGNATURE
SWORN TO AND SIGNED BEFORE ME THIS DATE	NOTARY PUBLIC	COMMISSION EXPIRES
DATE	AGENCY REPRESENTATIVE (NAME/TITLE)	SIGNATURE

CERTIFICATION OF PAYMENT AND ARREARAGE INFORMATION

The information provided in Part V, ORDER AND PAYMENT INFORMATION, is an accurate and true account of the arrearage owed by defendant/respondent, based on: ☐ OFFICIAL AGENCY/COURT RECORDS   ☐ PERSONAL KNOWLEDGE

DATE	NAME/TITLE, AGENCY OR COURT	SIGNATURE
SWORN TO AND SIGNED BEFORE ME THIS DATE	NOTARY PUBLIC	COMMISSION EXPIRES

Form OS 548 (3/87)

GENERAL TESTIMONY FOR URESA
PAGE 12 OF 12 PAGES

RESPONDING JURISDICTION COURT/ADM. AGENCY COPY

The paternity affidavit summarizes the evidence to be used by the responding jurisdiction to establish paternity where requested in the URESA petition. IT SUPPLEMENTS BUT DOES NOT TAKE THE PLACE OF THE URESA PETITION. All information for the paternity affidavit must be completed or furnished by the natural mother, properly signed by the mother and notarized in order to provide the responding state with facts upon which to establish paternity.

COURT/ADMINISTRATIVE AGENCY IDENTIFICATION AND CASE NUMBER

PLAINTIFF/PETITIONER

VS

DEFENDANT/RESPONDENT

☐ IV-D   ☐ NON IV-D

OTHER REFERENCE NUMBER

PATERNITY AFFIDAVIT

The undersigned, on oath, under penalty of perjury deposes and alleges the following:

1. I am the natural mother of the child of defendant/respondent named below:

CHILD'S NAME	DATE OF BIRTH	STATE OF BIRTH

DATE OF CONCEPTION	FULL TERM PREGNANCY ☐ YES ☐ NO	STATE OF CONCEPTION

2. This affidavit is filed to support a request to establish paternity of the above named child.

3. The child was conceived as a result of sexual intercourse with defendant/respondent during the time stated above, and defendant/respondent is the natural father of the child.

4. I ☐ did ☐ did not have sexual intercourse with any other man during the time the child was conceived.

If so - Name _____

I do not believe he is the father, because:

5. NAME _____ is the legally presumed father

and lives at (address) _____
He is not the natural father, because:

6. The following facts support my allegations of paternity against defendant/respondent:

	YES	NO	DON'T KNOW
a. We lived together from _____ to _____			
b. I have always asserted that defendant/respondent is the father of the child as follows:			
c. Defendant/Respondent has admitted he is the father of the child as follows:			

Form OS 549 (3/87)

PATERNITY AFFADAVIT
PAGE 1 OF 3 PAGES

RESPONDING JURISDICTION COURT/ADM. AGENCY

PATERNITY AFFIDAVIT

CASE NUMBER

6. Alleged facts (continued)	YES	NO	DON'T KNOW
d. Defendant/Respondent visited me and the child at the hospital during birth.			
e. Defendant/Respondent was present at the birth of the child.			
f. I told defendant/respondent he was the father of the child. His reaction was:			
g. Defendant/Respondent offered to pay for an abortion/medical expenses.			
h. The child resembles the defendant/respondent as follows:			
i. Defendant/Respondent is named on the birth certificate. ☐ Copy attached.			
j. Defendant/Respondent has never denied he is the father, although he has knowledge of the child.			
k. Defendant/Respondent has acknowledged in writing that he is the father of the child as follows: (attach copies)			
l. Defendant/Respondent has provided food, clothing, or financial support for the child.			
m. Defendant/Respondent lived with the child from to			
n. Defendant/Respondent visited the child. (state where and when)			
o. Defendant/Respondent sent cards/correspondence to me regarding the pregnancy and birth of the child as follows: (attach copies)			
p. Defendant/Respondent claimed the child on his tax returns.			
q. Defendant/Respondent provided gifts for the child as follows:			

r. Other:

7. Birth and medical expenses were paid by

in the amount of $

RESPONDING JURISDICTION COURT/ADM. AGENCY

PATERNITY AFFIDAVIT

CASE NUMBER

8. Witnesses to my relationship with defendant/respondent are:

NAME AND ADDRESS	NAME AND ADDRESS

9. The following additional information will be helpful in establishing paternity:

All of the information and facts contained in this PATERNITY AFFIDAVIT are true and correct to my best knowledge and belief.

DATE	SIGNATURE OF MOTHER	
SWORN TO AND SIGNED BEFORE ME THIS DATE	NOTARY PUBLIC	COMMISSION EXPIRES

The Order and Judgment form is for use by the judge/hearing officer who decides the case in the responding jurisdiction. This form includes a statement of the relevant findings, the order as issued by the trier of fact, sets up a payment schedule for the defendant/respondent. In any case which establishes an order for support, this form provides for wage withholding.

COURT/ADMINISTRATIVE AGENCY IDENTIFICATION AND CASE NUMBER

PLAINTIFF/PETITIONER

VS

DEFENDANT/RESPONDENT

☐ IV-D   ☐ NON IV-D

OTHER REFERENCE NUMBER

ORDER AND JUDGMENT

This matter was heard on (date) _____ before _____
with the following persons present:

Petitioner: ☐ present   ☐ not present Represented by: _____

Respondent: ☐ present   ☐ not present Represented by: _____

After considering all of the evidence, the Court/Administrative Agency FINDS:

1. ☐ That the defendant/respondent could not be located for service of process.

2. ☐ That the Court/Administrative Agency has jurisdiction of the parties and subject matter of this case.

3. ☐ That the defendant/respondent is not obligated to pay support on the following grounds:

4. ☐ That the defendant/respondent is the parent of the following child(ren):

NAME	DATE OF BIRTH

5. ☐ That the defendant/respondent owes a duty of support to the following dependents:

NAME	DATE OF BIRTH	RELATIONSHIP TO DEFENDANT/RESPONDENT

6. ☐ That $ _____ per _____ is a reasonable amount of support for defendant/respondent to pay.

7. ☐ That the defendant/respondent is in arrears in the amount of $ _____ as of _____ .

8. ☐ That the defendant/respondent owes reimbursement in the amount of $ _____ as of _____ .

Form OS 551 (3/87)

ORDER AND JUDGMENT
PAGE 1 OF 3 PAGES

RESPONDING JURISDICTION COURT/ADM. AGENCY

ORDER AND JUDGMENT

CASE NUMBER

Findings (continued)

INCOME	AMOUNT	PER
GROSS		
NET		

9. ☐ That the defendant/respondent's income is: ....

10. ☐ The Court/Administrative Agency further finds that:

THEREFORE, It is hereby ordered that:

1. ☐ This petition and supporting documents be returned to the initiating jurisdiction for location of the defendant/respondent.

2. ☐ This case be dismissed.

3. ☐ The defendant/respondent is the parent of the following child(ren):

NAME	DATE OF BIRTH

4. ☐ Judgment is entered in favor of plaintiff/petitioner, _____
and against defendant/respondent in the amount of $ _____ for arrearages.

5. ☐ Judgment is entered in favor of plaintiff/petitioner, _____
and against defendant/respondent in the amount of $ _____ for reimbursement.

6. ☐ The defendant/respondent shall pay $ _____ per _____
beginning _____ , to be paid as follows:

A.

PAYEE #1 (NAME AND ADDRESS)	FOR	AMOUNT
	CHILD SUPPORT	
	CHILD SUPPORT ARREARAGE	
	REIMBURSEMENT	
	SPOUSAL SUPPORT	
	SPOUSAL SUPPORT ARREARAGE	
	PAYEE #1 TOTAL	$

B.

PAYEE #2 (NAME AND ADDRESS)	FOR	AMOUNT
	CHILD SUPPORT	
	CHILD SUPPORT ARREARAGE	
	REIMBURSEMENT	
	SPOUSAL SUPPORT	
	SPOUSAL SUPPORT ARREARAGE	
	PAYEE #2 TOTAL	$

7. ☐ The defendant/respondent shall provide health insurance coverage for the child(ren) and provide assistance in obtaining payment for insured services.

Form OS 551 (3/87)

RESPONDING JURISDICTION COURT/ADM. AGENCY

ORDER AND JUDGMENT

CASE NUMBER

Order/Judgment (continued)

8. ☐ The defendant/respondent shall pay medical expenses, including dental and ophthalmological services for the child(ren) as follows:

9. ☐ The defendant/respondent shall pay and judgment is entered in favor of:

PAYEE (NAME AND ADDRESS)	FOR	AMOUNT
	COURT COSTS	
	COST OF PATERNITY TESTS	
	PLAINTIFF/PETITIONER'S ATTORNEY'S FEES	
	OTHER: (BOND)	
	TOTAL JUDGMENT	$

(NAME OF BONDSMAN IF APPLICABLE)

10. ☐ The defendant/respondent shall notify the Court/Administrative Agency of any change of address/employment within 10 days.

11. ☐ It is further ordered that:

12. ☒ NOTICE: This is an income withholding order. Support payments in arrears by _____ days may be withheld from income without further order of any court or further application for services.

DATE	PRESIDING OFFICER
DATE	JUDGE

Form OS 551 (3/87)

RESPONDING JURISDICTION COURT/ADM. AGENCY

COURT/ADMINISTRATIVE AGENCY IDENTIFICATION AND CASE NUMBER

PLAINTIFF/ PETITIONER

VS

DEFENDANT/RESPONDENT

☐ IV-D   ☐ NON IV-D

OTHER REFERENCE NUMBER

CERTIFICATE AND ORDER

The undersigned, _____ _____ ,
Judge/Presiding Officer of the above named Court/Administrative Agency, hereby certifies as follows:

1. On (date) _____ a petition was filed by the plaintiff/petitioner in this Court/Administrative Agency in a proceeding against the defendant/respondent under the provisions of the reciprocal support statute seeking support of the dependents named in the attached petition.

2. The defendant/respondent is believed to be residing in your jurisdiction at:

3. In the opinion of the undersigned Judge/Presiding Officer, the enclosed petition and testimony set forth facts from which it may be determined that the defendant/respondent owes a duty of support to the named dependents and that such petition should be dealt with according to law.

4. All payments should be made payable to and sent to:

WHEREFORE, it is ORDERED that three copies of this Certificate, with the petition, testimony, and the required copies of this state's reciprocal support statute, be transmitted to:

DATE	SIGNATURE (JUDGE/PRESIDING OFFICER)

Form OS 552 (3/87)

RESPONDING FILE COPY

CERTIFICATE AND ORDER
PAGE 1 OF 1 PAGE

State Agencies Administering Child Support Programs Under Title IV-D of the Social Security Act

Child Support Enforcement Division
Department of Human Resources
64 North Union Street
Montgomery, **Alabama** 36130
(205) 242-2734
(205) 294-9300 (information)

Child Support Enforcement Division
Department of Revenue
4th Floor
550 West 7th Avenue
Anchorage, **Alaska** 99501
(907) 276-3441

Assistance Attorney General
P.O. Box 7
Pago Pago, American Samoa 96799
(684) 633-4163

Child Support Enforcement Administration
Department of Economic Security
2222 W. Encanto
P.O. Box 6123—Site Code 776A
Phoenix, **Arizona** 85005
(602) 252-0236

Division of Child Support Enforcement
Arkansas Social Services
P.O. Box 3358
Little Rock, **Arkansas** 72203
(501) 682-8398

Child Support Program Management Branch
Department of Social Services
744 P Street—Mail Stop 9-011
Sacramento, **California** 95814
(916) 322-8495

Division of Child Support Enforcement
Department of Social Services

1575 Sherman Street
Denver, **Colorado** 80203-1714
(303) 866-5994

Bureau of Child Support Enforcement
Department of Human Resources
1049 Asylum Avenue
Hartford, **Connecticut** 06105
(203) 566-3053
(203) 566-4429 (information)

Divison of Child Support Enforcement
Department of Health & Social Services
P.O. Box 904
New Castle, **Delaware** 19720
(302) 421-8300

Office of Paternity and Child Support Enforcement
Department of Human Services
3rd Floor—Suite 3013
425 I Street, N.W.
Washington, D.C. 20001
(202) 724-5610   (FTS 724-8820)

Office of Child Support Enforcement
Department of Health and Rehabilitative Services
1317 Winewood Boulevard—Bldg. 3
Tallahassee, **Florida** 32399-0700
(904) 488-9900

Office of Child Support Recovery
State Department of Human Resources
878 Peachtree Street, N.E. Room 529
Atlanta, **Georgia** 30309
(404) 894-4119

Office of the Attorney General
Child Support Enforcement Office
Union Bank Building, Suite 309
194 Hernan Cortez Avenue

Agana, **Guam** 96910
(671) 477-2036

Child Support Enforcement Agency
Department of the Attorney General
P.O. Box 1860
Honolulu, **Hawaii** 96805-1860
(808) 548-5779

Bureau of Child Support Enforcement
Department of Health and Welfare
450 West State Street
Towers Building—7th Floor
Boise, **Idaho** 83720
(208) 334-5710
(208) 334-5787 (information)

Division of Child Support Enforcement
Department of Public Aid
Prescott E. Bloom Building
P.O. Box 19405
201 South Grand Avenue East
Springfield, **Illinois** 62794-9405
(217) 782-1366
(217) 782-1380 (information)

Child Support Division
Department of Public Welfare
141 South Meridian Street
4th Floor
Indianapolis, **Indiana** 46225
(317) 232-4885
(317) 232-3447 (information)

Bureau of Collections
Department of Human Services
Hoover Building—5th Floor
Des Moines, **Iowa** 50319
(515) 281-5580

Child Support Enforcement Program
Department of Social & Rehabilitation Services
300 South West Oakley St. Biddle Building
P.O. Box 497
Topeka, **Kansas** 66603
(913) 296-3237

Division of Child Support Enforcement
Department of Social Insurance
Cabinet for Human Resources
6th Floor East
275 East Main Street
Frankfort, **Kentucky** 40621
(502) 564-2285

Support Enforcement Services
Department of Social Services
Post Office Box 94065
Baton Rouge, **Louisiana** 70804
(504) 342-4780

Support Enforcement and Location Unit
Bureau of Social Welfare
Department of Human Services
State House, Station 11
Augusta, **Maine** 04333
(207) 289-2886

Child Support Enforcement Administration
Department of Human Resources
311 West Saratoga Street
Baltimore, **Maryland** 21201
(301) 333-3979

Department of Revenue
Child Support Enforcement Division
215 First Street
Cambridge, **Massachusetts** 02124
(617) 621-4200

Office of Child Support
Department of Social Services
P.O. Box 30037
300 South Capitol Avenue
Suite 621
Lansing, **Michigan** 48909
(517) 373-7570
(517) 373-3692 (information)

Office of Child Support Enforcement
Department of Human Services
444 Lafayette Road—4th Floor
St. Paul, **Minnesota** 55155-3846
(612) 296-2499
(612) 296–2567 (information)

Child Support Division
State Department of Public Welfare
P.O. Box 352
515 East Amite Street
Jackson, **Mississippi** 39205
(601) 354-0341 ext. 503

Division of Child Support Enforcement
Department of Social Services
P.O. Box 1527
Jefferson City, **Missouri** 65102-1527
(314) 751-4301

Child Support Enforcement Division
Department of Social and Rehabilitation Services
P.O. Box 5955
Helena, **Montana** 59604
(406) 444-4614

Child Support Enforcement Office
Department of Social Services
P.O. Box 95026
Lincoln, **Nebraska** 68509
(402) 471-9125
(402) 471-9157 (information)

Child Support Enforcement Program
Department of Human Resources
2527 North Carson Street
Capital Complex
Carson City, Nevada 89710
(702) 885-4744

Office of Child Support Enforcement Services
Division of Welfare
Health and Welfare Building
6 Hazen Drive
Concord, New Hampshire 03301
(603) 271-4426
(603) 271-4427 (information)

Department of Human Services
Division of Economic Assistance
Office of Child Support & Paternity Programs
CN 716
Trenton, New Jersey 08625
(609) 588-2401

Department of Human Services Department
Child Support Enforcement Division
2nd Floor, Channel 2 Bldg.
2009 South Pacheco
Santa Fe, New Mexico 87505
(505) 827-7200

Office of Child Support Enforcement
New York State Department of Social Services
P.O. Box 14
1 Commerce Plaza
Albany, New York 12260
(518) 474-9081

Child Support Enforcement Section
Division of Social Services
Department of Human Resources
437 North Harrington Street
Raleigh, North Carolina 27603-1393
(919) 733-4120

Child Support Enforcement Agency
Department of Human Services
State Capitol
Bismark, North Dakota 58505
(701) 224-3582

Bureau of Child Support
Department of Human Services
State Office Tower—27th Floor
30 East Broad Street
Columbus, Ohio 43266-0423
(614) 466-3233

Child Support Enforcement Division
Department of Human Services
P.O. Box 25352
Oklahoma City, Oklahoma 73125
(405) 424-5871

Recovery Services Section
Adult and Family Services Division
Department of Human Resources
P.O. Box 14506
Salem, Oregon 97309
(503) 378-5439
(503) 373-1297 (information)

Bureau of Child Support Enforcement
Department of Public Welfare
P.O. Box 8018
Harrisburg, Pennsylvania 17105
(717) 787-3672

Child Support Enforcement Program
Department of Social Services
CALL Box 3349
San Juan, Puerto Rico 00904
(809) 722-4731

Bureau of Family Support
Department of Human Services
77 Dorrance Street
Providence, Rhode Island 02903
(401) 277-2409
(401) 277-2847 (information)

Child Support Enforcement Division
Department of Social Services
P.O. Box 1520
Columbia, South Carolina 29202-9988
(803) 737-5870
(803) 737-5875 (information)

Office of Child Support Enforcement
Department of Social Services
700 Governors Drive
Pierre, South Dakota 57501-2291
(605) 773-3641

Child Support Services
Department of Human Services
Citizens Plaza Building 12th Floor
400 Deaderick Street
Nashville, Tennessee (37219)
(615) 741-1820
(615) 741-2441 (information)

Child Support Enforcement Division
Attorney General's Office
P.O. Box 12548
Austin, Texas 78711-2548
(512) 463-2181

Office of Recovery Services
Department of Social Services
120 North 200 West
P.O. Box 45011
Salt Lake City, Utah 84145-0011
(801) 538-4402
(801) 538-4400 (information)

Child Support Division
Department of Social Welfare
103 South Main Street
Waterbury, **Vermont** 05676
(802) 241-2910

Support and Paternity Division
Department of Law
46 Norre Gade
St. Thomas, **Virgin Islands** 00801
(809) 776-0372

Division of Support Enforcement Program
Department of Social Services
8007 Discovery Drive
Richmond, **Virginia** 23288
(804) 662-9297
(800) 468-8894 (information)

Office of Support Enforcement
Department of Social and Health Services
Post Office Box 9162. MS HJ-31
(712 Pear Street, SE)
Olympia, **Washington** 98504
(206) 586-6111

Child Advocate Office
Department of Human Services
1900 Washington Street, East
Charleston, **West Virginia** 25305
(304) 348-3780

Division of Economic Support
Bureau of Child Support
1 West Wilson St., Room 382
P.O. Box 7935
Madison, **Wisconsin** 53707-7935
(608) 266-1175
(608) 266-9909 (information)

Child Support Enforcement Section
Division of Health and Social Services
Hathaway Building
Cheyenne, **Wyoming** 82002
(307) 777-7892
(307) 777-6948 (information)

Divorce, Marriage, Birth and Death Records

Where to Write for Vital Records (DHHS Publication No. (PHS) 87-1142)

Where to Write for Vital Records

An official certificate of every birth, death, marriage, and divorce should be on file in the locality where the event occurred. The Federal Government does not maintain files or indexes of these records. These records are filed permanently either in a State vital statistics office or in a city, county, or other local office.

To obtain a certified copy of any of the certificates, write or go to the vital statistics office in the State or area where the event occurred. Addresses and fees are given for each event in the State or area concerned.

To ensure that you receive an accurate record for your requests and that your request is filled with all due speed, please follow the steps outlined below for the information in which you are interested:

- Write to the appropriate office to have your request filled.

- Under the appropriate office, information has been included for birth and death records concerning whether the State will accept checks or money orders and to whom they should be made payable. This same information would apply when marriage and divorce records are available from the State office. However, it is impossible for us to list fees and addresses for all county offices where marriage and divorce records may be obtained.

- For all certified copies requested, make check or money order payable for the correct amount for the number of copies you wish to obtain. Cash is not recommended because the office cannot refund cash lost in transit.

- All fees are subject to change. A telephone number has been included in the information for each State for use in verifying the current fee.

- Type or print all names and addresses in the letter.

- Give the following facts when writing for **birth or death records:**
  1. Full name of person whose record is being requested.
  2. Sex.
  3. Parent's names, including maiden name of mother.

4. Month, day, and year of birth or death.

5. Place of birth or death (city or town, county, and State; and name of hospital, if known).

6. Purpose for which copy is needed.

7. Relationship to person whose record is being requested.

- Give the following facts when writing for **marriage records:**

  1. Full names of bride and groom.

  2. Month, day, and year of marriage.

  3. Place of marriage (city or town, county, and State).

  4. Purpose for which copy is needed.

  5. Relationship to persons whose record is being requested.

- Give the following facts when writing for **divorce records:**

  1. Full names of husband and wife.

  2. Date of divorce or annulment.

  3. Place of divorce or annulment.

  4. Type of final decree.

  5. Purpose for which copy is needed.

  6. Relationship to persons whose record is being requested.

Foreign or High-Sea Births and Deaths and Certificates of Citizenship

Birth Records of Persons Born in Foreign Countries who are U.S. Citizens at Birth

Birth of U.S. citizens in foreign countries should be reported to the nearest American consular office as soon after the birth as possible on the Consular Report of Birth (Form FS-240). This report should be prepared and filed by one of the parents. However, the physician or midwife attending the birth or any other person having knowledge of the facts can prepare the report.

Documentary evidence is required to establish citizenship. Consular offices provide complete information on what evidence is needed. The Consular Report of Birth is a sworn statement of facts of birth. When approved, it establishes in documentary form the child's acquisition of U.S. citizenship. It has the same value as proof of citizenship as the Certificate of Citizenship issued by the Immigration and Naturalization Service.

A $13.00 fee is charged for reporting the birth. The original document is filed in the Passport Services, Correspondence Branch, U.S. Department of State, Washington, DC 20524. The parents are given a certified copy of the Consular Report of Birth (Form FS-240) and a short form, Certification of Birth (Form DS-1350 or Form FS-545).

To obtain a copy of a report of the birth in a foreign country of a U.S. citizen, write to Passport Services, Correspondence Branch, U.S. Department of State, Washington, DC 20524. State the full name of the child at birth, date of birth, place of birth, and names of parents. Also include any information about the U.S. passport on which the child's name was first included. Sign the request and state the relationship to the person whose record is being requested and the reason for the request.

The fee for each copy is $4.00. Enclose a check or money order made payable to the U.S. Department of State. Fee may be subject to change.

The Department of State issues two types of copies from the Consular Report of Birth (Form FS-240):

1. A full copy of Form FS-240 as it was filed.
2. A short form, Certification of Birth (Form DS-1350), which shows only the name and sex of child and the date and place of birth.

Records of Birth and Death Occurring on Vessels or Aircraft on the High Seas

When a birth or death occurs on the high seas, whether in an aircraft or on a vessel, the determination of where the record is filed is decided by the direction in which the vessel or aircraft was headed at the time the event occurred.

1. If the vessel or aircraft was outbound or docked or landed at a foreign port, requests for copies of the record should be made to the U.S. Department of State, Washington, DC 20520.
2. If the vessel or aircraft was inbound and the first port of entry was in the United States, write to the registration authority in the city where the vessel or aircraft docked or landed in the United States.
3. If the vessel was of U.S. registry, contact the U.S. Coast Guard facility at the port of entry.

Records Maintained by Foreign Countries

Most, but not all, foreign countries record birth and deaths. It is not feasible to list in this publication all foreign vital records offices, the charges they make for copies of records, or the information they may require to locate a record. However, most foreign countries will provide certification of births and deaths occurring within their boundaries.

U.S. citizens who need a copy of a foreign birth or death record may obtain assistance by writing to the Office of Overseas Citizens Services, U.S. Department of State, Washington, DC 20520.

Aliens residing in the United States who seek records of these events should contact their nearest consular office.

The information on both forms is valid. The Certification of Birth may be obtained in a name subsequently acquired by adoption or legitimation after proof is submitted to establish that such an action legally took place.

Birth Records of Alien Children Adopted by U.S. Citizens

Birth certifications for alien children adopted by U.S. citizens and lawfully admitted to the United States may be obtained from the Immigration and Naturalization Service (INS) if the birth information is on file.

Certification may be issued for children under 21 years of age who were born in a foreign country. Requests must be submitted on INS Form G-641, which can be obtained from any INS office. (Address can be found in a telephone directory.) For Certification of Birth Data (INS Form G-350), a $15.00 search fee, paid by check or money order, should accompany INS Form G-641.

Certification can be issued in the new name of an adopted or legitimated child after proof of an adoption or legitimation is submitted to INS. Because it may be issued for a child who has not yet become a U.S. citizen, this certification (Form G-350) is not proof of U.S. nationality.

Certificate of Citizenship

U.S. citizens who were born abroad and later naturalized or who were born in a foreign country to a U.S. citizen (parent or parents) may apply for a certificate of citizenship pursuant to the provisions of Section 341 of the Immigration and Nationality Act. Application can be made for this document in the United States at the nearest office of the Immigration and Naturalization Service (INS). The INS will issue a certification of citizenship for the person if proof of citizenship is submitted and the person is within the United States. The decision whether to apply for a certificate of citizenship is optional; its possession is not mandatory because a valid U.S. passport or a form FS-240 has the same evidentiary status.

Death Records of U.S. Citizens Who Die in Foreign Countries

The death of a U.S. citizen in a foreign country is normally reported to the nearest U.S. consular office. The consul prepares the official "Report of the Death of an American Citizen Abroad" (Form OF-180), and a copy of the Report of Death is filed permanently in the U.S. Department of State (see exceptions below.)

To obtain a copy of a report, write to Passport Services, Correspondence Branch, U.S. Department of State, Washington, DC 20524. The fee for a copy is $4.00. Fee may be subject to change.

Exception: Reports of deaths of members of the Armed Forces of the United States are made only to the branch of the service to which the person was attached at the time of death—Army, Navy, Air Force, or Coast Guard. In these cases, requests for copies of records should be directed as follows.
For members of the Army, Navy, or Air Force:

Secretary of Defense
Washington, DC 20301
For members of the Coast Guard:

Commandment, P.S.
U.S. Coast Guard
Washington, DC 20226

Place of Event	Cost of copy	Address	Remarks
ALABAMA			
Birth or Death	$7.00	Bureau of Vital Statistics State Department of Public Health Montgomery, AL 36130	State office has had records since January 1908. Additional copies at same time are $2.00 each. Fee for special searches is $5.00 per hour.
			Money order should be made payable to **Alabama Bureau of Vital Statistics.** To verify current fees, the telephone number is area code **205-261-5033.**
Marriage	$5.00	Same as Birth or Death	State office has had records since August 1936.
	Varies	See remarks	Probate Judge in county where license was issued.
Divorce	$5.00	Same as Birth or Death	State office has had records since January 1950.
	Varies	See remarks	Clerk or Register of Court of Equity in county where divorce was granted.
ALASKA			
Birth or Death	$7.00	Department of Health and Social Services Bureau of Vital Statistics P.O. Box H-02G Juneau, AK 99811-0675	State office has had records since January 1913. Additional copies requested at same time are $2.00 each.
			Money order should be made payable to **Bureau of Vital Records.** Personal checks are not accepted. To verify current fees, the telephone number is area code **907-465-3391.** This will be a **recorded** message.
Marriage	$5.00	Same as Birth or Death.	State office has had records since 1913.
Divorce	$5.00	Same as Birth or Death	State office has had records since 1950.
	Varies	See remarks	Clerk of Superior Court in judicial district where divorce was granted. Juneau and Ketchikan (First District), Nome (Second District), Anchorage (Third District), Fairbanks (Fourth District).
AMERICAN SAMOA			
Birth or death	$2.00	Registrar of Vital Statistics Vital Statistics Section Government of American Samoa Pago Pago, AS 96799	Registrar has had records since 1900.
			Money order should be made payable to **ASG Treasurer, Government of American Samoa 96799.** Personal checks are not accepted. To verify current fees, the telephone is area code **684-633-1222, extension 214.**
Marriage	$2.00	Same as Birth or Death	Personal identification required before records will be sent.
Divorce	$1.00	High Court of American Samoa Tutuila, AS 96799	

Record	Cost	Where to Write	Remarks
ARIZONA			
Birth (long form)	$5.00	Vital Records Section Arizona Department of Health Services P.O. Box 3887 Phoenix, AZ 85030	State office has had records since July 1909 and abstract of records filed in counties before then. Check or money order should be made payable to **Arizona Department of Health Services.** Personal checks are accepted. To verify current fees, the telephone number is area code **602-255-1080.** This will be a **recorded** message. Applicants must submit a copy of picture identification or have their request notarized.
Birth (short form)	$3.00		
Death	$5.00		
Marriage	Varies	See remarks	Clerk of Superior Court in county where license was issued.
Divorce	Varies	See remarks	Clerk of Superior County in county where divorce was granted.
ARKANSAS			
Birth	$5.00	Division of Vital Records Arkansas Department of Health 4815 West Markham Street Little Rock, AR 72201	State office has had records since February 1914 and some original Little Rock and Fort Smith records from 1881. Additional copies of death record, when requested at the same time, are $1.00 each. Check or money order should be made payable to **Arkansas Department of Health.** Personal checks are accepted. To verify current fees, the telephone number is area code **501-661-2336.** This will be a **recorded** message.
Death	$4.00		
Marriage	$5.00	Same as Birth or Death	Records since 1917.
	$2.00	See remarks	Full certified copy may be obtained from County Clerk in county where license was issued.
Divorce	$5.00	Same as Birth or Death	Copies since 1923.
	Varies	See remarks	Full certified copy may be obtained from Circuit or Chancery Clerk in county where divorce was granted.
CALIFORNIA			
Birth	$11.00	Vital Statistics Section Department of Health Services 410 N Street Sacramento, CA 95814	State office has had records since July 1905. For earlier records, write to County Recorder in county where event occurred. Check or money order should be made payable to **State Registrar, Department of Health Services** or **Vital Statistics.** Personal checks are accepted. To verify current fees, the telephone number is area code **916-445-2684.**
Death	$7.00		
Marriage	$11.00	Same as Birth or Death	State office has had records since July 1905. For earlier records, write to County Recorder in county where event occurred.
Divorce	$11.00	Same as Birth or Death	Fee is for search and identification of county where certified copy can be obtained. Certified copies are not available from State Health Department.
	Varies	See remarks	Clerk of Superior Court in county where divorce was granted.

Place of Event	Cost of copy	Address	Remarks
CANAL ZONE **Birth** or **Death**	$2.00	Panama Canal Commission Vital Statistics Clerk APO Miami, FL 34011	Records available from May 1904 to September 1979.
Marriage	$1.00	Same as Birth or Death	Records available from May 1904 to September 1979.
Divorce	$0.50	Same as Birth or Death	Records available from May 1904 to September 1979.
COLORADO **Birth** or **Death**	$6.00 Regular service $10.00 Priority service	Vital Records Section Colorado Department of Health 4210 East 11th Avenue Denver, CO 80220	State office has had death records since 1900 and birth records since 1910. State office also has birth records for some counties for years before 1910. Regular service means the record is mailed within 4 weeks. Priority service means the record is mailed within 5 days. Check or money order should be made payable to **Vital Records.** Personal checks are accepted. To verify current fees, the telephone number is area code **303-320-8474.** For a recorded message call **303-320-8333.**
Marriage	See remarks	Same as Birth or Death	Statewide index of records for 1900–39 and 1975 to present. Inquiries will be forwarded to appropriate office. Fee for verification is $6.00. Certified copies are not available from State Health Department.
	Varies	See remarks	County Clerk in county where license was issued.
Divorce	See remarks	Same as Birth or Death	Statewide index of records for 1900–39 and 1968 to present. Inquiries will be forwarded to appropriate office. Fee for verification is $6.00. Certified copies are not available from State Health Department.
	Varies	See remarks	Clerk of District Court in county where divorce was granted.
CONNECTICUT **Birth** or **Death** Short form	$3.00 $2.00	Department of Health Services Vital Records Section Division of Health Statistics State Department of Health 150 Washington Street Hartford, CT 06106	State office has had records since July 1897. For earlier records, write to Registrar of Vital Statistics in town or city where event occurred. Check or money order should be made payable to **Department of Health Services.** Personal checks are accepted. To verify current fees, the telephone number is area code **203-566-1124.**
Marriage	$3.00	Same as Birth or Death	Records since July 1897.
	$3.00	See remarks	Registrar of Vital Statistics in town where license was issued.
Divorce	See remarks	Same as Birth or Death	Index of records since 1947. Inquiries will be forwarded to appropriate office. Certified copies are not available from State office.
	Varies	See remarks	Clerk of Superior Court in county where divorce was granted.

DELAWARE

Type	Cost	Address	Remarks
Birth or Death	$5.00	Office of Vital Statistics Division of Public Health P.O. Box 637 Dover, DE 19903	State office has records for 1861–63 and since 1881 but no records for 1864–80. Additional copies of the same record requested at the same time are $3.00 each. Check or money order should be made payable to **Office of Vital Statistics.** Personal checks are accepted. To verify current fees, the telephone number is area code **302-736-4721.**
Marriage	$5.00	Same as Birth or Death	Records since 1847. Additional copies of the same record requested at the same time are $3.00 each.
Divorce	See Remarks	Same as Birth or Death	Records since 1935. Inquiries will be forwarded to appropriate office. Fee for search and verification of essential facts of divorce is $5.00 for each 5-year period searched. Certified copies are not available from State office.
	$2.00	See remarks	Prothonotary in county where divorce was granted up to 1975. For divorces granted after 1975 the parties concerned should contact Family Court in county where divorce was granted.

DISTRICT OF COLUMBIA

Type	Cost	Address	Remarks
Birth or Death	$8.00	Vital Records Branch Room 3009 425 I Street, NW Washington, DC 20001	Office has had death records since 1855 and birth records since 1874 but no death records were filed during the Civil War. Check or money order should be made payable to **D.C. Treasurer.** Personal checks are accepted. To verify current fees, the telephone number is area code **202-727-5316.** This will be a recorded message.
Marriage	$5.00	Same as Birth or Death	
	$5.00	Marriage Bureau 515 5th Street, NW Washington, DC 20001	Records since January 1982.
Divorce	$2.00	Clerk, Superior Court for the District of Columbia, Family Division 500 Indiana Avenue, NW Washington, DC 20001	Records since September 16, 1956.
	Varies	Clerk, U.S. District Court for the District of Columbia Washington, DC 20001	Records before September 16, 1956.

Place of Event	Cost of copy	Address	Remarks
FLORIDA **Birth** **Death**	$6.50 $4.00	Department of Health and Rehabilitative Services Office of Vital Statistics P.O. Box 210 Jacksonville, FL 32231–0042	State office has some birth records dating back to April 1865 and some death records dating back to August 1877. The majority of records date from January 1917. (If the exact date is unknown, the fee is $6.50 (births) or $2.50 (deaths) for the first year searched and $1.00 for each additional year up to a maximum of $25.00. Fee includes one certification of record if found or certified statement stating record not on file.) Additional copies are $2.00 each when requested at the same time. Check or money order should be made payable to **Office of Vital Statistics.** Personal checks are accepted. To verify current fees, the telephone number is area code **904-359-6900.** This will be a **recorded** message.
Marriage	$2.50	Same as Birth or Death	Records since June 6, 1927. (If the exact date is unknown, the fee is $2.50 for the first year searched and $1.00 for each additional year up to a maximum of $25.00. Fee includes one copy of record if found or certified statement stating record not on file.) Additional copies are $2.00 each when requested at the same time.
Divorce	$2.50	Same as Birth or Death	Records since June 6, 1927. (If the exact date is unknown, the fee is $2.50 for the first year searched and $1.00 for each additional year up to a maximum of $25.00. Fee includes one copy of record if found or certified statement stating record not on file.) Additional copies are $2.00 each when requested at the same time.
GEORGIA **Birth** or **Death**	$3.00	Georgia Department of Human Resources Vital Records Unit Room 217-H 47 Trinity Avenue, SW Atlanta, GA 30334	State office has had records since January 1919. For earlier records in Atlanta or Savannah, write to County Health Department in county where event occurred. Additional copies of same record ordered at same time are $1.00 each except birth cards, which are $2.00 each. Money order should be made payable to **Vital Records, GA. DHR.** Personal checks are not accepted. To verify current fees, the telephone number is area code **404-656-4900.** This is a **recorded** message.
Marriage	$3.00	Same as Birth or Death	Centralized State records since June 9, 1952. Certified copies are not issued at State office. Inquiries will be forwarded to appropriate Probate Judge in county where license was issued.
	$3.00	See remarks	Probate Judge in county where license was issued.

	Office	Fee	Remarks
Divorce	See remarks	Varies	Centralized State records since June 9, 1952. Certified copies are issued at State office. Inquiries before June 9, 1952, will be forwarded to appropriate Clerk of Superior Court in county where divorce was granted.
	See remarks	$3.00	Clerk of Superior Court in county where divorce was granted.
GUAM			
Birth or **Death**	Office of Vital Statistics, Department of Public Health and Social Services, Government of Guam, P.O. Box 2816, Agana, GU, M.I. 96910	$2.00	Office has had records since October 16, 1901. Money order should be made payable to **Treasurer of Guam.** Personal checks are not accepted. To verify current fees, the telephone number is area code **671-734-3050.**
Marriage	Same as Birth or Death	$2.00	
Divorce	Clerk, Superior Court of Guam, Agana, GU, M.I. 96910	Varies	
HAWAII			
Birth or **Death**	Research and Statistics Office, State Department of Health, P.O. Box 3378, Honolulu, HI 96801	$2.00	State office has had records since 1853. Check or money order should be made payable to **State Department of Health.** Personal checks are accepted for the correct amount only. To verify current fees, the telephone number is area code **808-548-5819.** This is a **recorded** message.
Marriage	Same as Birth or Death	$2.00	Records since July 1951.
Divorce	Same as Birth or Death	$2.00	Circuit Court in county where divorce was granted.
	See remarks		
IDAHO			
Birth or **Death**	Bureau of Vital Statistics, Standards, and Local Health Services, State Department of Health and Welfare, Statehouse, Boise, ID 83720	$8.00	State office has had records since 1911. For records from 1907 to 1911, write to County Recorder in county where event occurred. Check or money order should be made payable to **Idaho Vital Statistics.** Personal checks are accepted. To verify current fees, the telephone number is area code **208-334-5988.** This is a **recorded** message.
Marriage	Same as Birth or Death	$6.00	Records since 1947. Earlier records are with County Recorder in county where license was issued.
	See remarks	Varies	County Recorder in county where license was issued.
Divorce	Same as Birth or Death	$6.00	Records since January 1947. Earlier records are with County Recorder in county where divorce was granted.
	See remarks	Varies	County Records in county where divorce was granted.

Place of Event	Cost of copy	Address	Remarks
ILLINOIS			
Birth or **Death**	$15.00 certified copy $10.00 certification	Division of Vital Records State Department of Health 605 West Jefferson Street Springfield, IL 62702	State office has had records since January 1916. For earlier records and for copies of State records since January 1916, write to County Clerk in county where event occurred. (The fee for a search of the files is $5.00. If the record is found, one certification is issued at no additional charge. Additional certifications of the same record ordered at the same time are $2.00 each. The fee for a full certified copy is $10.00. Additional certified copies of the same record ordered at the same time are $2.00 each.) Money order or certified check should be made payable to **Illinois Department of Health.** To verify current fees, the telephone number is area code **217-782-6553.**
Marriage	See remarks	Same as Birth or Death	Records since January 1962. All items may be verified (fee $5.00). Inquiries will be forwarded to appropriate office. Certified copies are not available from State office.
	$5.00	See remarks	County Clerk in county where license was issued.
Divorce	See remarks	Same as Birth or Death	Records since January 1962. Some items may be verified (fee $5.00). Certified copies are not available from State office.
	Varies	See remarks	Clerk of Circuit Court county where divorce was granted;
INDIANA			
Birth **Death**	$6.00 $4.00	Division of Vital Records State Board of Health 1330 West Michigan Street P.O. Box 1964 Indianapolis, IN 46206–1964	State office has had birth records since October 1907 and death records since 1900. Additional copies of same record ordered at same time are $1.00 each. For earlier records, write to Health Officer in city or county where event occurred. Check or money order should be made payable to **Indiana State Board of Health.** Personal checks are accepted. To verify current fees, the telephone number is **317-633-0274.**
Marriage	See remarks	Same as Birth or Death	Marriage Index since 1958. Certified copies are not available from State Health Department.
	Varies	See remarks	Clerk of Circuit Court or Clerk of Superior Court in county where license was issued.
Divorce	Varies	See remarks	County Clerk in county where divorce was granted.
IOWA			
Birth or **Death**	$6.00	Iowa Department of Public Health Vital Records Section Lucas Office Building Des Moines, IA 50319	State office has had records since July 1880. Check or money order should be made payable to **Iowa Department of Public Health.** To verify current fees, the telephone number is area code **515-281-5871.** This will be a **recorded** message.

Type	Cost of Copy	Address	Remarks
Marriage	$6.00	Same as Birth or Death	State office has had records since July 1880. Brief statistical record only since 1906. Inquiries will be forwarded to appropriate office. Certified copies are not available from State Health Department.
Divorce	See remarks	Same as Birth or Death	Clerk of District Court in county where divorce was granted.
KANSAS **Birth or Death**	$6.00	Office of Vital Statistics Kansas State Department of Health and Environment 900 Jackson Street Topeka, KS 66612–1290	State office has had records since July 1911. For earlier records, write to County Clerk in county where event occurred. Additional copies of same record ordered at same time are $3.00 each. Check or money order should be made payable to **State Registrar of Vital Statistics.** Personal checks are accepted. To verify current fees, the telephone number is area code **913-296-1400.**
Marriage	$6.00 Varies	Same as Birth or Death See remarks	State office has had records since May 1913. District Judge in county where license was issued.
Divorce	$6.00 Varies	Same as Birth or Death See remarks	State office has had records since July 1951. Clerk of District Court in county where divorce was granted.
KENTUCKY **Birth** / **Death**	$5.00 $4.00	Office of Vital Statistics Department of Health Services 275 East Main Street Frankfort, KY 40621	State office has had records since January 1911 and some records for the cities of Louisville, Lexington, Covington, and Newport before then. Check or money order should be made payable to **Kentucky State Treasurer.** Personal checks are accepted. To verify current fees, the telephone number is area code **502-564-4212.**
Marriage	$4.00 Varies	Same as Birth or Death See remarks	Records since June 1958. Clerk of County Court in county where license was issued.
Divorce	$4.00 Varies	Same as Birth or Death See remarks	Records since June 1958. Clerk of Circuit Court in county where decree was issued.
LOUISIANA **Birth (long form)** / **Birth (short form)** / **Death**	$8.00 $5.00 $5.00	Division of Vital Records Office of Health Services and Environmental Quality P.O. Box 60630 New Orleans, LA 70160	State office has had records since July 1914. Birth records for City of New Orleans are available from 1790, and death records from 1803. Check or money order should be made payable to **Vital Records.** Personal checks are accepted. To verify current fees, the telephone number is area code **504-568-5175.**
Marriage Orleans Parish / Other Parishes	$5.00 Varies	Same as Birth or Death See remarks	Certified copies are issued by Clerk of Court in parish where license was issued.
Divorce	Varies	See remarks	Clerk of Court in parish where divorce was granted. For Orleans Parish, copies may be obtained from State office for $2.00

Place of Event	Cost of copy	Address	Remarks
MAINE			
Birth or **Death**	$5.00	Office of Vital Records Human Services Building Station 11 State House Augusta, ME 04333	State office has had records since 1892. For earlier records, write to the municipality where the event occurred. Additional copies of same record ordered at same time are $2.00 each. Check or money order should be made payable to **Treasurer, State of Maine.** Personal checks are accepted. To verify current fees, the telephone number is area code **207-289-3181.**
Marriage	$5.00	Same as Birth or Death	Additional copies of same record ordered at same time are $2.00 each.
	$2.00	See remarks	Town Clerk in town where license was issued.
Divorce	$2.00	Same as Birth or Death	Records since January 1892.
	$5.00	See remarks	Clerk of District Court in judicial division where divorce was granted.
MARYLAND			
Birth or **Death**	$4.00	Division of Vital Records State Department of Health and Mental Hygiene State Office Building P.O. Box 13146 201 West Preston Street Baltimore, MD 21203	State office has had records since August 1898. Records for City of Baltimore are available from January 1875. Check or money order should be made payable to **Department of Health and Mental Hygiene.** Personal checks are accepted. To verify current fees, the telephone number is area code **301-225-5988.** This will be a **recorded** message.
Marriage	$3.00	Same as Birth or Death	Records since June 1951.
	Varies	See remarks	Clerk of Circuit Court in county where license was issued or Clerk of Court of Common Pleas of Baltimore City (for licenses issued in City of Baltimore).
Divorce	$3.00	Same as Birth or Death	Records since January 1961. Certified copies are not available from State office. Some items may be verified. Inquiries will be forwarded to appropriate office.
	Varies	See remarks	Clerk of Circuit Court in county where divorce was granted.
MASSACHUSETTS			
Birth or **Death**	$6.00	Registry of Vital Records and Statistics 150 Treemont Street, Room B-3 Boston, MA 02111	State office has had records since 1896. For earlier records, write to the State Archives, State House, Boston, MA. Check or money order should be made payable to **Commonwealth of Massachusetts.** Personal checks are accepted. To verify current fees, the telephone number is area code **617-727-0110.**
Marriage	$3.00	Same as Birth or Death	Records since 1891.

Record	Cost of Copy	Address	Remarks
Divorce	See remarks	Same as Birth or Death	Index only since 1952. Inquirer will be directed where to send request. Certified copies are not available from State office.
	$3.00	See remarks	Registrar of Probate Court in county where divorce was granted.
MICHIGAN Birth or Death	$10.00	Office of the State Registrar and Center for Health Statistics Michigan Department of Public Health 3500 North Logan Street Lansing, MI 48909	State office has had records since 1867. Copies of records since 1867 may also be obtained from County Clerk in county where event occurred. Fees vary from county to county. Detroit records may be obtained from the City of Detroit Health Department for births occurring since 1893 and for deaths since 1897. Check or money order should be made payable to **State of Michigan.** Personal checks are accepted. To verify current fees, the telephone number is area code **517-335-8655.** This will be a **recorded** message.
Marriage	$10.00	Same as Birth or Death	Records since April 1867.
	Varies	See remarks	County Clerk in county where license was issued.
Divorce	$10.00	Same as Birth or Death	Records since 1897.
	Varies	See remarks	County Clerk in county where divorce was granted.
MINNESOTA Birth Death	$11.00 $8.00	Minnesota Department of Health Section of Vital Statistics 717 Delaware Street, SE P.O. Box 9441 Minneapolis, MN 55440	State office has had records since January 1908. Copies of earlier records may be obtained from Court Administrator in county where event occurred or from the St. Paul City Health Department if the event occurred in St. Paul. Additional copies of the birth record when ordered at the same time are $5.00 each. Additional copies of the death record when ordered at the same time are $2.00 each. Check or money order should be made payable to **Treasurer, State of Minnesota.** Personal checks are accepted. To verify current fees, the telephone number is area code **612-623-5121.** This will be a **recorded** message.
Marriage	See remarks	Same as Birth or Death	Statewide index since January 1958. Inquiries will be forwarded to appropriate office. Certified copies are not available from State Department of Health.
	$8.00	See remarks	Court Administrator in county where license was issued. Additional copies of the marriage record when ordered at the same time are $2.00 each.
Divorce	See remarks	Same as Birth or Death	Index since January 1970. Certified copies are not available from State office.
	$8.00	See remarks	Court Administrator in county where divorce was granted.

Place of Event	Cost of copy	Address	Remarks
MISSISSIPPI			
Birth	$10.00	Vital Records	State office has had records since 1912. Full copies of birth certificates obtained within 1 year after the event are $5.00. Additional copies of same record ordered at same time are $1.00 each.
Birth (short form)	$5.00	State Board of Health	
Death	$5.00	P.O. Box 1700	
		Jackson, MS 39215–1700	For out-of-State requests only bank or postal money orders are accepted and should be made payable to **Mississippi State Department of Health.** Personal checks are accepted for in-State requests only. To verify current fees, the telephone number is area code **601-354-6606.** A **recorded** message may be reached on area code **601-354-6600.**
Marriage	$5.00	Same as Birth or Death	Statistical records only from January 1926 to July 1, 1938, and since January 1942.
	$3.00	See remarks	Circuit Clerk in county where license was issued.
Divorce	See remarks $0.50 per page plus $1.00 for certification	Same as Birth or Death	Records since January 1926. Certified copies are not available from State office. Inquiries will be forwarded to appropriate office.
	Varies	See remarks	Chancery Clerk in county where divorce was granted.
MISSOURI			
Birth or Death	$4.00	Department of Health Bureau of Vital Records P.O. Box 570 Jefferson City, MO 65102	State office has had records since January 1910. If event occurred in St. Louis (City), St. Louis County, or Kansas City before 1910, write to the City or County Health Department. Copies of these records are $3.00 each in St. Louis City and County. In Kansas City, $6.00 for first copy and $3.00 for each additional copy ordered at same time.
			Check or money order should be made payable to **Missouri Department of Health.** Personal checks are accepted. To verify current fees on **Birth** records, the telephone number is area code **314-751-6387;** for **Death** records, area code **314-751-6376.**
Marriage	No fee	Same as Birth or Death	Indexes since July 1948. Correspondent will be referred to appropriate Recorder of Deeds in county where license was issued.
	Varies	See remarks	Recorder of Deeds in county where license was issued.
Divorce	See remarks	Same as Birth or Death	Indexes since July 1948. Certified copies are not available from State Health Department. Inquiries will be forwarded to appropriate office.
	Varies	See remarks	Clerk of Circuit Court in county where divorce was granted.

MONTANA

Birth or **Death**

Bureau of Records and Statistics
State Department of Health and
Environmental Sciences
Helena, MT 59620

$5.00

State office has had records since late 1907.

Check or money order should be made payable to **Montana Department of Health and Environmental Sciences.** Personal checks are accepted. To verify current fees, the telephone number is area code **406-444-2614.**

Marriage

Same as Birth or Death

See remarks

Records since July 1943. Some items may be verified. Inquiries will be forwarded to appropriate office. Apply to county where license was issued if known. Certified copies are not available from State office

See remarks

Varies

Clerk of District Court in county where license was issued.

Divorce

Same as Birth or Death

See remarks

Records since July 1943. Some items may be verified. Inquiries will be forwarded to appropriate office. Apply to court where divorce was granted if known. Certified copies are not available from State office.

See remarks

Varies

Clerk of District Court in county where divorce was granted.

NEBRASKA

Birth
Death

Bureau of Vital Statistics
State Department of Health
301 Centennial Mall South
P.O. Box 95007
Lincoln, NE 68509–5007

$6.00
$5.00

State office has had records since late 1904. If birth occurred before then, write the State office for information.

Check or money order should be made payable to **Bureau of Vital Statistics.** Personal checks are accepted. To verify current fees, the telephone number is area code **402-471-2871.**

Marriage

Same as Birth or Death

$5.00

Records since January 1909.

See remarks

Varies

County Court in county where license was issued.

Divorce

Same as Birth or Death

$5.00

Records since January 1909.

See remarks

Varies

Clerk of District Court in county where divorce was granted.

NEVADA

Birth or **Death**

Division of Health—Vital Statistics
Capitol Complex
Carson City, NV 89710

$7.00

State office has had records since July 1904. For earlier records, write to County Recorder in county where event occurred. Additional copies of death records ordered at the same time are $4.00 for second and third copies, $3.00 each for the next three copies, and $2.00 each for any additional copies.

Check or money order should be made payable to **Section of Vital Statistics.** Personal checks are accepted. To verify current fees, the telephone number is area code **702-885-4480.**

Marriage

Same as Birth or Death

See remarks

Indexes since January 1968. Certified copies are not available from State Health Department. Inquiries will be forwarded to appropriate office.

See remarks

Varies

County Recorder in county where license was issued.

Place of Event	Cost of copy	Address	Remarks
Divorce	See remarks	Same as Birth or Death	Indexes since January 1968. Certified copies are not available from State Health Department. Inquiries will be forwarded to appropriate office.
	Varies	See remarks	County Clerk in county where divorce was granted.
NEW HAMPSHIRE **Birth** or **Death**	$3.00	Bureau of Vital Records Health and Human Services Building 6 Hazen Drive Concord, NH 03301	State office has had records since 1640. Copies of records may be obtained from State office or from City or Town Clerk in place where event occurred. Check or money order should be made payable to **Treasurer, State of New Hampshire.** Personal checks are accepted. To verify current fees, the telephone number is area code **603-271-4654.**
Marriage	$3.00	Same as Birth or Death	Records since 1640.
	Varies	See remarks	Town Clerk in town where license was issued.
Divorce	$3.00	Same as Birth or Death	Records since 1808.
	Varies	See remarks	Clerk of Superior Court where divorce was granted.
NEW JERSEY **Birth** or **Death**	$4.00	State Department of Health Bureau of Vital Statistics CN 360 Trenton, NJ 08625	State office has had records since June 1878. Additional copies of same record ordered at same time are $2.00 each. If the exact date is unknown, the fee is an additional $1.00.
		Archives and History Bureau State Library Division State Department of Education Trenton, NJ 08625	For records from May 1848 to May 1878. Check or money order should be made payable to **New Jersey State Registrar** or **New Jersey State Department of Health.** Personal checks are accepted. To verify current fees, the telephone number is area code **609-292-4087.**
Marriage	$4.00	Same as Birth or Death	If the exact date is unknown, the fee is an additional $1.00 per year searched.
	$2.00	Archives and History Bureau State Library Division State Department of Education Trenton, NJ 08625	For records from May 1848 to May 1878.
Divorce	$2.00	Superior Court Chancery Division State House Annex Room 320 CN 971 Trenton, NJ 08625	The fee is for the first four pages. Additional pages cost $0.50 each.

New Mexico

Record	Cost of Copy	Address	Remarks
Birth or **Death**	$5.00	Vital Statistics Bureau New Mexico Health Services Division P.O. Box 968 Santa Fe, NM 87504–0968	State office has had records since 1920, and delayed records since 1880. Check or money order should be made payable to **Vital Statistics Bureau.** Personal checks are accepted. To verify current fees, the telephone number is area code **505-827-2338.** This will be a **recorded** message.
Marriage	Varies	See remarks	County Clerk in county where license was issued.
Divorce	Varies	See remarks	Clerk of Superior Court where divorce was granted.

New York (except New York City)

Record	Cost of Copy	Address	Remarks
Birth or **Death**	$15.00	Bureau of Vital Records State Department of Health Empire State Plaza Tower Building Albany, NY 12237	State office has had records since 1880. For records before 1914 in Albany, Buffalo, and Yonkers, or before 1880 in any other city, write to Registrar of Vital Statistics in city where event occurred. For the rest of the State, except New York City, write to State office. Check or money order should be made payable to **New York State Department of Health.** Personal checks are accepted. To verify current fees, the telephone number is area code **518-474-3075.** This will be a **recorded** message.
Marriage	$5.00 $5.00	Same as Birth or Death See remarks	Records from 1880 to present. For records from 1880–1907 and licenses issued in the cities of Albany, Buffalo, or Yonkers, apply to—Albany: City Clerk, City Hall, Albany, NY 12207; Buffalo: City Clerk, City Hall, Buffalo, NY 14202; Yonkers: Registrar of Vital Statistics, Health Center Building, Yonkers, NY 10701.
Divorce	$5.00 Varies	Same as Birth or Death See remarks	Records since January 1963. County Clerk in county where divorce was granted.

New York City

Record	Cost of Copy	Address	Remarks
Birth or **Death**	$5.00	Bureau of Vital Records Department of Health of New York City 125 Worth Street New York, NY 10013	Office has had birth records since 1898 and death records since 1920. For Old City of New York (Manhattan and part of the Bronx) birth records for 1865–97 and death records for 1865–1919 write to Archives Division, Department of Records and Information Services, 31 Chambers Street, New York, NY 10007. Money order should be made payable to **New York City Department of Health.** To verify current fees, the telephone number is area code **212-619-4530.** This will be a **recorded** message.

Place of Event	Cost of copy	Address	Remarks
Marriage			
New	$10.00	See remarks	Records from 1847 to 1865. Archives Division, Department of Records and information Services, 31 Chambers Street, York, NY 10007, except Brooklyn records for this period which are filed with County Clerk's Office, King County, Supreme Court Building, Brooklyn, NY 11201. Additional copies of same record ordered at same time are $5.00 each.
	$10.00	See remarks	Records from 1866 to 1907. City Clerk's Office in borough where marriage was performed.
	$10.00	See remarks	Records from 1908 to May 12, 1943. New York City residents write to City Clerk's Office in the borough of bride's residence; nonresidents write to City Clerk's Office in borough where license was obtained.
	$10.00	See remarks	Records since May 13, 1943. City Clerk's Office in borough where license was issued.
Bronx Borough	$10.00	City Clerk's Office 1780 Grand Concourse Bronx, NY 10457	
Brooklyn Borough	$10.00	City Clerk's Office Municipal Building Brooklyn, NY 11201	
Manhattan Borough	$10.00	City Clerk's Office Municipal Building New York, NY 10007	
Queens Borough	$10.00	City Clerk's Office 120–55 Queens Boulevard Kew Gardens, NY 11424	
Staten Island Borough (no longer called Richmond)	$10.00	City Clerk's Office Staten Island Borough Hall Staten Island, NY 10301	
Divorce			See New York State
NORTH CAROLINA Birth or Death	$5.00	Department of Human Resources Division of Health Services Vital Records Branch P.O. Box 2091 Raleigh, NC 27602	State office has had birth records since October 1913 and death records since January 1, 1930. Death records from 1913 through 1929 are available from Archives and Records Section, State Records Center, 215 North Blount Street, Raleigh, NC 27602. Check or money order should be made payable to **Vital Records Branch.** Personal checks are accepted. To verify current the telephone number is area code **919-733-3526.**

fees,

Type	Address	Cost	Remarks
Marriage	Same as Birth or Death	$5.00	Records since January 1962.
	See remarks	$3.00	Registrar of Deeds in county where marriage was performed.
Divorce	Same as Birth or Death	$5.00	Records since January 1958.
	See remarks	Varies	Clerk of Superior Court where divorce was granted.
NORTH DAKOTA			
Birth	Division of Vital Records State Department of Health Office of Statistical Services Bismarck, ND 58505	$7.00	State office has had some records since July 1893. Years from 1894 to 1920 are incomplete. Additional copies of birth records are $4.00 each; death records are $2.00 each.
Death		$5.00	Money order should be made payable to **North Dakota State Department of Health.** To verify current fees, the telephone number is area code **701-224-2360.**
Marriage	Same as Birth or Death	$5.00	Records since July 1925. Requests for earlier records will be forwarded to appropriate office. Additional copies are $2.00 each.
	See remarks	Varies	County Judge in county where license was issued.
Divorce	Same as Birth or Death	See	Index of records since July 1949. Some items may be verified. Certified copies are not available from State Health Department. Inquiries will be forwarded to appropriate office.
	See remarks	Varies	Clerk of District Court in county where divorce was granted.
OHIO			
Birth or Death	Division of Vital Statistics Ohio Department of Health G-20 Ohio Department Building 65 South Front Street Columbus, OH 43266-0333	$7.00	State office has had records since December 20, 1908. For earlier records, write to Probate Court in county where event occurred.
			Check or money order should be made payable to **State Treasurer.** Personal checks are accepted. To verify current fees, the telephone number is area code **614-466-2531.**
Marriage	Same as Birth or Death	See remarks	Records since September 1949. All items may be verified. Certified copies are not available from State Health Department. Inquiries will be referred to appropriate office.
	See remarks	Varies	Probate Judge in county where license was issued.
Divorce	Same as Birth or Death	See remarks	Records since September 1949. All items may be verified. Certified copies are not available from State Health Department. Inquiries will be forwarded to appropriate office.
	See remarks	Varies	Clerk of Court of Common Pleas in county where divorce was granted.

Place of Event	Cost of copy	Address	Remarks
OKLAHOMA **Birth** or **Death**	$5.00	Vital Records Section State Department of Health Northeast 10th Street and Stonewall P.O. Box 53551 Oklahoma City, OK 73152	State office has had records since October 1908. Check or money order should be made payable to **Oklahoma State Department of Health.** Personal checks are accepted. To verify current fees, the telephone number is area code **405-271-4040.**
Marriage	Varies	See remarks	Clerk of Court in county where license was issued.
Divorce	Varies	See remarks	Clerk of Court in county where divorce was granted.
OREGON **Birth** or **Death**	$8.00	Oregon State Health Division Vital Statistics Section P.O. Box 116 Portland, OR 97207	State office has had records since January 1903. Some earlier records for the City of Portland since approximately 1880 are available from the Oregon State Archives, 1005 Broadway, NE, Salem, OR 97310.
Heirloom Birth	$25.00	Same as Birth or Death	Presentation style calligraphy certificate suitable for framing. Check or money order should be made payable to **Oregon State Health Division.** To verify current fees, the telephone number is area code **503-229-5710.** This will be a **recorded** message.
Marriage	$8.00	Same as Birth or Death	Records since January 1906.
	Varies	See remarks	County Clerk in county where license was issued. County Clerks also have some records before 1906.
Divorce	$8.00	Same as Birth or Death	Records since 1925.
	Varies	See remarks	County Clerk in county where divorce was granted. County Clerks also have some records before 1925.
PENNSYLVANIA **Birth**	$4.00	Division of Vital Records State Department of Health Central Building 101 South Mercer Street P.O. Box 1528 New Castle, PA 16103	State office has had records since January 1906. For earlier records, write to Register of Wills, Orphans Court, in county seat where event occurred. Persons born in Pittsburgh from 1870 to 1905 or in Allegheny City, now part of Pittsburgh, from 1882 to 1905 should write to Office of Biostatistics, Pittsburgh Health Department, City-County Building, Pittsburgh, PA 15219. For events occurring in City of Philadelphia from 1860 to 1915, write to Vital Statistics, Philadelphia Department of Public Health, City Hall Annex, Philadelphia, PA 19107.
Wallet card	$5.00		
Death	$3.00		Check or money order should be made payable to **Vital Records.** Personal checks are accepted. To verify current fees, the telephone number is area code **412-656-3100.**

	Address	Cost	Remarks
Marriage	Same as Birth or Death	See remarks	Records since January 1906. Certified copies are not available from State Health Department. Inquiries will be forwarded to appropriate office.
	See remarks	Varies	Marriage License Clerks, County Court House, in county where license was issued.
Divorce	Same as Birth or Death	Varies	Records since January 1946. Certified copies are not available from State Health Department. Inquiries will be forwarded to appropriate office.
	See remarks	Varies	Prothonotary, Court House, in county seat where divorce was granted.
PUERTO RICO **Birth** or **Death**	Division of Demographic Registry and Vital Statistics Department of Health San Juan, PR 00908	$2.00	Central office has had records since July 22, 1931. Copies of earlier records may be obtained by writing to local Registrar (Registrador Demografico) in municipality where event occurred or by writing to central office for information. Money order should be made payable to **Secretary of the Treasury.** Personal checks are not accepted. To verify current fees, the telephone number is area code **809-728-4300.**
Marriage	Same as Birth or Death	$2.00	
Divorce	Same as Birth or Death	$2.00	
	See remarks		Superior Court where divorce was granted.
RHODE ISLAND **Birth** or **Death**	Division of Vital Records State Health Department Room 101, Cannon Building 3 Capitol Hill Providence, RI 02908–5097	$5.00	State office has had records since 1853. For earlier records, write to Town Clerk in town where event occurred. Additional copies of the same record ordered at the same time are $3.00 each. Money order should be made payable to **General Treasurer, State of Rhode Island.** To verify current fees, the telephone number is area code **401-277-2811.** This will be a **recorded** message.
Marriage	Same as Birth or Death	$5.00	Records since January 1853. Additional copies of the same record ordered at the same time are $3.00 each.
Divorce	Clerk of Family Court 1 Dorrance Plaza Providence, RI 02903	$1.00	

Place of Event	Cost of copy	Address	Remarks
SOUTH CAROLINA			
Birth or Death	$6.00	Office of Vital Records and Public Health Statistics S.C. Department of Health and Environmental Control 2600 Bull Street Columbia, SC 29201	State office has had records since January 1915. City of Charleston births from 1877 and deaths from 1821 are on file at Charleston County Health Department. Ledger entries of Florence City births and deaths from 1895 to 1914 are on file at Florence County Health Department. Ledger entries of Newberry City births and deaths from the late 1800's are on file at Newberry County Health Department. These are the only early records obtainable.
births			Check or money order should be made payable to Office **of Vital Records.** Personal checks are accepted. To verify current fees, the telephone number is area code **803-734-4830.**
Marriage	$5.00	Same as Birth or Death	Records since July 1950.
	Varies	See remarks	Records since July 1911. Probate Judge in county where license was issued.
Divorce	$5.00	Same as Birth or Death	Records since July 1962.
	Varies	See remarks	Records since April 1949. Clerk of county where petition was filed.
SOUTH DAKOTA			
Birth or Death	$5.00	State Department of Health Center for Health Policy and Statistics Vital Records 523 E. Capitol Pierre, SD 57501	State office has had records since July 1905 and access to other records for some events that occurred before then. Money order should be made payable to **South Dakota Department of Health.** To verify current fees, the telephone number is area code **605-773-3355.**
Marriage	$5.00	Same as Birth or Death	Records since July 1905.
	$5.00	See remarks	County Treasurer in county where license was issued.
Divorce	$5.00	Same as Birth or Death	Records since July 1905.
	Varies	See remarks	Clerk of Court in county where divorce was granted.
TENNESSEE			
Birth (long form)	$6.00	Tennessee Vital Records Department of Health and Environment Cordell Hull Building Nashville, TN 37219–5402	State office has had birth records for entire State since January 1914, for Nashville since June 1881, for Knoxville since July 1881, and for Chattanooga since January 1882. State office has had death records for entire State since January 1914, for Nashville since July 1874, for Knoxville since July 1887, and for Chattanooga since March 6, 1872. Birth and death enumeration records by school district are available for July 1908 through June 1912. For Memphis birth records from April 1874 through December 1887 and November 1898 to January 1, 1914, and for Memphis death records from May 1848 to January 1, 1914, write to Memphis-Shelby County Health Department, Division of Vital Records, Memphis, TN 38105.
Birth (short form)	$4.00		
Death	$5.00		

Check or money order should be made payable to **Tennessee Vital Records**. Personal checks are accepted. To verify current fees, the telephone number is area code **615-741-1763**. In Tennessee call **1-800-423-1901**.

Record	Fee	Office / Address	Remarks
Marriage	$4.00	Same as Birth or Death	Records since July 1945. County Clerk in county where license was issued.
Divorce	$4.00	Same as Birth or Death	Records since July 1945. Clerk of Court in county where divorce was granted.

TEXAS

Record	Fee	Office / Address	Remarks
Birth or **Death**	$8.00	Bureau of Vital Statistics, Texas Department of Health, 1100 West 49th Street, Austin, TX 78756–3191	State office has had records since 1903. Additional copies of same record ordered at same time are $2.00 each. Check or money order should be made payable to **Texas Department of Health**. Personal checks are accepted. To verify current fees, the telephone number is area code **512-458-7380**.
Marriage	See remarks	Same as Birth or Death	Records since January 1966. Certified copies are not available from State office. Fee for search and verification of essential facts of marriage is $2.00. County Clerk in county where license was issued.
Divorce	See remarks	Same as Birth or Death	Records since January 1968. Certified copies are not available from State office. Fee for search and verification of essential facts of divorce is $2.00 Clerk of District Court in County where divorce was granted.

TRUST TERRITORY OF THE PACIFIC ISLANDS

Birth or **Death**

Area	Fee	Office / Address
Commonwealth of Northern Mariana Islands	$2.50	Commonwealth Courts, Commonwealth Governments, Saipan, CM 96950
Republic of the Marshall Islands	$0.25 plus $0.10 per 100 words	Chief Clerk of Supreme Courts, Republic of the Marshall Islands, Majuro, Marshall Islands 96960
Republic of Palau	$0.25 plus $0.10 per 100 words	Chief Clerk of Supreme Courts, Republic of Palau, Koror, Palau, W.C.I. 96940
Federated States of Micronesia	$0.25 plus $0.10 per 100 words	Clerk of Courts, State of Truk, FSM, Moen, Truk, E.C.I. 96942

Courts have had records since November 12, 1952. Beginning in 1950, a few records have been filed with the Hawaii Bureau of Vital Statistics. If not sure of the area in which the event occurred, write to the Director of Health Services, Trust Territory of the Pacific Islands, Saipan, Northern Mariana Islands 96950 to have the inquiry referred to the correct area.

Money order should be made payable to **Clerk of Courts** in area where inquiries are made. Personal checks are not accepted.

Place of Event	Cost of copy	Address	Remarks
		Clerk of Courts State of Ponape, FSM Kolonia, Ponape, E.C.I. 96941	
		Clerk of Courts State of Kosrae, FSM Lelu, Losrae, E.C.I. 96944	
		Clerk of Courts State of Yap, FSM Colonia, Yap, W.C.I. 96943	
Marriage	Varies	See remarks	Clerk of Court in district where marriage was performed.
Divorce	Varies	See remarks	Clerk of Court in district where divorce was granted.
UTAH			
Birth	$10.00	Bureau of Vital Records	State office has had records since 1905. If event occurred from 1890 to 1904 in Salt Lake City or Ogden, write to City Board of Health.
Death	$8.00	Utah Department of Health 288 North 1460 West P.O. Box 16700 Salt Lake City, UT 84116–0700	For records elsewhere in the State from 1898 to 1904, write to County Clerk in county where event occurred. Additional copies, when requested at the same time, are $3.00 each. Check or money order should be made payable to **Utah Department of Health**. Personal checks are accepted. To verify current fees, the telephone number is area code **801-538-6105.**
Marriage	$7.00	Same as Birth or Death	State office has had records since 1978. Only short form certified copies are available.
	Varies	See remarks	County Clerk in county where license was issued.
Divorce	$7.00	Same as Birth or Death	State office has had records since 1978. Only short form certified copies are available.
	Varies	See remarks	County Clerk in county where divorce was granted.
VERMONT			
Birth or **Death**	$5.00	Vermont Department of Health Vital Records Section Box 70 60 Main Street Burlington, VT 05402	State has had records since 1955. Check or money order should be made payable to **Vermont Department of Health**. Personal checks are accepted. To verify current fees, the telephone number is area code **802-863-7275.**
Birth, Death, or Marriage	$5.00	Division of Public Records 6 Baldwin Street Montpelier, VT 05602	Records prior to 1955.

Record	Cost	Send request to	Remarks
Marriage	$5.00	Same as Birth or Death	State has had records since 1955.
	$5.00	See remarks	Town Clerk in town where license was issued.
Divorce	$5.00	Same as Birth or Death	State has had records since 1968.
	$5.00	See remarks	Town Clerk in town where divorce was granted.
VIRGINIA **Birth** or **Death**	$5.00	Division of Vital Records State Health Department P.O. Box 1000 Richmond, VA 23208–1000	State office has had records from January 1853 to December 1896 and since June 14, 1912. For records between those dates, write to the Health Department in the city where event occurred. Check or money order should be made payable to **State Health Department.** Personal checks are accepted. To verify current fees, the telephone number is area code **804-786-6228.**
Marriage	$5.00	Same as Birth or Death	Records since January 1853.
	Varies	See remarks	Clerk of Court in county or city where license was issued.
Divorce	$5.00	Same as Birth or Death	Records since January 1918.
	Varies	See remarks	Clerk of Court in county or city where divorce was granted.
VIRGIN ISLANDS **Birth or Death** St. Croix	$10.00	Registrar of Vital Statistics Charles Harwood Memorial Hospital St. Croix, VI 00820	Registrar has had birth and death records on file since 1840.
St. Thomas and St. John	$10.00	Registrar of Vital Statistics Charlotte Amalie St. Thomas, VI 00802	Registrar has had birth records on file since July 1906 and death records since January 1906. Money order for birth and death records should be made payable to **Bureau of Vital Statistics.** Personal checks are not accepted.
Marriage	See remarks	Bureau of Vital Records and Statistical Services Virgin Islands Department of Health Charlotte Amalie St. Thomas, VI 00801	Certified copies are not available. Inquiries will be forwarded to appropriate office.
St. Croix	$2.00	Chief Deputy Clerk Territorial Court of the Virgin Islands P.O. Box 929 Christiansted St. Croix, VI 00820	
St. Thomas and St. John	$2.00	Clerk of the Territorial Court of the Virgin Islands P.O. Box 70 Charlotte Amalie St. Croix, VI 00801	

Place of Event	Cost of copy	Address	Remarks
Divorce	See remarks	Same as Marriage	Certified copies are not available. Inquiries will be forwarded to appropriate office.
St. Croix	$5.00	Same as Marriage	Money order for marriage and divorce records should be made payable to **Territorial Court of the Virgin Islands.** Personal checks are not accepted.
St. Thomas St. John	$5.00	Same as Marriage	
WASHINGTON **Birth** or **Death**	$11.00	Vital Records P.O. Box 9709, ET-11 Olympia, WA 98504–9709	State office has had records since July 1907. For King, Pierce, and Spokane counties copies may also be obtained from county health departments. County Auditor of county of birth has registered births prior to July 1907.
			Money order should be made payable to **Vital Records.** To verify current fees, the telephone number is area code **206-753-5396.** Recorded messages for out of State, call **1-800-551-0562;** in State, call **1-800-331-0680.**
Marriage	$6.00	Same as Birth or Death	State office has had records since January 1968.
	$2.00	See remarks	County Auditor in county where license was issued.
Divorce	$6.00	Same as Birth or Death	State office has had records since January 1968.
	Varies	See remarks	County Clerk in county where divorce was granted.
WEST VIRGINIA **Birth** or **Death**	$5.00	Division of Vital Statistics State Department of Health State Office Building No. 3 Charleston, WV 25305	State office has had records since January 1917. For earlier records, write to Clerk of County Court in county where event occurred.
			Check or money order should be made payable to **Division of Vital Statistics.** Personal checks are accepted. To verify current fees, the telephone number is area code **304-348-2931.**
Marriage	$5.00	Same as Birth or Death	Records since 1921. Certified copies available from 1964.
	Varies	See remarks	County Clerk in county where license was issued.
Divorce	See remarks	Same as Birth or Death	Index since 1968. Some items may be verified (fee $5.00). Certified copies are not available form State office.
	Varies	See remarks	Clerk of Circuit Court, Chancery Side, in county where divorce was granted.

WISCONSIN

Birth	$7.00	Bureau of Health Statistics	State office has scattered records earlier than 1857. Records before October 1, 1907, are very incomplete. Additional copies of the same record ordered at the same time are $2.00 each.
Death	$5.00	Wisconsin Department of Health	Check or money order should be made payable to **Center for Health Statistics.** Personal checks are accepted. To verify current fees, the telephone number is area code **608-266-1371.**
		P.O. Box 309	
		Madison, WI 53701	
Marriage	$5.00	Same as Birth or Death	Records since April 1836. Records before October 1, 1907, are incomplete. Additional copies of the same record ordered at the same time are $2.00 each.
Divorce	$5.00	Same as Birth or Death	Records since October 1907. Additional copies of the same record ordered at the same time are $2.00 each.

WYOMING

Birth	$5.00	Vital Records Services	State office has had records since July 1909.
Death	$3.00	Division of Health and Medical Services	Money order should be made payable to **Vital Records Services.** To verify current fees, the telephone number is area code **307-777-7591.**
		Hathaway Building	
		Cheyenne, WY 82002	
Marriage	$5.00	Same as Birth or Death	Records since May 1941.
	Varies	See remarks	County Clerk in county where license was issued.
Divorce	$5.00	Same as Birth or Death	Records since May 1941.
	Varies	See remarks	Clerk of District Court where divorce took place.

Organizations and Resources

Academy of Family Mediators
P.O. Box 10501
Eugene, OR 10501
503-345-1205

AIDS Hotline
800-342-AIDS

American Academy of Matrimonial Lawyers
20 N. Michigan Ave., Suite 540
Chicago, IL 60602
312-263-6477

American Arbitration Association
140 W. 51st St.
New York, NY 10020
212-484-4000

American Association for Marriage and Family
    Therapy
1717 K. St., NW, Suite 407
Wash. D.C. 20006
202-429-1825

American Association for Protecting Children
2725 East Hampden Ave.
Denver, CO 80231
303-695-0811

American Association of Retired Persons
1909 K. St., NW
Wash. D.C. 20049
202-872-4700

American Association of Sex Educators, Counselors,
    and Therapists
11 DuPont Circle, Suite 220
Wash. D.C. 20036
202-462-1171

American Bar Association
Family Law Section
750 N. Lake Shore Dr.
Chicago, IL 60611
312-988-5584

American College of Nurse-Midwives
1522 K. St., NW, Suite 1120

Wash. D.C. 20005
202-347-5445

American Fertility Institute
2140 11th Ave., South, Suite 200
Birmingham, AL 35205
205-933-8494

Association for Voluntary Sterilization, Inc.
122 E. 42nd St.
New York, NY 10017
212-573-8322

Association of Family and Conciliation Courts
329 W. Wilson St.
Madison, WI 53703
608-251-4001

AZT Hotline
800-843-9388

Center for Dispute Settlement
1666 Connecticut Ave., NW, Suite 501
Wash. D.C. 20009
202-265-9572

Center for Surrogate Parenting, Inc.
8383 Wilshire Blvd., Suite 750
Beverly Hills, CA 90211
213-655-1974

Center for Women Policy Studies
2000 P. St., NW, #508
Wash. D.C. 20036
202-872-1770

Centers for Disease Control
Technical Information Services
Atlanta, GA 30333
404-329-3311

Child Find of America, Inc.
P.O. Box 277
New Paltz, NY 12561
914-255-1848
800-I-AM-LOST

Child Welfare League of American
440 1st St., NW

Wash. D.C. 20001
202-638-2952

Community Dispute Services
140 W. 51st St.
New York, NY 10020
212-484-4000

Divorce Mediation Services
Association of Family and Conciliation Courts
1227 Spruce St.
Boulder, CO
303-447-8116

Equal Rights Advocates
1370 Mission St.
San Francisco, CA 94103
415-621-0505

Family Law Council
P.O. Box 217
Fair Lawn, NJ 07410

Federal Parent Locator Service
Department of Health and Human Services
Office of Child Support Enforcement
Wash. D.C. 20201
202-245-1647

Herpes Resource Information
260 Sheridan Ave.
Palo Alto, CA 94302
415-328-7710

Institute for Reproductive Medicine
Eastern Virginia Medical School
Norfolk General Hospital
825 Fairfax Ave.
Norfolk, VA 23507
804-446-8948

Joint Custody Association
10606 Wilkins Ave.
Los Angeles, CA 90024
213-475-5352

Mothers without Custody
P.O. Box 56762
Houston, TX 77256
301-552-2319

National Abortion Rights Action League
1101 14th St., NW
Wash. D.C. 20005
202-371-0779
202-347-7774

National Academy of Conciliators
5530 Wisconsin Ave., Suite 1130
Chevy Chase, MD 20815
301-654-6515

National Association of Counsel for Children
1205 Oneida St.
Denver, CO 80220
303-321-3963

National Center on Child Abuse and Neglect
Department of Health and Social Services
P.O. Box 1182
Wash. D.C. 20013
202-245-0586

National Center for Mediation Education
2083 West St., Suite 3C
Annapolis, MD 21401
301-261-8445

National Center for Missing and Exploited Children
1835 K. St., NW, Suite 600
Wash. D.C. 20006
202-634-9821
800-843-5678

National Center for Youth law
114 Sansome St., Suite 900
San Francisco, CA 94104
415-543-3307

National Center on Women & Family Law, Inc.
799 Broadway, Rm. 402
New York, NY 10003
212-674-8200

National Child Support Enforcement Association
444 N. Capitol, NW, Suite 613
Wash. D.C. 20001
202-624-8180

National Clearinghouse on Marital and Date Rape
2325 Oak
Berkeley, CA 94708
415-548-1770

National Coalition Against Domestic Violence
P.O. Box 15127
Wash. D.C. 20003
202-293-8860
800-333-SAFE

National Committee for Adoption
1930 17th St., NW
Wash. D.C. 20009
202-328-1200

National Committee for Prevention of Child Abuse
2001 O. St., NW
Wash. D.C. 20036
202-965-1900
312-663-3520
800-422-4453

National Council of Juvenile and Family Court Judges
University of Nevada
P.O. Box 8970
Reno, NV 89507
702-784-6012

National Gay and Lesbian Task Force
80 5th Ave., Suite 1601
New York, NY 10011
800-221-7044

National Gay Rights Advocates
540 Castro St.
San Francisco, CA 94114
415-863-3624

National Institute for Dispute Resolution
1901 L. St., Suite 600
Wash. D.C. 20036
202-466-4764

National Juvenile Court Services Association
University of Nevada
P.O. Box 8970
Reno, NV 89507
702-784-4859

National Organization for Changing Men
P.O. Box 451
Watseka, IL 60970
815-347-2279

National Organization for Men, Inc.
381 Park Ave. S.
New York, NY 10016

National Organization for Women
425 13th St., NW
Wash. D.C. 20004
202-347-2279

National Resource Center for Child Advocacy
  and Protection
American Bar Association
1800 M. St., NW
Wash. D.C. 20036
202-331-2250

National Resource Center on Child Abuse and Neglect
9725 East Hampden Ave.
Denver, CO 80231
303-695-0811

National Right to Life Committee
419 7th St., NW
Wash. D.C. 20045
202-626-8800

National Runaway Switchboard
800-621-4000

National VD Hotline
800-227-8922
800-982-5883 (CA)

North American Council on Adoptable Children
1346 Connecticut Ave., NW, Suite 229
Wash. D.C. 20036
202-466-7570

Office of Citizens Consular Services
Department of State
2201 C. St., NW, Rm. 4817
Wash. D.C. 20520
202-647-3666

Women's Bureau
The Work and Family Clearinghouse
Department of Labor
Division of Information and Publications
Wash. D.C. 20210
202-523-6652

Women's Equity Action League
1250 I. St., NW, Suite 305
Wash. D.C. 20005
202-898-1588

Women Organized Against Sexual Harassment
2437 Edwards St.
Berkeley, CA 94702

Single Mothers by Choice
P.O. Box 7788, FDR Station
New York, NY 10150
212-988-0993

Stepfamily Association of American, Inc.
28 Allegheny Ave., Suite 1307
Baltimore, MD 21204
301-823-7570

Overseas Citizen Services
Department of State
Wash. D.C. 20520
202-647-3666
202-647-5225

Parents and Friends of Lesbians and Gays
P.O. Box 24565
Los Angeles, CA 90024
213-472-8952

Parents without Partners International
8807 Colesville Rd.
Silver Spring, MD 20910
301-588-9354

Pension Rights Center
1346 Connecticut Ave., NW, Rm. 1019
Wash. D.C. 20036
202-296-3776

Planned Parenthood Federation of America
810 7th Ave.
New York, NY 10019
212-541-7800
202-785-3351

Select Committee on Children, Youth, and Families
U.S. House of Representatives

House Office Building Annex 2, Room H2-385
Wash. D.C. 20515

Sex Information and Education Council of the United
    States
80 5th Ave.
New York, NY 10011
212-929-2300

Abandonment See Desertion.

Abduction The unlawful taking away of another.

Absolute Divorce See Divorce.

Abuse Physically harming a person.

Abuse of Process A tort with the following elements: (1) a use of civil or criminal proceedings, (2) for an improper or ulterior purpose, (3) resulting in actual damage. For example, you have someone arrested in order to pressure him to marry your daughter, whom he impregnated. The purpose of the criminal law is not to encourage marriage.

Acceptance An assent or acquiescence to an offer.

Acknowledgement A formal recognition or affirmation that something is genuine.

Actuary A statistician. A person skilled in mathematical calculations to determine insurance risks.

Adjudicate To decide by judicial process; to judge.

Adjusted Basis See Tax Basis.

Adjusted Gross Income The total amount received after making allowed deductions.

Administrative Agency A part of the executive branch of government whose function is to execute or carry out the law.

Administrator A person appointed by a court to manage or administer the estate of a deceased, often when no valid will exists. See also Personal Representative.

Adoption The legal process by which an adoptive parent assumes all the rights and duties of the natural (i.e., biological) parent. The latter's parental rights are terminated.

Adoption by Estoppel See Equitable Adoption, Estoppel.

Adultery Voluntary sexual intercourse between a married person and someone to whom he or she is not married.

Adversarial Proceeding A proceeding in court or at an agency where both parties to a dispute can appear and argue their opposing positions.

AFDC Aid to Families with Dependent Children, a public assistance program.

Affidavit A written statement of facts under oath or affirmation.

Affinity Relationship by marriage rather than by blood.

Affirmative Defense A defense that raises new facts not in the plaintiff's complaint.

Agency A relationship in which one person acts for another or represents another by the latter's express or implied authority. See also Administrative Agency.

Aggravated Damages Money paid to cover special circumstances, e.g., the presence of malice, that justify an increase in the amount paid.

Aggrieved Party The party who has been wronged.

Alienation of Affections A tort that is committed when the defendant diminishes the marital relationship between the plaintiff and the latter's spouse.

Alimony Money or other property paid in fulfillment of a duty to support one's spouse after a separation or divorce. Note, however, that the Internal Revenue Service uses a broader definition of alimony for purposes of determining whether it is *deductible,* depending on the date the alimony is paid.

Alimony in Gross Lump-sum alimony.

A Mensa et Thoro See Legal Separation.

American Bar Association A voluntary, national organization of attorneys.

American Digest System See Digest. The American Digest System is the most comprehensive digest in existence. It covers almost every court in the country.

American Jurisprudence, 2d A national legal encyclopedia.

American Law Reports A set of reporters that contain selected opinions from many different courts. Following each opinion there is a research paper—called an *annotation*—that gives a survey of the law on a particular issue found in the opinion.

Amnesty Forgiveness; a general pardon from the state.

Annotated   Organized by subject matter with research references or other commentary.

Annotation   Commentary. Also, a research paper that gives a survey of the law on a particular issue. The annotations are printed in volumes of *American Law Reports*.

Annuity   A fixed sum payable to an individual at specified intervals for a specific period of time or for life.

Annulment   A declaration that a valid marriage never existed.

Antenuptial Agreement   A contract made between two individuals about to be married that resolves support, property division, and related matters in the event of the death of one of the marries or the dissolution of the marriage. Also called a *prenuptial agreement* and a *premarital agreement*.

Appearance   Formally going before a court.

Appellant   The party bringing an appeal because of disagreement with the ruling of a lower tribunal.

Appellee   The party against whom an appeal is brought.

Appreciation   An increase in value.

Arbitration   The process of submitting a dispute to a third party outside the judicial system who will resolve the dispute for the parties.

Arm's Length, At   As between two strangers who are looking out for their own self-interests.

Arraignment   Bringing the accused before a court to hear the criminal charges and to enter a plea thereto.

Arrears, Arrearages   Payments that are due but have not been made.

Artificial Insemination   The impregnation of a woman by a method other than sexual intercourse.

Assignee   The person to whom ownership or rights are transferred. See also Assigns.

Assignment   The transfer of ownership or other rights.

Assignor   The person who transfers ownership or rights to another.

Assigns   As a noun, it is a synonym for *assignees,* who are person to whom ownership or other rights have been or will be transferred. As a verb, it means to transfer ownership or other rights.

Assisted Conception   A pregnancy resulting from (1) fertilizing an egg of a woman with sperm of a man by means other than sexual intercourse, or (2) implanting an embryo. The sperm is not that of her husband.

Attachment   A court authorization of the seizure of the defendant's property so that it can be used to satisfy a judgment against him or her.

Attorney Work Product   The following material is protected from discovery: (1) the private memoranda of an attorney, and (2) mental impressions or personal recollections prepared or formed by an attorney in anticipation of litigation or for trial.

Attorney-Client Privilege   The right of a client to refuse to answer questions that would disclose communications between the client and his or her attorney. The purpose of the communication must be the facilitation of legal services from the attorney to the client. The client can also prevent the attorney from making such disclosures.

A Vinculo Matrimonii   See Divorce.

Banns of Marriage   A public announcement of a proposed marriage.

Basis   See Tax Basis.

Bastardy   Pertaining to a child born before his or her parents were married, or born to parents who never married.

Battered Wife Syndrome   Psychological helplessness because of a wife's financial dependence, loneliness, guilt, shame, and fear of reprisal from her husband who has repeatedly battered her in the past.

Beneficiary   The person named in a document such as a will or insurance policy to receive property or other benefit.

Bequest   A gift of personal property in a will.

Betrothal   A mutual promise to marry.

BFOQ   See Bona Fide Occupational Qualification.

Bias   A predisposition to act in a certain way. A preconceived idea of how something should be decided.

Bigamy   Entering or attempting to enter a marriage when a prior marriage is still valid.

Bilateral Divorce   A divorce granted by a court when both the husband and the wife are present before the court.

Bill   A proposed statute offered for passage by the legislature.

Biological Parent   One's natural parent; a parent by blood.

Bird's Nest Custody   Joint custody where the child remains in one home and each parent moves in and out during alternating periods of time.

Black Market Adoptions   An adoption that involves

a payment beyond reasonable expenses in order to facilitate the adoption.

Blue Book See Uniform System of Citation.

Boilerplate Standard language in legal documents that is identical in documents of a like nature; language often used in documents having a definite meaning in the same context without variation.

Bona Fide Occupational Qualification (BFOQ) Sex discrimination that is reasonably necessary for the operation of a particular business or enterprise.

Canon 1. A rule of behavior. 2. A maxim or guideline.

Canon Law Church or ecclesiastical law.

Canons of Ethics Rules that embody standards of conduct. In the legal profession, the canons of ethics are often referred to as a Code of Ethics or as a Code of Professional Responsibility that governs attorneys. The current canon of ethics of the American Bar Association are found within the Model Rules of Professional Responsibility.

Capacity The legal power to do something. The ability to understand the nature and effects of one's actions or inactions.

Capital Improvements Structural improvements on property, as opposed to ordinary maintenance work.

Caption of Complaint The heading or beginning of the complaint that contains the name of the court, the names of the parties, their litigation status, and the name of the document, e.g., Complaint for Divorce.

CARTWHEEL A technique designed to assist you to use indexes and tables of contents. By identifying broader, narrower, and other related words, cartwheeling helps you increase the number of words to check in these indexes and tables.

Case Law The body of law found in court opinions. See Court Opinion.

Cause of Action The facts that give a person a right to judicial relief. A legally acceptable reason for suing.

Challenge for Cause The elimination of a prospective juror during *voir dire,* which is the jury selection process, for a specific reason such as bias.

Chambers A judge's private office.

Chattel See Personal Property.

Chose in Action The right to recover something through a lawsuit.

Citation The "address" where you can find a document in a library, e.g., the volume and page number of a reporter where an opinion can be found.

Civil contempt See Contempt of Court.

Civil Fraud See Fraud.

Civil Procedure The body of law governing the methods and practices of civil litigation.

Closed Case File The file of a client whose case is no longer being worked on.

Code A book or set of books that contains rules or laws organized by subject matter. The state code, also called the *state statutory code,* is a collection of statutes written by the state legislature organized by subject matter.

Code of Ethics See Canons of Ethics.

Code of Regulations Laws written by administrative agencies organized by subject matter.

Cohabitation Living together as husband and wife whether or not the parties are married. See also Contract Cohabitation.

Collateral Attack A nondirect attack or challenge to the validity of a judgment. An attack brought in a different proceeding.

Collusion An agreement between a husband and wife in a divorce proceeding that one or both will lie to the court in order to facilitate the obtaining of the divorce.

Comity The court's decision to give effect to the laws and judicial decisions of another state as a matter of deference and mutual respect even if no obligation exists to do so.

Commingling Funds Placing general law firm funds into the same account that contains the funds of a client.

Common Law Judge-made law created in the absence of other controlling law such as statutory law.

Common Law Marriage The marriage of two people who have not gone through a ceremonial marriage. They have agreed to be husband and wife, lived together as husband and wife, and held themselves out to the public as husband and wife.

Common-Law Property Property acquired during the marriage in a state other than a community-property state. Upon divorce, the parties are given an equitable, but not necessarily equal, division of such property. At one time, however, common-law property was given to the party who had legal title to the property.

Common Representation See Multiple Representation.

Community Property Property in which each spouse has a one-half interest because it was acquired during the marriage, regardless of who has title to the property. Excluded is property acquired by gift or inheritance, which is the separate property of the spouse who receives it.

Competence The knowledge and skill that is reasonably necessary to represent a particular person.

Complaint A document filed in court by one party suing another that states a grievance, called a *cause of action,* against the other party.

Conciliation The resolution or settlement of a dispute in an amicable manner. A Conciliation Service is a court-authorized process whereby a counselor attempts to determine if parties filing for divorce can be reconciled, and if not, whether they can agree on the resolution of support, custody, and property-division issues.

Concurrent Jurisdiction When two or more courts have the power to hear the same kind of case, each court has concurrent jurisdiction over such a case.

Condonation An express or implied forgiveness by the innocent spouse of the marital fault committed by the other spouse.

Confidence A confidence is any information protected by the attorney-client privilege. A *secret* is any information gained in the professional relationship if the client has requested that it be held secret or if its disclosure would embarrass or be detrimental to the client.

Confidentiality The ethical obligation not to disclose information relating to the representation of a client.

Conflict of Interest Being pulled in two different directions at the same time, resulting in a significant potential that one of the participants will be placed at a disadvantage. Divided loyalties.

Conjugal Pertaining to marriage; appropriate for married persons.

Connivance A willingness or a consent by one spouse that a marital wrong be done by the other spouse.

Consanguinity Relationship by blood; kinship.

Conservator A person appointed by the court to manage the affairs of an adult who is not competent to do so on his or her own.

Consideration Something of value that is exchanged between the parties, e.g., an exchange of promises to do or to refrain from doing something.

Consortium Companionship, love, affection, sexual relationship, and services that a person enjoys with and from his or her spouse. See Loss of Consortium.

Constitution The basic legal document of a government that allocates power among the three branches of the government, and that may also enumerate fundamental rights of individuals.

Constructive Desertion The conduct of the spouse who stayed home justified the other spouse's departure; or the spouse who stayed home refuses a sincere offer of reconciliation from the other spouse who initially left.

Constructive Trust A trust created by operation of law against one who has improperly obtained legal possession of or legal rights to property through fraud, duress, abuse of confidence, or other unconscionable conduct. See also Trust.

Consumer Price Index A monthly report by the U.S. Bureau of Labor Statistics that tracks the price level of a group of goods and services purchased by the average consumer.

Consummation Sexual intercourse for the first time between spouses.

Contempt of Court Obstructing or assailing the authority or dignity of the court such as by intentionally violating a court order. The purpose of a *civil* contempt proceeding is to compel future compliance with a court order. The purpose of a *criminal* contempt proceeding is to punish the offender.

Contested Litigated; argued by all sides because of the presence of serious disputes.

Contingency An event that may or may not occur.

Contingent Fee When an attorney receives a contingent fee for services rendered, the amount of the fee, if any, will depend on the outcome of the case. (The fee is often a percentage of what the client wins.) A *fixed* fee, on the other hand, is a flat sum, an hourly rate, or a combination, regardless of the outcome of the case.

Continuance The postponement or adjournment of a proceeding to a later date.

Contract An enforceable agreement. The elements of a contract are (1) offer, (2) acceptance, and (3) consideration. The parties must have the legal capacity to enter a contract.

Contract Cohabitation A contract made between two individuals who intend to stay unmarried indefinitely that covers financial and related matters while living together, and upon death or earlier separation.

Conversion 1. The unauthorized exercise of dominion and control over someone's personal property. 2. Once a judicial separation has been in place for a designated period of time, the parties can ask a court for a divorce on that basis alone. The latter is called a *convertible divorce.*

Conveyance The transfer of an interest in land.

Co-parenting Two individuals who share the task of raising a child. Usually, at least one of the individuals is not a biological parent of the child. Sometimes, however, co-parenting refers to two biological parents who have joint custody of the child.

Co-respondent   The person who allegedly had sexual intercourse with a defendant charged with adultery.

Corpus Juris Secundum   An national legal encyclopedia.

Corroboration   Additional evidence beyond that provided by the word of the plaintiff alone.

Count   A separate and independent claim or charge in a pleading such as a complaint.

Counterclaim   A claim made by the defendant against the plaintiff.

Court Opinion   The written explanation by a court of why it reached a certain conclusion or holding.

Covenant   A promise or agreement.

Credit Clouding   To notify a creditor or credit bureau that a debtor is delinquent on certain debts.

Criminal Contempt   See Contempt of Court.

Criminal Conversation   A tort committed by having sex with the plaintiff's spouse.

Criminal Fraud   See Fraud.

Criminal Law   The body of law covering acts declared to be crimes by the legislature for statutory crimes, or by the courts for common law crimes.

Curtesy   During his life, a surviving husband has the right to use the property of his deceased wife. Some states imposed the requirement that she die leaving issue capable of inheriting the estate.

Custodial Parent   The parent with physical custody of the child.

Compensatory Damages   Money paid to make the plaintiff whole. The payment is for actual loss or injury. The objective is to place the plaintiff in the position he or she would have been in if no loss or injury occurred. Included are out-of-pocket expenses, loss of income, pain and suffering, etc.

Damages   Money paid because of a wrongful injury or loss to person or property.

Decedent   The person who has died, the deceased.

Deep Pocket   The person who probably has sufficient resources to pay damages if a judgment is awarded by the court.

Default   Obtained because the other side failed to appear or contest the matter.

Defendant   The party against whom a claim is brought.

Defense   Allegations of fact or legal theories offered to offset or defeat claims or demands.

Defined Benefit Plan   A pension plan where the amount of the benefit is fixed but not the amount of the contribution.

Defined Contribution Plan   A pension plan where the amount of the contribution is generally fixed but the amount of the benefit is not.

Deposition   A pretrial discovery device, usually conducted outside the courtroom, during which one party questions the other party or a witness for the other party.

Depository Library, Federal   A library that receives certain law books from the federal government free (e.g., the United States Code), in exchange for which the library must allow the public to have access to those books.

Depreciation   A decrease in value.

Derivative Actions   A suit whose success is dependent on the success of a separate suit.

Descent   Acquiring property by inheritance rather than by will; acquiring property from a decedent who died intestate.

Desertion   One spouse voluntarily but without justification leaves another (who does not consent to the departure) for an uninterrupted period of time with the intent not to return to resume cohabitation. Also called *abandonment*. See Constructive Desertion.

Devise   Land acquired by will. The person to whom land is given by will is the devisee.

Digest   1. Sets of books that contain small paragraph summaries of court opinions. 2. A summary of a document or a series of documents.

Direct Attack   A challenge to the validity of a judgment made in a proceeding brought specifically for that purpose, e.g., an appeal of a judgment brought immediately after it was rendered by the trial court.

Disaffirm Contracts   The right of a minor to repudiate and refuse to perform a contract he or she has entered.

Disbursement   Payment.

Discipline   The imposition of correction or punishment.

Discovery   Steps that a party can take before trial to obtain information from the other side in order to prepare for trial.

Distributive Share   The portion of an estate that a person receives from a person who dies intestate, i.e., without leaving a valid will.

Divided Custody   See Split Custody.

Divided Loyalty   Representing a client when a conflict of interest exists. See Conflict of Interest.

Divisible Divorce   A divorce decree that is enforceable in another state only in part. That part of a divorce decree that dissolves the marriage is enforceable (if the plaintiff was domiciled in the state), but that part of the divorce that ordered alimony, child support, or a property division is not (if the court did not have personal jurisdiction over the defendant).

Divorce   A declaration that a marriage has been dissolved so that the parties are no longer married to each other. Also called an *absolute divorce,* and a *divorce a vinculo matrimonii.*

Divorce Kits   A package of do-it-yourself materials containing standard forms and written instructions on how to obtain a divorce without an attorney.

DNA   Deoxyribonucleic acid. A constituent of living cell nuclei.

Docket Number   A docket is a list or calendar of cases to be tried or heard at a specific term of the court. Cases on this list are assigned a number.

Doctor-Patient Privilege   The right of a patient to refuse to disclose any confidential (private) communications with his or her doctor that relate to the medical care. The patient can also prevent the doctor from making such disclosures.

Domestic Partnership   Two unmarried individuals who live together in a close personal relationship and who have registered as domestic partners. Some cities require that they also agree to be jointly responsible for basic living expenses.

Domicile   The place where a person has been physically present with the intent to make that place a permanent home; the place to which one intends to return when away. A residence, on the other hand, is simply the place where you are living at a particular time. A person can have more than one residence, but generally can have only one domicile.

Domicile of Choice   A domicile chosen by a person with the legal capacity to choose.

Domiciliary   One who is domiciled in a particular state.

Donor/Donee   See Gift.

Dower   During her life, a surviving wife has the right to use one third of all the real estate her deceased husband owned or acquired during the marriage which her issue, if any, could have inherited.

Draft   1. As a verb, draft means to write a document, e.g., a letter, contract, or memorandum. 2. As a noun, it means a version of a document that is not yet final or ready for distribution.

Dual Divorce   A divorce granted to both the husband and the wife.

Duress   Coercion; acting under the pressure of an unlawful act or threat.

Election against Will   Obtaining a designated share of a deceased spouse's estate in spite of what the latter provided or failed to provide for the surviving spouse in a will. A forced share of a decedent's estate.

Element   A portion of a rule that is a precondition to the applicability of the entire rule.

Element in Contention   The portion of a rule (i.e., the element) that will form the basis of a legal issue because of disagreement between the parties on interpreting or applying that element to the facts of the case.

Emancipation   The relinquishment of control over a child by his or her parent or legal guardian.

Encumber   To impose a burden, claim, or liability on something.

Enoch Arden Doctrine   The presumption that a spouse is dead after being missing for a designated number of years.

Equitable Adoption   For some purposes (e.g., determining heirship) a child will be considered the adopted child of a person who made a contract to adopt the child but who failed to go through the formal adoption procedures. Also called *adoption by estoppel.*

Equitable Distribution   The fair, but not necessarily equal, division between former spouses of all property acquired during the marriage regardless of which spouse holds title to any of the property.

Equitable Estoppel   See Estoppel.

Escalation Clause   A provision in a contract or other document that provides for an increase or decrease in the amount to be paid based upon a factor over which the parties do not have complete control.

Escrow   Property (e.g., money, stock, deed) delivered by one person (called the *grantor, promisor,* or *obligor*) to another (e.g., a bank, an escrow agent) to be held by the latter until a designated condition or contingency occurs, at which time the property is to be delivered to the person for whose benefit the escrow was established (called the *grantee, promisee, obligee,* or *beneficiary*).

Estate   All the property left by the decedent from which any debts must be paid and gifts completed.

Estoppel   Stopping. Equitable estoppel is the prevention of a party, due to his or her conduct, from asserting a right to the detriment of another who was entitled to rely on that conduct.

Ethics   Standards of conduct embodied within rules that govern an organization, occupation, or profession.

Et Ux   And wife.

Evidence   Anything offered to establish the existence or nonexistence of a fact in dispute.

Ex Parte Divorce   A divorce rendered by a court when only one of the spouses was present in the state. The court did not have personal jurisdiction over the defendant.

Exclusive Jurisdiction   A court has exclusive jurisdiction when only that court has the power to hear a certain kind of case.

Executed   Carried out according to its terms.

Execution of Judgment   The process of carrying out or satisfying the judgment of a court. Using a writ of execution, a court officer (e.g., a sheriff) is commanded to seize the property of the losing litigant, sell it, and pay the winning litigant out of the proceeds.

Executor   A person designated in a will to carry out the terms of the will and handle related matters. If a female, this person is sometimes called an *executrix*. See also Personal Representative.

Executory   Unperformed as yet.

Executrix   See Executor.

Exemplary Damages   See Punitive Damages.

Extradition   The process by which a state or country turns over an individual who has been accused or convicted of a crime to another state or country.

Facilitation of Divorce   That which makes a divorce easier to obtain.

Fact Particularization   A technique of identifying a series of questions to be answered by interviewing and investigation. The questions cover the details on participants, incidents, places, times, etc.

Fair Market Value   The amount that a willing buyer would pay a willing seller for property, neither being under any compulsion to buy or sell and both having reasonable knowledge of or access to the relevant facts.

False Arrest   An arrest of an individual without a privilege to do so.

False Imprisonment   A tort with the following elements: (1) the defendant performs an act that completely confines the plaintiff within fixed boundaries set by the defendant; (2) the defendant intends the confinement; (3) the defendant causes the confinement; and (4) the plaintiff is either conscious of the confinement or is harmed by it.

Family Purpose Doctrine   The owner of a car who makes it available for family use will be liable for injuries caused while a member of the immediate family is using the car with the owner's consent for a family purpose at the time of the accident.

Fault Grounds   Marital wrongs that will justify the granting of a divorce, e.g., adultery.

Fee Splitting   1. A single bill to the client covering the fee of two or more attorneys who are not in the same firm. 2. Receiving part of a fee because of making a referral of the client.

Fiduciary   Pertaining to someone who owes another good faith, loyalty, trust, and candor.

Filiation   A judicial determination of paternity. The relation of child to father.

Filius Nullius   The son or child of nobody. The status of an illegitimate child at common law.

Fixed Fee   See Contingent Fee.

Flowchart   An overview of the step-by-step process by which something is done.

Forced Share   See Election against Will.

Foreign Divorce   A divorce obtained in another state or country.

Formbook   A practical treatise or manual containing standard forms along with checklists, summaries of the law, etc. See also Treatise.

Fornication   Sexual intercourse between unmarried persons.

Forum Non Conveniens   The discretionary power of a court to decline the exercise of its jurisdiction when it would be more convenient and the ends of justice would be better served if the action were tried in another court.

Forum Shopping   To travel from court to court until you find a court that will provide a ruling that is favorable to you.

Forum State   The state in which the parties are now litigating a case.

Foster Home   A temporary home for a child when his or her own family cannot provide care and when adoption is either not possible at the present time, or is under consideration.

Fraud   Fraud exists when the defendant knowingly makes a false statement of present fact that he or she intends the plaintiff to rely upon. The plaintiff must reasonably rely on the statement and be harmed thereby. This is *civil fraud*. *Criminal fraud* usually requires a willfulness or evil purpose. See also Statute of Frauds.

Friendly Divorce A divorce proceeding in which the husband and wife are not contesting the dissolution of the marriage, nor anything related thereto. An uncontested divorce.

Front Loading Making substantial "alimony" payments shortly after the separation or divorce in an attempt to disguise property division as deductible alimony.

Full Faith and Credit One state must recognize the legislative acts, public records, and judicial decisions of another state.

Garnishment A proceeding whereby a debtor's money or other property under the control of another is given to a third person to whom the debtor owes a debt.

Get A bill of divorcement in a Jewish divorce.

Gift The voluntary delivery of something with the present intent to transfer title and control, for which no payment or consideration is made. Once the item is accepted, the gift is irrevocable. The person making the gift is the *donor*. The person receiving it is the *donee*.

Goodwill The reputation of a business which causes it to generate additional customers.

Gross Income The total amount received or earned before deductions.

Guarantee A warranty or assurance that a particular result will be achieved.

Guardian ad Litem A special guardian appointed by the court to represent the interests of another, often to defend an action or to bring an action.

Guardianship The legal right to the custody of an individual.

Hearsay Testimony in court of a statement made by another out of court when the statement is being offered to assert the truth of the matter in the statement.

Heart-Balm Cause of Action The heart-balm causes of action are breach of promise to marry, alienation of affections, criminal conversation, enticement, and seduction. Heart-balm statutes have abolished these causes of action.

Heir One who receives property by inheritance rather than by will.

Hold Harmless In the event of trouble, to relieve someone of responsibility or liability.

Home State The state where the child has lived for at least six consecutive months or since birth if the child is less than six months old.

Homestead One's dwelling house along with adjoining land and buildings.

Hornbooks A text that summarizes an area of the law, usually with commentary and extensive footnotes. See also Treatise.

Husband-Wife Privilege See Marital Communications.

Illegitimate Child A child born when his or her parents are not married to each other.

Illicit Cohabitation Sexual intercourse between unmarried persons who are living together. See also Cohabitation.

Imminent Near at hand; about to happen; immediate.

Immunity See Tort Immunity.

Implied Contract A contract not created or evidenced by an explicit agreement of the parties but inferred as a matter of reason and justice from their conduct and the surrounding circumstances.

In Camera In the judge's private chambers.

Incest Sexual intercourse between two people who are too closely related to each other as defined by statute.

Incorrigible Habitually disobedient and and disruptive.

In Forma Pauperis As a poor person. As such, certain filing fees are waived.

In Loco Parentis Standing in the place of a parent.

In Personam Jurisdiction See Personal Jurisdiction.

In Rem Jurisdiction The power of the court to make a decision affecting a particular *res*, which is a thing or status.

In Vitro Fertilization A process by which a sperm and an egg are joined in a laboratory and the fertilized egg is implanted in the woman.

Inchoate Begun but not completed; partial.

Incident to Closely connected to something else.

Incompatibility A no-fault ground for divorce that exists when there is such discord between the husband and wife that it is impossible for them to live together in a normal marital relationship.

Indemnify To compensate or reimburse someone; to secure someone against loss or damage.

Idemnity The right to have another person pay you the amount you were forced to pay.

Independent Professional Judgment Advice given by

an attorney who is not subject to a conflict of interest. See Conflict of Interest.

Inheritance Property received from someone who dies without leaving a valid will. The state determines who receives such property.

Injunction A court order requiring a person to do or to refrain from doing a particular thing.

Instrument A formal document such as a deed, mortgage, will, or contract.

Intake Memorandum A document on a new client containing the basic facts about the client and about the case. The facts are obtained from the initial interview of the client.

Intentional Torts Torts other than negligence and strict liability, e.g., assault, battery.

Intercept Program A procedure by which the government seizes designated benefits owed to a parent in order to cover the latter's delinquent child support payments.

Interlocutory Not final; interim.

Interoffice Memorandum of Law See Memorandum, Memorandum of Law. *Interoffice* simply means that the memo is internal; it was not written for anyone outside of the office or organization.

Interrogatories A written set of questions sent before trial by one party to another in order to help the former prepare for trial.

Interspousal Between or pertaining to husband and wife.

Intestate Dying without leaving a valid will.

Intestate Succession Obtaining property of a deceased who did not leave a valid will.

Intrafamily Torts Torts committed by one family member on another.

Irreconcilable Differences A no-fault ground for divorce that exists when there is such discord between the husband and wife that there has been an irremediable breakdown of the marriage.

Irremediable Breakdown See Irreconcilable Differences.

Irrevocable That which cannot be changed or undone.

Issue 1. Everyone who has descended from a common ancestor. 2. A legal question. See also Legal Periodical.

Joint Custody Each parent shares legal custody and/or shares physical custody, often over alternating, but not necessarily equal, periods of time. Also called *shared custody*.

Joint Tenancy Property owned by two or more persons in undivided equal shares with a right of survivorship. See Survivorship.

Joint Venture An association of persons who jointly undertake an enterprise, each having an equal right to control the enterprise.

Judgment Debtor/Judgment Creditor The person who loses and therefore must pay a money judgment is the judgment debtor. The winner is the judgment creditor.

Judicial Separation See Legal Separation.

Jurisdiction 1. The power of a court to act in a particular case. 2. The geographic area over which a particular court has authority. See also Concurrent Jurisdiction, Exclusive Jurisdiction, In Rem Jurisdiction, Personal Jurisdiction, and Subject-Matter Jurisdiction.

Juvenile Delinquent A young person under a designated age whose conduct would constitute a crime if performed by an adult.

Law Review/Law Journal A law review is a legal periodical published by a law school. Also called a law journal. See Legal Periodical.

Legal Analysis The application of rules of law to facts in order to answer a legal question or issue.

Legal Capacity See Capacity.

Legal Custody The right and duty to make decisions about raising a child.

Legal Encyclopedias A multi-volume set of books that summarize almost every area of the law.

Legal Issue A question of law. See also Legal Analysis.

Legal Malpractice See Malpractice.

Legal Periodical An ongoing publication of commentary on the law, usually scholarly in nature. It is published by law schools, bar associations, and commercial companies. The periodical is printed in pamphlet form as an *issue*. Later, subscribers often place sets of issues in bound volumes.

Legal Separation A declaration that parties can live separate and apart even though they are still married to each other. Also called a *legal separation*, a *judicial separation*, a *limited divorce*, a *divorce a mensa et thoro*, and a *separation from bed and board*.

Legatee A person to whom property (usually personal property) is given by will.

Legitimacy The status or condition of being born in wedlock.

Legitimation The process by which an illegitimate child becomes a legitimate child.

Levy To seize in order to satisfy a claim.

Lexis A legal data base for computer research.

Liabilities That which one owes; debts.

Lien A security or encumbrance on property; a claim or charge on property for the payment of a debt or other obligation.

Limited Divorce See Legal Separation.

Living Apart A no-fault ground for divorce that exists when a husband and wife have lived separately for a designated period of consecutive time.

Long Arm Jurisdiction The power that a court obtains over a nonresident defendant who has such sufficient purposeful contact with the state that it is fair and reasonable for the state to adjudicate a dispute involving the defendant.

Loose-Leaf Service A law book published as a three-ring binder containing pages that can be inserted and removed with relative ease.

Lord Mansfield's Rule The testimony of either spouse is inadmissible on the question of whether the husband had access to the wife at the time of conception since such evidence would tend to bastardize (i.e., declare illegitimate) the child.

Loss of Consortium A tort action for the loss of or the interference with the companionship, love, affection, sexual relationship, and services that the plaintiff enjoyed with his or her spouse before the latter was injured by the defendant.

Loss of Services A tort action for the loss of or the interference with the right of a parent to control the services and earnings of his or her child because of the injury inflicted on the child by the defendant.

Lucid Interval A period of time during which a person has the mental capacity to understand what he or she is doing.

Maintenance Food, clothing, shelter, and other necessaries of life.

Majority A designated age of legal adulthood in the state, usually eighteen or twenty-one.

Malice Animosity; the intent to inflict injury.

Malicious Prosecution A tort with the following elements: (1) to initiate or procure the initiation of legal proceedings—civil or criminal, (2) without probable cause, (3) with malice, and (4) the proceedings terminate in favor of the person against whom the proceedings were brought.

Malpractice Professional wrongdoing. Legal malpractice normally refers to negligence by an attorney.

Manual A practical treatise often containing standard forms along with checklists, summaries of the law, etc. Sometimes called a *Practice Manual*. See also Treatise.

Marital Communications Those communications between a husband and wife while cohabiting. According to the privilege for marital communications, or the husband-wife privilege, one spouse cannot disclose in court any confidential communications that occurred between the spouses during the marriage.

Market Value See Fair Market Value.

Married Women's Property Acts Statutes that removed all or most of the legal disabilities imposed on women with respect to the disposition of their property.

Mediation The process of submitting a dispute to a third party outside the judicial system who will help the parties reach their own resolution of the dispute. The mediator will not hand the parties a decision.

Memorandum A memorandum is any writing or notation sent to a person or to a file. It can be a highly formal and lengthy document or a simple one-line note. The plural of memorandum is *memoranda*.

Memoradum of Law A written analysis in which the writer tries to answer a legal question or issue by the application of rules of law to facts.

Meretricious Vulgar; unlawful, usually pertaining to sexual relations.

Microfilm Reels or cassettes that contain images or photographs that have been greatly reduced in size. Many law books and periodicals have been placed on microfilm.

Migratory Divorce A divorce obtained in a state to which one or both of the parties traveled before returning to their original state.

Minimum Fee Schedule A list of fees announced by the bar association that an attorney *must* charge, at a minimum, for designated services rendered. Charging lower than the minimum would be unethical. (Today, minimum fee schedules are illegal.)

Minor Someone under the age of majority in the state, which is usually eighteen or twenty-one.

Miscegenation The marriage of persons of different races.

Model Rules of Professional Responsibility See Canon of Ethics.

Mortgage An interest in land that provides security for the performance of a duty or the payment of a debt.

Multiple Representation Representing more than one party in a transaction or proceeding. The parties may actually or nominally be on opposite sides. Also called *common representation*.

National Conference of Commissioners on Uniform State Laws   See Uniform Laws.

Necessaries   The basic items needed by family members in order to maintain a standard of living. These items can be purchased and charged to the spouse who has failed to provide them.

Neglect   The failure to provide support, medical care, education, moral example, discipline, and other necessaries.

Negligence   A duty that is breached by the failure to use reasonable care, causing harm to the plaintiff.

Nisi   Not final; interim

No-Fault Divorce   A divorce granted on one of the no-fault grounds for divorce. See Irreconcilable Differences, Incompatibility, Living Apart.

Non-Engagement Letter   A letter to a person stating that you are declining the request to represent him or her.

Nonage   Below the required minimum age.

Noncustodial Parent   The parent with visitation rights who does not have custody of the child.

Nonmolestation Clause   A clause in an agreement that the parties will not bother each other.

Notes to Decisions   Small paragraph summaries of court opinions that have interpreted a particular statute. These paragraphs are printed after the text of the statute within annotated codes.

Nuisance   An unreasonable interference with the use and enjoyment of land.

Obligor/Obligee   The person who has an obligation is the obligor. The person to whom this obligation is owed is the obligee.

Offer   To present something that can be accepted or rejected.

Open Adoption   An adoption in which the natural parent maintains certain kinds of contact with his or her child after the latter is adopted.

Operation of Law   A result that occurs because the law mandates the result, not because the parties have agreed to produce the result.

Opinion   See Court Opinion.

Order to Show Cause (OSC)   An order telling a person to appear in court and explain why a certain order should not be entered.

Palimony   A nonlegal term that means payments made by one nonmarried party to another after they cease living together, usually because of an enforceable contract to do so while they were together.

Paralegal   A person with legal skills who works under the supervision of an attorney or who is otherwise authorized to use those skills.

Parent Locator Service   A government agency that helps locate parents who are delinquent in child support payments.

Paternity   Fatherhood.

Pendente Lite   While the litigation is still going on.

Peremptory Challenges   The elimination of a prospective juror during *voir dire*, which is the jury selection process. No reason need be given.

Periodic Payments   A payment of a fixed amount for an indefinite period, or the payment of an indefinite amount for a fixed or indefinite period.

Personal Jurisdiction   The power that a court obtains over an individual after proper service of process on him or her. The court's power to render a decision that binds the individual defendant. Also called *in personam jurisdiction*.

Personal Property   Everything, other than real property, that can be owned. Also called *chattels*.

Personal Representative   An executor or administrator of the estate of the deceased. Someone who formally acts on behalf of the estate of the deceased.

Petition   A formal request that the court take some action.

Physical Custody   The parent with whom the child actually lives has physical custody.

Plaintiff   The party bringing a claim against another.

Pleading   A formal allegation or position, usually in writing, that states a party's claim, defense, or other response. Examples of pleadings are complaint, answer, etc.

Pocket Part   A pocket in the inside back cover of some bound volumes. In this pocket you will find pamphlets that update the bound volume.

Polygamy   The practice of having more than one spouse at the same time, usually more than two.

Post-Nuptial   After marriage. See Separation Agreement.

Practice Manuals   See Manual.

Practice of Law   Assisting another to secure his or her legal rights. See Unauthorized Practice of Law.

Prayer   A formal request.

Premarital Agreement   See Antenuptial Agreement.

Prenuptial   Before marriage. See Antenuptial Agreement.

Preponderance of Evidence   A standard of proof that is established if it is more likely than not that a fact is as alleged.

Present value   The amount of money an individual would have to be given now in order to produce or generate a certain amount of money in a designated period of time.

Presents, These   This legal document.

Presumption   An assumption of fact that can be drawn when another fact or set of facts is established. The presumption is *rebuttable* if a party can introduce evidence to show that the assumption is false.

Price Fixing   An agreement by competing individuals or firms on the setting of price ranges or levels.

Primary Authority   Any *law* that a court could rely on in reaching its conclusion, e.g., a constitutional provision, statute, regulation, ordinance, other court opinion.

Privilege   A benefit, advantage, or right enjoyed by an individual.

Privilege against Self-Incrimination   The right to refuse to answer questions that directly or indirectly connect the individual to a crime.

Probate   A court proceeding at which a will is proved to be valid or invalid.

Probation   Restricted and supervised living in the community in lieu of institutionalization.

Procedural Law   The technical rules that set forth the steps required to litigate a case before a court or administrative agency.

Proctor   A person appointed for a particular purpose, e.g., protect the interests of a child.

Professional Responsibility   See Canons of Ethics.

Pro Hac Vice   For this particular occasion.

Proof of Service   A statement that service of process on the defendant has been made.

Property Division   The distribution of property accumulated by the parties as a result of their joint efforts during the marriage.

Pro Se Divorce   A divorce obtained when a party represents himself or herself.

Prosecute   To commence and carry forward a lawsuit.

Protective Order   A court order directing a person to refrain from harming or harassing another.

Provocation   The plaintiff incited the acts constituting the marital wrong by the other spouse.

Proxy Marriage   The performance of a valid marriage ceremony through agents because one or both of the parties are absent.

Public Assistance   Welfare or other forms of financial help from the government to the poor.

Punitive Damages   Money paid to punish the wrongdoer and/or to deter others. The amount is beyond what is needed to compensate the aggrieved party. Also called *exemplary damages*.

Putative   Alleged or reputed.

Putative Marriage   A marriage contracted in good faith and in ignorance (on one or both sides) of an impediment that renders the marriage unlawful.

QDRO   See Qualified Domestic Relations Order.

Qualified Domestic Relations Order   A court order that allows a nonemployee to reach pension benefits of an employee or former employee.

Quantum Meruit   "As much as he deserves." Valuable services are rendered or materials are furnished by the plaintiff, and accepted, used, or enjoyed by the defendant under such circumstances that the plaintiff reasonably expected to be paid. A promise to pay is implied in order to avoid unjust enrichment.

Quasi Contract   A contract created by the law to avoid unjust enrichment.

Quasi-Community Property   Real or personal property, wherever situated, that was acquired by either spouse while domiciled outside a community property state that would have been community property if it had been acquired in a community-property state.

Quasi-Marital Property   Property that will be treated as having been acquired or improved while the parties were married even though the marriage was never valid.

Quitclaim   A release or giving up of whatever claim or title you have in property. You are turning over whatever you have, without guaranteeing anything.

Real Property/Real Estate   Land and anything permanently attached to the land.

Realize   To obtain something actually, rather than on paper only.

Reasonable   See Unreasonable.

Rebuttable Presumption   See Presumption.

Recapture Rule   The recalculation of a tax liability when the parties have improperly attempted to disguise a property division as alimony through frontloading. See Front Loading.

Receivership The court appointment of someone to control and manage the defendant's property in order to ensure compliance with a court order.

Reconciliation The full resumption of the marital relationship.

Recrimination The party seeking the divorce (the plaintiff) has also committed a serious marital wrong.

Regional Digest See Digest. A regional digest contains summaries of opinions written by courts in a designated cluster of states. The full text of the opinions is found in the corresponding regional reporter for the digest.

Regional Reporter The volumes that contain the full text of opinions from courts within a designated cluster of states.

Regulation A law enacted by an administrative agency.

Rehabilitative Alimony Alimony for a limited time until the recipient can get back on his or her feet and become self-sufficient.

Remise To give up or release.

Reporters The volumes that contain the full text of court opinions.

Reprimand A form of public discipline by which an attorney's conduct is declared to have been improper, but that does not limit his or her right to practice law.

Request for Admissions A statement of fact sent by one party to another, asking the latter to agree or disagree with the statement.

Res A thing or object; a status.

Rescission The cancellation of something.

Res Judicata When a judgment on its merits has been rendered, the parties cannot relitigate the same dispute.

Respondeat Superior "Let the master answer," e.g., the employer is liable for the conduct of the employee while acting within the scope of employment.

Respondent The defendant; the person against whom a claim is made.

Restatement of Torts A treatise written by the American Law Institute that articulates the law of torts.

Restraining Order A form of injunction issued ex parte to restrain the defendant from doing a threatened act.

Resulting Trust A trust implied in law from the intention of the parties. A trust that arises when a person transfers property under circumstances that raise the inference that he or she did not intend the transferee to actually receive any interest in the property. See also Trust.

Retainer The act of hiring an attorney. The contract by which a prospective client hires an attorney. The contract should state the nature of the services to be rendered and the cost thereof.

Rules of Professional Responsibility See Canons of Ethics.

Sanction A penalty for an infraction or violation. See also Discipline.

Secondary Authority Any *nonlaw* that a court could rely on in reaching its conclusion, e.g., an article in a legal periodical, a treatise.

Secret See Confidence.

Self-Incrimination See Privilege against Self-Incrimination.

Separate Maintenance Court-ordered support while the spouses are separated.

Separate Property Property totally owned by one spouse only; noncommunity property.

Separation Agreement A contract between spouses who have separated or who are about to separate in which the terms of their separation are spelled out, e.g., support obligations, child custody, division of property accumulated during the marriage. The agreement may or may not be later incorporated and merged in a divorce decree. Also called a post-nuptial contract.

Service of Process Providing a formal notice to the defendant that orders him or her to appear in court in order to answer the allegations in the claims made by the plaintiff.

Settlor See Trust.

Severable That which can be removed from the whole and survive separately without destroying that which remains.

Severally Individually, separately.

Shared Custody See Joint Custody.

Shepardize To use the set of law books called *Shepard's Citations* in order to obtain specific information about a document, e.g., whether an opinion has been overruled, or whether a statute has been repealed.

Sole Custody One parent has physical and legal custody.

Sole Proprietorship A form of business in which one person owns all the assets.

Solemnization The performance of a formal ceremony in public.

Solicitation Asking or urging someone to do something.

Specialization The development of experience and expertise in a particular area of practice.

Specific Performance A remedy for breach of contract that forces the wrongdoing party to complete the contract as promised.

Split Custody 1. One parent has legal custody, with physical custody going to each parent during alternating periods when the child lives with him or her. 2. Each parent receives sole custody of at least one sibling with visitation rights as to the other siblings. The latter definition is also referred to as *divided custody.*

Standard Form A frequently used format for a document or instrument.

Standing The right to bring a case before a court.

Statute An act of the legislature declaring, commanding, or prohibiting something.

Statute of Frauds The requirement that certain kinds of transactions be in writing in order to be enforceable.

Statute of Limitations The time within which a suit must be brought. If it is brought after this time, it is barred.

Statutory Code See Code.

Stepparent A person who marries the natural mother or father of a child, but who is not one of the child's natural parents.

Stipulation An agreement between the parties on a matter so that evidence on the matter does not have to be introduced at the trial.

Subject-Matter Jurisdiction The power of the court to hear a particular category or kind of case; its authority to make rulings on certain subject matters.

Subpoena A command to appear in court.

Substantive Law The rights and duties imposed by law (e.g., the duty to pay child support) other than procedural rights and duties.

Substituted Service Service of process other than by handing the process documents to the defendant in person, e.g. service by mail.

Succession Obtaining property of the deceased, usually when there is no will.

Summary Dissolution A divorce obtained in an expedited manner because of the lack of controversy between the husband and wife.

Summons A service-of-process document commanding the defendant to appear in court.

Supervised Visitation Visitation by a parent with his or her child while another adult (other than the custodial parent) is present.

Surety Bond The obligation of a guarantor to pay a second party upon default by a third party in the performance the third party owes the second party.

Surrogate Mothers A woman who is artificially inseminated with the semen of a man who is not her husband, with the understanding that she will surrender the baby at birth to the father and his wife.

Survivorship, Right of Becoming automatically entitled to property by reason of the death of one of the other joint tenants. The interest of the deceased passes to the other joint tenants, and not to the estate of the deceased. See Joint Tenancy.

System An organized way of accomplishing a task that seeks to be more efficient than alternative methods.

Talak "I divorce you." Words spoken by a husband to his wife in a Moslem divorce.

Tax Basis One's initial capital investment in property. An adjusted basis is calculated after making allowed adjustments and deductions to the initial capital investment, e.g., an increase in the basis because of a capital improvement.

Tenancy by Entireties When a husband and wife have a joint tenancy in property, it is called a tenancy by the entireties. See Joint Tenancy, Survivorship.

Tenancy in Common Property owned by two or more persons in shares that may or may not be equal, with no right of survivorship. Each tenant in common has a right to possession of the property. See also Survivorship.

Tender-Years Presumption A young child is presumed to be better off with its mother than with its father.

Termination of Parental Rights A judicial declaration that a parent shall no longer have a right to participate in decisions affecting the welfare of the child.

Testate Dying with a valid will.

Testator The person who has died leaving a valid will.

Tort Wrongful conduct (other than a crime or a breach of contract) that has caused harm to person or property.

Tort Immunity One who enjoys a tort immunity cannot be sued for what would otherwise be a tort.

Transferor/Transferee The person who transfers property is the transferor; the person to whom property is transferred is the transferee.

Transitory Divorce A divorce granted in a state where neither spouse was domiciled at the time.

Treatise Any book written by a private individual (or by a public official writing in a nonofficial capacity) that provides an overview of and commentary on an area of the law. Hornbooks, manuals, and formbooks are treatises.

Trespass   Wrongfully intruding on land in possession of another.

Trimester   Three months.

Trust   When property is in trust, its legal title is held by one party (the trustee) for the benefit of another (the beneficiary). The creator of the trust is called the settlor.

Unauthorized Practice of Law   Performing functions that only attorneys are allowed to perform. Violating the state statute on who can practice law. Engaging in legal tasks without attorney supervision and/or without special authorization to engage in such tasks.

Uncontested   See Friendly Divorce.

Undertaking   A promise, engagement, or enterprise.

Unethical Conduct   See Ethics, Canons of Ethics.

Uniform Laws   Proposed statutes written by the National Conference of Commissioners on Uniform State Laws. The proposals are submitted to state legislatures for consideration.

Uniform System of Citation   The bible of citation form—also called the *blue book*. See Citation.

Unreasonable   That which is contrary to the behavior of an ordinary, prudent person under the same circumstances.

URESA   Uniform Reciprocal Enforcement of Support Act.

Venue   The place of the trial. When more than one court has jurisdiction to hear a case, the choice of the court is called the *choice of venue*.

Verification of Complaint   A sworn statement that the contents of the complaint are true.

Vested   That which you have a fixed right to receive; it cannot be forfeited or taken away by a contingency or condition.

Viability   The stage of fetal development when the life of an unborn child may be continued indefinitely outside the womb by natural or artificial support systems.

Vicarious Liability   One person is liable solely because of the wrong committed by someone else.

Visitation   The right of a noncustodial parent to visit and spend time with his or her children.

Void   Invalid whether or not a court declares it so.

Void ab Initio   Invalid from the time it started.

Voidable   Invalid only if a court declares it so.

Voir Dire   Jury selection.

Ward   An individual under the care of a court-appointed guardian.

Welfare   See Public Assistance.

Westlaw   A legal data base for computer research.

Will   A document that specifies the disposition of one's property and provides related instructions upon death.

Words and Phrases   A multi-volume legal dictionary. The definitions come from court opinions.

Work Product, Attorney   See Attorney Work Product.

Writ of Execution   See Execution of Judgment.

Wrongful Birth   An action by parents of an unwanted deformed child for their own damages. The defendant wrongfully caused the birth.

Wrongful Life   An action by or on behalf of an unwanted deformed child for its own damages. The defendant wrongfully caused the birth.

Wrongful Pregnancy   An action by parents of a healthy child that they did not want. The defendant wrongfully caused the birth. Also called *wrongful conception*.

INDEX

■ M

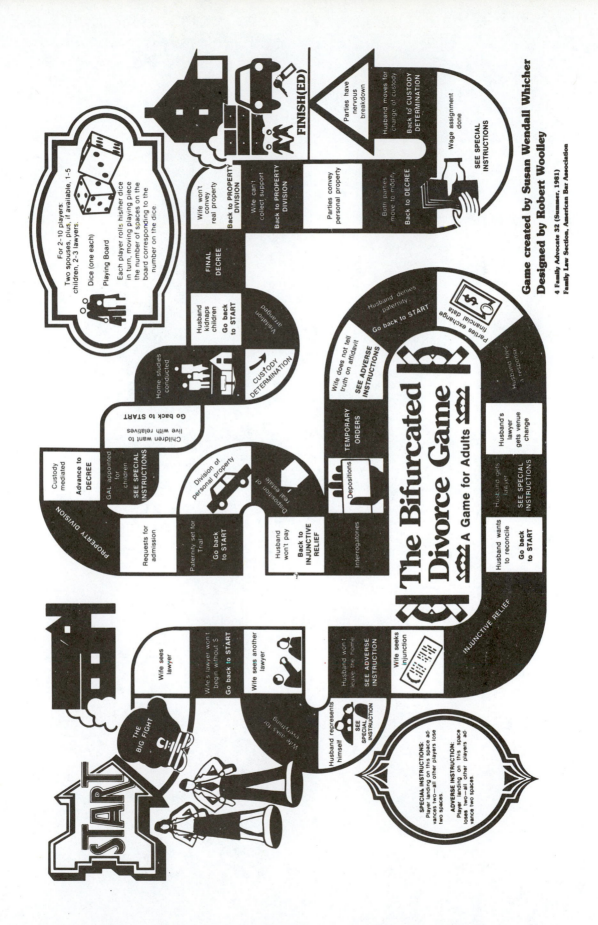

The Bifurcated Divorce Game
🐟 A Game for Adults 🐟

Game created by Susan Wendall Whicher
Designed by Robert Woolley

4 Family Advocate 32 (Summer, 1981)
Family Law Section, American Bar Association

START

THE BIG FIGHT

FINISH(ED)

Wife sees lawyer

Wife's lawyer won't begin without $ Go back to START

Wife sees another lawyer

Husband won't leave the home SEE ADVERSE INSTRUCTION

Wife seeks injunction

Wife asks for everything

Husband represents himself SEE SPECIAL INSTRUCTION

INJUNCTIVE RELIEF

Husband wants to reconcile Go back to START

Husband gets lawyer SEE SPECIAL INSTRUCTIONS

Husband's lawyer gets venue change

Husband files a response

Parties exchange financial data

Husband denies paternity Go back to START

Wife does not tell truth on affidavit SEE ADVERSE INSTRUCTIONS

TEMPORARY ORDERS

Depositions

Interrogatories

Husband won't pay Back to INJUNCTIVE RELIEF

Disposition of real estate

Division of personal property

Paternity set for Trial Go back to START

Requests for admission

PROPERTY DIVISION

GAL appointed for children SEE SPECIAL INSTRUCTIONS

Children want to live with relatives Go back to START

Custody mediated Advance to DECREE

Home studies conducted

CUSTODY DETERMINATION

Husband kidnaps children Go back to START

Visitation arranged

FINAL DECREE

Wife won't convey real property Back to PROPERTY DIVISION

Wife can't collect support Back to PROPERTY DIVISION

Parties convey personal property Back to DECREE

Both parties move to modify Back to DECREE

Wife moves for change of custody Back to CUSTODY DETERMINATION

Husband moves for change of custody Back to CUSTODY DETERMINATION

Parties have nervous breakdown

Wage assignment done SEE SPECIAL INSTRUCTIONS

For 2-10 players:
Two spouses, plus, if available, 1-5 children, 2-3 lawyers.

Dice (one each)

Playing Board

Each player rolls his/her dice in turn, moving playing piece the number of spaces on the board corresponding to the number on the dice

SPECIAL INSTRUCTIONS: Player landing on this space advances two—all other players lose two spaces.

ADVERSE INSTRUCTION: Player landing on this space loses two—all other players advance two spaces.